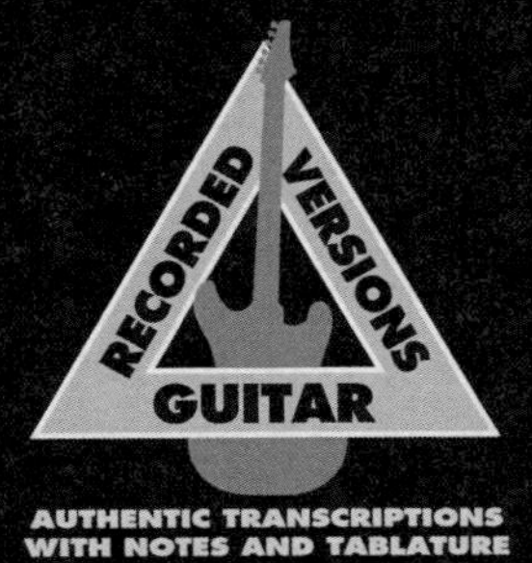

AUTHENTIC TRANSCRIPTIONS WITH NOTES AND TABLATURE

COHEED AN[...]A

GOOD APOLLO I'M BURNING STAR IV | VOLUME [...]NESS

Music transcriptions by Addi Booth and Andrew Moore

ISBN 978-1-4234-0920-5

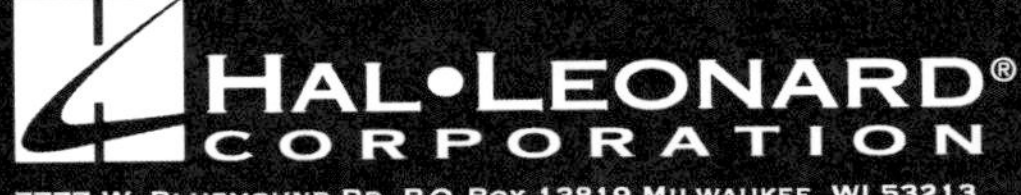

7777 W. BLUEMOUND RD. P.O. BOX 13819 MILWAUKEE, WI 53213

In Australia Contact:
Hal Leonard Australia Pty. Ltd.
4 Lentara Court
Cheltenham, Victoria, 3192 Australia
Email: ausadmin@halleonard.com

Visit Hal Leonard Online at
www.halleonard.com

Keeping the Blade

Words and Music by Claudio Sanchez and Joshua Eppard

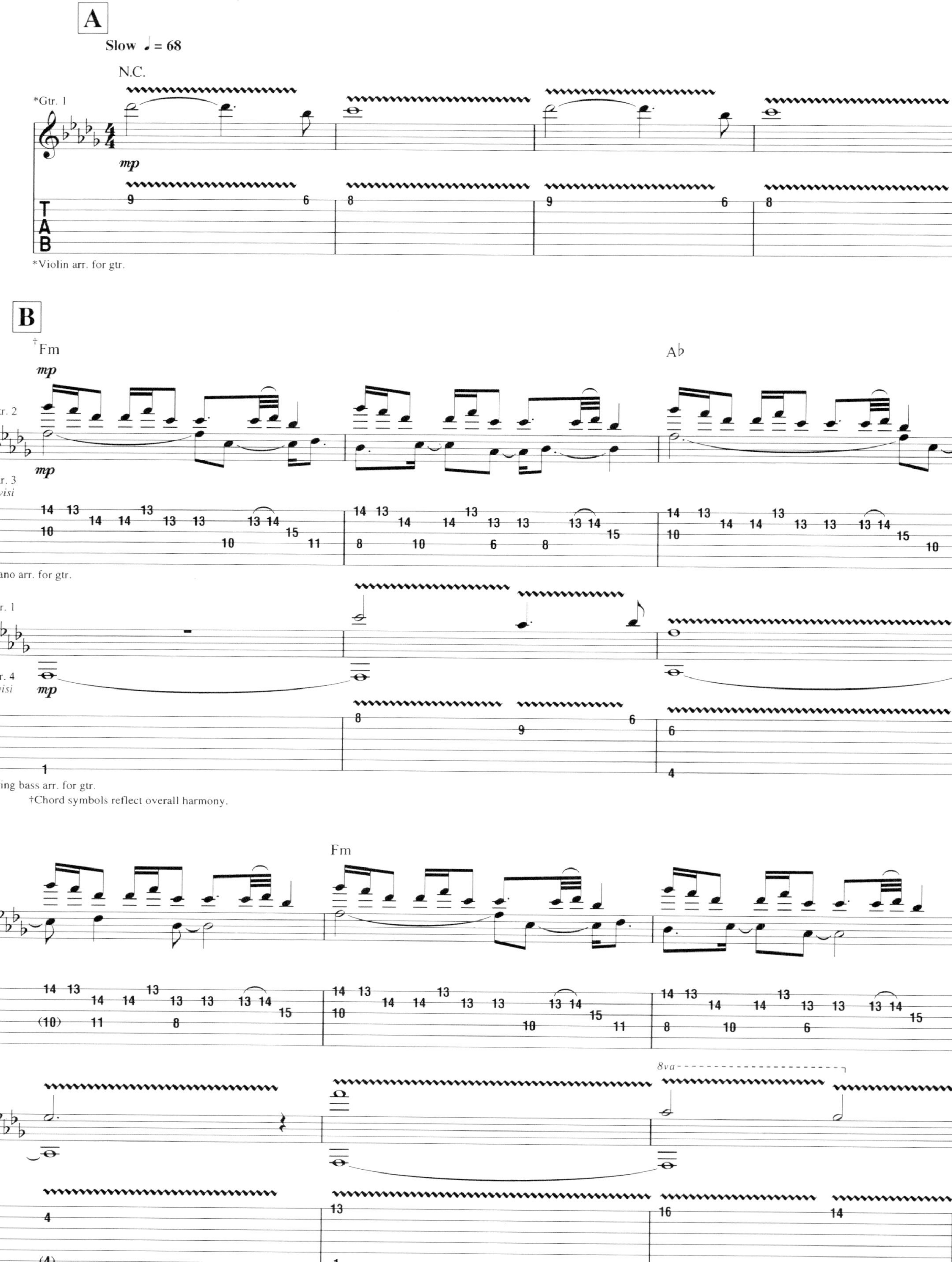

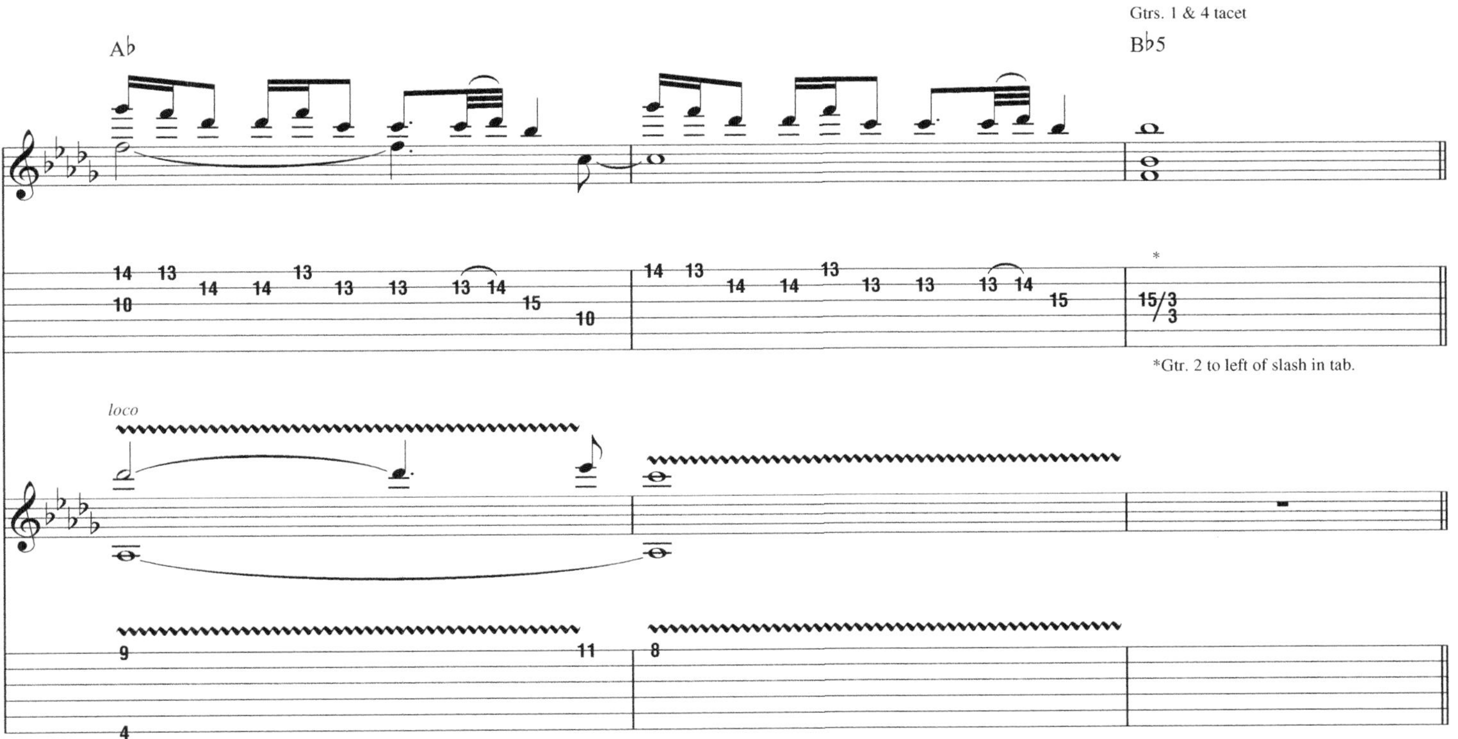
Gtrs. 1 & 4 tacet
A♭
B♭5
*Gtr. 2 to left of slash in tab.
loco

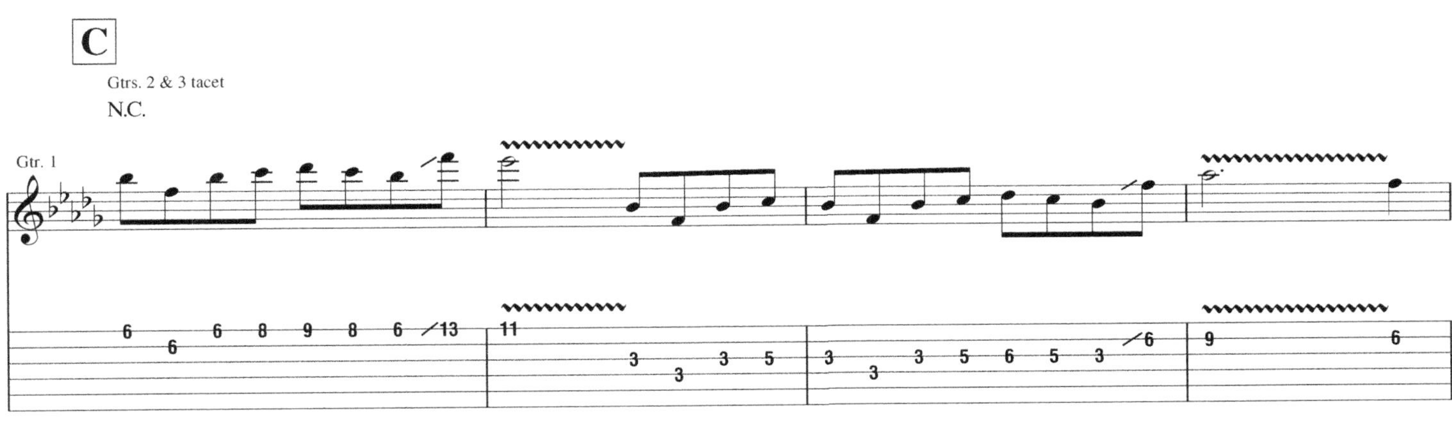
C
Gtrs. 2 & 3 tacet
N.C.
Gtr. 1

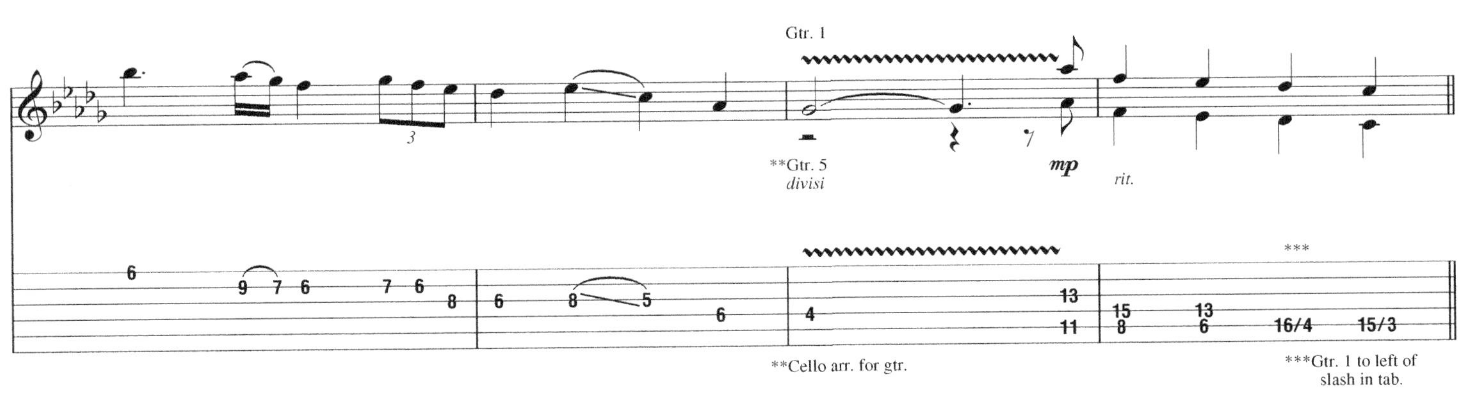
Gtr. 1
**Gtr. 5
divisi
mp
rit.
**Cello arr. for gtr.
***Gtr. 1 to left of slash in tab.

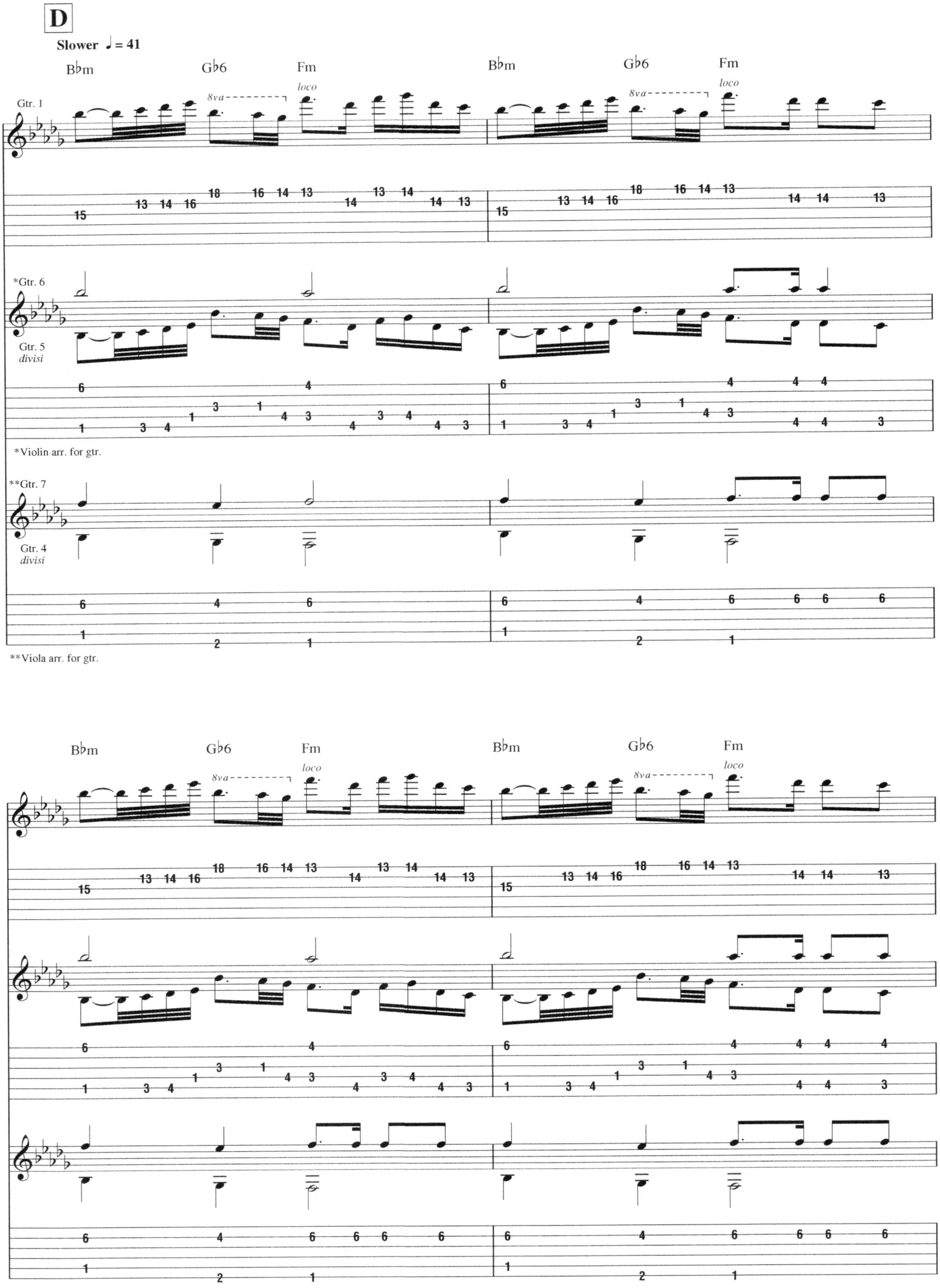

D

Slower ♩ = 41

B♭m G♭6 Fm B♭m G♭6 Fm

8va loco 8va loco

Gtr. 1

*Gtr. 6

Gtr. 5 *divisi*

*Violin arr. for gtr.

**Gtr. 7

Gtr. 4 *divisi*

**Viola arr. for gtr.

B♭m G♭6 Fm B♭m G♭6 Fm

8va loco 8va loco

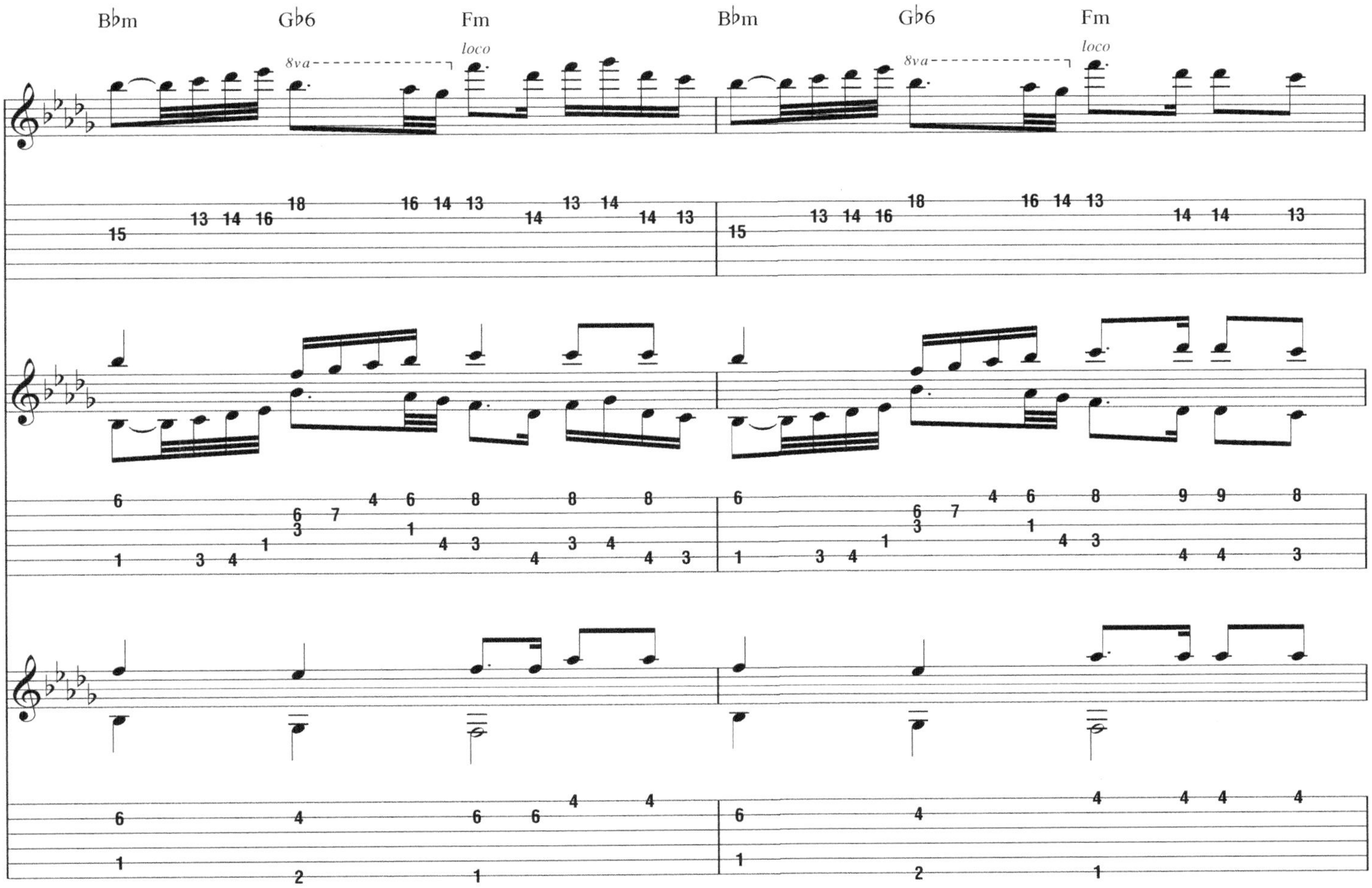

B♭m G♭6 Fm B♭m G♭6 Fm

8va loco 8va loco

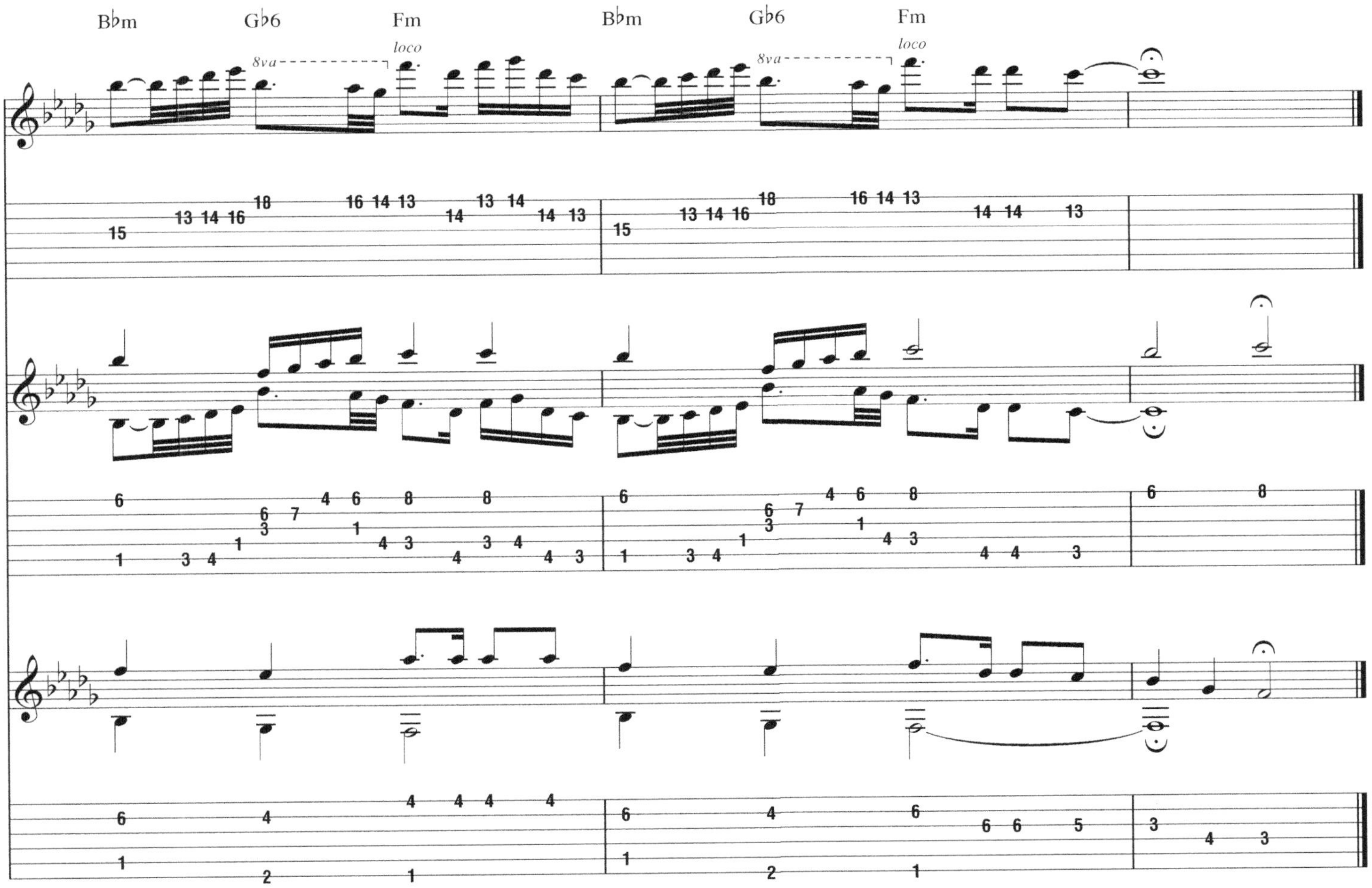

B♭m G♭6 Fm B♭m G♭6 Fm

8va loco 8va loco

Always & Never

Words and Music by Claudio Sanchez

Tune down 1/2 step, drop D tuning:
(low to high) D♭-A♭-D♭-G♭-B♭-E♭

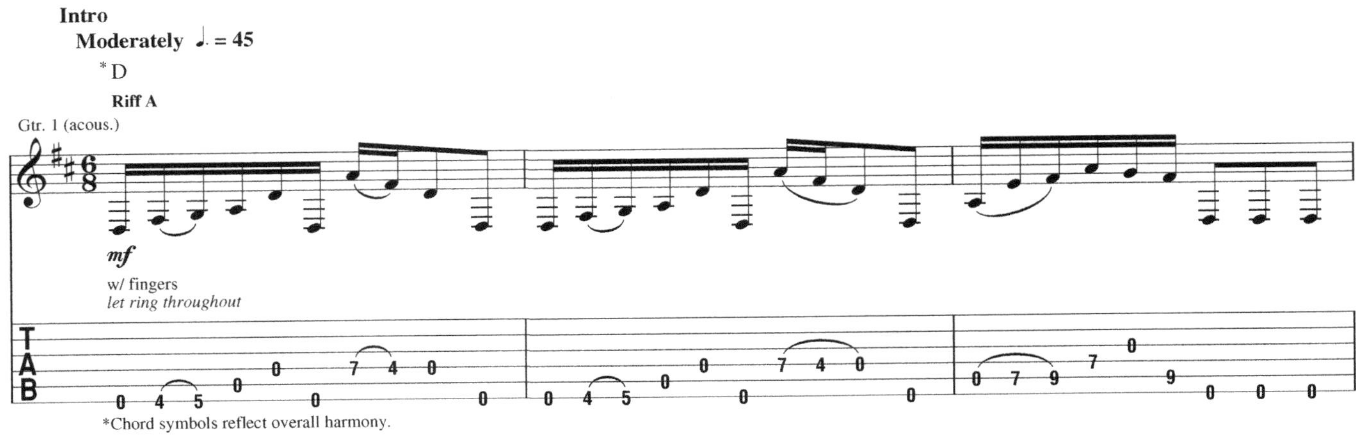

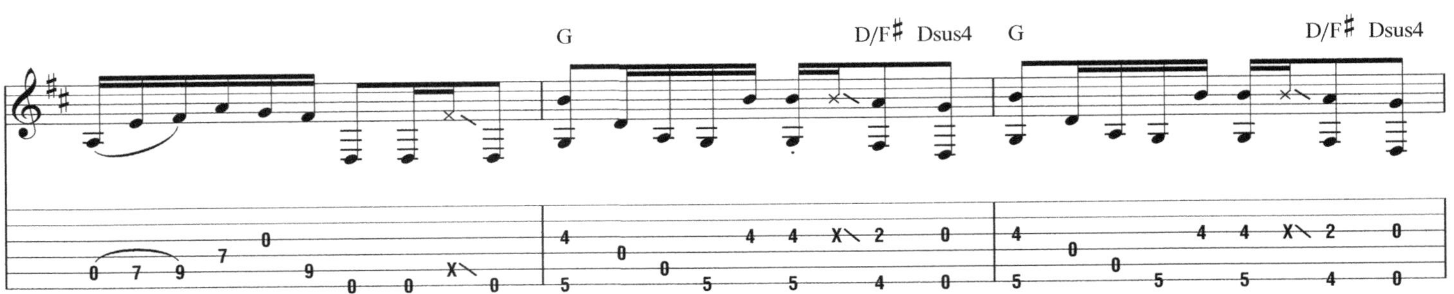

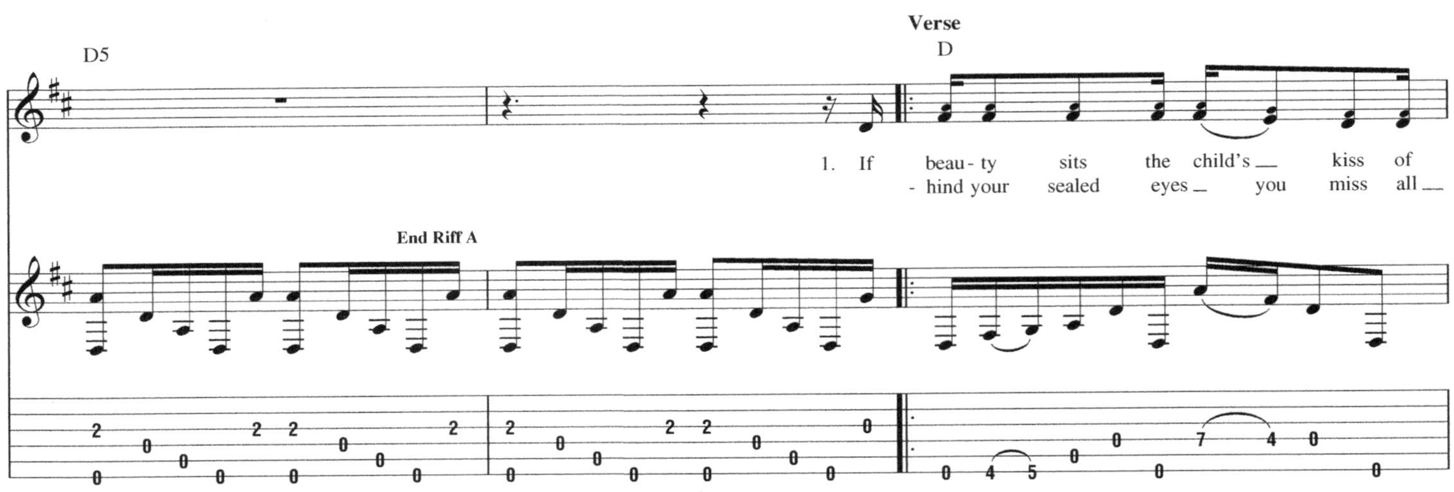

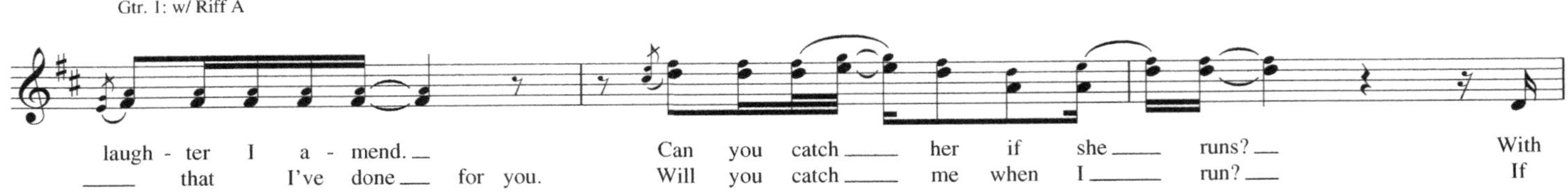

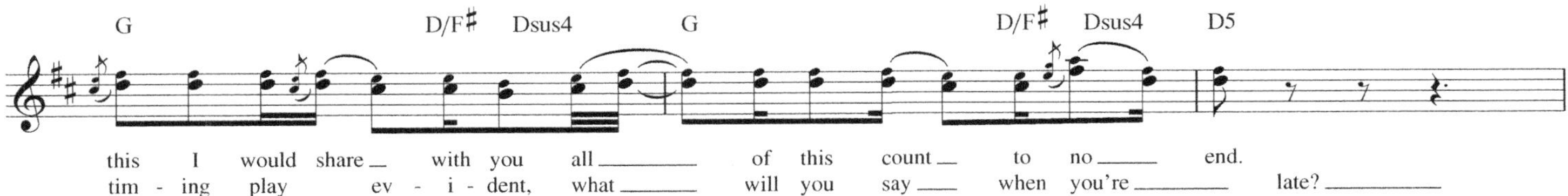
G
D/F♯
Dsus4
G
D/F♯
Dsus4
D5
this I would share with you all of this count to no end.
tim - ing play ev - i - dent, what will you say when you're late?

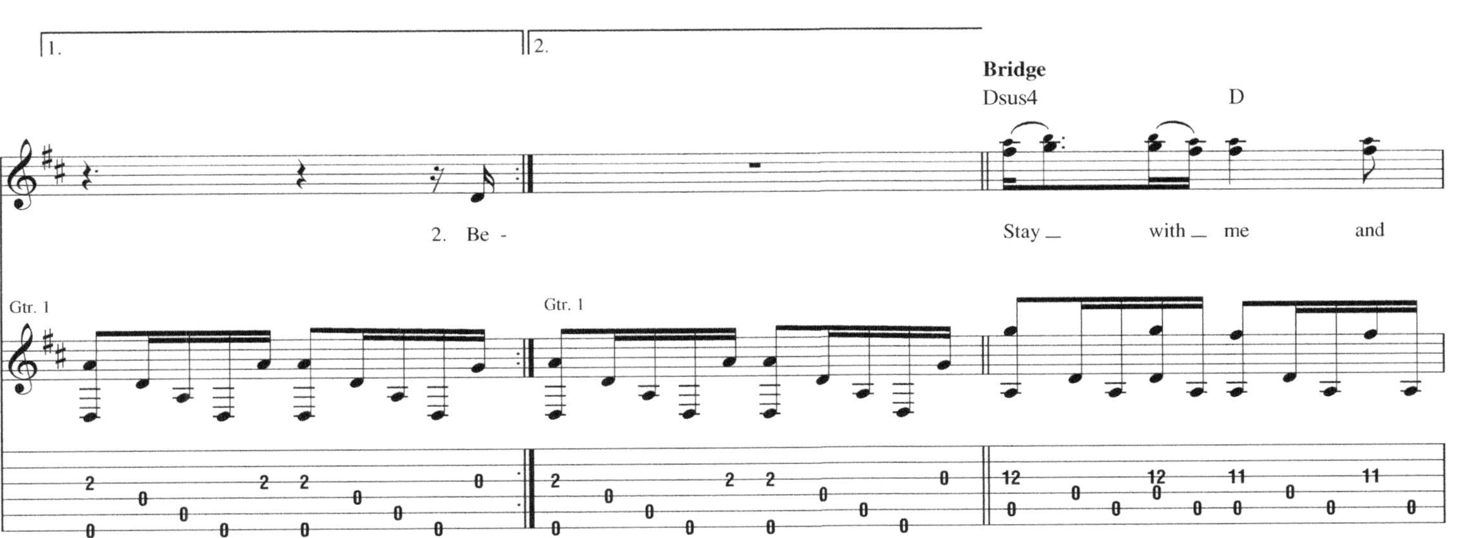
1.
2.
Bridge
Dsus4
D
2. Be -
Stay with me and
Gtr. 1
Gtr. 1

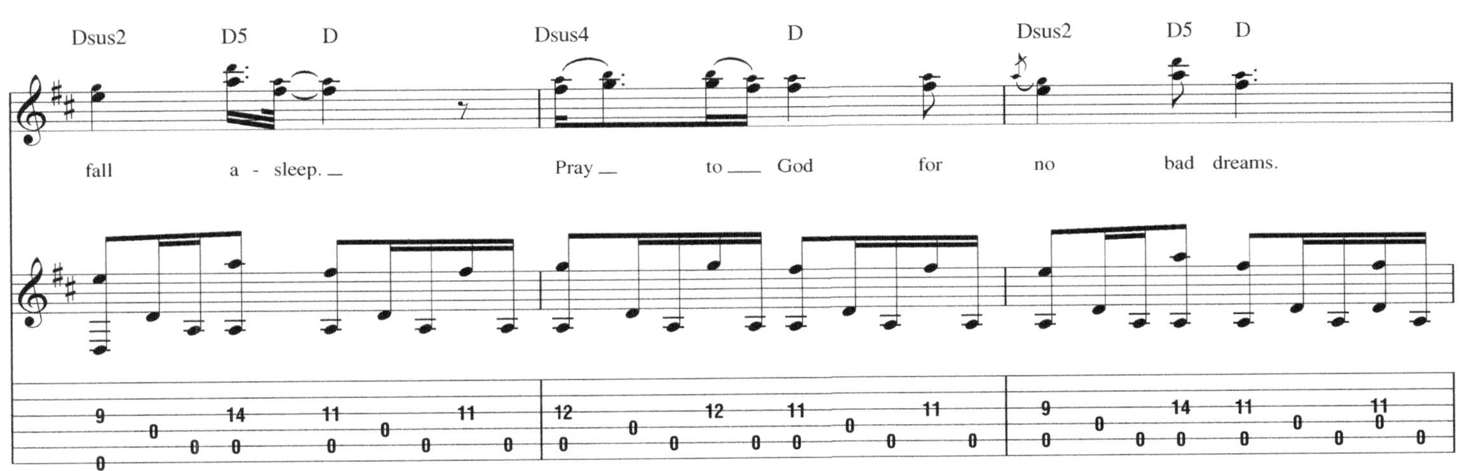
Dsus2
D5
D
Dsus4
D
Dsus2
D5
D
fall a - sleep. Pray to God for no bad dreams.

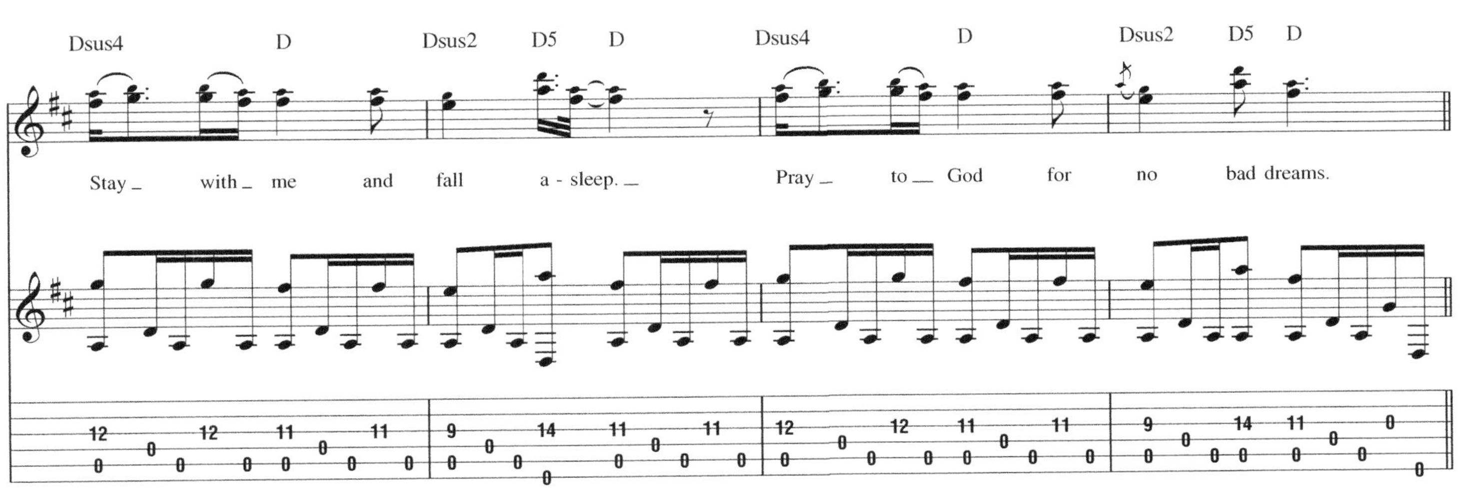
Dsus4
D
Dsus2
D5
D
Dsus4
D
Dsus2
D5
D
Stay with me and fall a - sleep. Pray to God for no bad dreams.

To Coda

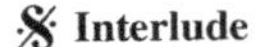

Interlude

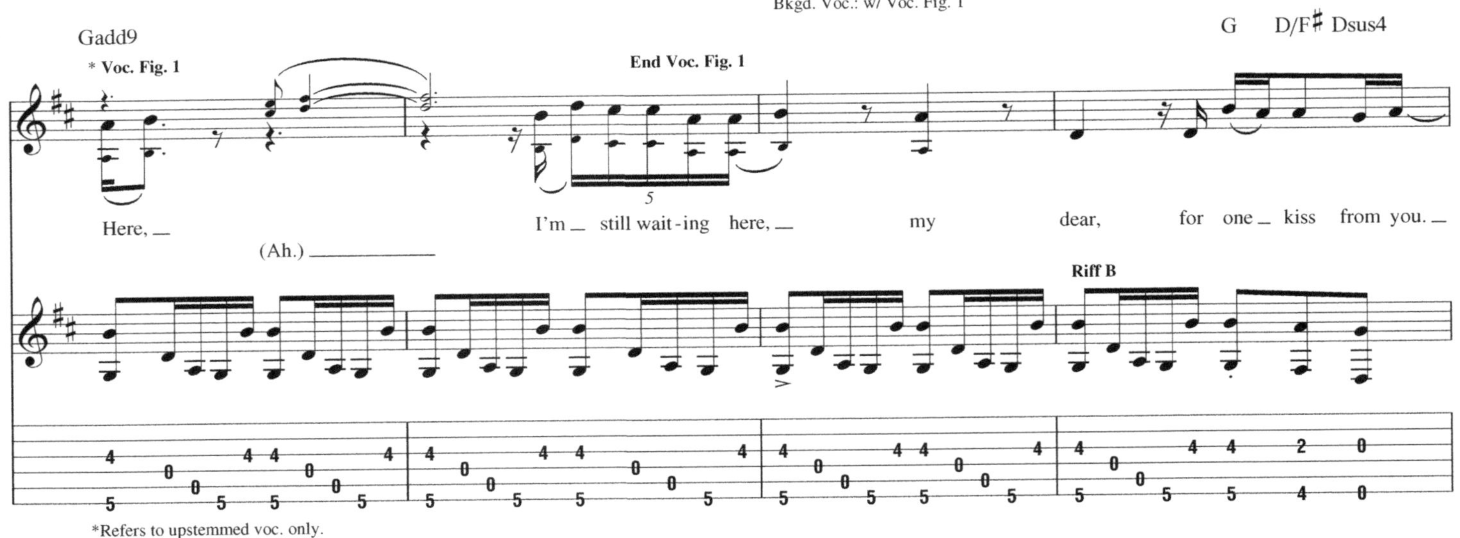

D.S. al Coda

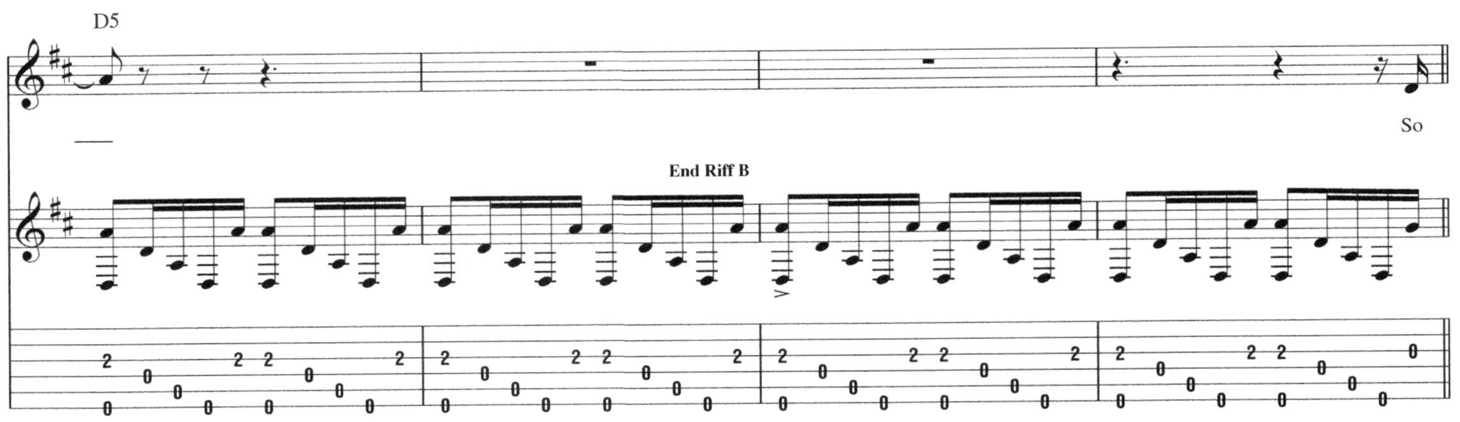

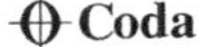

Coda

Outro

Gtr. 1: w/ Riff B

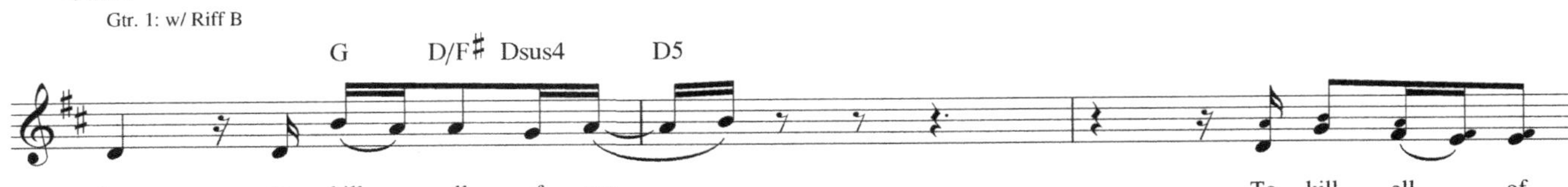

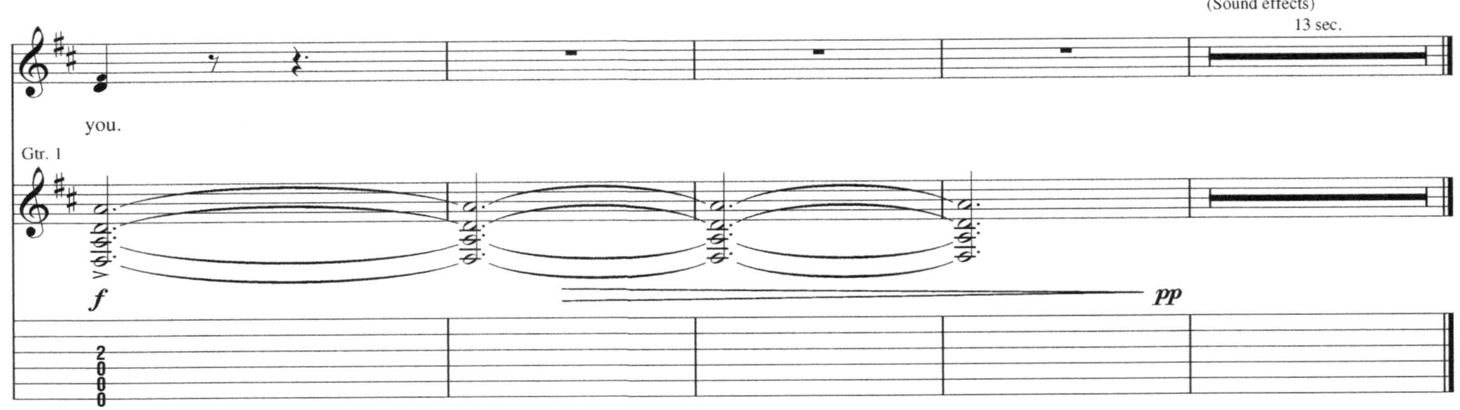

Welcome Home

Words and Music by Claudio Sanchez, Michael Todd, Joshua Eppard and Travis Stever

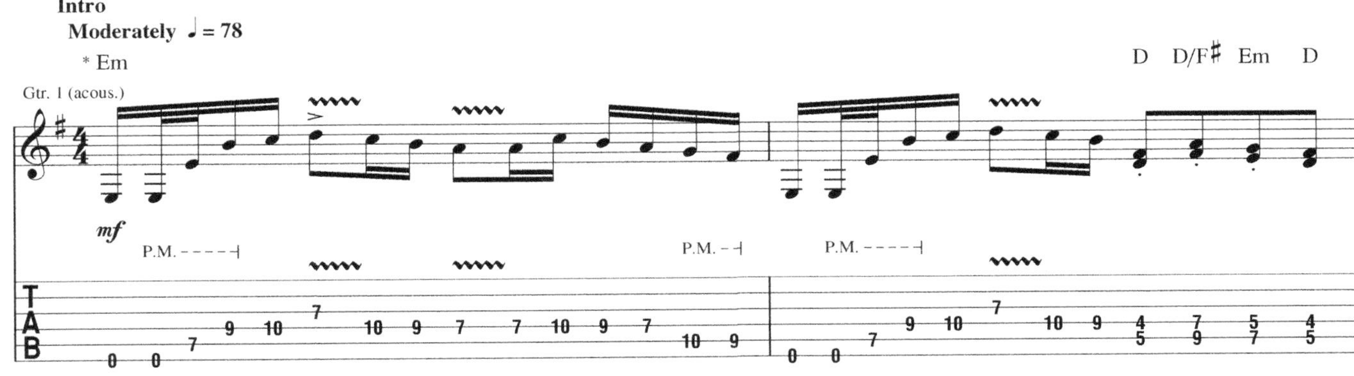

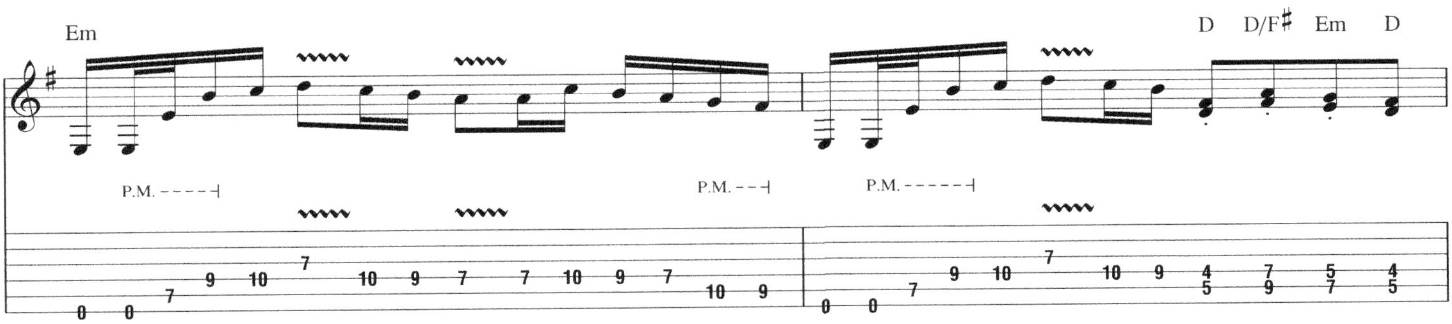

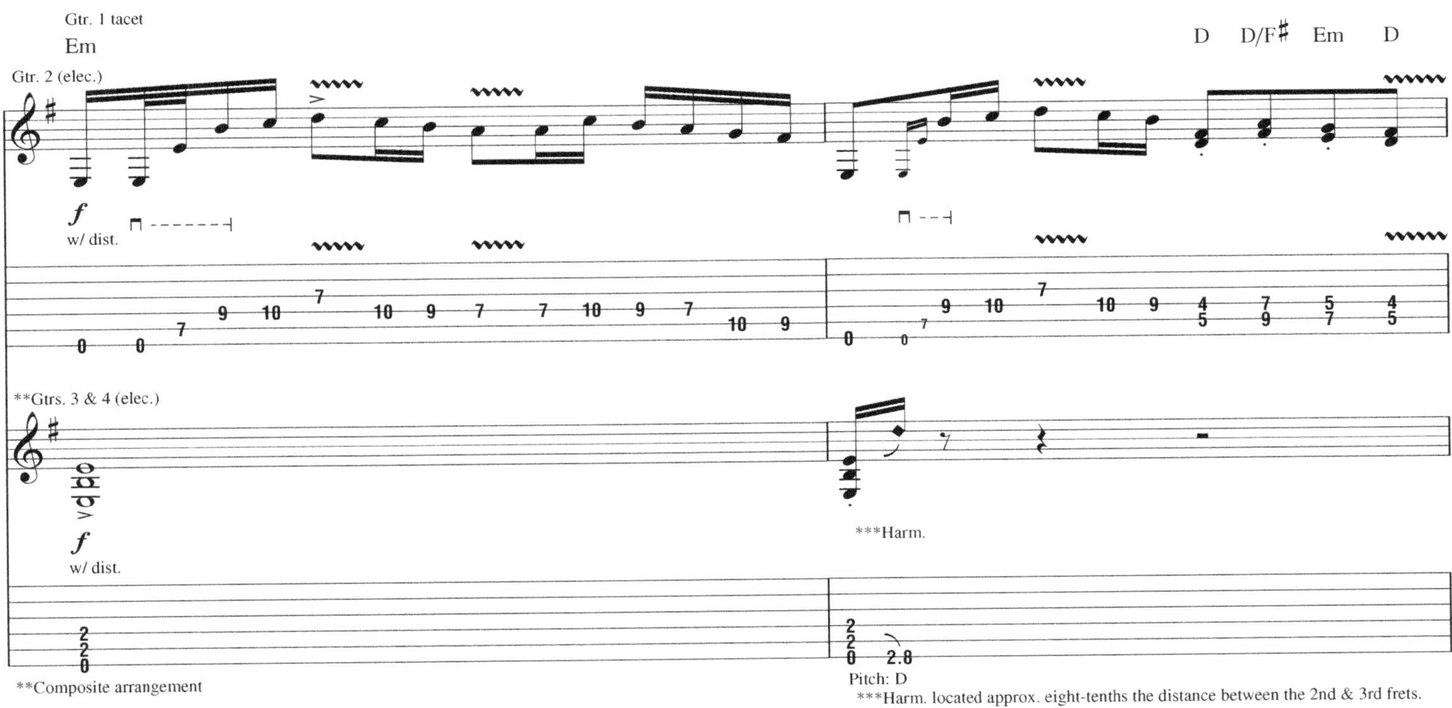

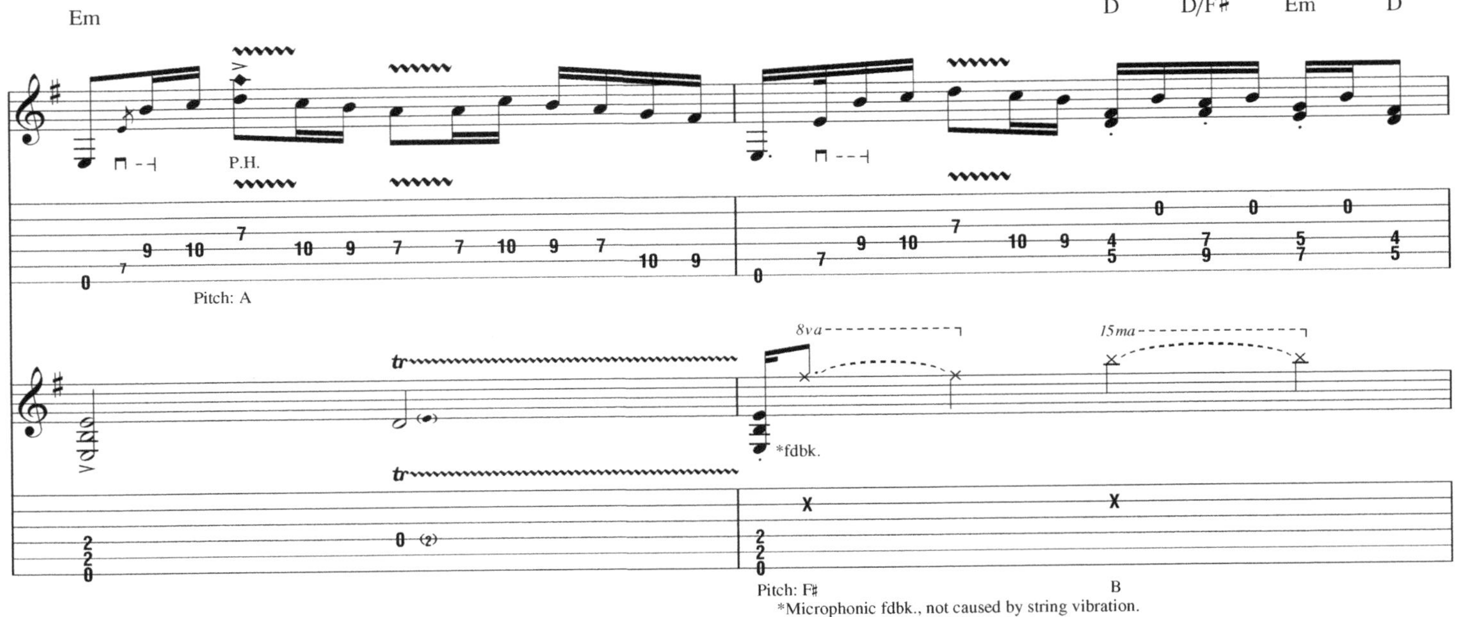
Em
D
D/F♯
Em
D
P.H.
Pitch: A
8va
15ma
tr
*fdbk.
Pitch: F♯
B
*Microphonic fdbk., not caused by string vibration.

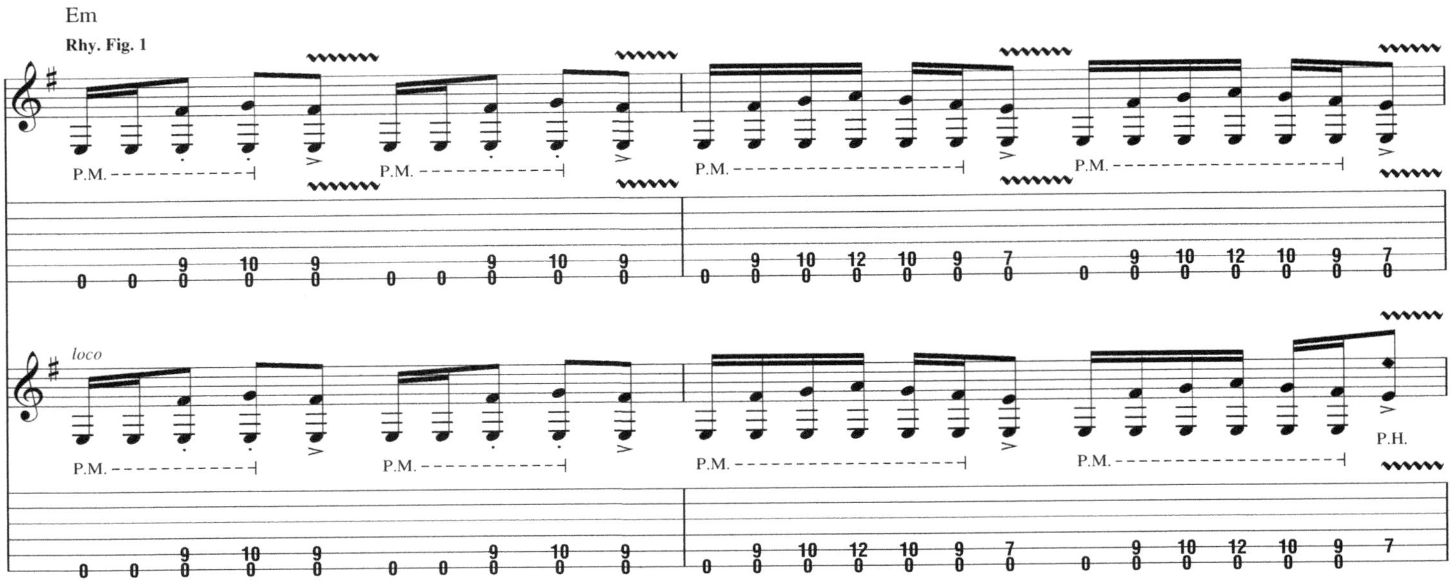
Em
Rhy. Fig. 1
P.M.
loco
P.H.

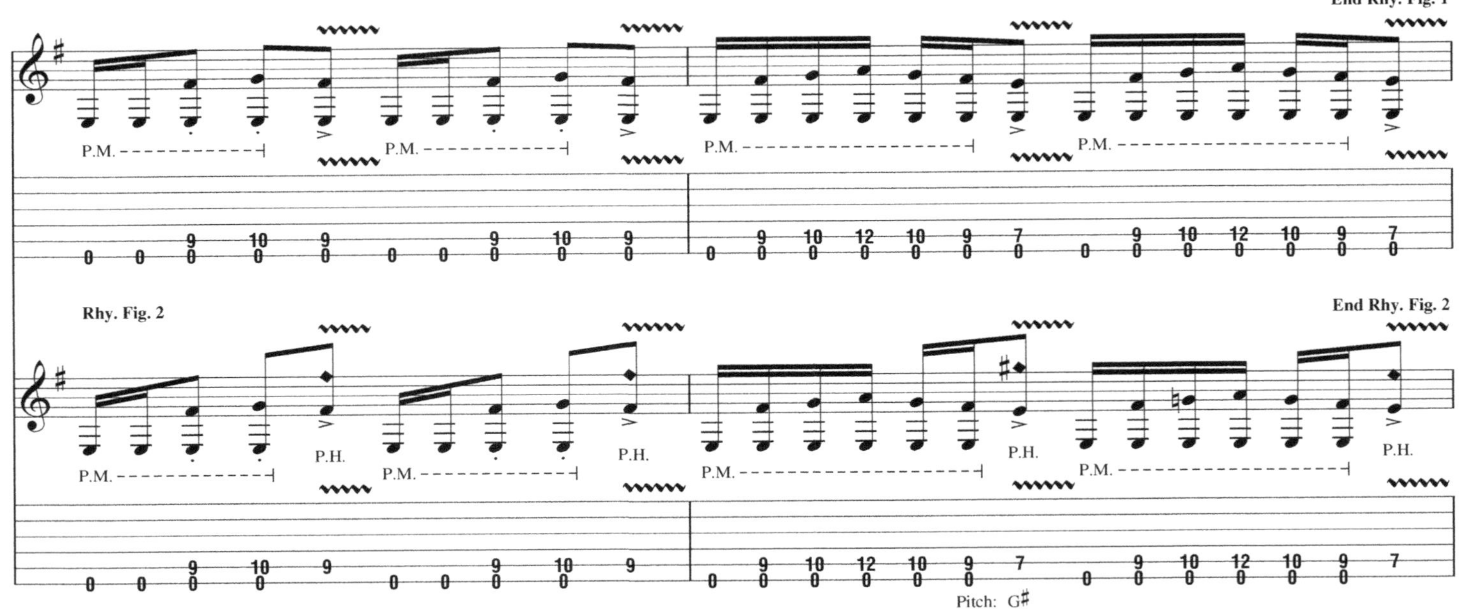
End Rhy. Fig. 1
P.M.
Rhy. Fig. 2
End Rhy. Fig. 2
P.H.
Pitch: G♯

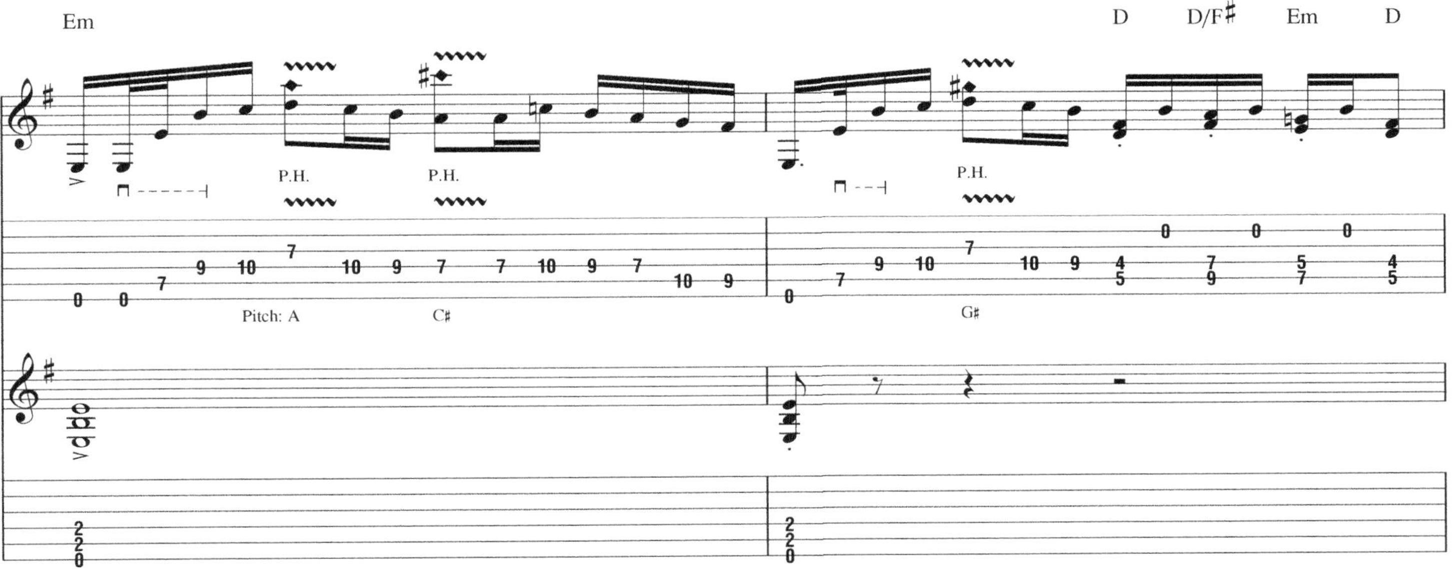
Em
D
D/F♯
Em
D
P.H.
P.H.
P.H.
Pitch: A
C♯
G♯

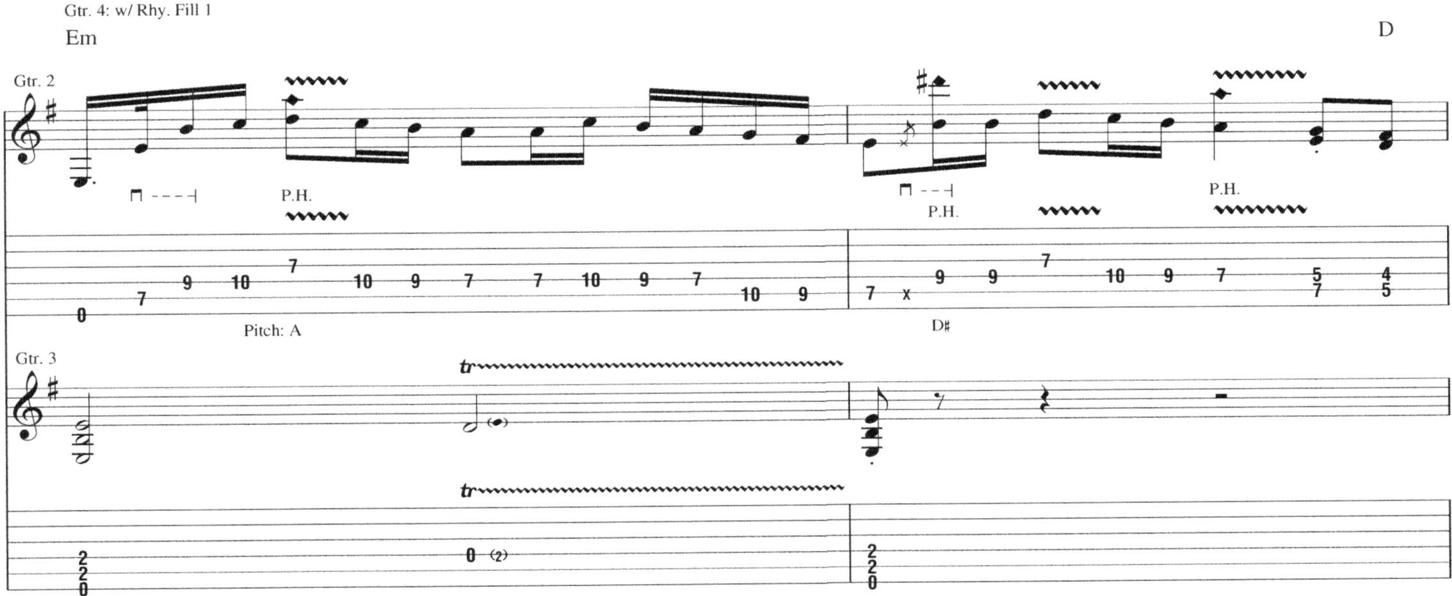
Gtr. 4: w/ Rhy. Fill 1
Em
D
Gtr. 2
P.H.
P.H.
P.H.
Pitch: A
D♯
Gtr. 3

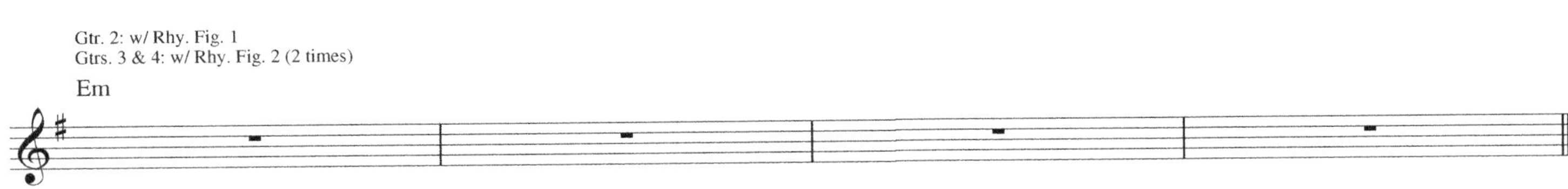
Gtr. 2: w/ Rhy. Fig. 1
Gtrs. 3 & 4: w/ Rhy. Fig. 2 (2 times)
Em

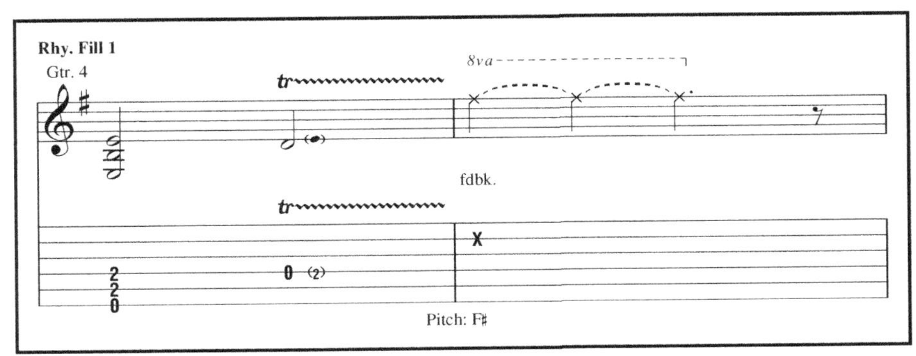
Rhy. Fill 1
Gtr. 4
8va
fdbk.
Pitch: F♯

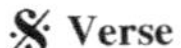
Verse

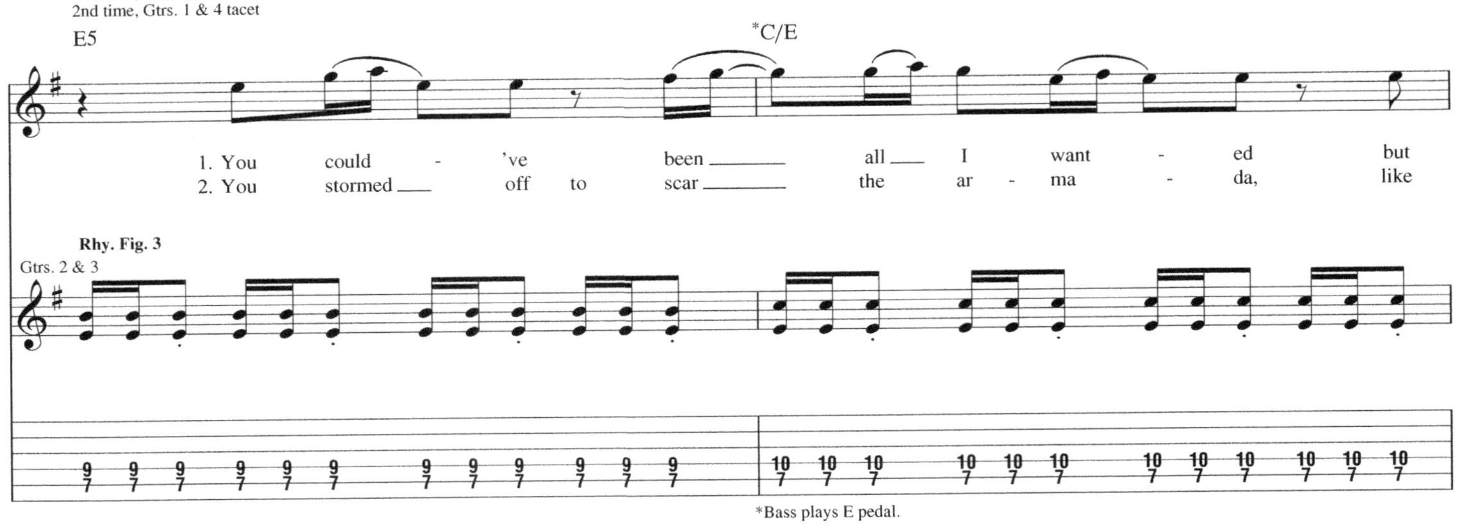
2nd time, Lead Voc.: w/ Voc. Fill 1
2nd time, Gtrs. 1 & 4 tacet
E5
*C/E
1. You could - 've been all I want - ed but
2. You stormed off to scar the ar - ma - da, like
Rhy. Fig. 3
Gtrs. 2 & 3
*Bass plays E pedal.

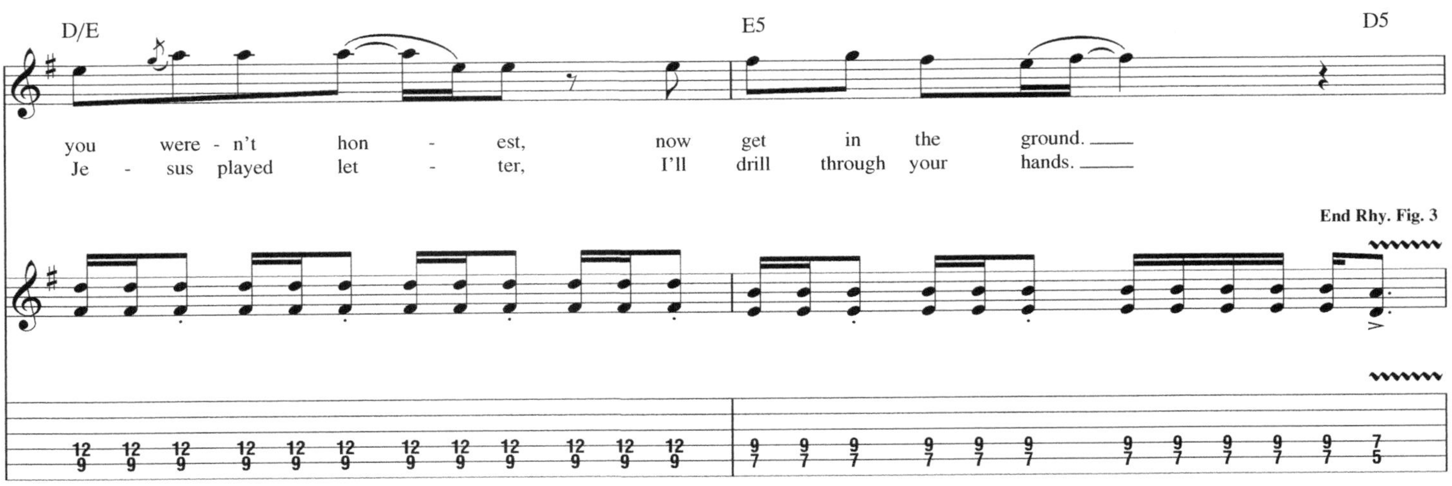
D/E
E5
D5
you were - n't hon - est, now get in the ground.
Je - sus played let - ter, I'll drill through your hands.
End Rhy. Fig. 3

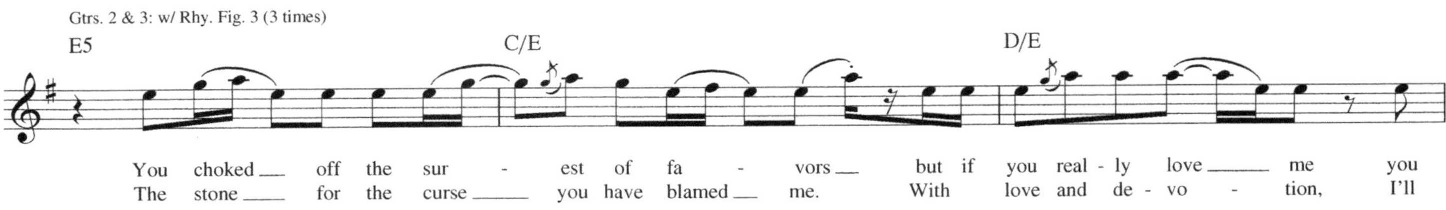
Gtrs. 2 & 3: w/ Rhy. Fig. 3 (3 times)
E5
C/E
D/E
You choked off the sur - est of fa - vors but if you real - ly love me you
The stone for the curse you have blamed me. With love and de - vo - tion, I'll

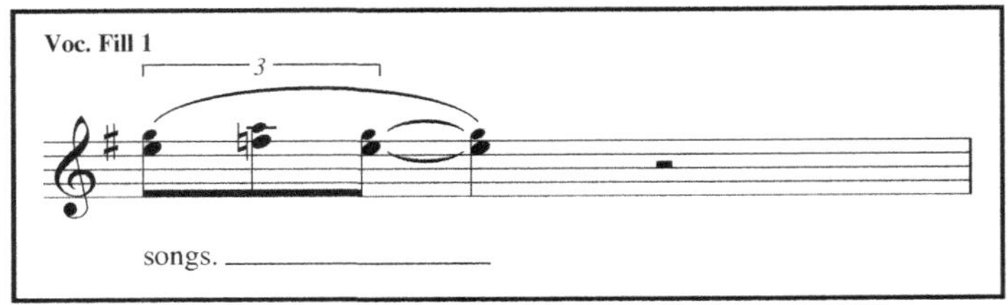
Voc. Fill 1
3
songs.

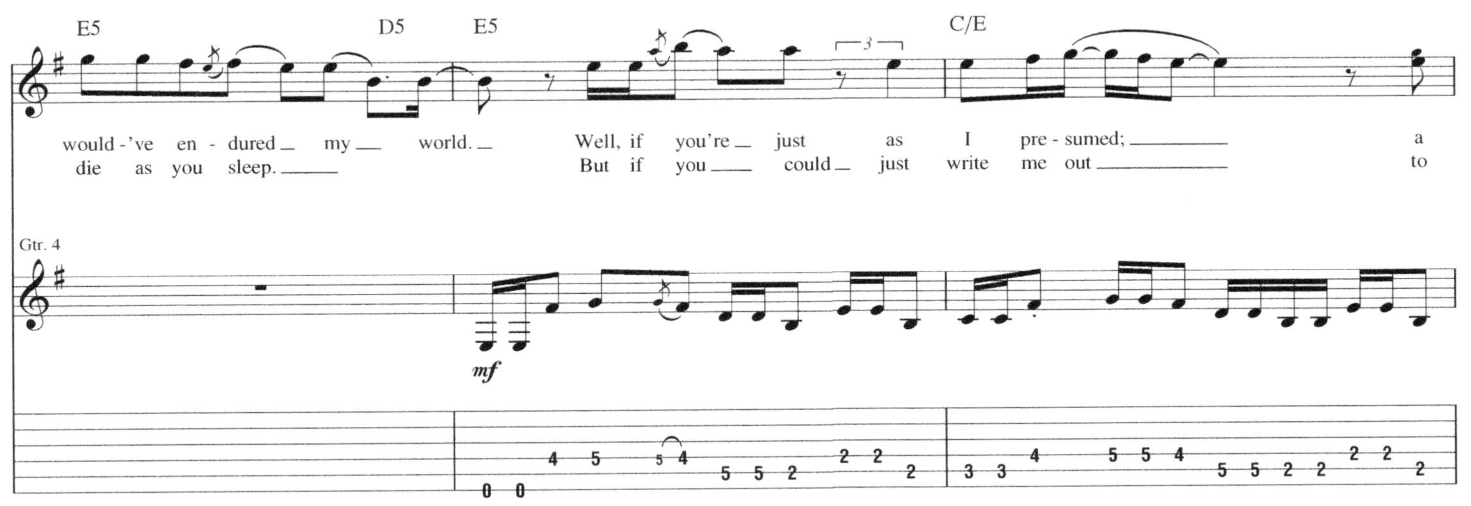
E5
D5
E5
C/E
would-'ve en-dured my world.
Well, if you're just as I pre-sumed;
a
die as you sleep.
But if you could just write me out
to
Gtr. 4
mf

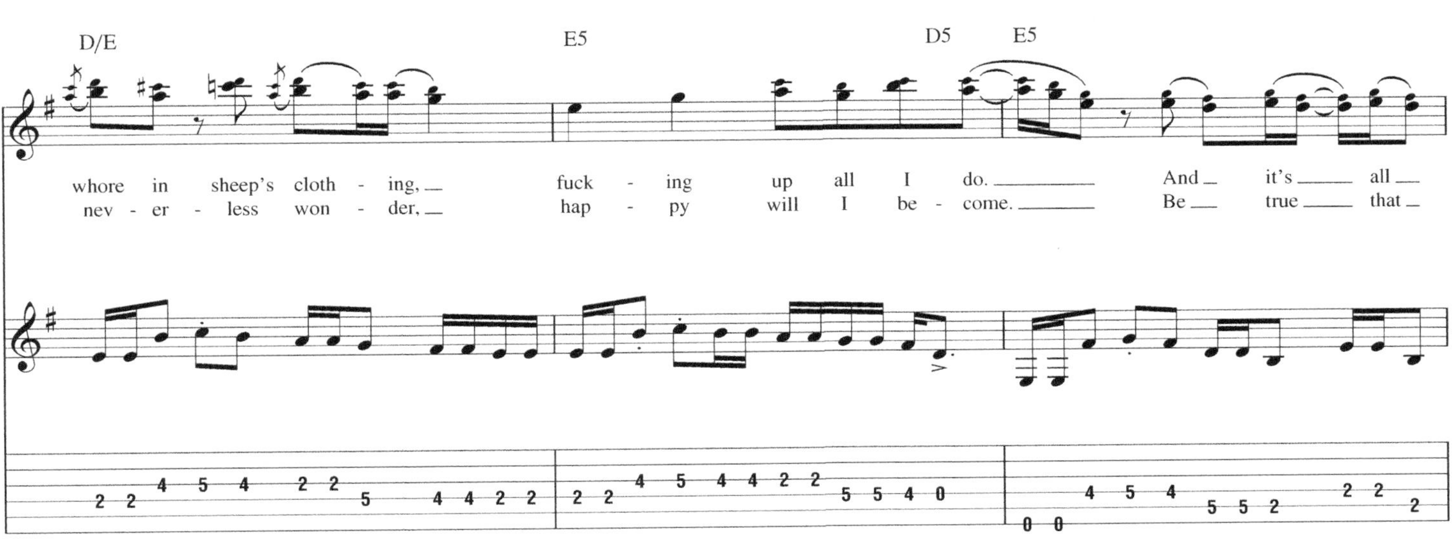
D/E
E5
D5
E5
whore in sheep's cloth-ing,
fuck-ing up all I do.
And it's all
nev-er-less won-der,
hap-py will I be-come.
Be true that

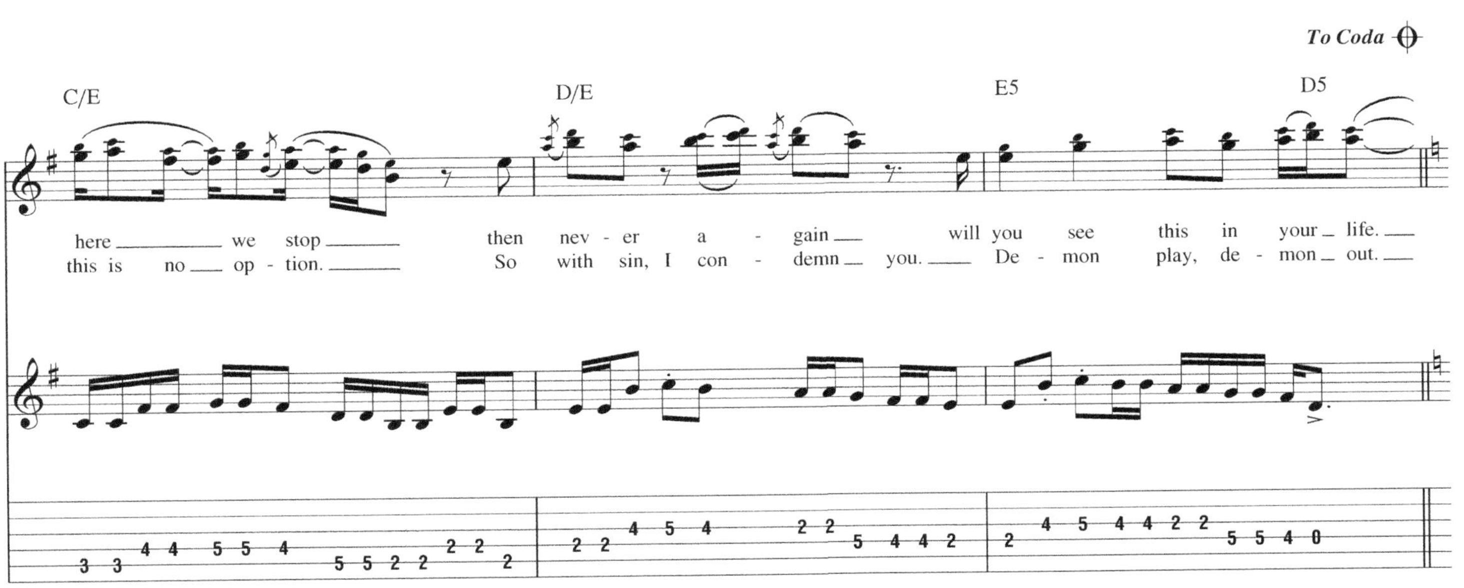
To Coda
C/E
D/E
E5
D5
here we stop
then nev-er a-gain will you see this in your life.
this is no op-tion.
So with sin, I con-demn you. De-mon play, de-mon out.

Chorus

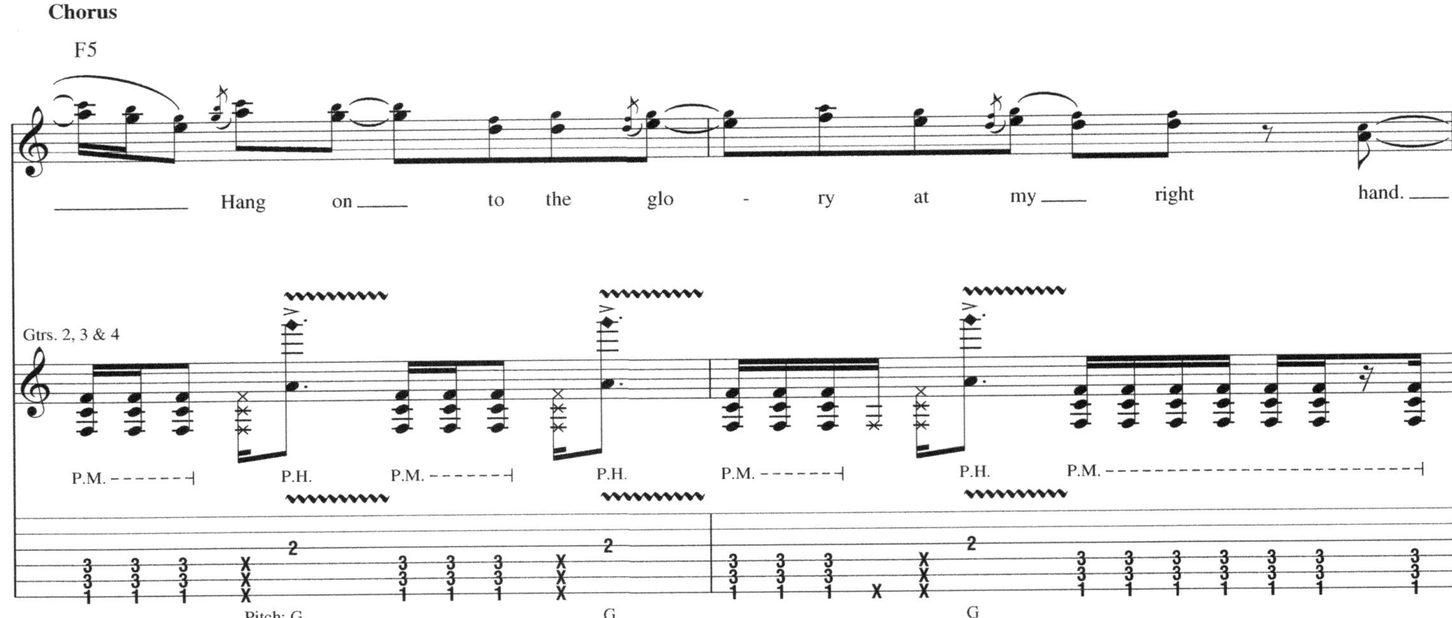
F5
Hang on to the glo - ry at my right hand.
Gtrs. 2, 3 & 4
P.M.
P.H.
Pitch: G
G
G

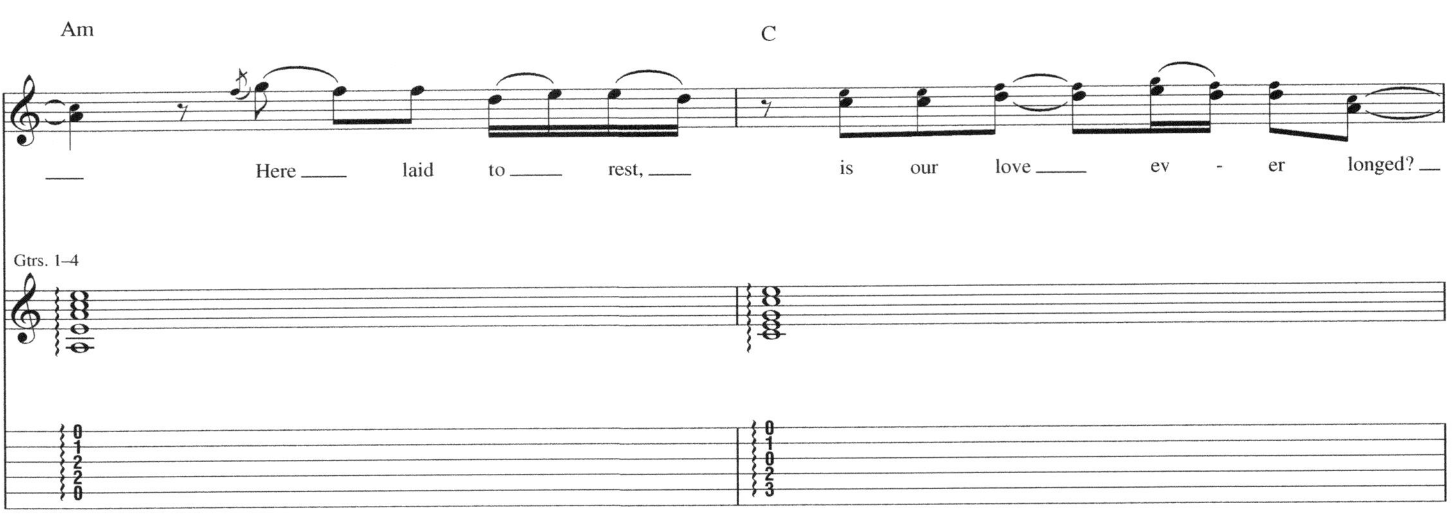
Am
C
Here laid to rest, is our love ev - er longed?
Gtrs. 1–4

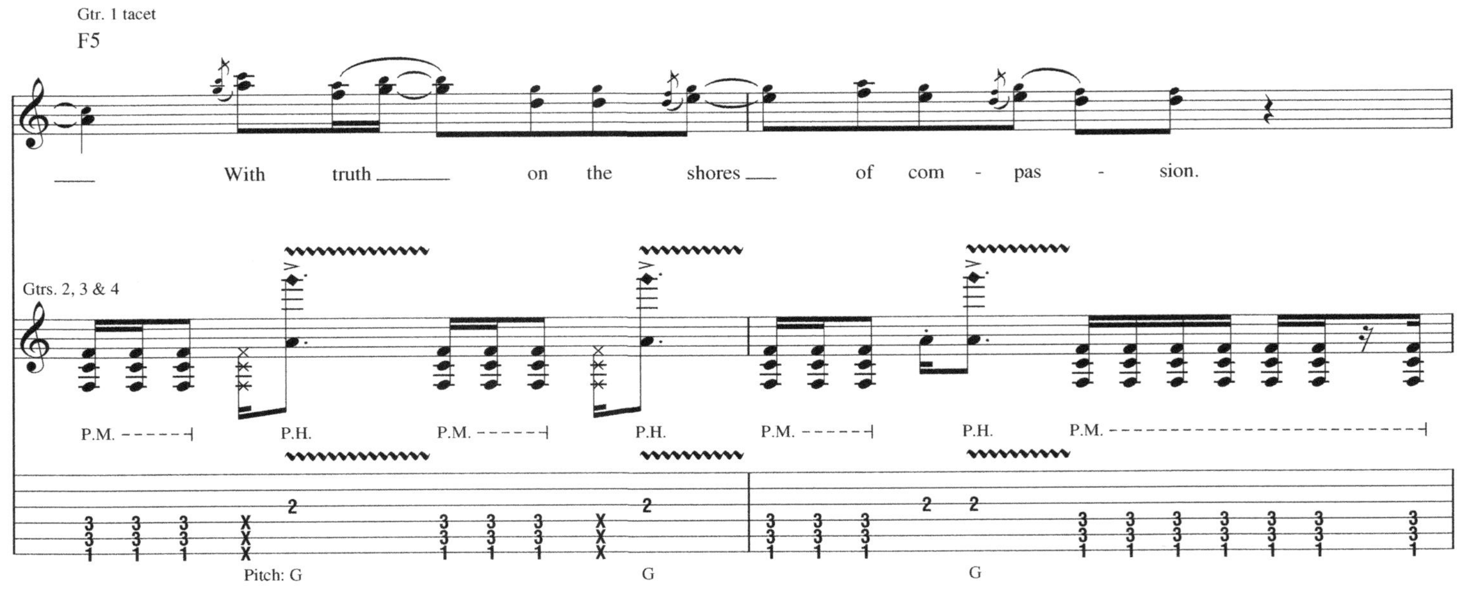
Gtr. 1 tacet
F5
With truth on the shores of com - pas - sion.
Gtrs. 2, 3 & 4
P.M.
P.H.
Pitch: G
G
G

D.S. al Coda

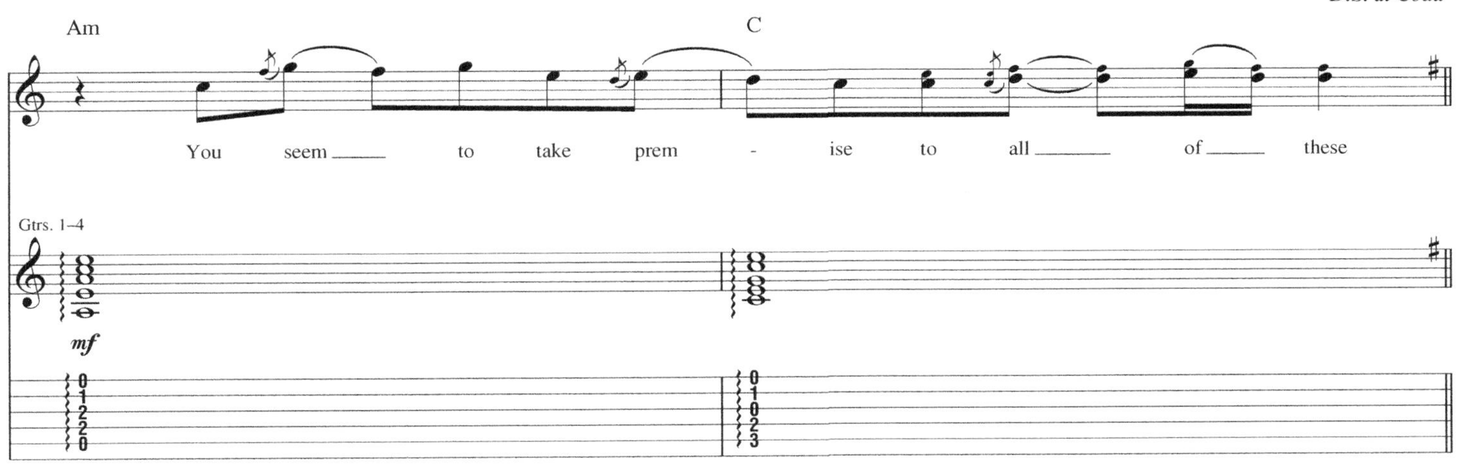

Coda

Chorus

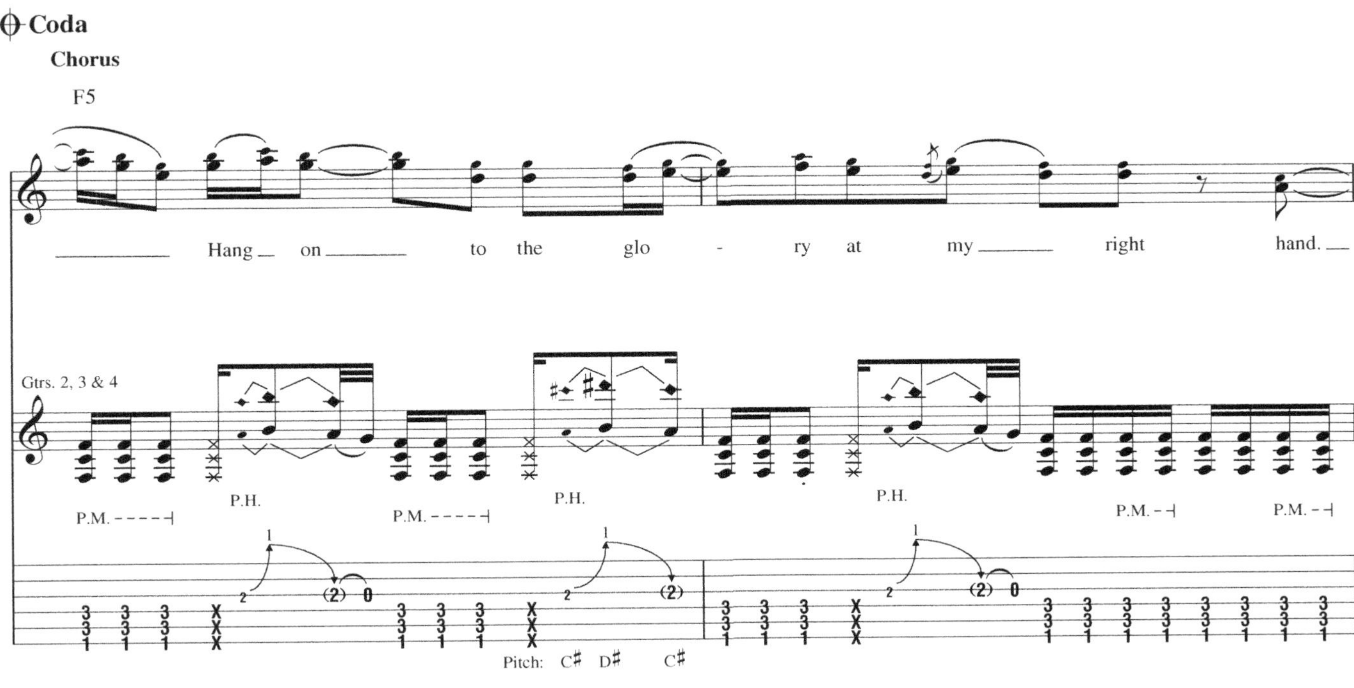

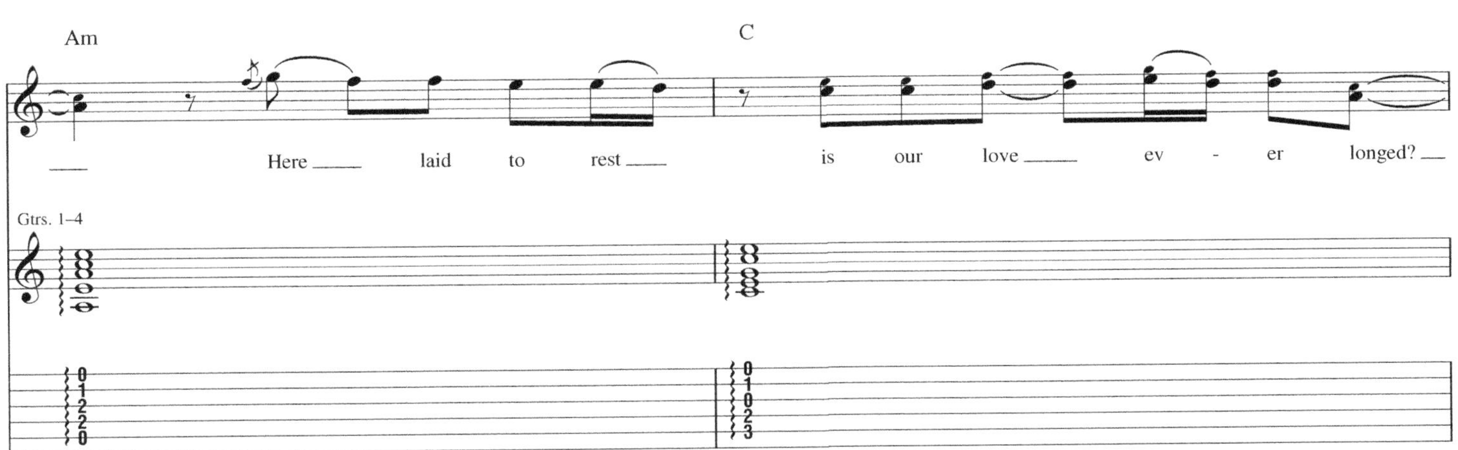

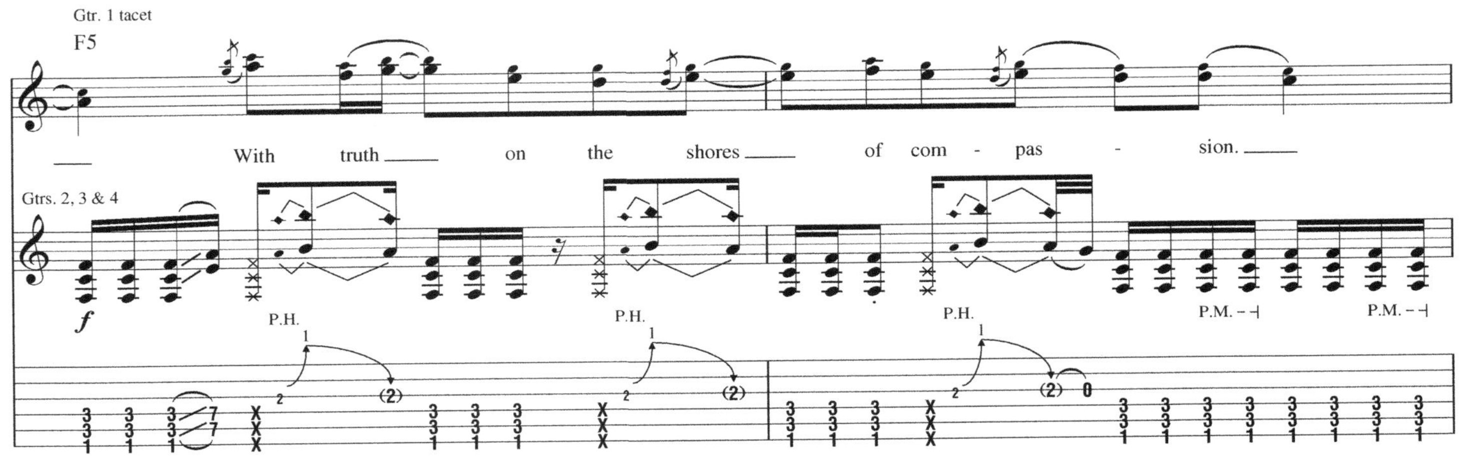

Gtr. 1 tacet
F5
With truth on the shores of com - pas - sion.
Gtrs. 2, 3 & 4
P.H.
P.H.
P.H.
P.M.
P.M.

Bridge

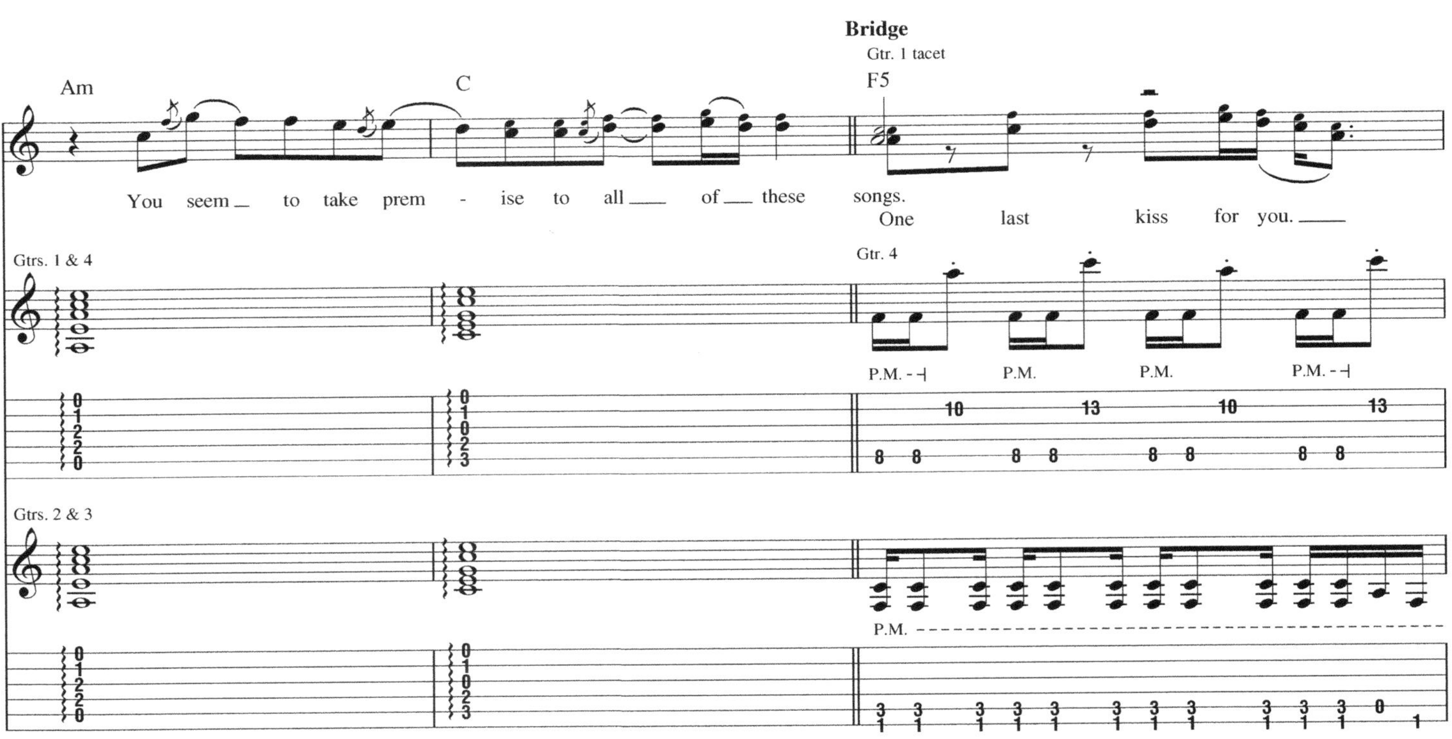

Am
C
Gtr. 1 tacet
F5
You seem to take prem - ise to all of these songs.
One last kiss for you.
Gtrs. 1 & 4
Gtr. 4
P.M.
P.M.
P.M.
P.M.
Gtrs. 2 & 3
P.M.

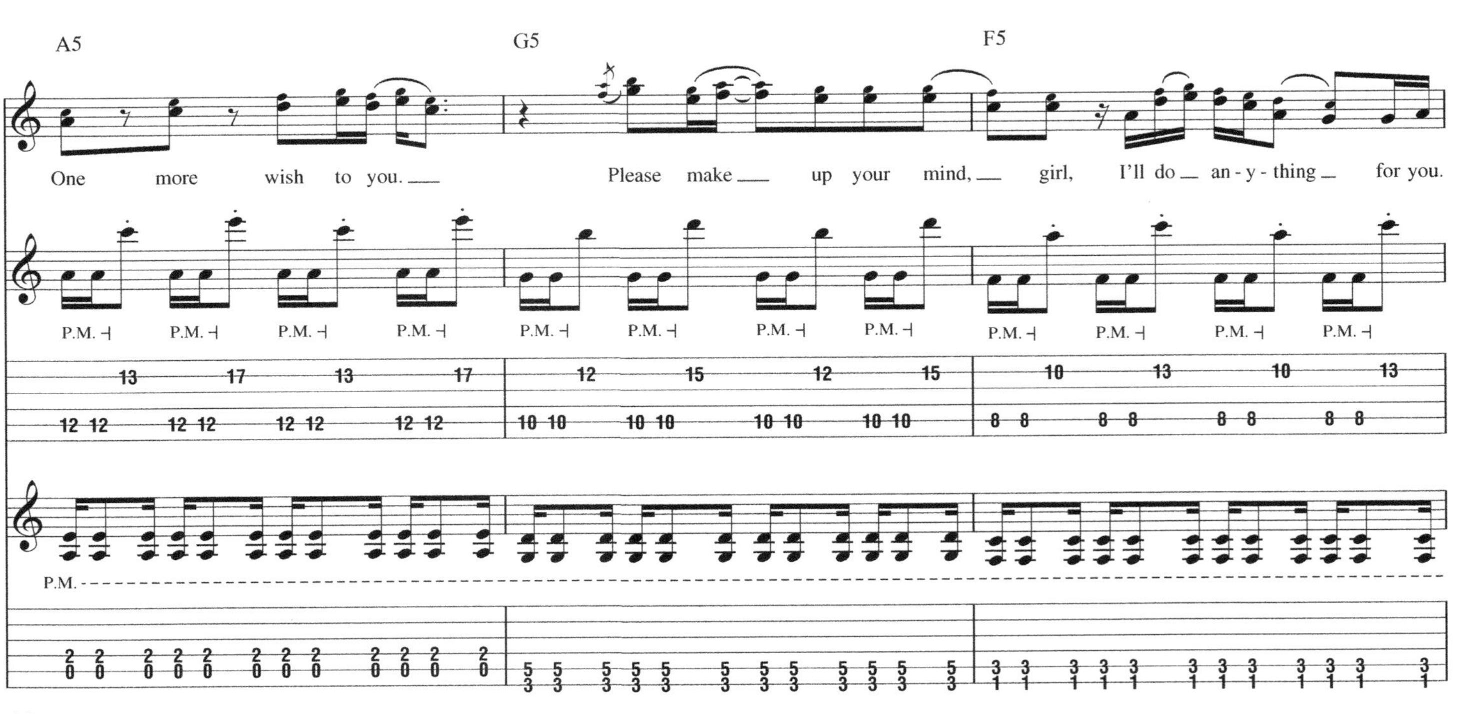

A5
G5
F5
One more wish to you.
Please make up your mind, girl, I'll do an - y - thing for you.
P.M.

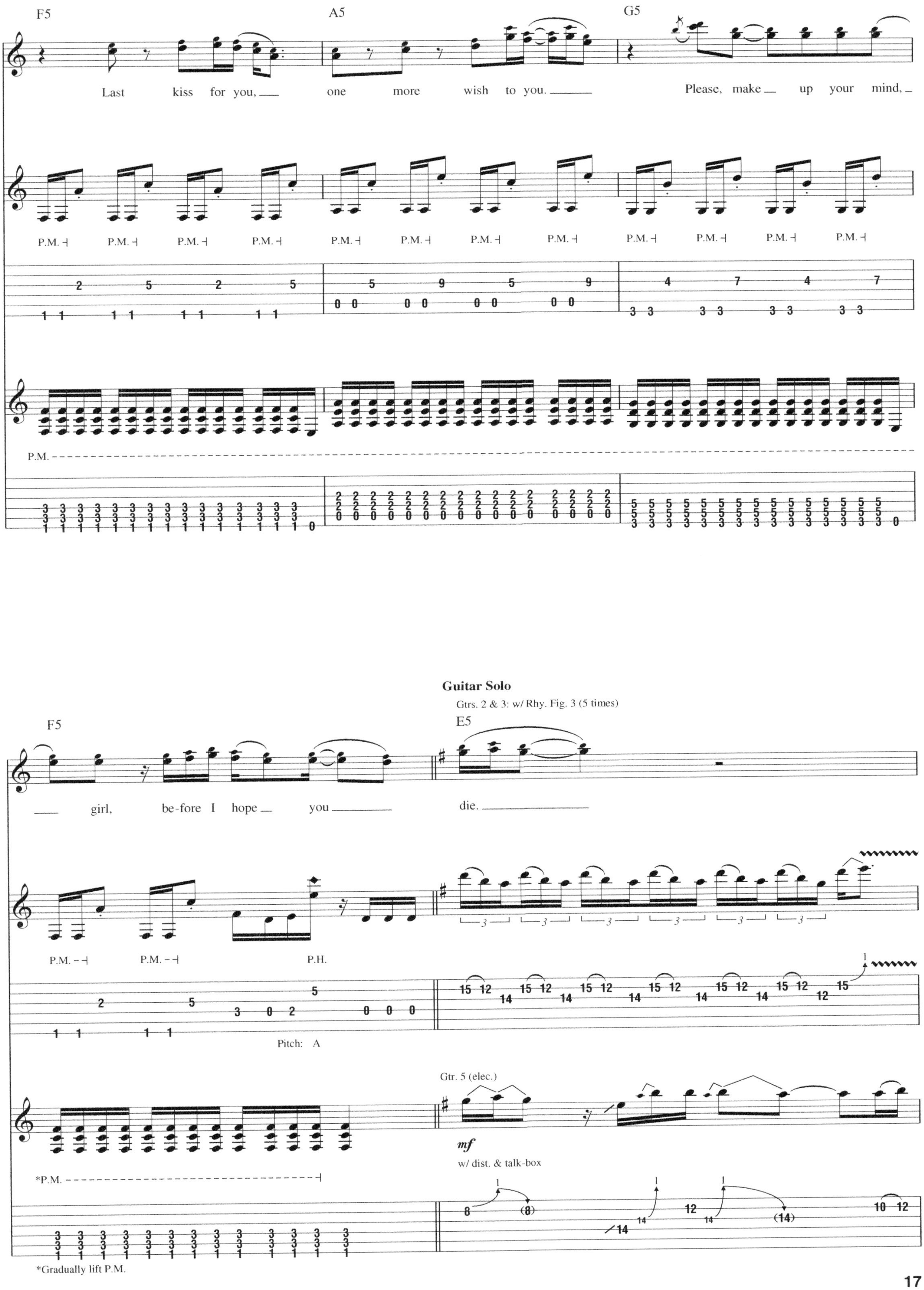

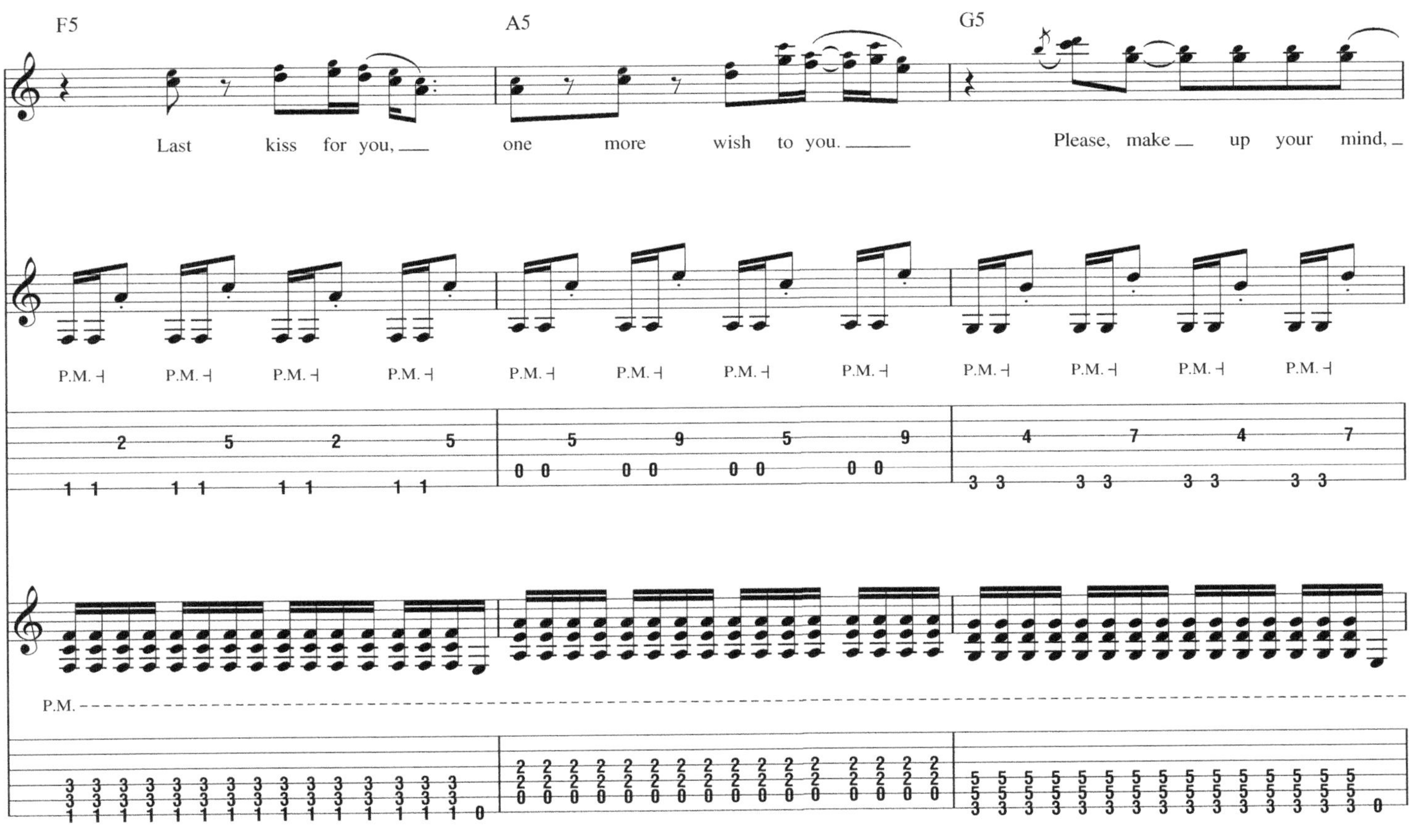

F5

Guitar Solo

Gtrs. 2 & 3: w/ Rhy. Fig. 3 (5 times)

E5

girl, be-fore I hope you die.

P.M. P.M. P.H.

Pitch: A

Gtr. 5 (elec.)

mf

w/ dist. & talk-box

*P.M.

*Gradually lift P.M.

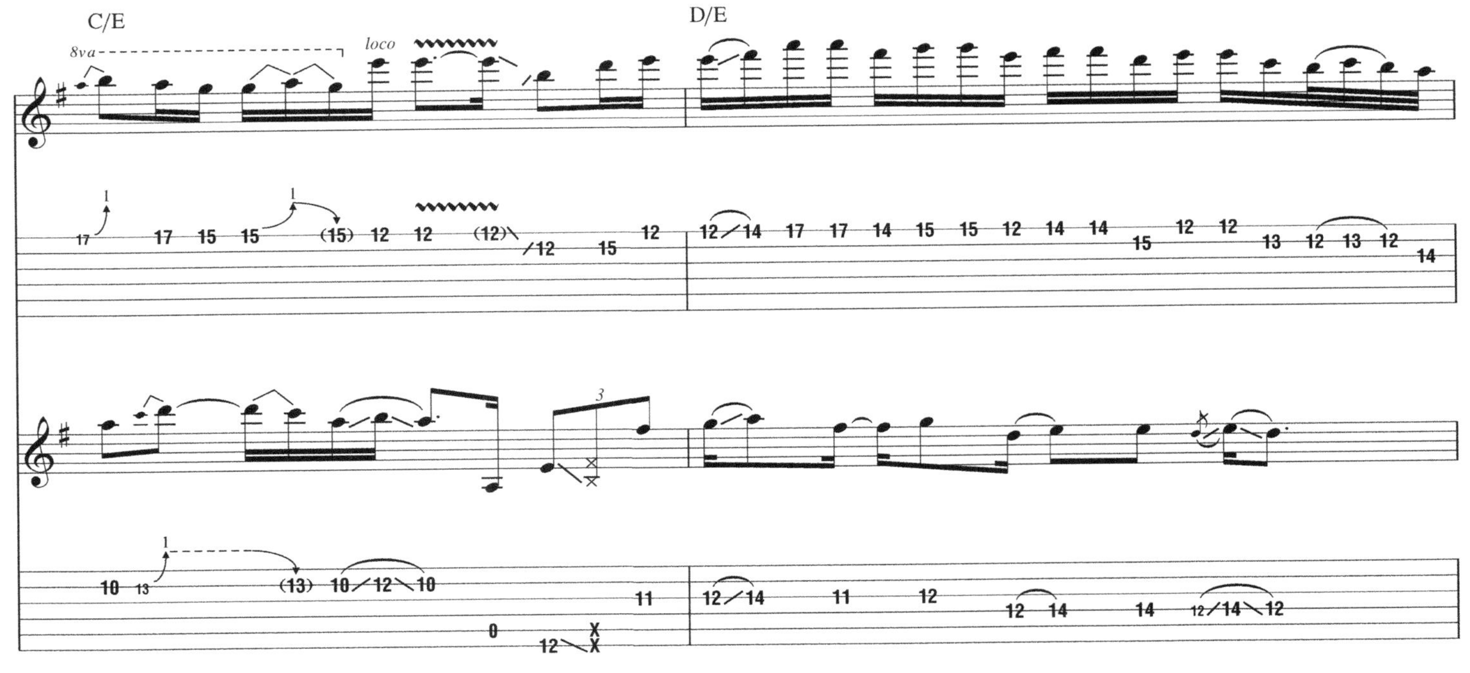
C/E
8va
loco
D/E

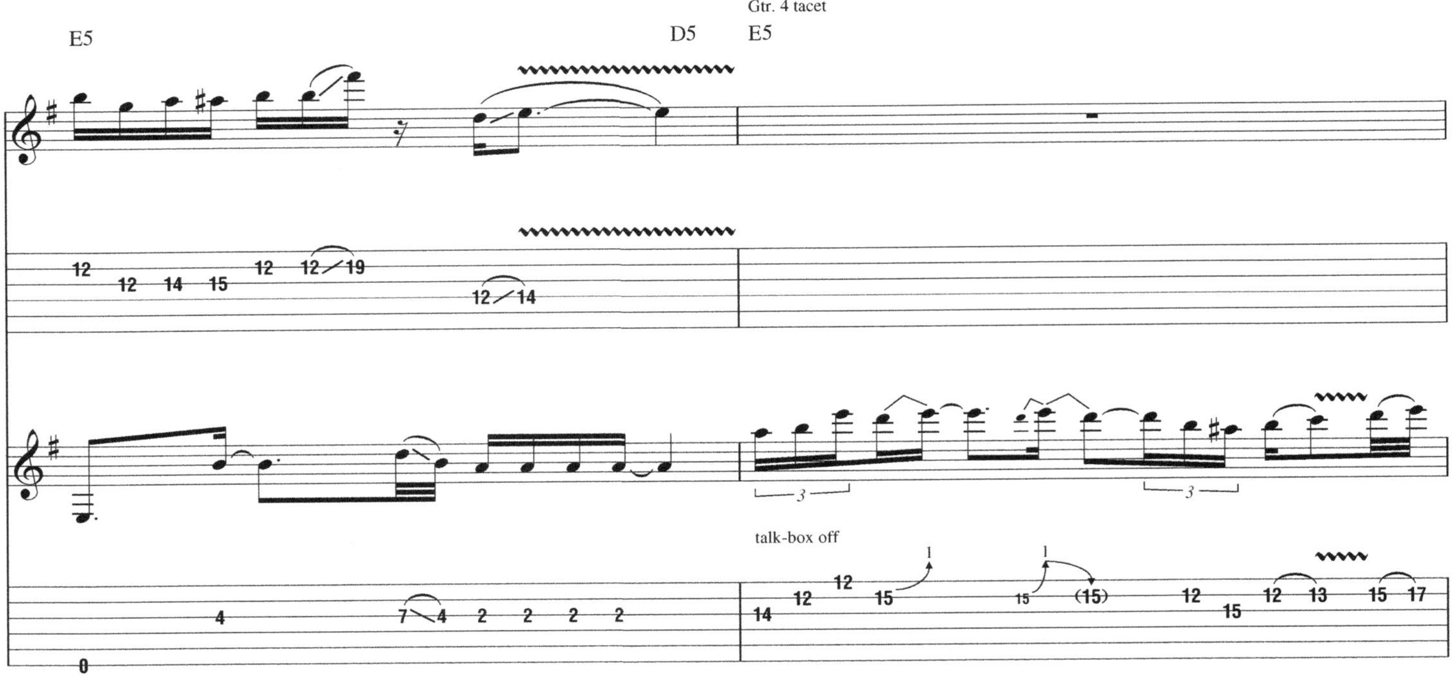
E5
D5
Gtr. 4 tacet
E5
talk-box off

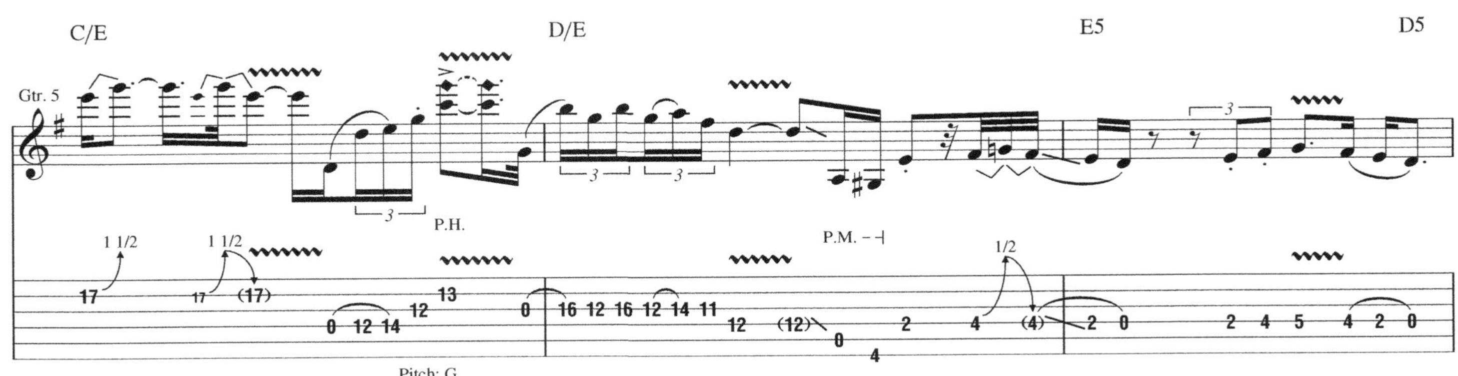
C/E
D/E
E5
D5
Gtr. 5
P.H.
P.M.
Pitch: G

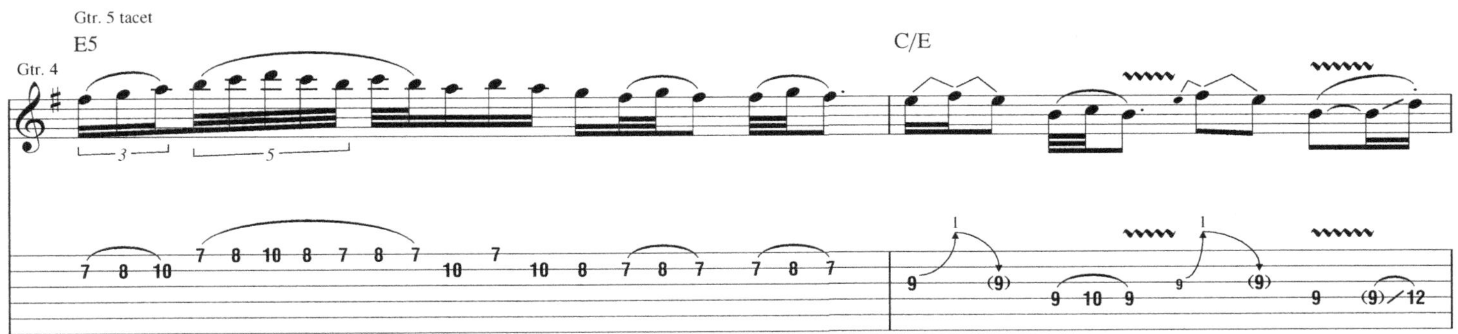
Gtr. 5 tacet
E5
C/E
Gtr. 4

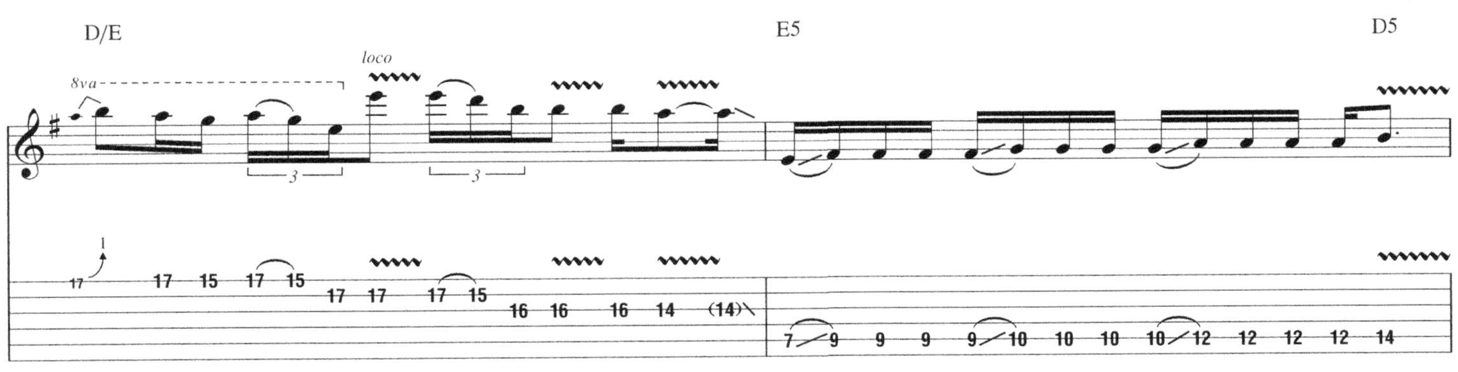
D/E
E5
D5
8va
loco

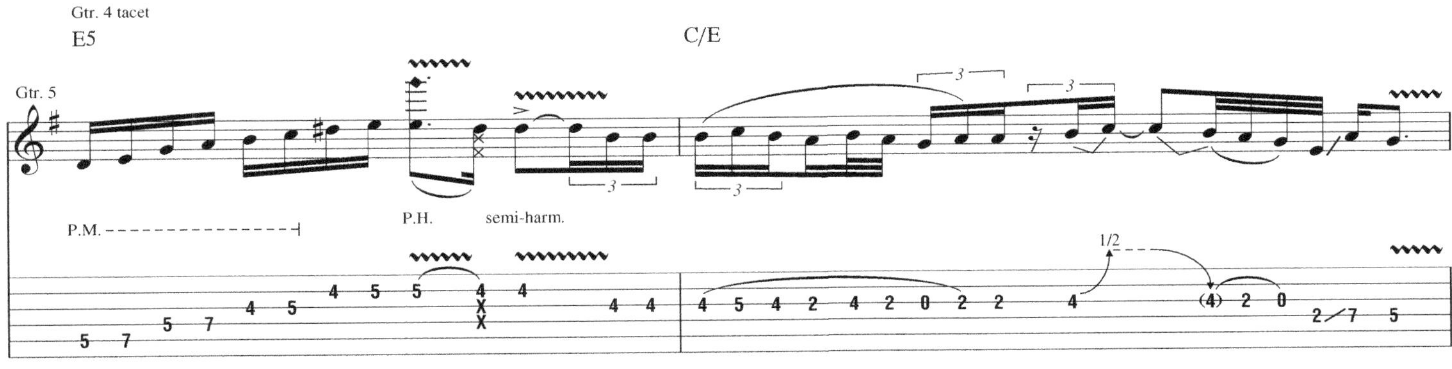
Gtr. 4 tacet
E5
C/E
Gtr. 5
P.M.
P.H.
semi-harm.

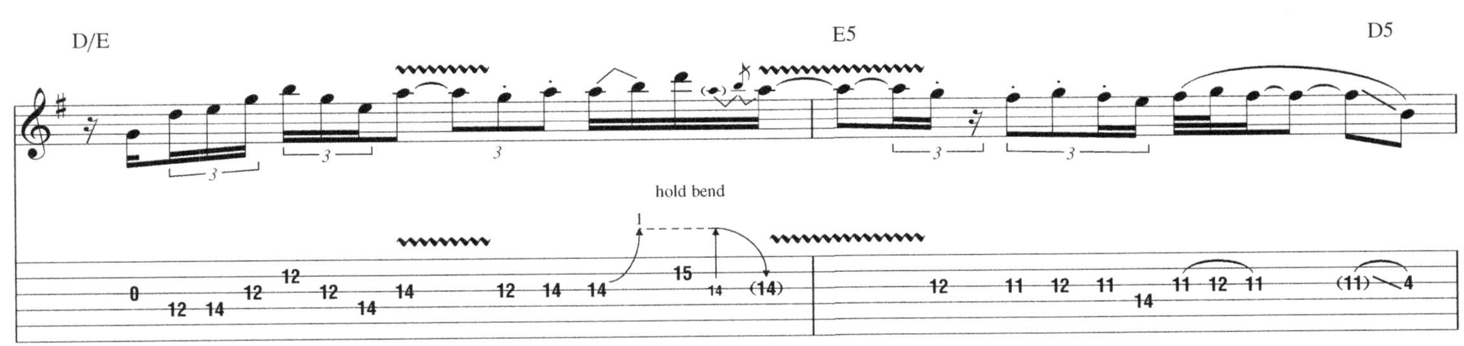
D/E
E5
D5
hold bend

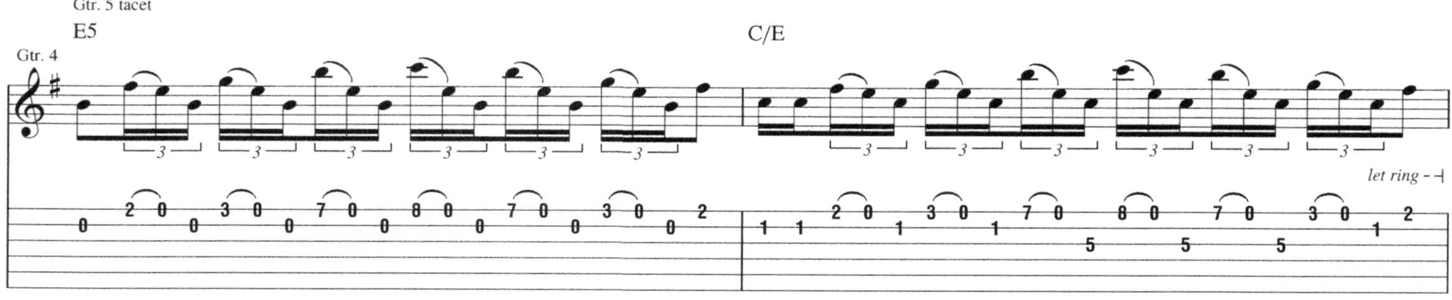
Gtr. 5 tacet
E5
C/E
Gtr. 4
let ring

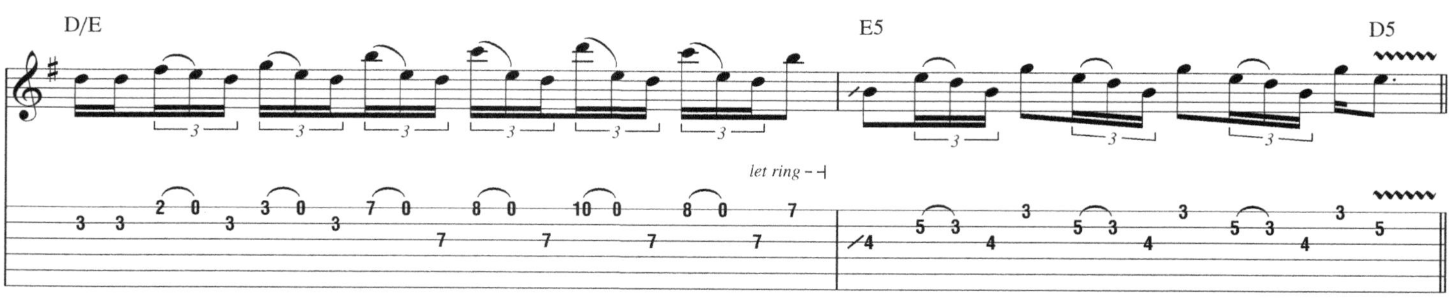
D/E
E5
D5
let ring

Outro

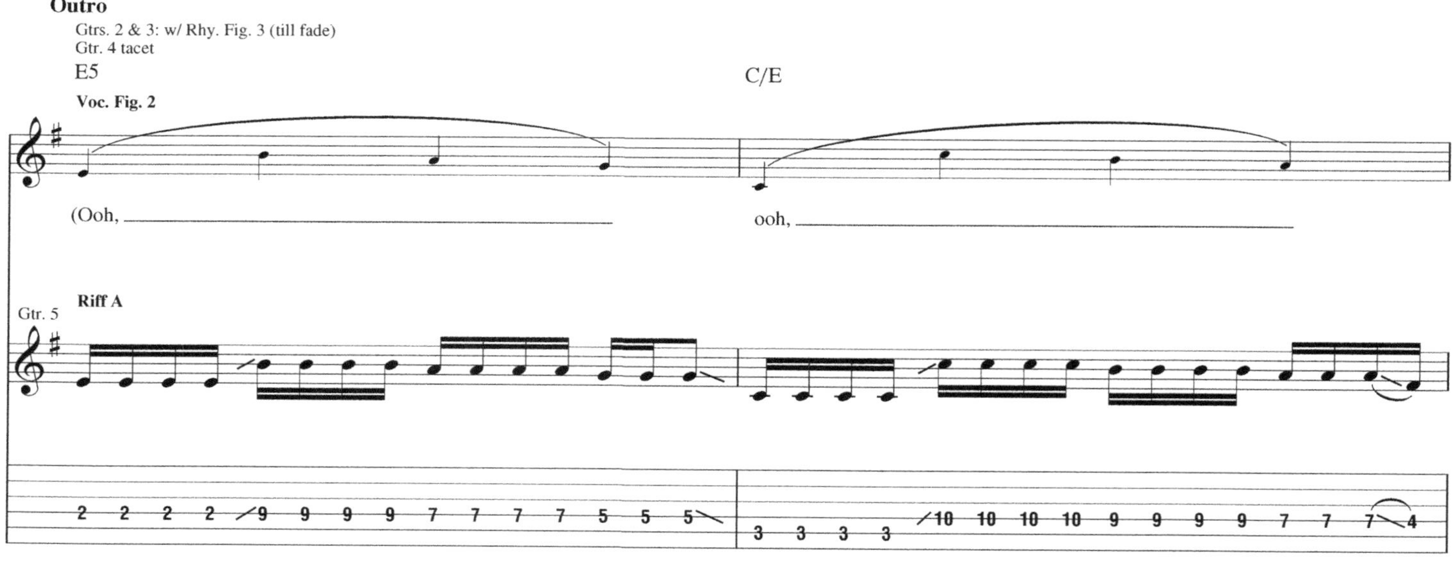
Gtrs. 2 & 3: w/ Rhy. Fig. 3 (till fade)
Gtr. 4 tacet
E5
C/E
Voc. Fig. 2
(Ooh,
ooh,
Riff A
Gtr. 5

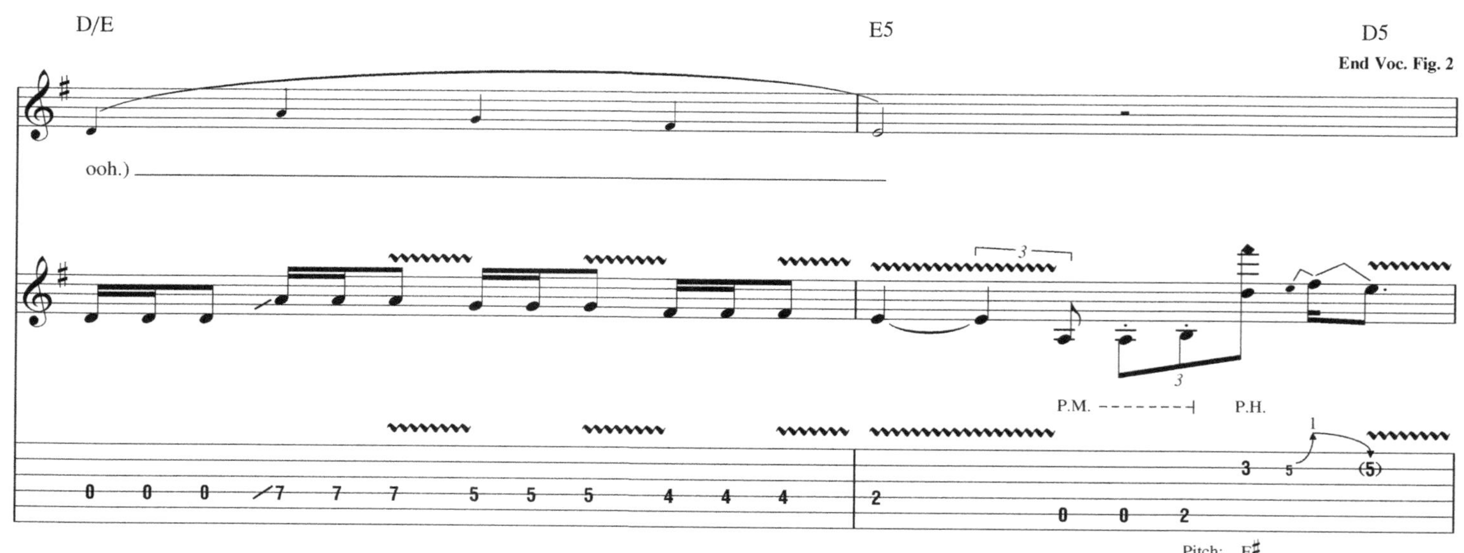
D/E
E5
D5
End Voc. Fig. 2
ooh.)
P.M.
P.H.
Pitch: F♯

Bkgd. Voc.: w/ Voc. Fig. 2 (till fade)

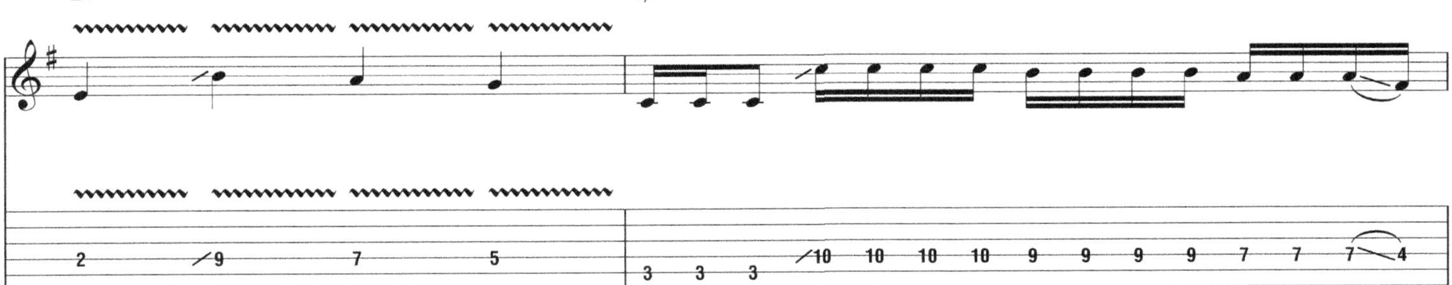
E5
C/E

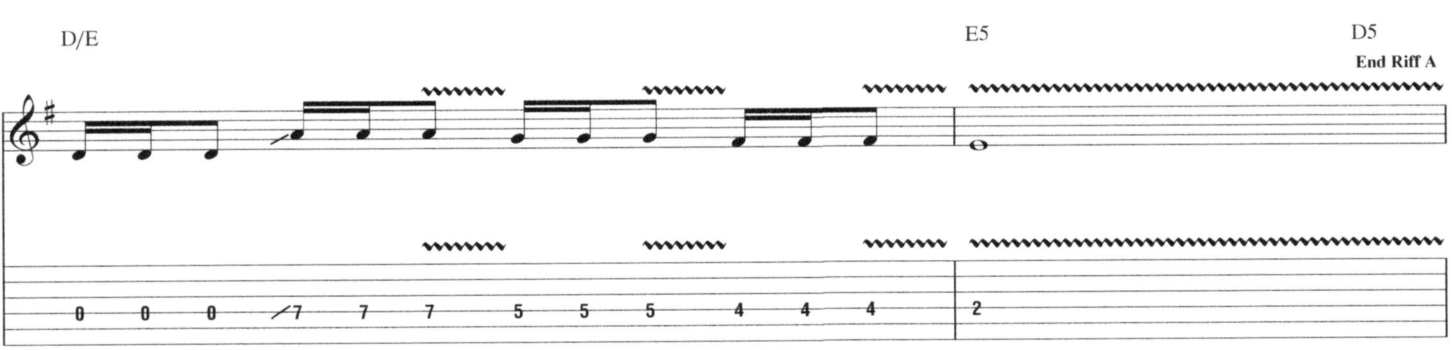
D/E
E5
D5
End Riff A

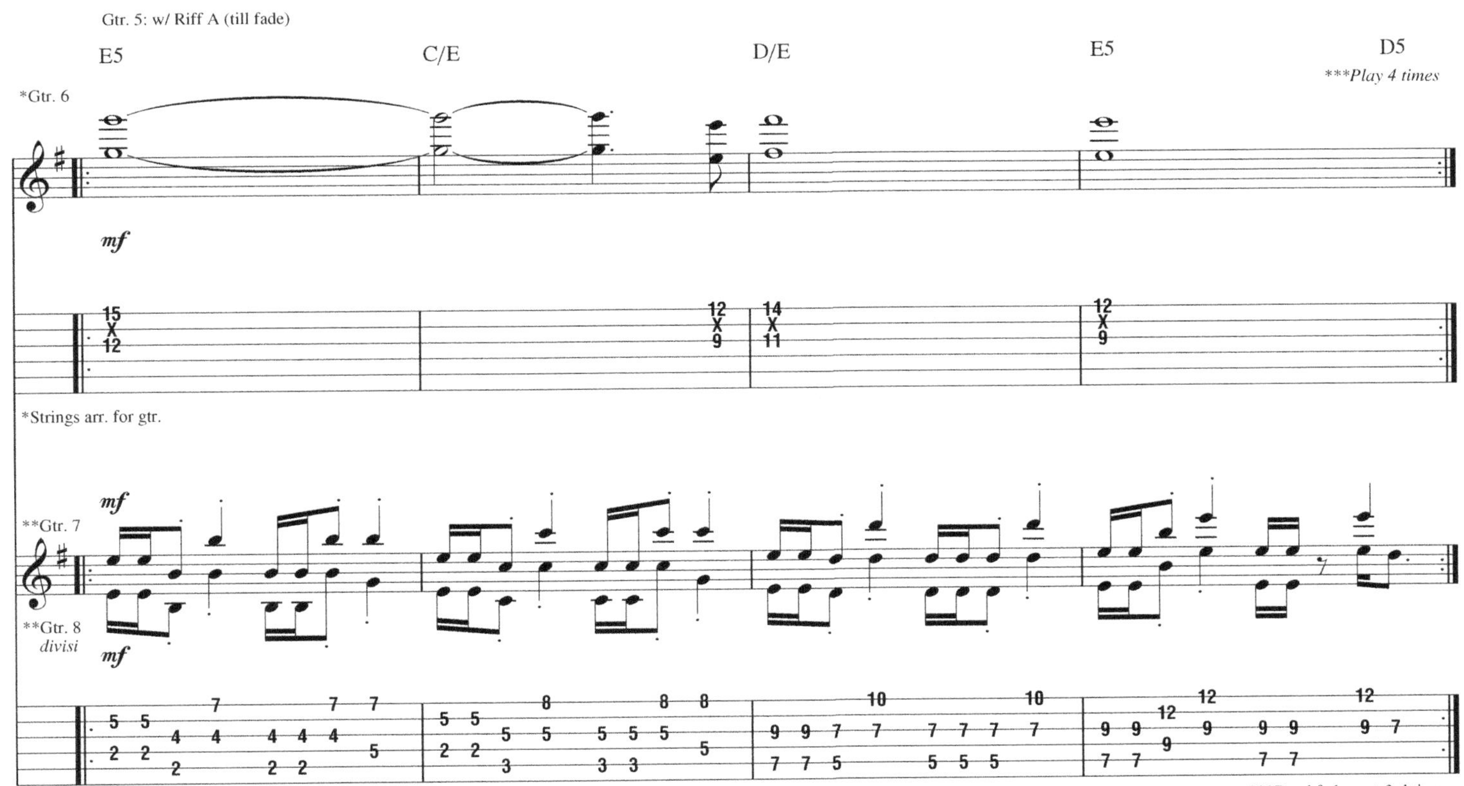
Gtr. 5: w/ Riff A (till fade)
E5
C/E
D/E
E5
D5
***Play 4 times
*Gtr. 6
mf
*Strings arr. for gtr.
**Gtr. 7
**Gtr. 8
divisi
**Strings arr. for gtr.
***Band fades out 3rd time.

Ten Speed (Of God's Blood & Burial)

Words and Music by Claudio Sanchez, Michael Todd, Joshua Eppard and Travis Stever

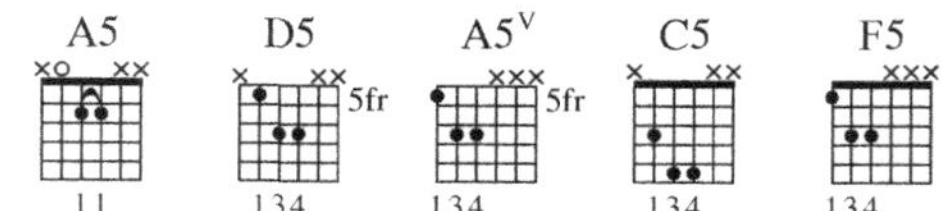

Tune down 1/2 step:
(low to high) E♭-A♭-D♭-G♭-B♭-E♭

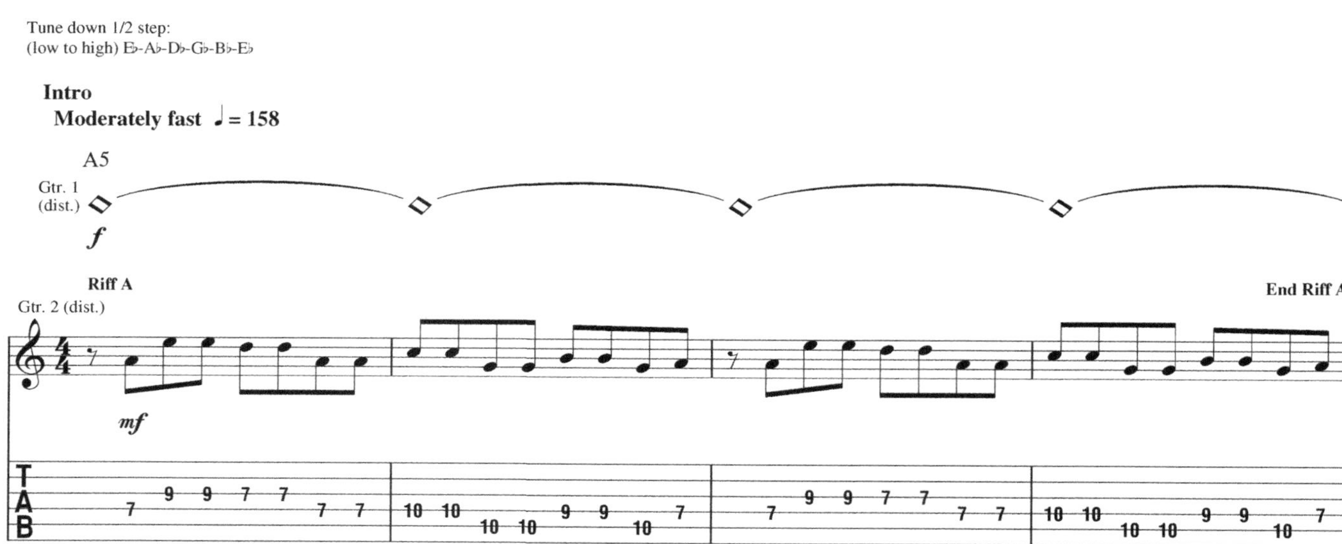

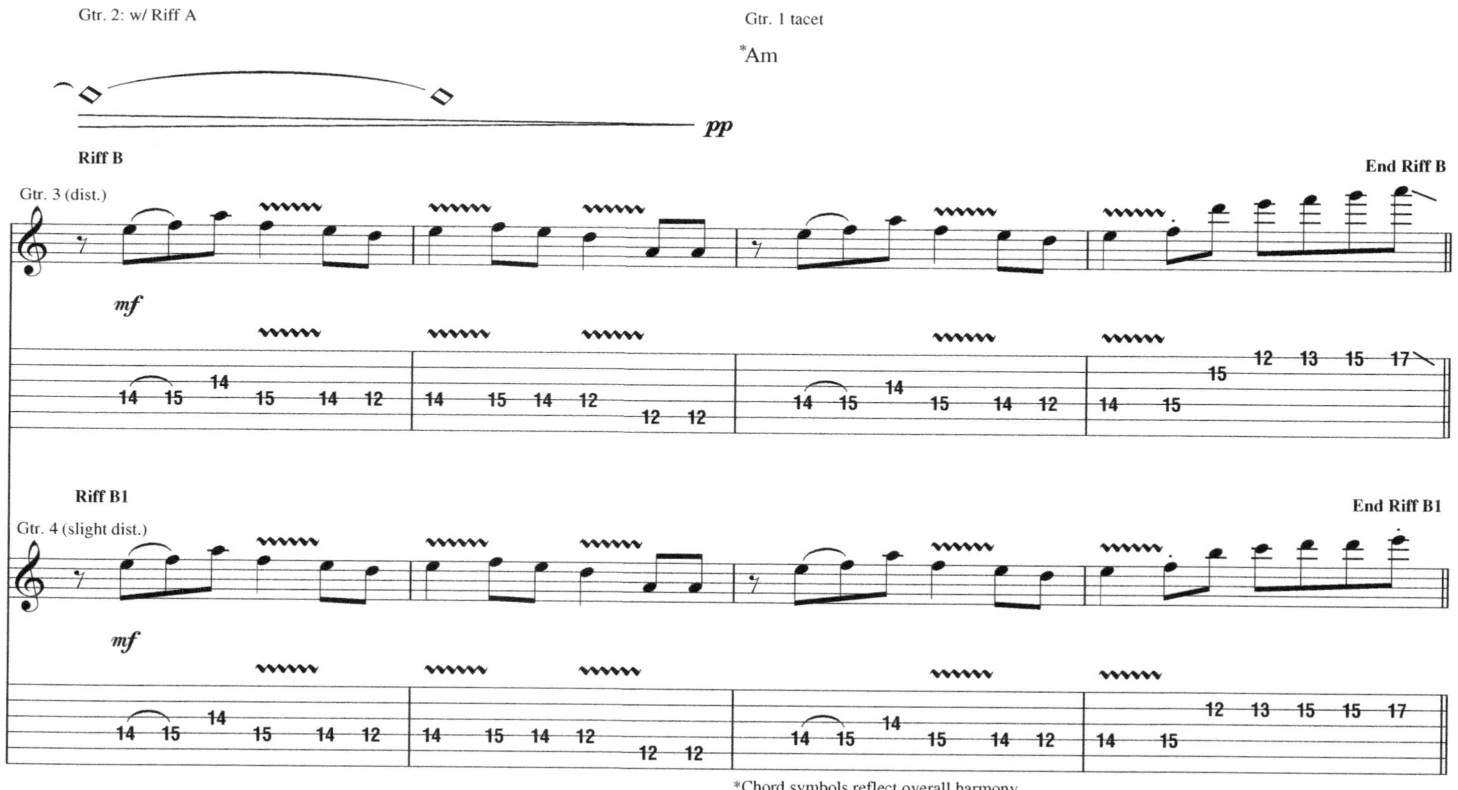

*Chord symbols reflect overall harmony.

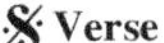 **Verse**

Gtr. 2: w/ Riff A (4 times)
Gtr. 3: w/ Riff B (3 3/4 times)
2nd time, Gtr. 1 tacet

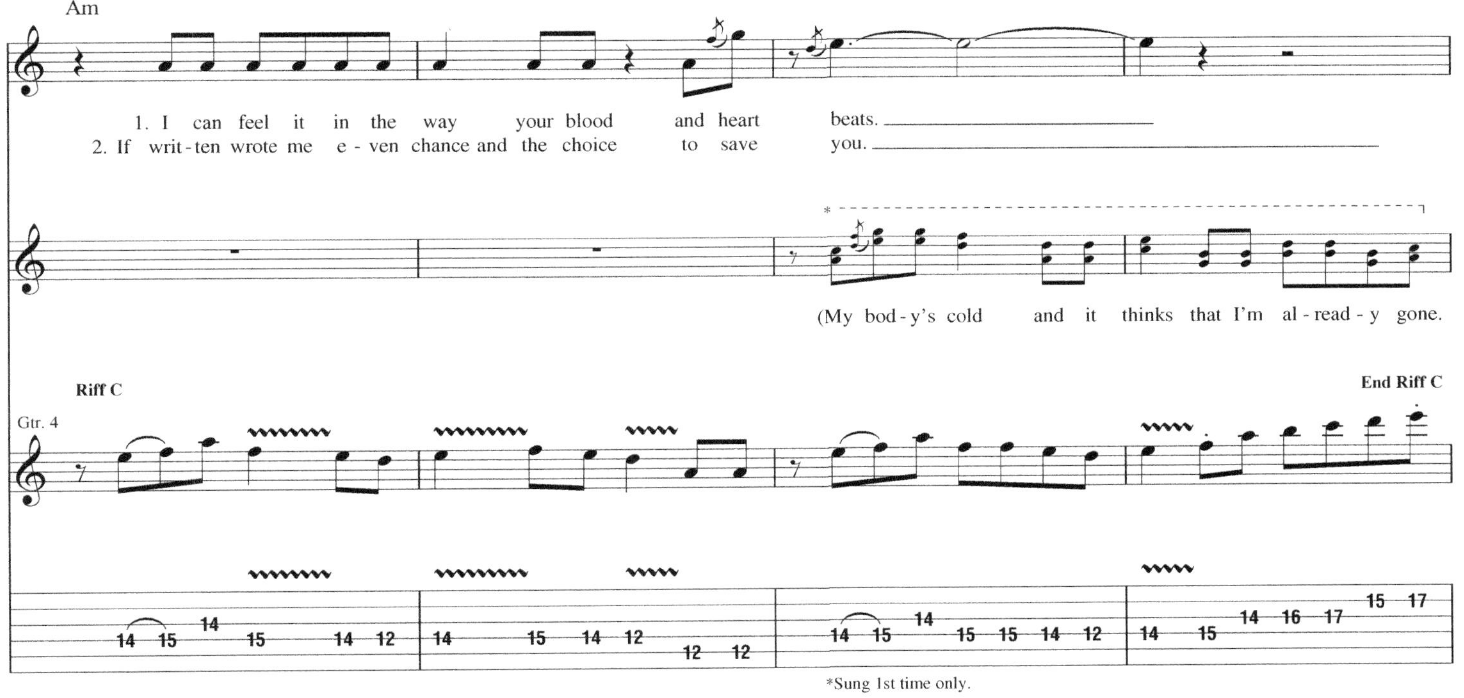

*Sung 1st time only.

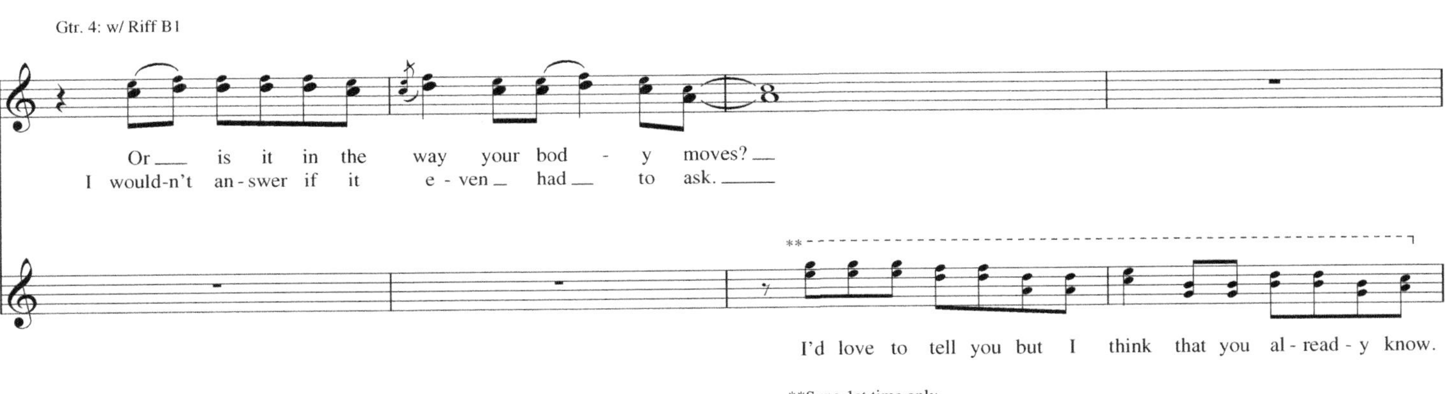

**Sung 1st time only.

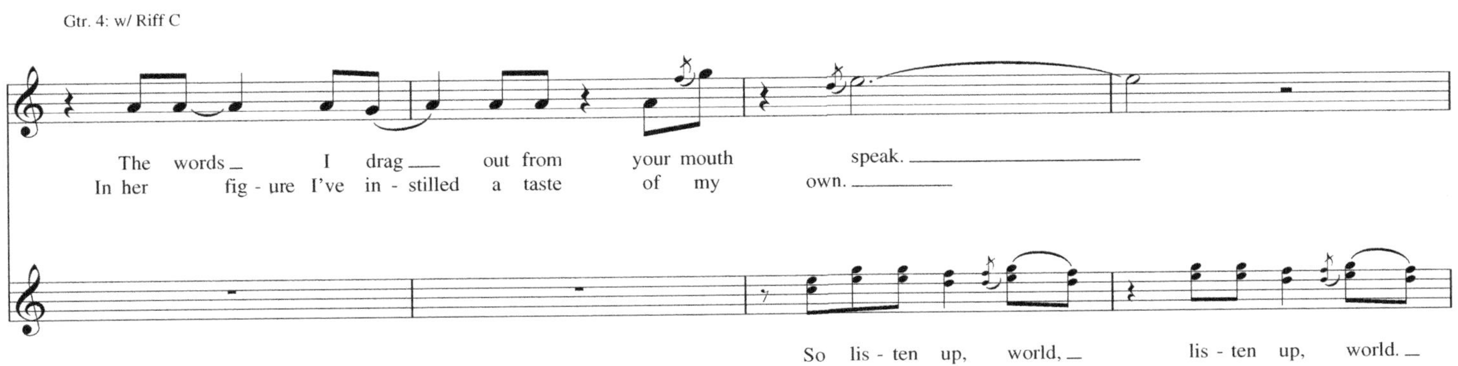

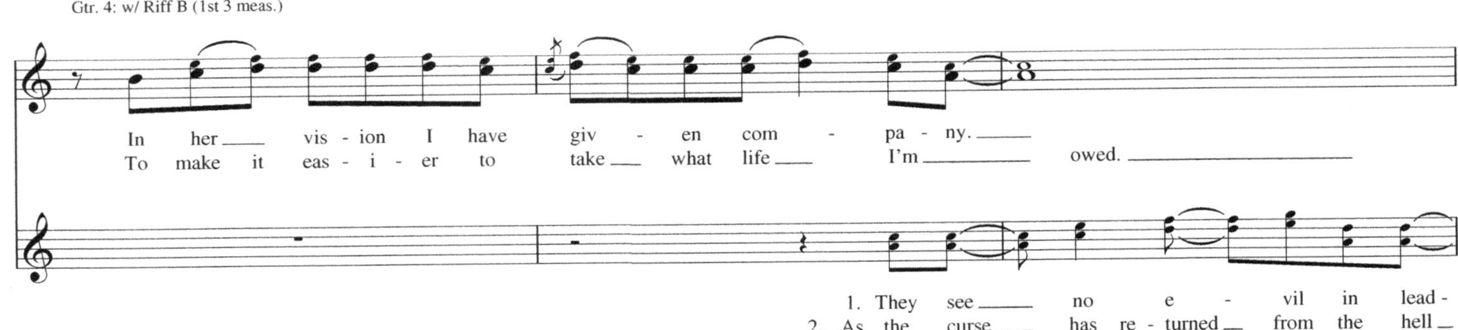

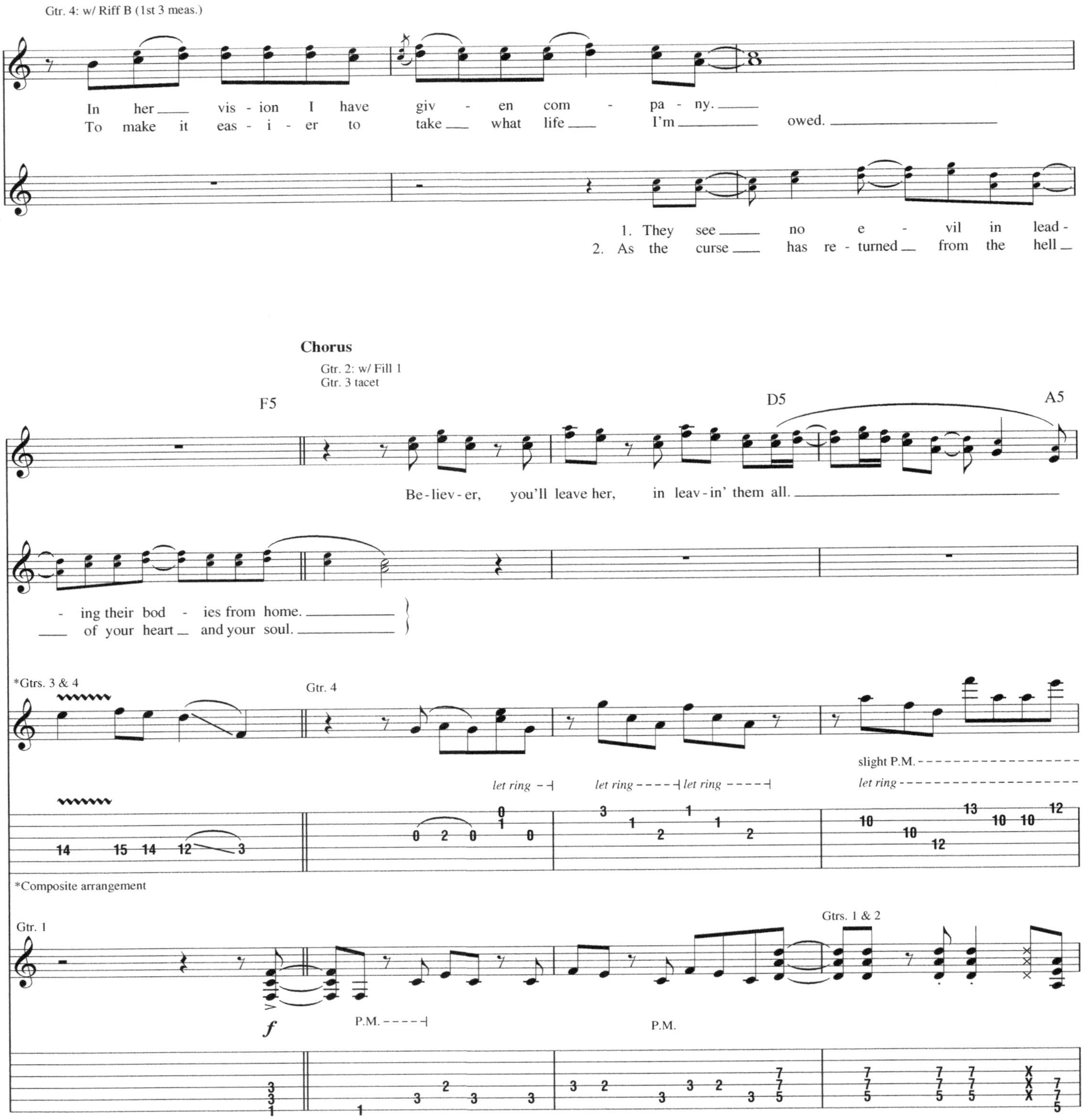

Chorus

Gtr. 2: w/ Fill 1
Gtr. 3 tacet

F5 D5 A5

Be - liev - er, you'll leave her, in leav - in' them all.

- ing their bod - ies from home.
of your heart and your soul.

*Gtrs. 3 & 4

Gtr. 4

let ring
let ring
let ring
slight P.M.
let ring

*Composite arrangement

Gtr. 1

f

P.M.

P.M.

Gtrs. 1 & 2

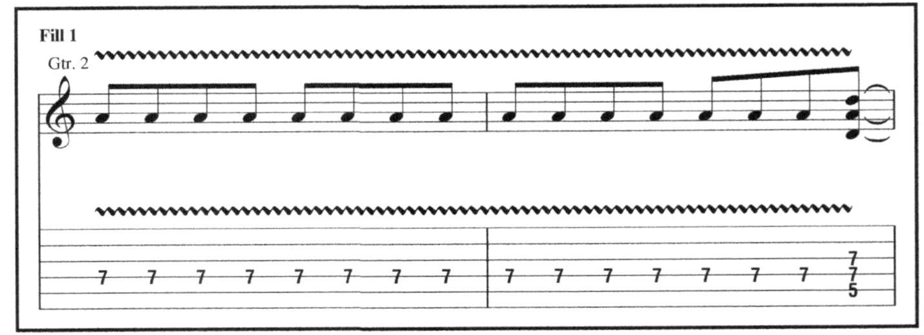

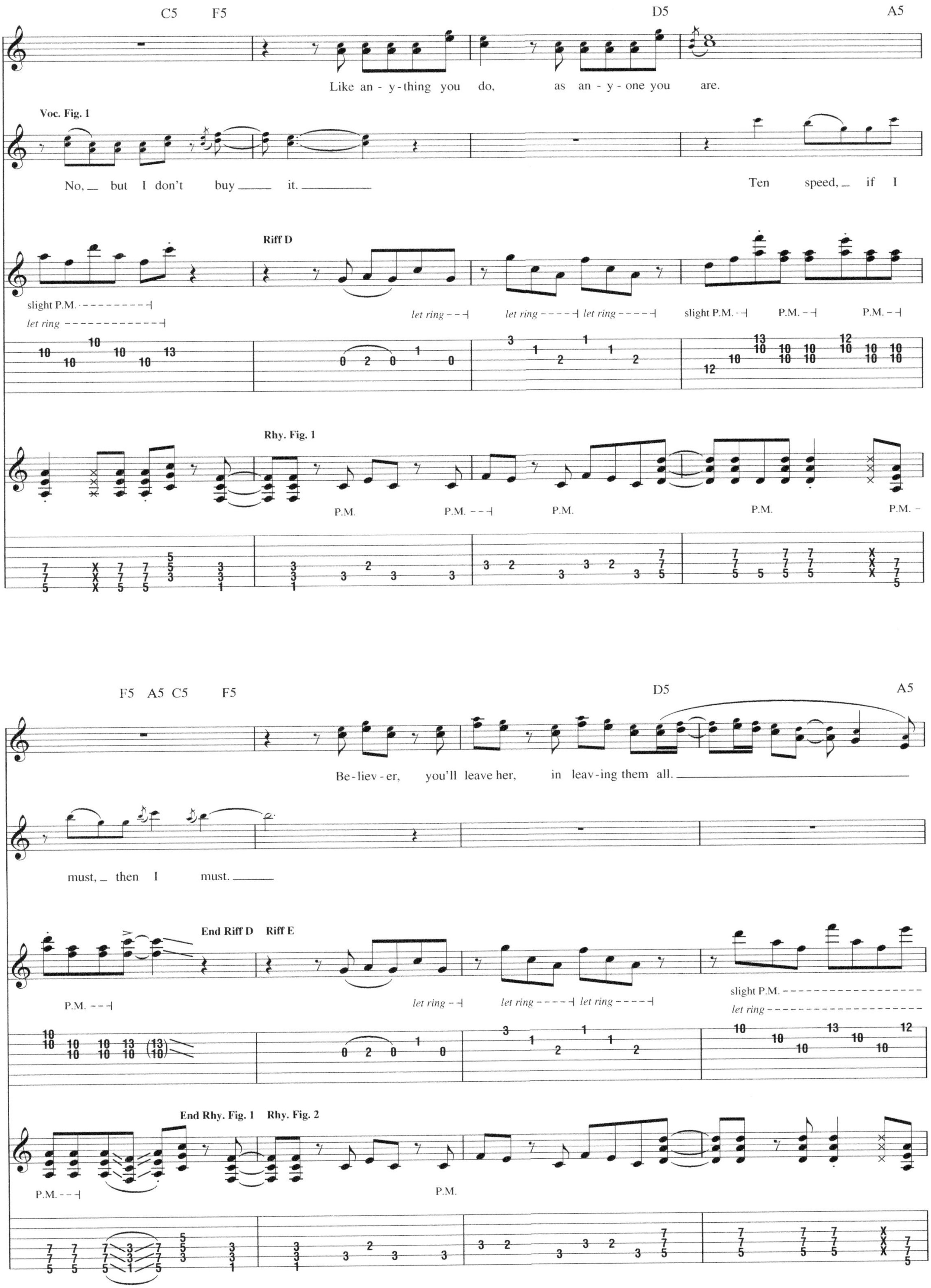

C5 F5 D5 A5

Like an - y - thing you do, as an - y - one you are.

Voc. Fig. 1

No, but I don't buy it.

Ten speed, if I

Riff D

slight P.M.

let ring

let ring let ring let ring slight P.M. P.M. P.M.

Rhy. Fig. 1

P.M. P.M. P.M. P.M. P.M.

F5 A5 C5 F5 D5 A5

Be - liev - er, you'll leave her, in leav - ing them all.

must, then I must.

End Riff D Riff E

P.M.

let ring let ring let ring

slight P.M.

let ring

End Rhy. Fig. 1 Rhy. Fig. 2

P.M. P.M.

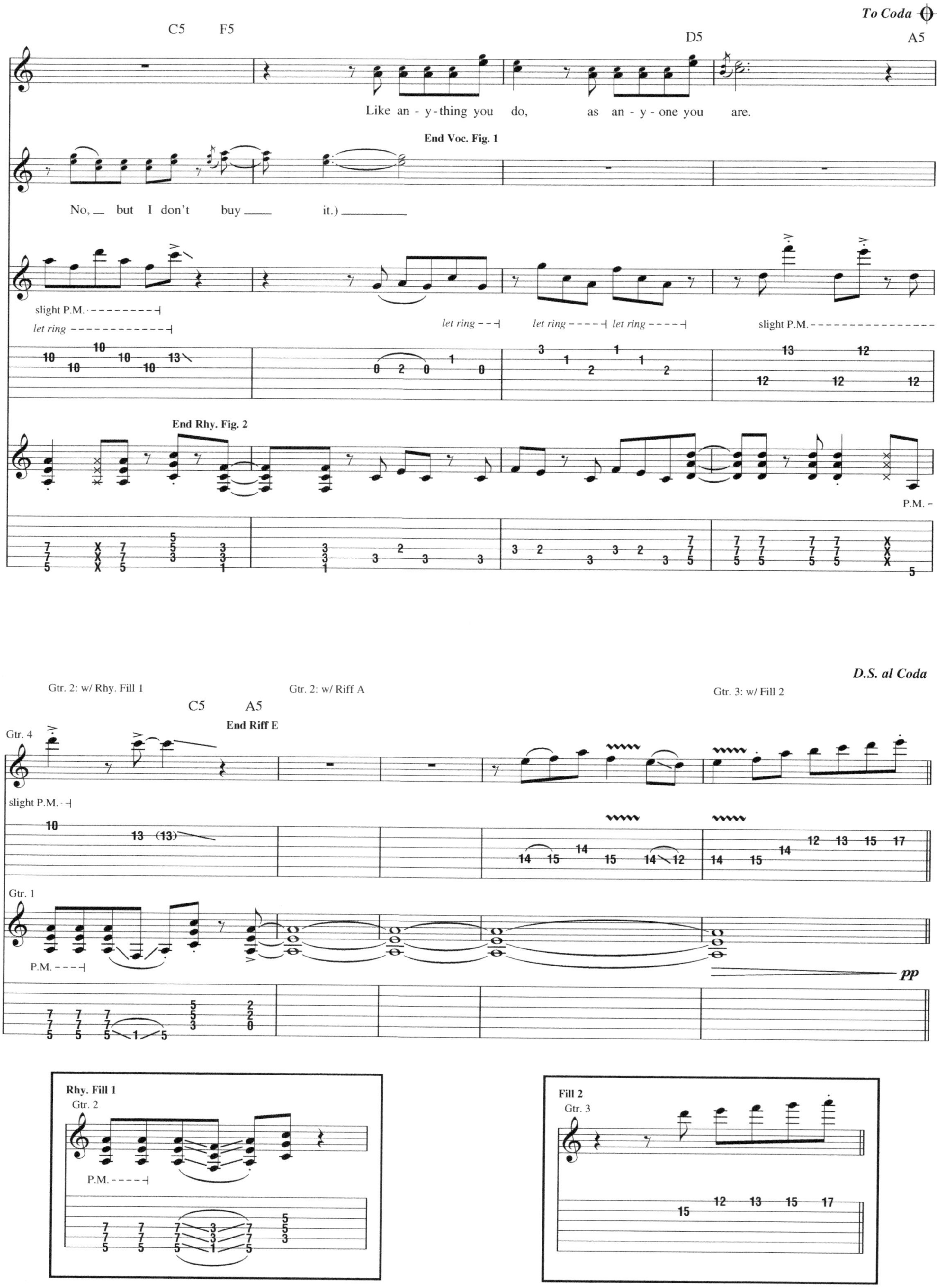

To Coda ⊕

C5 F5 D5 A5

Like an - y - thing you do, as an - y - one you are.

End Voc. Fig. 1

No, — but I don't buy — it.) —

slight P.M.

let ring

let ring

let ring

let ring

slight P.M.

End Rhy. Fig. 2

P.M.

D.S. al Coda

Gtr. 2: w/ Rhy. Fill 1

Gtr. 2: w/ Riff A

Gtr. 3: w/ Fill 2

C5 A5

End Riff E

Gtr. 4

slight P.M.

Gtr. 1

P.M.

pp

Rhy. Fill 1

Gtr. 2

P.M.

Fill 2

Gtr. 3

Coda

Guitar Solo

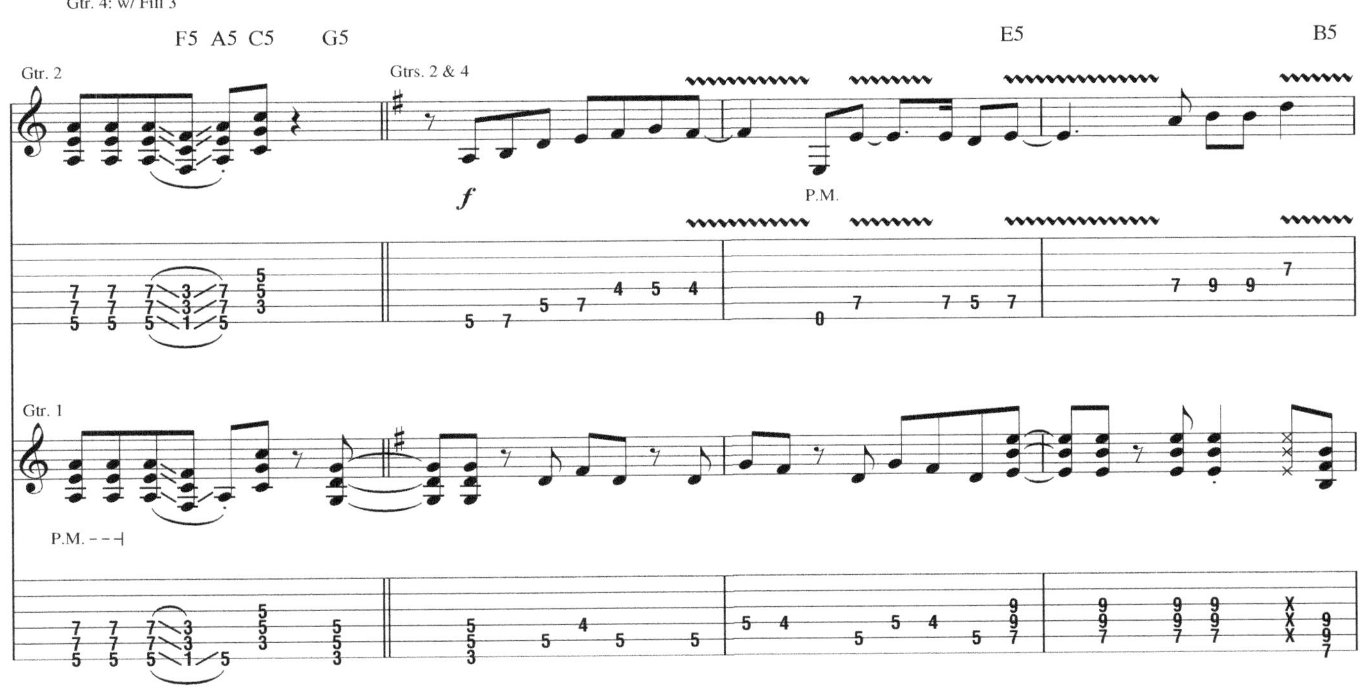

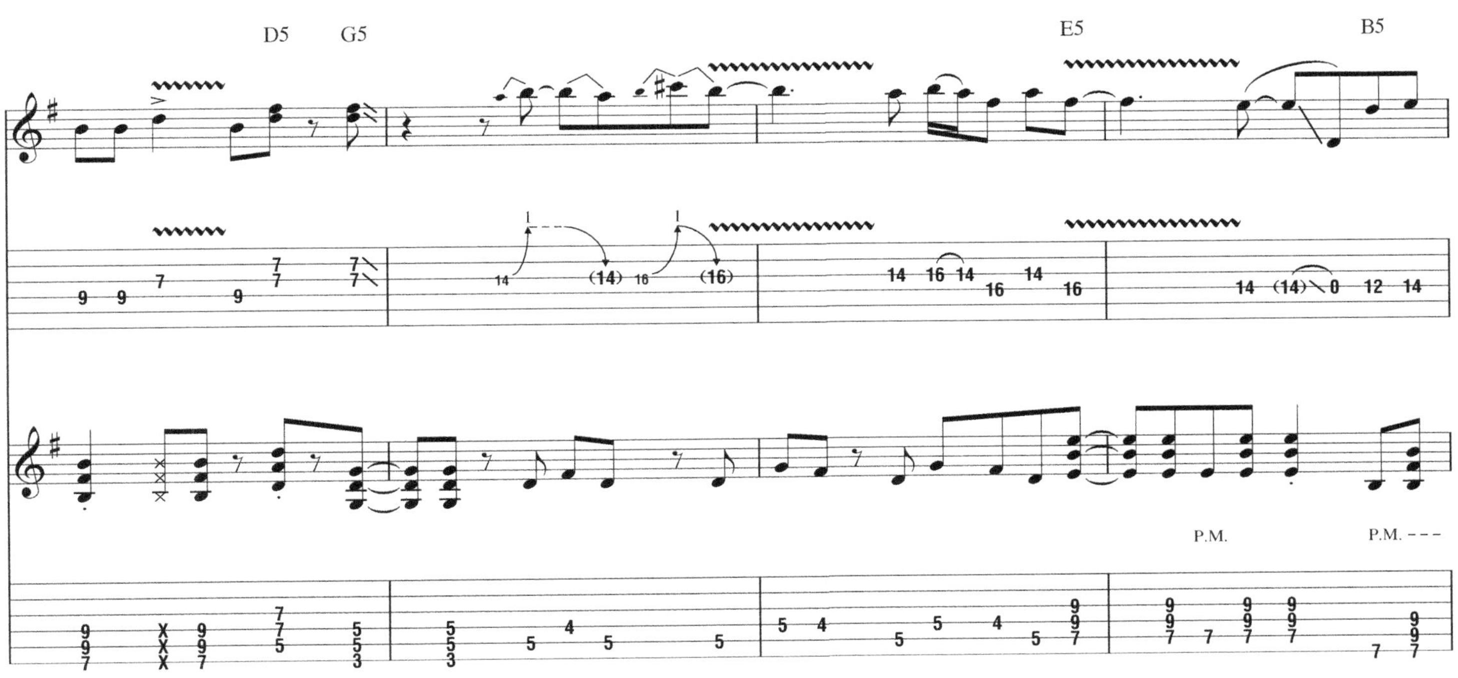

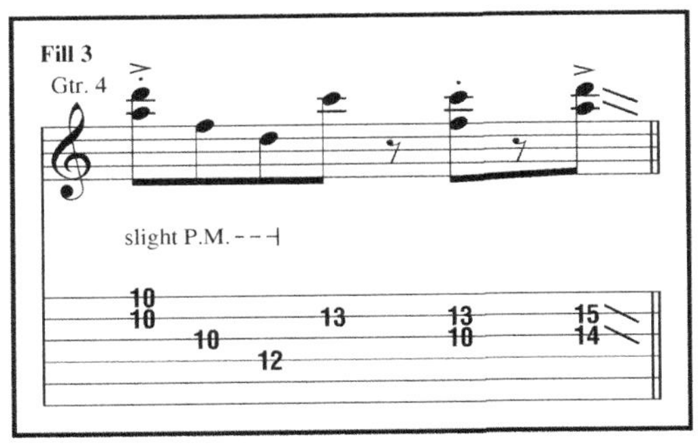

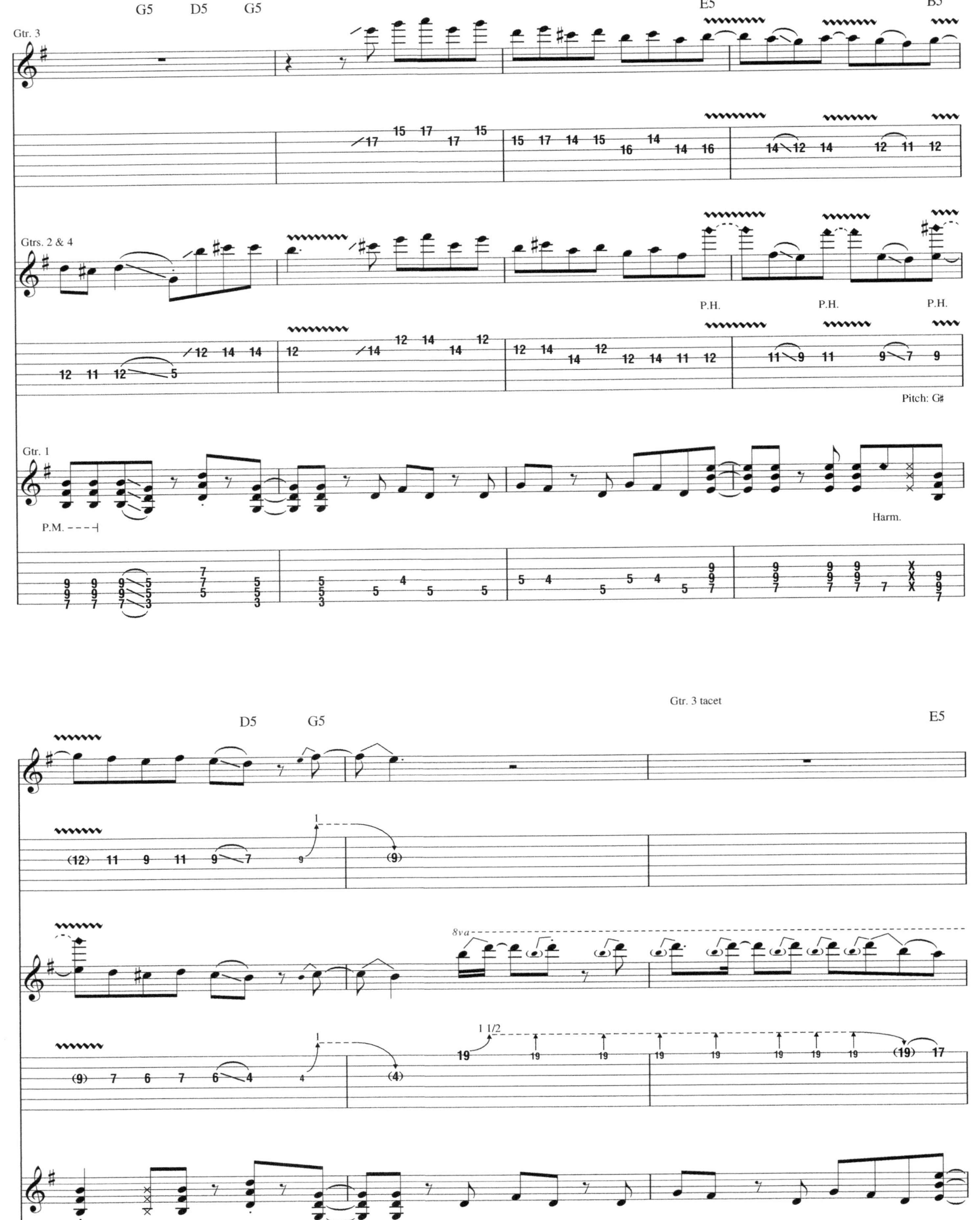
G5
D5
G5
E5
B5
Gtr. 3
Gtrs. 2 & 4
P.H.
P.H.
P.H.
Pitch: G♯
Gtr. 1
P.M.
Harm.
D5
G5
Gtr. 3 tacet
E5
8va
1 1/2

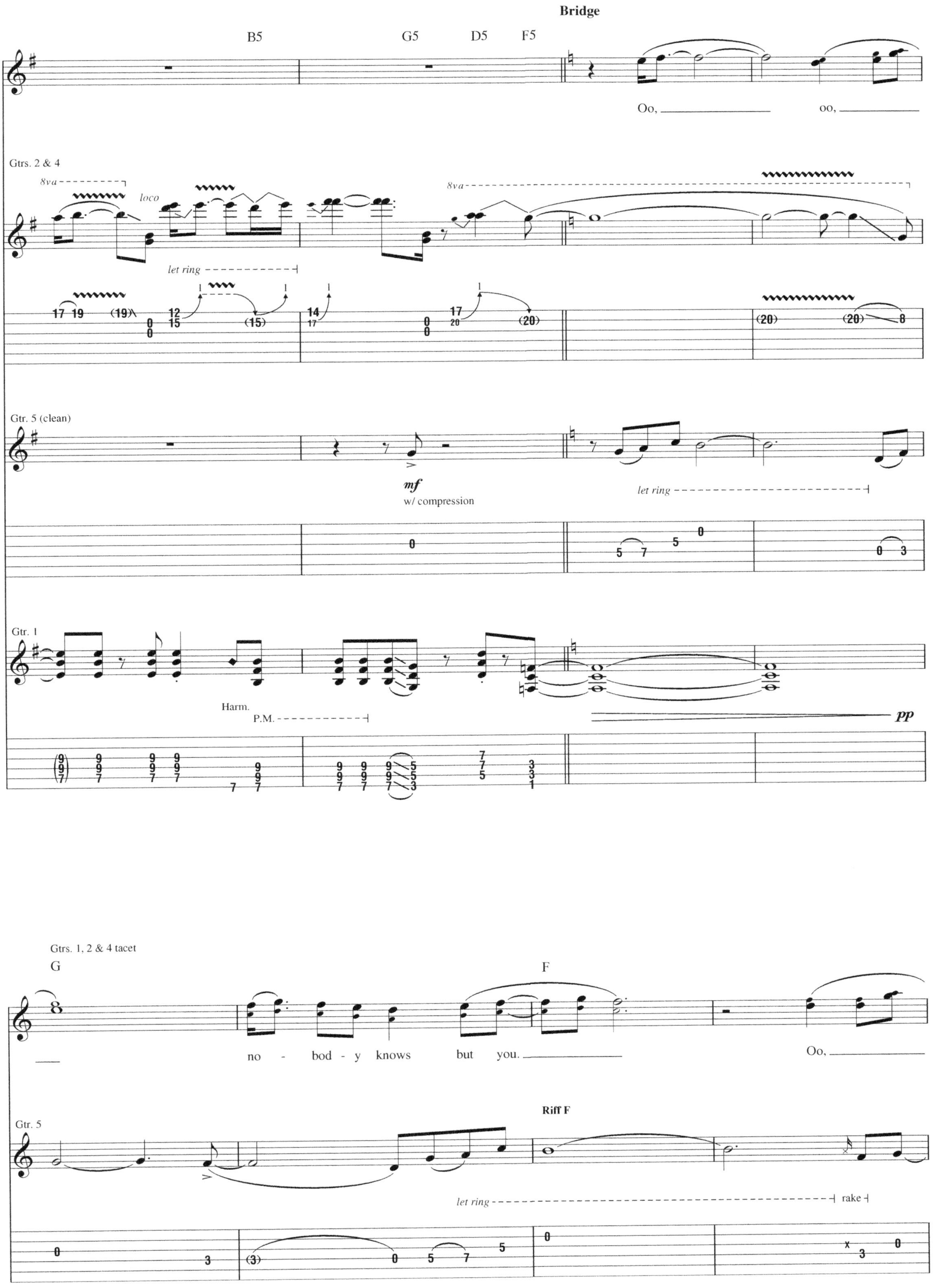

Bridge

B5 G5 D5 F5

Oo, oo,

Gtrs. 2 & 4

8va loco let ring 8va

Gtr. 5 (clean)

mf
w/ compression

let ring

Gtr. 1

Harm.
P.M.

pp

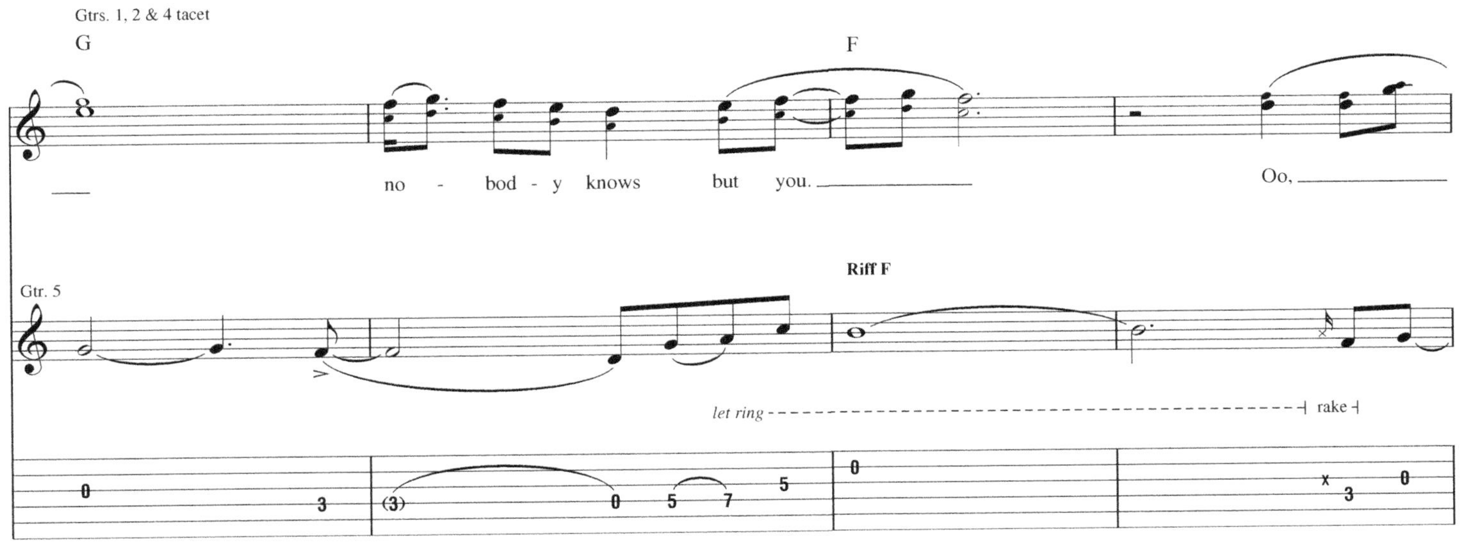

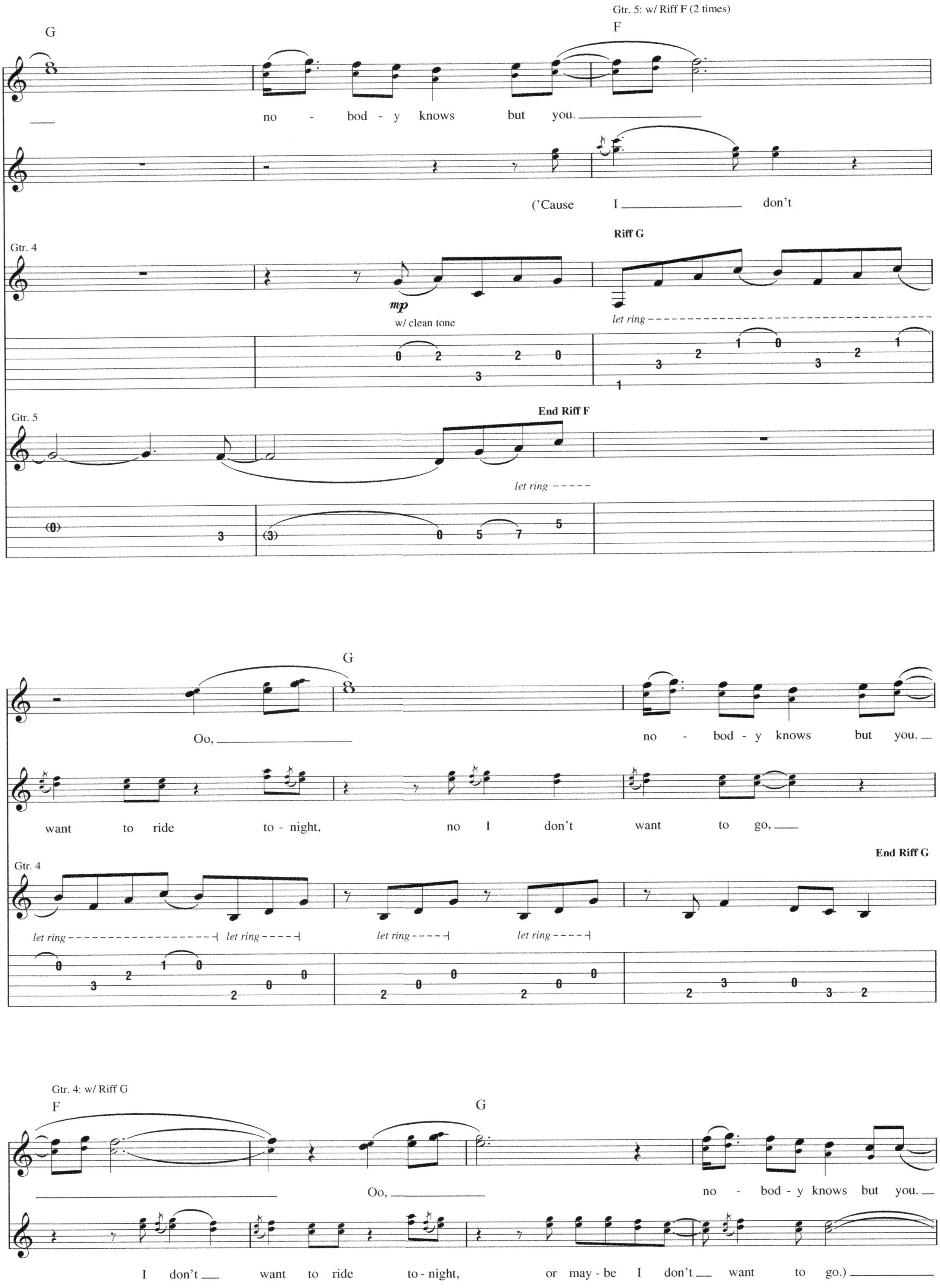

Gtr. 5: w/ Riff F (2 times)

G F

no - bod - y knows but you.

('Cause I don't

Gtr. 4 Riff G

mp

w/ clean tone

let ring

Gtr. 5 End Riff F

let ring

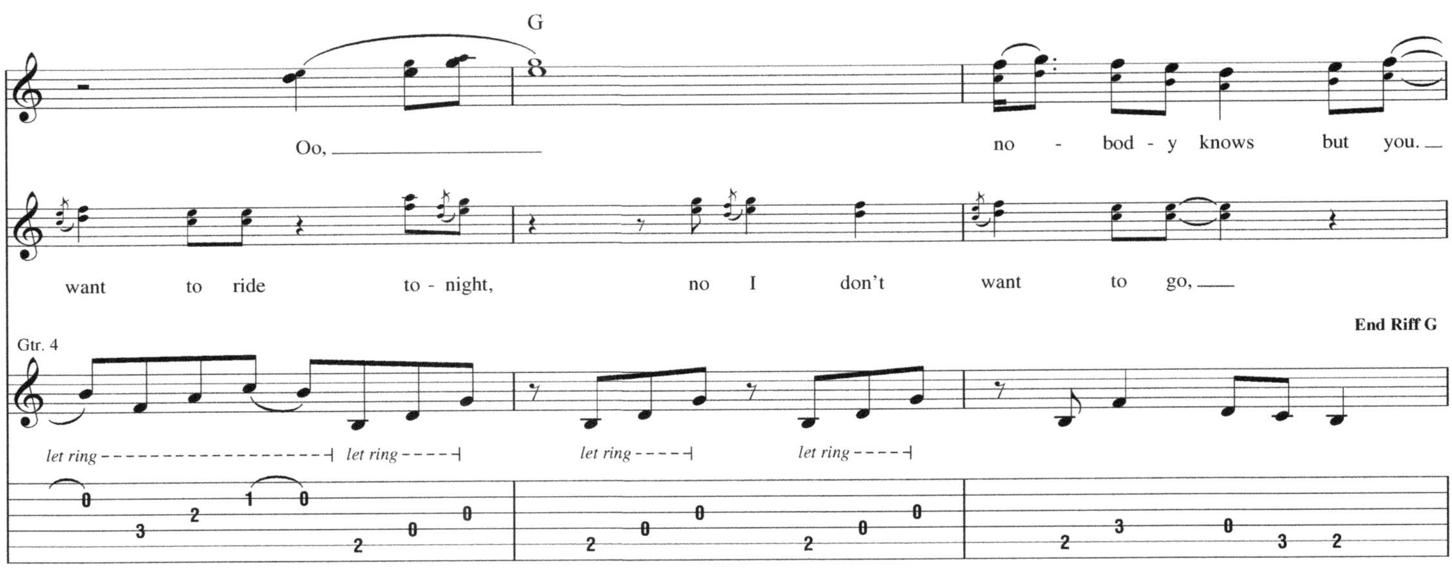

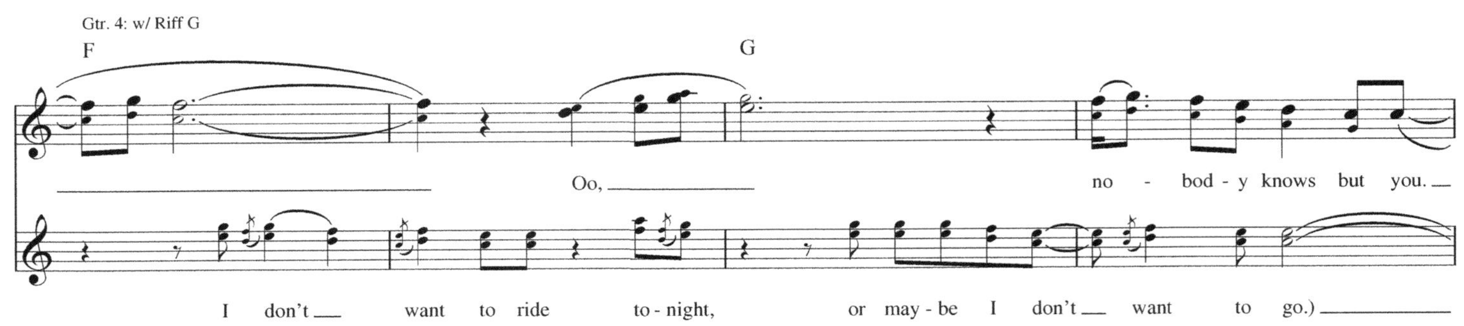

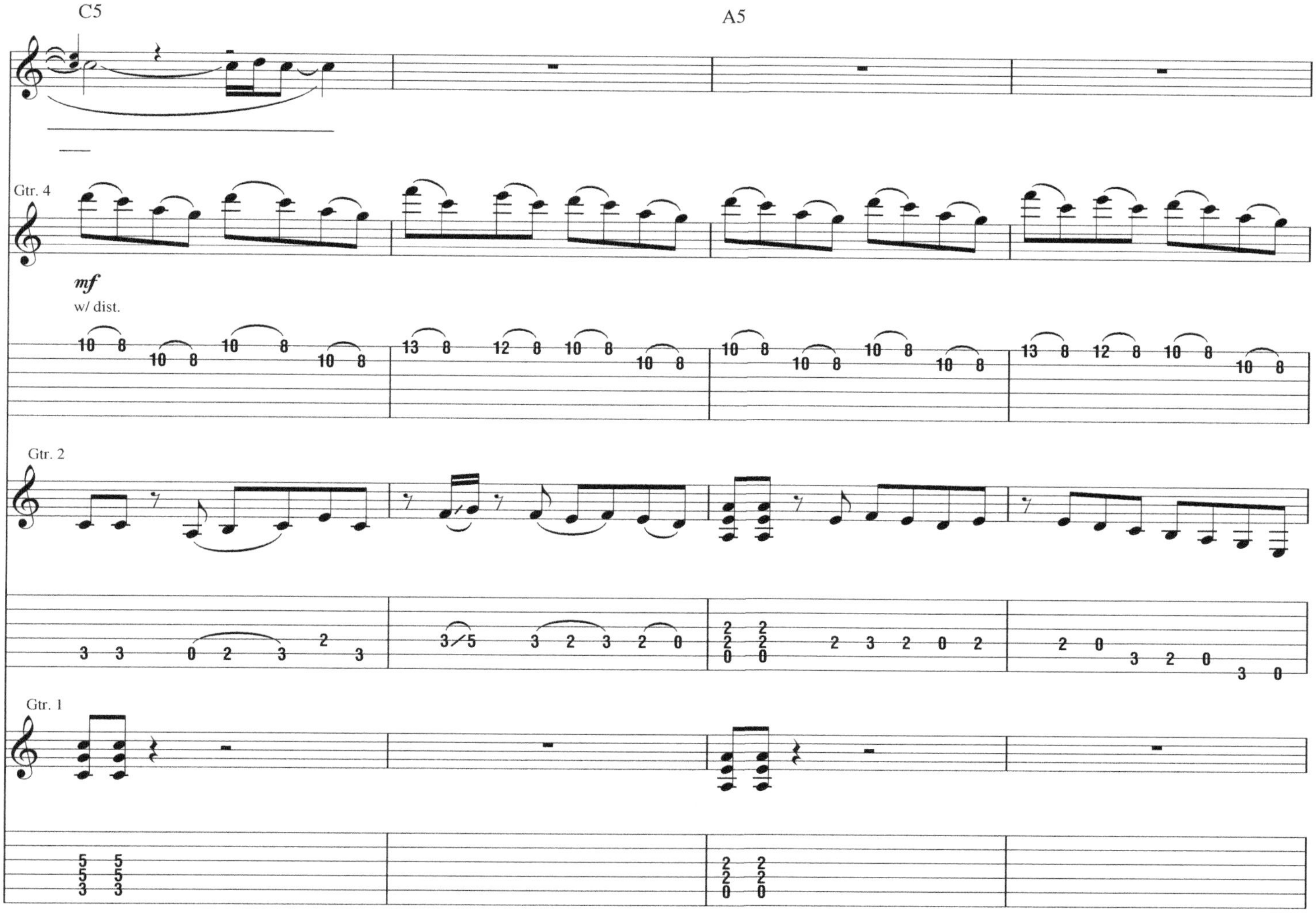

C5

A5

Gtr. 4

mf

w/ dist.

Gtr. 2

Gtr. 1

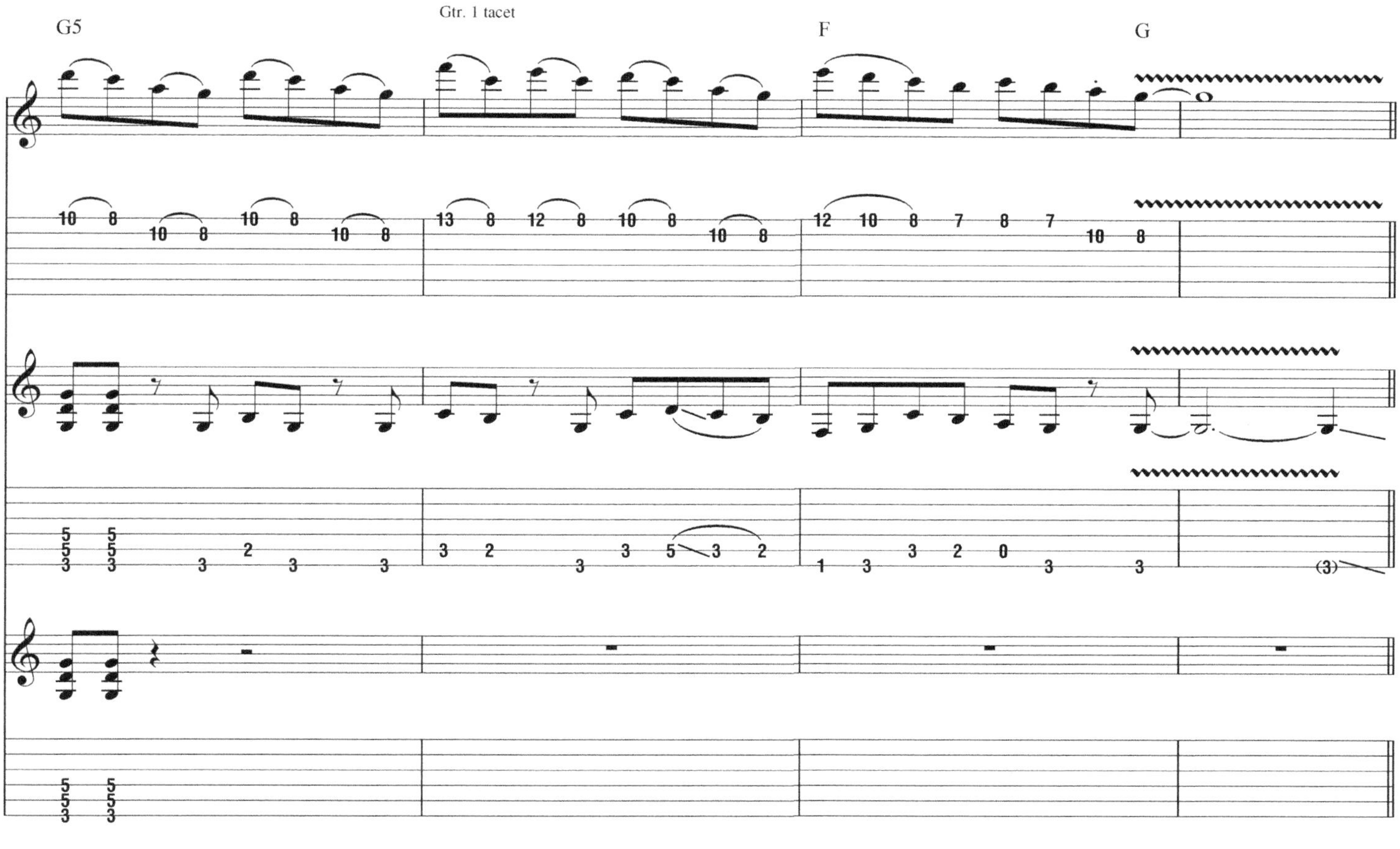

G5

Gtr. 1 tacet

F

G

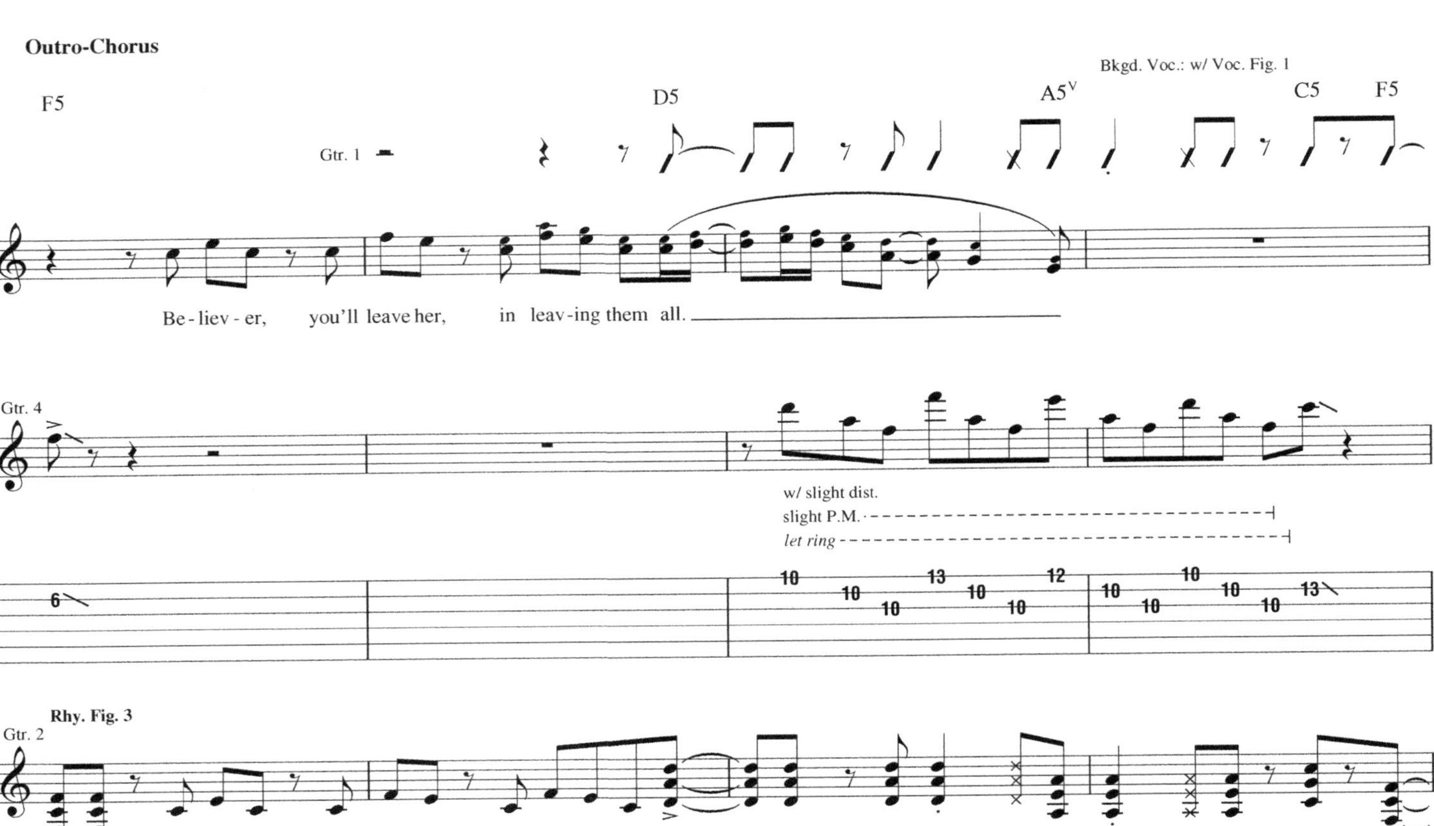
Outro-Chorus
Bkgd. Voc.: w/ Voc. Fig. 1
F5
D5
A5
C5
F5
Gtr. 1
Be - liev - er, you'll leave her, in leav - ing them all.
Gtr. 4
w/ slight dist.
slight P.M.
let ring
Rhy. Fig. 3
Gtr. 2
P.M.
P.M.

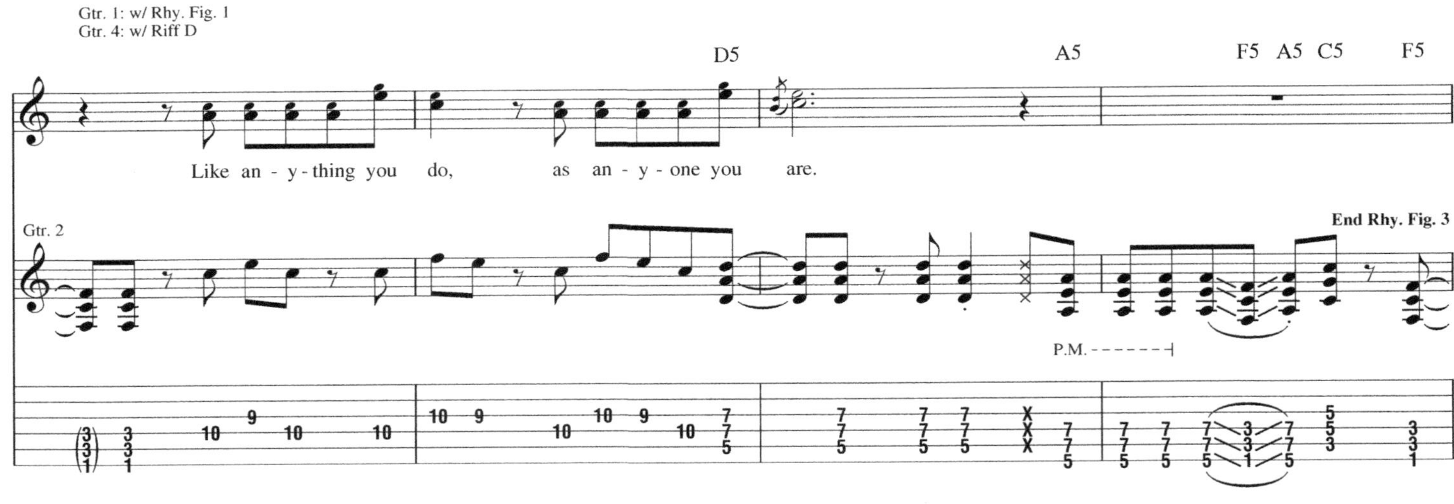
Gtr. 1: w/ Rhy. Fig. 1
Gtr. 4: w/ Riff D
D5
A5
F5 A5 C5
F5
Like an - y - thing you do, as an - y - one you are.
Gtr. 2
End Rhy. Fig. 3
P.M.

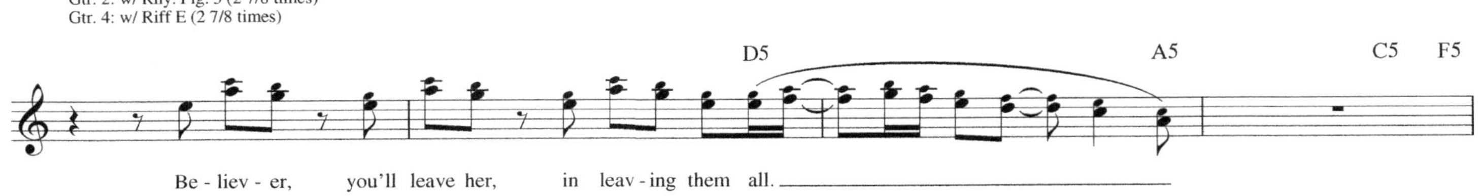
Gtr. 1: w/ Rhy. Fig. 2
Gtr. 2: w/ Rhy. Fig. 3 (2 7/8 times)
Gtr. 4: w/ Riff E (2 7/8 times)
D5
A5
C5
F5
Be - liev - er, you'll leave her, in leav - ing them all.

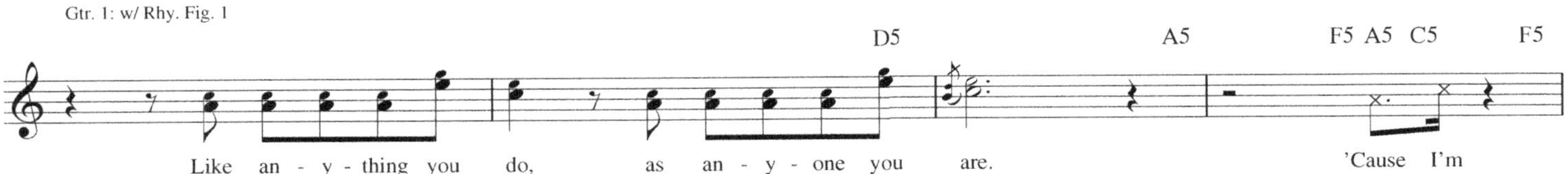
Gtr. 1: w/ Rhy. Fig. 1
D5
A5
F5 A5 C5
F5
Like an - y - thing you do, as an - y - one you are. 'Cause I'm

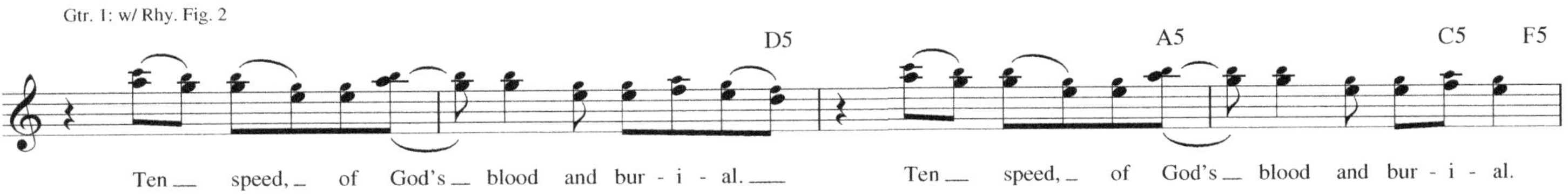
Gtr. 1: w/ Rhy. Fig. 2
D5
A5
C5
F5
Ten speed, of God's blood and bur - i - al. Ten speed, of God's blood and bur - i - al.

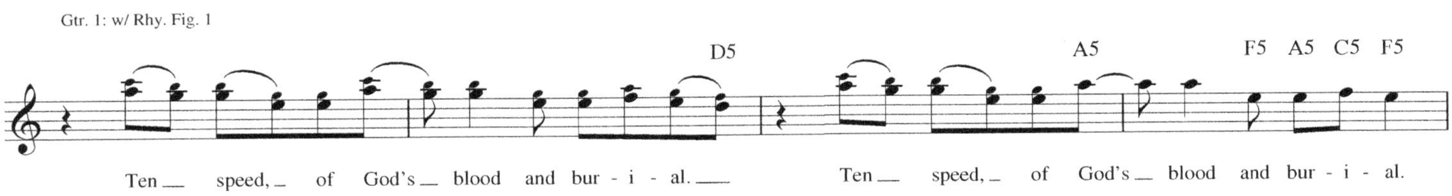
Gtr. 1: w/ Rhy. Fig. 1
D5
A5
F5 A5 C5 F5
Ten speed, of God's blood and bur - i - al. Ten speed, of God's blood and bur - i - al.

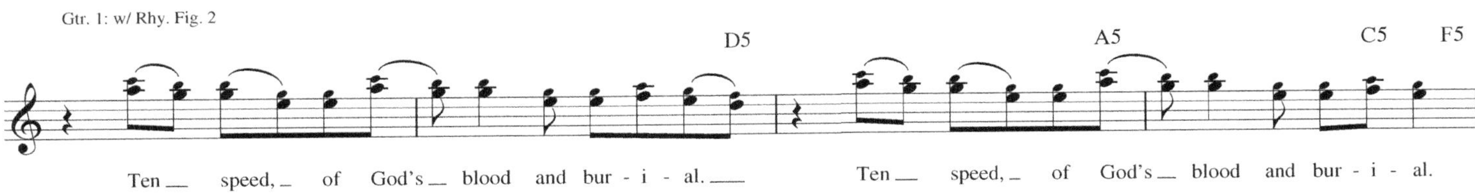
Gtr. 1: w/ Rhy. Fig. 2
D5
A5
C5
F5
Ten speed, of God's blood and bur - i - al. Ten speed, of God's blood and bur - i - al.

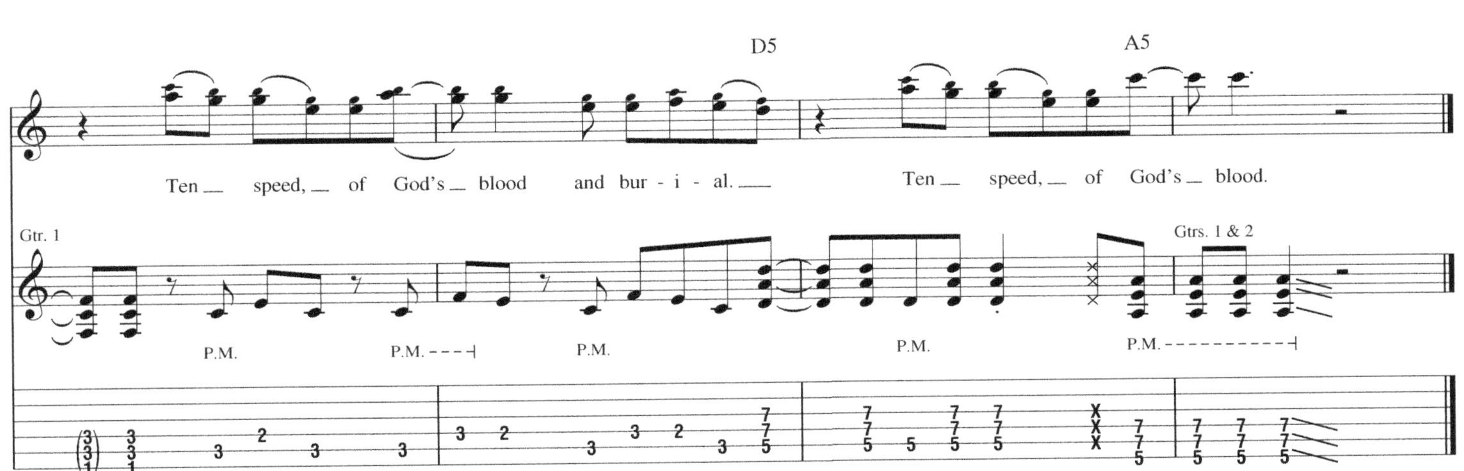
D5
A5
Ten speed, of God's blood and bur - i - al. Ten speed, of God's blood.
Gtr. 1
Gtrs. 1 & 2
P.M.
P.M.
P.M.
P.M.
P.M.

Crossing the Frame

Words and Music by Claudio Sanchez, Michael Todd, Joshua Eppard and Travis Stever

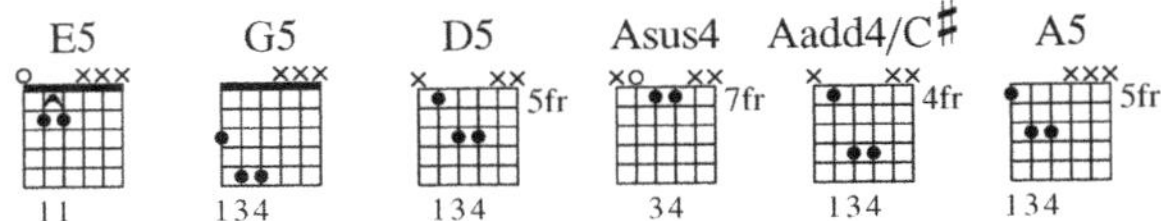

Tune down 1/2 step:
(low to high) E♭-A♭-D♭-G♭-B♭-E♭

Intro
Moderately fast ♩ = 160

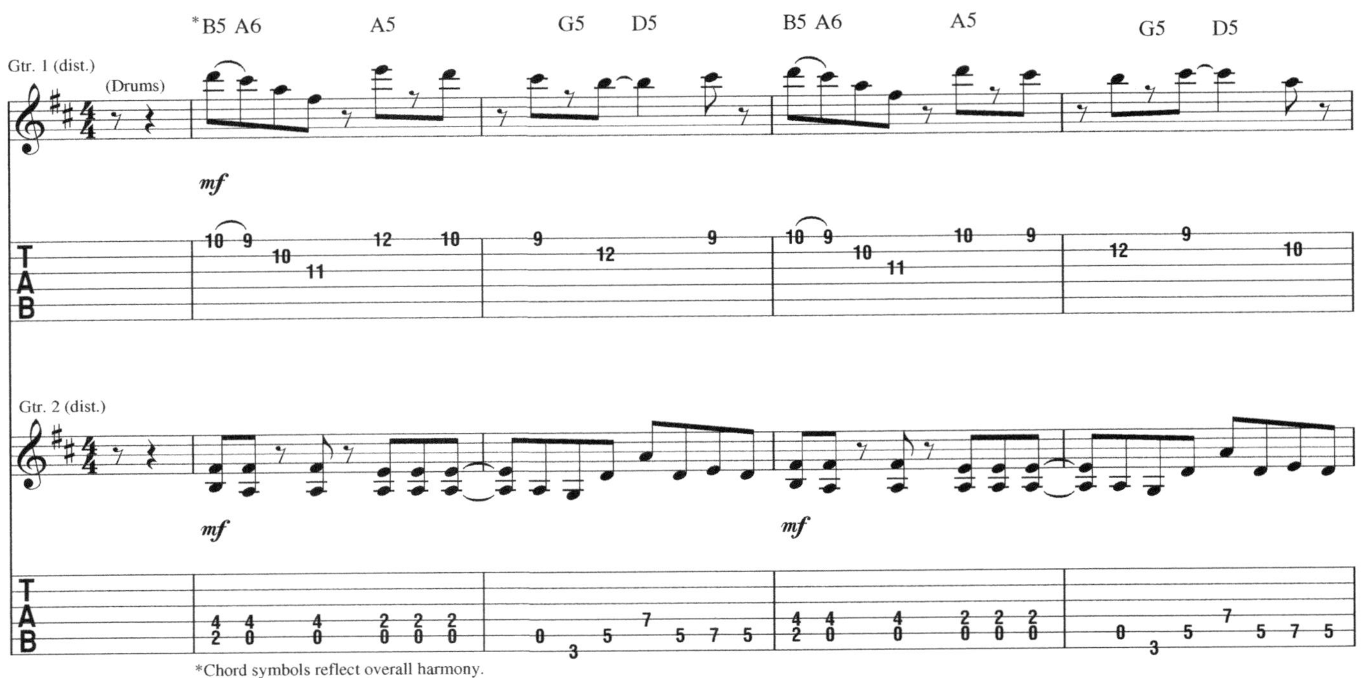

*Chord symbols reflect overall harmony.

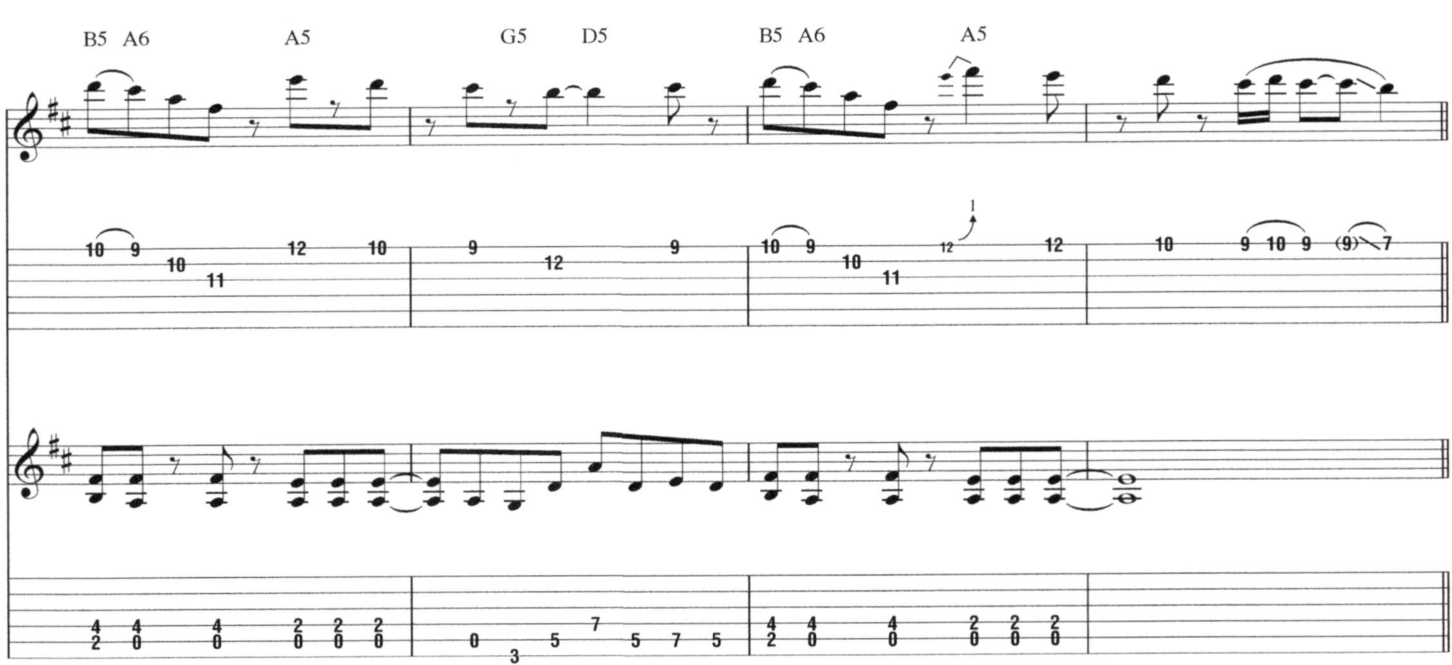

Verse

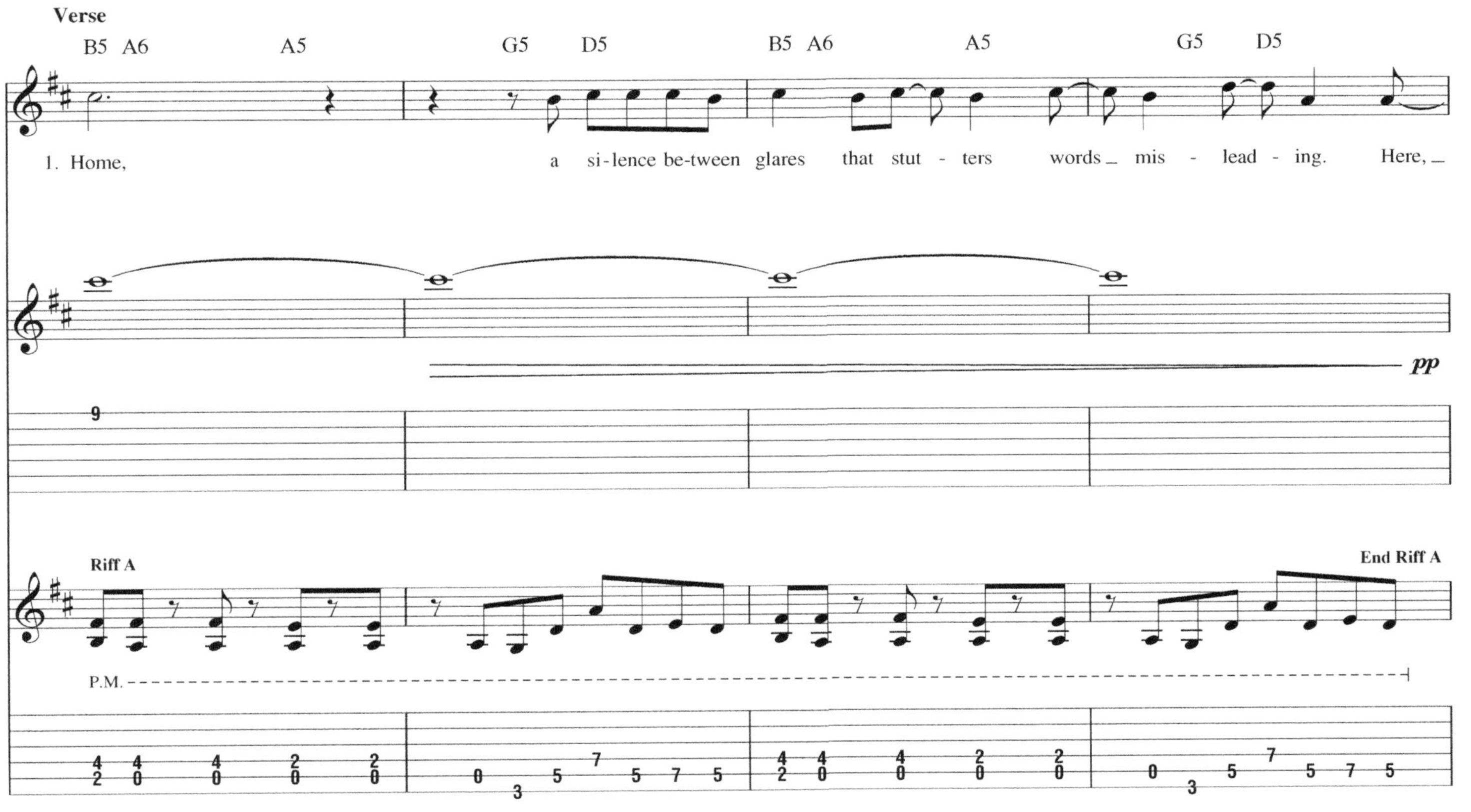

B5 A6 A5 G5 D5 B5 A6 A5 G5 D5
1. Home, a si-lence be-tween glares that stut - ters words_ mis - lead - ing. Here,_
pp
Riff A
End Riff A
P.M.

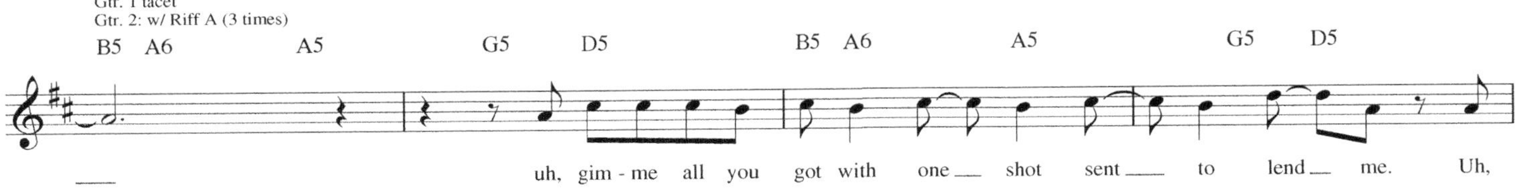

Gtr. 1 tacet
Gtr. 2: w/ Riff A (3 times)
B5 A6 A5 G5 D5 B5 A6 A5 G5 D5
uh, gim - me all you got with one_ shot sent_ to lend_ me. Uh,

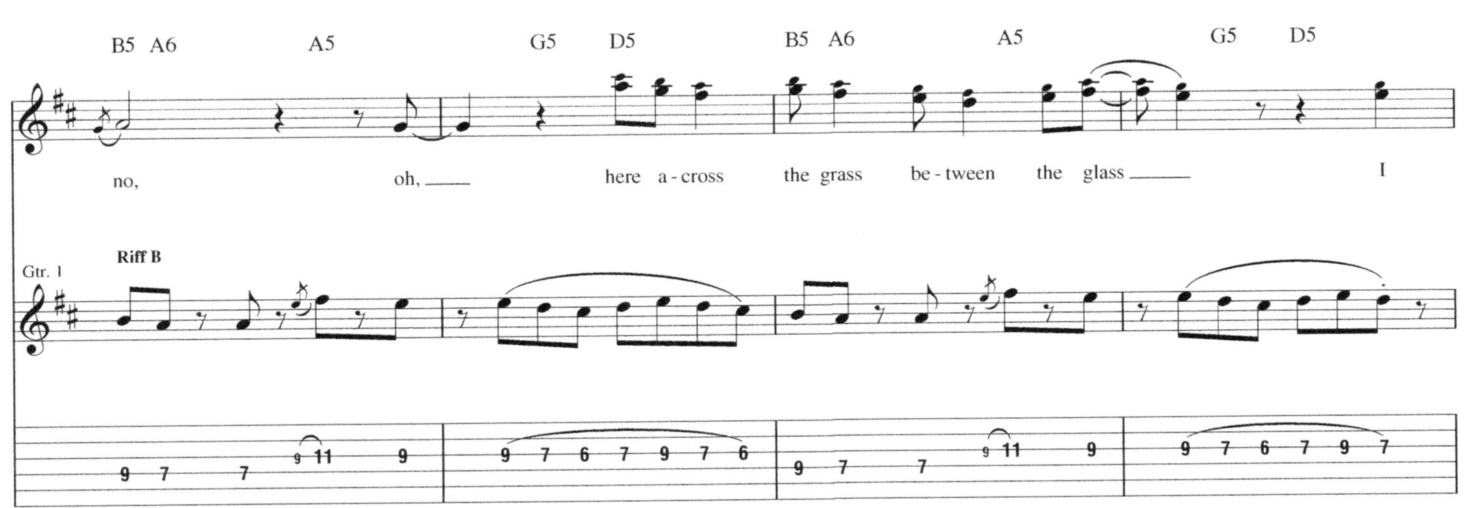

B5 A6 A5 G5 D5 B5 A6 A5 G5 D5
no, oh,_ here a-cross the grass be-tween the glass_ I
Riff B
Gtr. 1

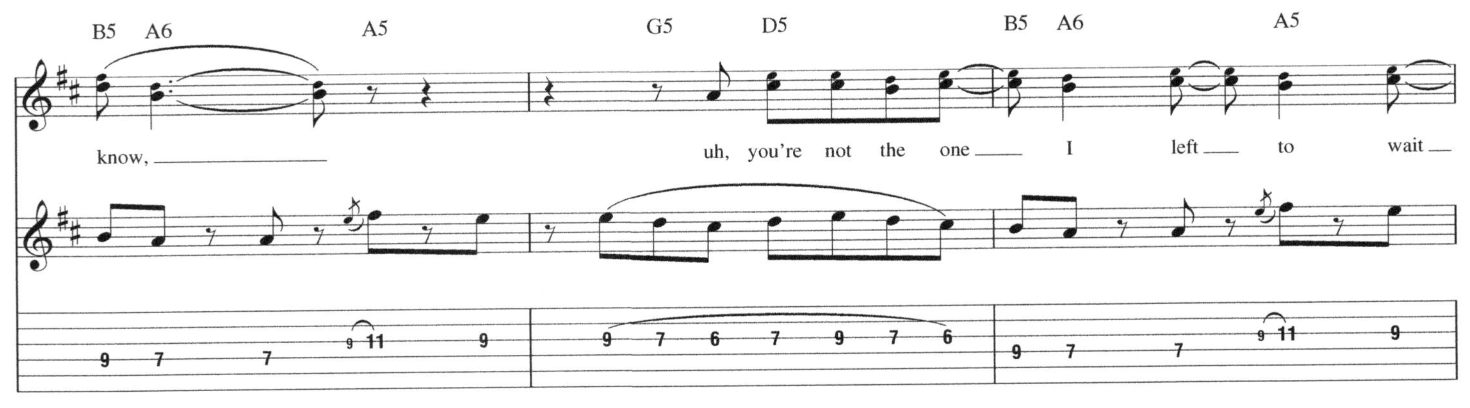
B5 A6 A5 G5 D5 B5 A6 A5
know, uh, you're not the one I left to wait

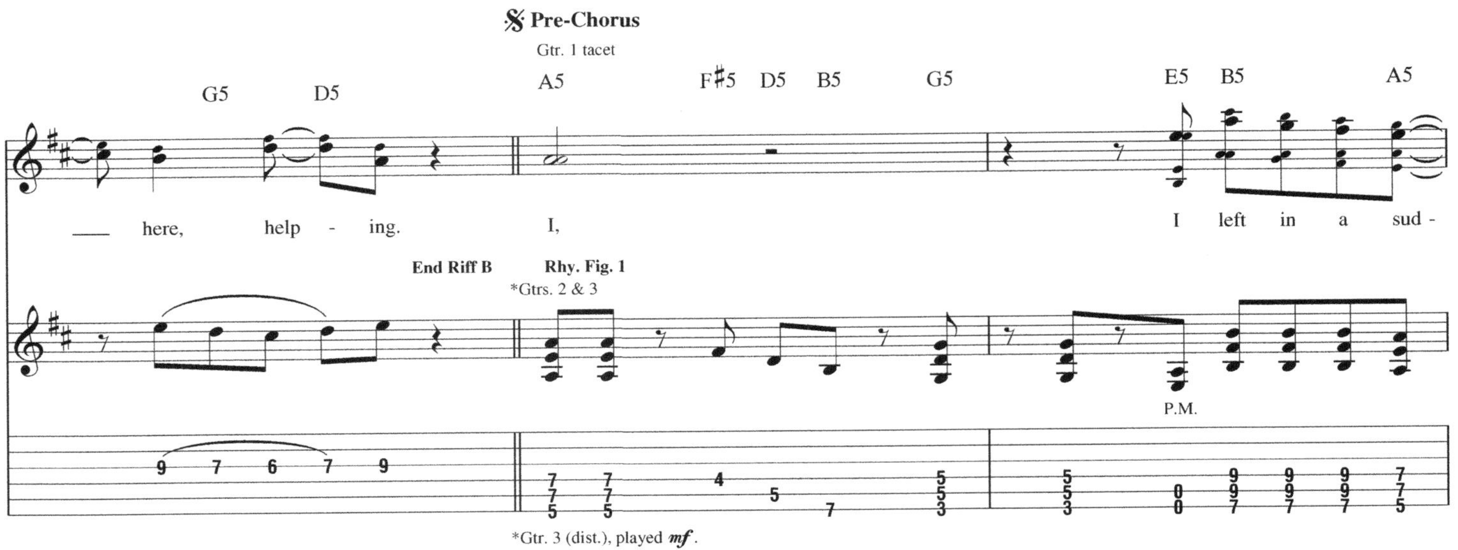
Pre-Chorus
Gtr. 1 tacet
G5 D5 A5 F#5 D5 B5 G5 E5 B5 A5
here, helping. I, I left in a sud-
End Riff B
Rhy. Fig. 1
*Gtrs. 2 & 3
P.M.
*Gtr. 3 (dist.), played mf.

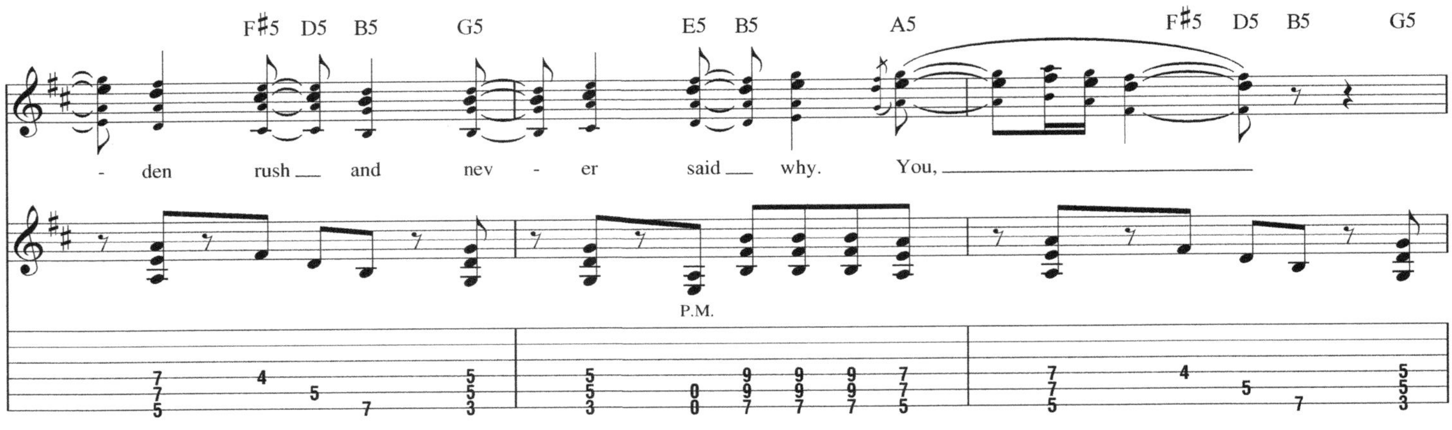
F#5 D5 B5 G5 E5 B5 A5 F#5 D5 B5 G5
-den rush and nev-er said why. You,
P.M.

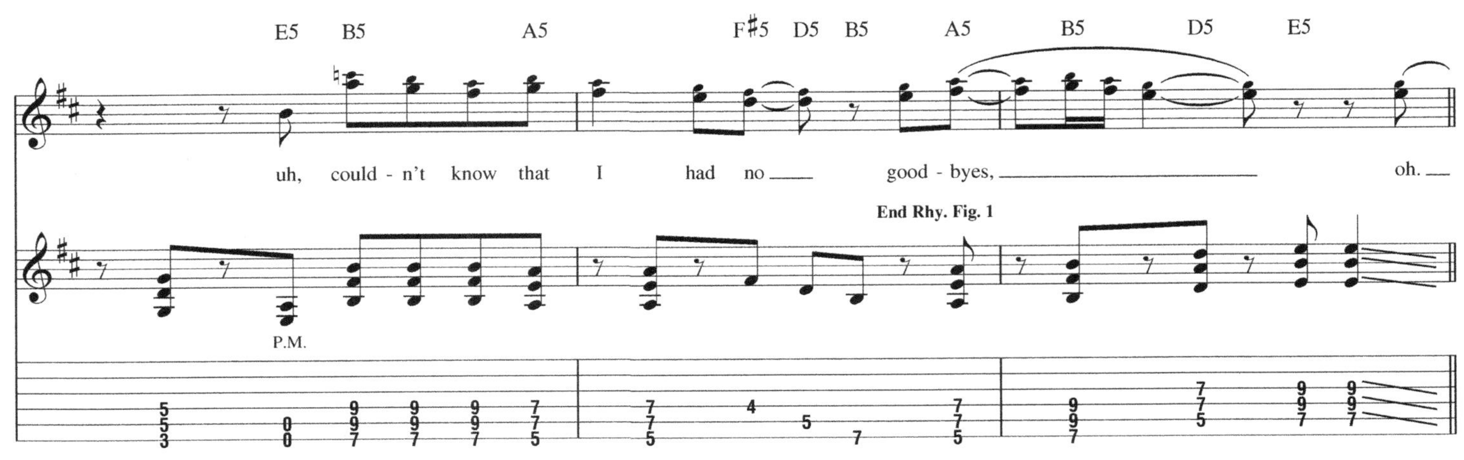
E5 B5 A5 F#5 D5 B5 A5 B5 D5 E5
uh, could-n't know that I had no good-byes, oh.
End Rhy. Fig. 1
P.M.

Chorus

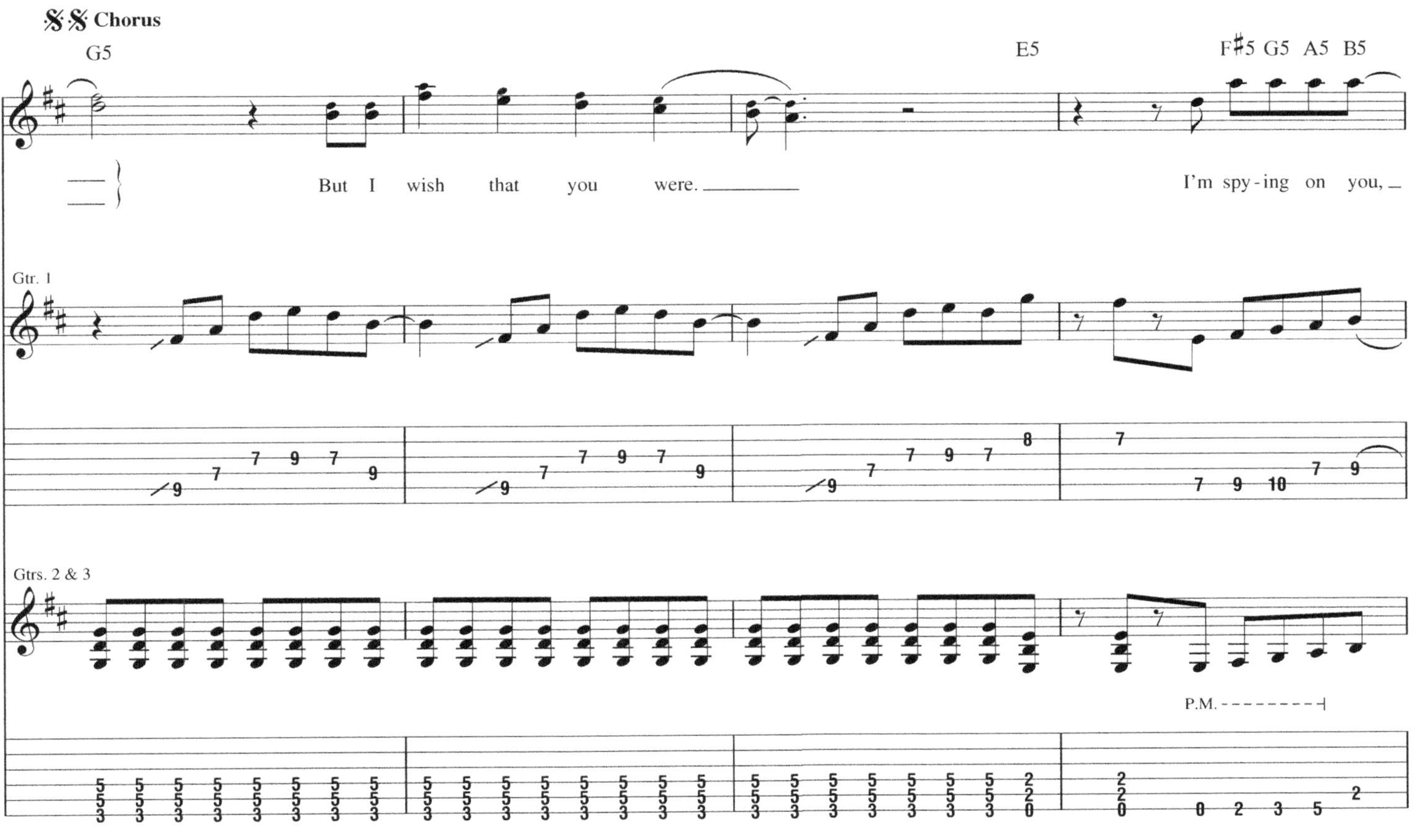
G5
E5
F♯5 G5 A5 B5
But I wish that you were.
I'm spy-ing on you,
Gtr. 1
Gtrs. 2 & 3
P.M.

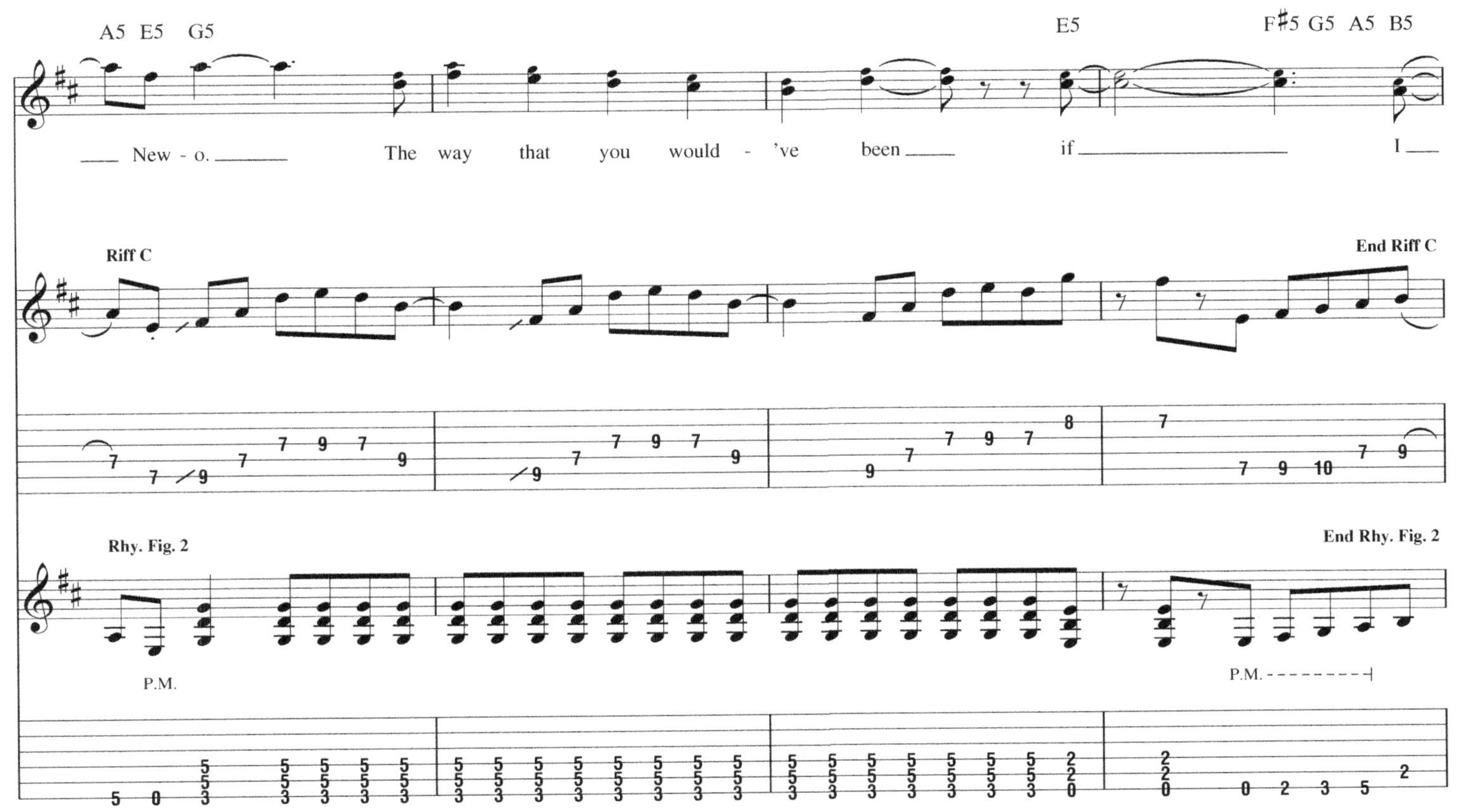
A5 E5 G5
E5
F♯5 G5 A5 B5
New - o.
The way that you would - 've been if I
Riff C
End Riff C
Rhy. Fig. 2
End Rhy. Fig. 2
P.M.
P.M.

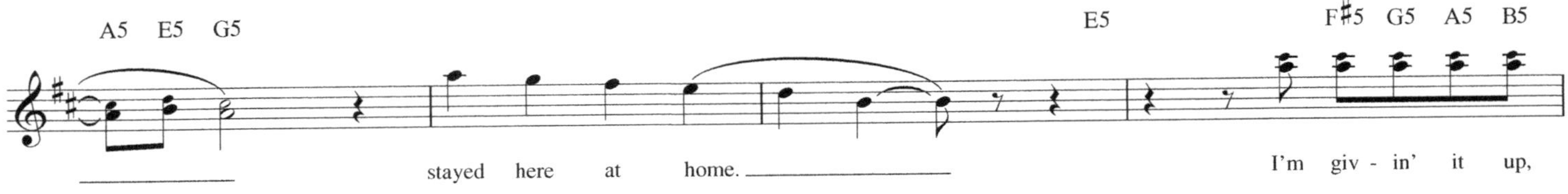
Gtr. 1: w/ Riff C
Gtrs. 2 & 3: w/ Rhy. Fig. 2 (1 3/4 times)
A5 E5 G5
E5
F♯5 G5 A5 B5
stayed here at home.
I'm giv - in' it up,

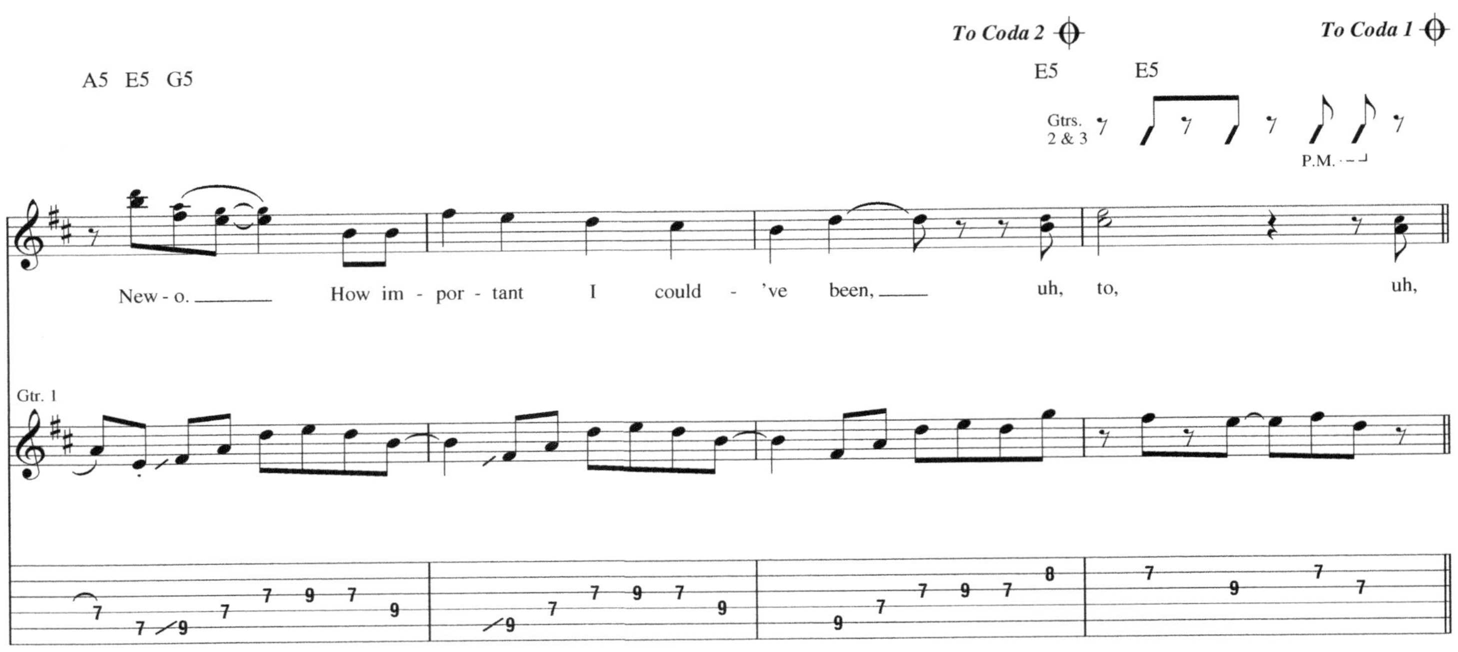
To Coda 2
To Coda 1
A5 E5 G5
E5 E5
Gtrs. 2 & 3
P.M.
New - o. How im - por - tant I could - 've been, uh, to, uh,
Gtr. 1

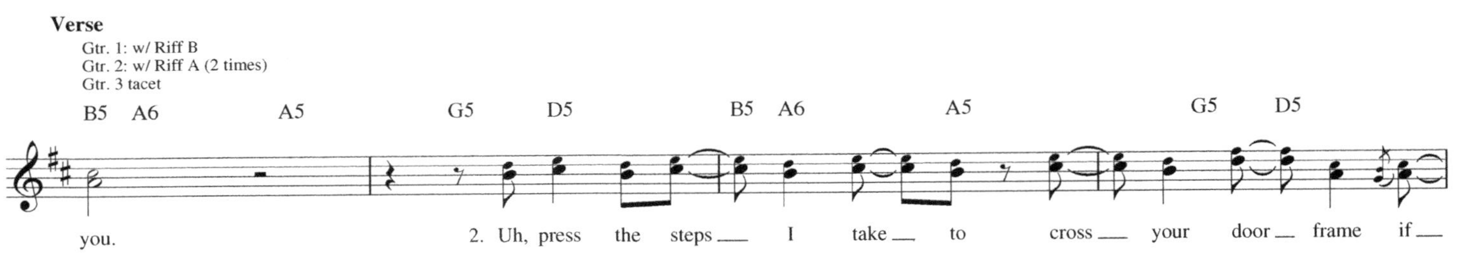
Verse
Gtr. 1: w/ Riff B
Gtr. 2: w/ Riff A (2 times)
Gtr. 3 tacet
B5 A6 A5 G5 D5 B5 A6 A5 G5 D5
you. 2. Uh, press the steps I take to cross your door frame if

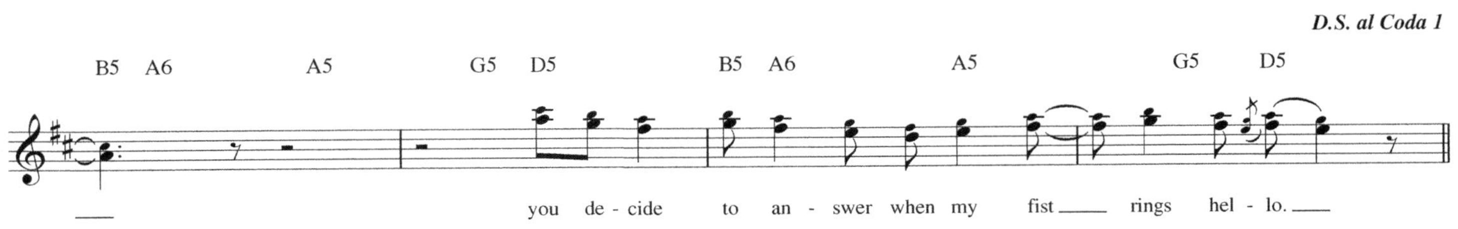
D.S. al Coda 1
B5 A6 A5 G5 D5 B5 A6 A5 G5 D5
you de - cide to an - swer when my fist rings hel - lo.

Coda 1

Bridge

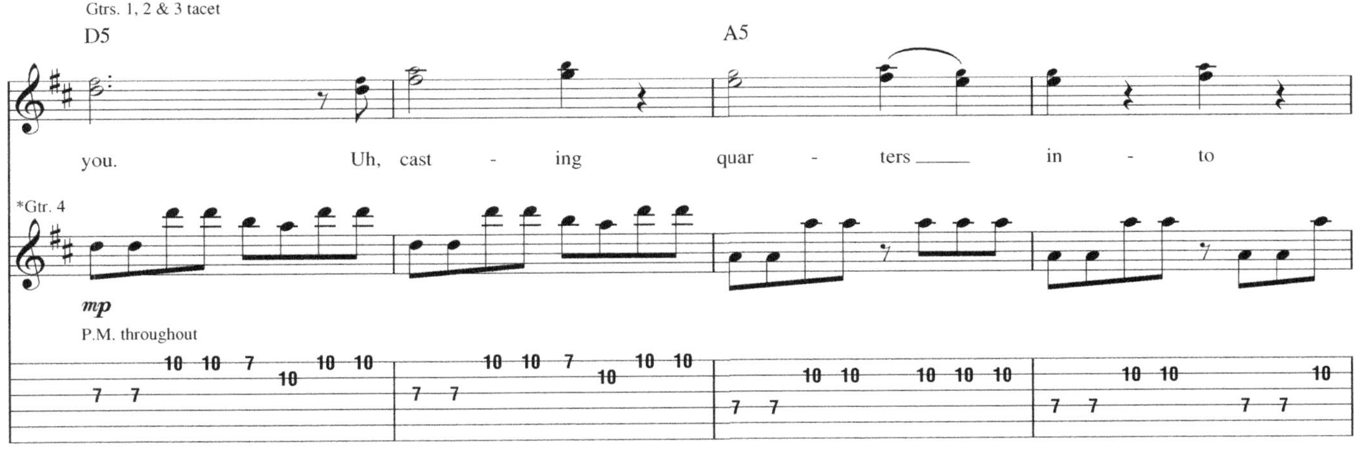

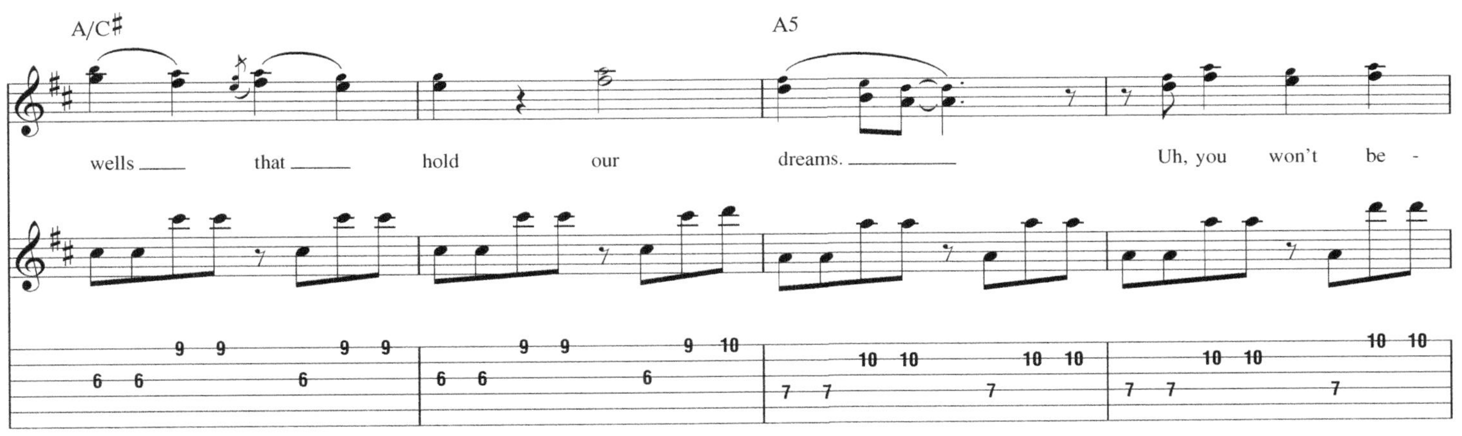

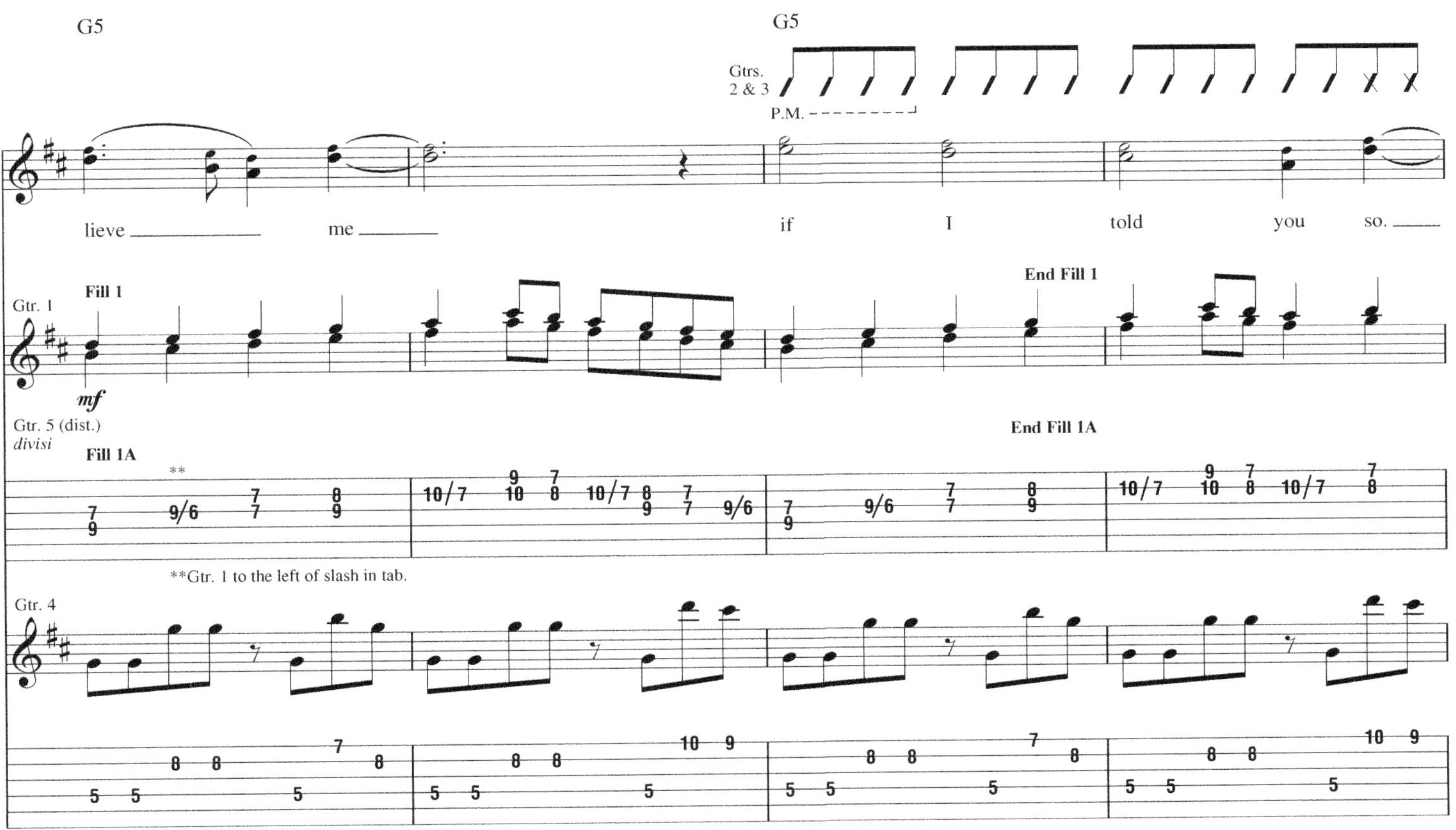

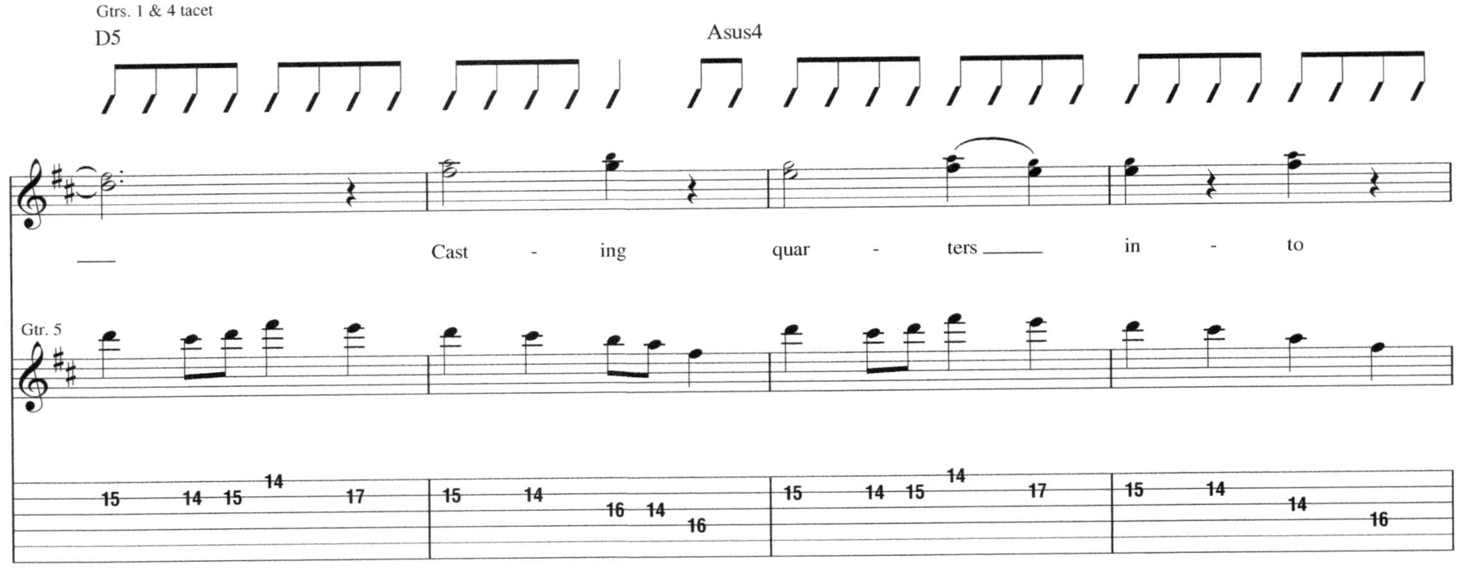
Gtrs. 1 & 4 tacet
D5
Asus4
Cast - ing quar - ters in - to
Gtr. 5

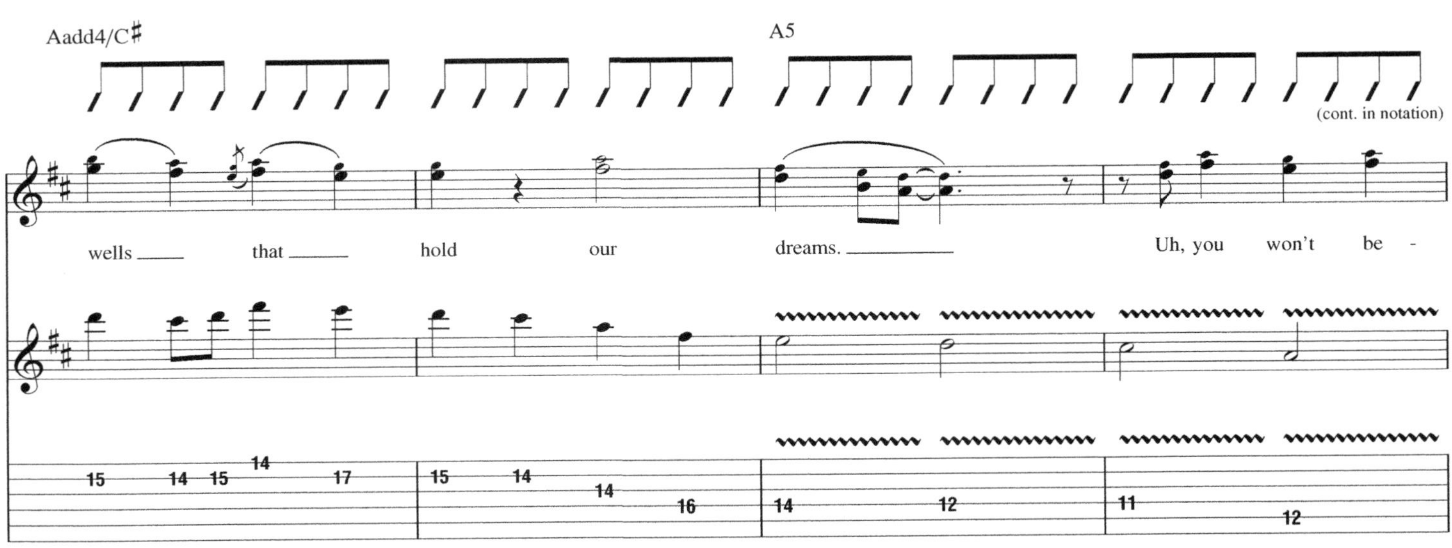
Aadd4/C♯
A5
(cont. in notation)
wells that hold our dreams. Uh, you won't be -

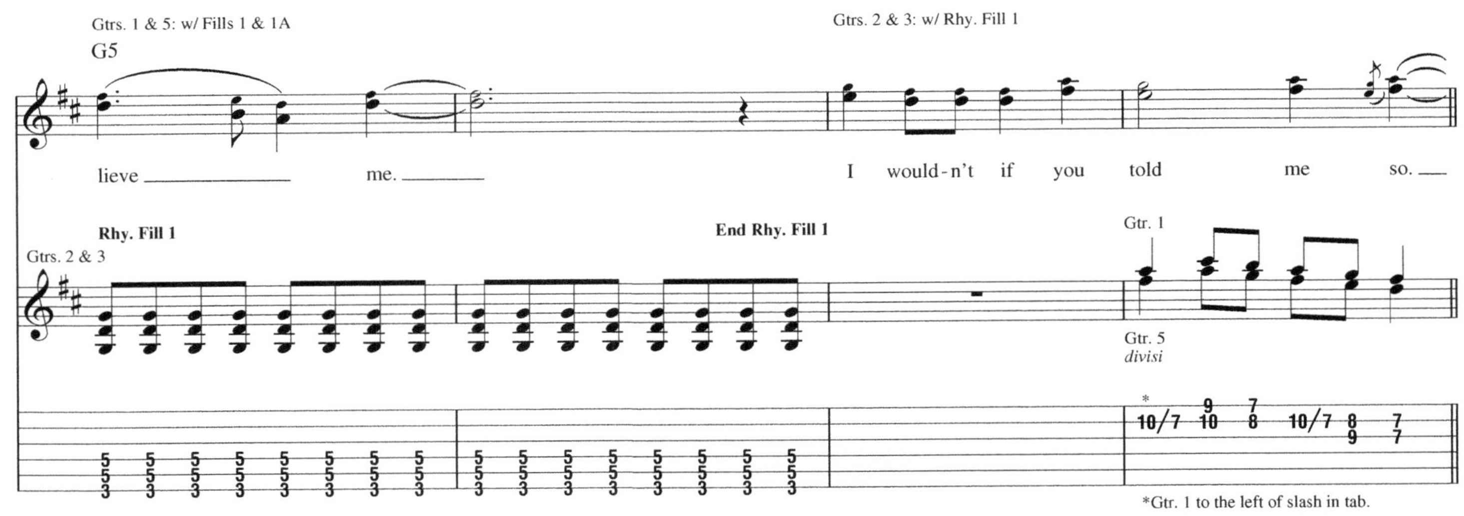
Gtrs. 1 & 5: w/ Fills 1 & 1A
G5
Gtrs. 2 & 3: w/ Rhy. Fill 1
lieve me. I would-n't if you told me so.
Rhy. Fill 1
Gtrs. 2 & 3
End Rhy. Fill 1
Gtr. 1
Gtr. 5
divisi
*Gtr. 1 to the left of slash in tab.

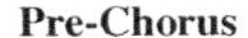
Pre-Chorus

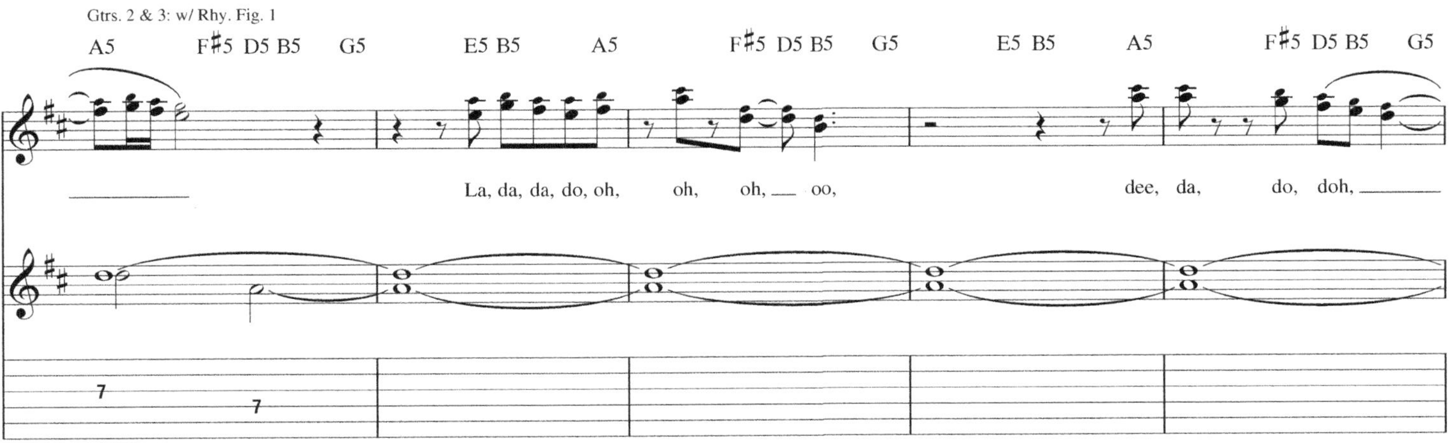
Gtrs. 2 & 3: w/ Rhy. Fig. 1
A5 F♯5 D5 B5 G5 E5 B5 A5 F♯5 D5 B5 G5 E5 B5 A5 F♯5 D5 B5 G5
La, da, da, do, oh, oh, oh, oo, dee, da, do, doh,

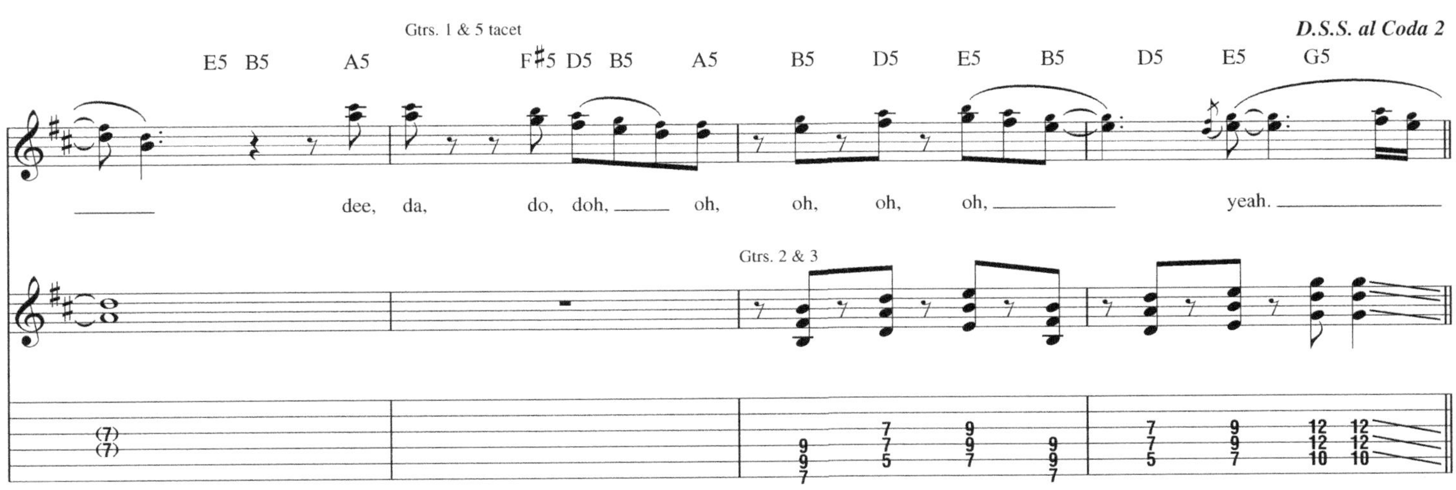
Gtrs. 1 & 5 tacet
D.S.S. al Coda 2
E5 B5 A5 F♯5 D5 B5 A5 B5 D5 E5 B5 D5 E5 G5
dee, da, do, doh, oh, oh, oh, oh, yeah.
Gtrs. 2 & 3

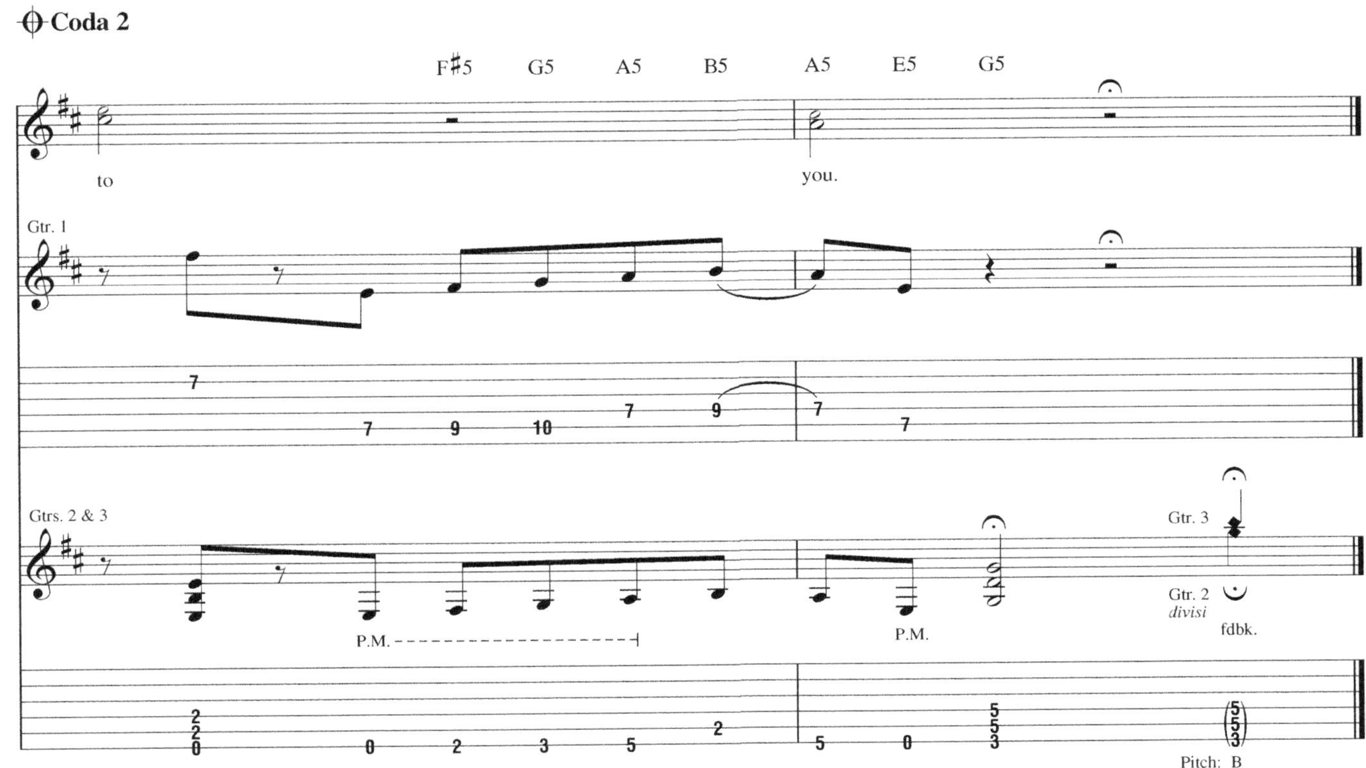
Coda 2
F♯5 G5 A5 B5 A5 E5 G5
to you.
Gtr. 1
Gtrs. 2 & 3
P.M.
P.M.
Gtr. 3
Gtr. 2
divisi
fdbk.
Pitch: B

Apollo I: The Writing Writer

Words and Music by Claudio Sanchez, Michael Todd, Joshua Eppard and Travis Stever

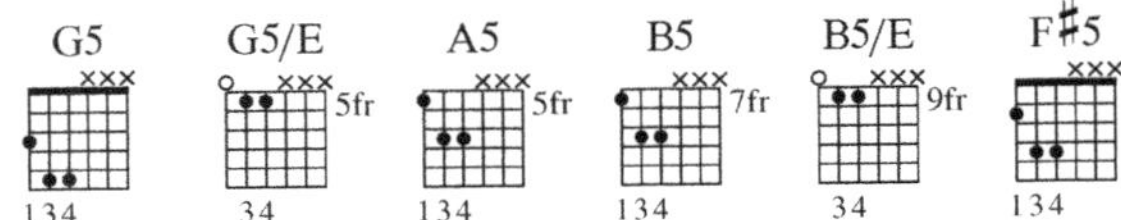

Tune down 1/2 step:
(low to high) E♭-A♭-D♭-G♭-B♭-E♭

Intro
Free time

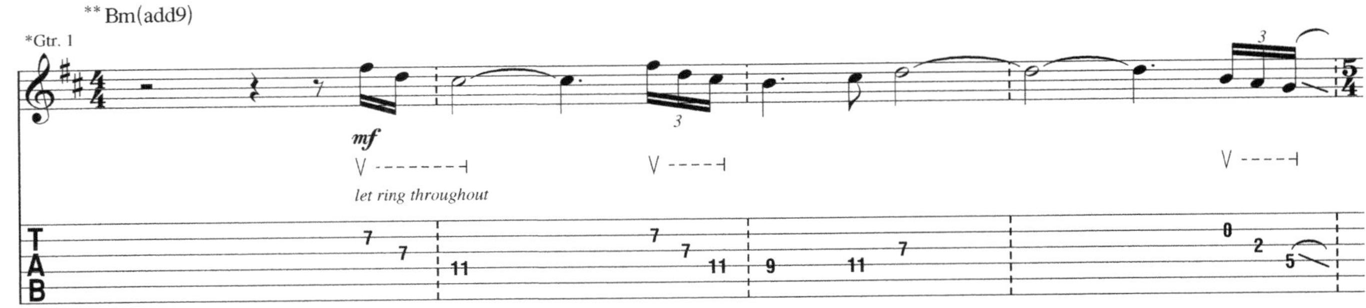

*Kybd. arr. for gtr.
**Chord symbols reflect overall harmony.

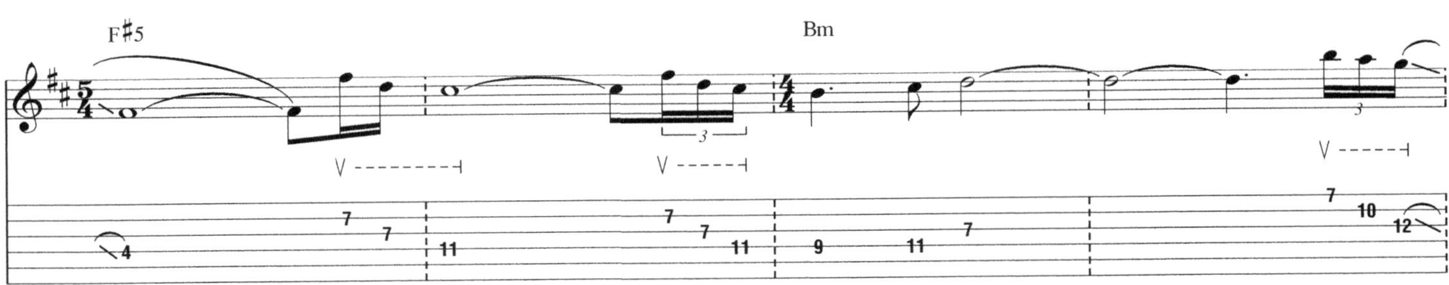

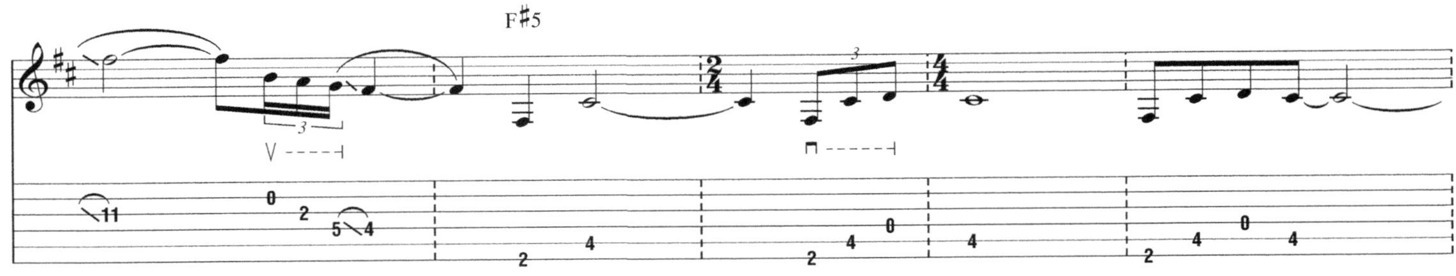

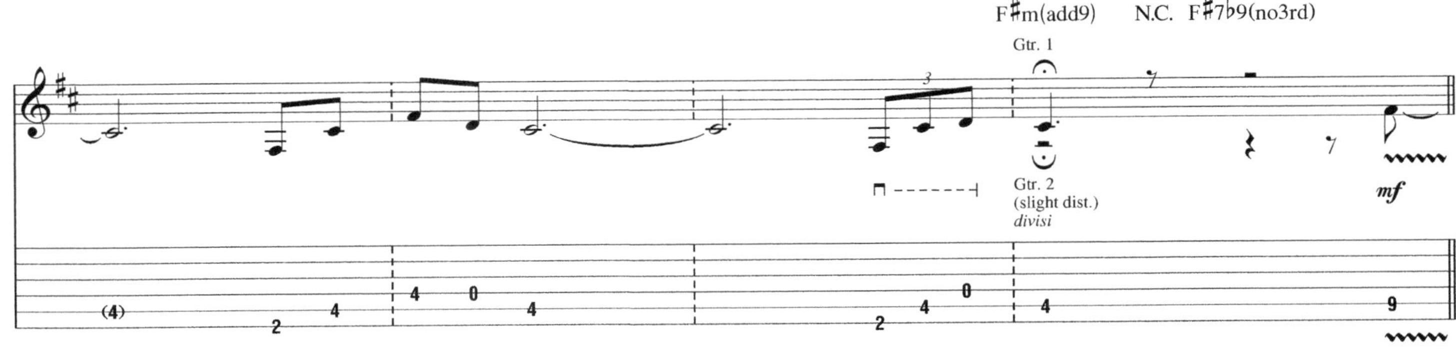

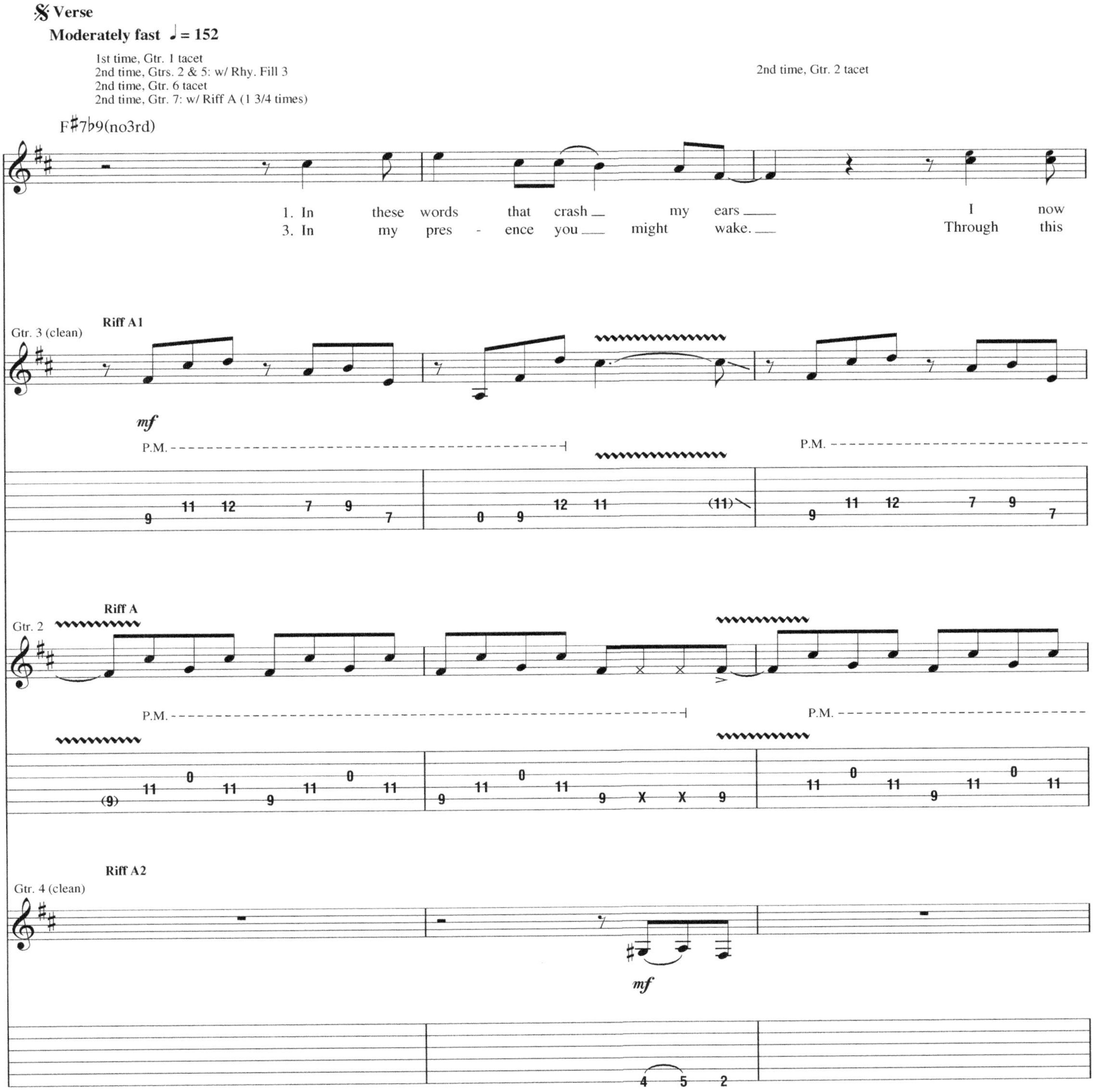

𝄋 Verse

Moderately fast ♩ = 152

1st time, Gtr. 1 tacet
2nd time, Gtrs. 2 & 5: w/ Rhy. Fill 3
2nd time, Gtr. 6 tacet
2nd time, Gtr. 7: w/ Riff A (1 3/4 times)

2nd time, Gtr. 2 tacet

F♯7♭9(no3rd)

1. In these words that crash __ my ears __ I now
3. In my pres - ence you __ might wake. __ Through this

Gtr. 3 (clean) **Riff A1**

mf

P.M. - ┤ P.M. - - - - - - - - - - - - -

Gtr. 2 **Riff A**

P.M. - ┤ P.M. - - - - - - - - - - - - -

Gtr. 4 (clean) **Riff A2**

mf

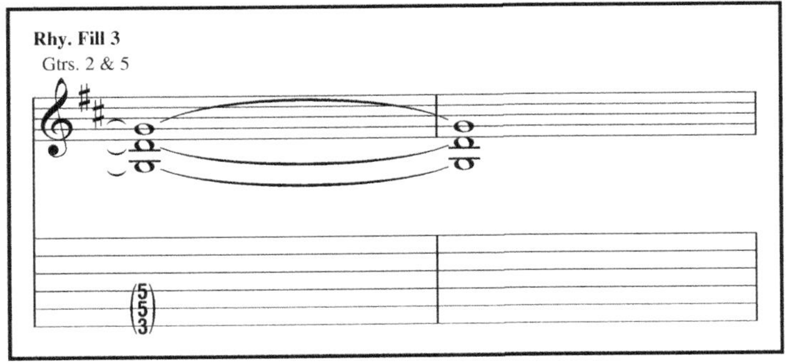

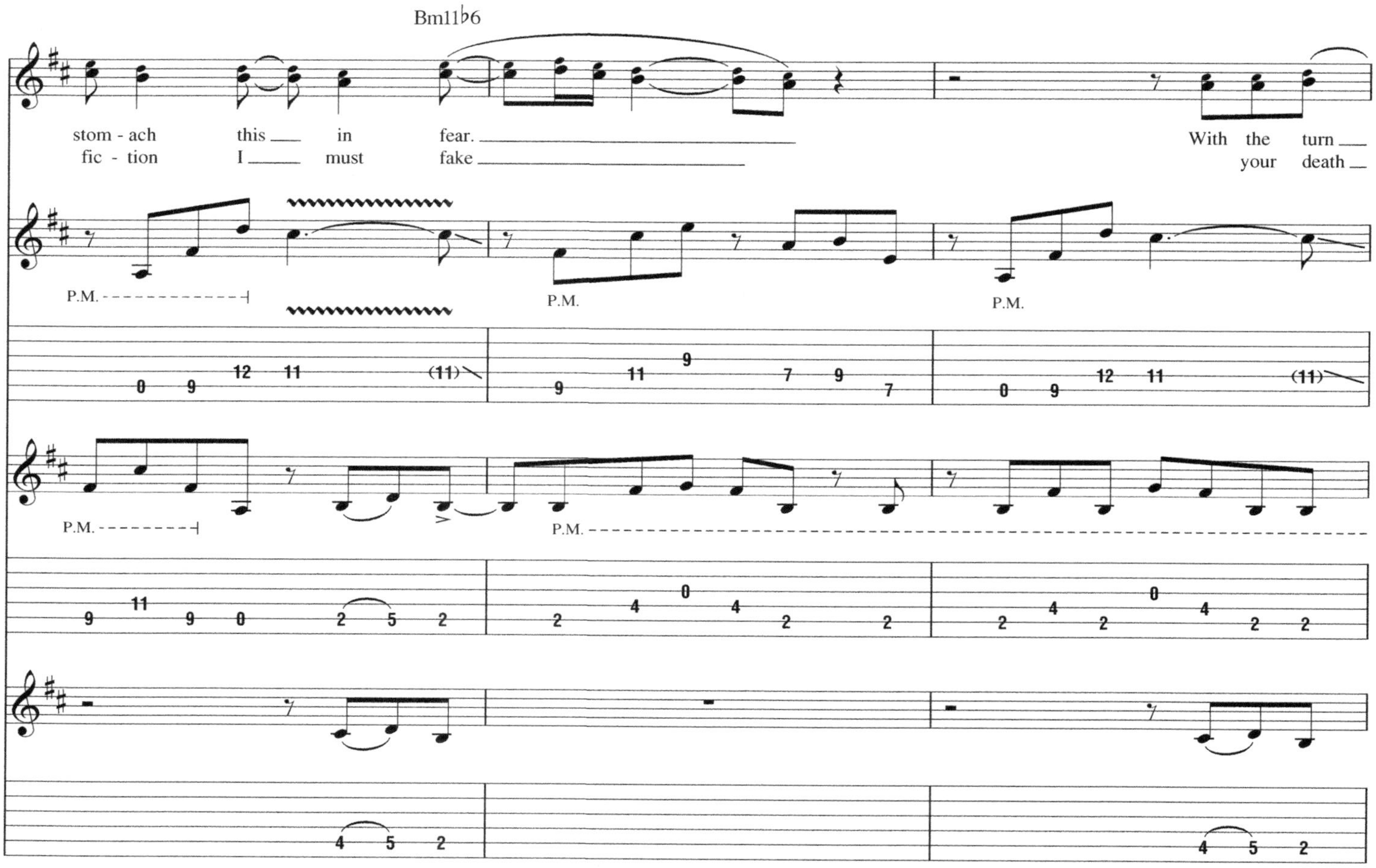

Bm11♭6

stom - ach this ___ in fear. ___
fic - tion I ___ must fake ___

With the turn ___
your death ___

P.M.

P.M.

P.M.

P.M.

P.M.

1st time, Gtr. 2: w/ Riff A
1st time, Gtr. 3: w/ Riff A1 (1st 7 meas.)
Gtr. 4: w/ Riff A2
2nd time, Gtr. 3: w/ Riff A1

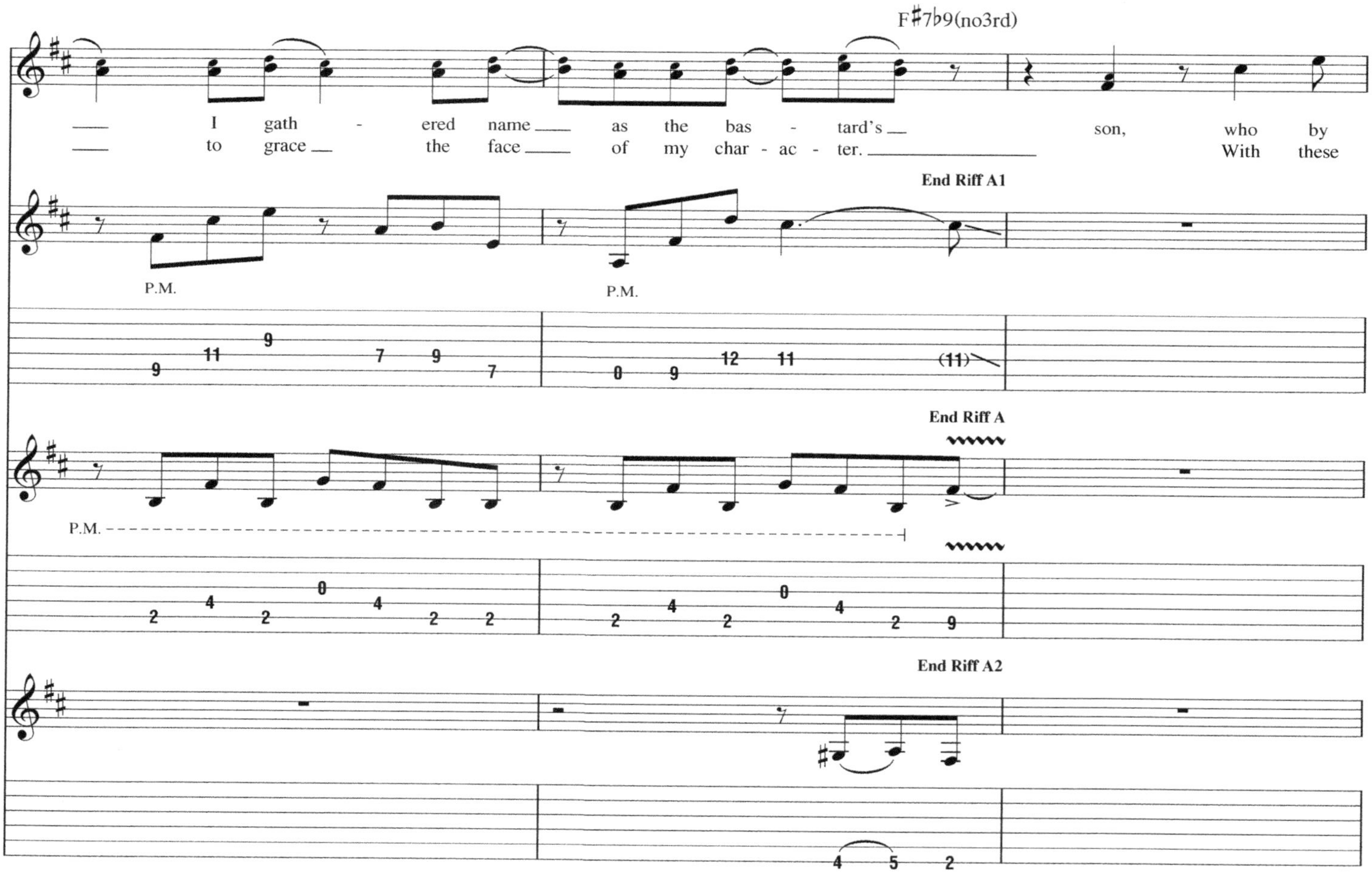

F♯7♭9(no3rd)

___ I gath - ered name ___ as the bas - tard's ___ son, who by
___ to grace ___ the face ___ of my char - ac - ter. ___ With these

End Riff A1

P.M.

P.M.

End Riff A

P.M.

End Riff A2

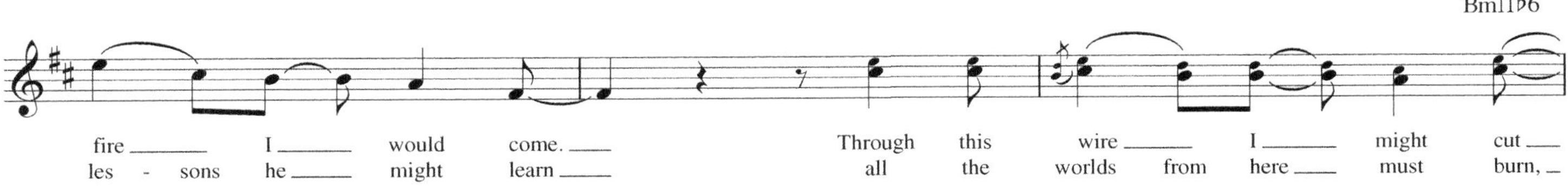

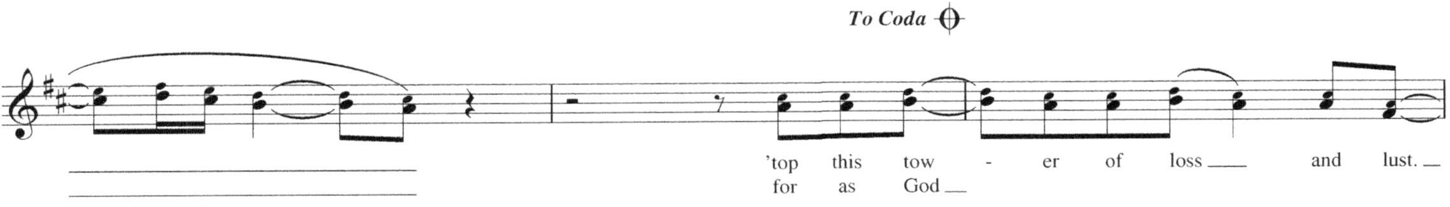

Verse

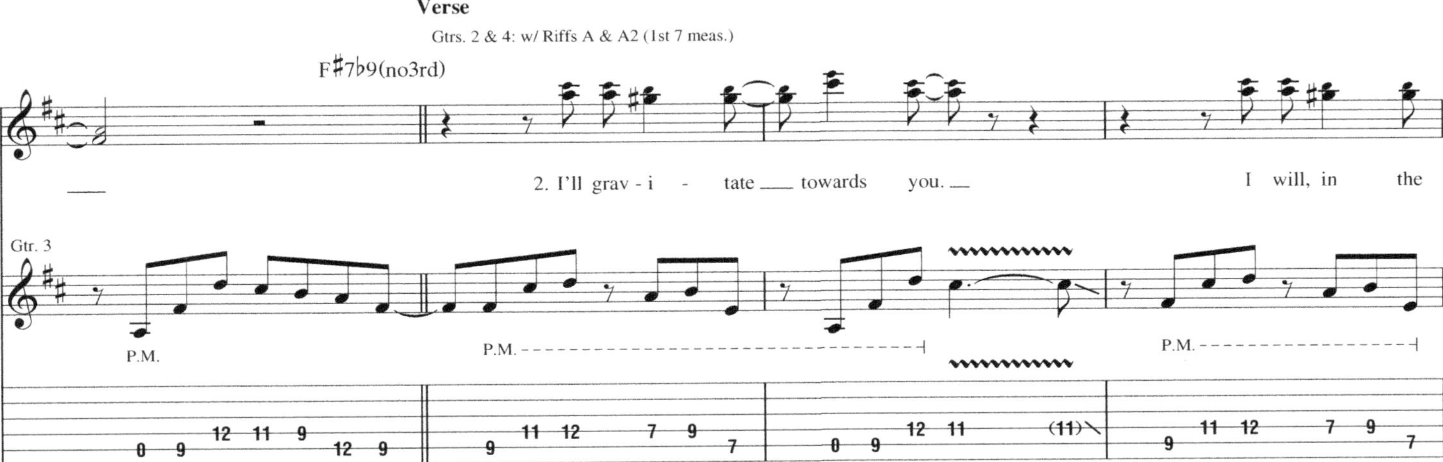

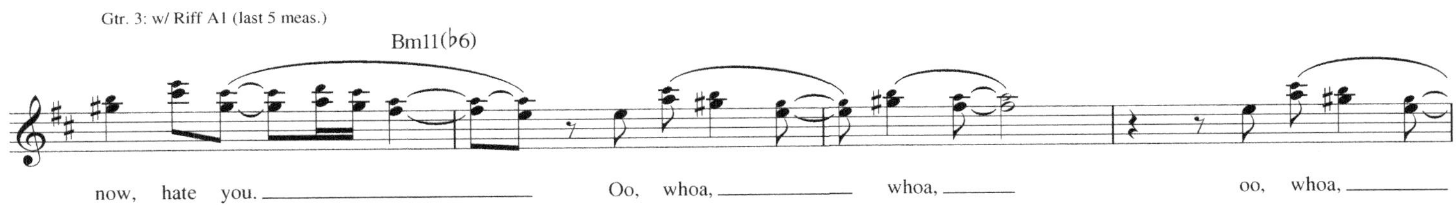

Pre-Chorus

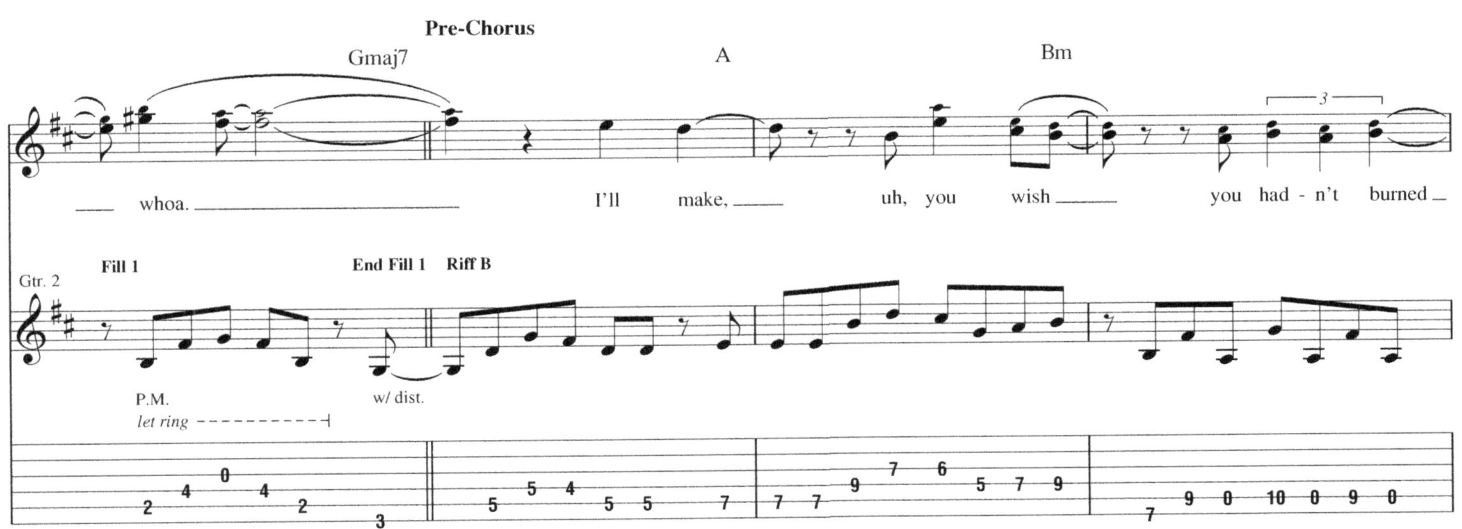

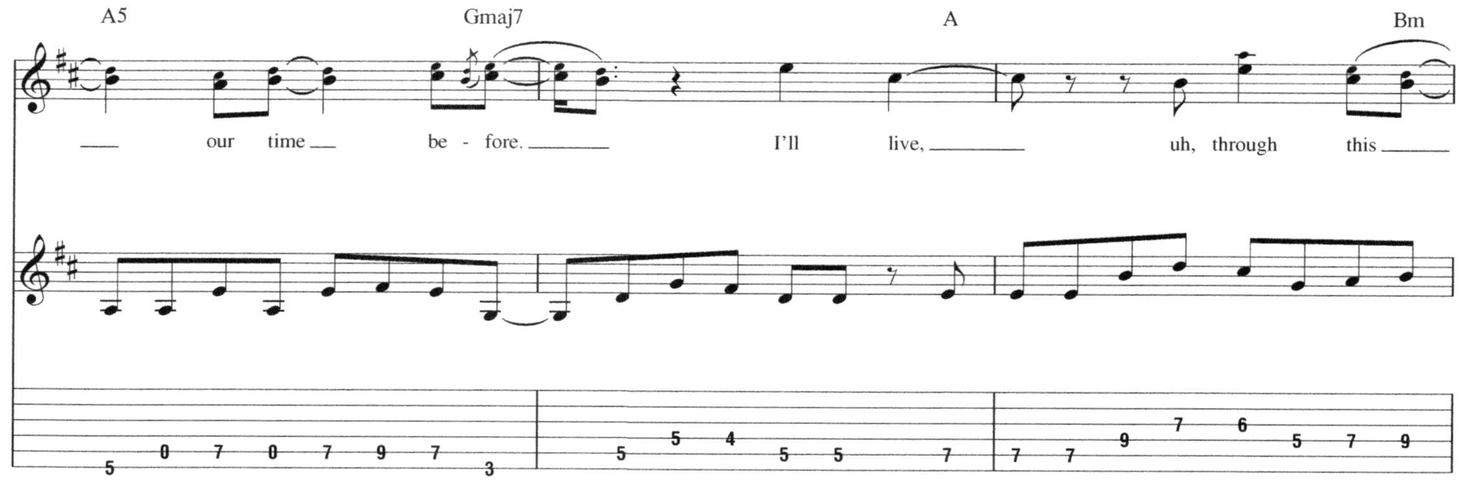
A5
Gmaj7
A
Bm
our time be - fore. I'll live, uh, through this
5 0 7 0 7 9 7 3
5 5 4 5 5 7
7 7 9 7 6 5 7 9

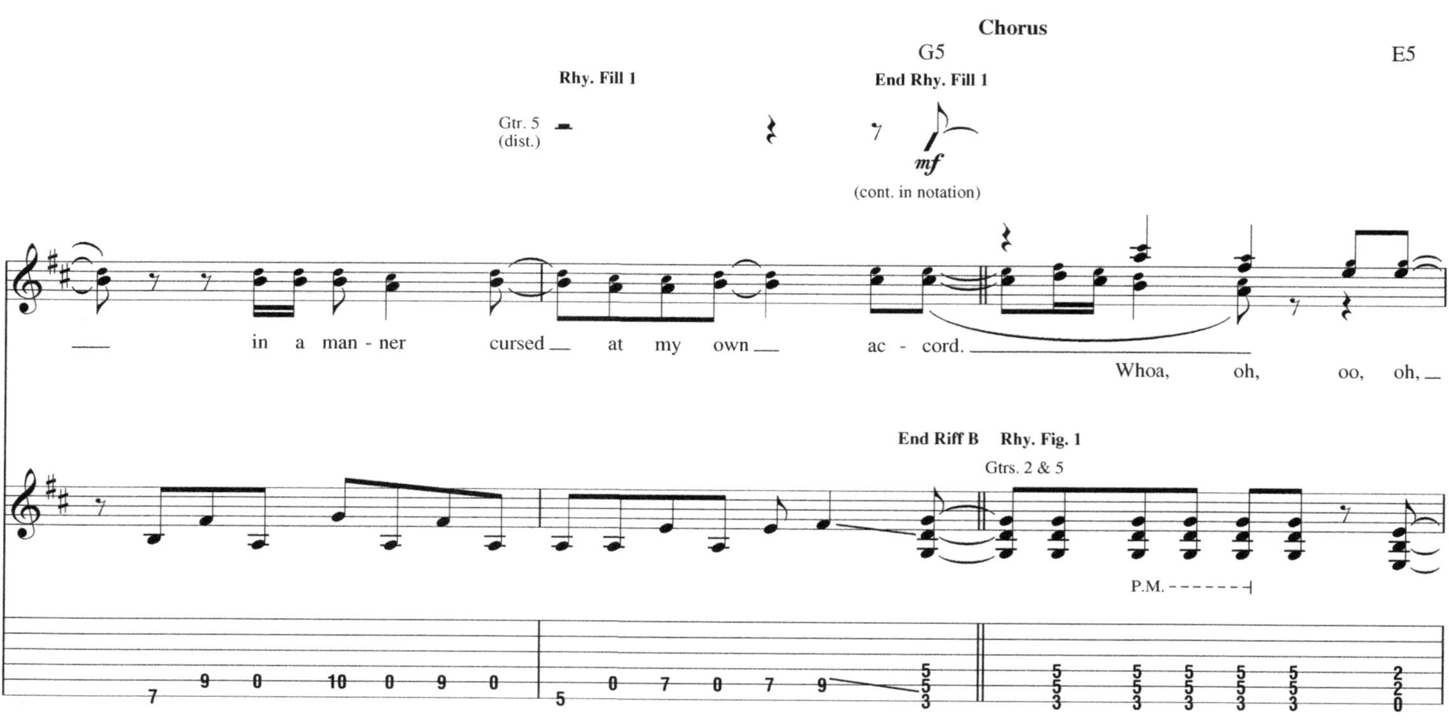
Chorus
G5
E5
Rhy. Fill 1
End Rhy. Fill 1
Gtr. 5 (dist.)
mf
(cont. in notation)
in a man - ner cursed at my own ac - cord.
Whoa, oh, oo, oh,
End Riff B
Rhy. Fig. 1
Gtrs. 2 & 5
P.M.

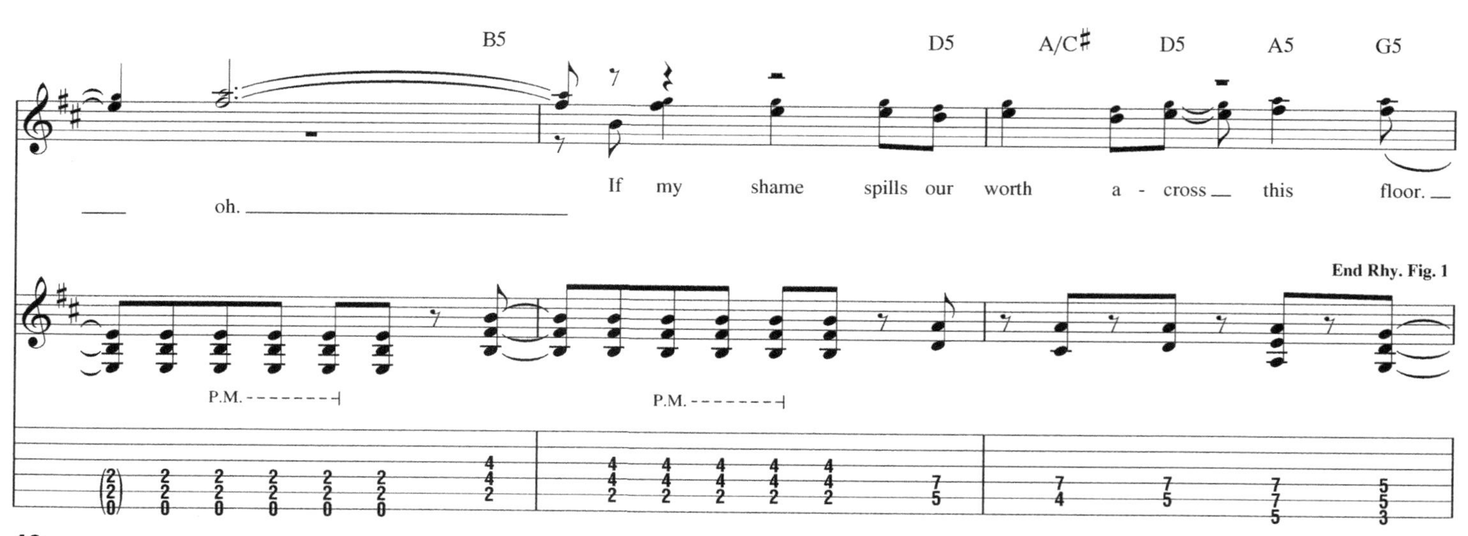
B5
D5
A/C♯
D5
A5
G5
oh.
If my shame spills our worth a - cross this floor.
End Rhy. Fig. 1
P.M.
P.M.

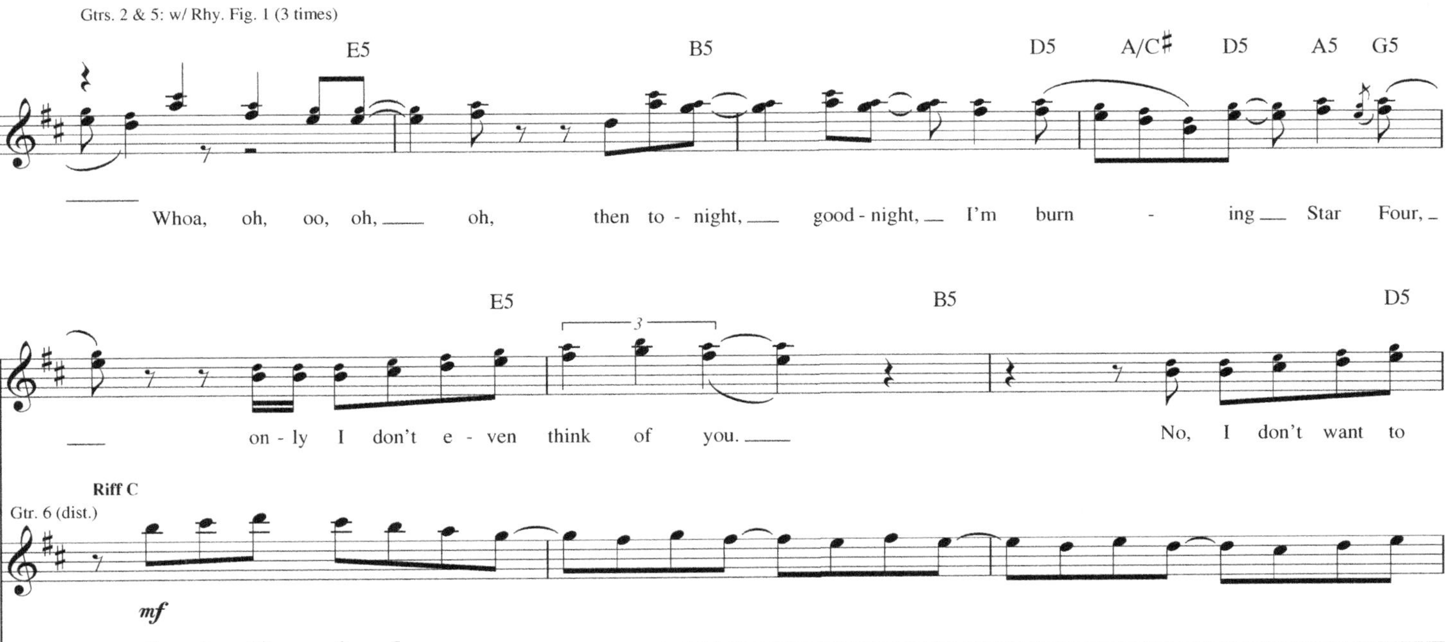

Gtrs. 2 & 5: w/ Rhy. Fig. 1 (3 times)
E5 B5 D5 A/C♯ D5 A5 G5
Whoa, oh, oo, oh, oh, then to - night, good - night, I'm burn - ing Star Four,
E5 B5 D5
only I don't e - ven think of you. No, I don't want to
Riff C
Gtr. 6 (dist.)
mf

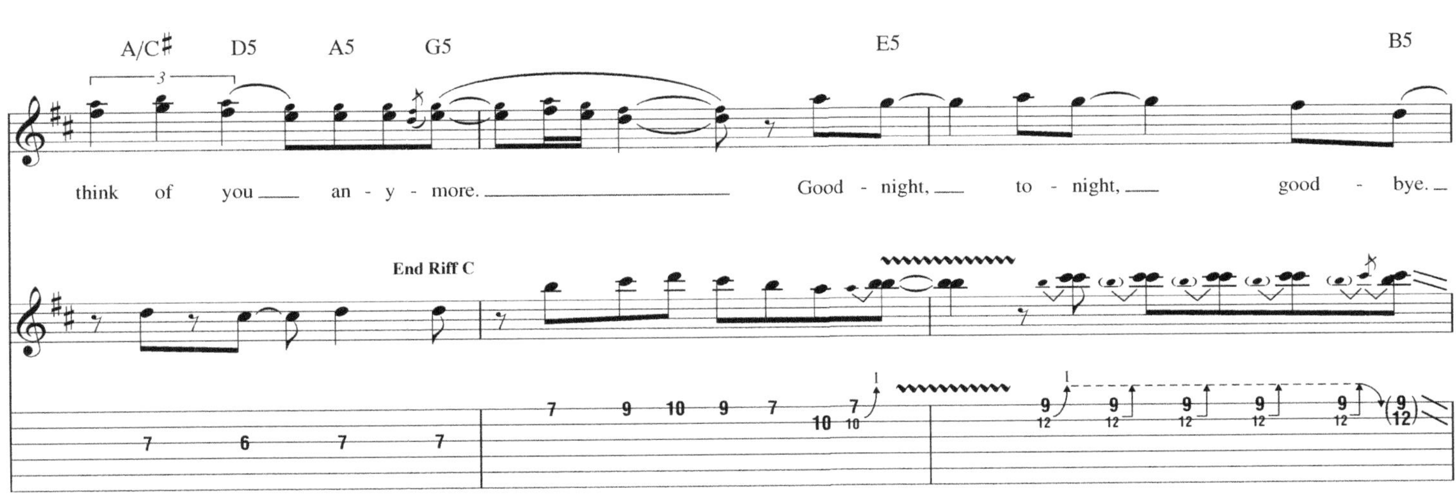

A/C♯ D5 A5 G5 E5 B5
think of you an - y - more. Good - night, to - night, good - bye.
End Riff C

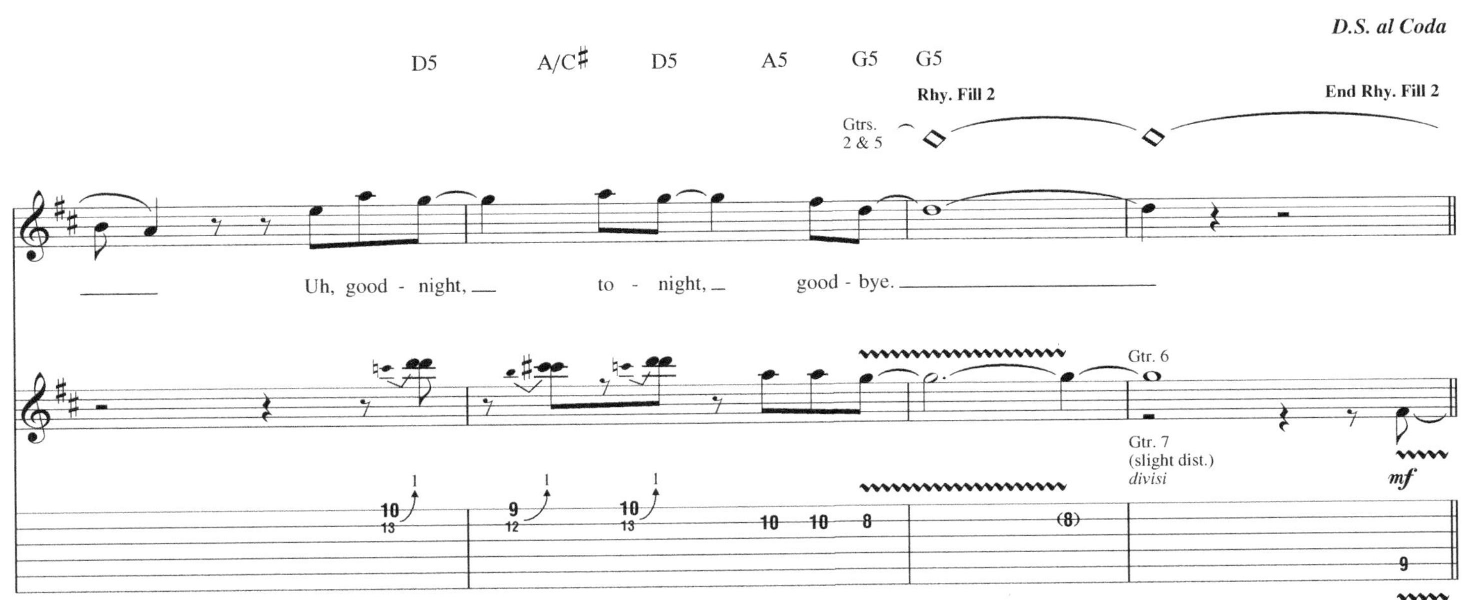

D.S. al Coda
D5 A/C♯ D5 A5 G5 G5
Rhy. Fill 2
End Rhy. Fill 2
Gtrs. 2 & 5
Uh, good - night, to - night, good - bye.
Gtr. 6
Gtr. 7 (slight dist.) divisi
mf

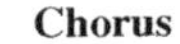
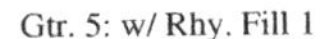
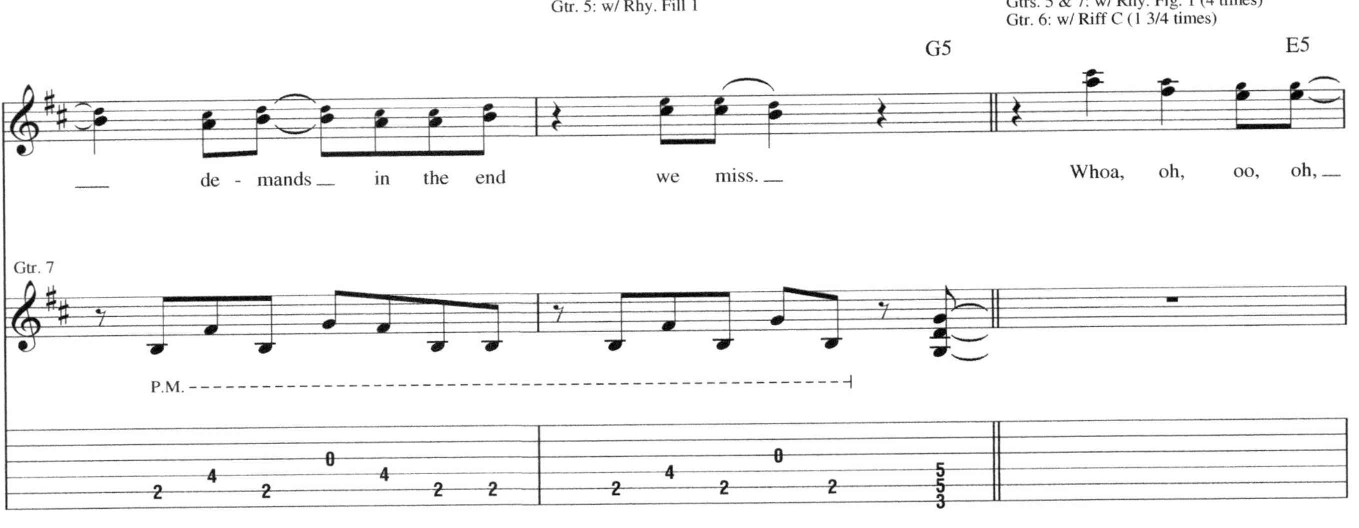
Coda
Chorus
Gtr. 5: w/ Rhy. Fill 1
Gtrs. 5 & 7: w/ Rhy. Fig. 1 (4 times)
Gtr. 6: w/ Riff C (1 3/4 times)
G5
E5
de - mands in the end we miss. Whoa, oh, oo, oh,
Gtr. 7
P.M.
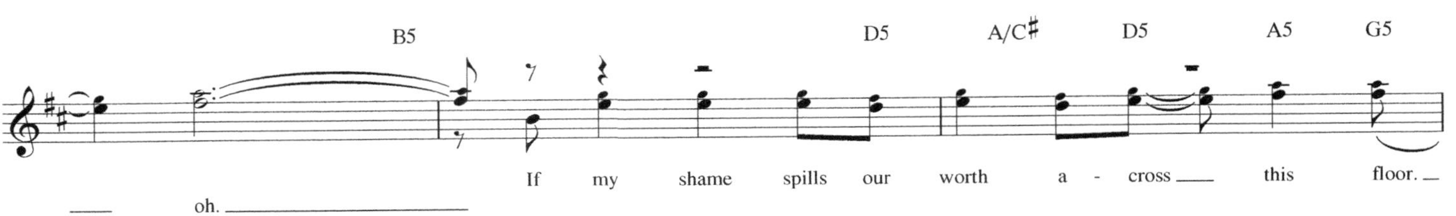
B5
D5
A/C♯
D5
A5
G5
oh.
If my shame spills our worth a - cross this floor.
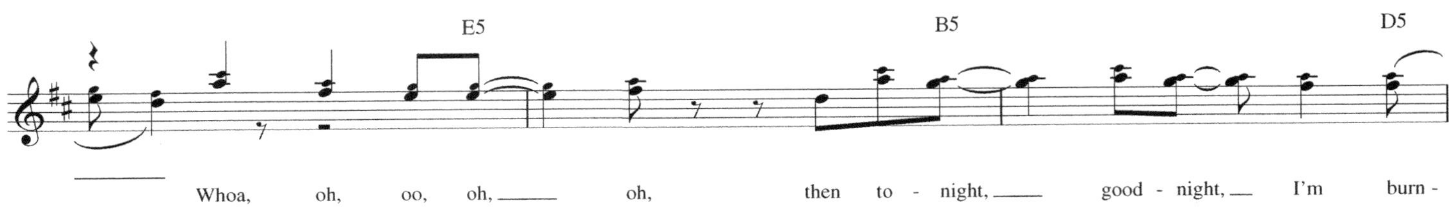
E5
B5
D5
Whoa, oh, oo, oh, oh, then to - night, good - night, I'm burn -
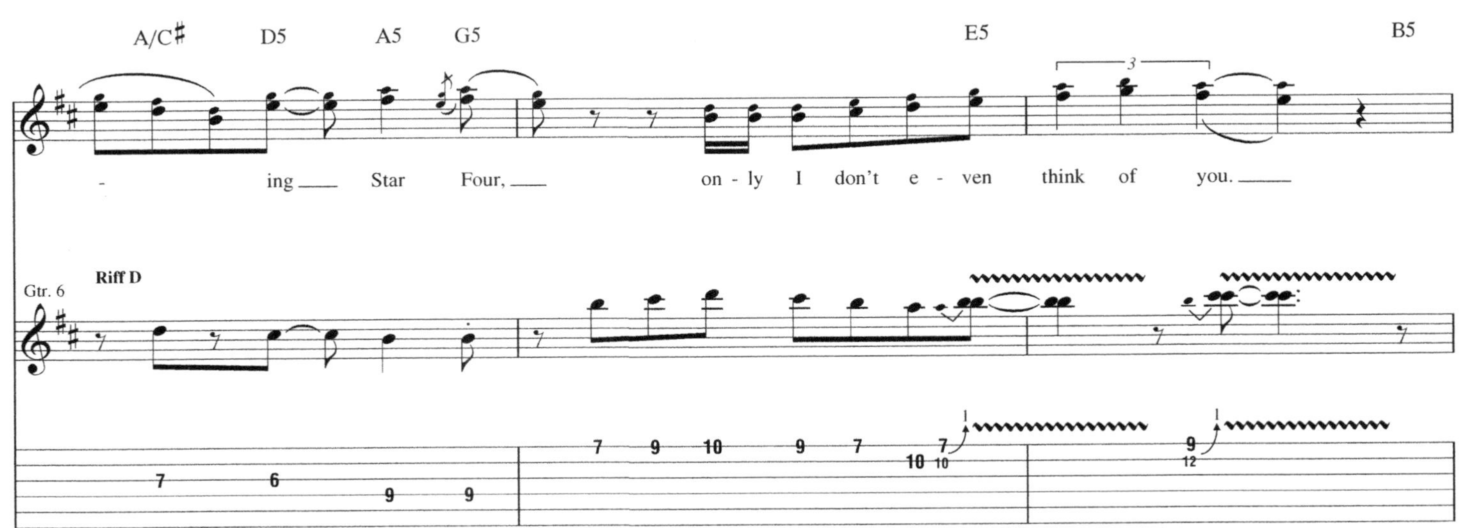
A/C♯
D5
A5
G5
E5
B5
- ing Star Four, on - ly I don't e - ven think of you.
Riff D
Gtr. 6

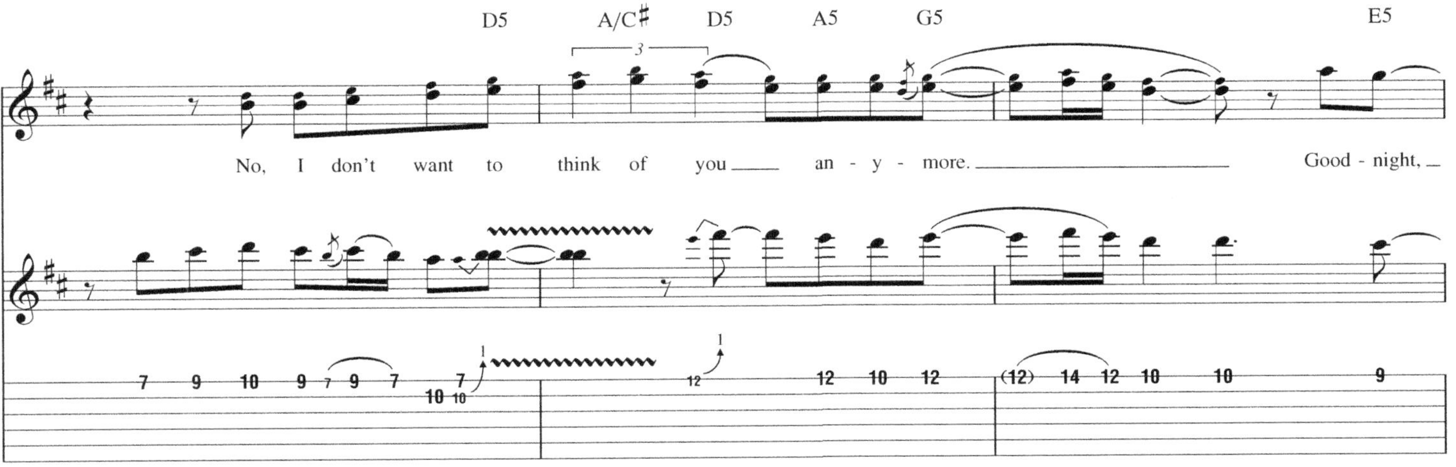
D5
A/C♯
D5
A5
G5
E5
No, I don't want to think of you anymore.
Good - night,

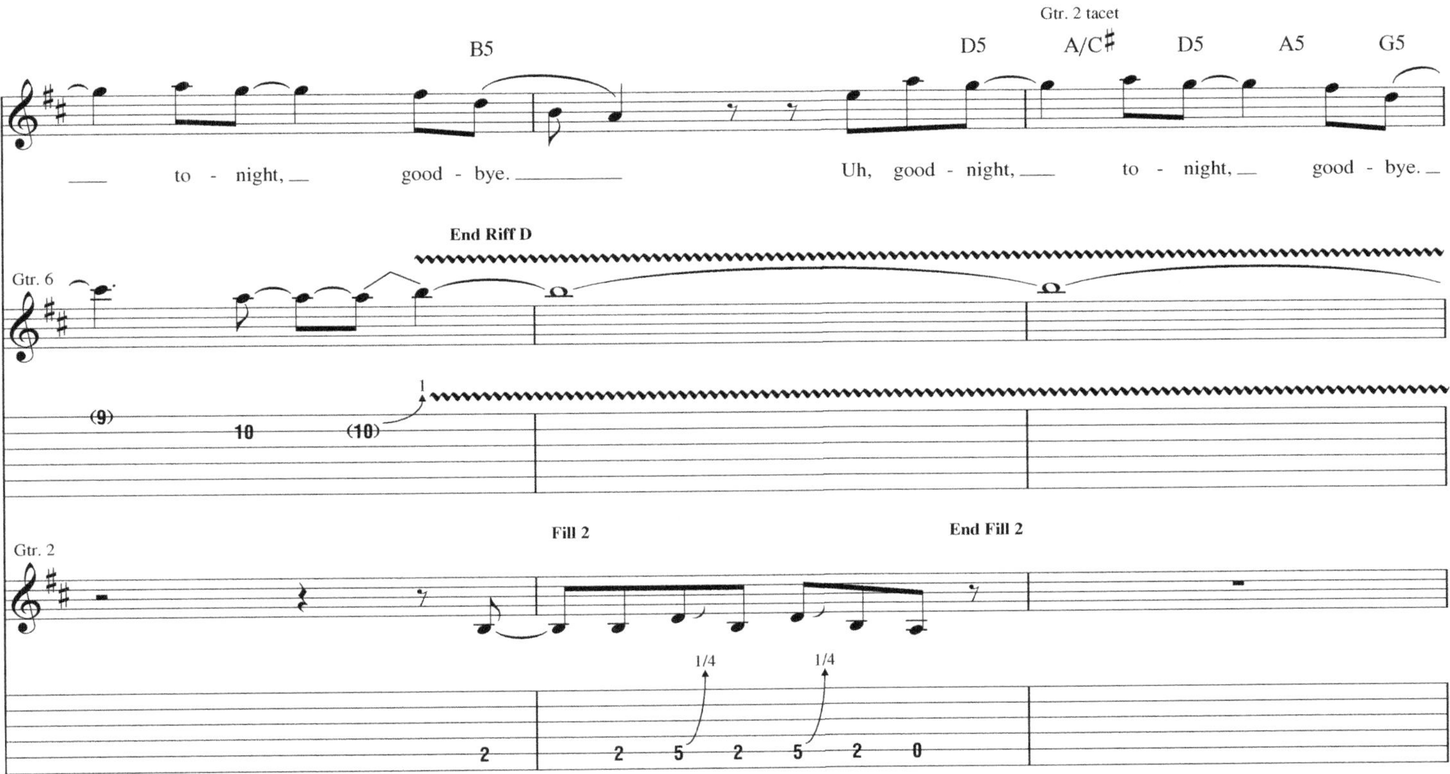
Gtr. 2 tacet
B5
D5
A/C♯
D5
A5
G5
to - night, good - bye.
Uh, good - night, to - night, good - bye.
End Riff D
Gtr. 6
Gtr. 2
Fill 2
End Fill 2
1/4
1/4

Interlude

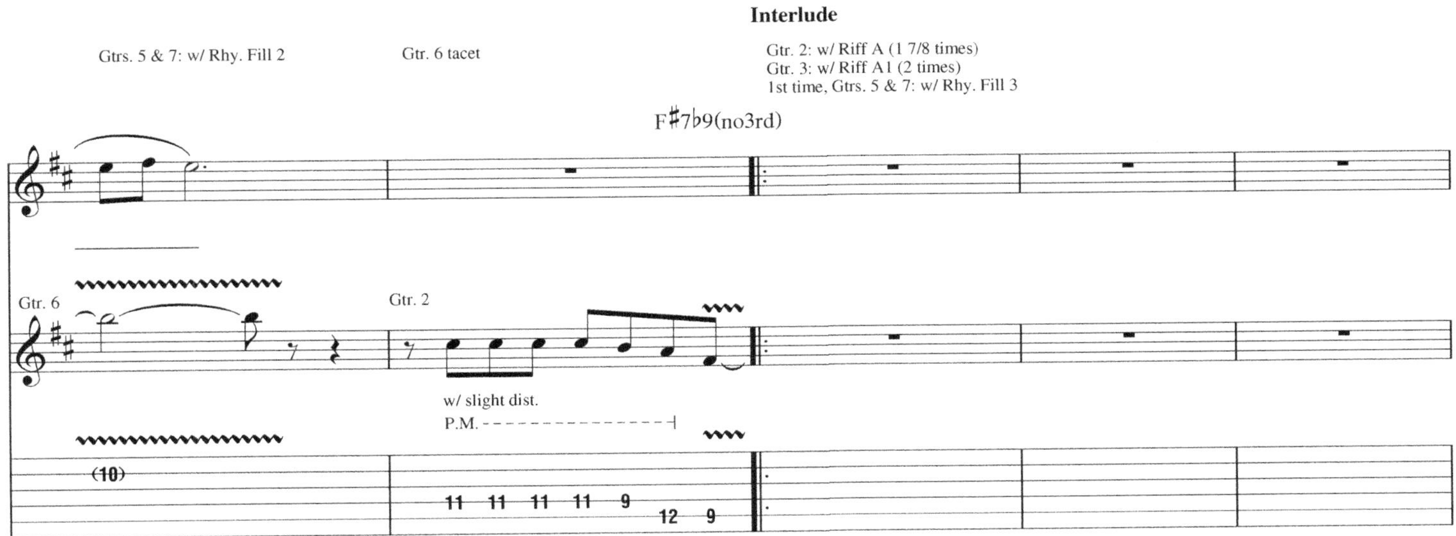
Gtrs. 5 & 7: w/ Rhy. Fill 2
Gtr. 6 tacet
Gtr. 2: w/ Riff A (1 7/8 times)
Gtr. 3: w/ Riff A1 (2 times)
1st time, Gtrs. 5 & 7: w/ Rhy. Fill 3
F♯7♭9(no3rd)
Gtr. 6
Gtr. 2
w/ slight dist.
P.M.

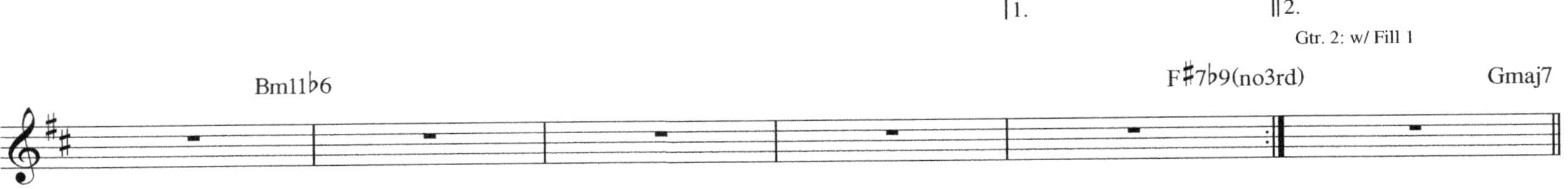

Pre-Chorus

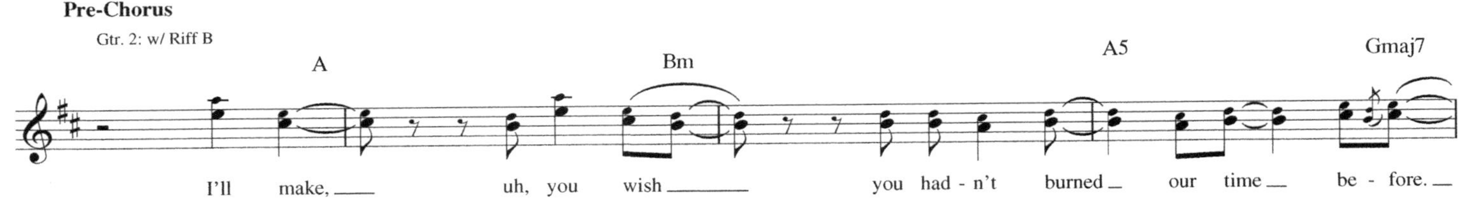

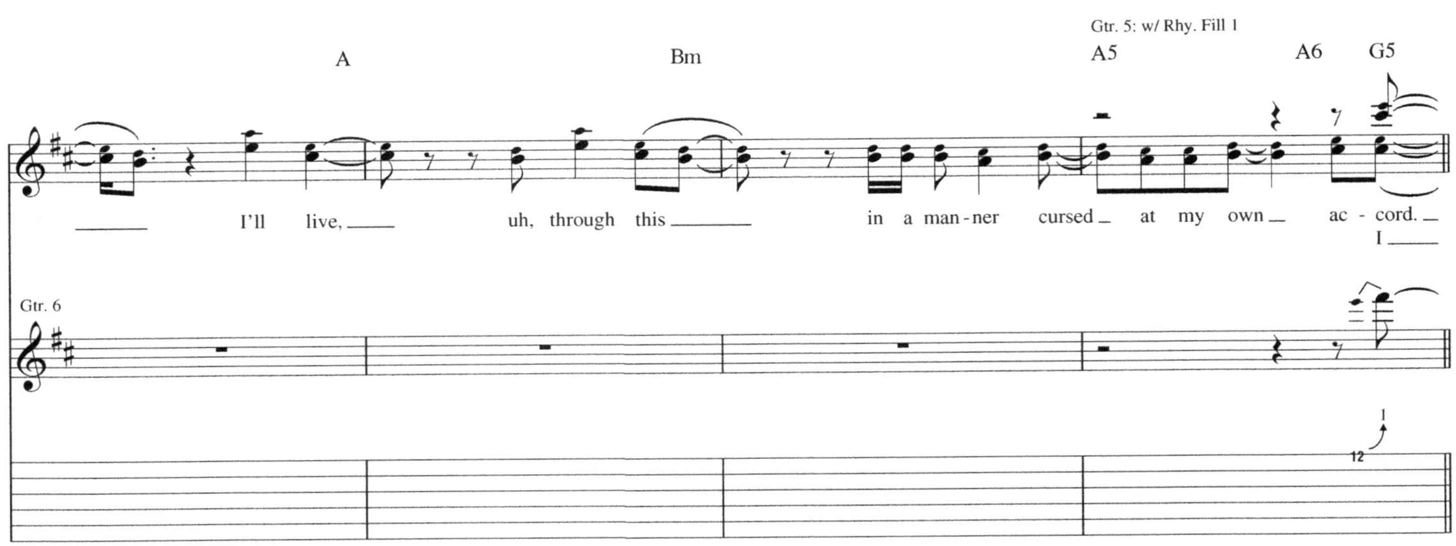

Bridge

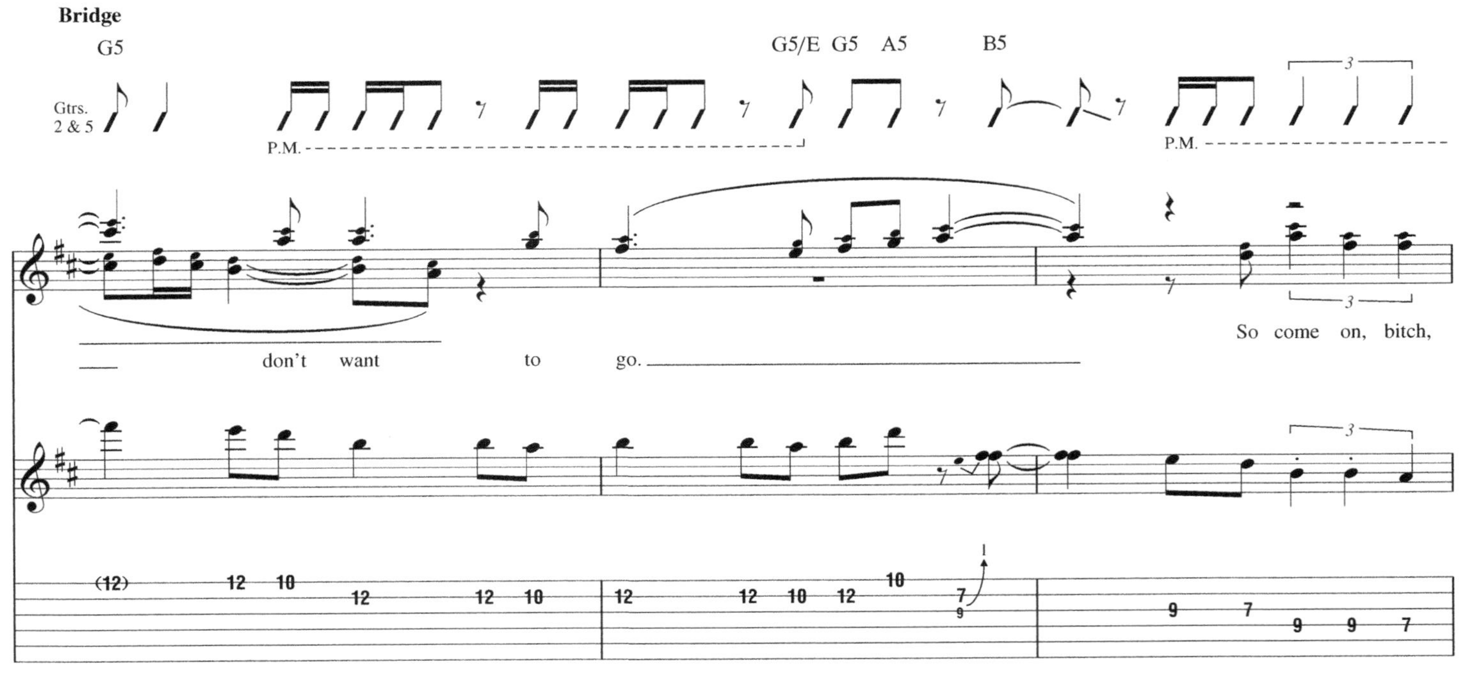

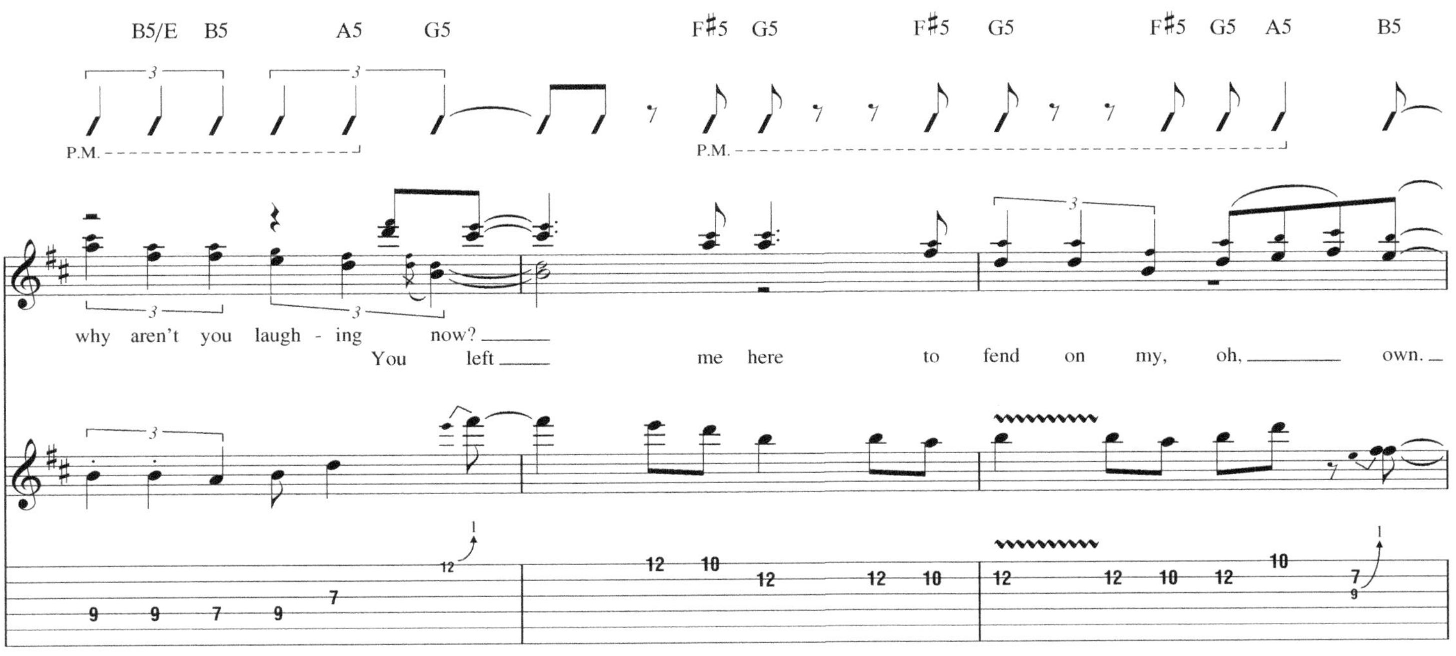

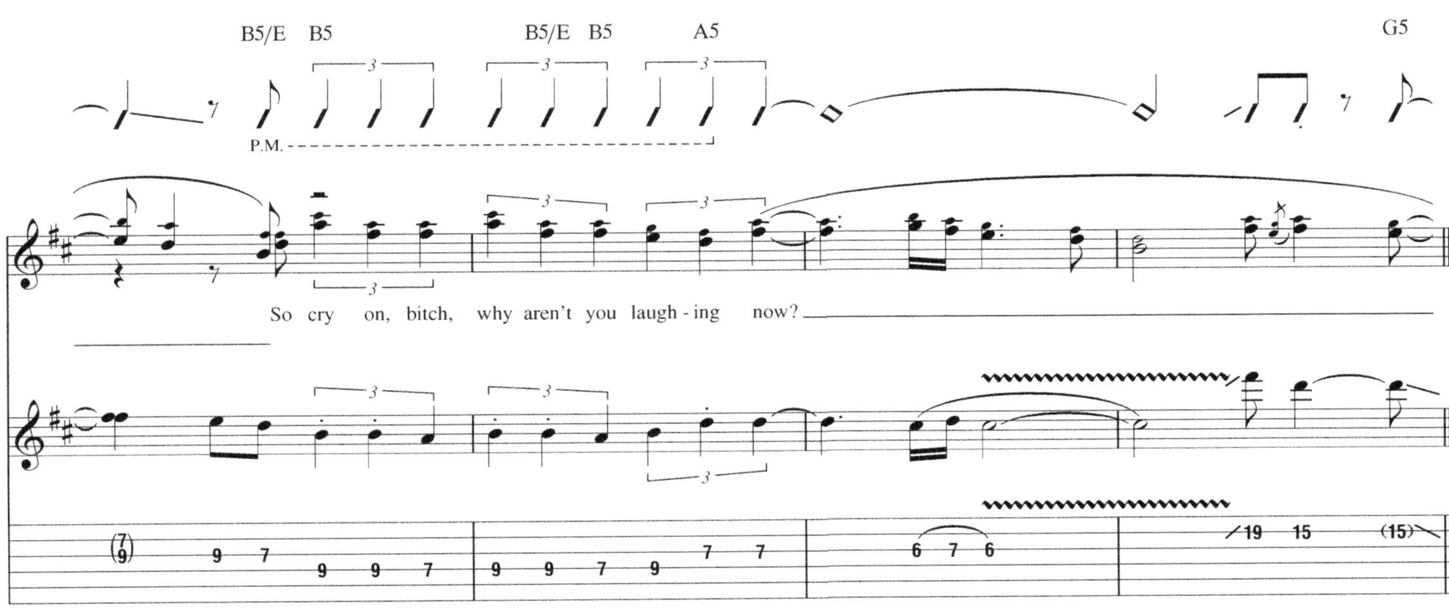

Chorus

Gtrs. 2 & 5: w/ Rhy. Fig. 1 (7 1/2 times)
Gtr. 6: w/ Riff C (1 3/4 times)

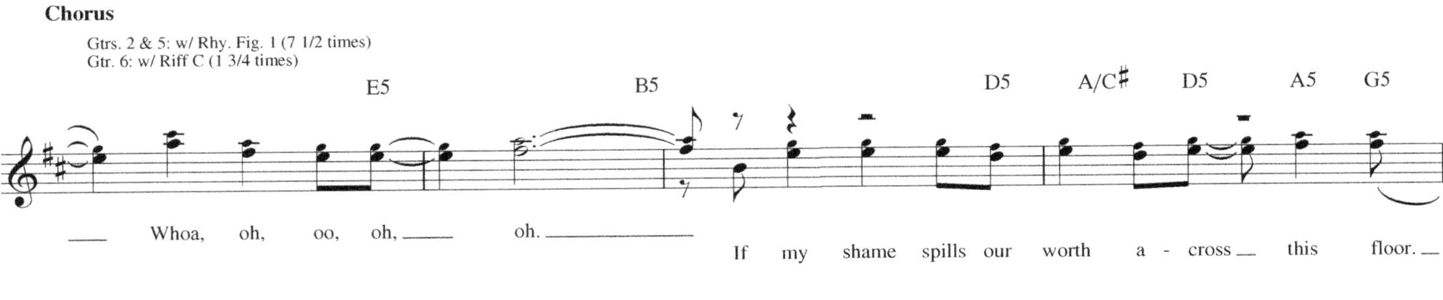

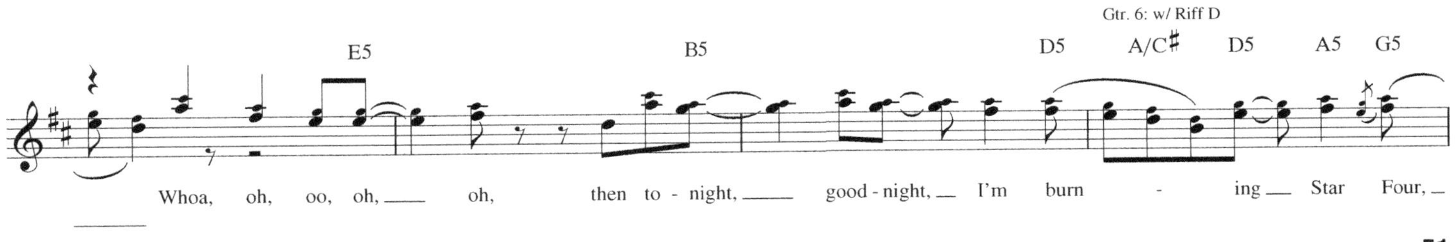

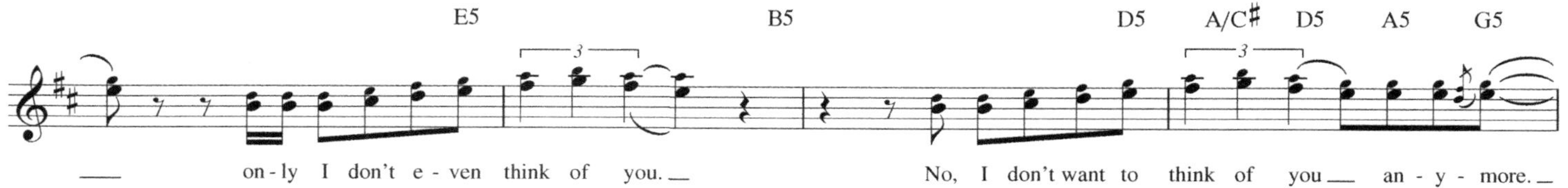
E5 B5 D5 A/C♯ D5 A5 G5
only I don't even think of you.
No, I don't want to think of you anymore.

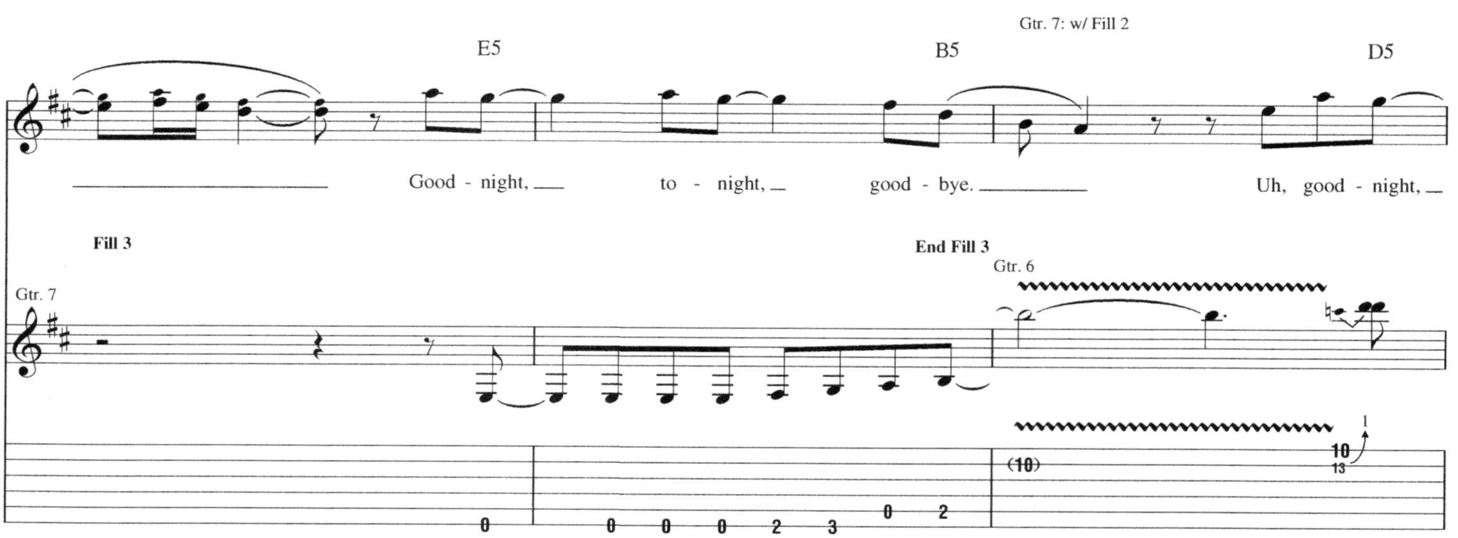
E5 Gtr. 7: w/ Fill 2 B5 D5
Goodnight, tonight, goodbye. Uh, goodnight,
Fill 3
End Fill 3
Gtr. 6
Gtr. 7

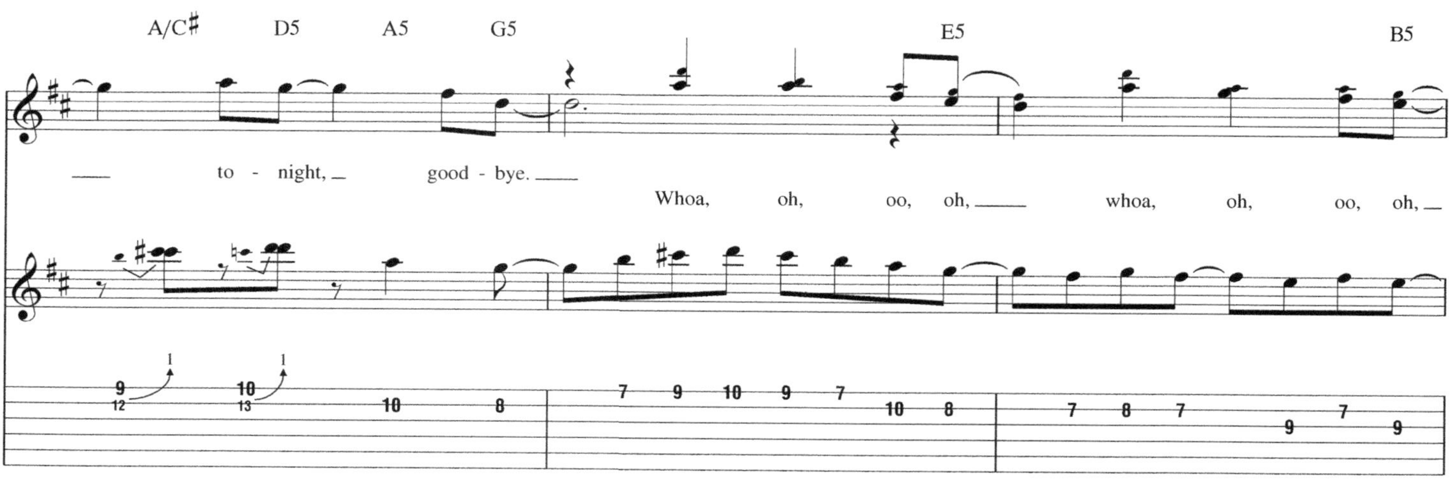
A/C♯ D5 A5 G5 E5 B5
tonight, goodbye.
Whoa, oh, oo, oh, whoa, oh, oo, oh,

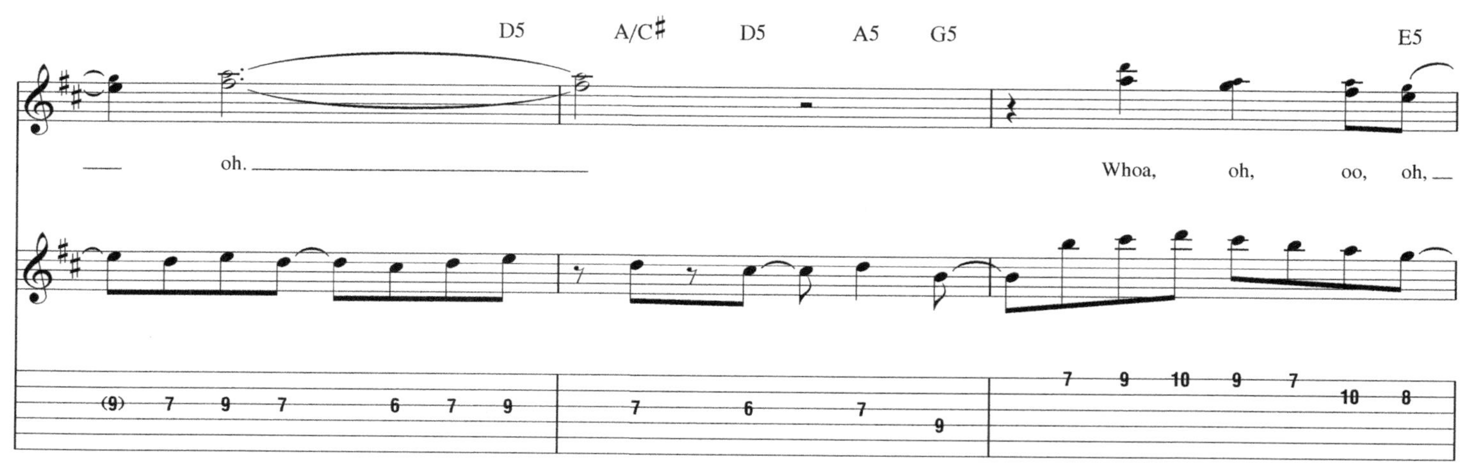
D5 A/C♯ D5 A5 G5 E5
oh.
Whoa, oh, oo, oh,

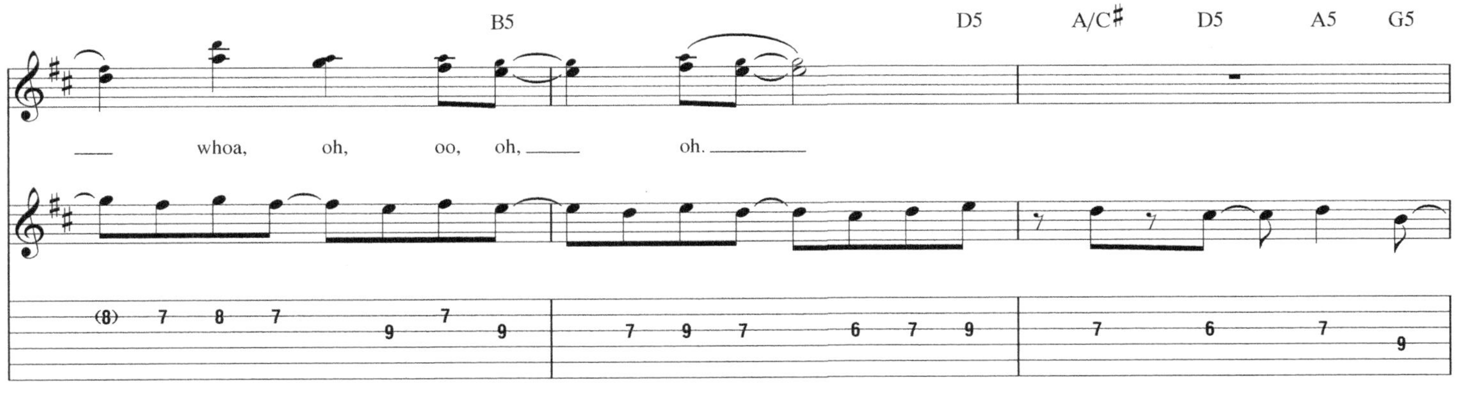
B5
D5
A/C♯
D5
A5
G5
whoa, oh, oo, oh, oh.

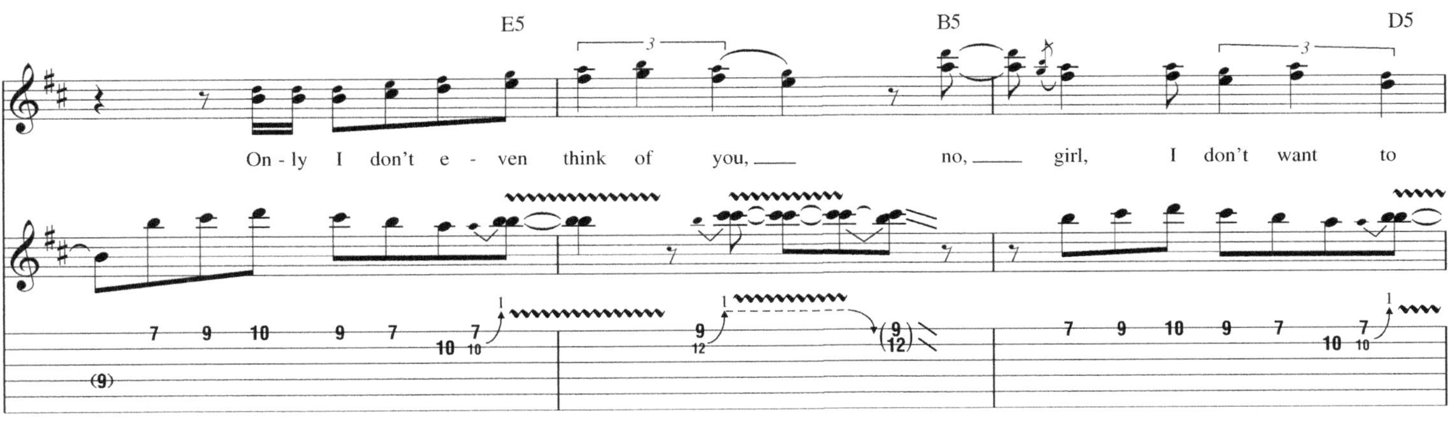
E5
B5
D5
On - ly I don't e - ven think of you, no, girl, I don't want to

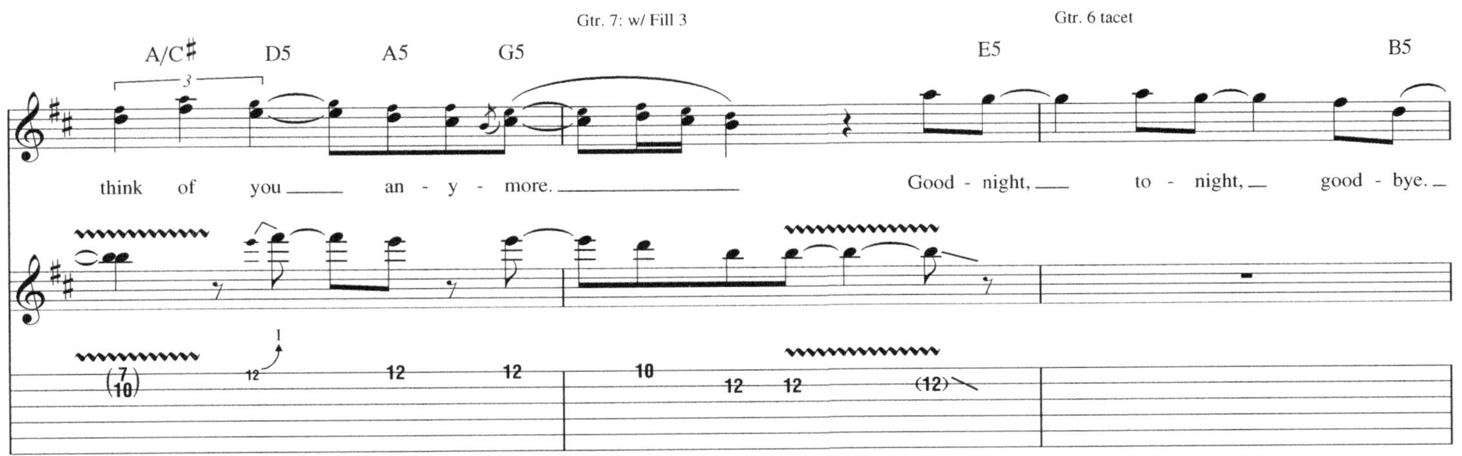
Gtr. 7: w/ Fill 3
Gtr. 6 tacet
A/C♯
D5
A5
G5
E5
B5
think of you an - y - more. Good - night, to - night, good - bye.

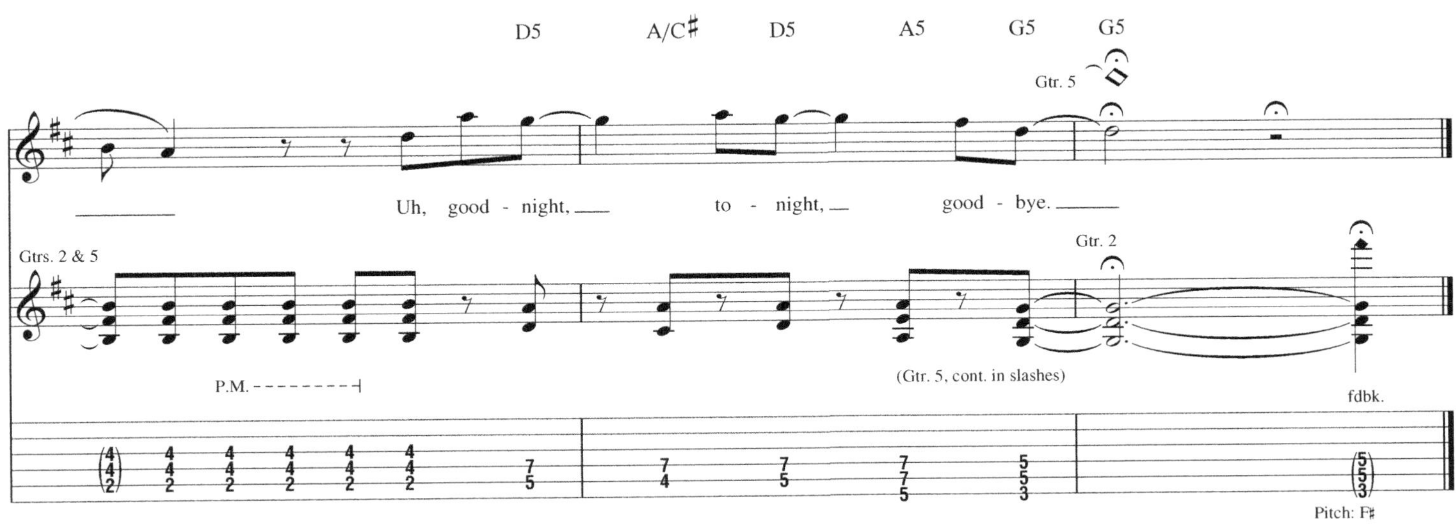
Gtr. 7: w/ Fill 2
D5
A/C♯
D5
A5
G5
G5
Gtr. 5
Uh, good - night, to - night, good - bye.
Gtrs. 2 & 5
Gtr. 2
P.M.
(Gtr. 5, cont. in slashes)
fdbk.
Pitch: F♯

Once Upon Your Dead Body

Words and Music by Claudio Sanchez, Michael Todd, Joshua Eppard and Travis Stever

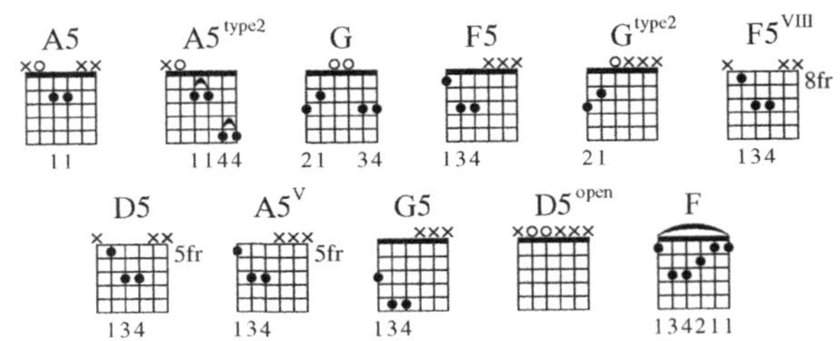

Tune down 1/2 step:
(low to high) E♭-A♭-D♭-G♭-B♭-E♭

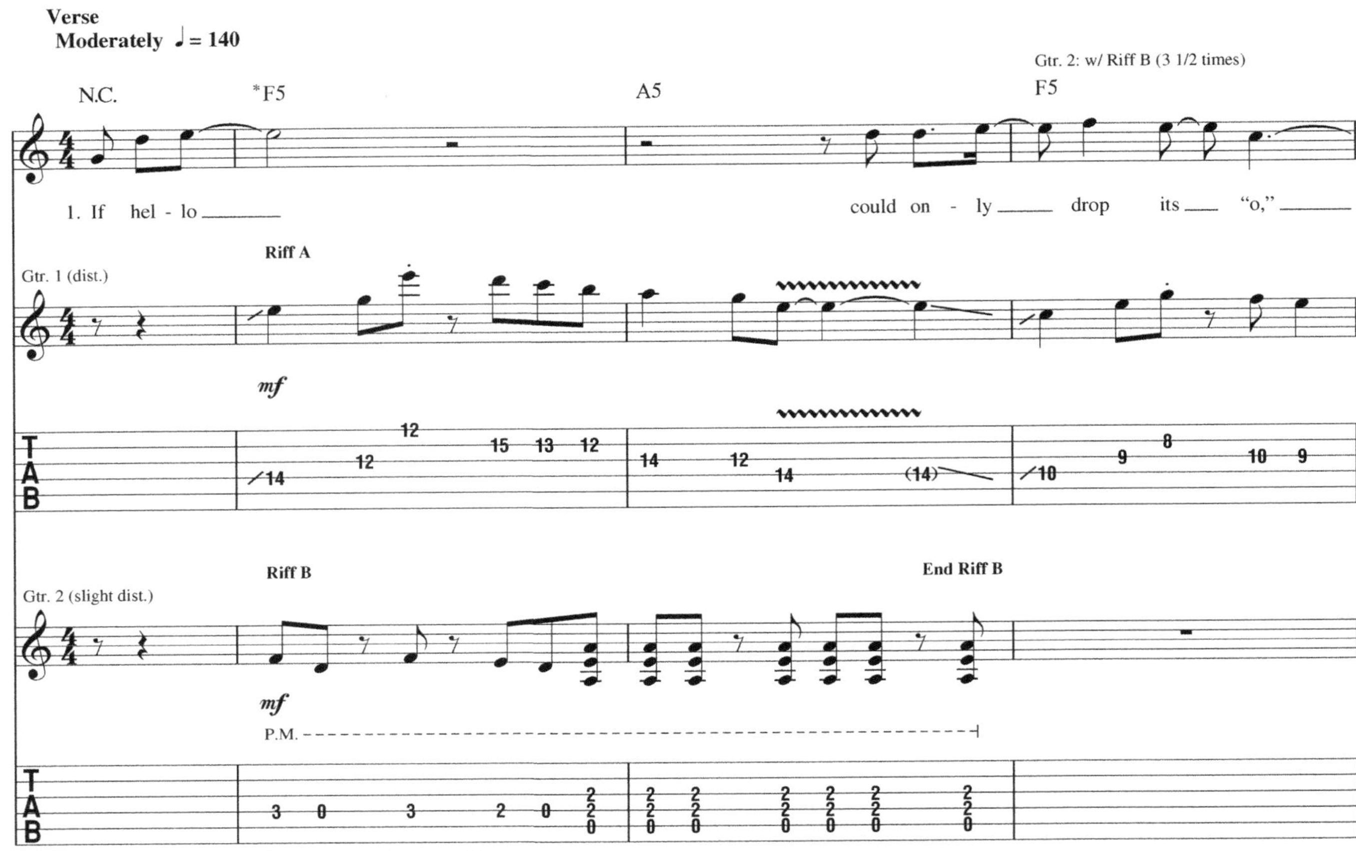

*Chord symbols reflect overall harmony.

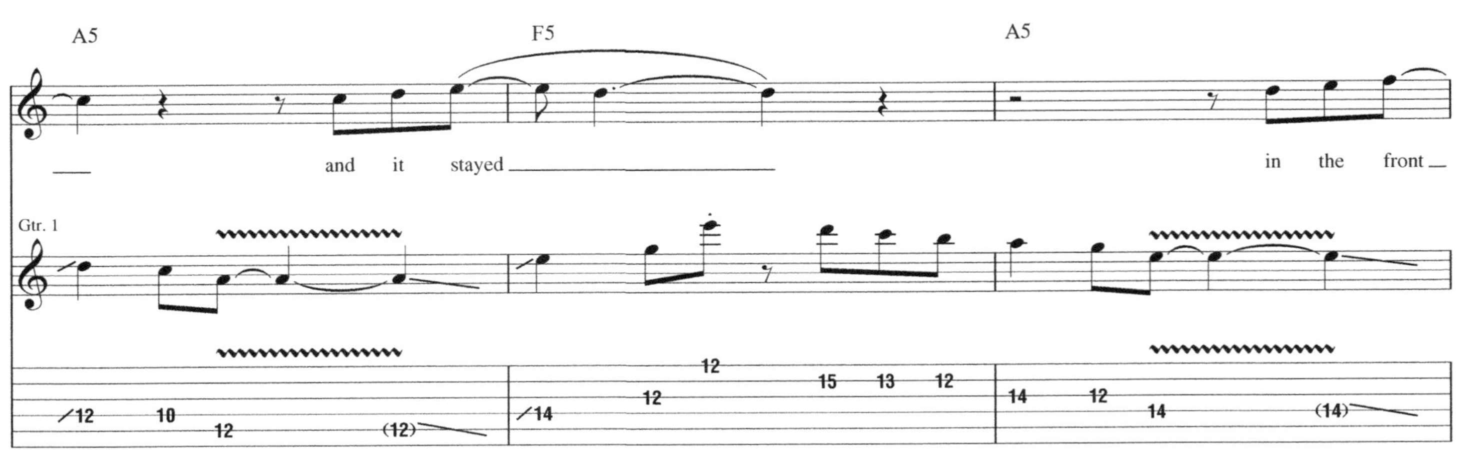

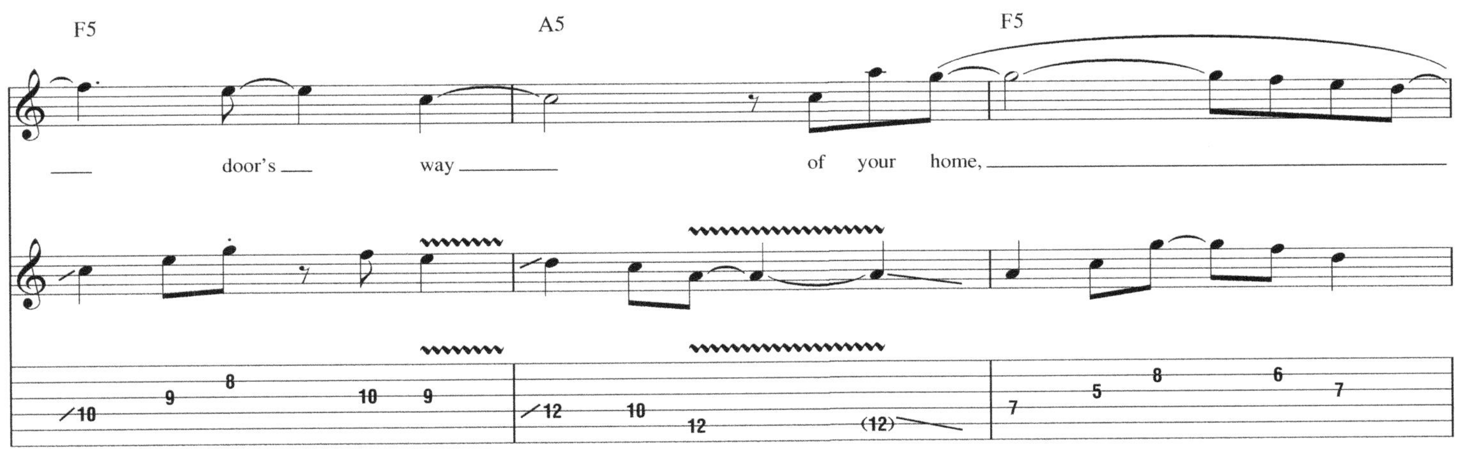

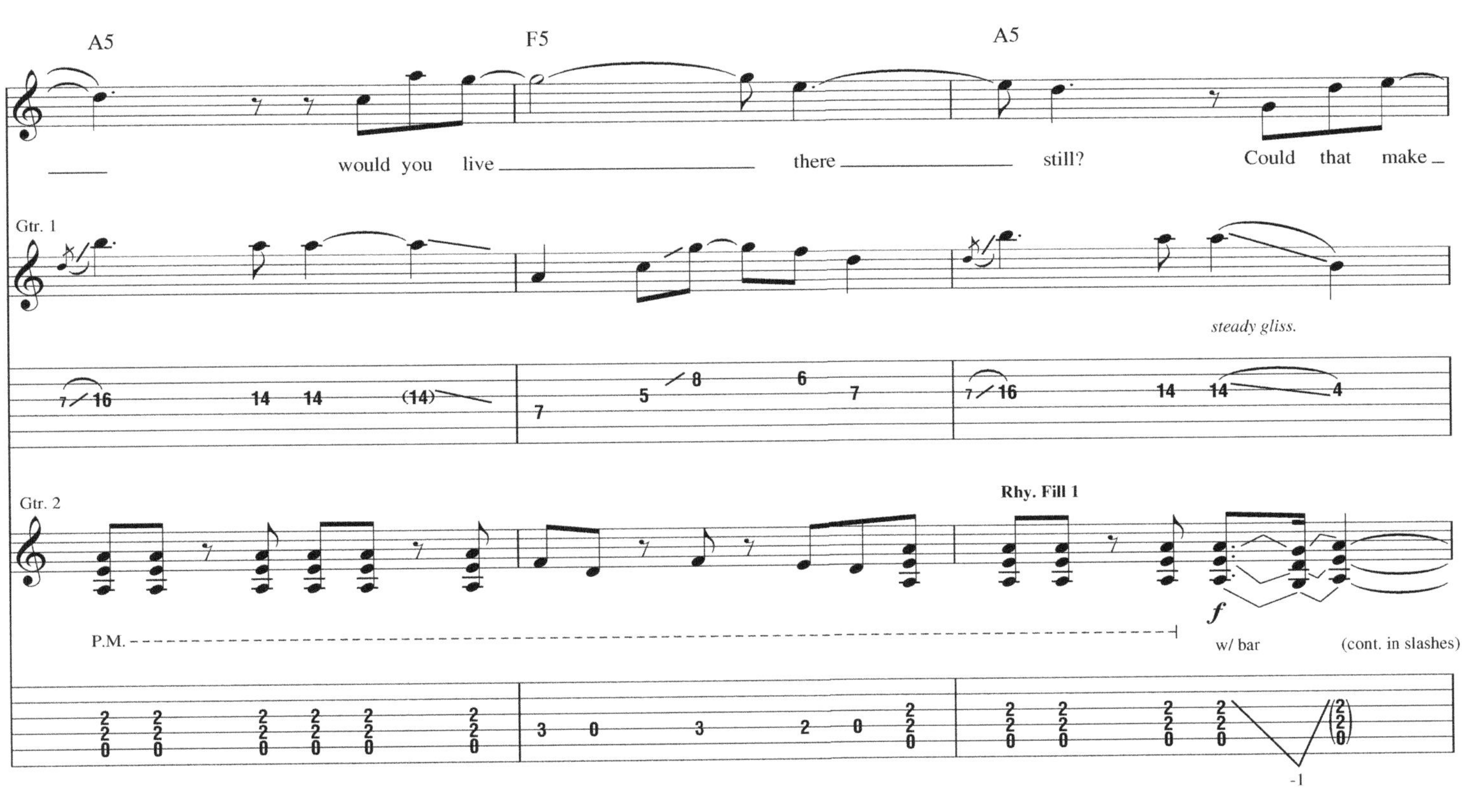

*Gtr. 3: w/ Riff B (1 1/2 times)

Gtr. 2 tacet

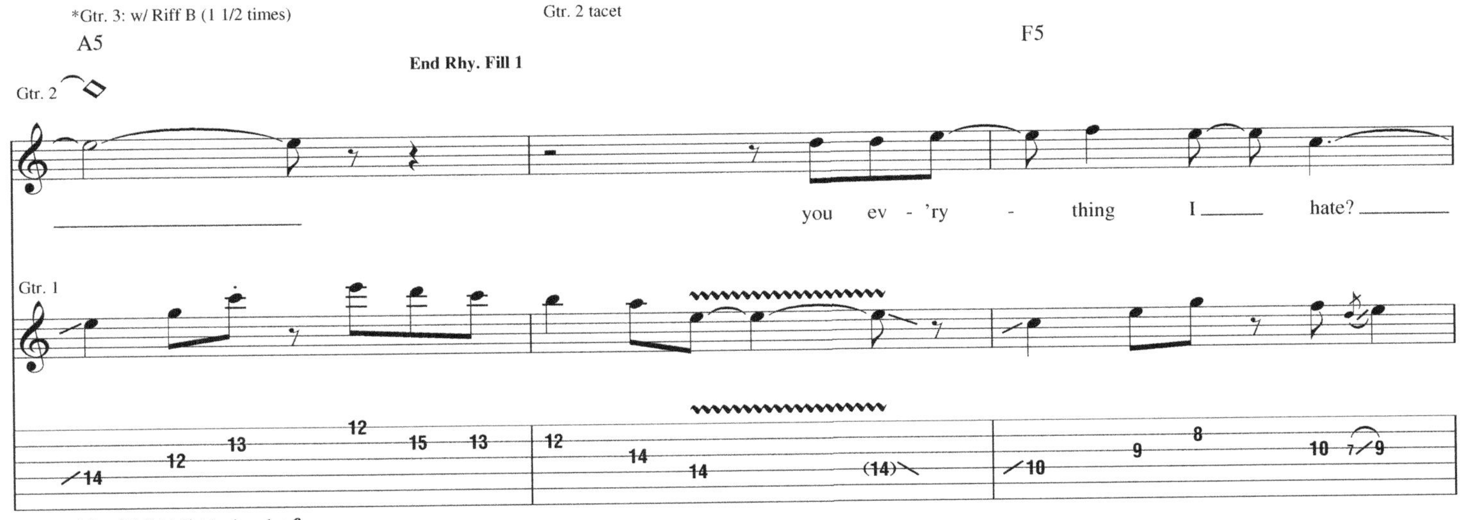

*Gtr. 3 (slight dist.), played *mf*.

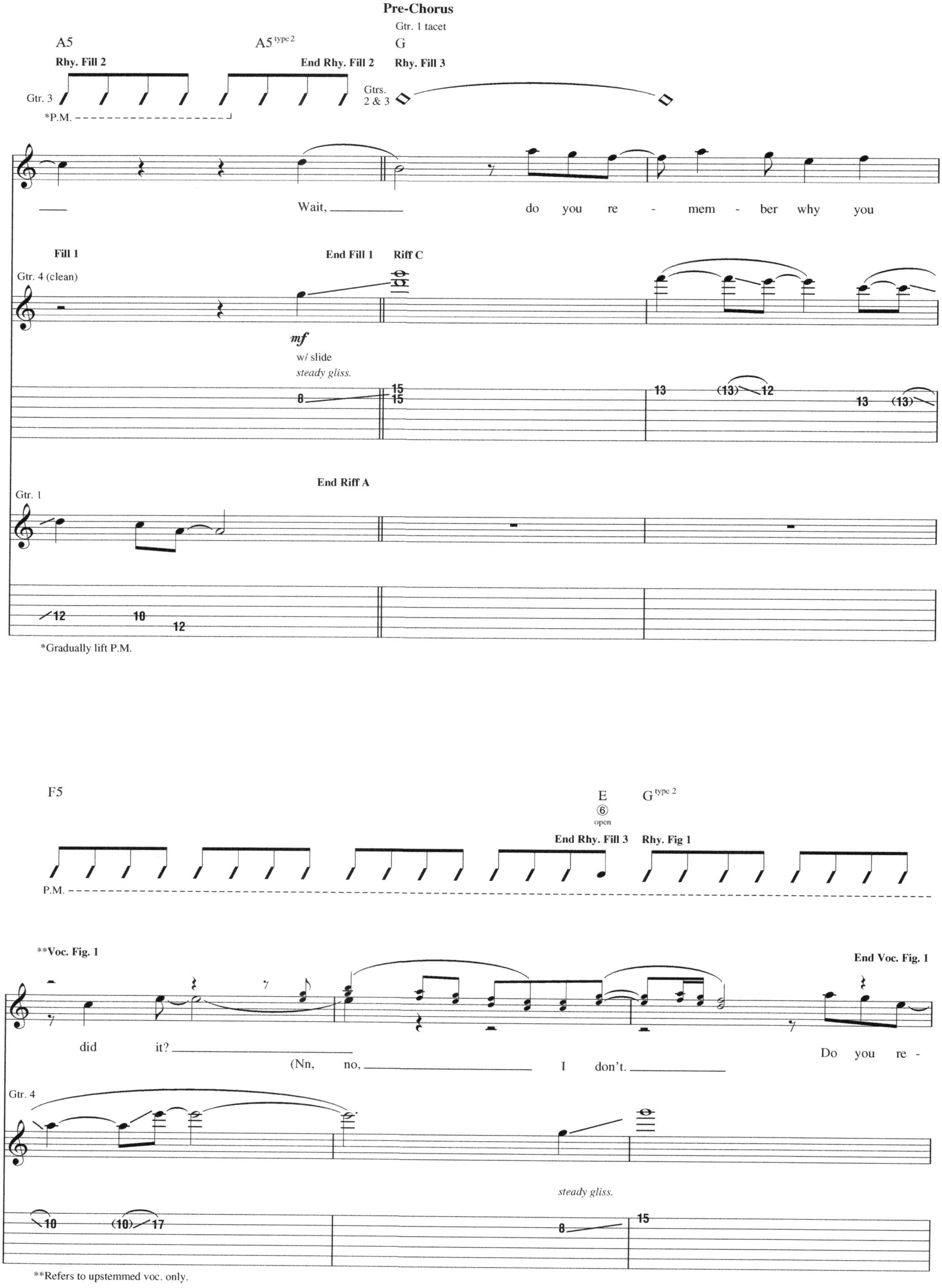

Pre-Chorus

Gtr. 1 tacet

A5 A5 type 2 G

Rhy. Fill 2 **End Rhy. Fill 2** **Rhy. Fill 3**

Gtr. 3 Gtrs. 2 & 3

*P.M.

Wait, do you re - mem - ber why you

Fill 1 **End Fill 1** **Riff C**

Gtr. 4 (clean)

mf

w/ slide

steady gliss.

8 15 15 13 (13) 12 13 (13)

End Riff A

Gtr. 1

12 10 12

*Gradually lift P.M.

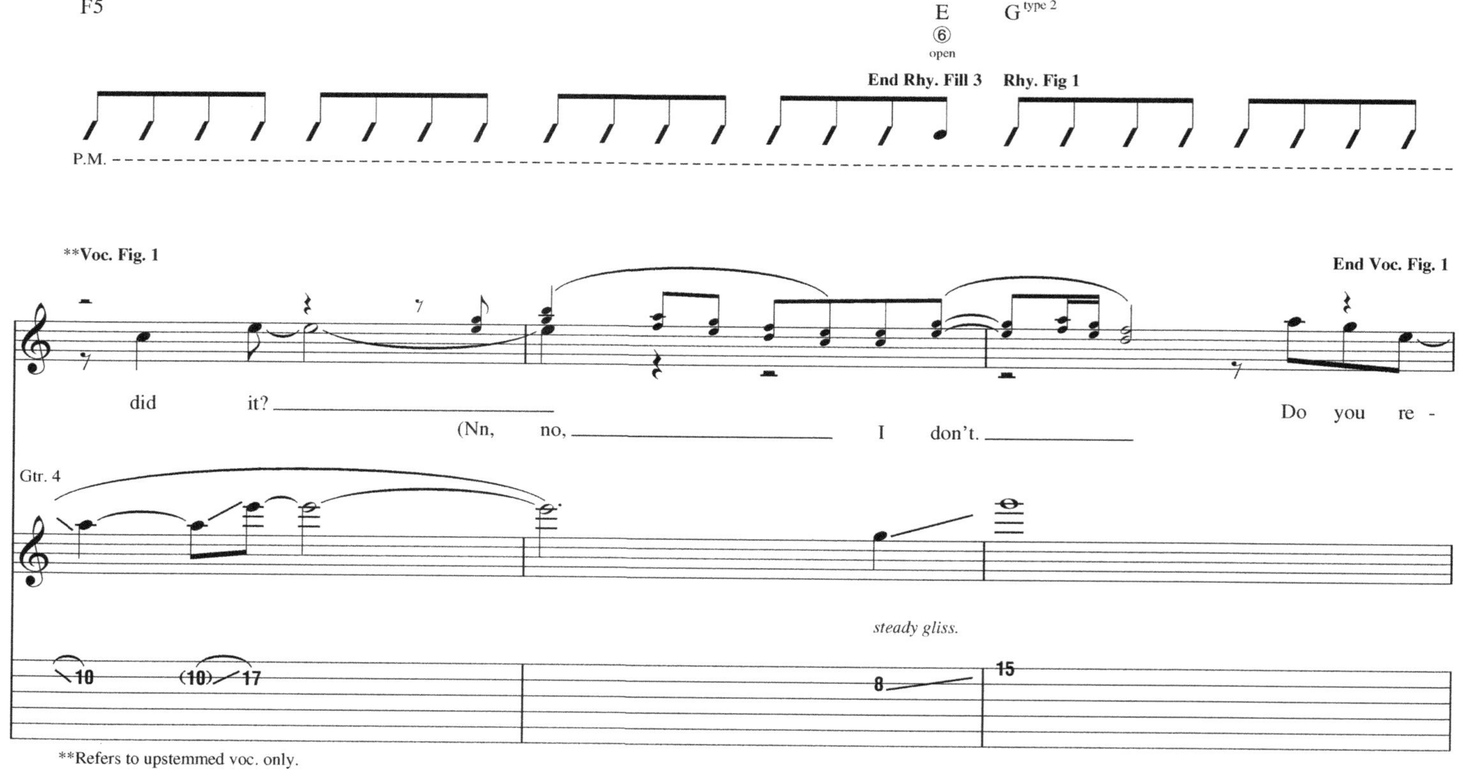

**Refers to upstemmed voc. only.

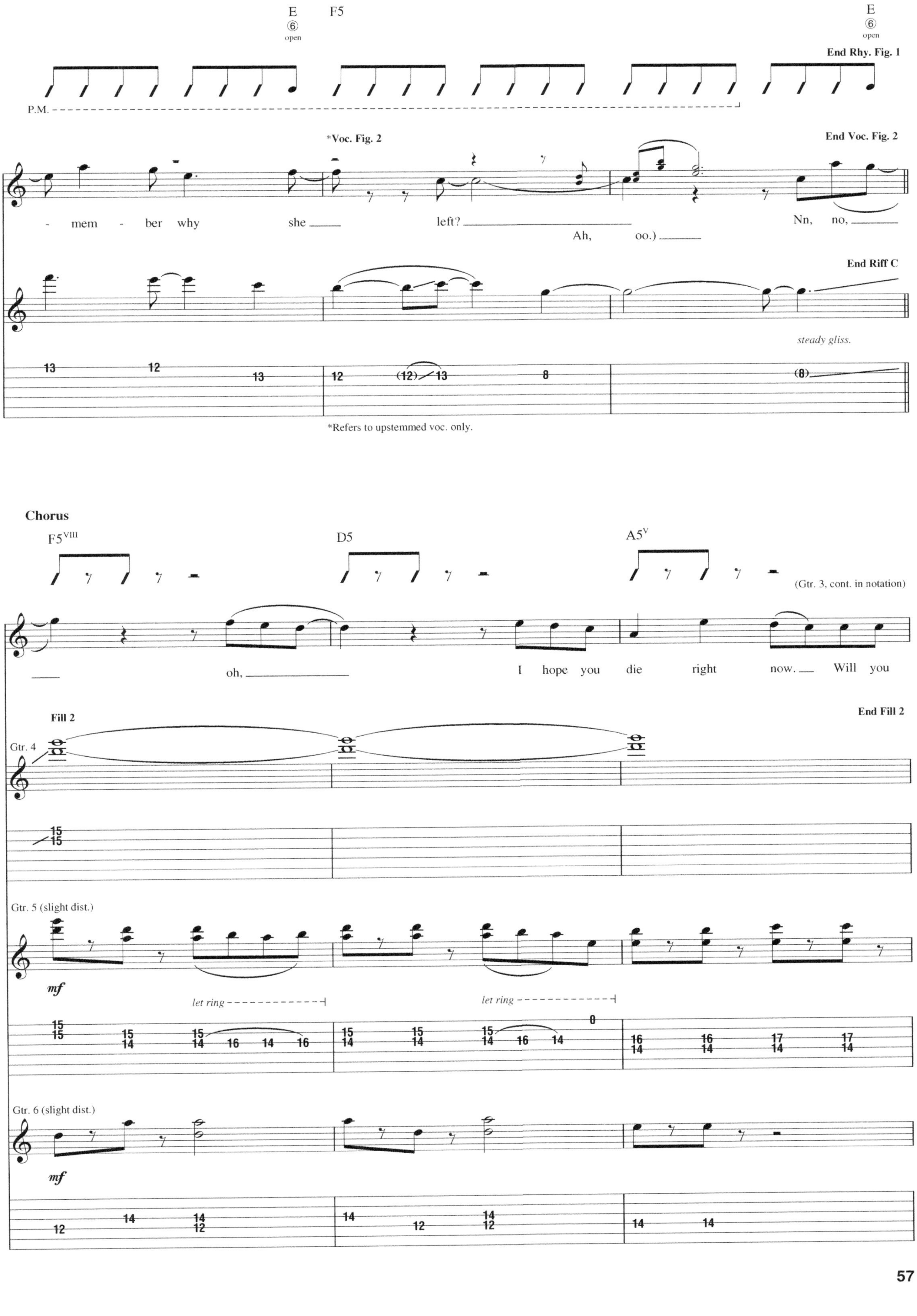

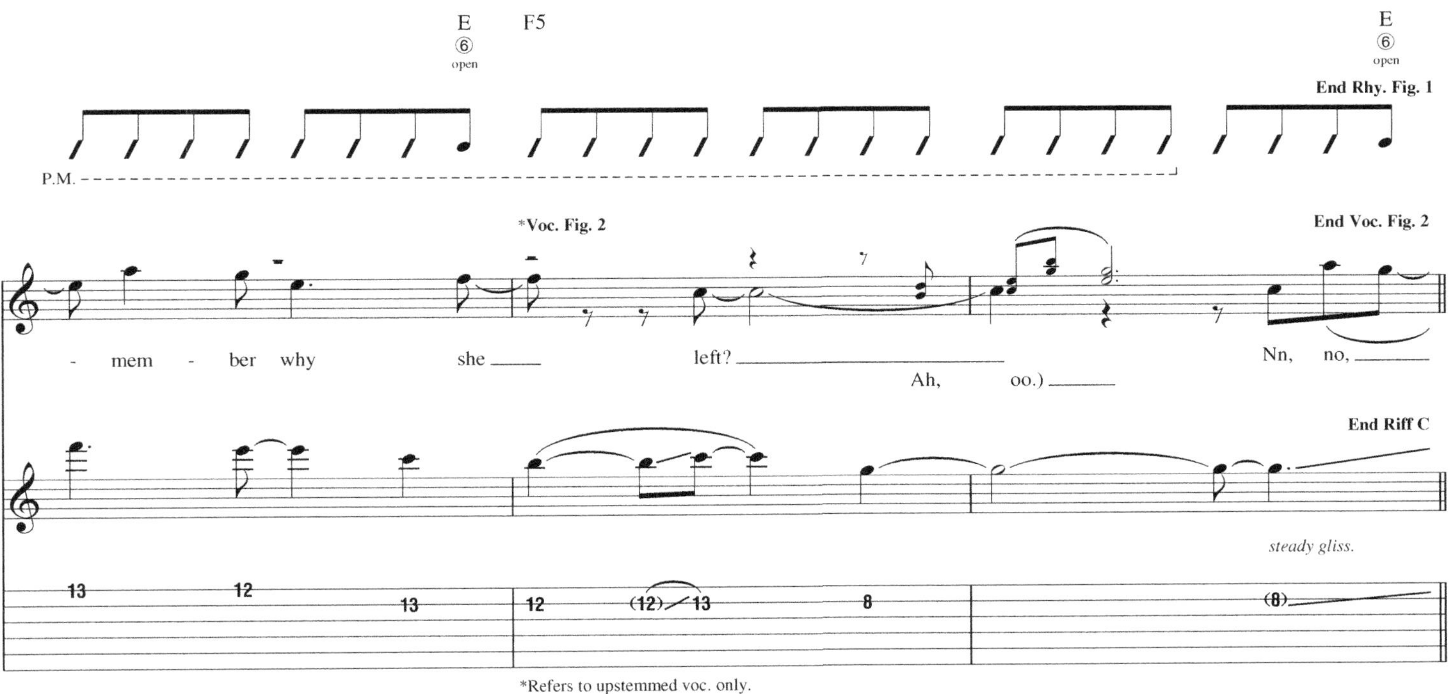

*Refers to upstemmed voc. only.

Chorus

F5^VIII D5 A5^V

(Gtr. 3, cont. in notation)

oh, I hope you die right now. Will you

Fill 2 End Fill 2

Gtr. 4

Gtr. 5 (slight dist.)

mf

let ring

Gtr. 6 (slight dist.)

mf

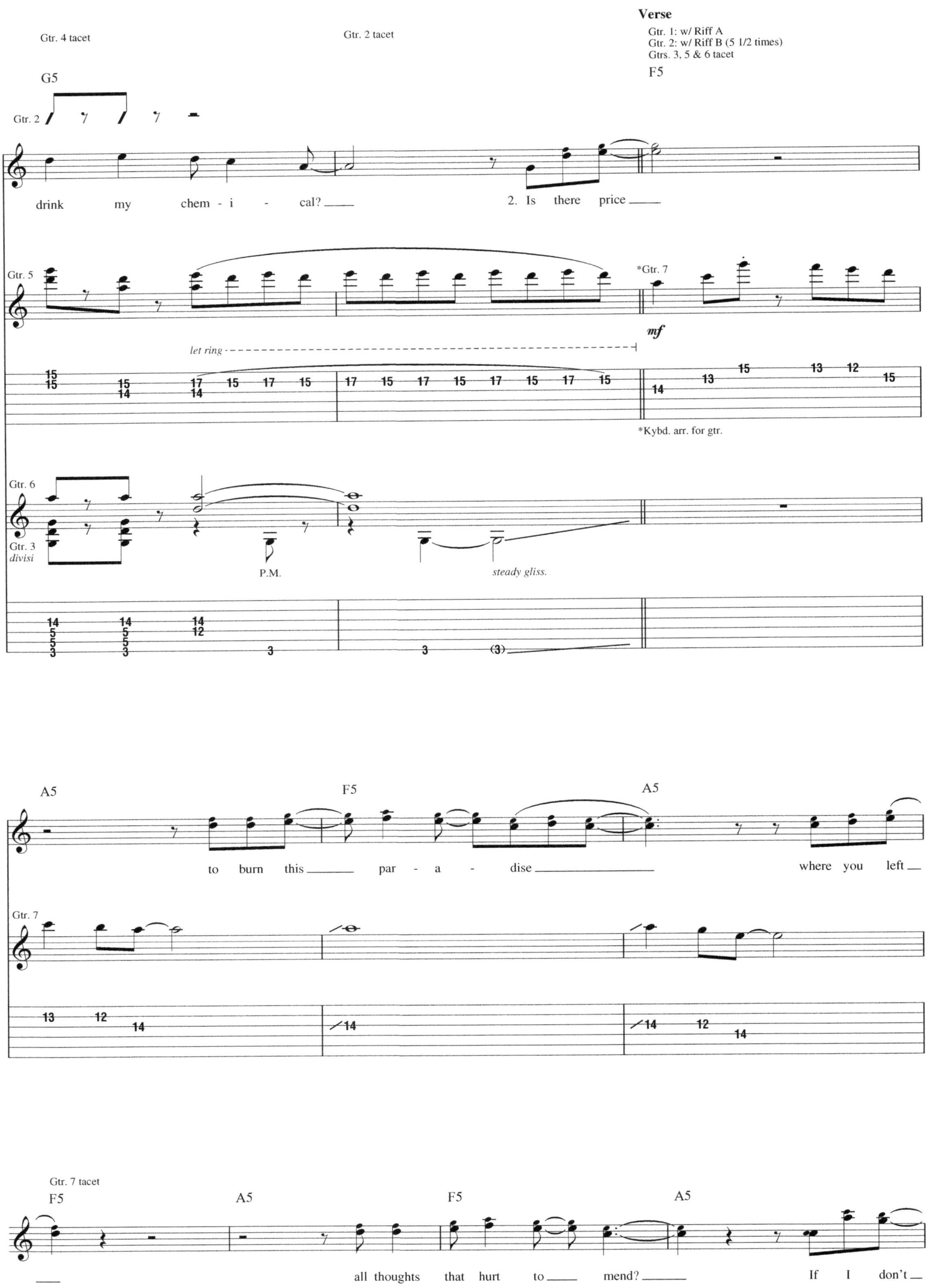

Gtr. 4 tacet

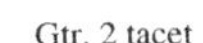

Verse

Gtr. 1: w/ Riff A
Gtr. 2: w/ Riff B (5 1/2 times)
Gtrs. 3, 5 & 6 tacet

G5 F5

Gtr. 2

drink my chem - i - cal? 2. Is there price

Gtr. 5 *Gtr. 7

mf

let ring

15 15 15 15 14 17 14 15 17 15 17 15 17 15 17 15 17 15 17 15 14 13 15 13 12 15

*Kybd. arr. for gtr.

Gtr. 6

Gtr. 3 *divisi*

P.M. *steady gliss.*

14 5 5 3 14 5 5 3 14 12 3 3 (3)

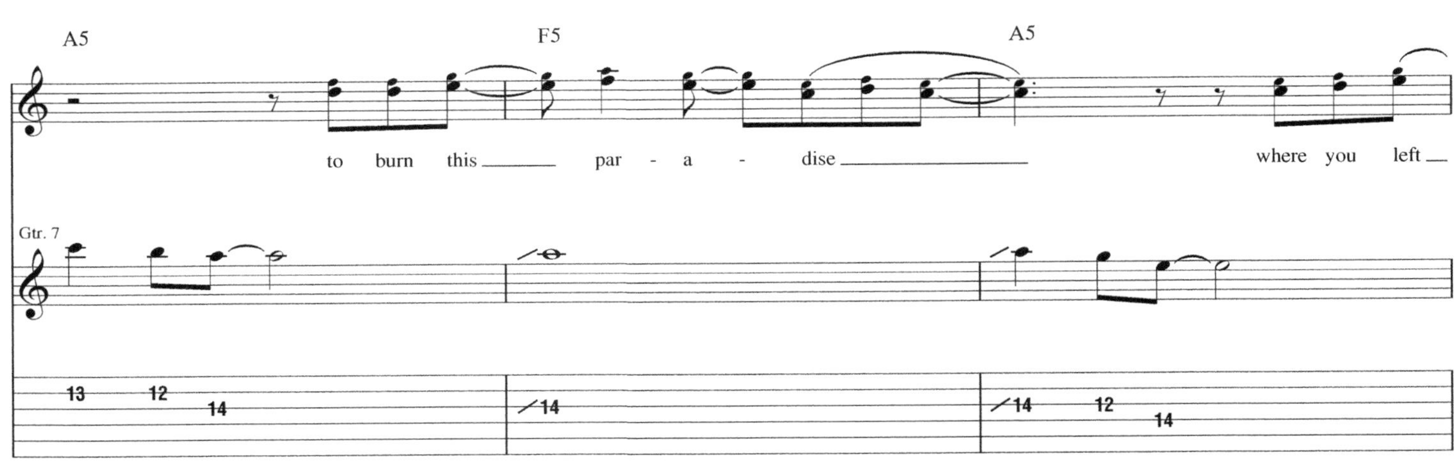

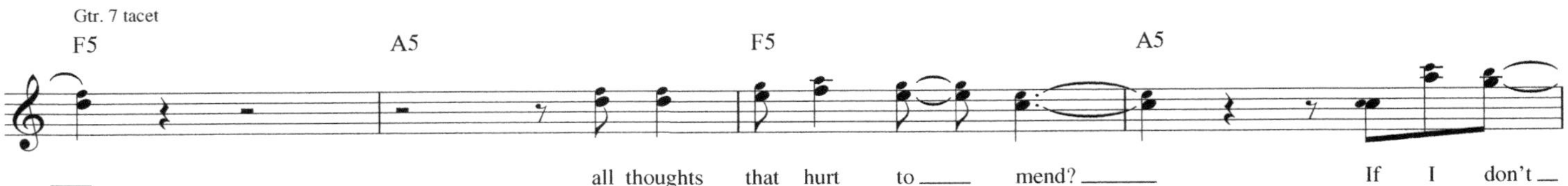

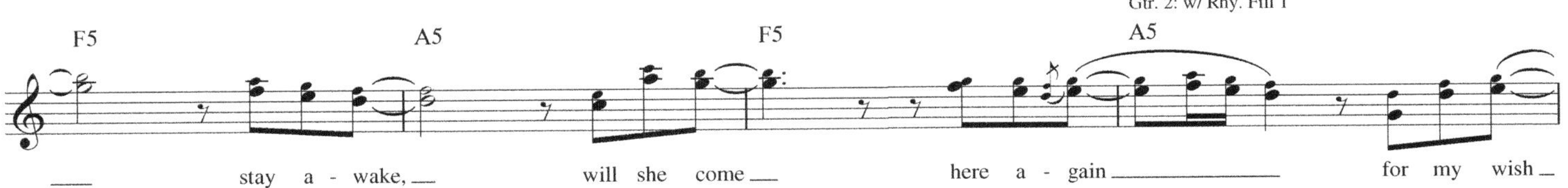

Gtr. 2: w/ Rhy. Fill 1
F5
A5
F5
A5
stay a - wake, will she come here a - gain for my wish

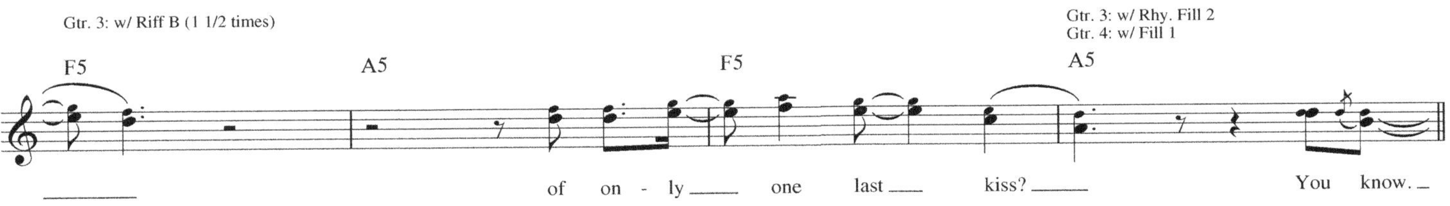

Gtr. 3: w/ Riff B (1 1/2 times)
Gtr. 3: w/ Rhy. Fill 2
Gtr. 4: w/ Fill 1
F5
A5
F5
A5
of on - ly one last kiss? You know.

Pre-Chorus

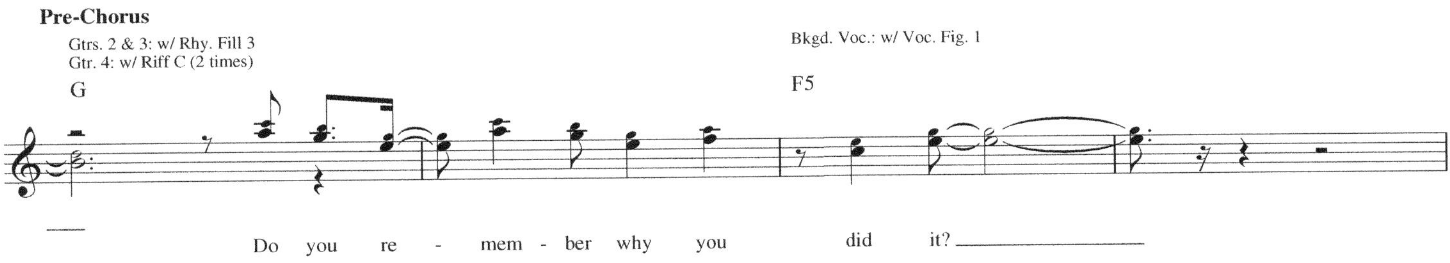

Gtrs. 2 & 3: w/ Rhy. Fill 3
Gtr. 4: w/ Riff C (2 times)
Bkgd. Voc.: w/ Voc. Fig. 1
G
F5
Do you re - mem - ber why you did it?

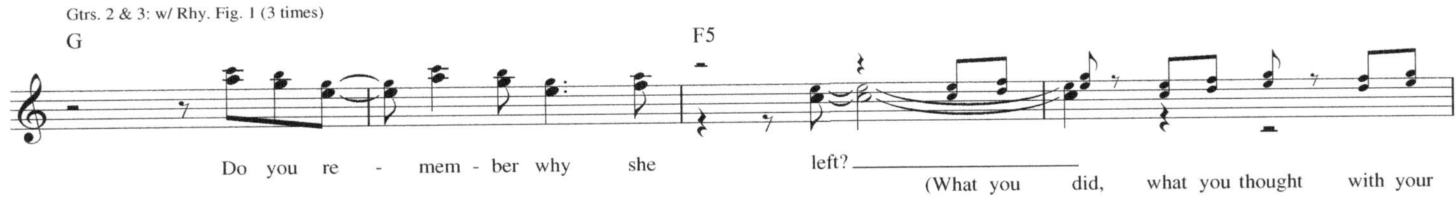

Gtrs. 2 & 3: w/ Rhy. Fig. 1 (3 times)
G
F5
Do you re - mem - ber why she left?
(What you did, what you thought with your

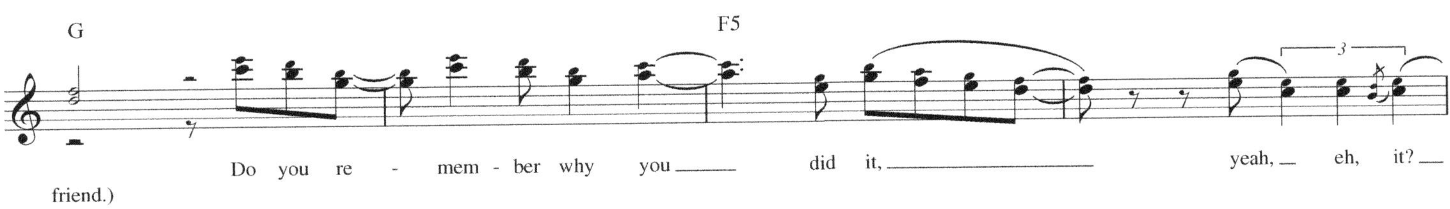

G
F5
Do you re - mem - ber why you did it, yeah, eh, it?
friend.)

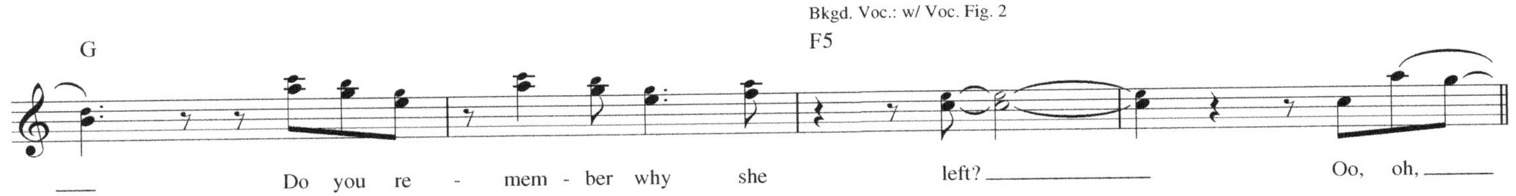

Bkgd. Voc.: w/ Voc. Fig. 2
G
F5
Do you re - mem - ber why she left? Oo, oh,

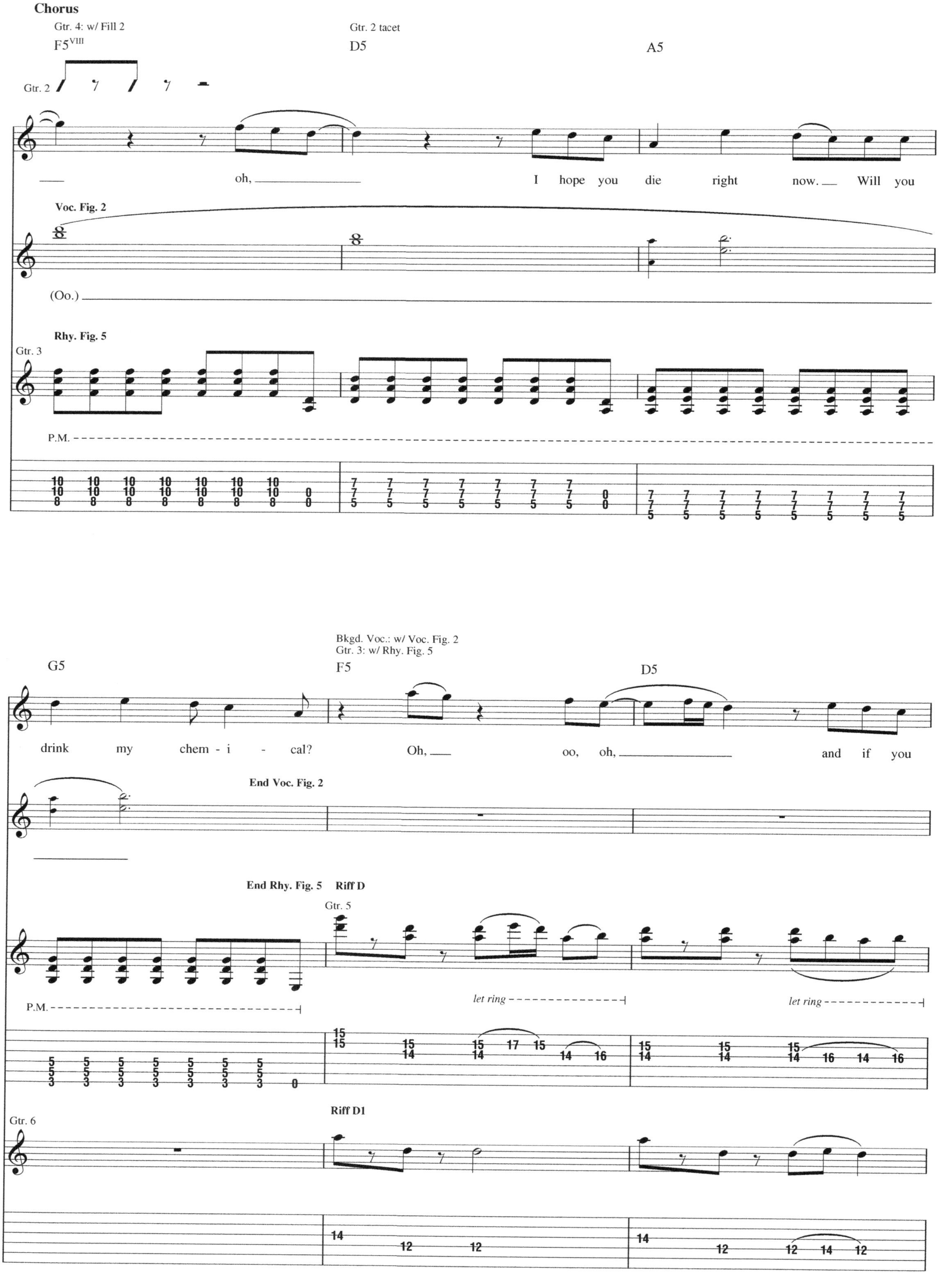

Chorus

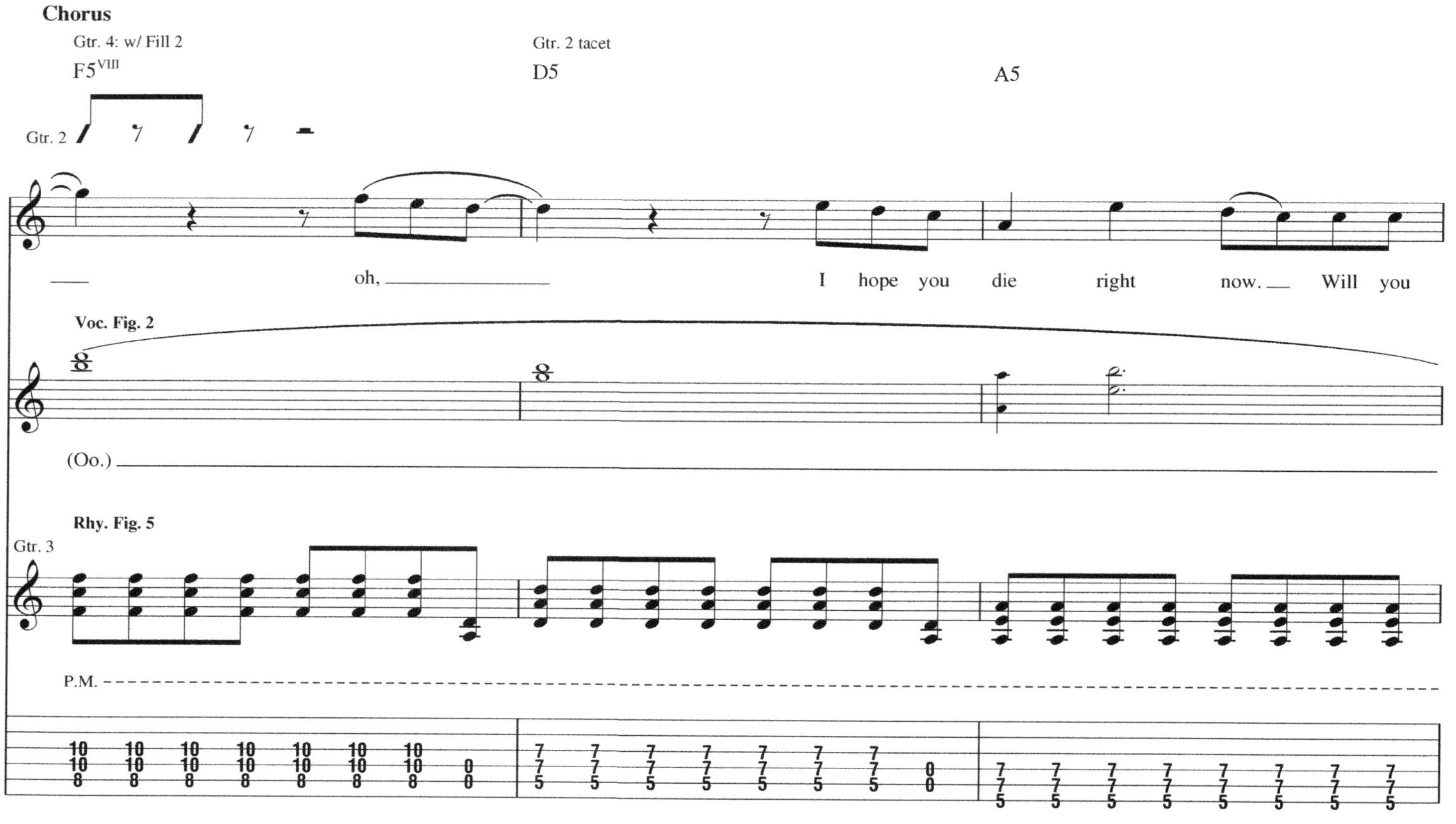

G5
Bkgd. Voc.: w/ Voc. Fig. 2
Gtr. 3: w/ Rhy. Fig. 5
F5
D5

drink my chem - i - cal? Oh, oo, oh, and if you

End Voc. Fig. 2

End Rhy. Fig. 5 Riff D

Gtr. 5

P.M.

let ring

let ring

Gtr. 6

Riff D1

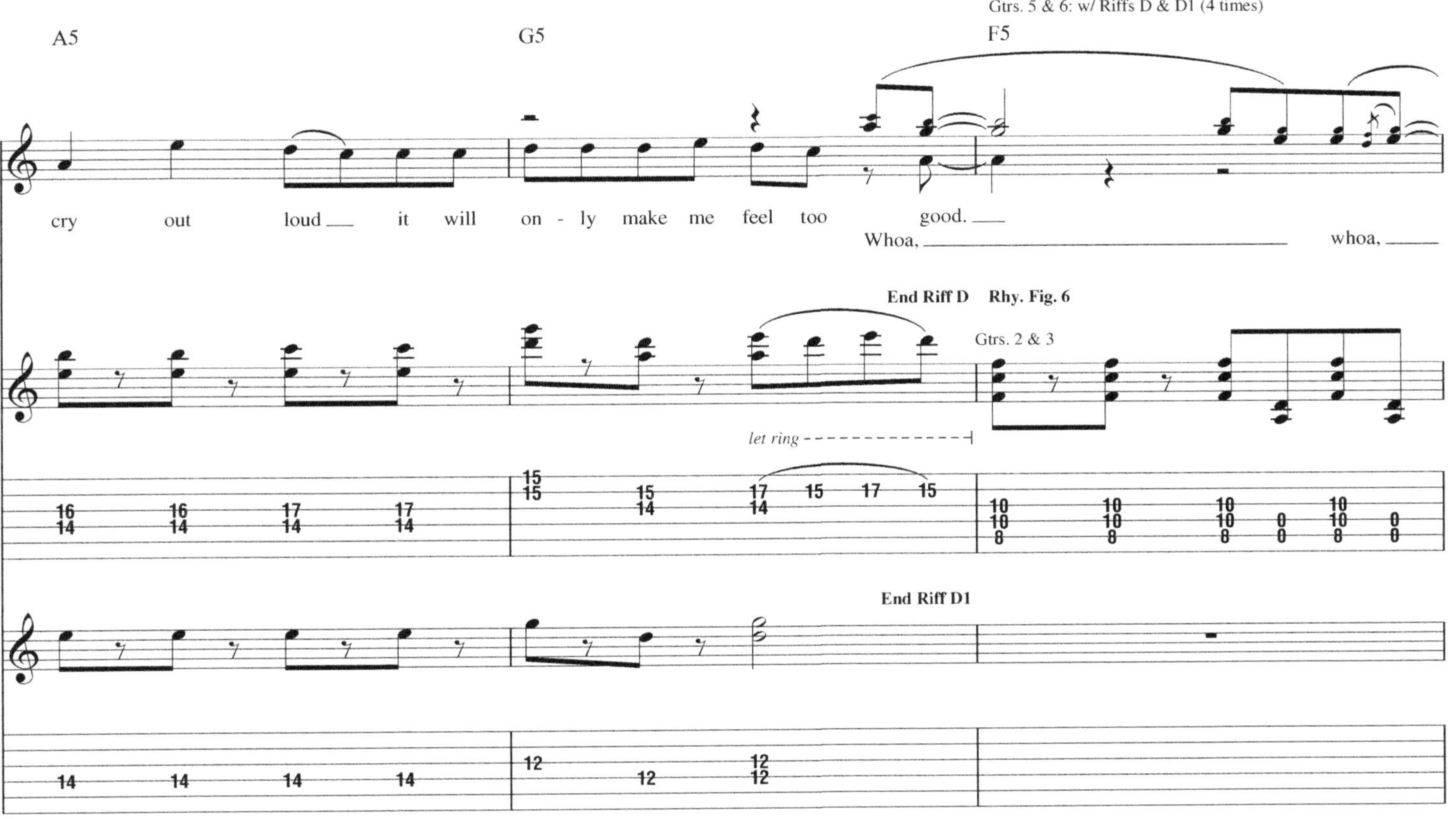
Gtrs. 5 & 6: w/ Riffs D & D1 (4 times)
A5
G5
F5
cry out loud it will only make me feel too good.
Whoa, whoa,
End Riff D
Rhy. Fig. 6
Gtrs. 2 & 3
let ring
End Riff D1
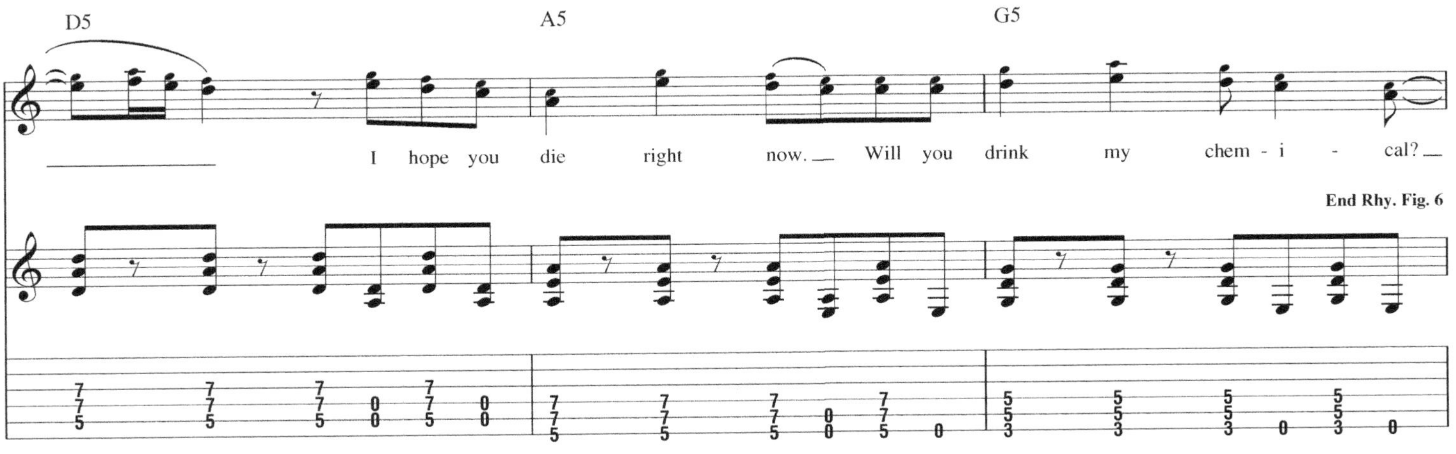
D5
A5
G5
I hope you die right now. Will you drink my chem-i-cal?
End Rhy. Fig. 6
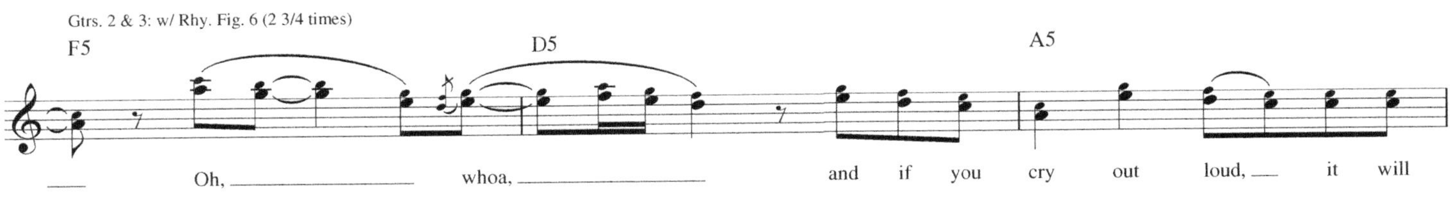
Gtrs. 2 & 3: w/ Rhy. Fig. 6 (2 3/4 times)
F5
D5
A5
Oh, whoa, and if you cry out loud, it will
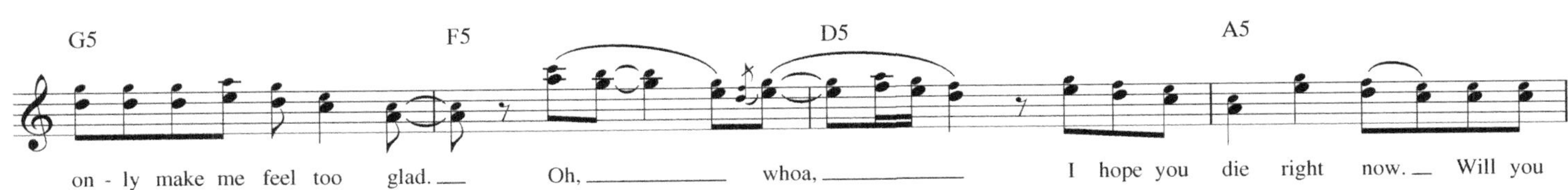
G5
F5
D5
A5
only make me feel too glad. Oh, whoa, I hope you die right now. Will you

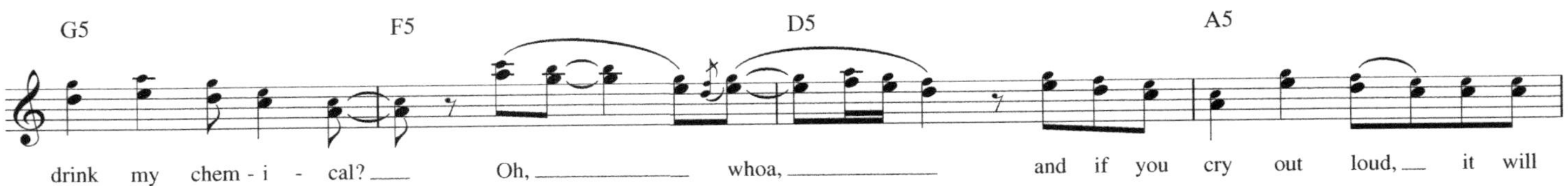
G5
F5
D5
A5
drink my chem - i - cal?
Oh,
whoa,
and if you cry out loud, it will

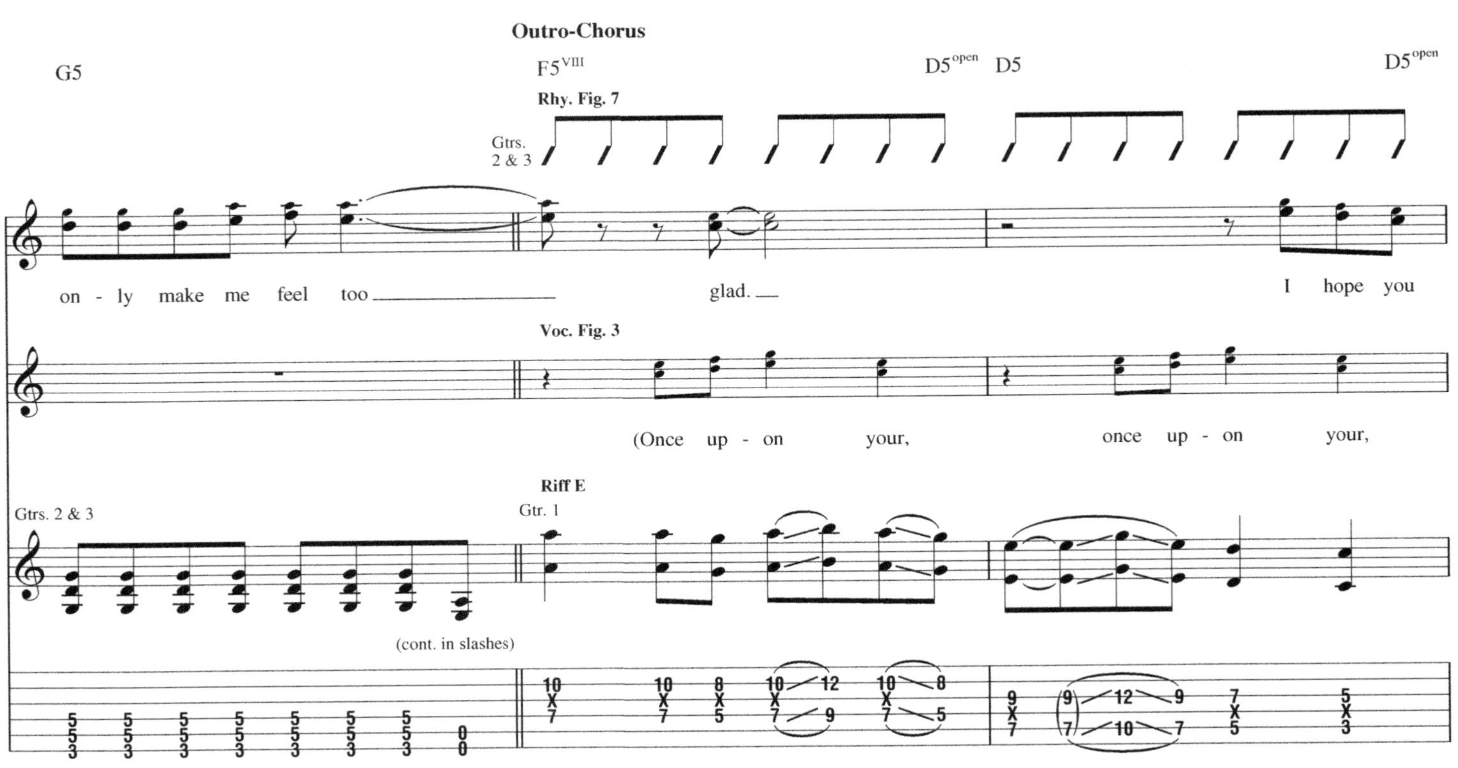
Outro-Chorus
G5
F5VIII
D5open
D5
D5open
Rhy. Fig. 7
Gtrs. 2 & 3
on - ly make me feel too
glad.
I hope you
Voc. Fig. 3
(Once up - on your,
once up - on your,
Riff E
Gtrs. 2 & 3
Gtr. 1
(cont. in slashes)

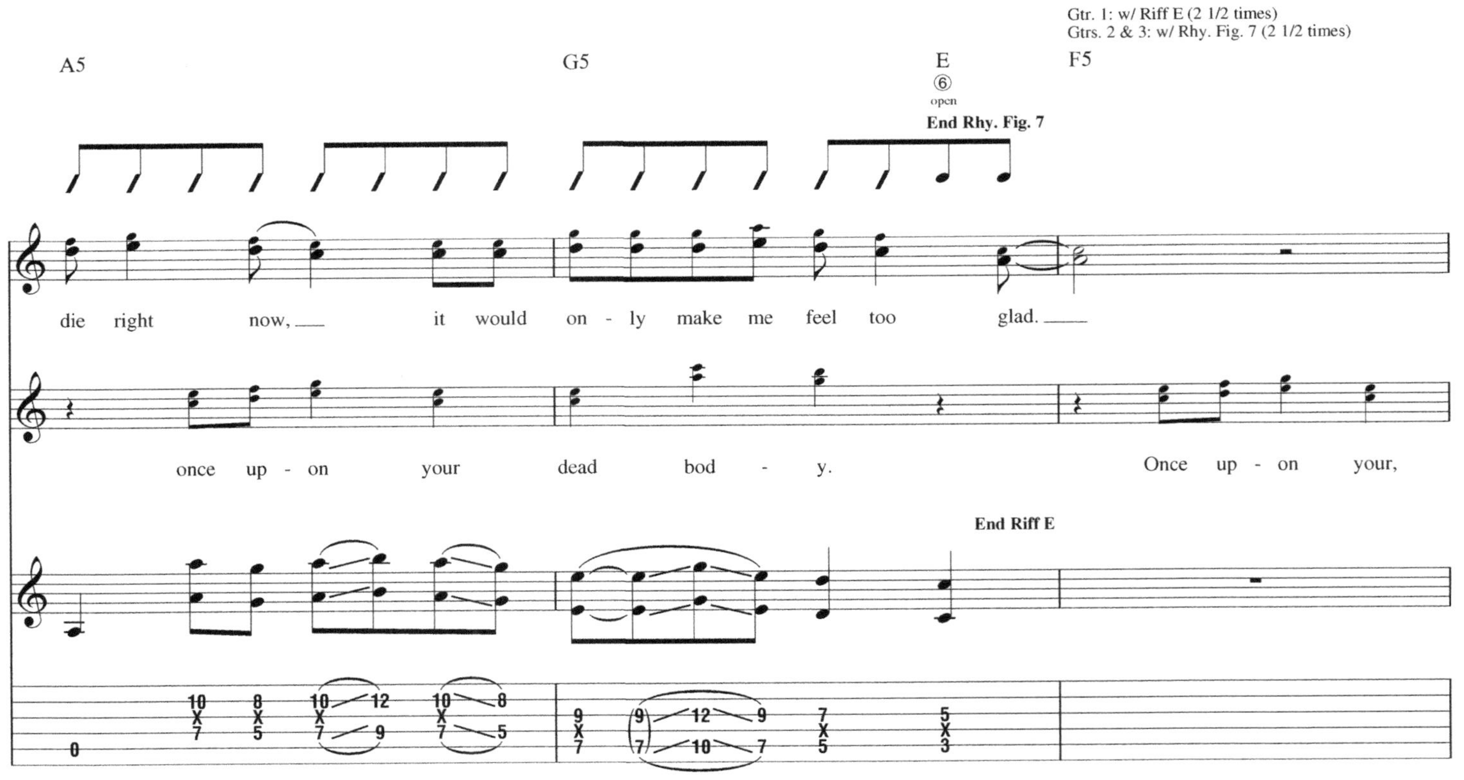
Gtr. 1: w/ Riff E (2 1/2 times)
Gtrs. 2 & 3: w/ Rhy. Fig. 7 (2 1/2 times)
A5
G5
E
⑥ open
F5
End Rhy. Fig. 7
die right now,
it would
on - ly make me feel too
glad.
once up - on your dead bod - y.
Once up - on your,
End Riff E

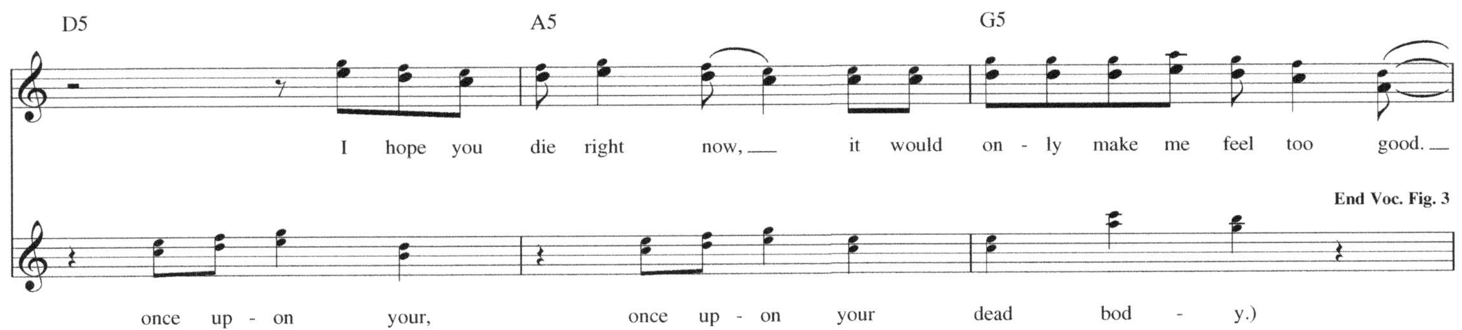

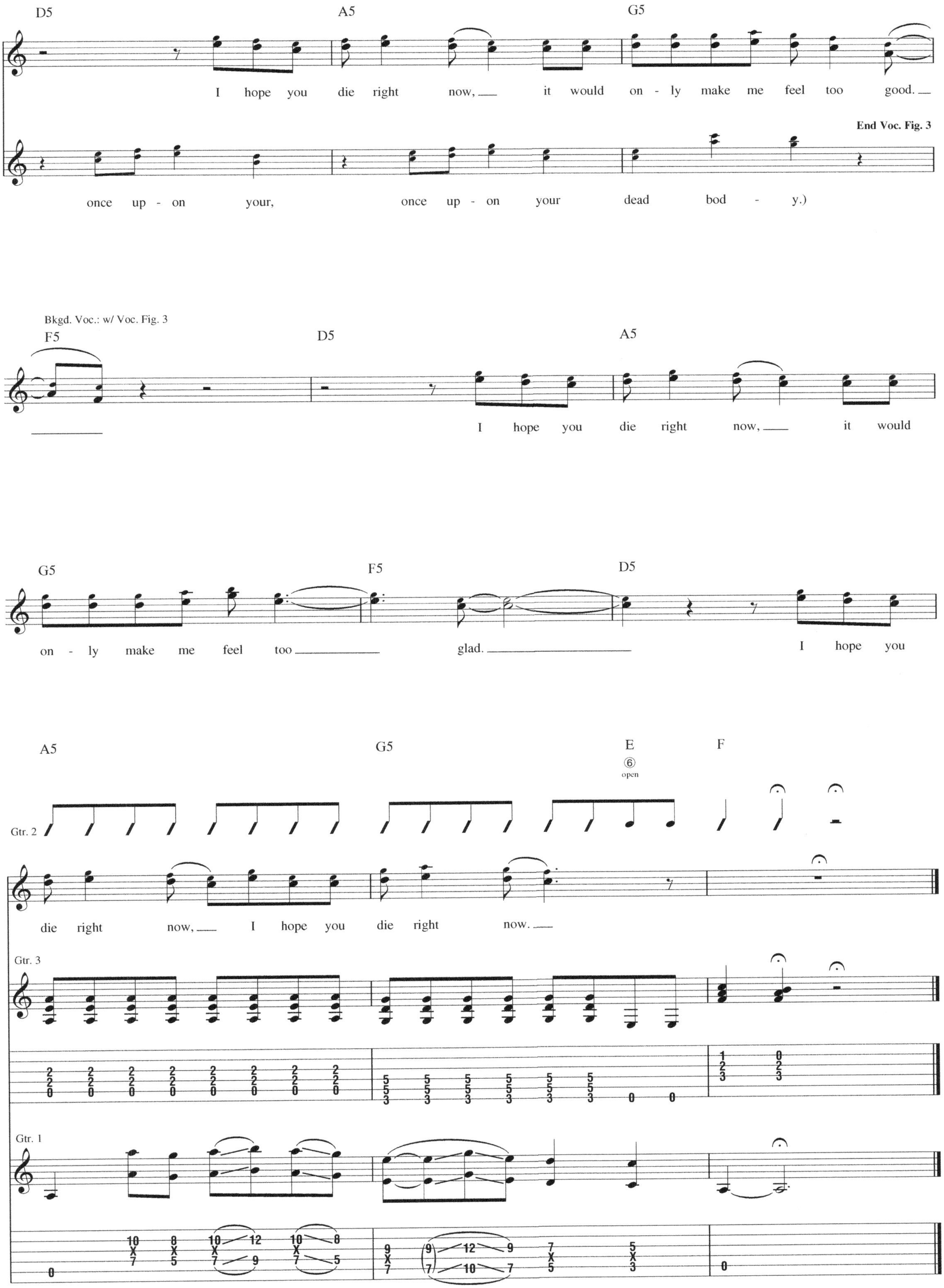

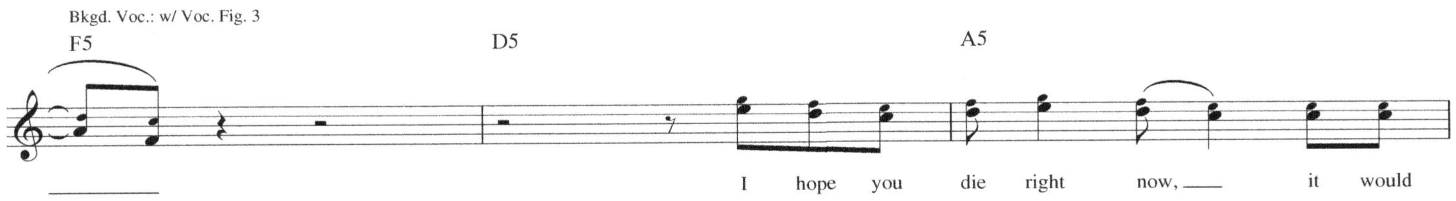

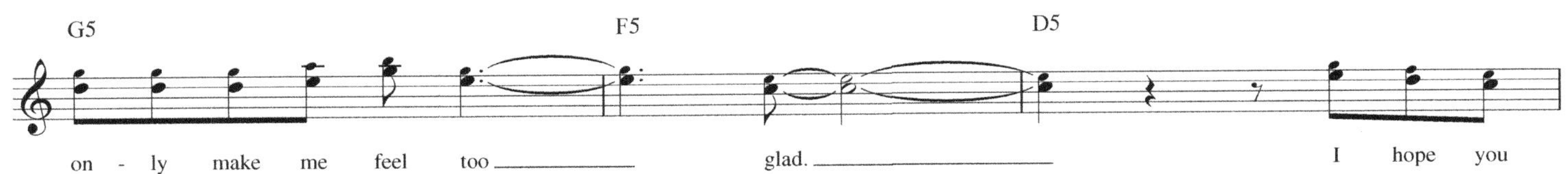

A5 G5 E ⑥ open F

Gtr. 2

die right now, I hope you die right now.

Gtr. 3

Gtr. 1

Wake Up

Words and Music by Claudio Sanchez, Michael Todd, Joshua Eppard and Travis Stever

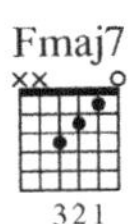

Tune down 1/2 step:
(low to high) E♭-A♭-D♭-G♭-B♭-E♭

Intro
Moderately slow ♩ = 72

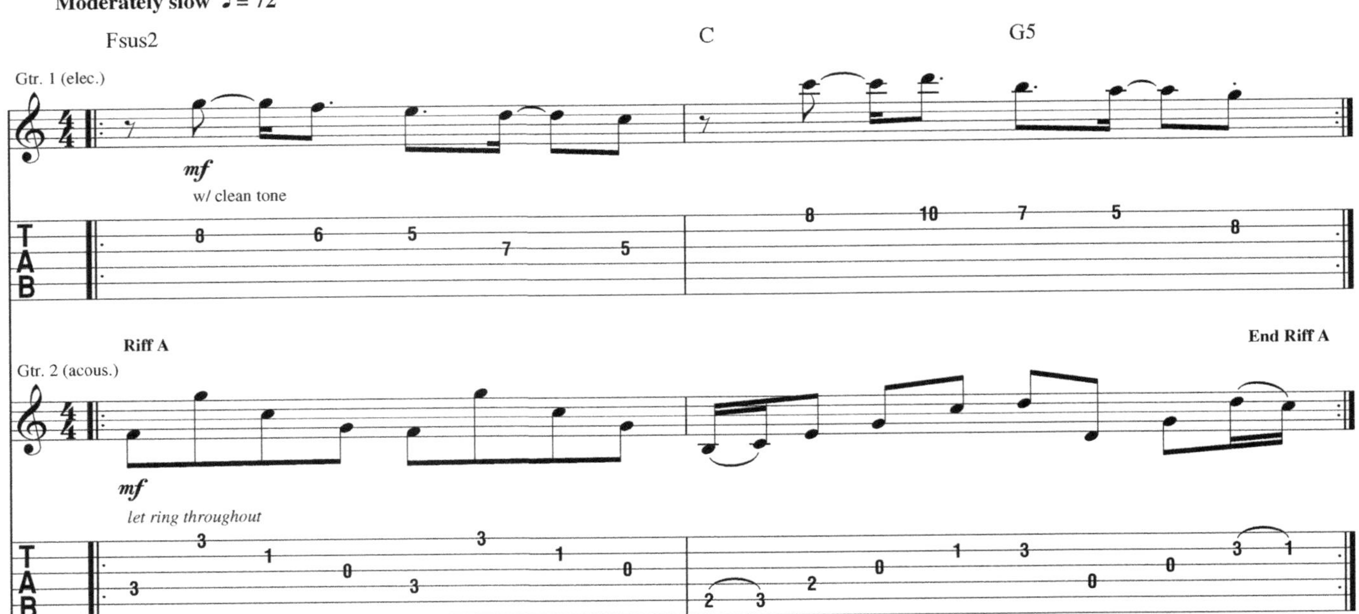

Verse

Gtr. 1 tacet
Gtr. 2: w/ Riff A (4 times)

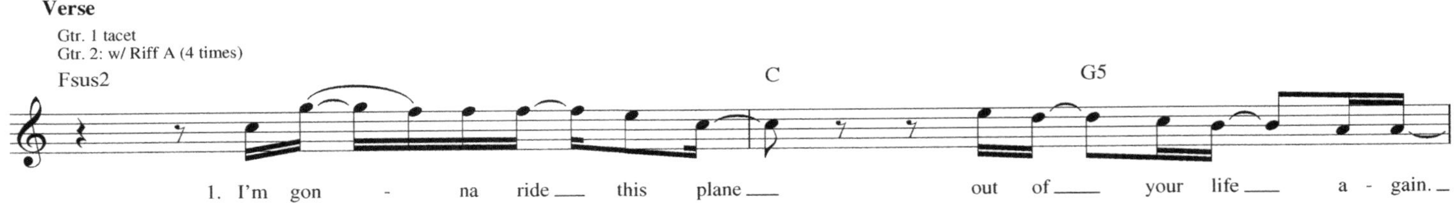

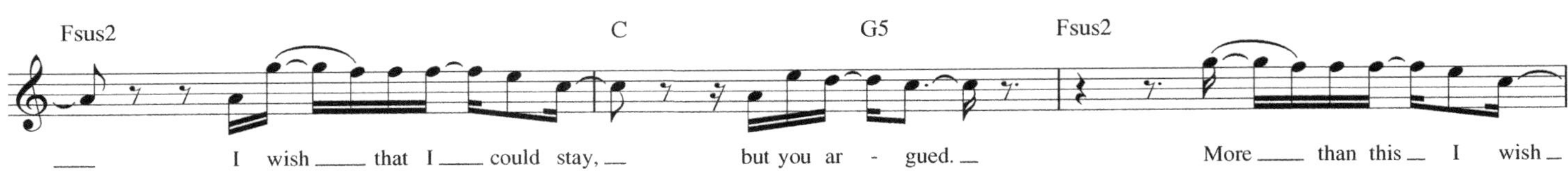

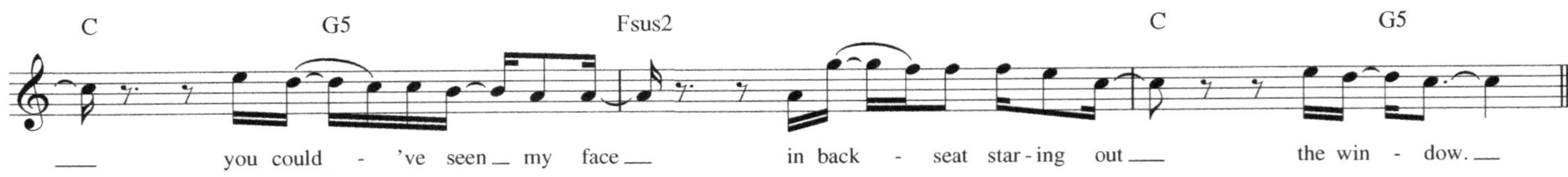

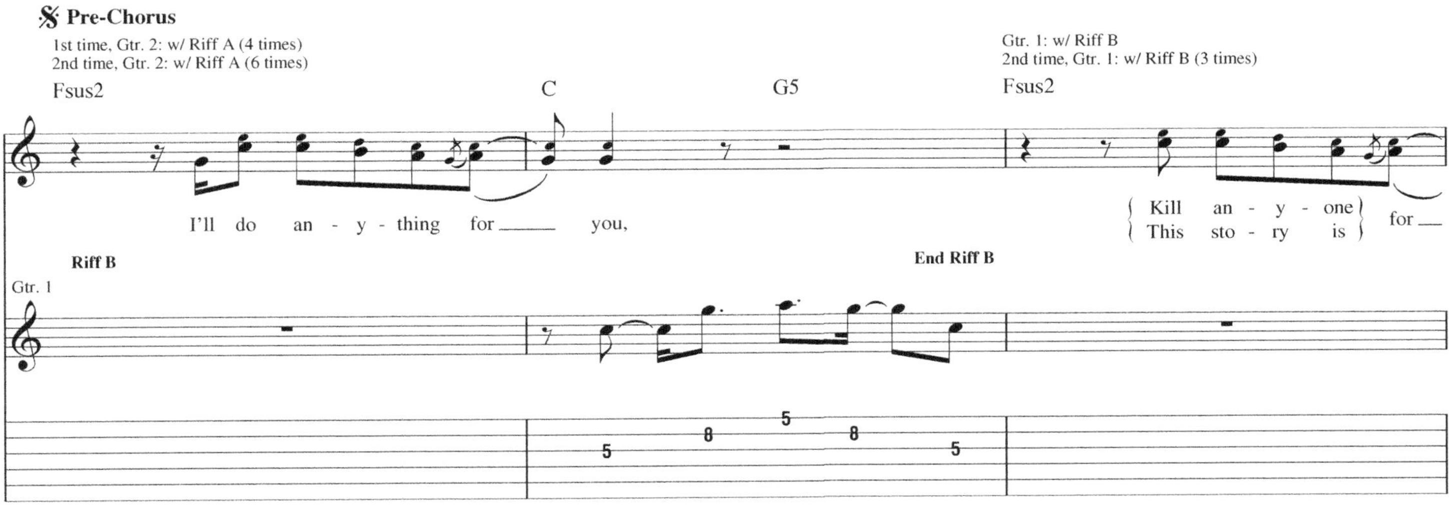
Pre-Chorus
1st time, Gtr. 2: w/ Riff A (4 times)
2nd time, Gtr. 2: w/ Riff A (6 times)
Gtr. 1: w/ Riff B
2nd time, Gtr. 1: w/ Riff B (3 times)
Fsus2
C
G5
Fsus2
I'll do an - y - thing for you,
Kill an - y - one
This sto - ry is
for
Riff B
Gtr. 1
End Riff B
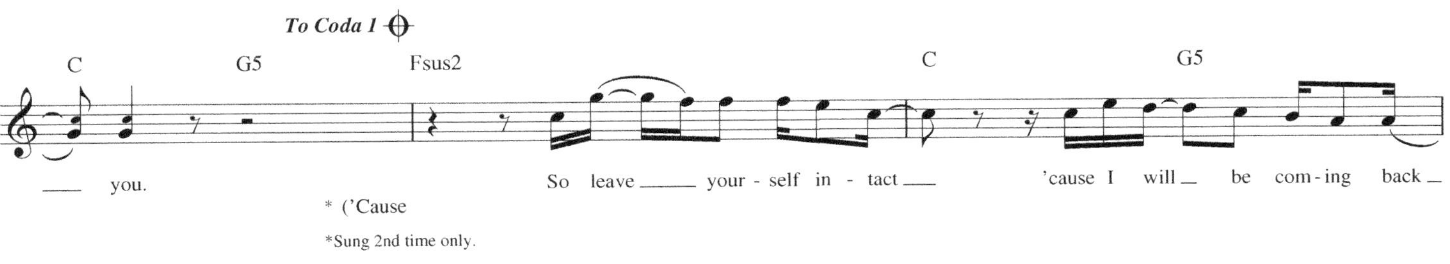
To Coda 1
C
G5
Fsus2
C
G5
you.
* ('Cause
So leave your - self in - tact 'cause I will be com - ing back
*Sung 2nd time only.
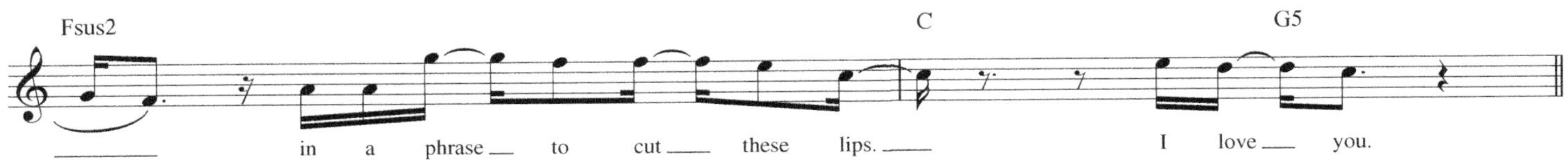
Fsus2
C
G5
in a phrase to cut these lips. I love you.
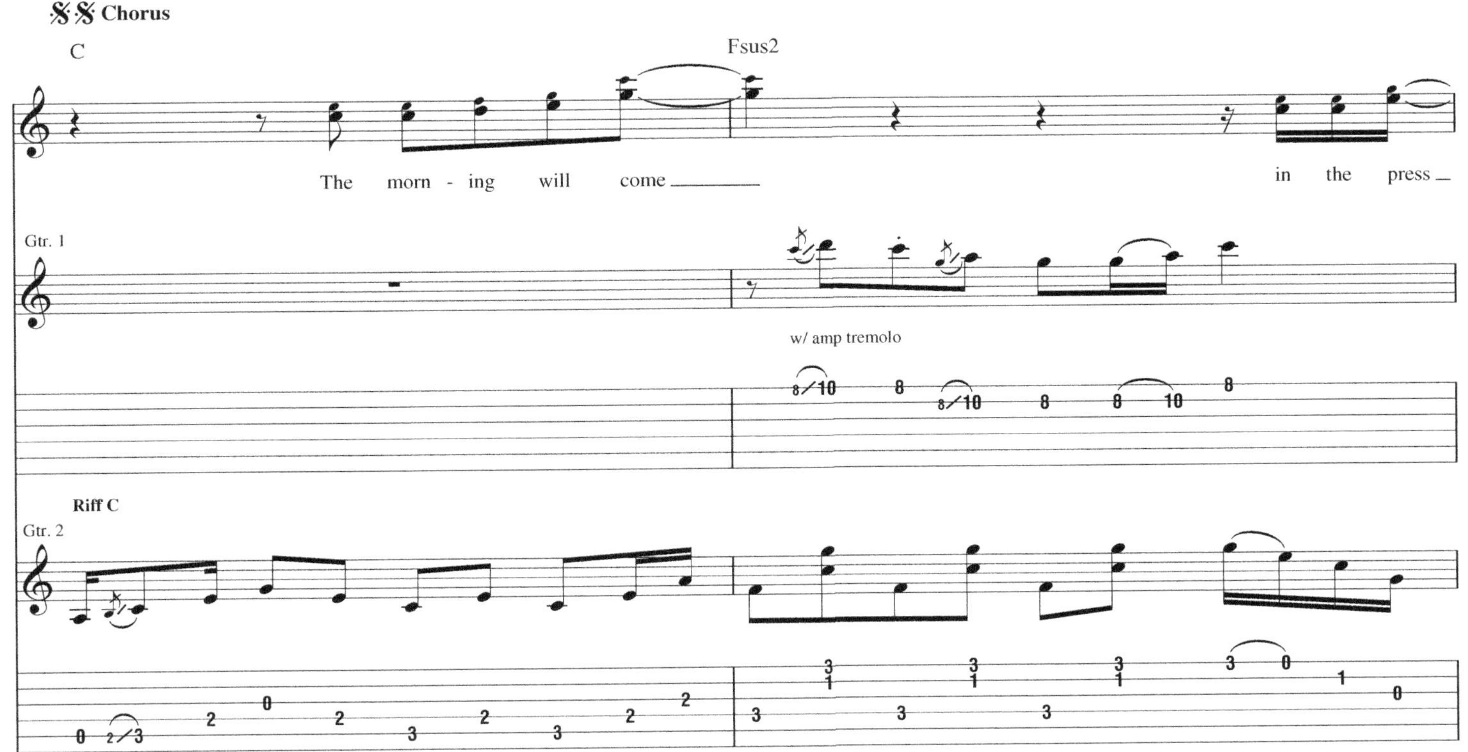
Chorus
C
Fsus2
The morn - ing will come in the press
Gtr. 1
w/ amp tremolo
Riff C
Gtr. 2

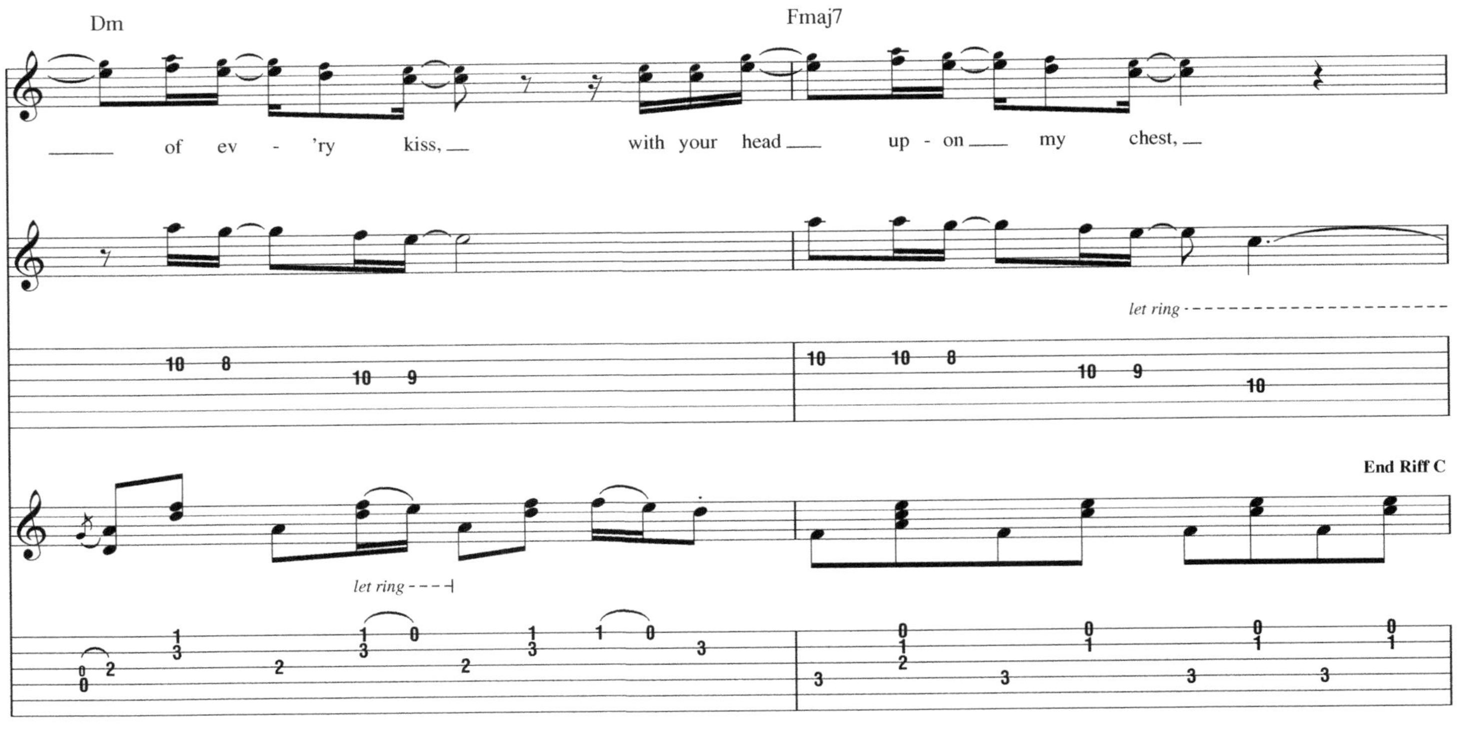
Dm
Fmaj7
of ev - 'ry kiss, with your head up - on my chest,
let ring
End Riff C
let ring

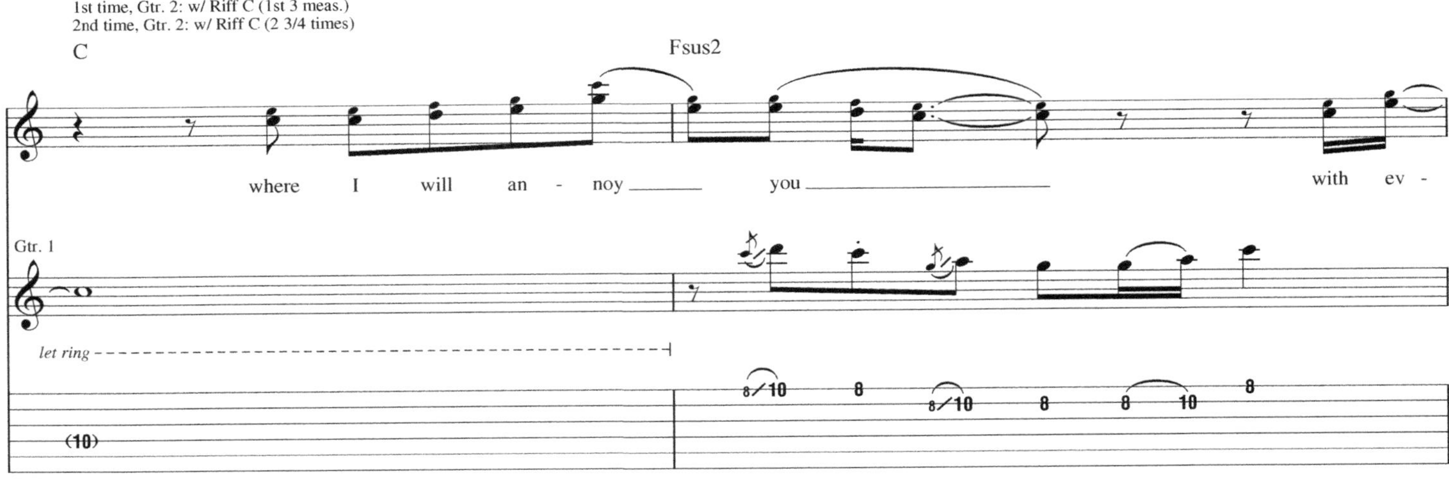
1st time, Gtr. 2: w/ Riff C (1st 3 meas.)
2nd time, Gtr. 2: w/ Riff C (2 3/4 times)
C
Fsus2
where I will an - noy you with ev -
Gtr. 1
let ring

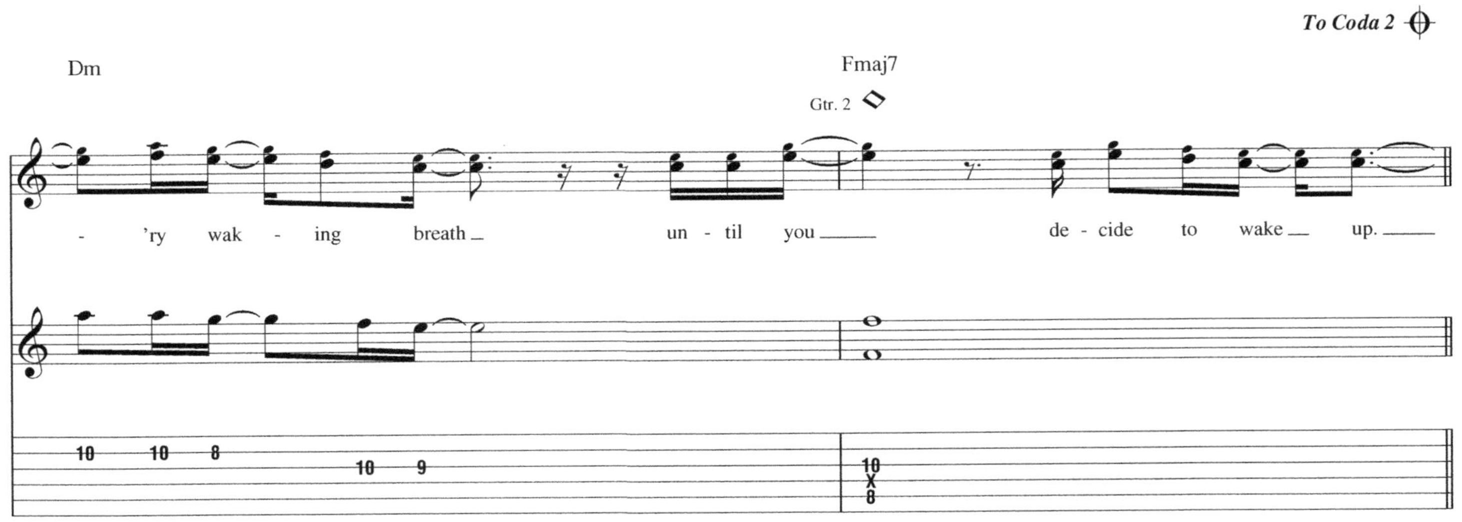
To Coda 2
Dm
Fmaj7
Gtr. 2
- 'ry wak - ing breath un - til you de - cide to wake up.

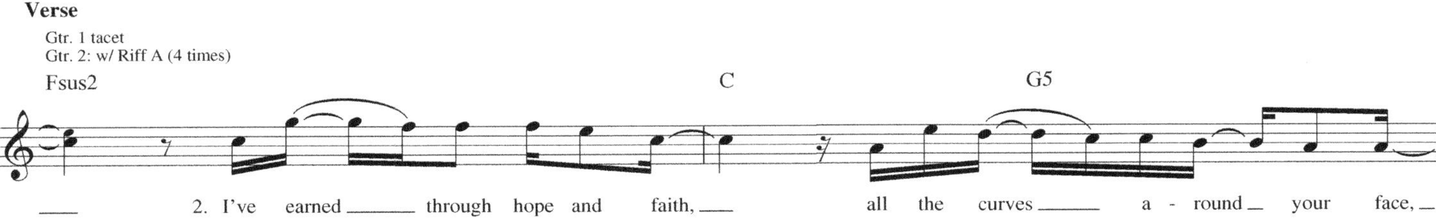
Verse
Gtr. 1 tacet
Gtr. 2: w/ Riff A (4 times)
Fsus2
C
G5
2. I've earned through hope and faith, all the curves a - round your face,

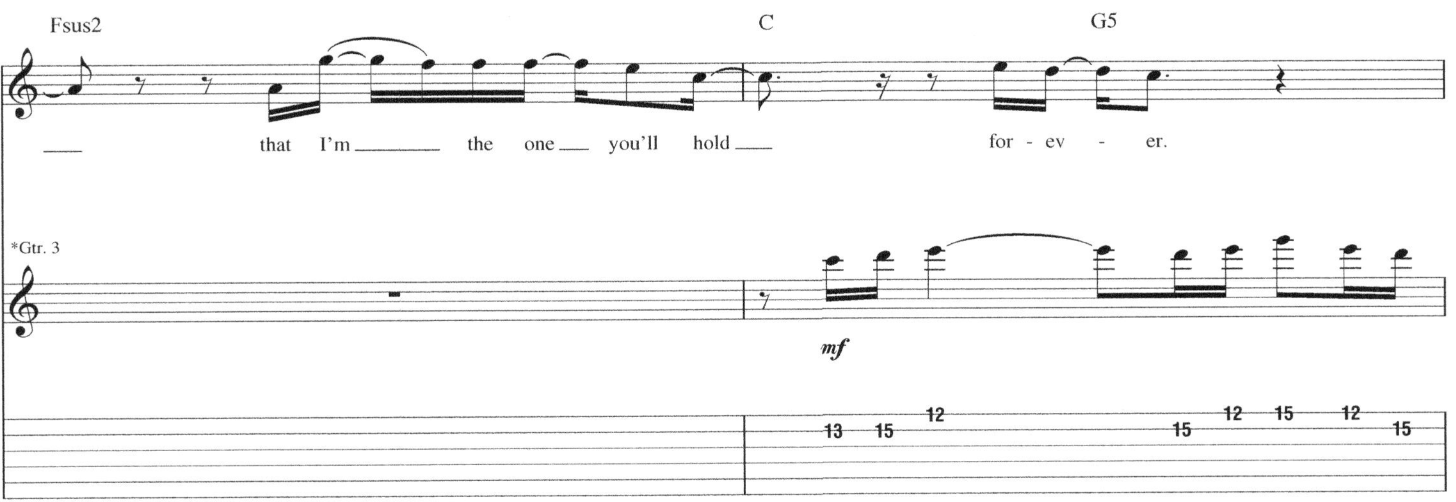
Fsus2
C
G5
that I'm the one you'll hold for - ev - er.
*Gtr. 3
mf
13 15 12 15 12 15 12 15
*Elec. piano arr. for gtr.

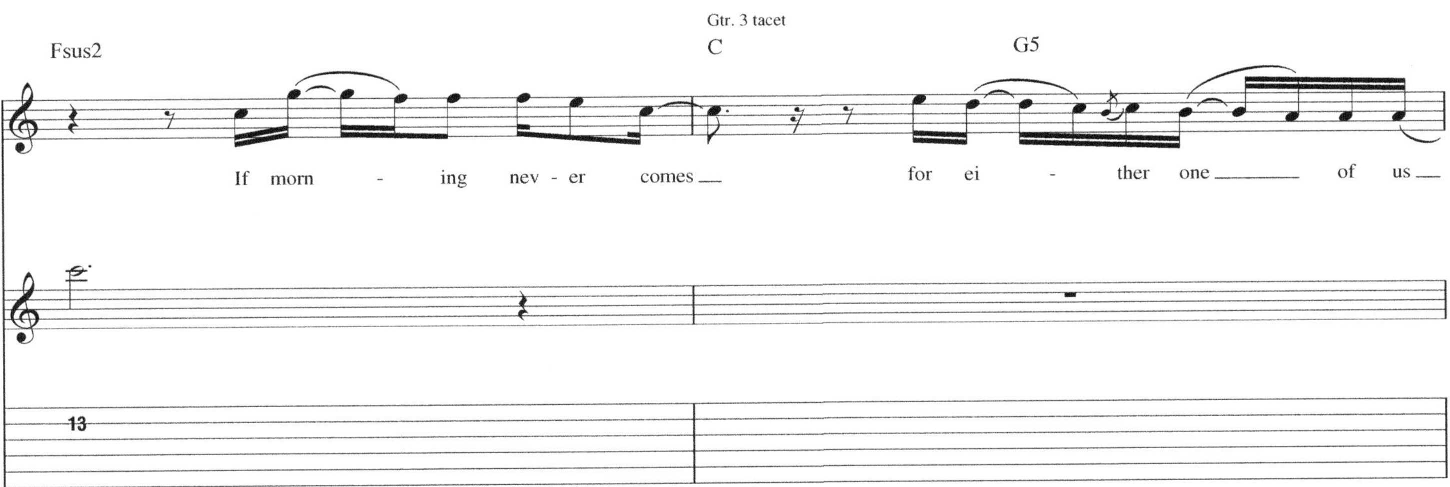
Gtr. 3 tacet
Fsus2
C
G5
If morn - ing nev - er comes for ei - ther one of us
13

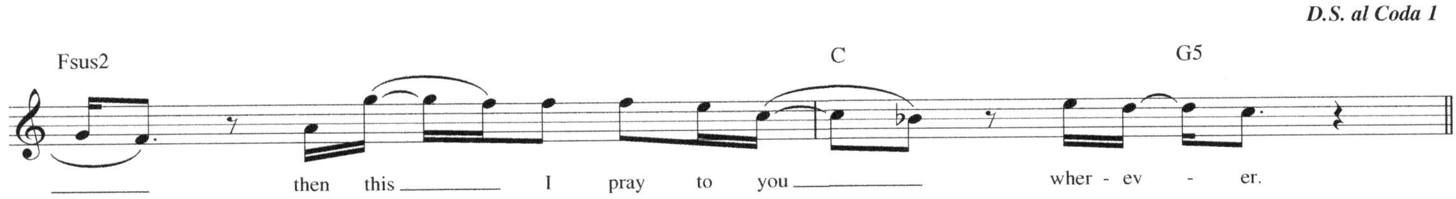
D.S. al Coda 1
Fsus2
C
G5
then this I pray to you wher - ev - er.

Coda 1

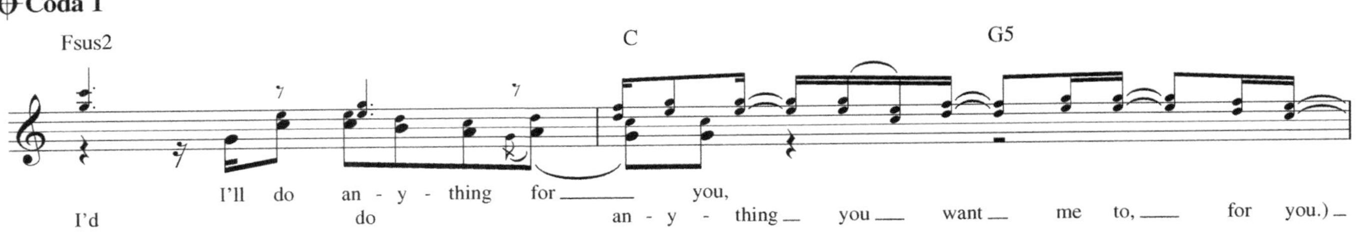

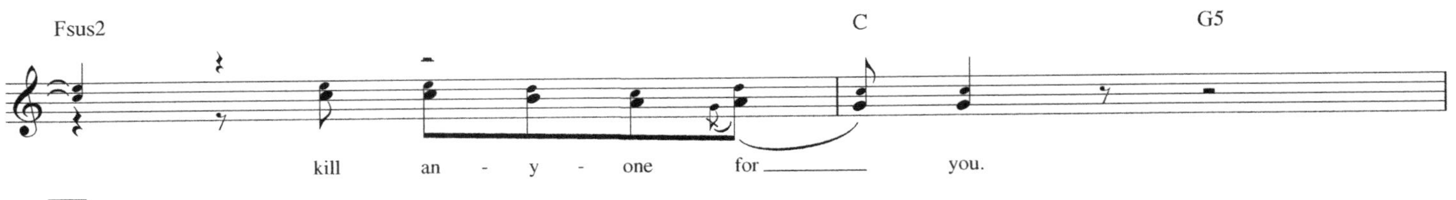

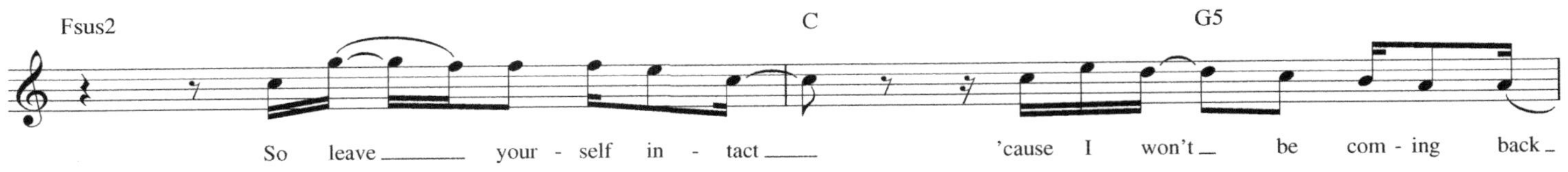

D.S.S. al Coda 2

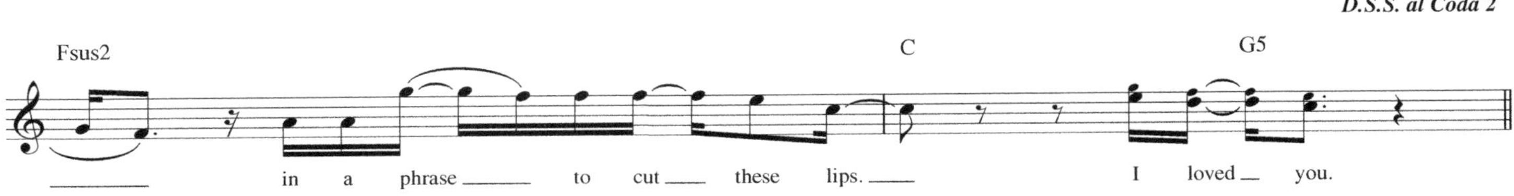

Coda 2

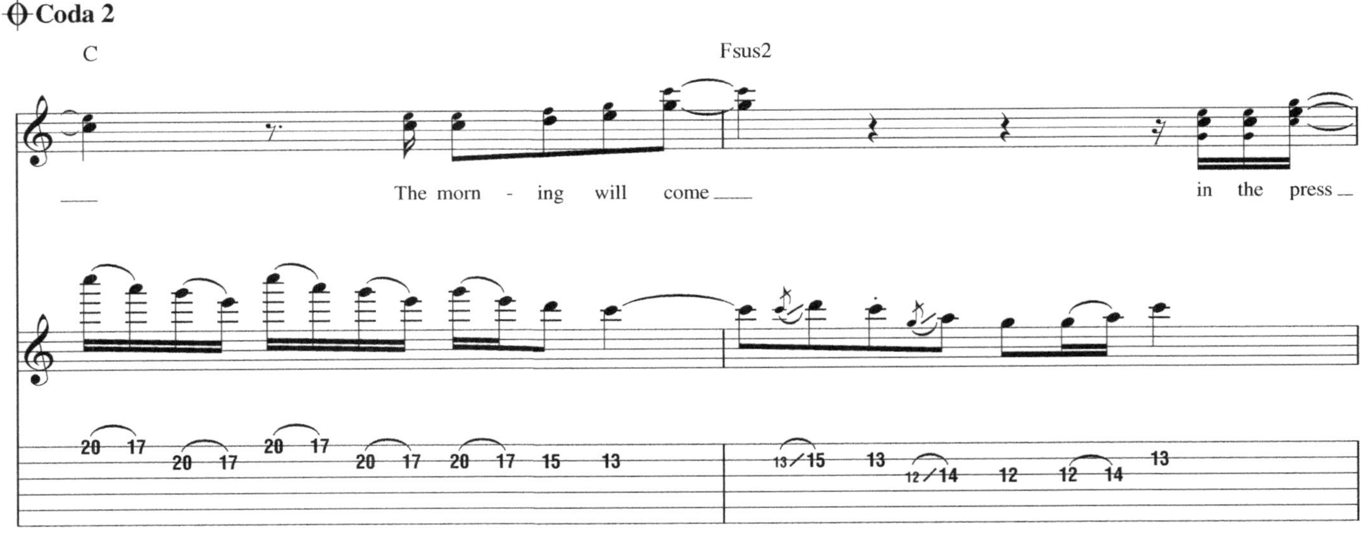

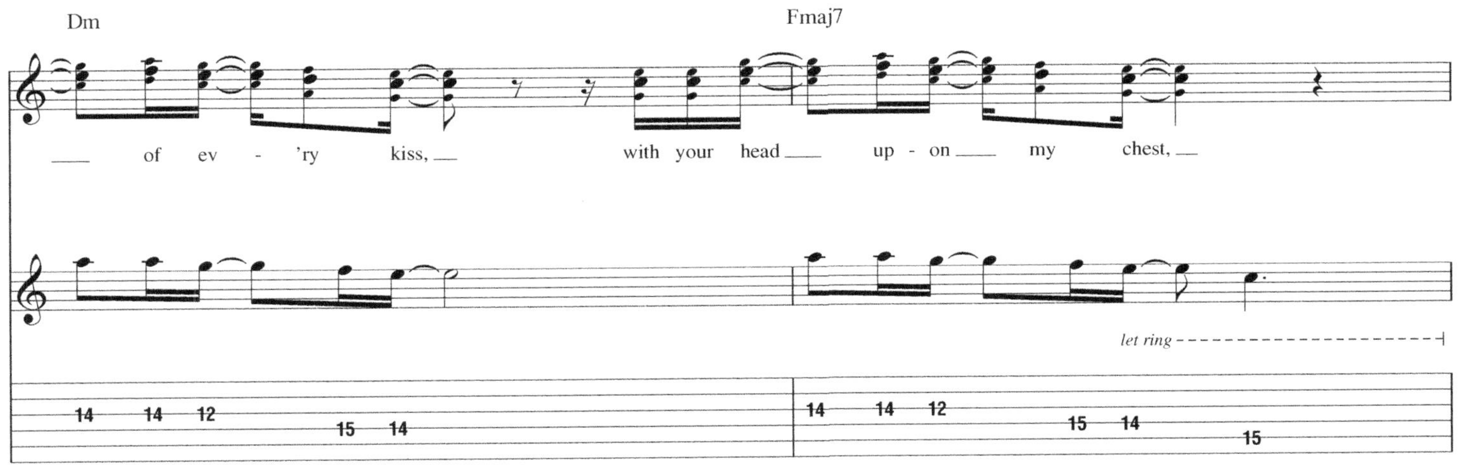
Dm
Fmaj7
of ev - 'ry kiss,
with your head
up - on
my chest,
let ring
14 14 12 15 14
14 14 12 15 14 15

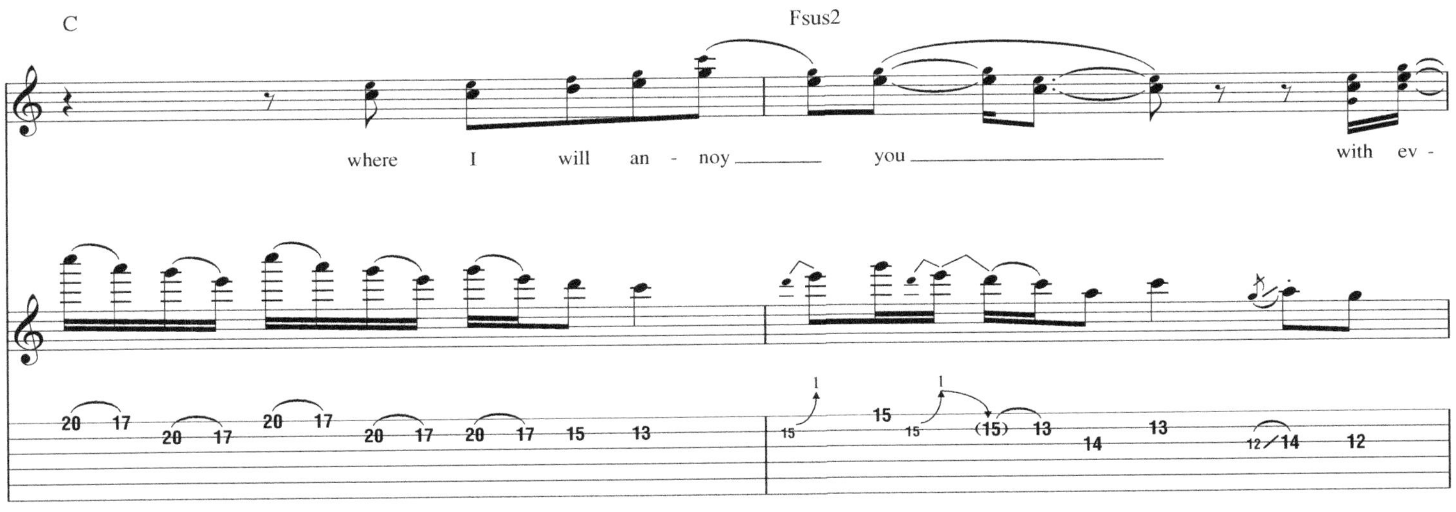
C
Fsus2
where I will an - noy
you
with ev -
20 17 20 17 20 17 20 17 20 17 15 13
1
15 15
1
15 (15) 13 14 13 12 14 12

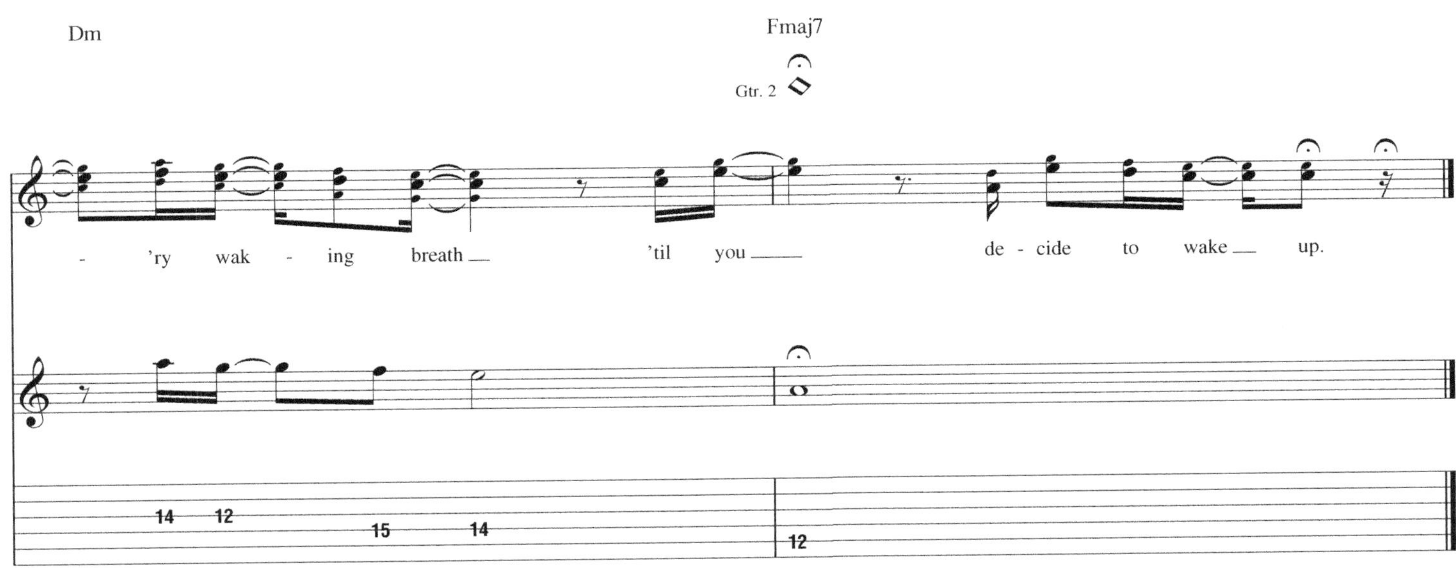
Dm
Fmaj7
Gtr. 2
- 'ry wak - ing breath
'til you
de - cide to wake up.
14 12 15 14
12

The Suffering

Words and Music by Claudio Sanchez, Michael Todd, Joshua Eppard and Travis Stever

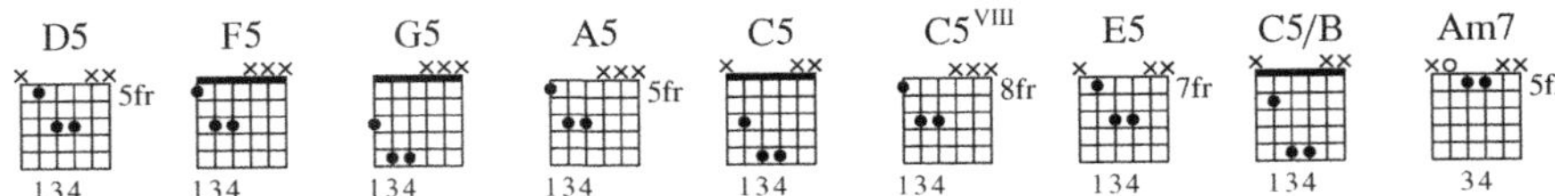

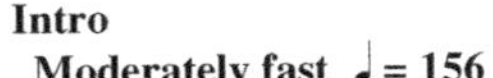

Intro
Moderately fast ♩ = 156

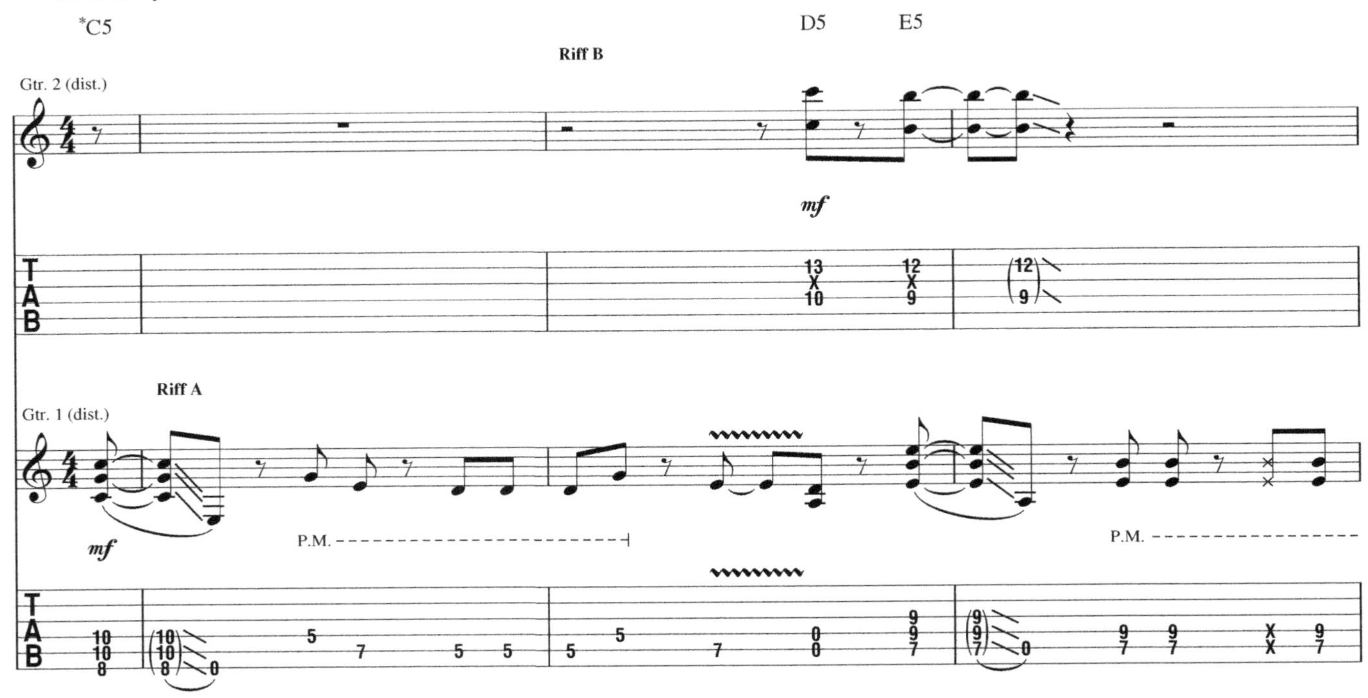

*Chord symbols reflect implied harmony.

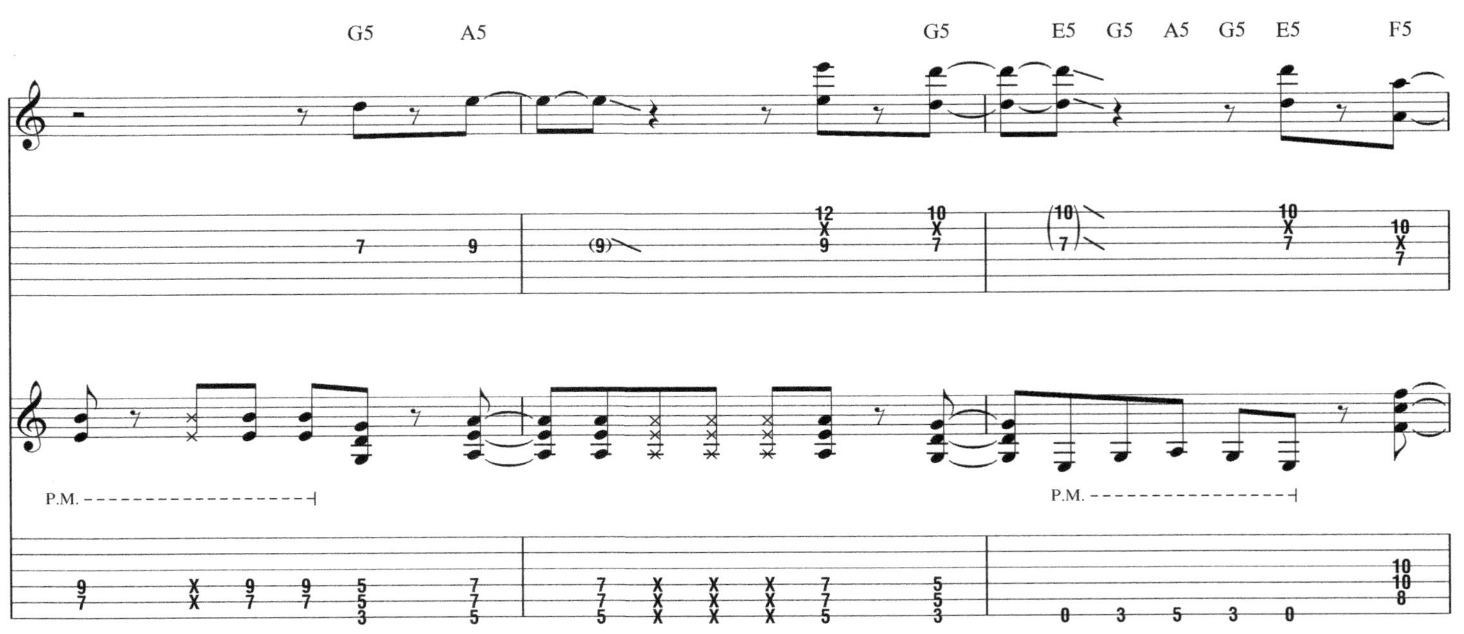

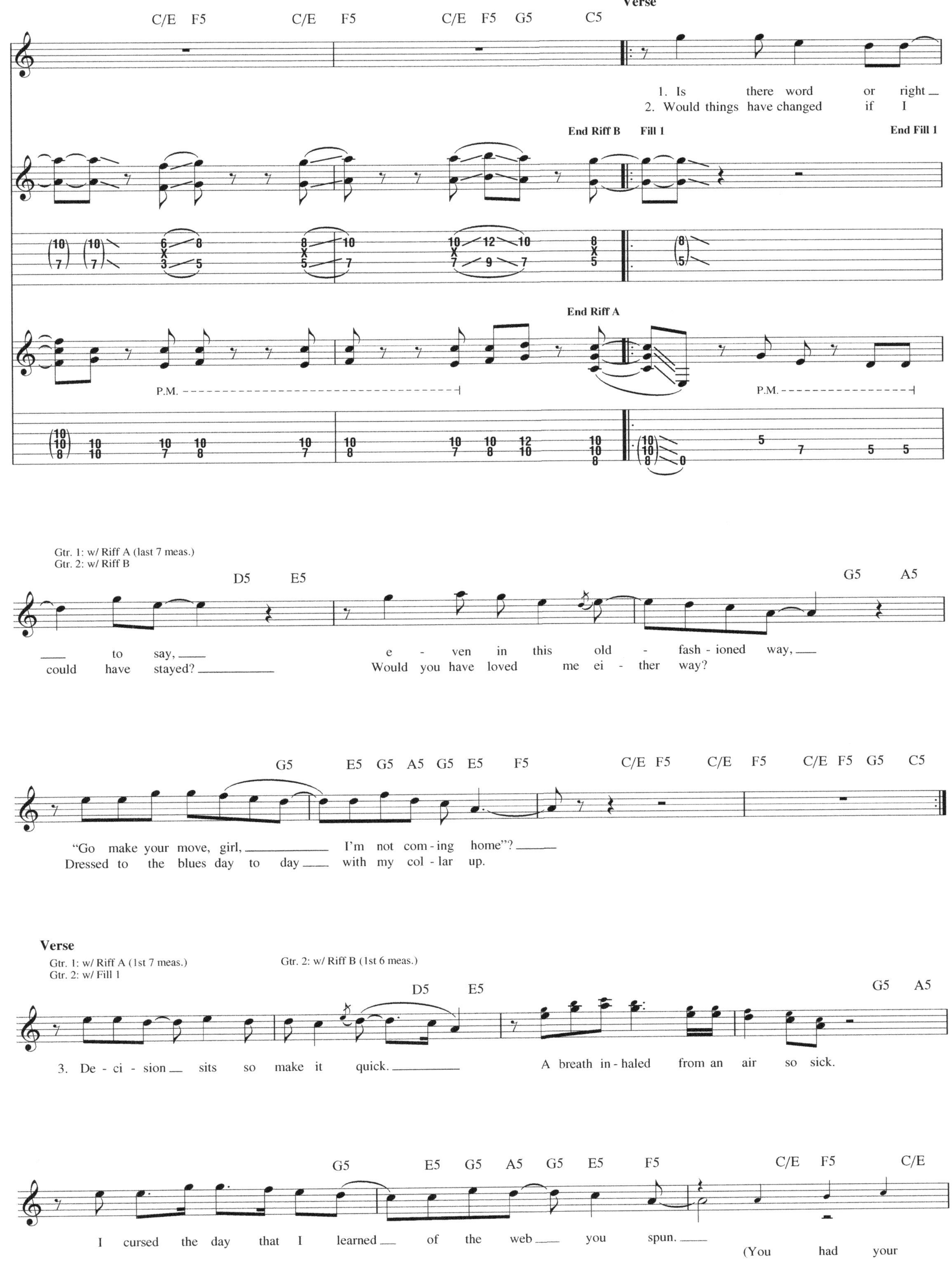
C/E F5 C/E F5 C/E F5 G5 C5
Verse
1. Is there word or right
2. Would things have changed if I
End Riff B
Fill 1
End Fill 1
End Riff A
P.M.
P.M.
Gtr. 1: w/ Riff A (last 7 meas.)
Gtr. 2: w/ Riff B
D5 E5
G5 A5
to say,
could have stayed?
e - ven in this old - fash - ioned way,
Would you have loved me ei - ther way?
G5 E5 G5 A5 G5 E5 F5 C/E F5 C/E F5 C/E F5 G5 C5
"Go make your move, girl, I'm not com - ing home"?
Dressed to the blues day to day with my col - lar up.
Verse
Gtr. 1: w/ Riff A (1st 7 meas.)
Gtr. 2: w/ Fill 1
Gtr. 2: w/ Riff B (1st 6 meas.)
D5 E5
G5 A5
3. De - ci - sion sits so make it quick.
A breath in - haled from an air so sick.
G5 E5 G5 A5 G5 E5 F5 C/E F5 C/E
I cursed the day that I learned of the web you spun.
(You had your

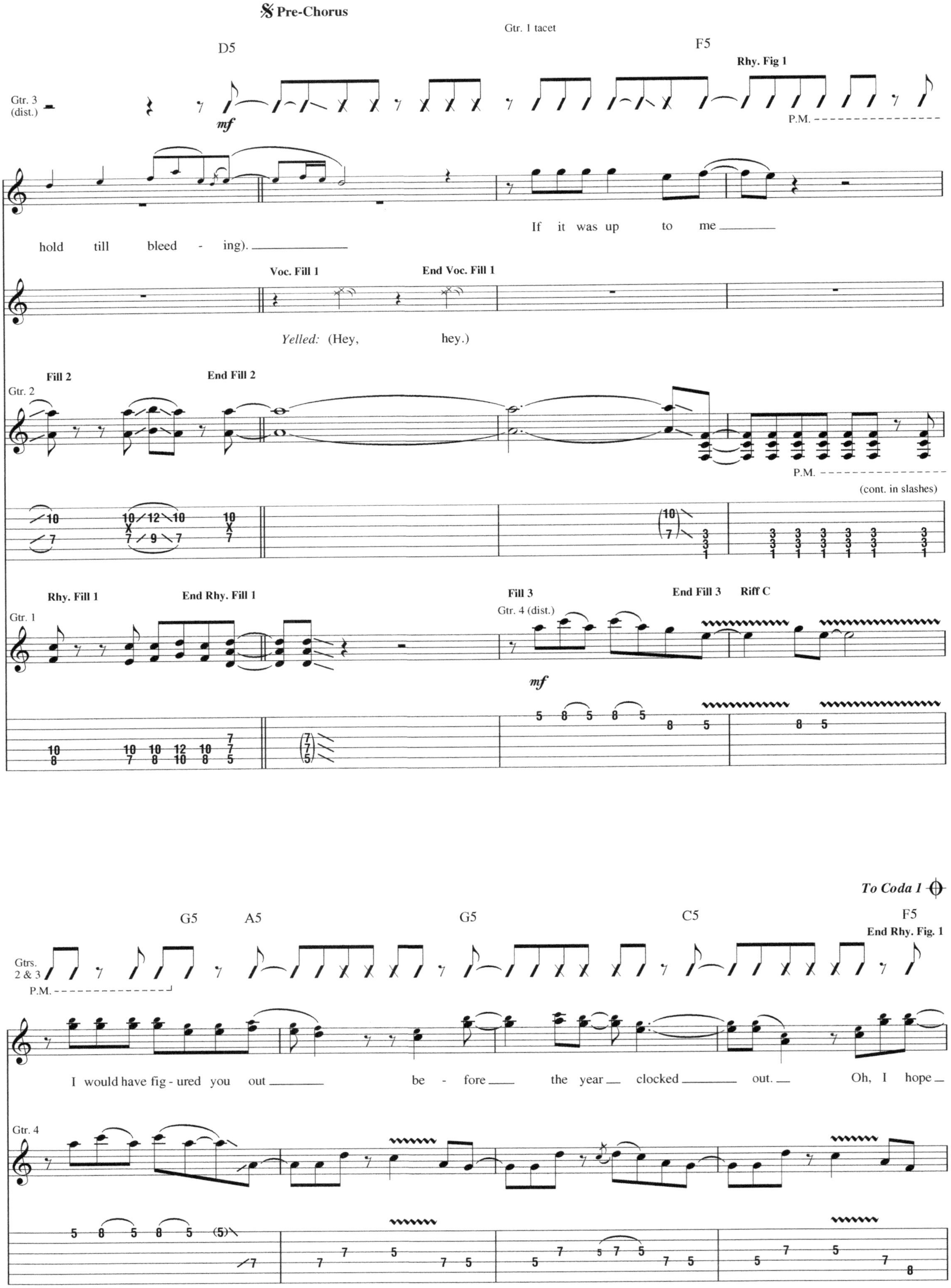

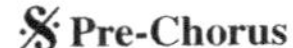

Pre-Chorus

Gtr. 1 tacet

D5 F5

Rhy. Fig 1

Gtr. 3 (dist.)

mf

P.M.

hold till bleed - ing). If it was up to me

Voc. Fill 1 End Voc. Fill 1

Yelled: (Hey, hey.)

Fill 2 End Fill 2

Gtr. 2

P.M.

(cont. in slashes)

Rhy. Fill 1 End Rhy. Fill 1

Gtr. 1

Fill 3 End Fill 3 Riff C

Gtr. 4 (dist.)

mf

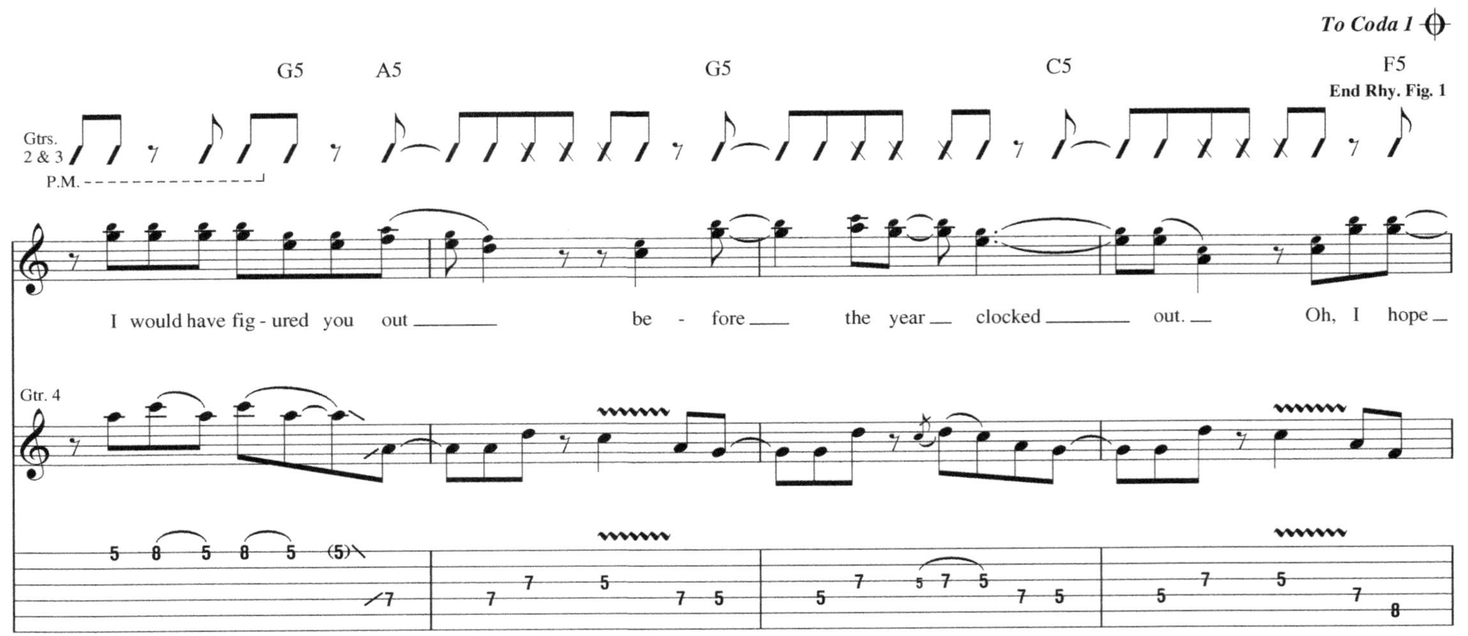

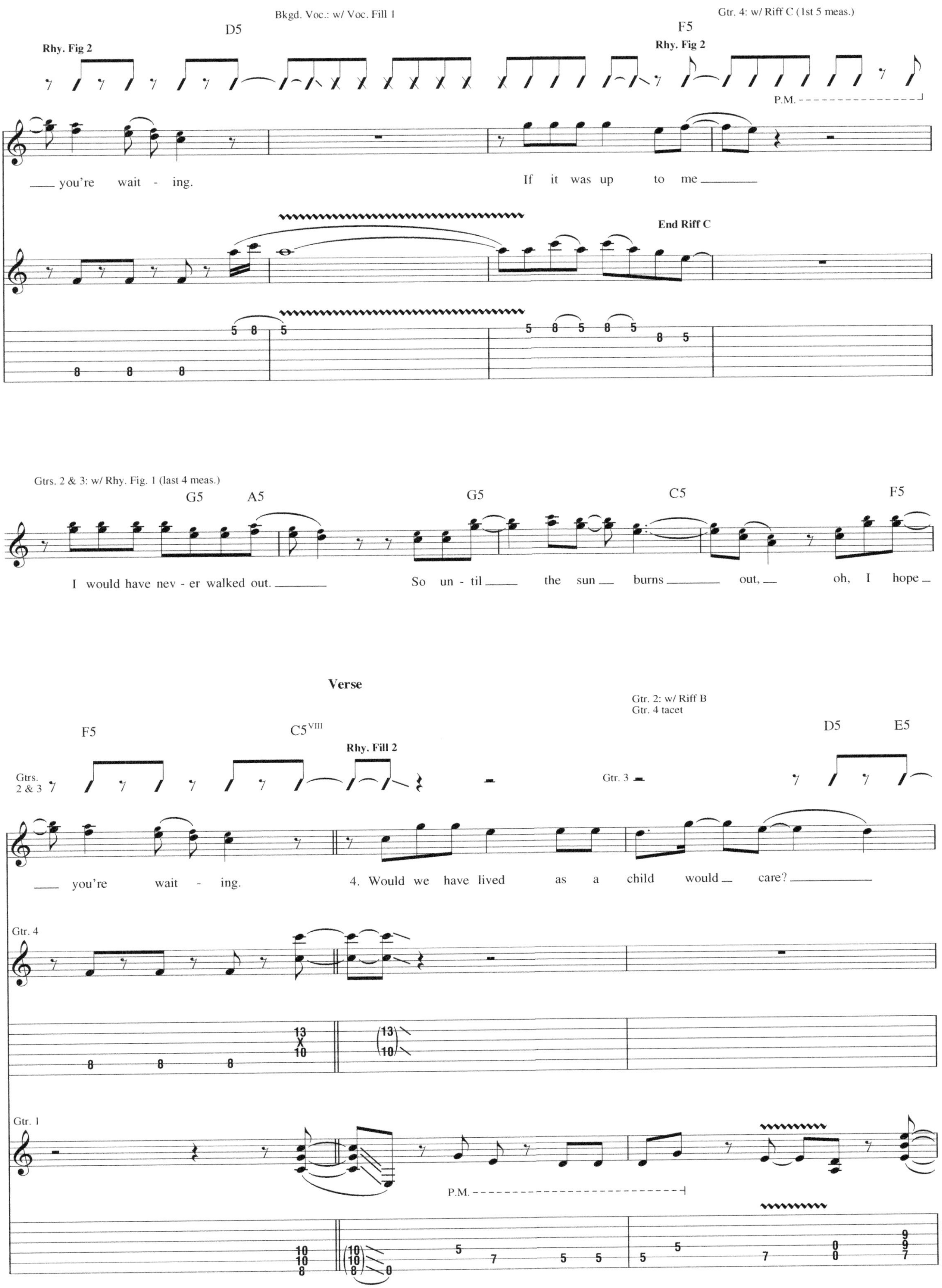

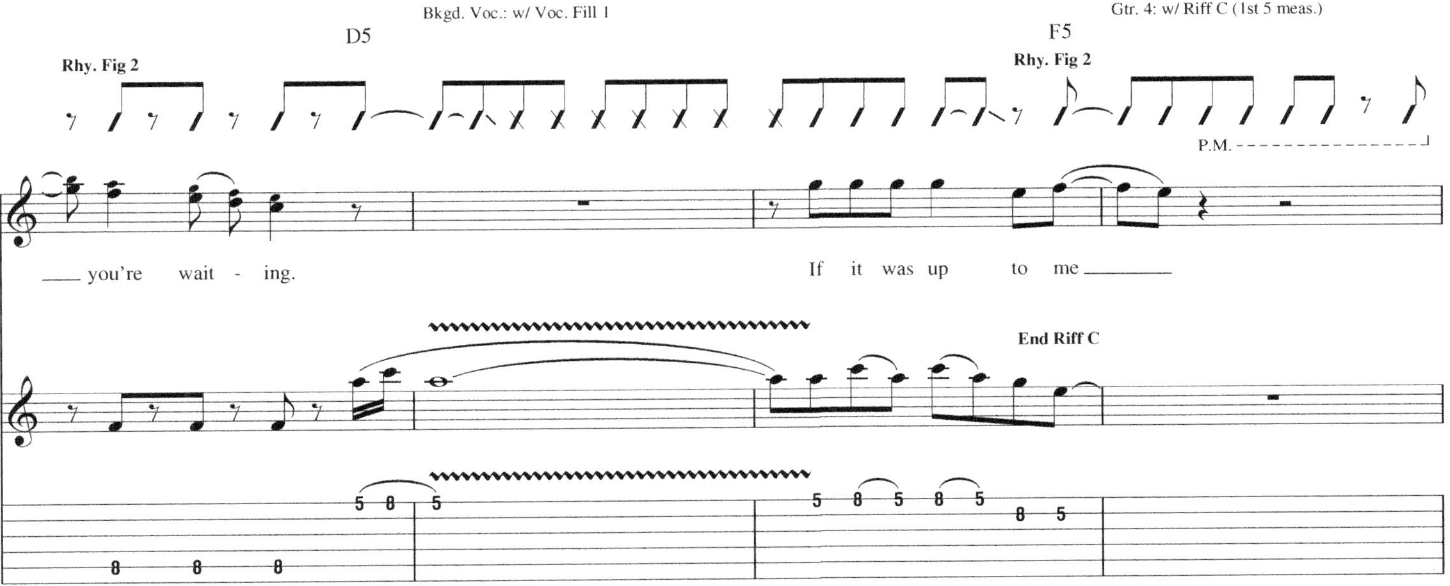

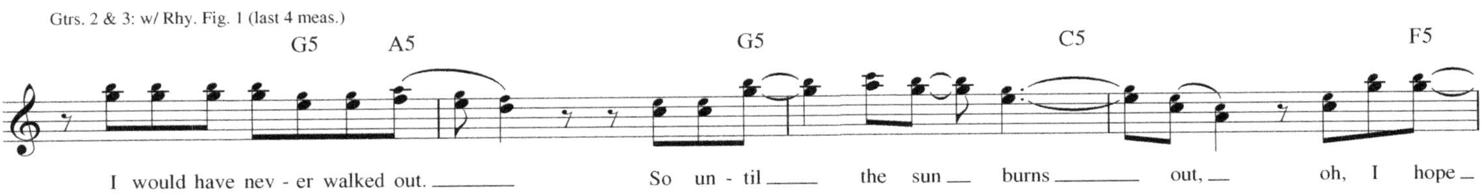

Verse

Gtr. 2: w/ Riff B
Gtr. 4 tacet

F5 C5VIII D5 E5

Rhy. Fill 2

Gtrs. 2 & 3

Gtr. 3

you're wait - ing. 4. Would we have lived as a child would care?

Gtr. 4

Gtr. 1

P.M.

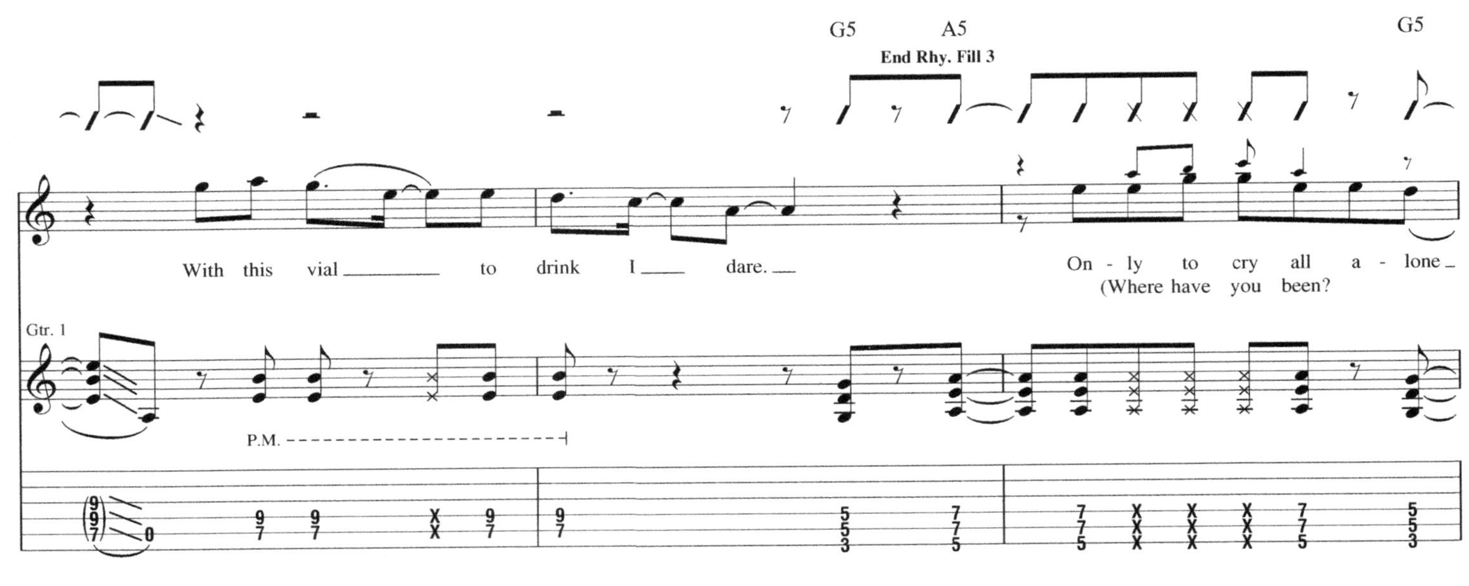
G5
A5
End Rhy. Fill 3
G5
With this vial to drink I dare.
On - ly to cry all a - lone
(Where have you been?
Gtr. 1
P.M.

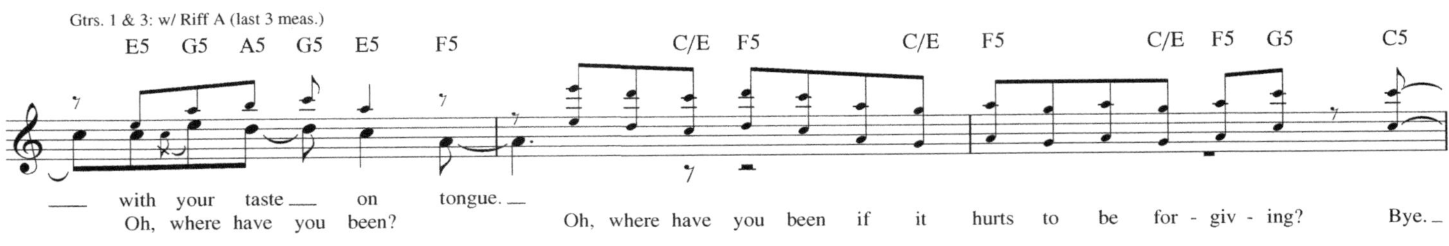
Gtrs. 1 & 3: w/ Riff A (last 3 meas.)
E5 G5 A5 G5 E5 F5 C/E F5 C/E F5 C/E F5 G5 C5
with your taste on tongue.
Oh, where have you been?
Oh, where have you been if it hurts to be for - giv - ing? Bye.

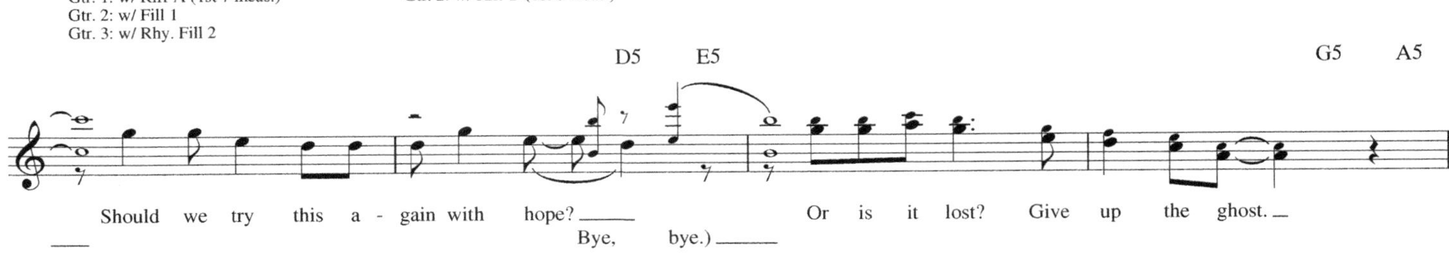
Gtr. 1: w/ Riff A (1st 7 meas.)
Gtr. 2: w/ Fill 1
Gtr. 3: w/ Rhy. Fill 2
Gtr. 2: w/ Riff B (1st 6 meas.)
D5 E5 G5 A5
Should we try this a - gain with hope?
Bye, bye.)
Or is it lost? Give up the ghost.

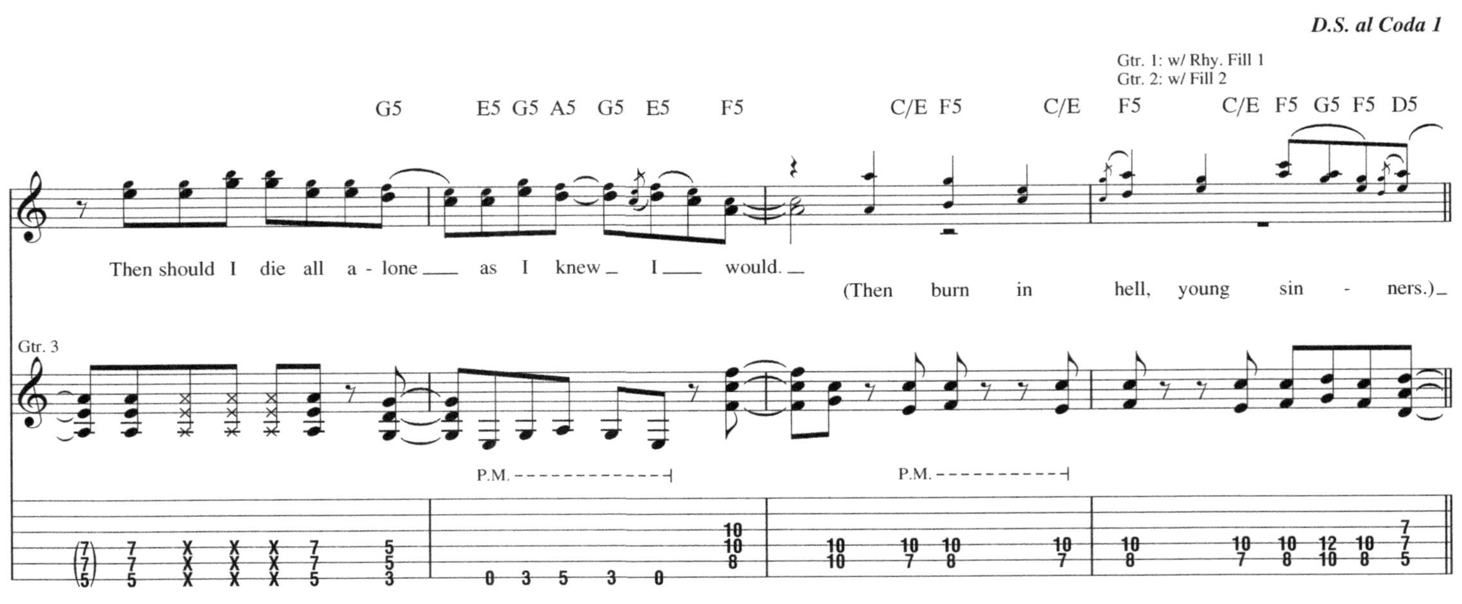
D.S. al Coda 1
Gtr. 1: w/ Rhy. Fill 1
Gtr. 2: w/ Fill 2
G5 E5 G5 A5 G5 E5 F5 C/E F5 C/E F5 C/E F5 G5 F5 D5
Then should I die all a - lone as I knew I would.
(Then burn in hell, young sin - ners.)
Gtr. 3
P.M.
P.M.

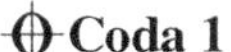

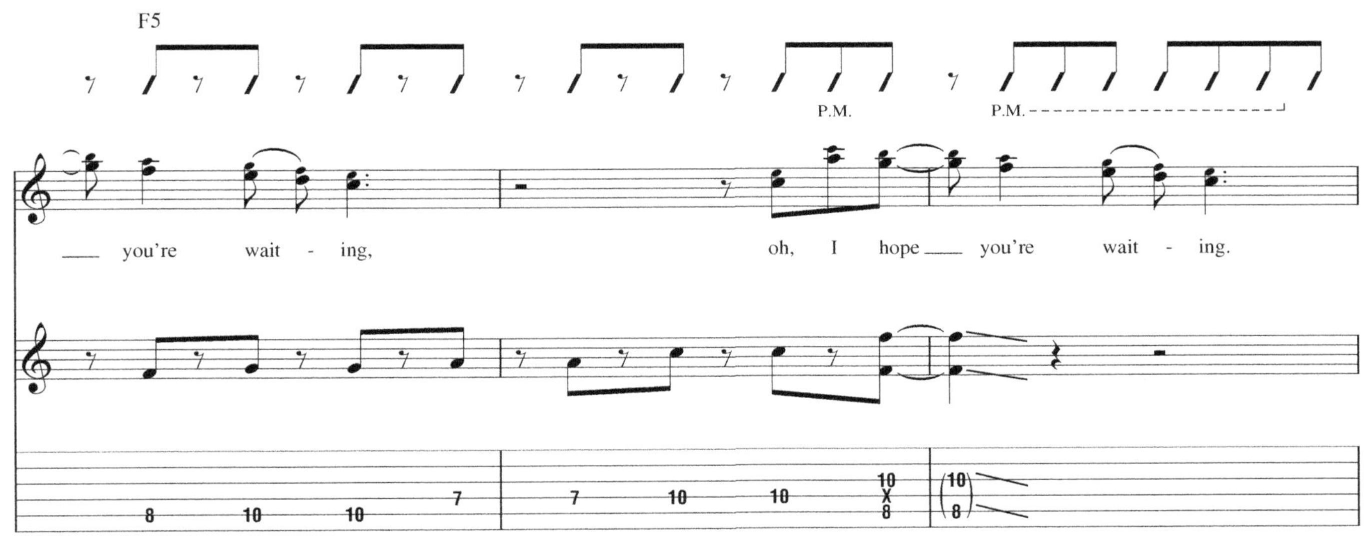
F5
P.M.
P.M.
you're wait - ing,
oh, I hope you're wait - ing.

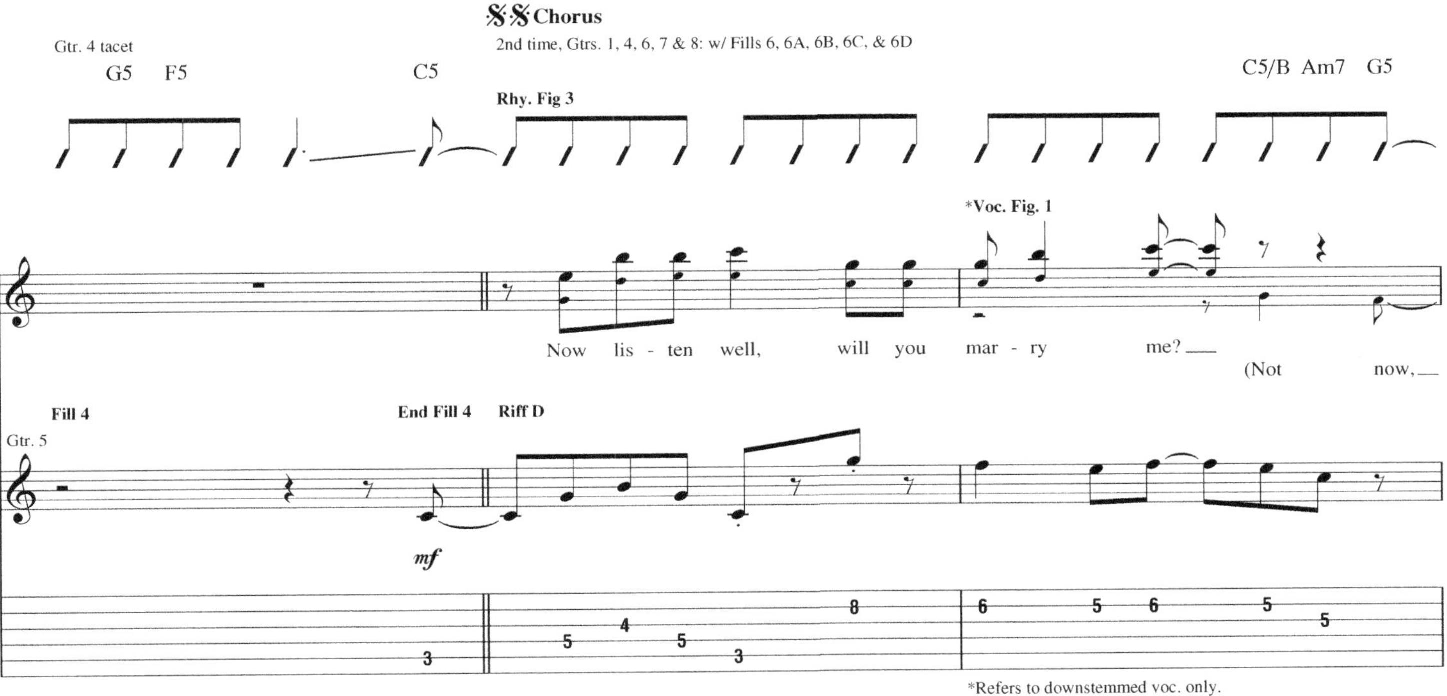
Chorus
Gtr. 4 tacet
2nd time, Gtrs. 1, 4, 6, 7 & 8: w/ Fills 6, 6A, 6B, 6C, & 6D
G5 F5 C5 C5/B Am7 G5
Rhy. Fig 3
*Voc. Fig. 1
Now lis - ten well, will you mar - ry me?
(Not now,
Fill 4
Gtr. 5
End Fill 4
Riff D
mf
*Refers to downstemmed voc. only.

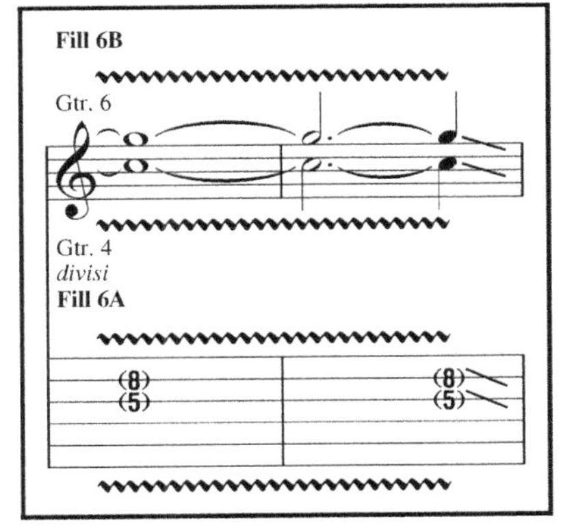
Fill 6B
Gtr. 6
Gtr. 4
divisi
Fill 6A

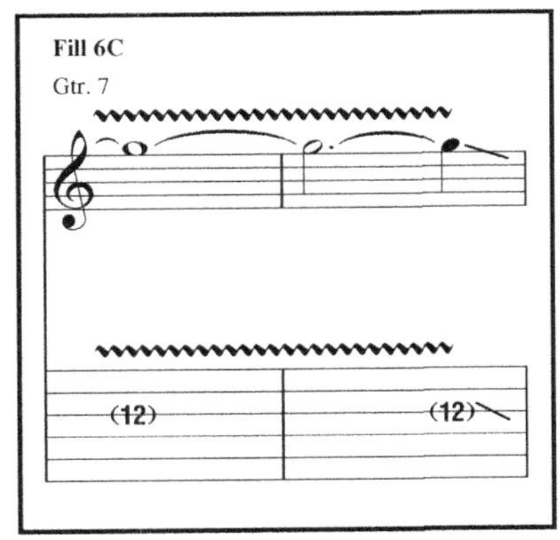
Fill 6C
Gtr. 7

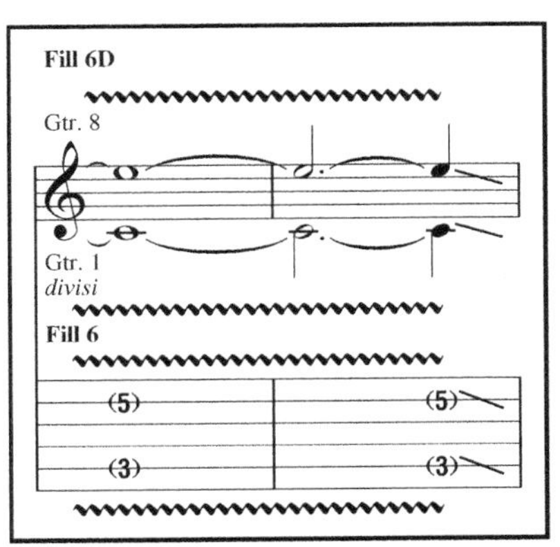
Fill 6D
Gtr. 8
Gtr. 1
divisi
Fill 6

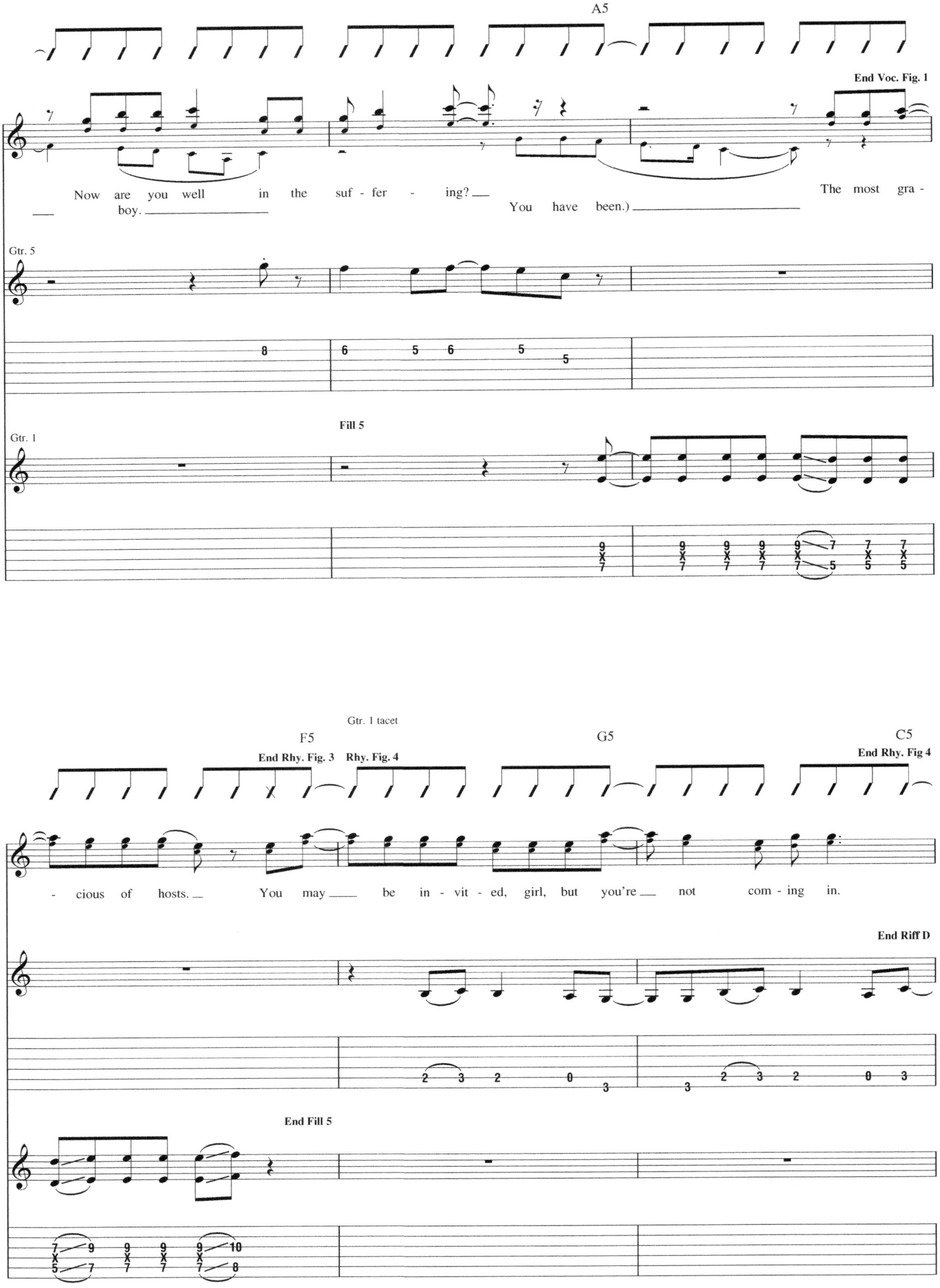

A5

End Voc. Fig. 1

Now are you well in the suf - fer - ing? The most gra -

boy. You have been.)

Gtr. 5

8 6 5 6 5 5

Gtr. 1

Fill 5

Gtr. 1 tacet

F5 G5 C5

End Rhy. Fig. 3 Rhy. Fig. 4 End Rhy. Fig 4

- cious of hosts. You may be in - vit - ed, girl, but you're not com - ing in.

End Riff D

2 3 2 0 3 3 2 3 2 0 3

End Fill 5

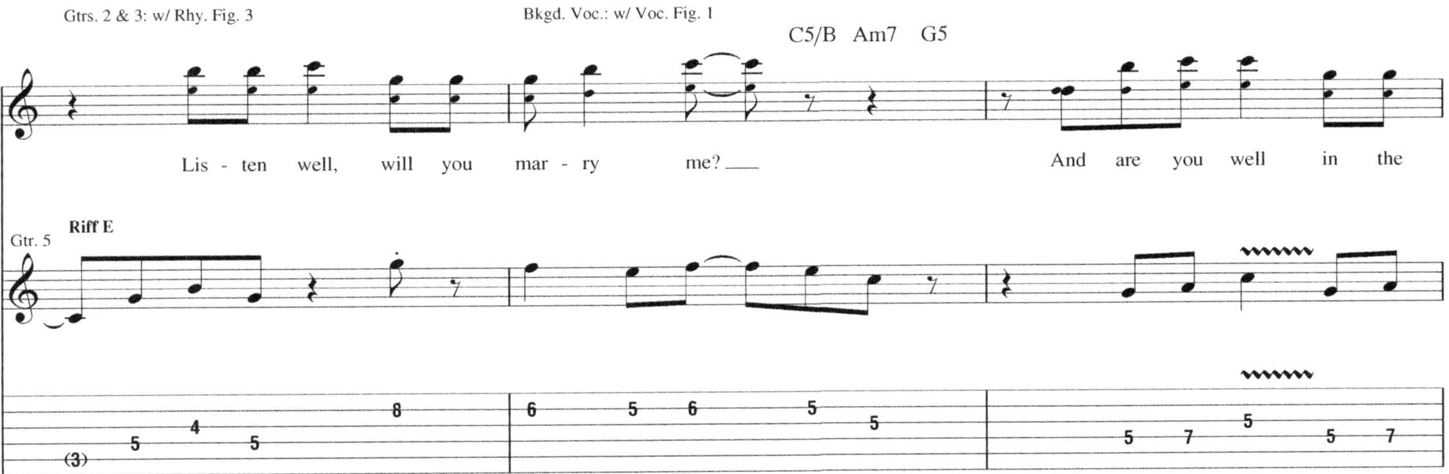
Gtrs. 2 & 3: w/ Rhy. Fig. 3
Bkgd. Voc.: w/ Voc. Fig. 1
C5/B Am7 G5
Lis - ten well, will you mar - ry me?
And are you well in the
Gtr. 5
Riff E

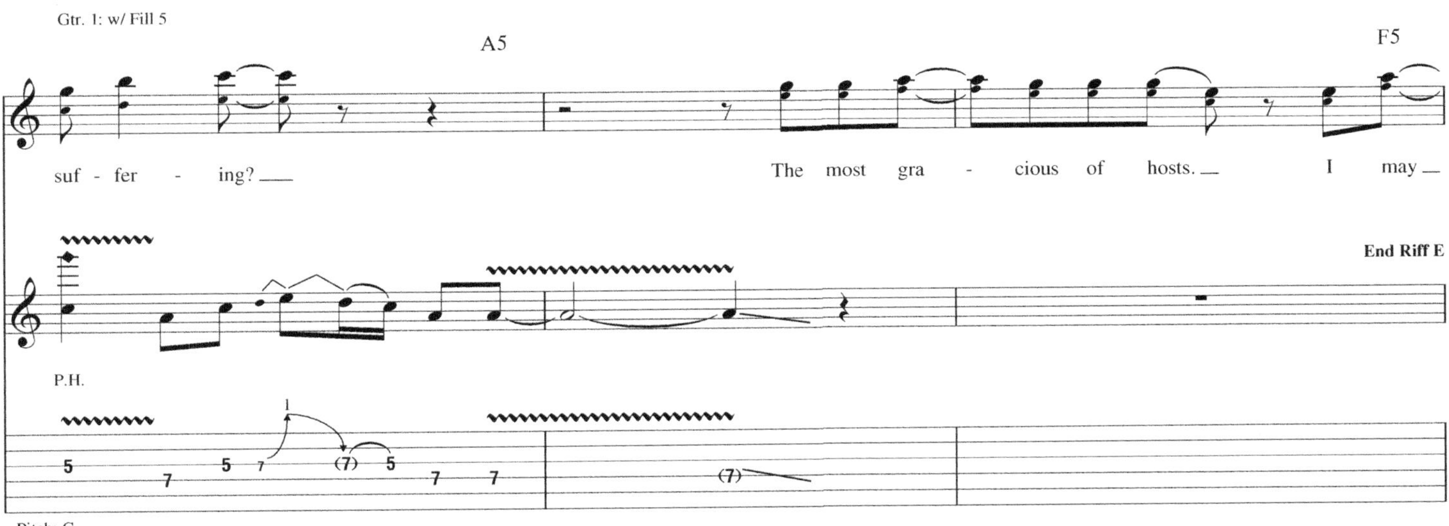
Gtr. 1: w/ Fill 5
A5
F5
suf - fer - ing?
The most gra - cious of hosts.
I may
End Riff E
P.H.
Pitch: G

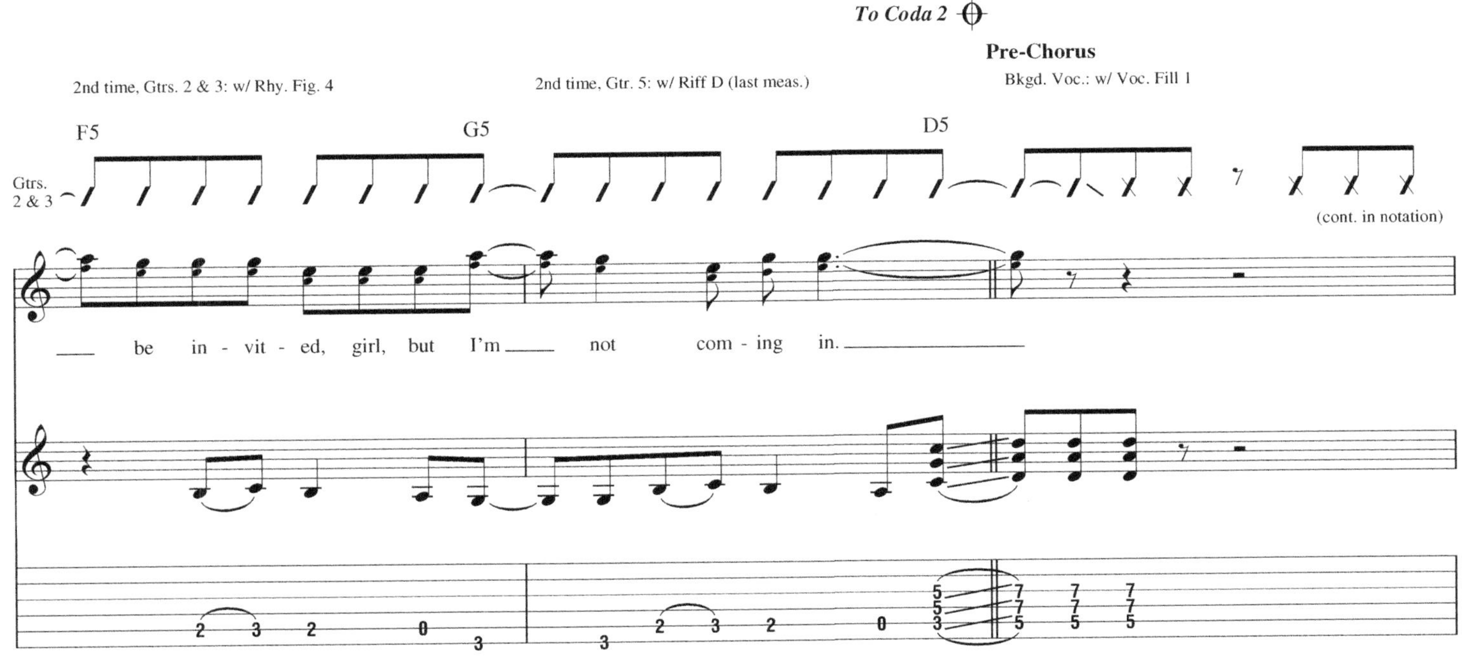
To Coda 2
Pre-Chorus
2nd time, Gtrs. 2 & 3: w/ Rhy. Fig. 4
2nd time, Gtr. 5: w/ Riff D (last meas.)
Bkgd. Voc.: w/ Voc. Fill 1
F5
G5
D5
Gtrs. 2 & 3
(cont. in notation)
be in - vit - ed, girl, but I'm not com - ing in.

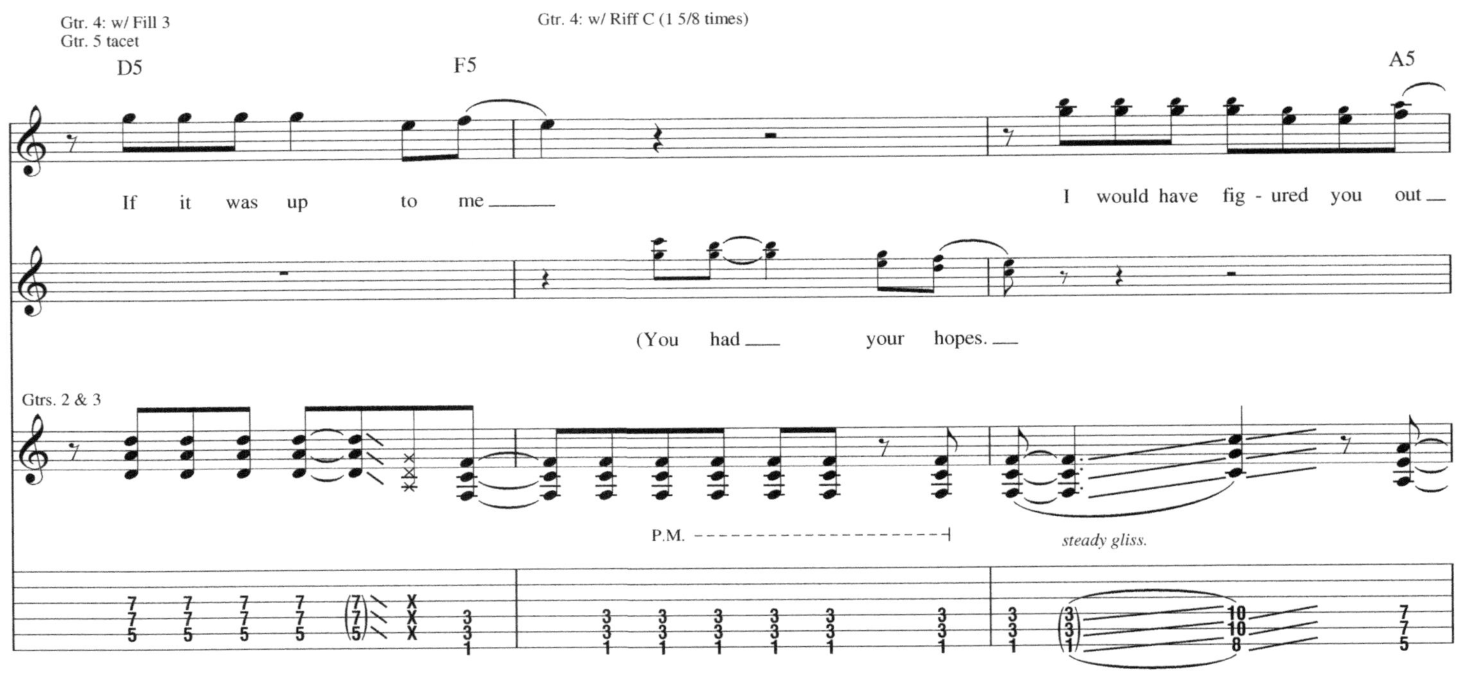
Gtr. 4: w/ Fill 3
Gtr. 5 tacet
Gtr. 4: w/ Riff C (1 5/8 times)
D5
F5
A5
If it was up to me
I would have fig - ured you out
(You had your hopes.
Gtrs. 2 & 3
P.M.
steady gliss.
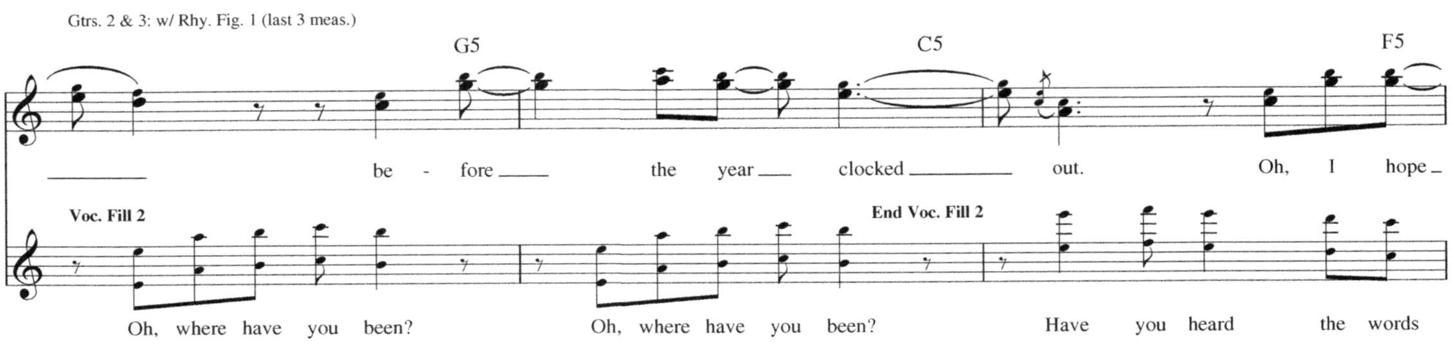
Gtrs. 2 & 3: w/ Rhy. Fig. 1 (last 3 meas.)
G5
C5
F5
be - fore the year clocked out.
Oh, I hope
Voc. Fill 2
End Voc. Fill 2
Oh, where have you been?
Oh, where have you been?
Have you heard the words
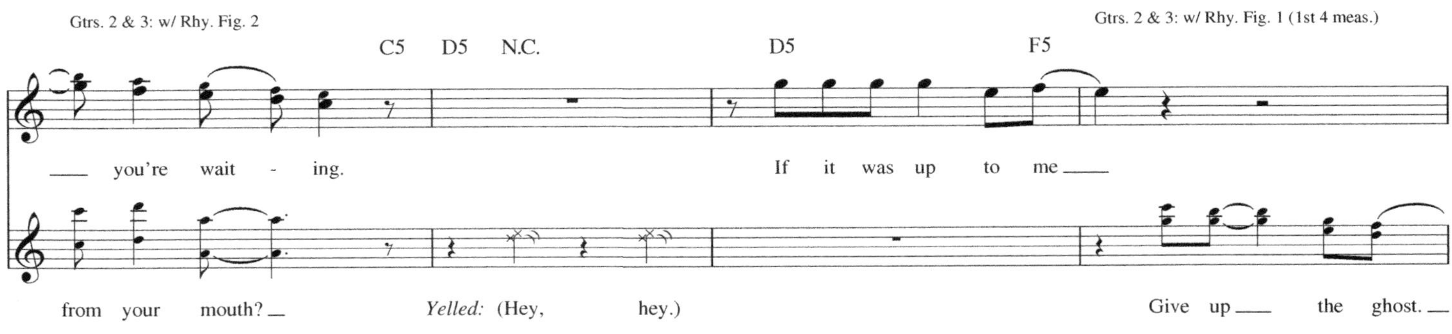
Gtrs. 2 & 3: w/ Rhy. Fig. 2
Gtrs. 2 & 3: w/ Rhy. Fig. 1 (1st 4 meas.)
C5 D5 N.C.
D5
F5
you're wait - ing.
If it was up to me
from your mouth?
Yelled: (Hey, hey.)
Give up the ghost.
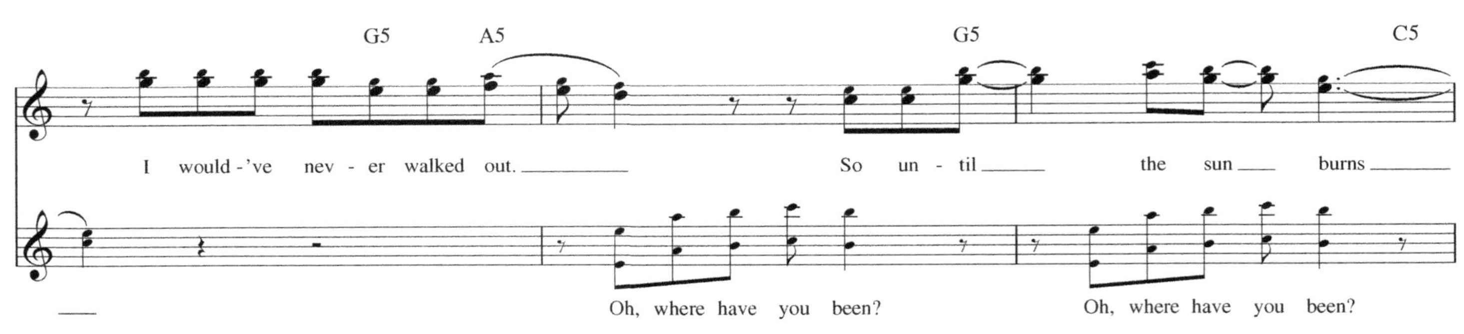
G5
A5
G5
C5
I would - 've nev - er walked out.
So un - til the sun burns
Oh, where have you been?
Oh, where have you been?

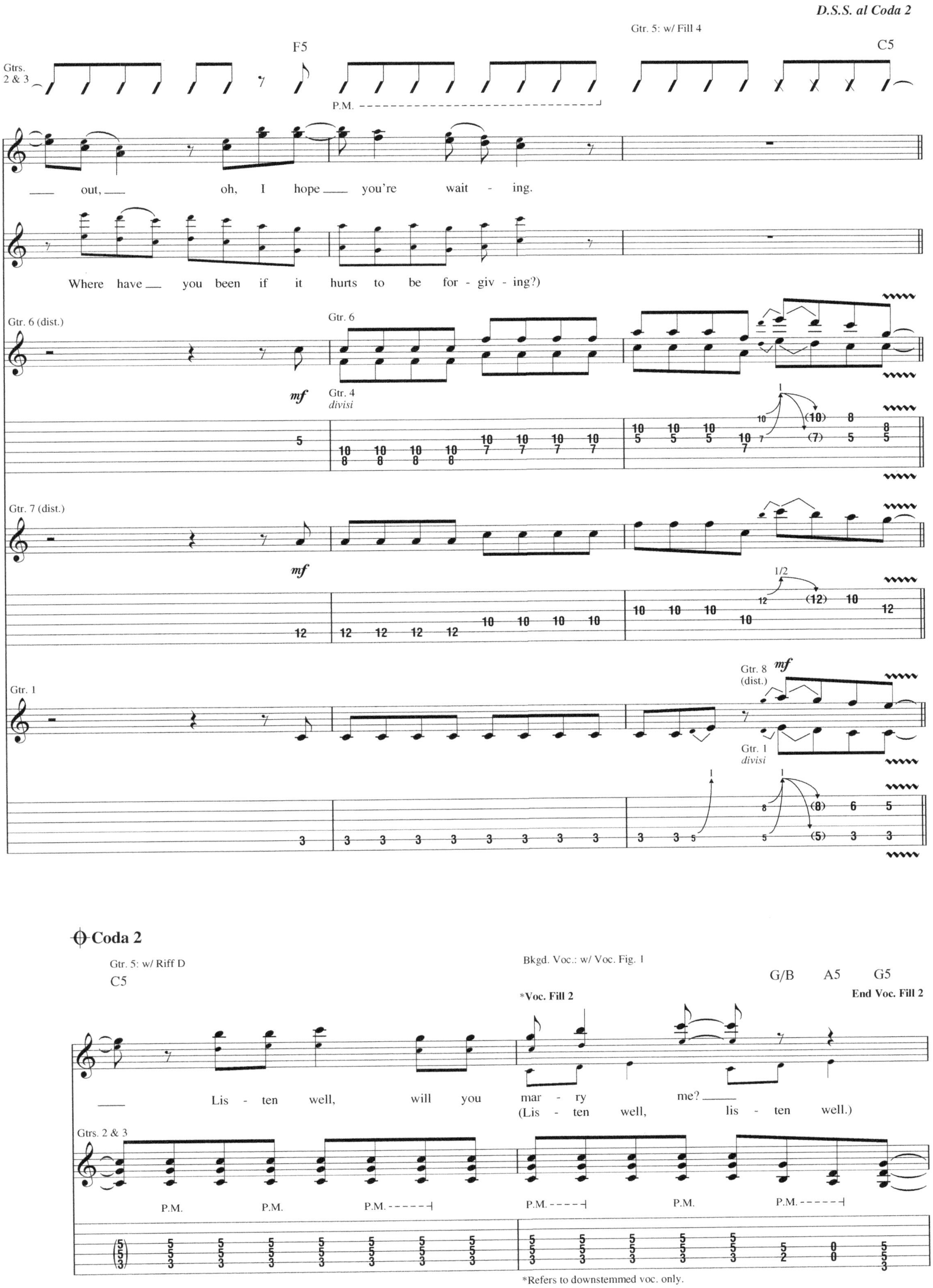

D.S.S. al Coda 2

Gtr. 5: w/ Fill 4

F5 C5

Gtrs. 2 & 3

P.M.

out, oh, I hope you're wait - ing.

Where have you been if it hurts to be for - giv - ing?)

Gtr. 6 (dist.)

Gtr. 6

mf

Gtr. 4 *divisi*

Gtr. 7 (dist.)

mf

Gtr. 1

Gtr. 8 (dist.) *mf*

Gtr. 1 *divisi*

Coda 2

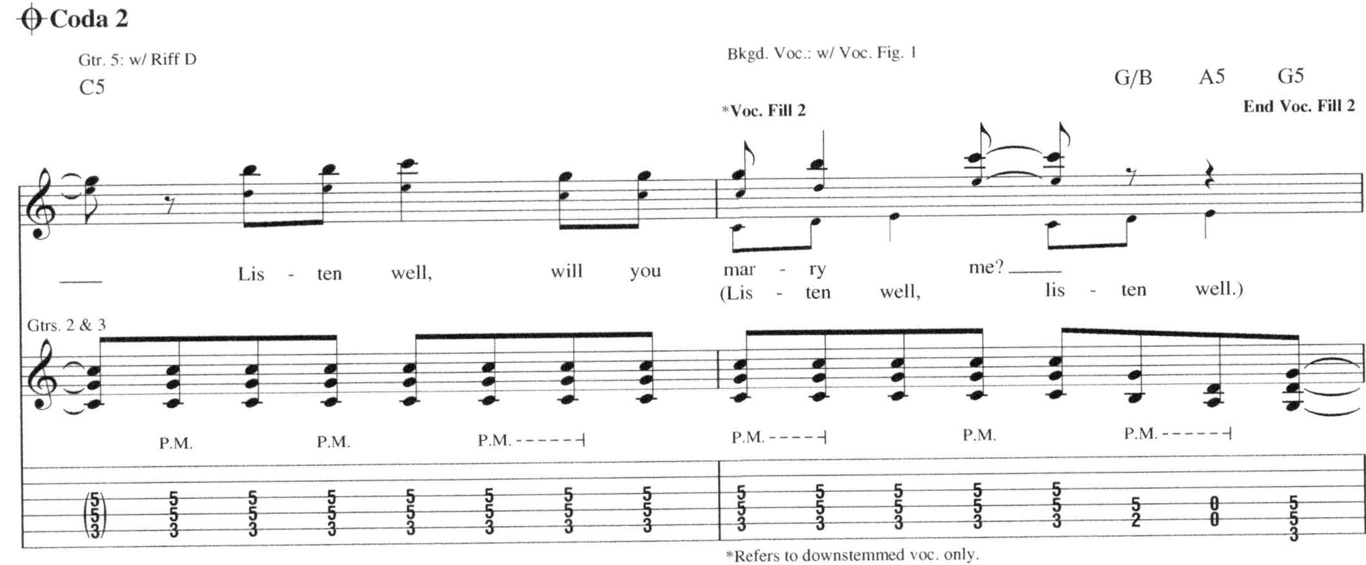

*Refers to downstemmed voc. only.

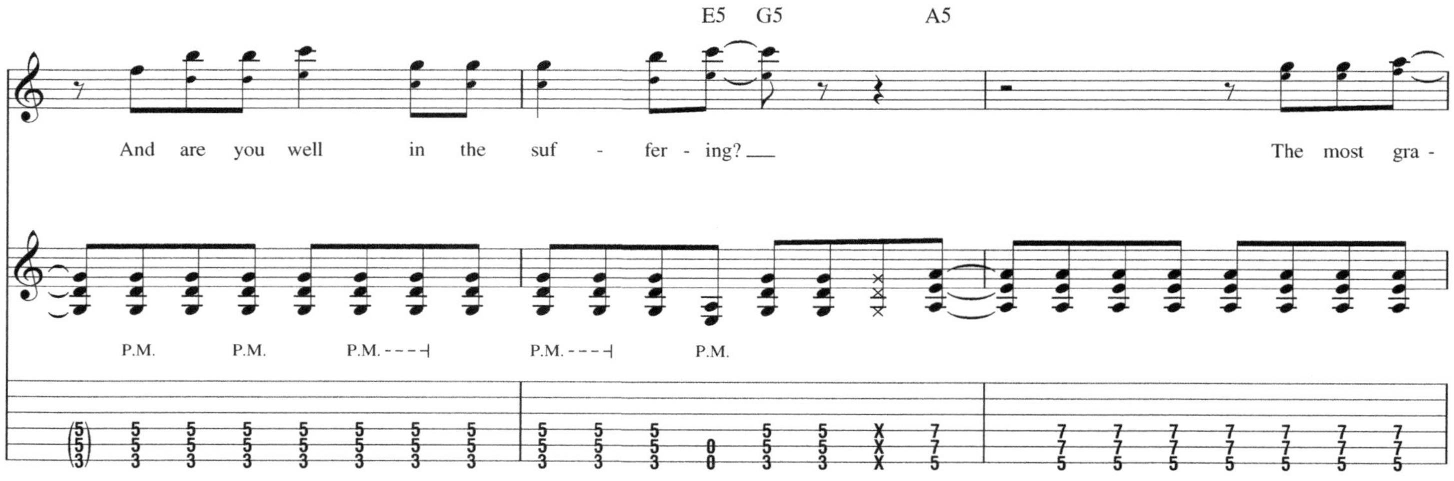
Bkgd. Voc.: w/ Voc. Fill 2
Gtr. 1: w/ Fill 5
E5 G5 A5
And are you well in the suf - fer - ing? The most gra -
P.M. P.M. P.M. P.M. P.M.

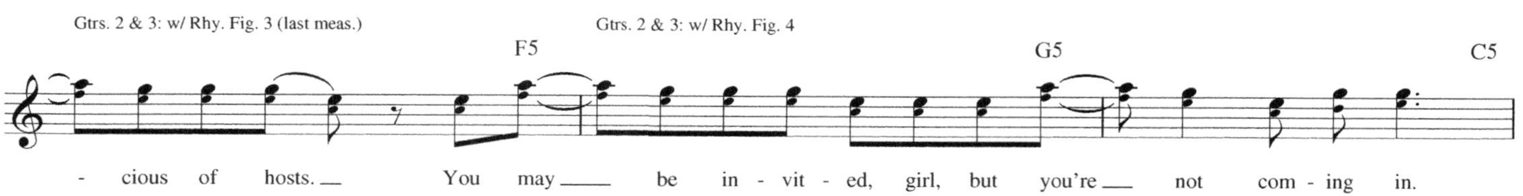
Gtrs. 2 & 3: w/ Rhy. Fig. 3 (last meas.)
Gtrs. 2 & 3: w/ Rhy. Fig. 4
F5 G5 C5
- cious of hosts. You may be in - vit - ed, girl, but you're not com - ing in.

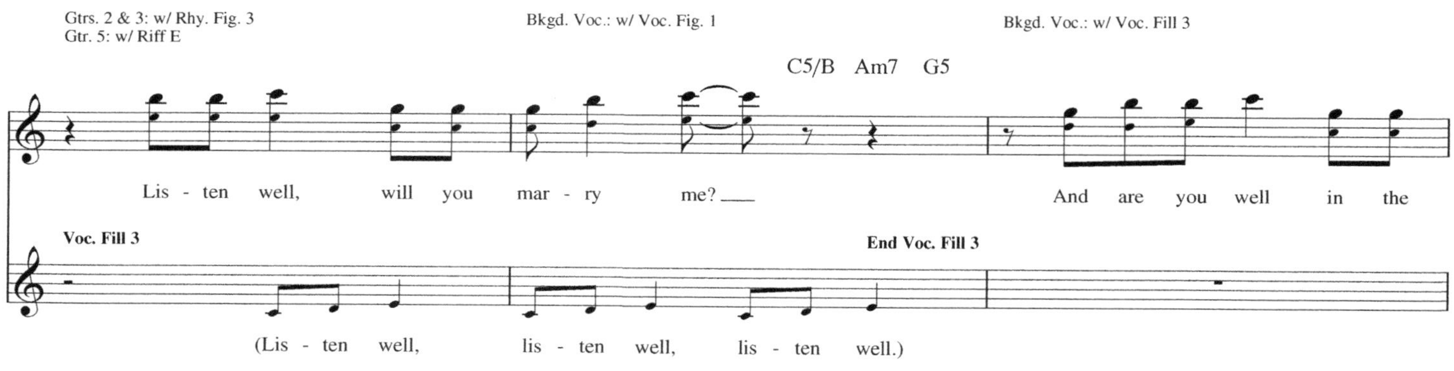
Gtrs. 2 & 3: w/ Rhy. Fig. 3
Gtr. 5: w/ Riff E
Bkgd. Voc.: w/ Voc. Fig. 1
Bkgd. Voc.: w/ Voc. Fill 3
C5/B Am7 G5
Lis - ten well, will you mar - ry me? And are you well in the
Voc. Fill 3
End Voc. Fill 3
(Lis - ten well, lis - ten well, lis - ten well.)

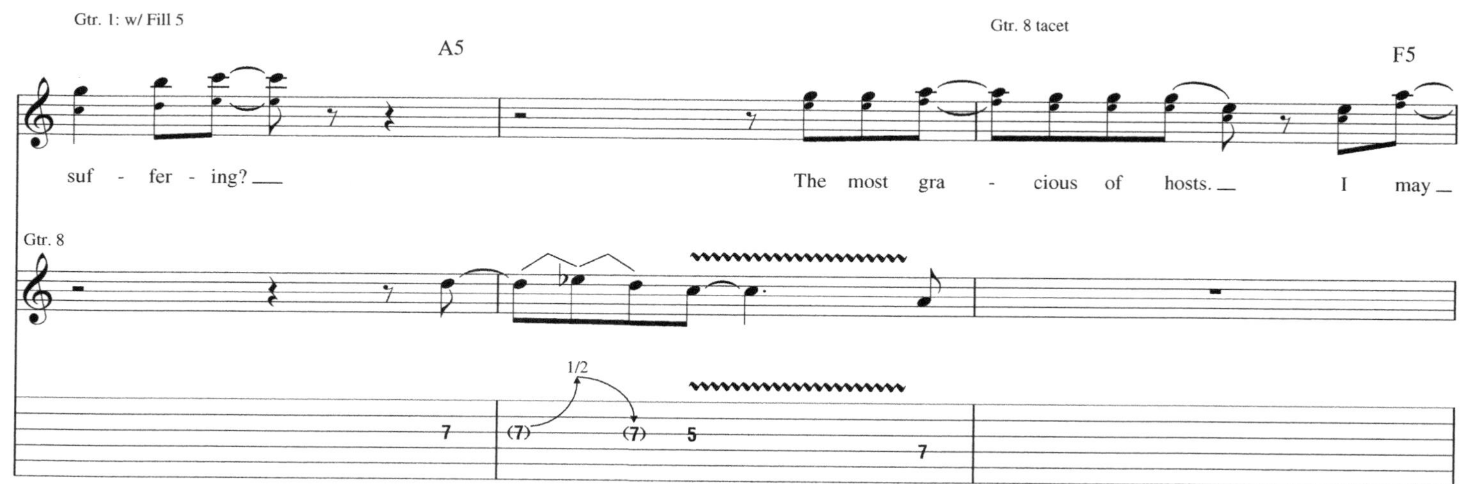
Gtr. 1: w/ Fill 5
Gtr. 8 tacet
A5 F5
suf - fer - ing? The most gra - cious of hosts. I may
Gtr. 8
1/2

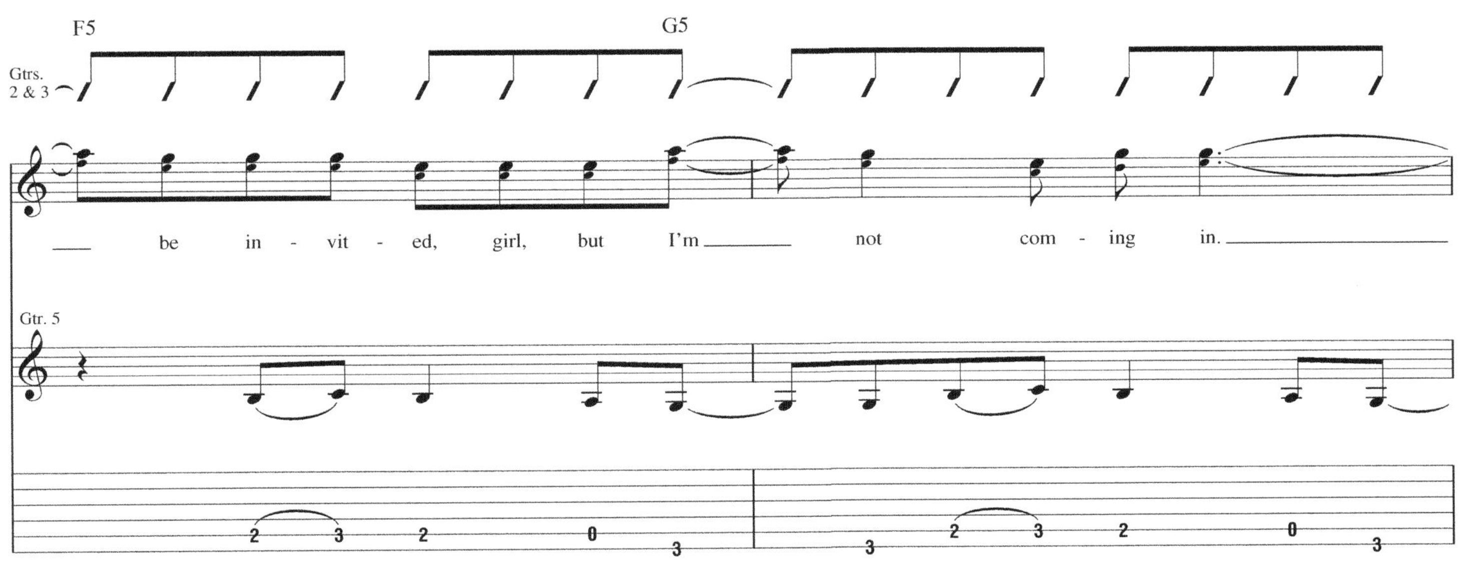
F5
G5
Gtrs. 2 & 3
be in - vit - ed, girl, but I'm not com - ing in.
Gtr. 5

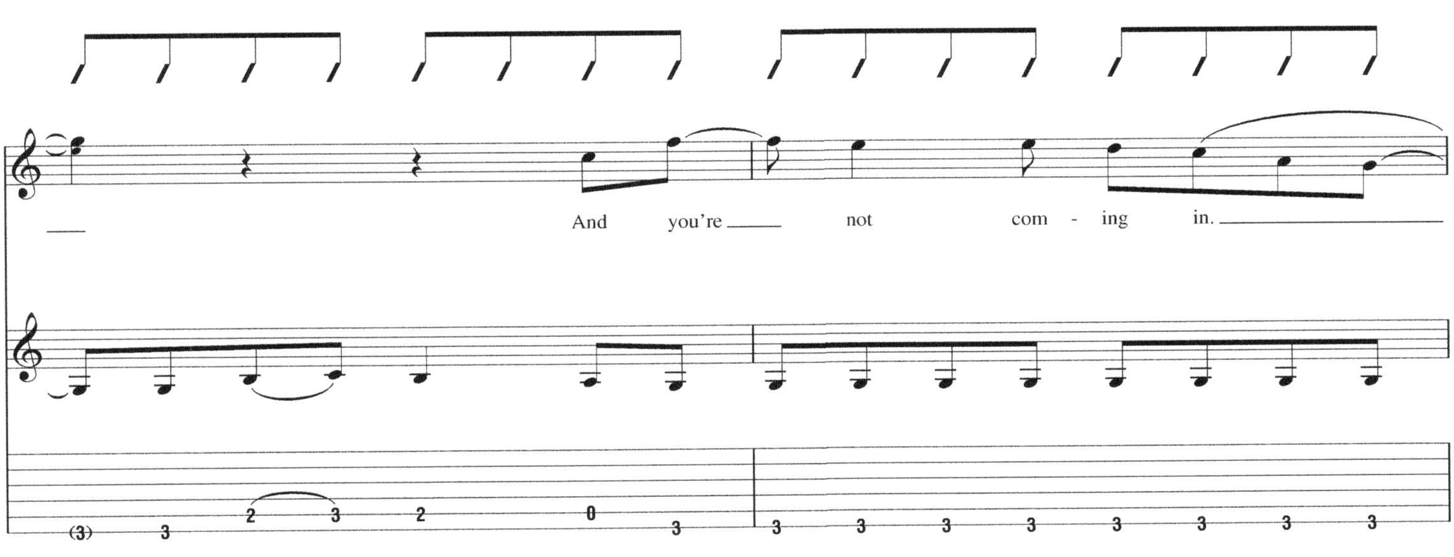
And you're not com - ing in.

Free time

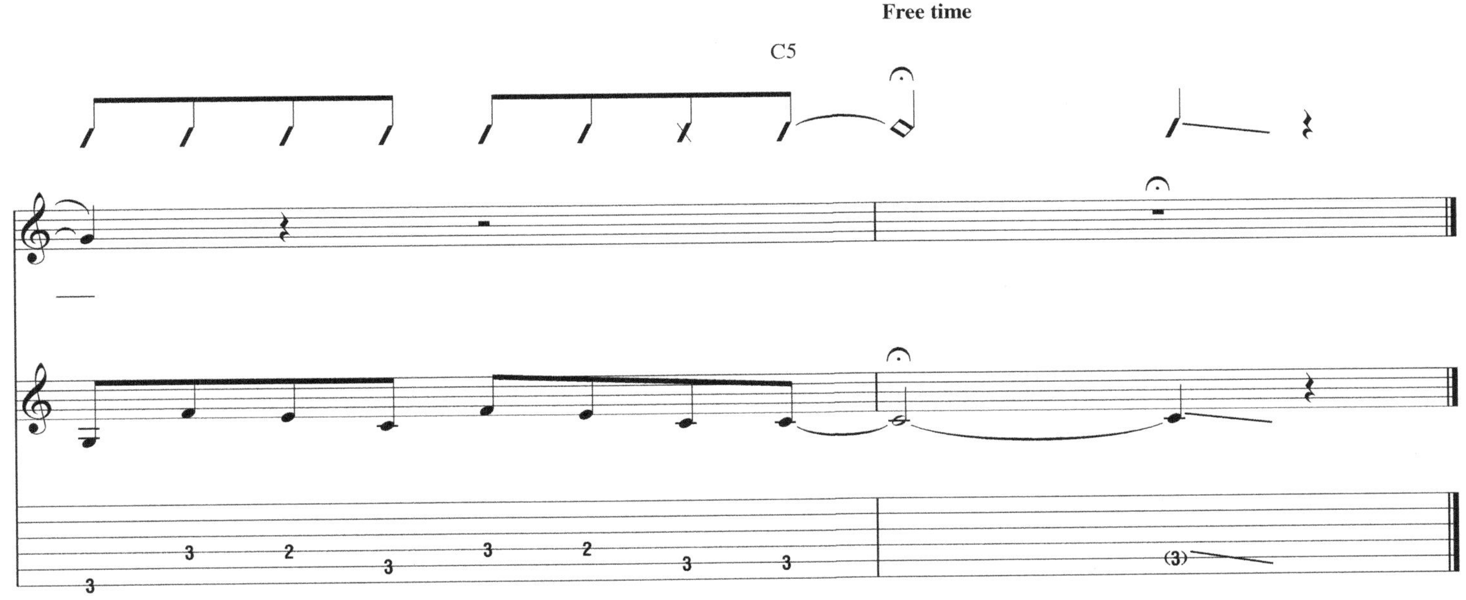
C5

Lying Lies & Dirty Secrets of Miss Erica Court

Words and Music by Claudio Sanchez, Michael Todd, Joshua Eppard and Travis Stever

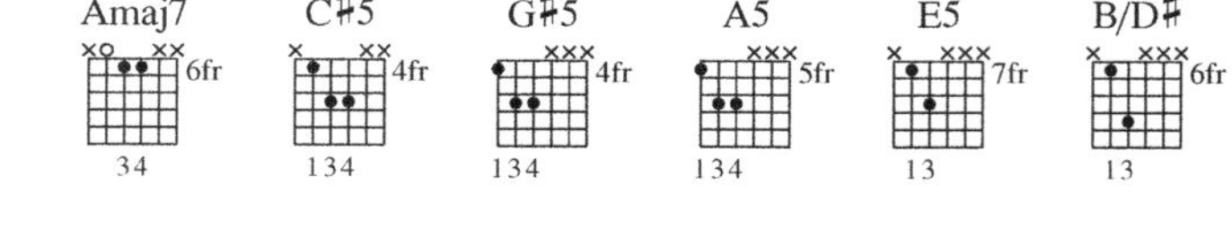

Tune down 1/2 step:
(low to high) E♭-A♭-D♭-G♭-B♭-E♭

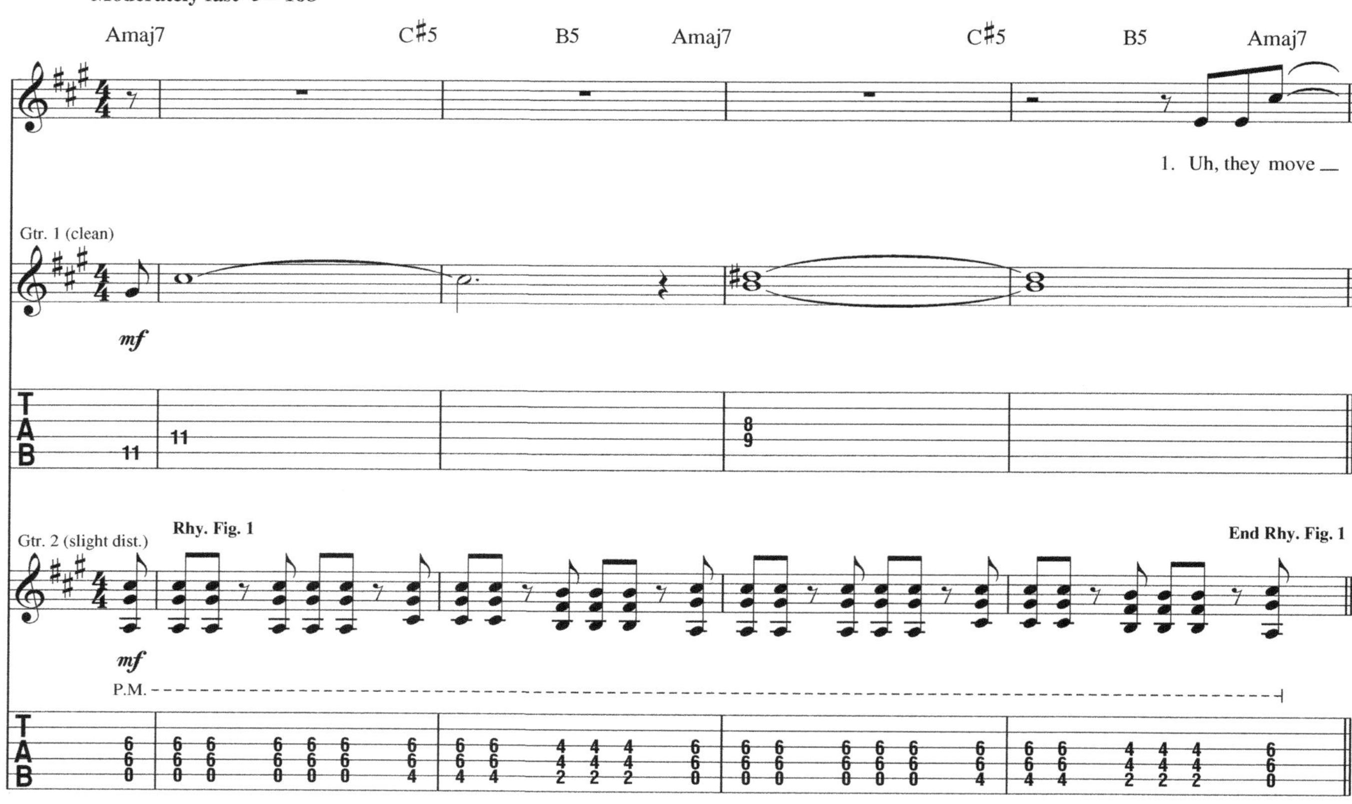

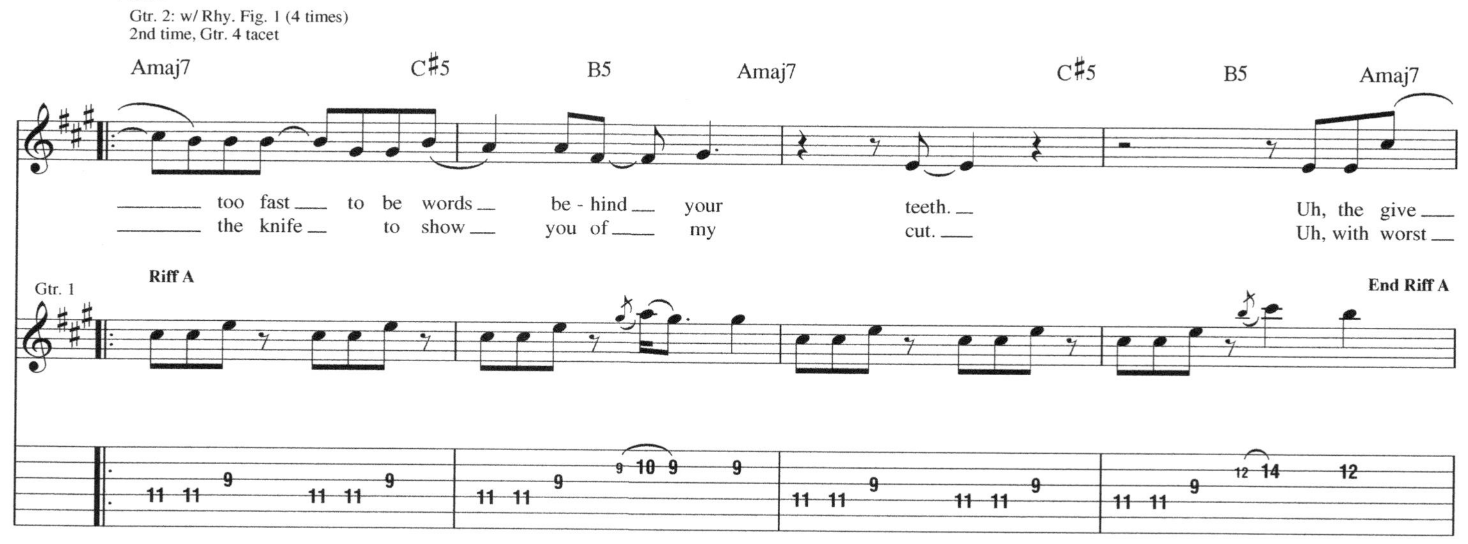

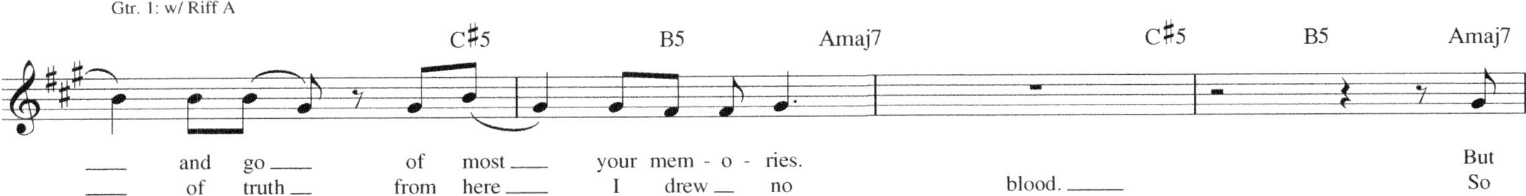
Gtr. 1: w/ Riff A
C♯5
B5
Amaj7
C♯5
B5
Amaj7
and go of most your mem - o - ries. But
of truth from here I drew no blood. So

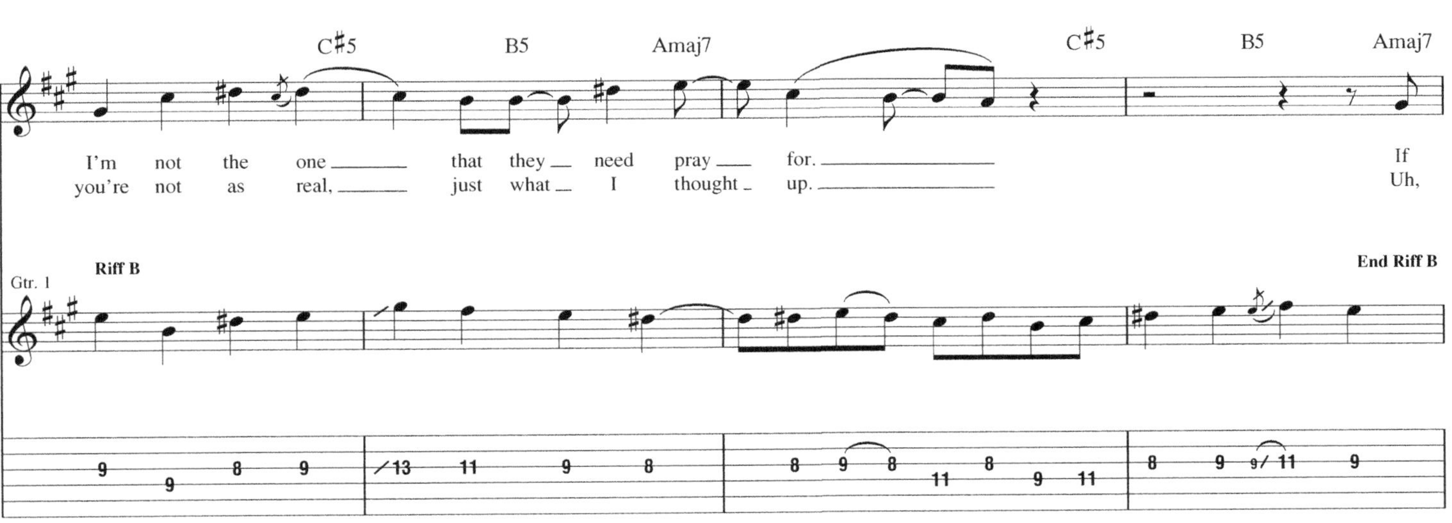
C♯5
B5
Amaj7
C♯5
B5
Amaj7
I'm not the one that they need pray for. If
you're not as real, just what I thought up. Uh,
Riff B
Gtr. 1
End Riff B

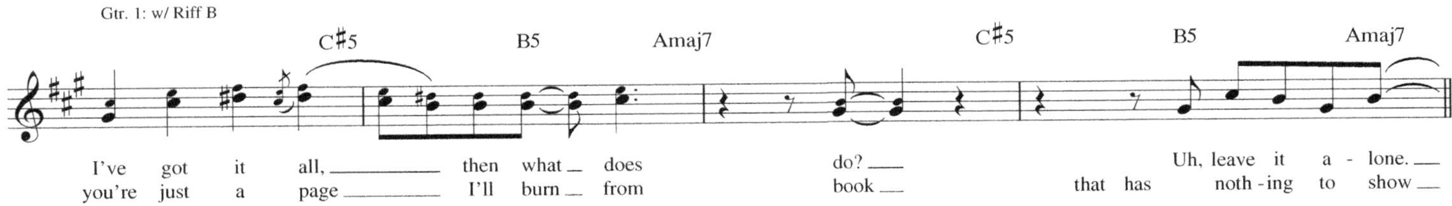
Gtr. 1: w/ Riff B
C♯5
B5
Amaj7
C♯5
B5
Amaj7
I've got it all, then what does do? Uh, leave it a - lone.
you're just a page I'll burn from book that has noth - ing to show

Pre-Chorus

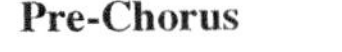
1st time, Gtr. 1: w/ Riff A

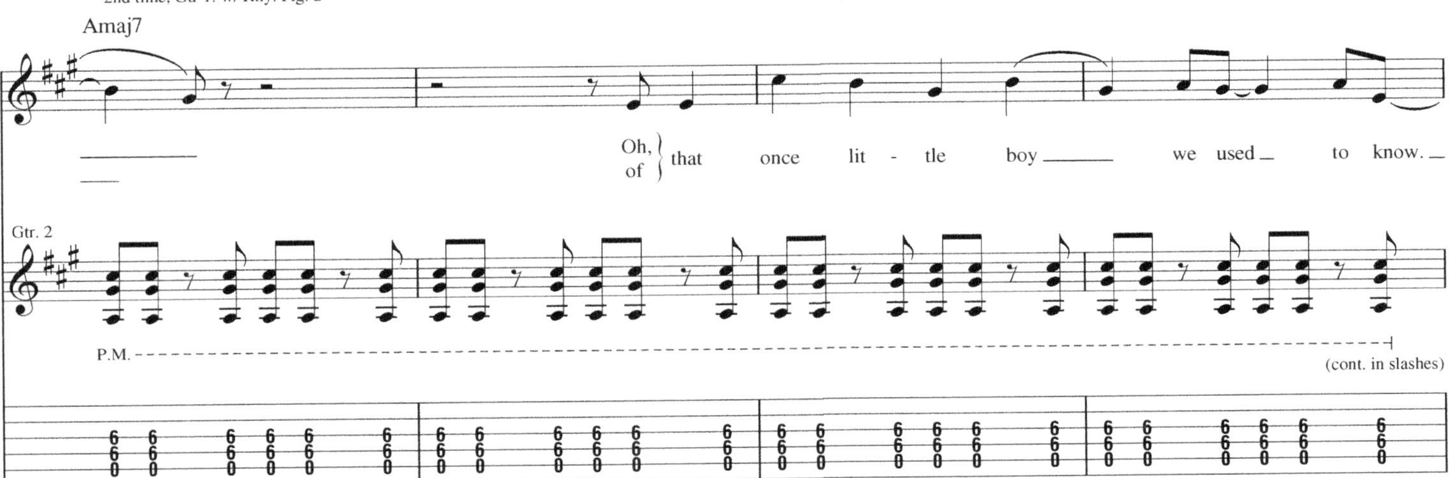
2nd time, Gtr 1: w/ Rhy. Fig. 2
Amaj7
Oh, of that once lit - tle boy we used to know.
Gtr. 2
P.M.
(cont. in slashes)

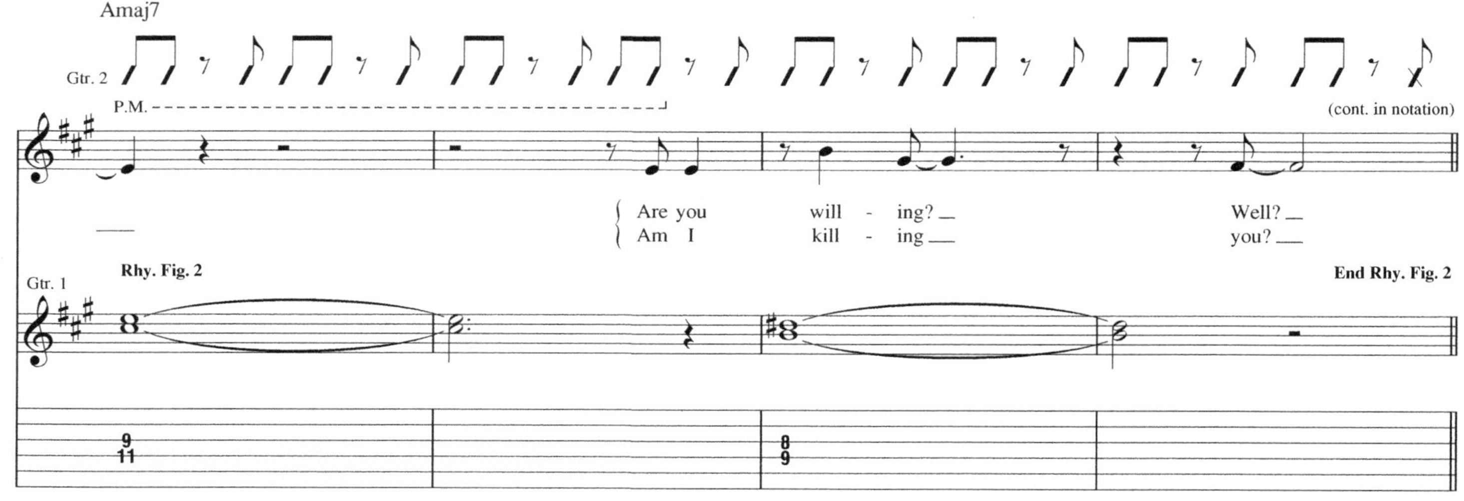

Chorus

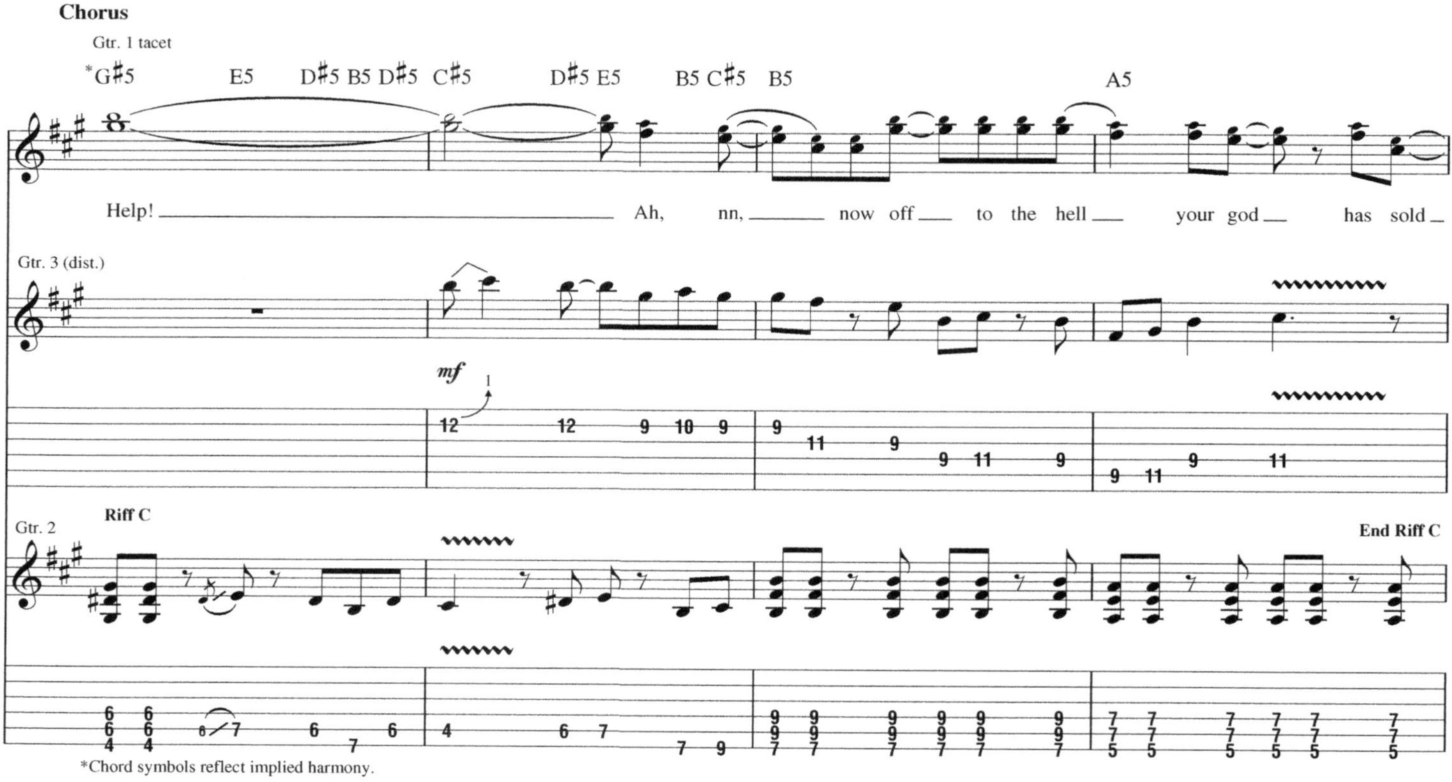

*Chord symbols reflect implied harmony.

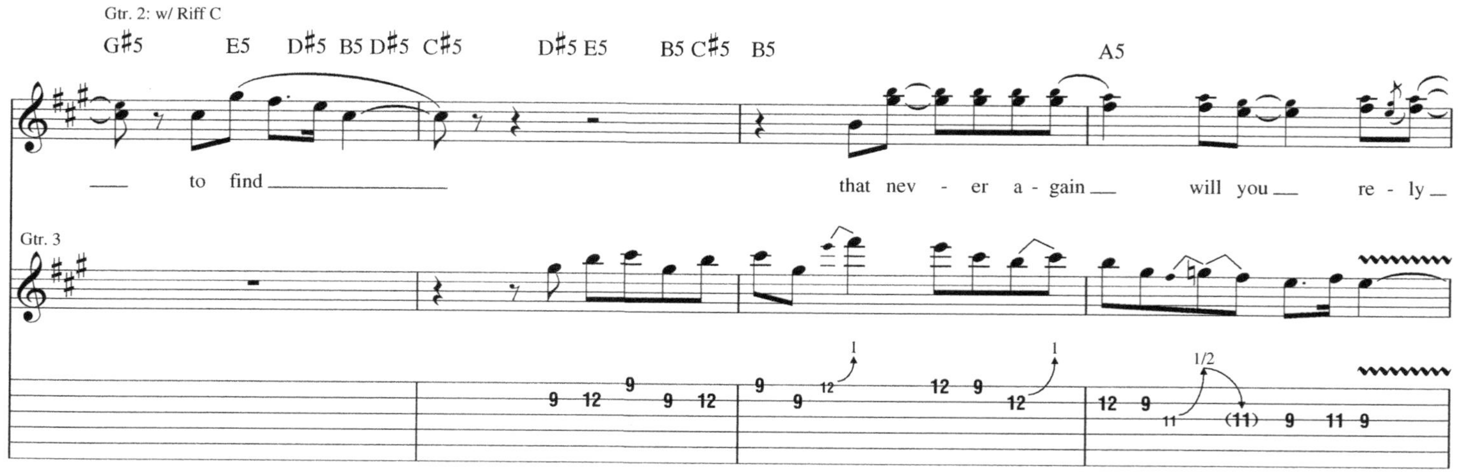

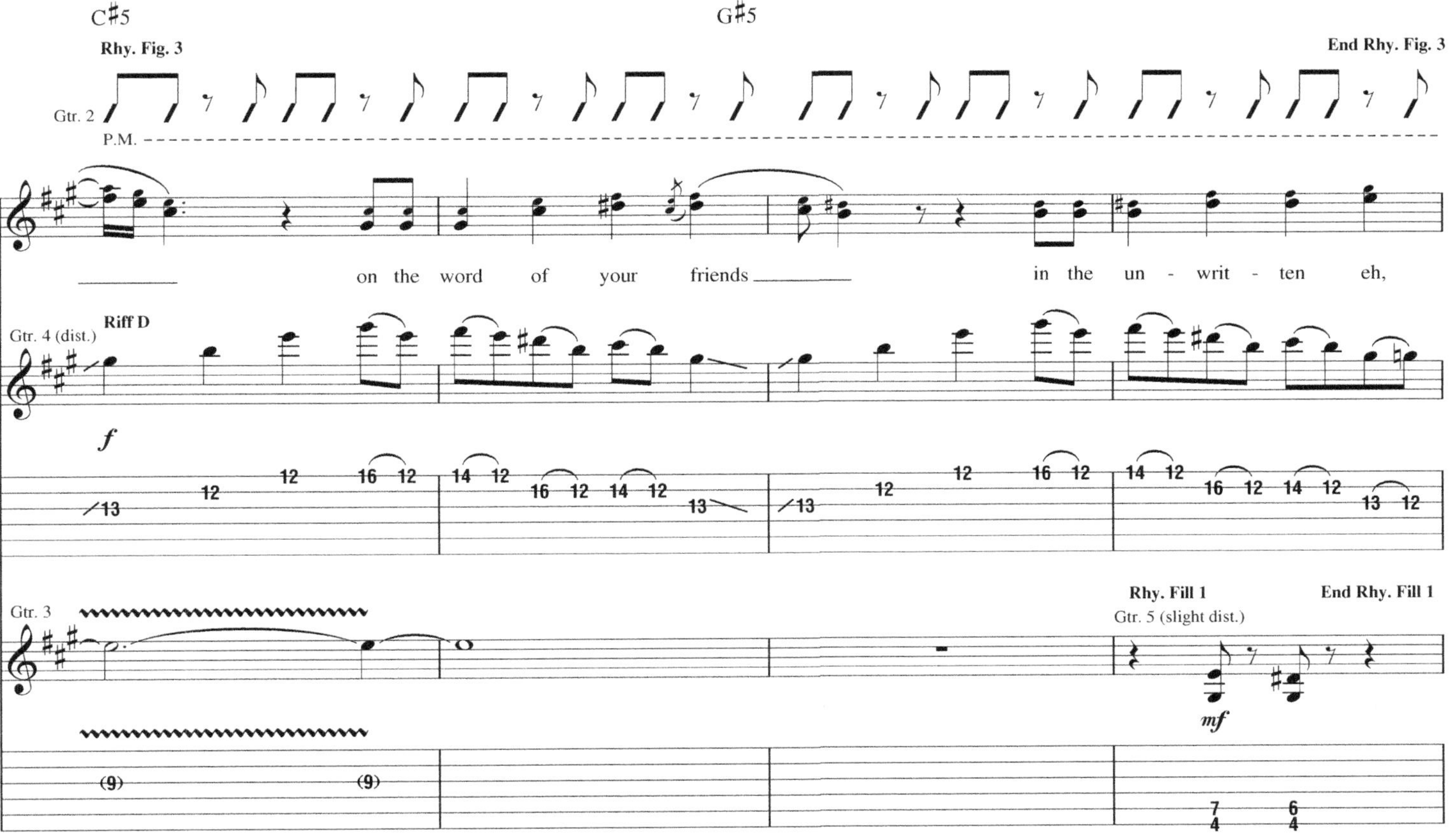
Gr. 3 tacet
C#5
G#5
Rhy. Fig. 3
End Rhy. Fig. 3
Gtr. 2
P.M.
on the word of your friends
in the un - writ - ten eh,
Riff D
Gtr. 4 (dist.)
f
Gtr. 3
Rhy. Fill 1
End Rhy. Fill 1
Gtr. 5 (slight dist.)
mf
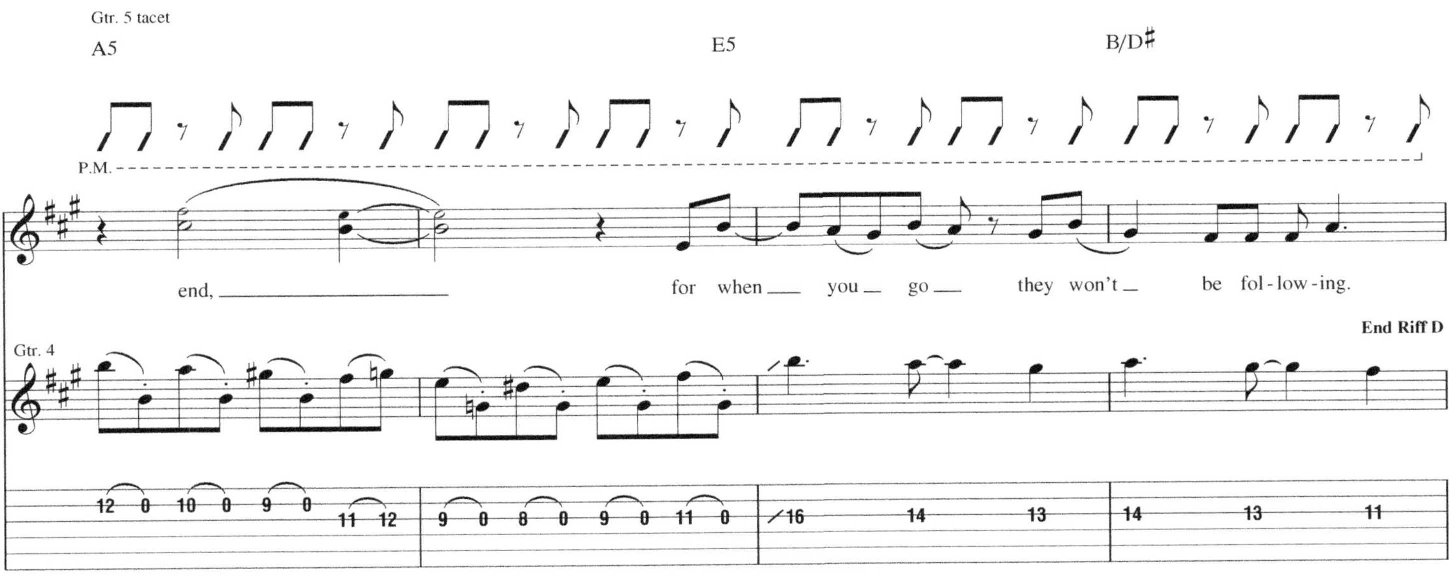
Gtr. 5 tacet
A5
E5
B/D#
P.M.
end,
for when you go they won't be fol-low-ing.
Gtr. 4
End Riff D
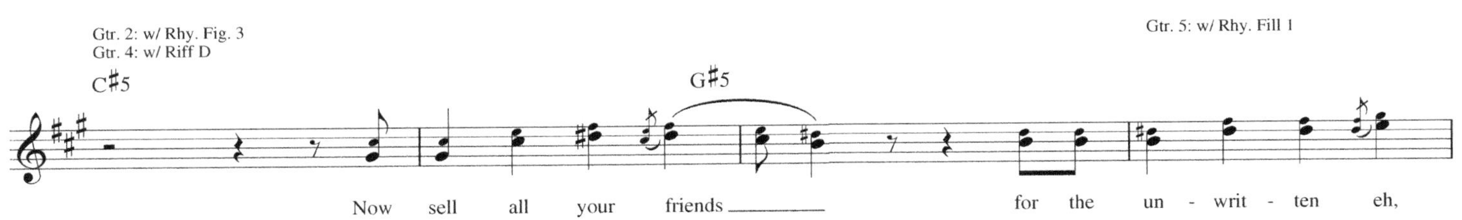
Gtr. 2: w/ Rhy. Fig. 3
Gtr. 4: w/ Riff D
Gtr. 5: w/ Rhy. Fill 1
C#5
G#5
Now sell all your friends
for the un - writ - ten eh,

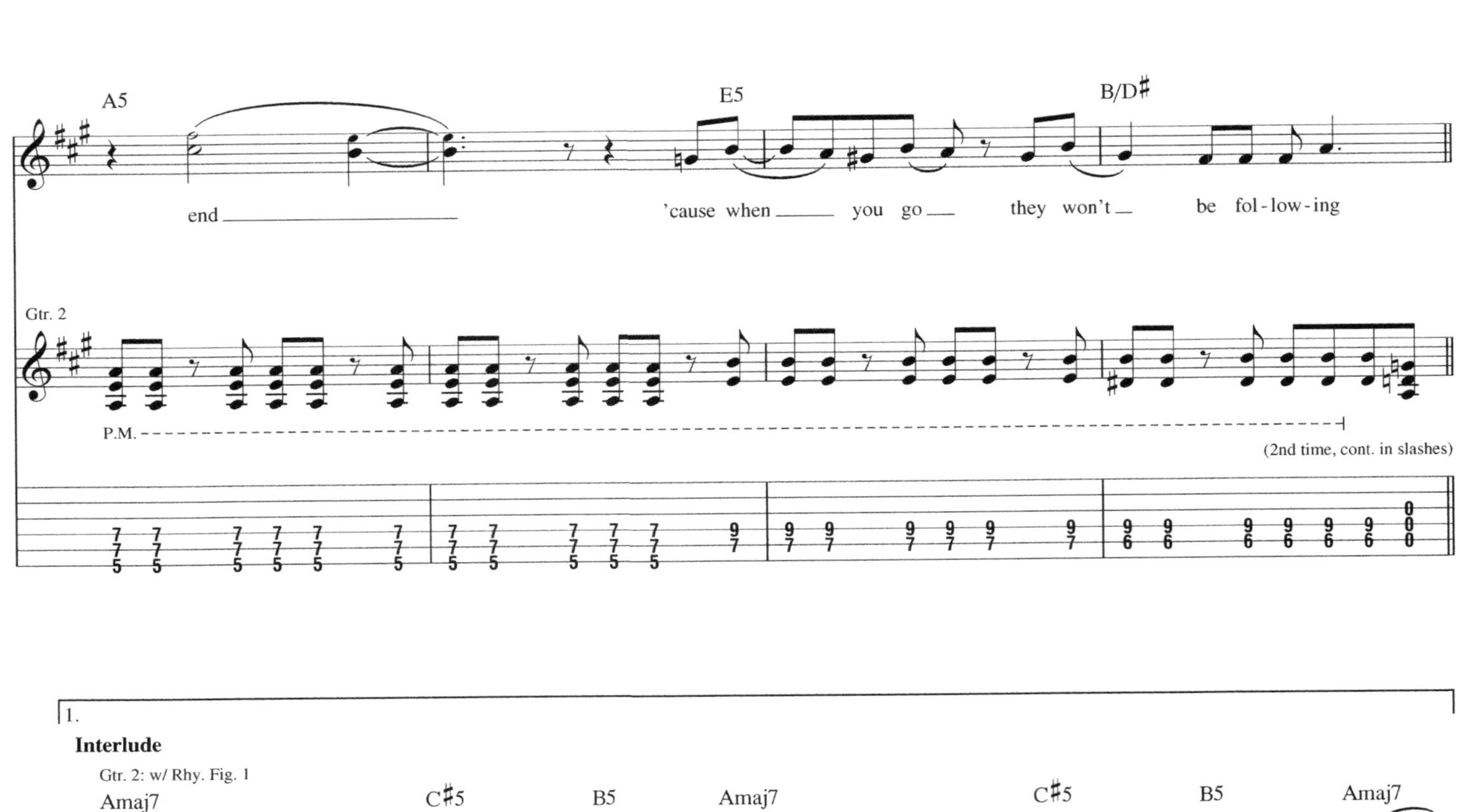
A5
E5
B/D♯
end
'cause when you go they won't be fol-low-ing
Gr. 2
P.M.
(2nd time, cont. in slashes)

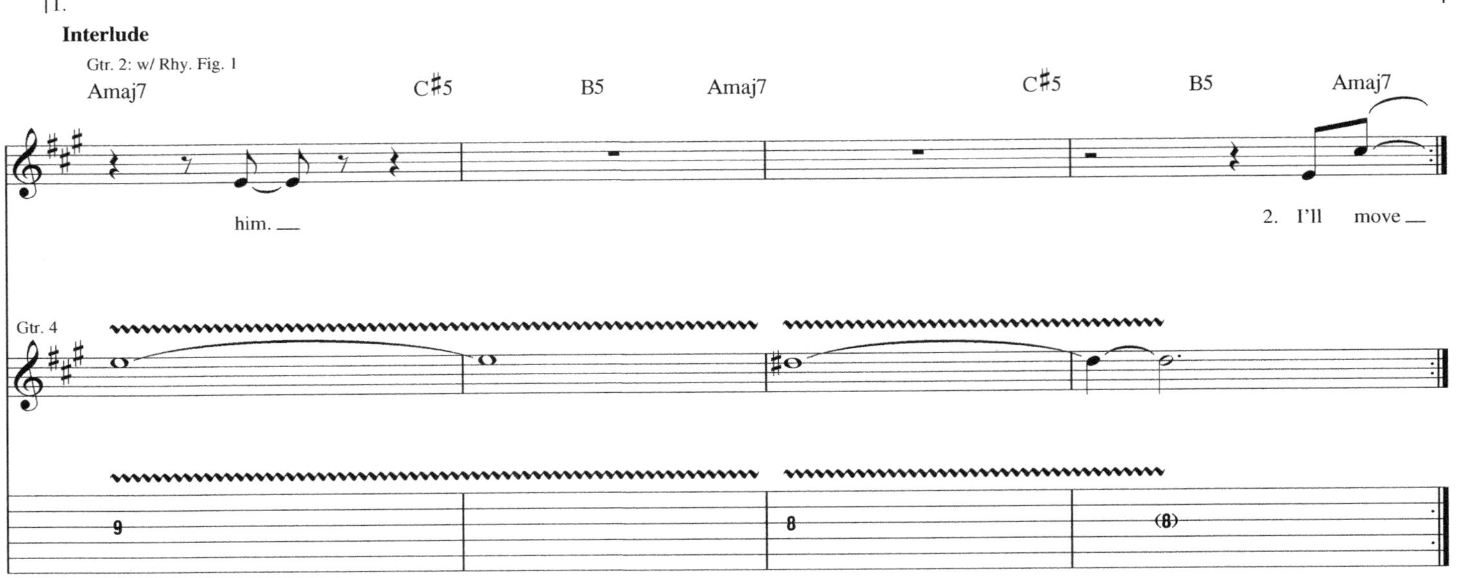
1.
Interlude
Gr. 2: w/ Rhy. Fig. 1
Amaj7
C♯5
B5
Amaj7
C♯5
B5
Amaj7
him.
2. I'll move
Gr. 4

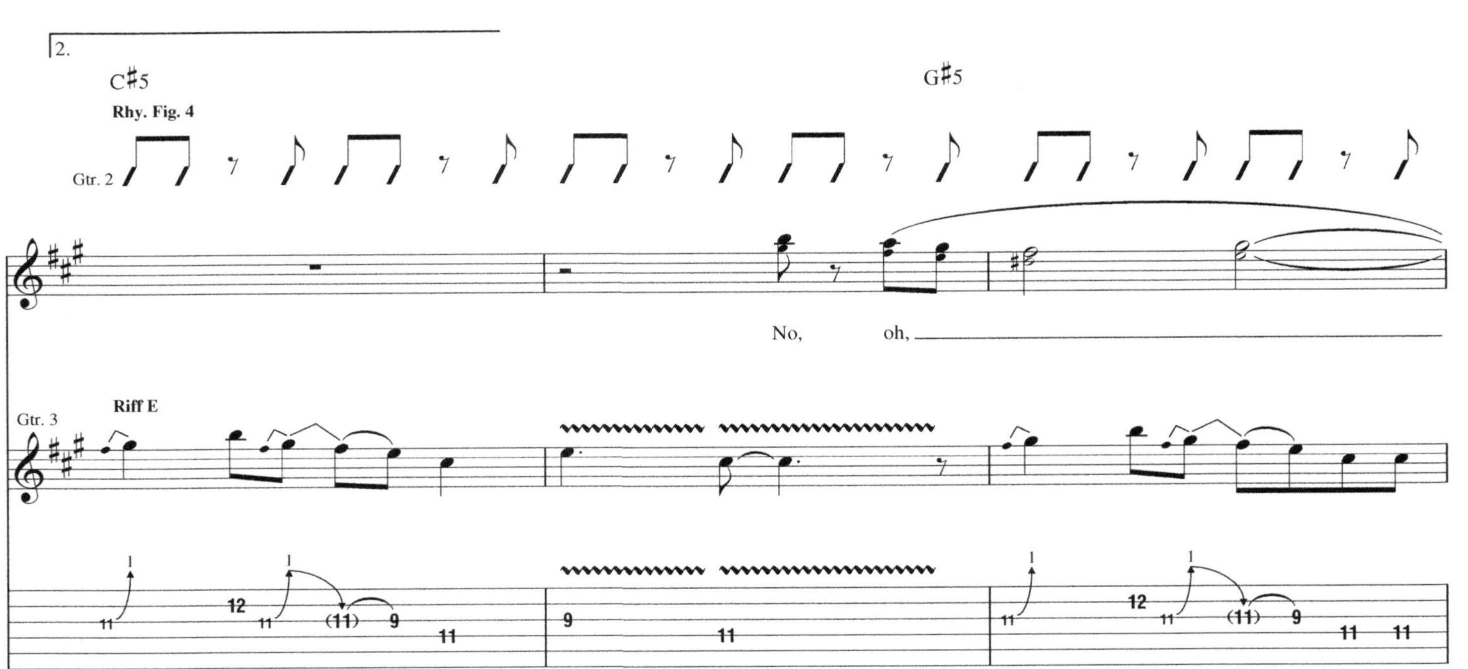
2.
C♯5
G♯5
Rhy. Fig. 4
Gr. 2
No, oh,
Riff E
Gr. 3

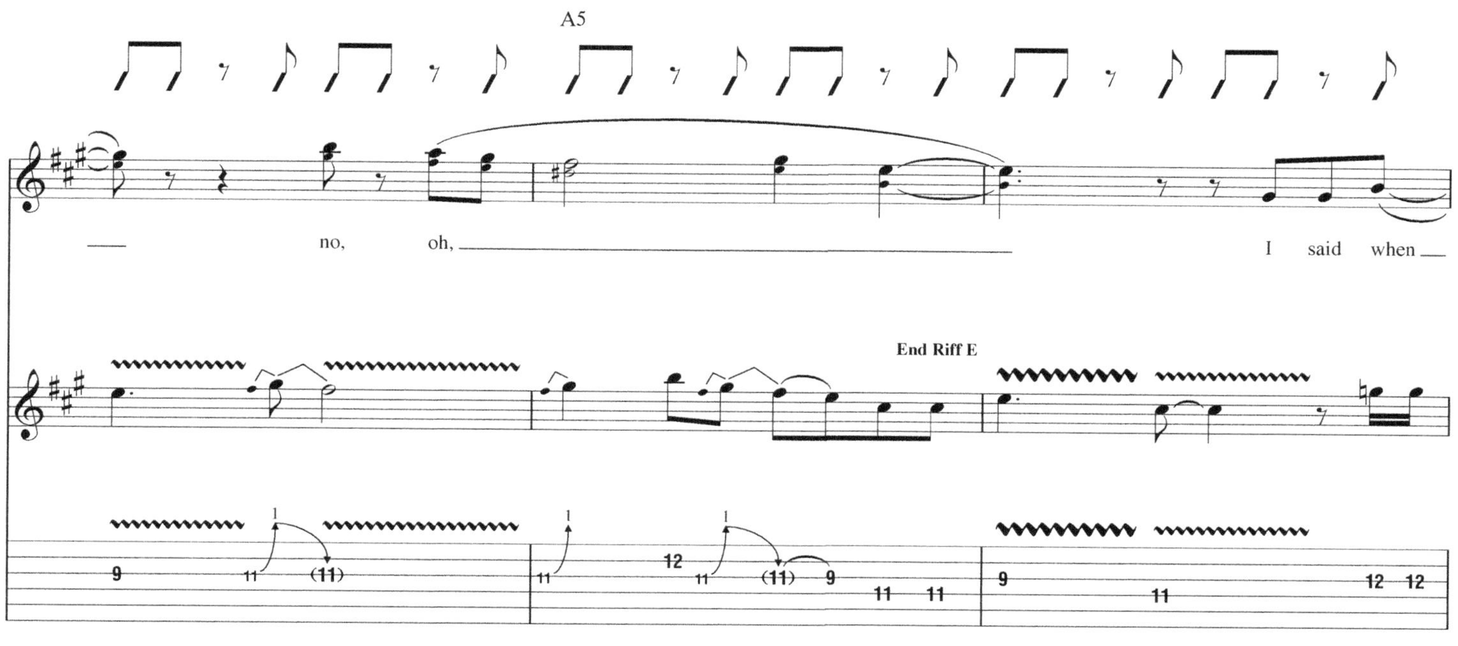
A5
no,
oh,
I said when
End Riff E

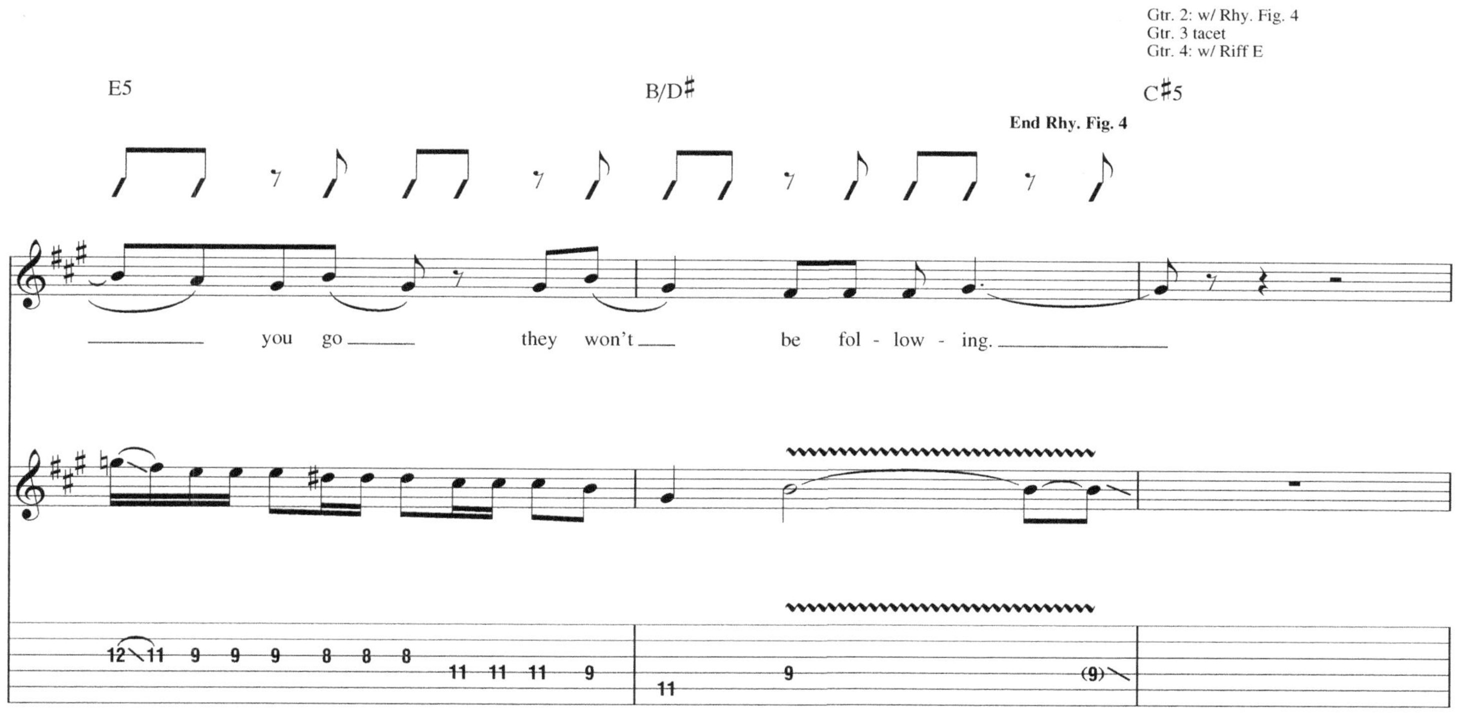
Gtr. 2: w/ Rhy. Fig. 4
Gtr. 3 tacet
Gtr. 4: w/ Riff E
E5
B/D♯
C♯5
End Rhy. Fig. 4
you go
they won't
be fol - low - ing.

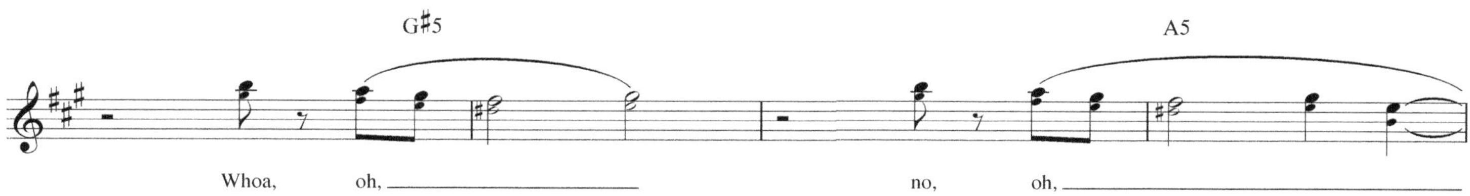
G♯5
A5
Whoa,
oh,
no,
oh,

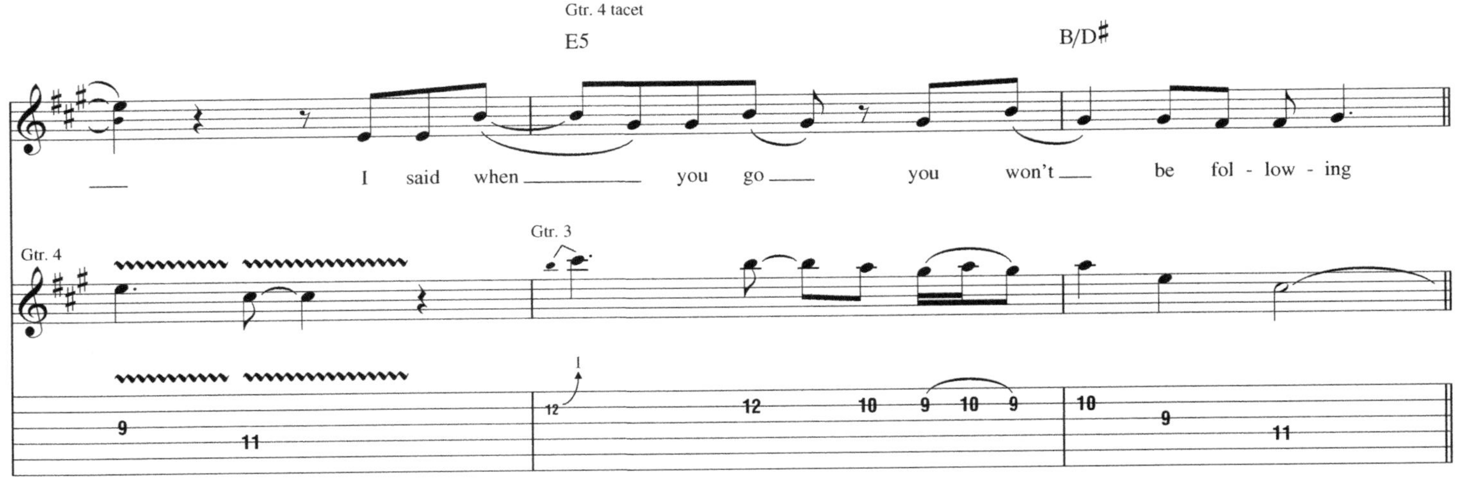
Gtr. 4 tacet
E5
B/D♯
I said when you go you won't be fol - low - ing
Gtr. 4
Gtr. 3

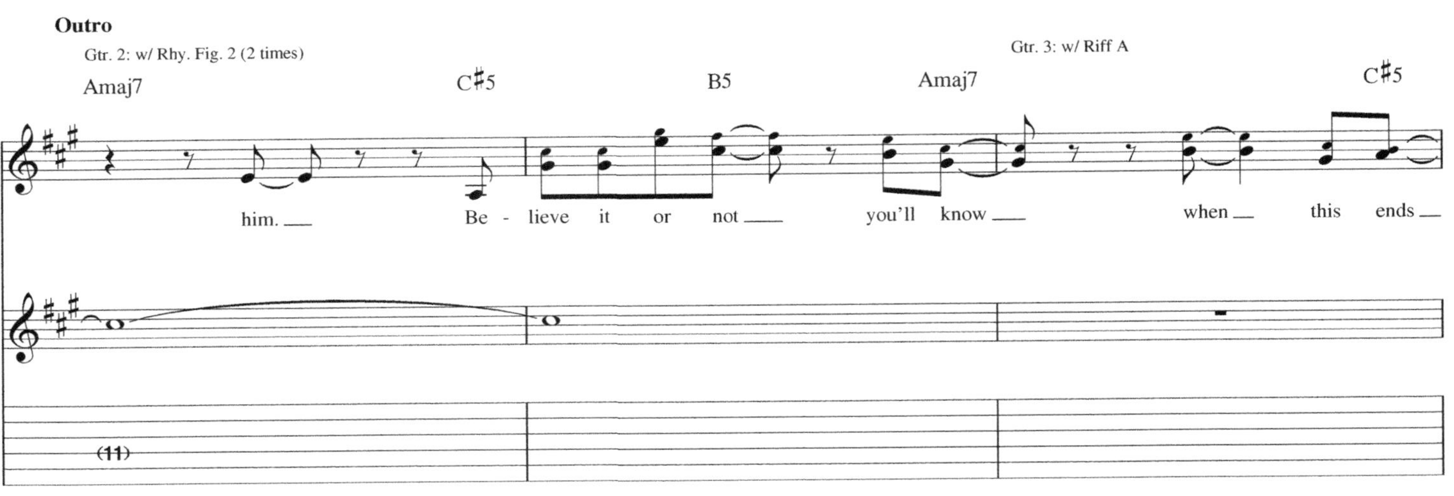
Outro
Gtr. 2: w/ Rhy. Fig. 2 (2 times)
Gtr. 3: w/ Riff A
Amaj7
C♯5
B5
Amaj7
C♯5
him. Be - lieve it or not you'll know when this ends

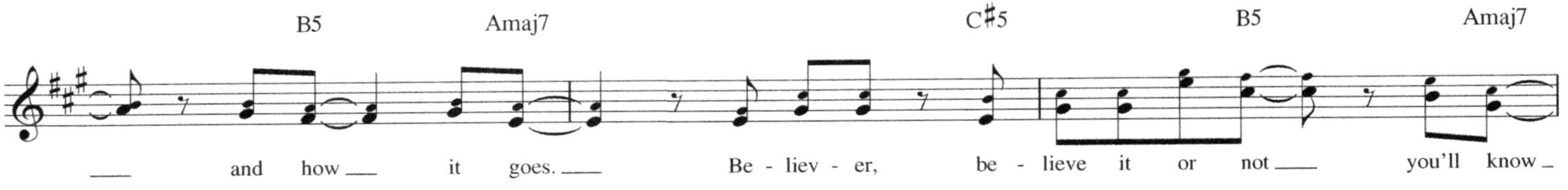
B5
Amaj7
C♯5
B5
Amaj7
and how it goes. Be - liev - er, be - lieve it or not you'll know

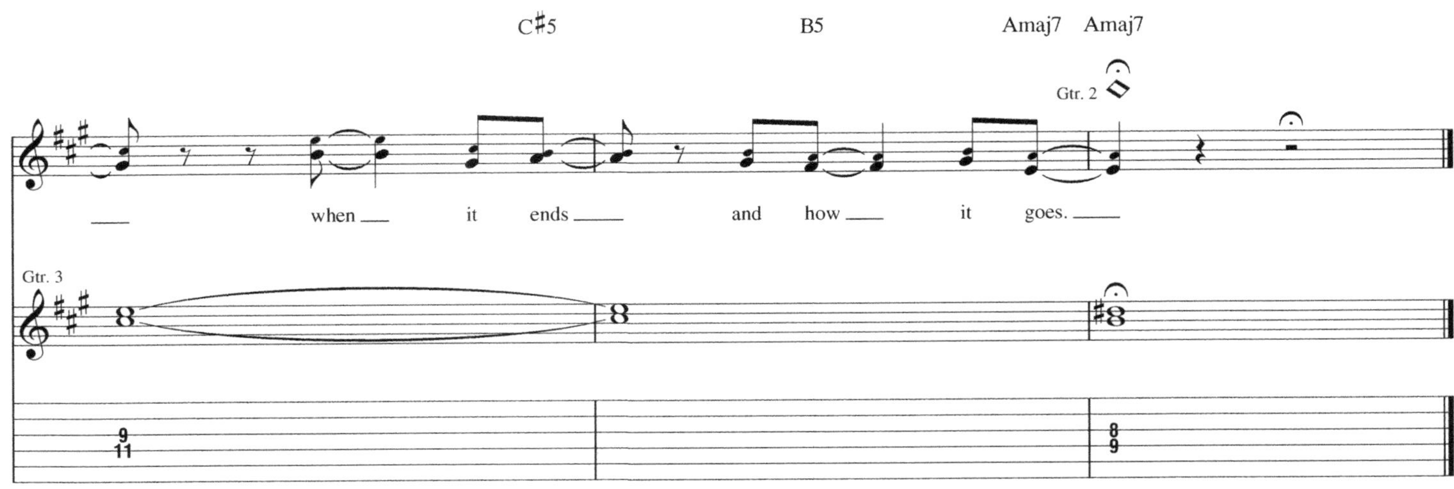
C♯5
B5
Amaj7
Amaj7
Gtr. 2
when it ends and how it goes.
Gtr. 3

Mother May I

Words and Music by Claudio Sanchez, Michael Todd, Joshua Eppard and Travis Stever

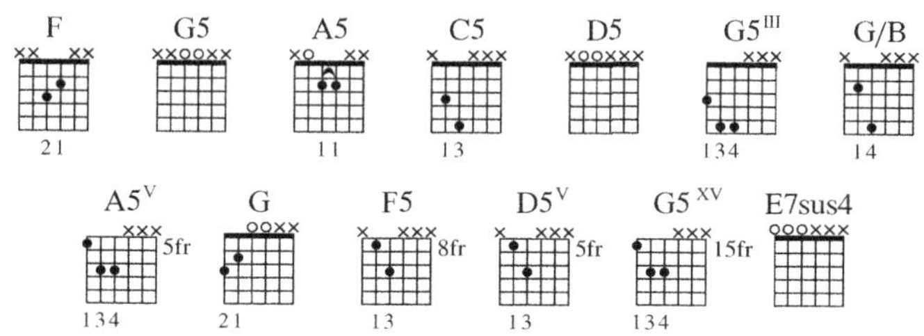

Tune down 1/2 step:
(low to high) E♭-A♭-D♭-G♭-B♭-E♭

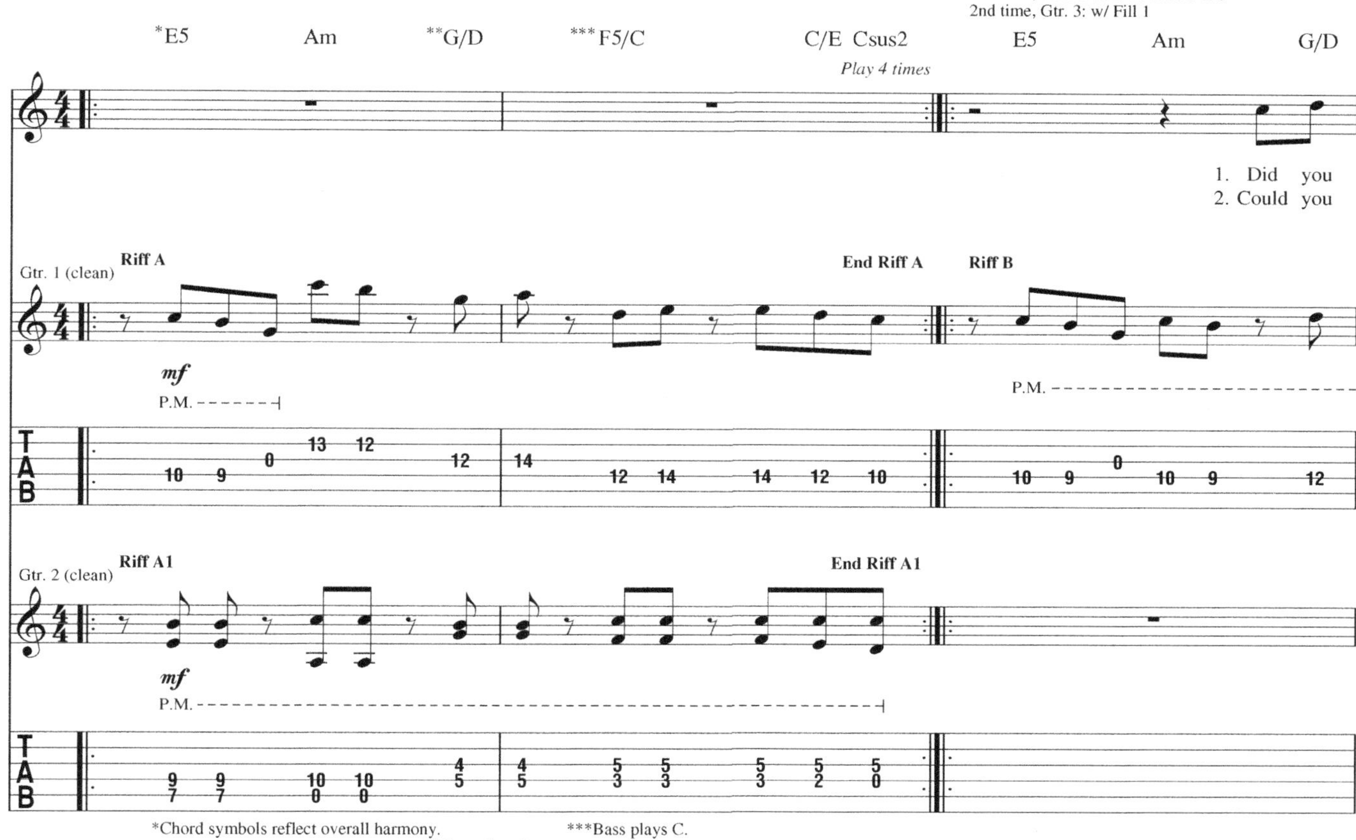

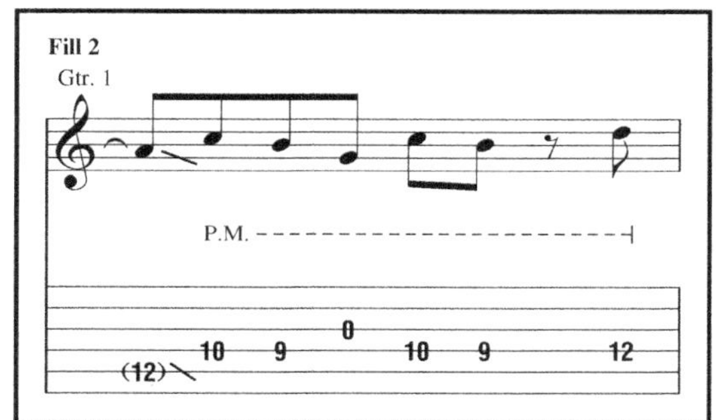

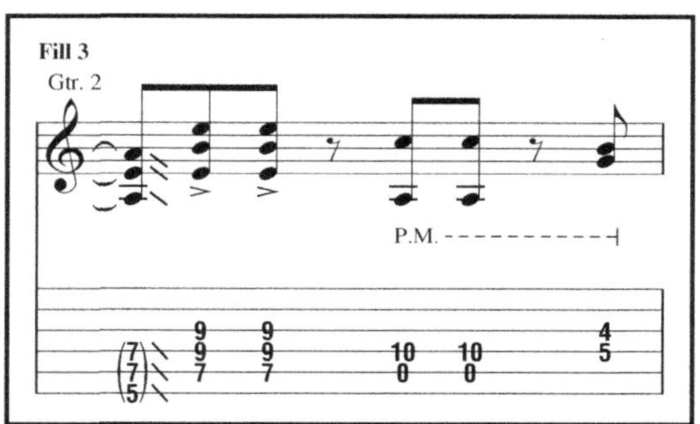

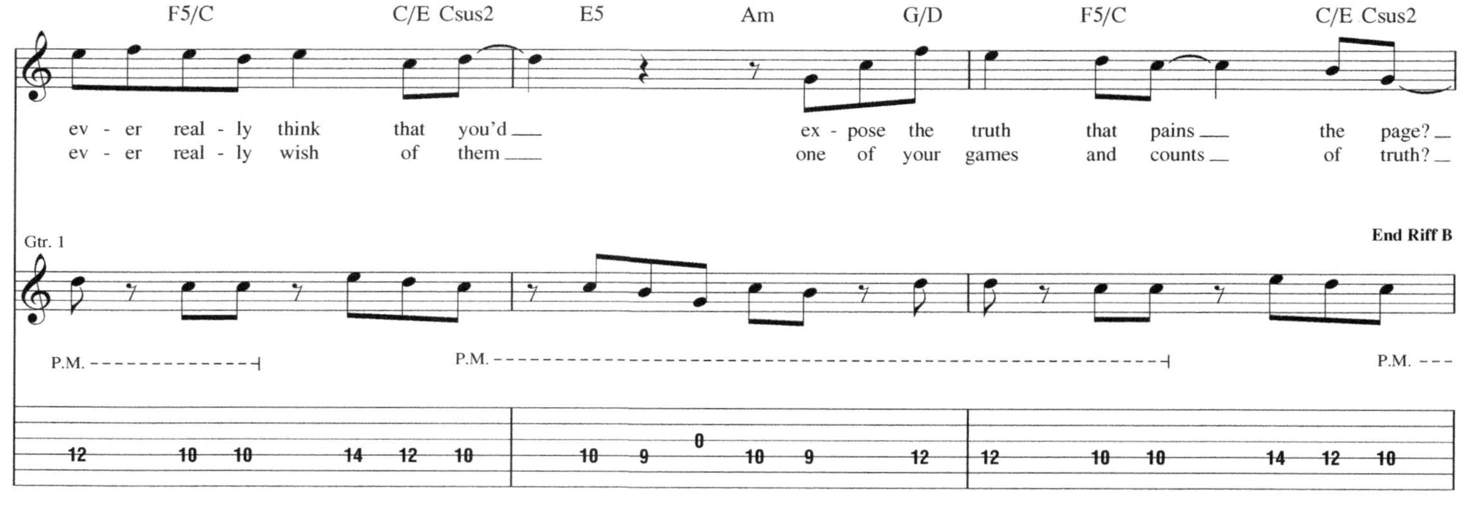
F5/C C/E Csus2 E5 Am G/D F5/C C/E Csus2
ev - er real - ly think that you'd ex - pose the truth that pains the page?
ev - er real - ly wish of them one of your games and counts of truth?
Gtr. 1
End Riff B
P.M.
P.M.
P.M.
12 10 10 14 12 10 10 9 0 10 9 12 12 10 10 14 12 10

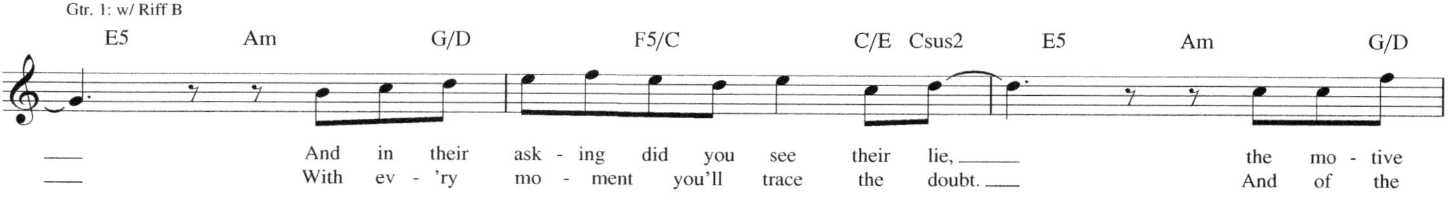
Gtr. 1: w/ Riff B
E5 Am G/D F5/C C/E Csus2 E5 Am G/D
And in their ask - ing did you see their lie, the mo - tive
With ev - 'ry mo - ment you'll trace the doubt. And of the

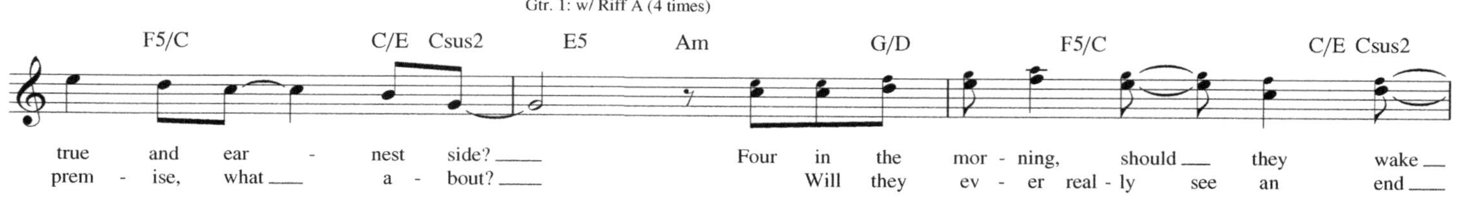
Gtr. 1: w/ Riff A (4 times)
F5/C C/E Csus2 E5 Am G/D F5/C C/E Csus2
true and ear - nest side? Four in the mor - ning, should they wake
prem - ise, what a - bout? Will they ev - er real - ly see an end

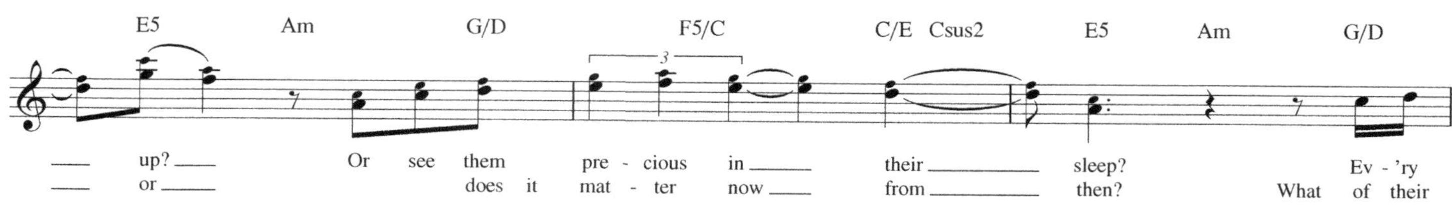
E5 Am G/D F5/C C/E Csus2 E5 Am G/D
3
up? Or see them pre - cious in their sleep? Ev - 'ry
or does it mat - ter now from then? What of their

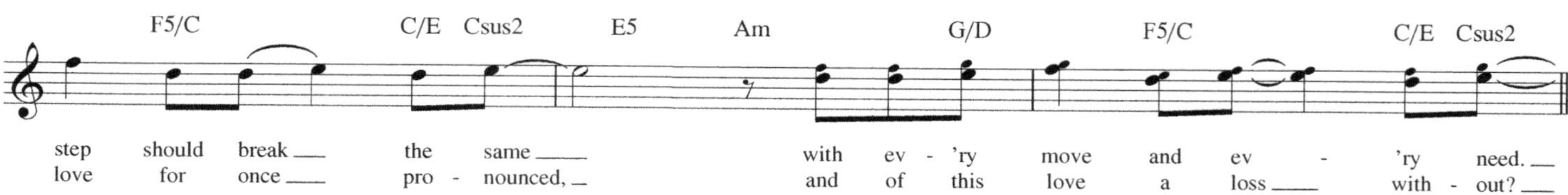
F5/C C/E Csus2 E5 Am G/D F5/C C/E Csus2
step should break the same with ev - 'ry move and ev - 'ry need.
love for once pro - nounced, and of this love a loss with - out?

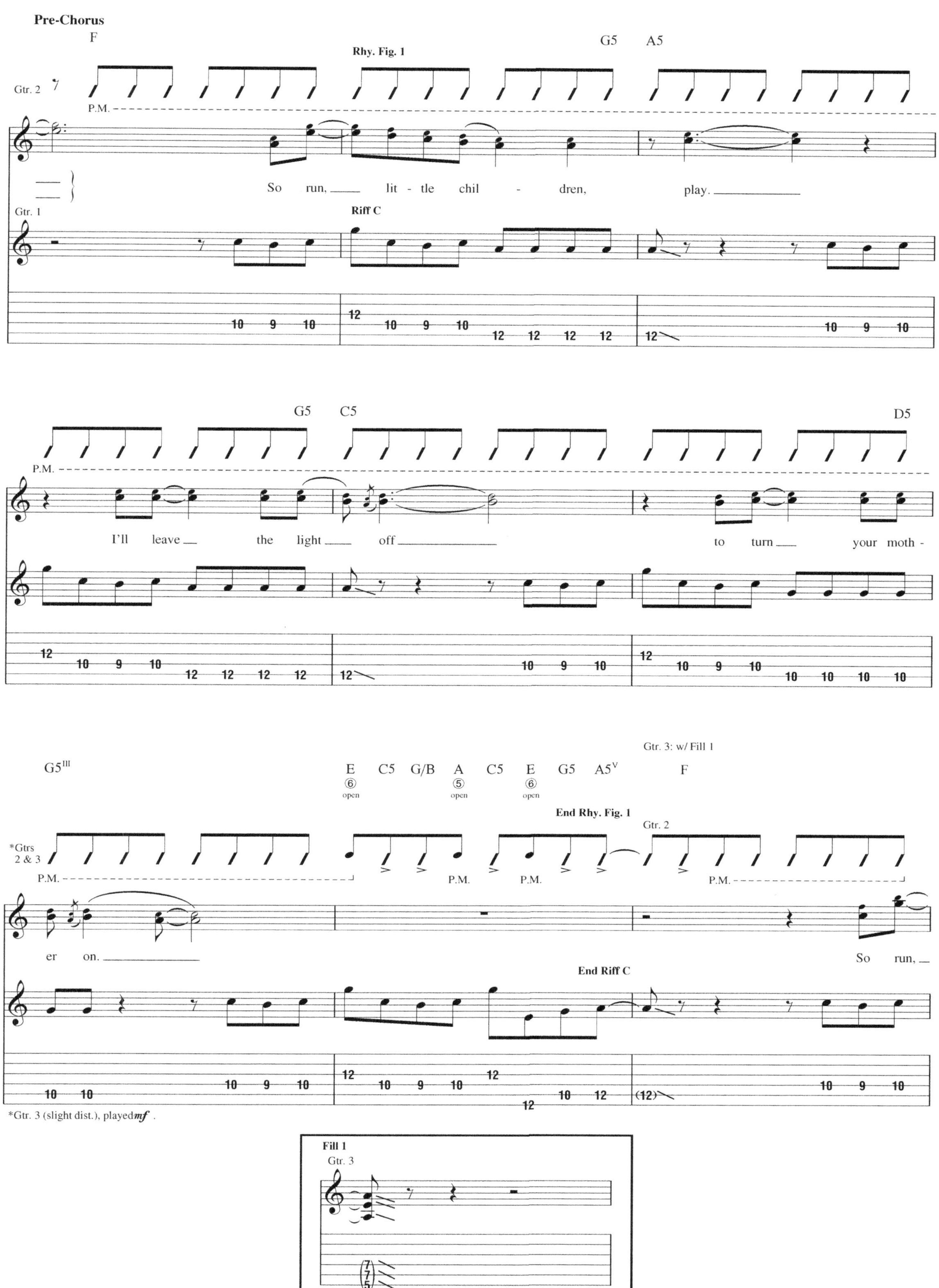

Pre-Chorus
F
Rhy. Fig. 1
G5 A5
Gtr. 2
P.M.
So run, little children, play.
Gtr. 1
Riff C
G5 C5
D5
P.M.
I'll leave the light off to turn your mother on.
Gtr. 3: w/ Fill 1
G5III
E ⑥ open C5 G/B A ⑤ open C5 E ⑥ open G5 A5V F
End Rhy. Fig. 1
Gtr. 2
*Gtrs 2 & 3
P.M.
er on.
So run,
End Riff C
*Gtr. 3 (slight dist.), played mf.
Fill 1
Gtr. 3

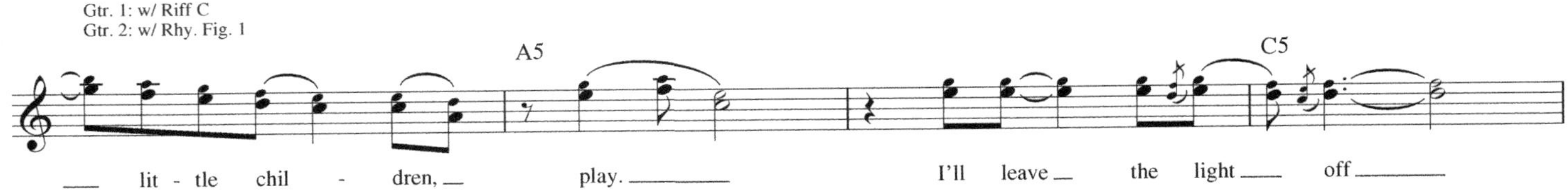
Gtr. 1: w/ Riff C
Gtr. 2: w/ Rhy. Fig. 1
A5
C5
lit - tle chil - dren,
play.
I'll leave the light off

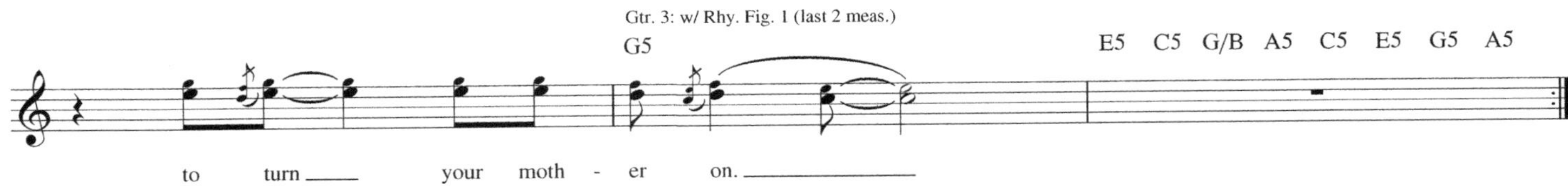
Gtr. 3: w/ Rhy. Fig. 1 (last 2 meas.)
G5
E5 C5 G/B A5 C5 E5 G5 A5
to turn your moth - er on.

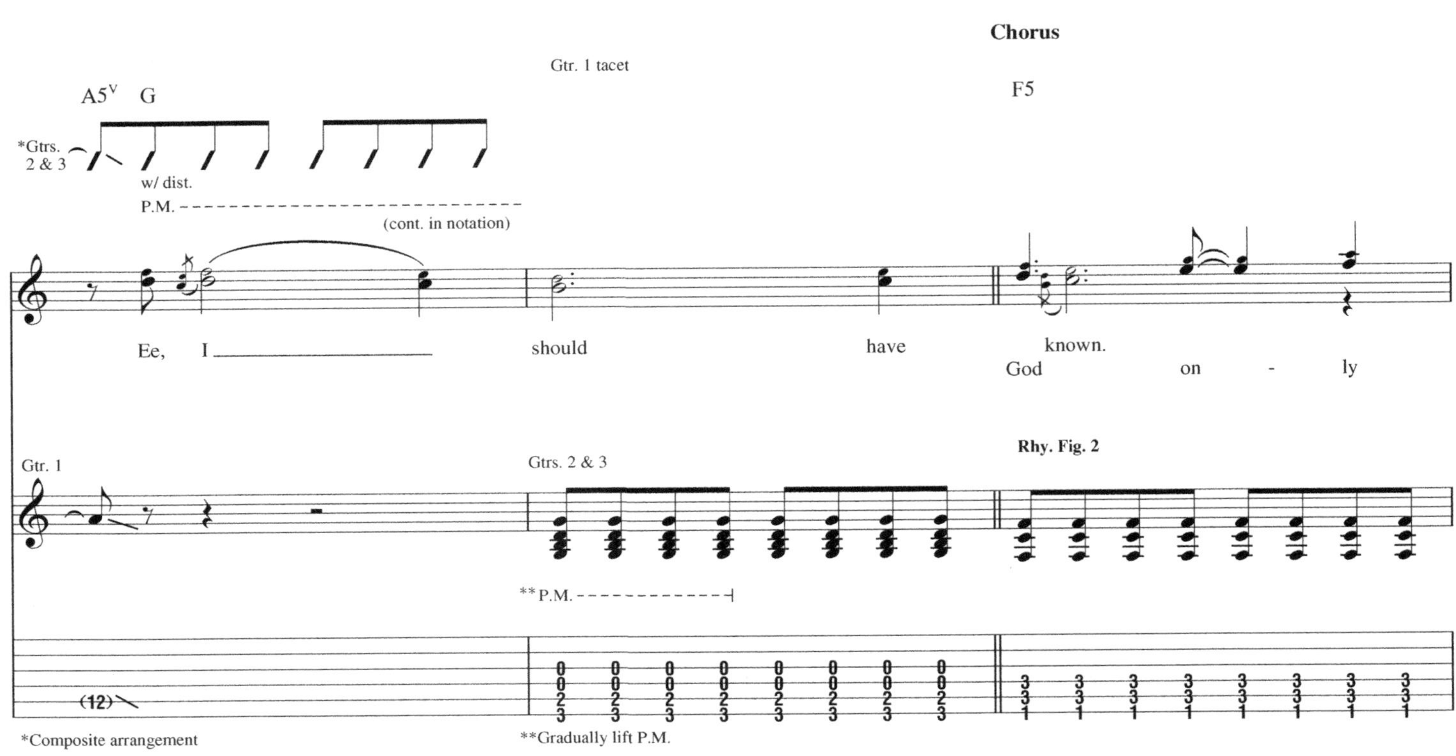
Chorus
Gtr. 1 tacet
A5 G
F5
*Gtrs. 2 & 3
w/ dist.
P.M.
(cont. in notation)
Ee, I should have known.
God on - ly
Gtr. 1
Gtrs. 2 & 3
Rhy. Fig. 2
**P.M.
*Composite arrangement
**Gradually lift P.M.

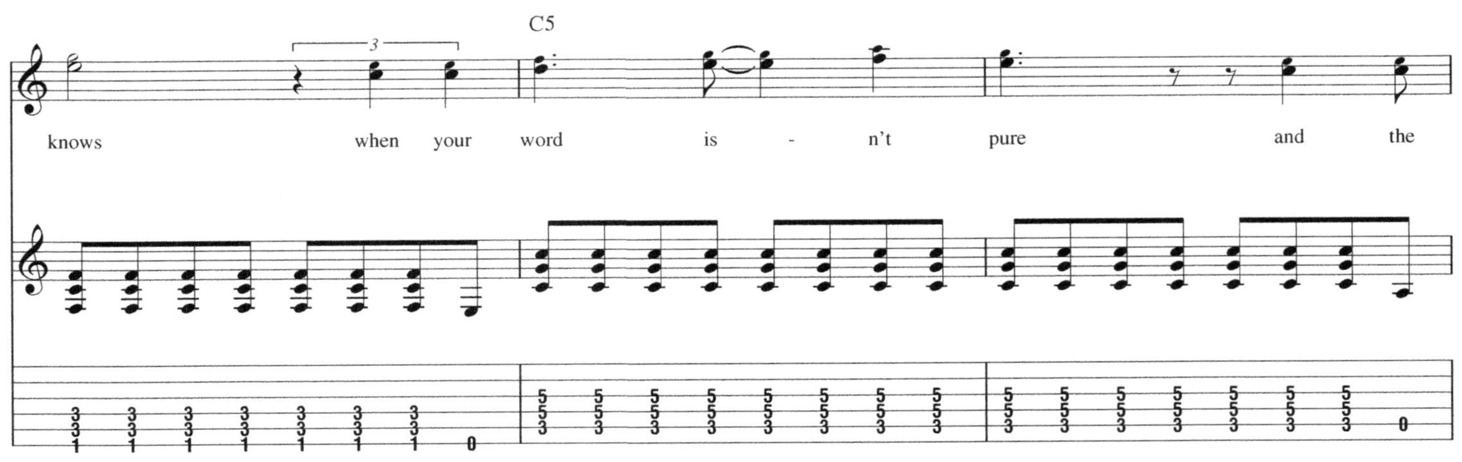
C5
knows when your word is - n't pure and the

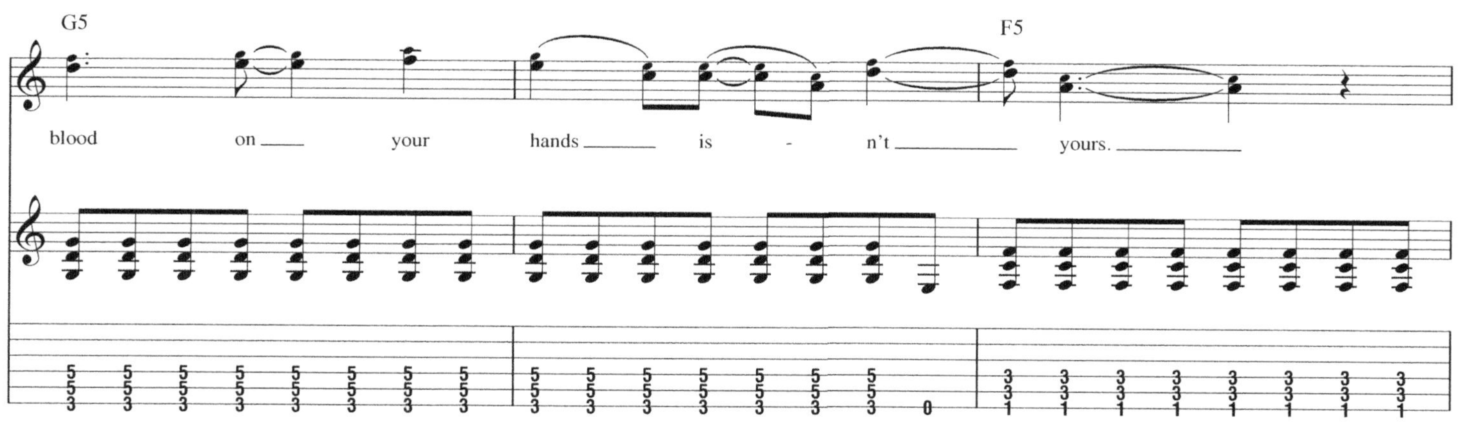
G5
F5
blood on your hands is - n't yours.

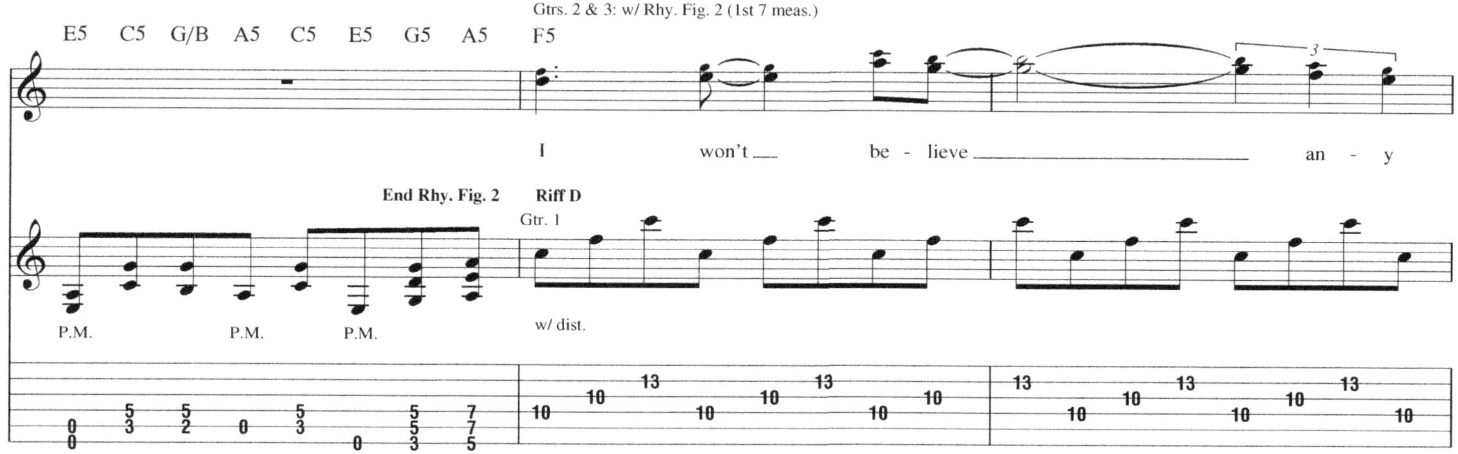
Gtrs. 2 & 3: w/ Rhy. Fig. 2 (1st 7 meas.)
E5 C5 G/B A5 C5 E5 G5 A5
F5
I won't be - lieve an - y
End Rhy. Fig. 2
Riff D
Gtr. 1
P.M.
P.M.
P.M.
w/ dist.

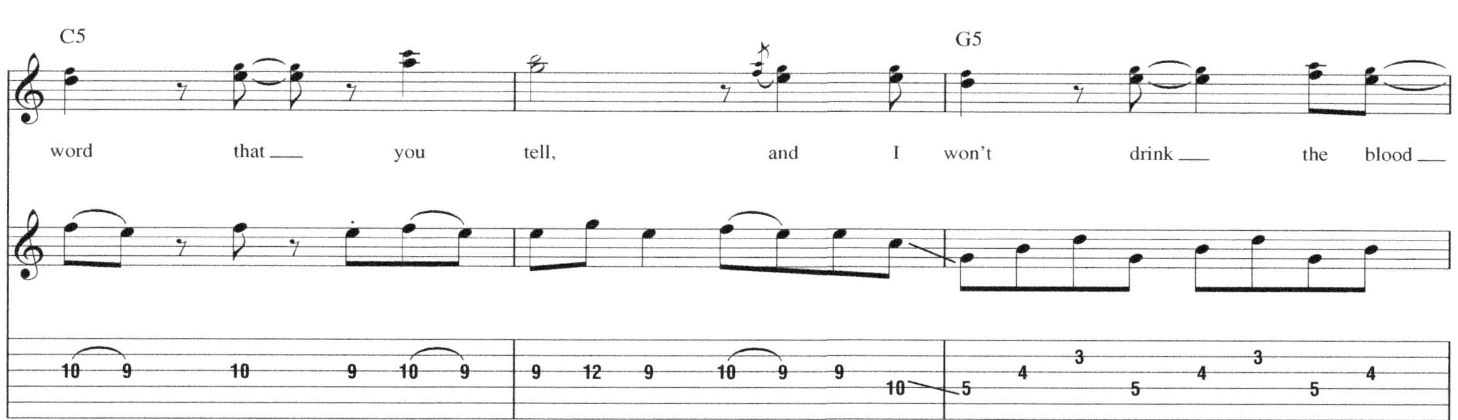
C5
G5
word that you tell, and I won't drink the blood

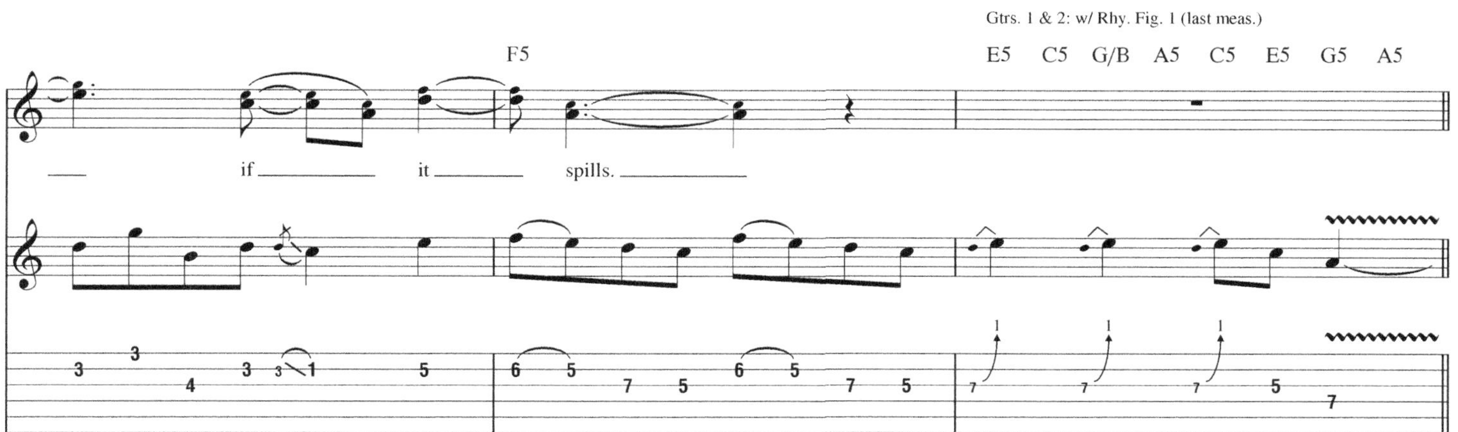
Gtrs. 1 & 2: w/ Rhy. Fig. 1 (last meas.)
F5
E5 C5 G/B A5 C5 E5 G5 A5
if it spills.

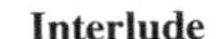

Interlude

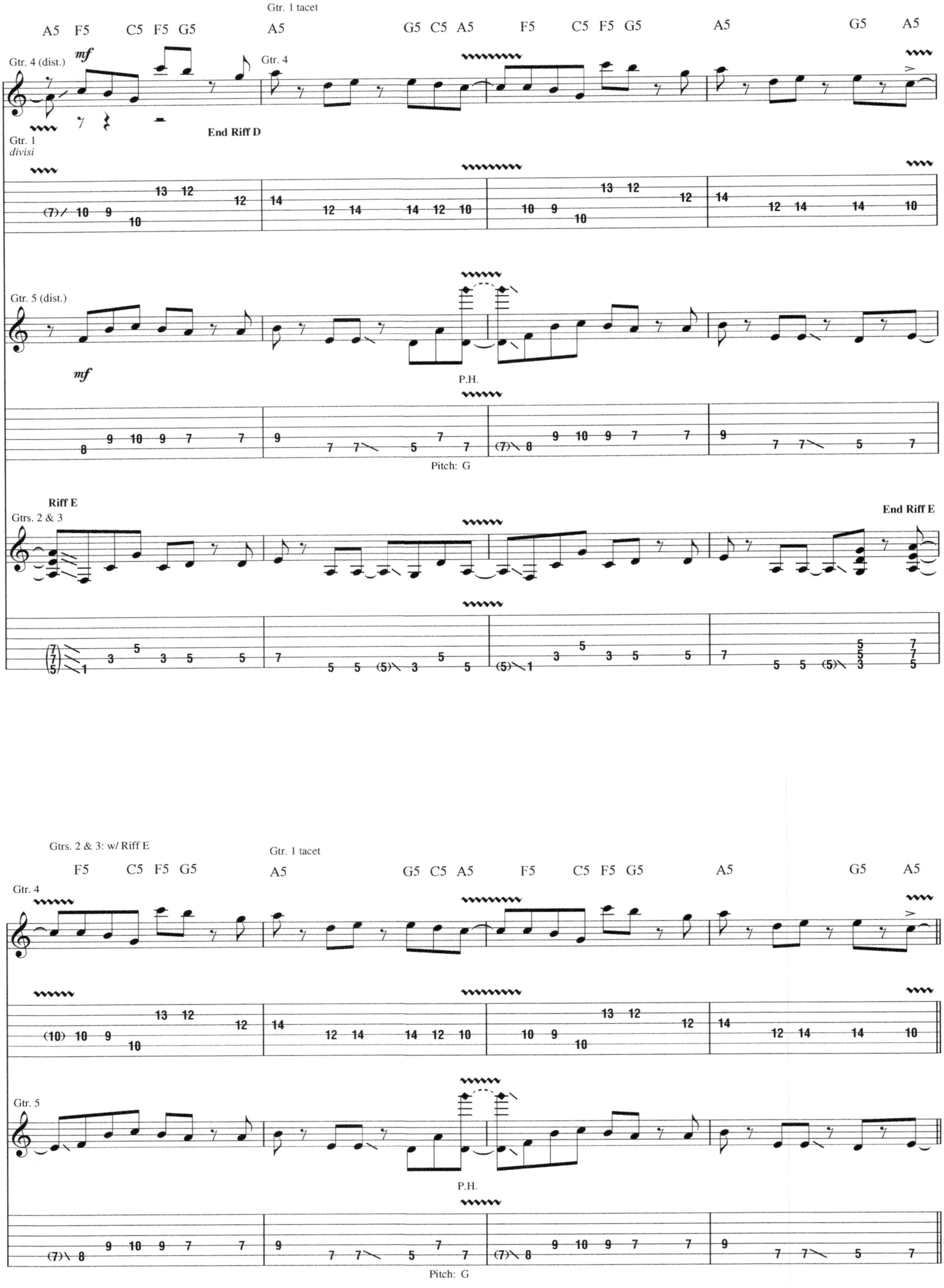

Gtr. 1 tacet

A5 F5 C5 F5 G5 A5 G5 C5 A5 F5 C5 F5 G5 A5 G5 A5

Gtr. 4 (dist.)

mf

Gtr. 4

End Riff D

Gtr. 1
divisi

Gtr. 5 (dist.)

mf

P.H.

Pitch: G

Riff E

Gtrs. 2 & 3

End Riff E

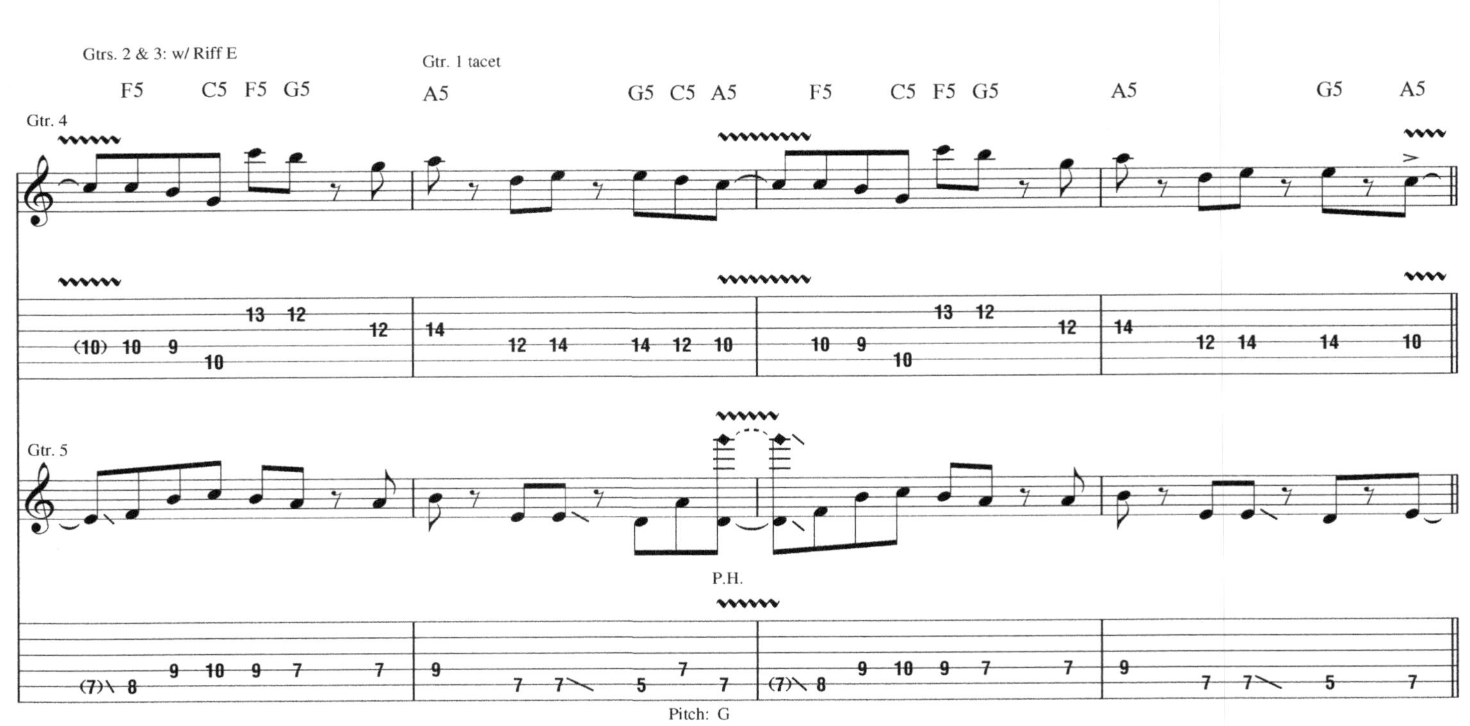

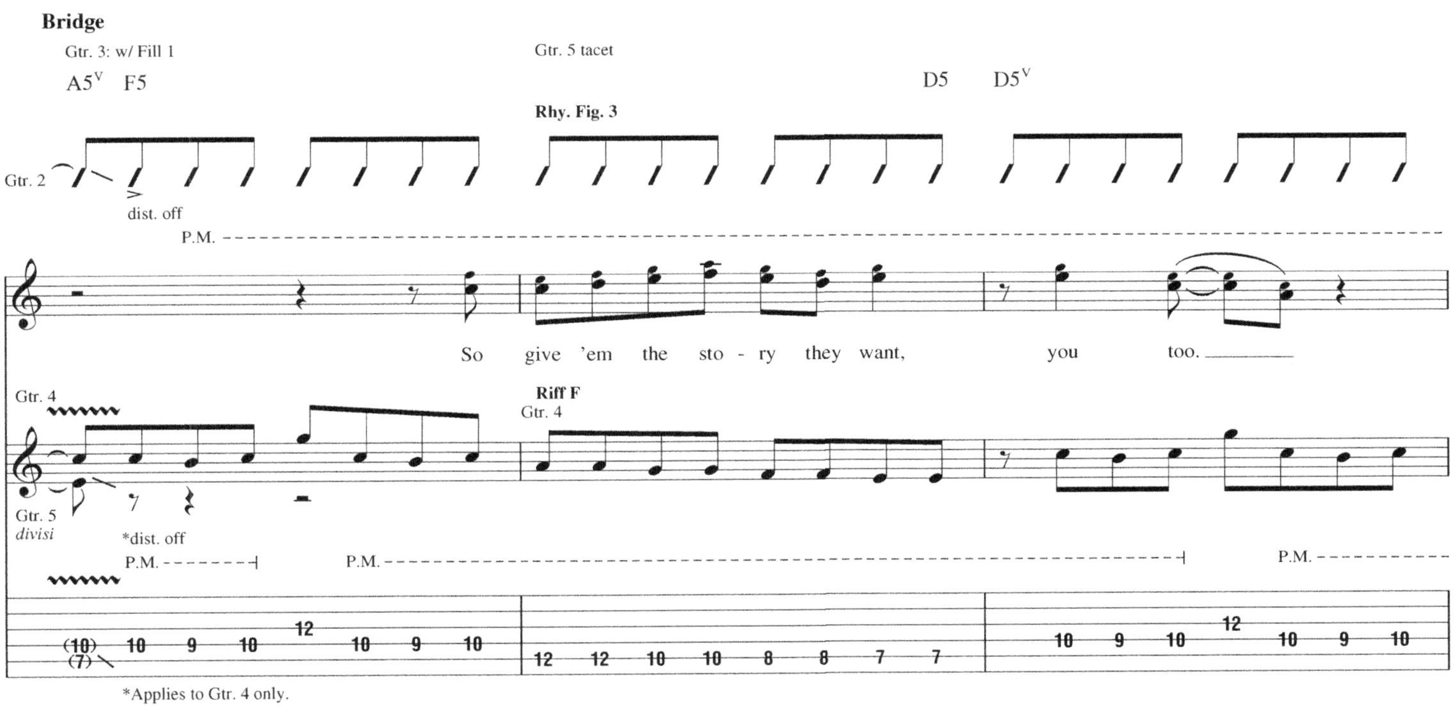
Bridge
Gtr. 3: w/ Fill 1
Gtr. 5 tacet
A5V F5
D5 D5V
Rhy. Fig. 3
Gtr. 2
dist. off
P.M.
So give 'em the sto - ry they want, you too.
Gtr. 4
Riff F
Gtr. 4
Gtr. 5
divisi
*dist. off
P.M.
P.M.
P.M.
*Applies to Gtr. 4 only.

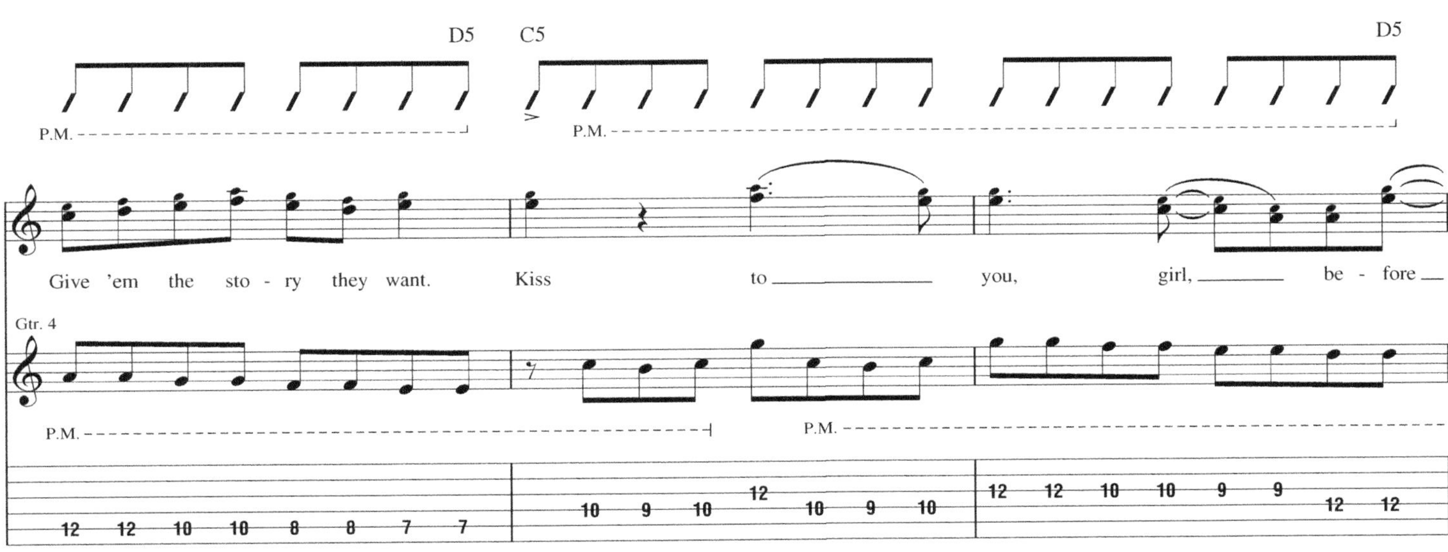
D5 C5
D5
P.M.
P.M.
Give 'em the sto - ry they want. Kiss to you, girl, be - fore
Gtr. 4
P.M.
P.M.

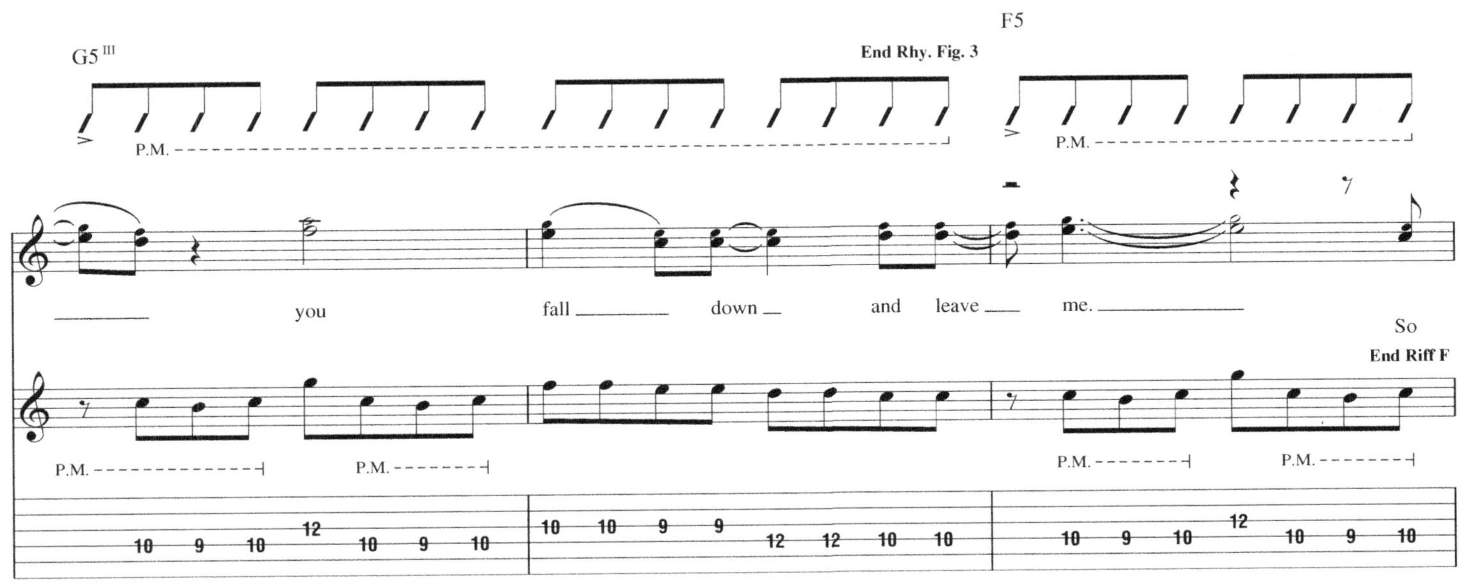
G5 III
F5
End Rhy. Fig. 3
P.M.
P.M.
you fall down and leave me.
So
End Riff F
P.M.
P.M.
P.M.
P.M.

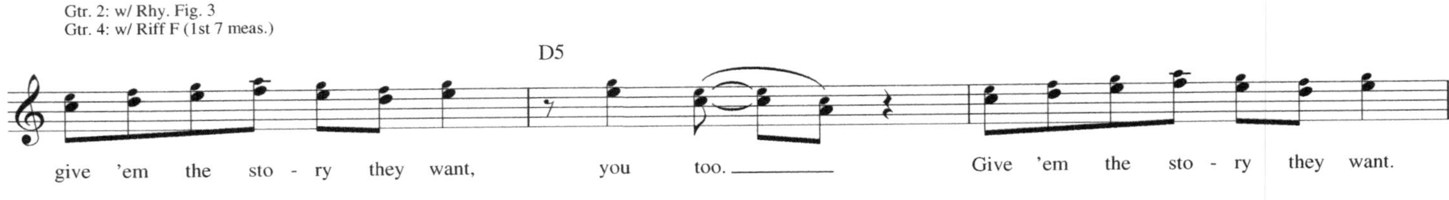
Gtr. 2: w/ Rhy. Fig. 3
Gtr. 4: w/ Riff F (1st 7 meas.)
D5
give 'em the sto - ry they want, you too.
Give 'em the sto - ry they want.

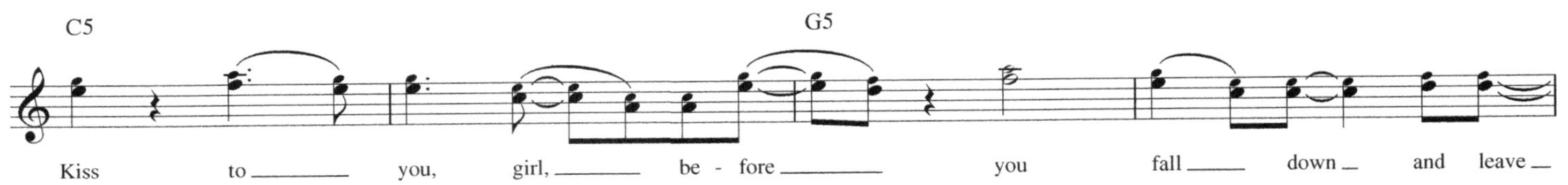
C5
G5
Kiss to you, girl, be - fore you fall down and leave

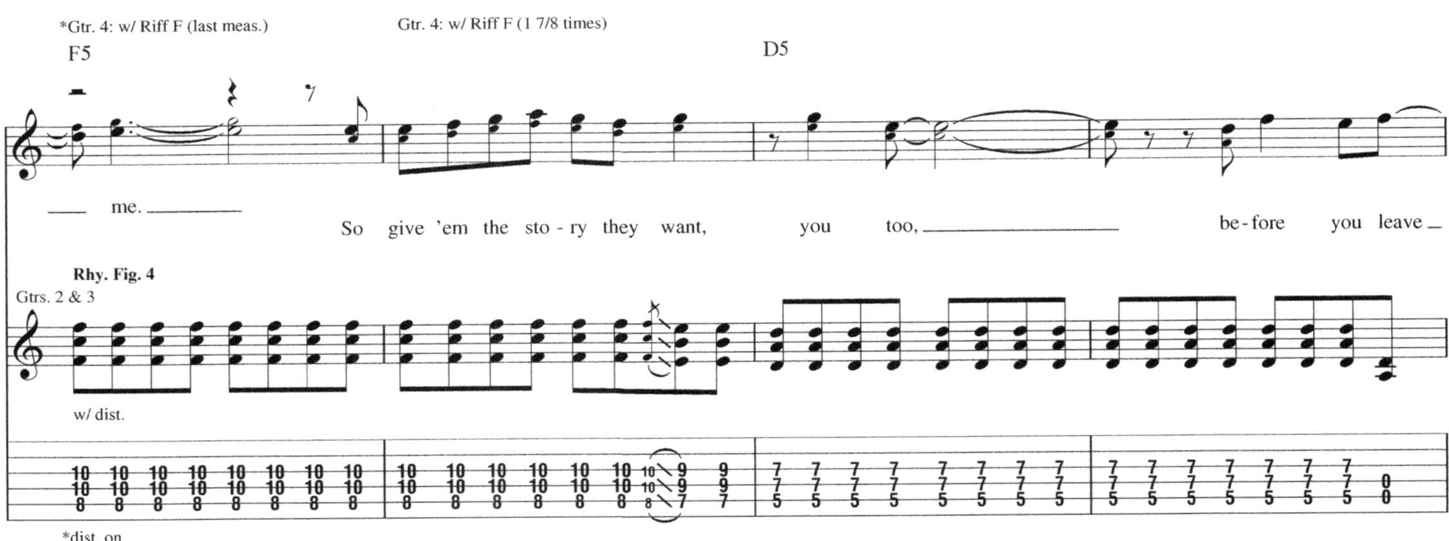
*Gtr. 4: w/ Riff F (last meas.)
Gtr. 4: w/ Riff F (1 7/8 times)
F5
D5
me. So give 'em the sto - ry they want, you too, be - fore you leave
Rhy. Fig. 4
Gtrs. 2 & 3
w/ dist.
*dist. on

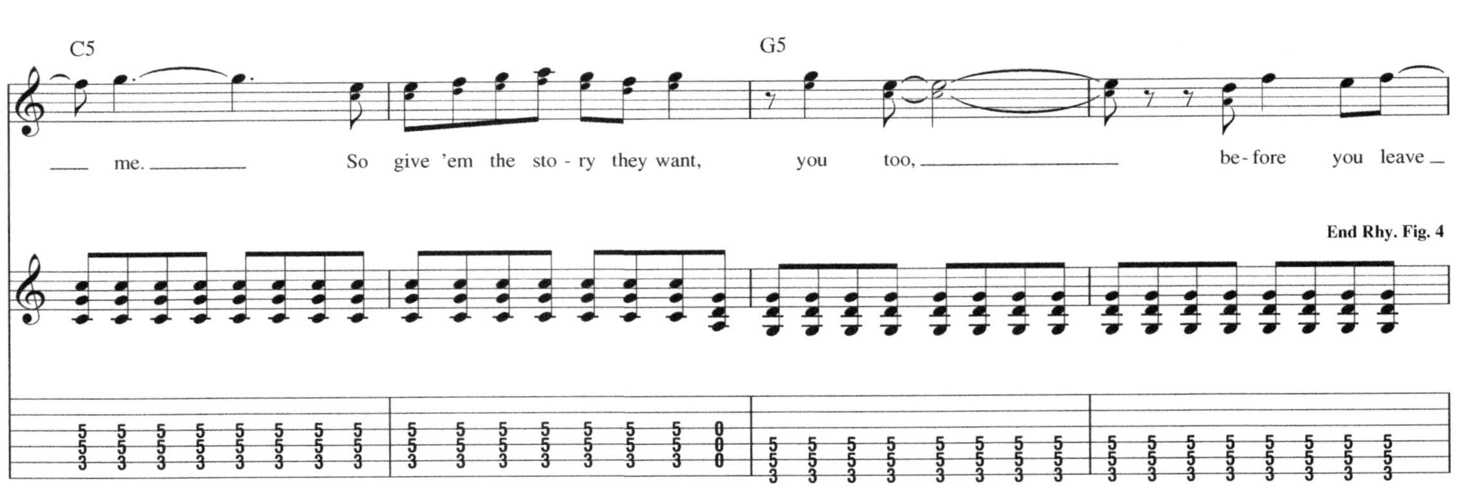
C5
G5
me. So give 'em the sto - ry they want, you too, be - fore you leave
End Rhy. Fig. 4

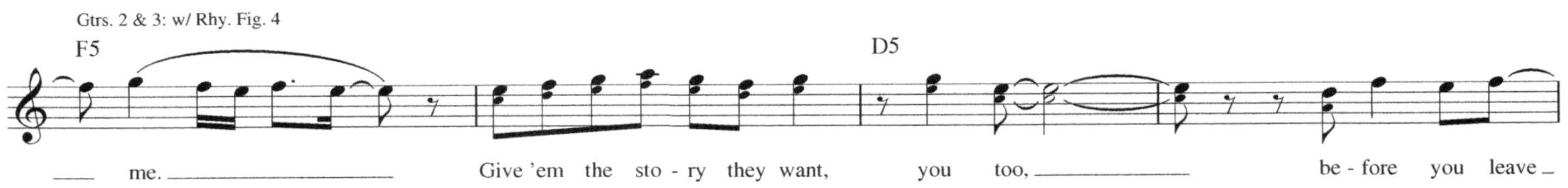
Gtrs. 2 & 3: w/ Rhy. Fig. 4
F5
D5
me. Give 'em the sto - ry they want, you too, be - fore you leave

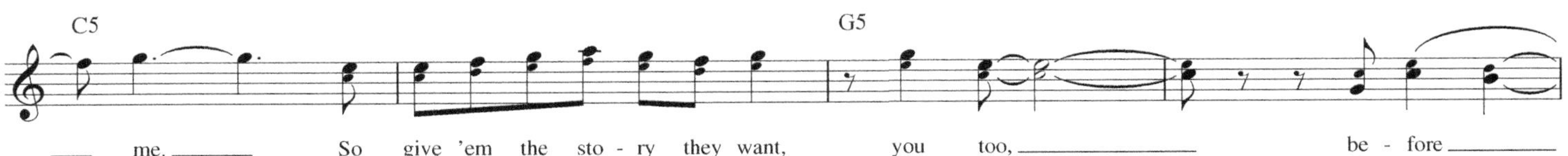

Chorus

Gtrs. 2 & 3: w/ Rhy. Fig. 2 (3 7/8 times)
Gtr. 4: w/ Riff D

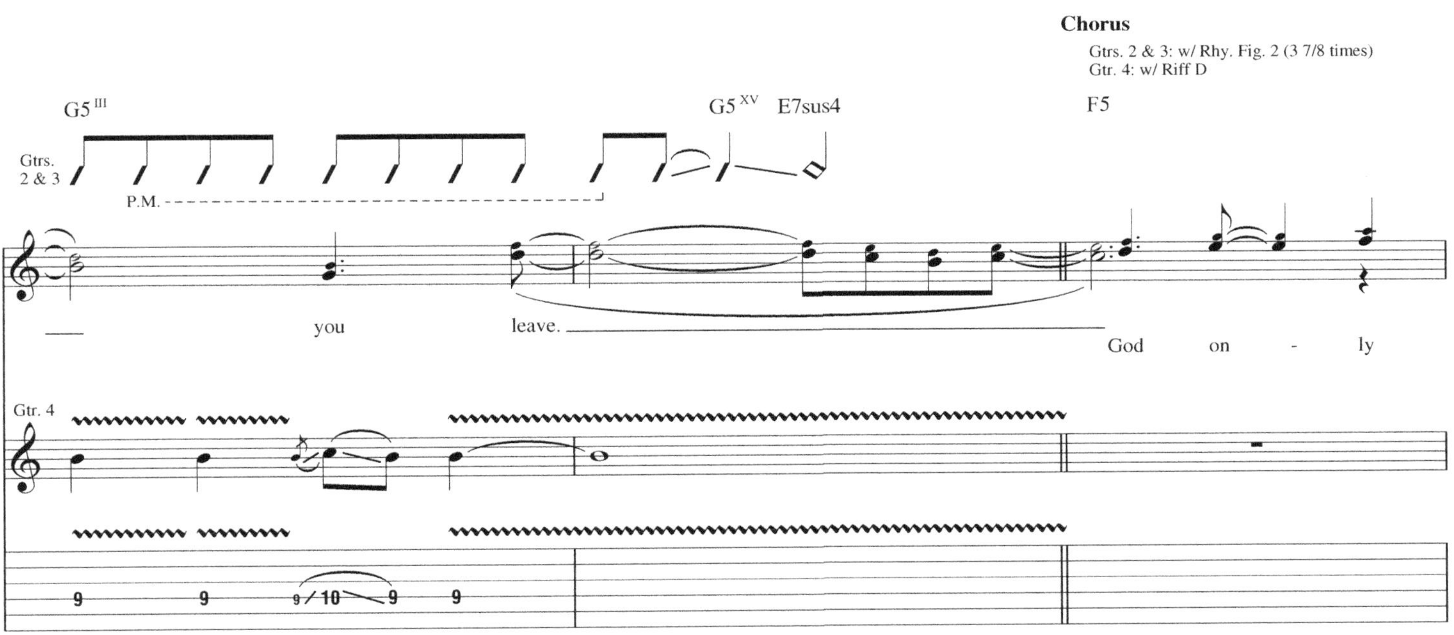

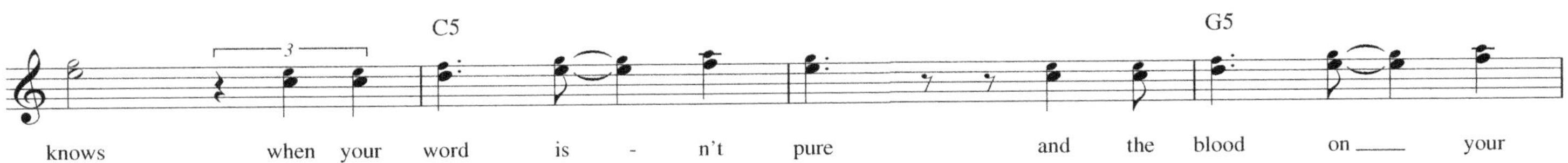

Gtr. 1: w/ Riff D

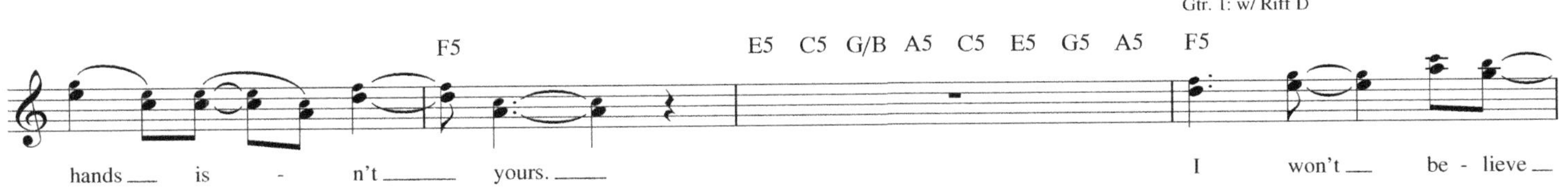

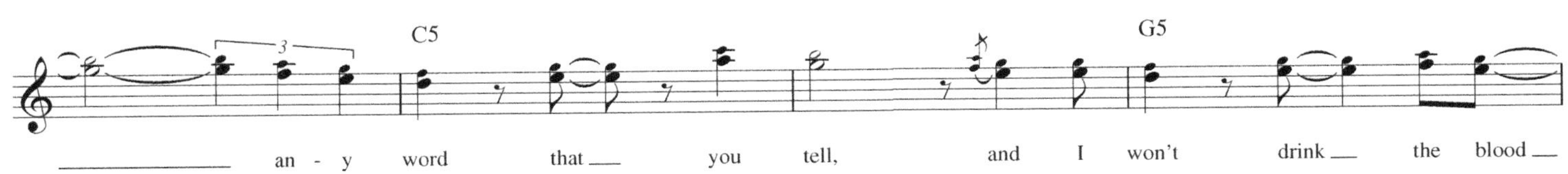

Gtr. 4: w/ Riff D

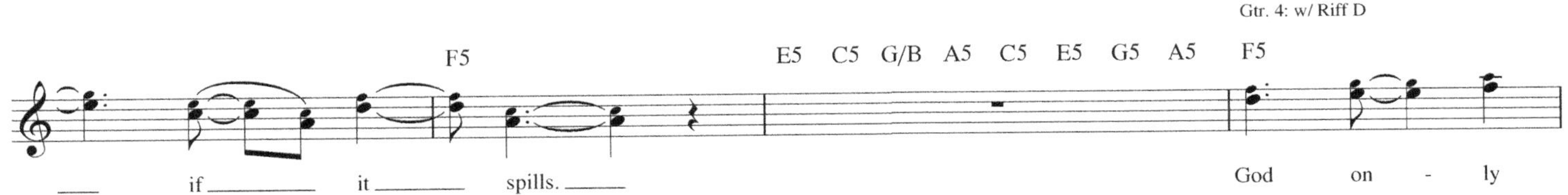

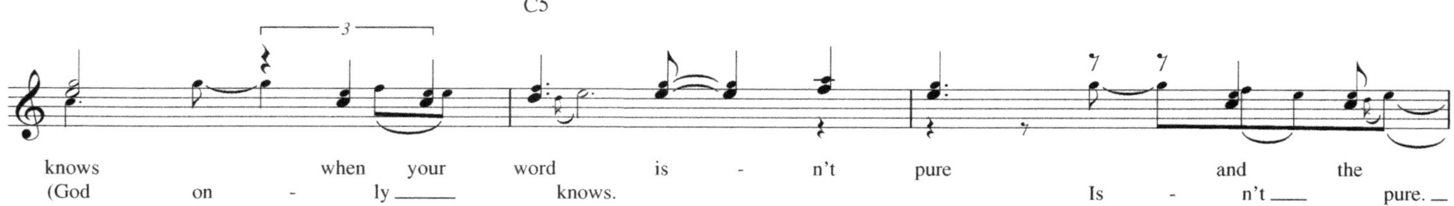
C5
knows when your word is - n't pure and the
(God on - ly knows. Is - n't pure.

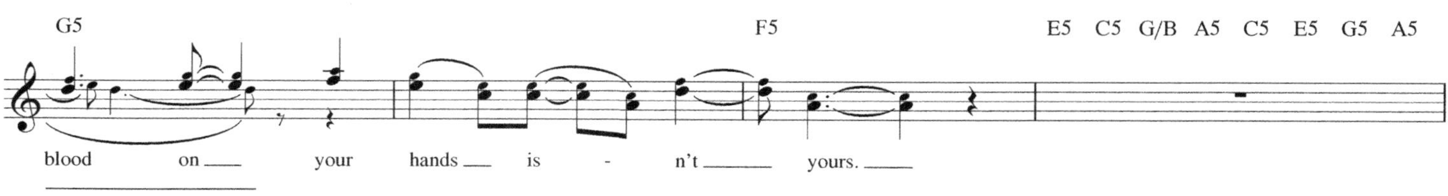
G5 F5 E5 C5 G/B A5 C5 E5 G5 A5
blood on your hands is - n't yours.

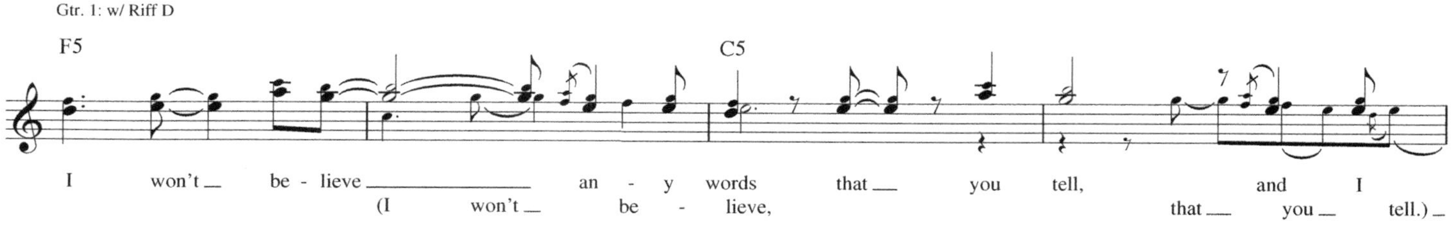
Gtr. 1: w/ Riff D
F5 C5
I won't be - lieve an - y words that you tell, and I
(I won't be - lieve, that you tell.)

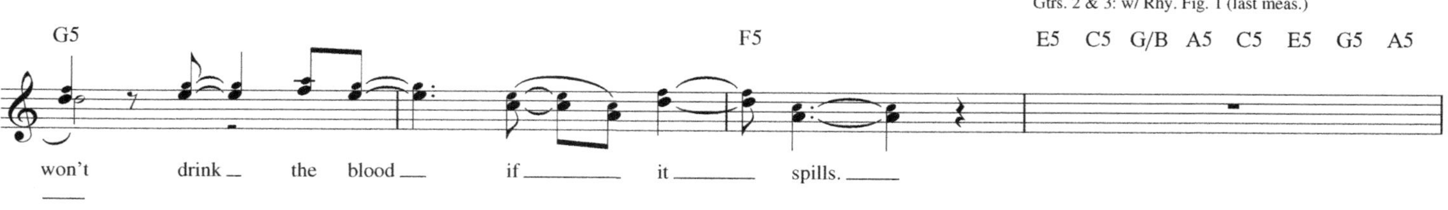
Gtrs. 2 & 3: w/ Rhy. Fig. 1 (last meas.)
G5 F5 E5 C5 G/B A5 C5 E5 G5 A5
won't drink the blood if it spills.

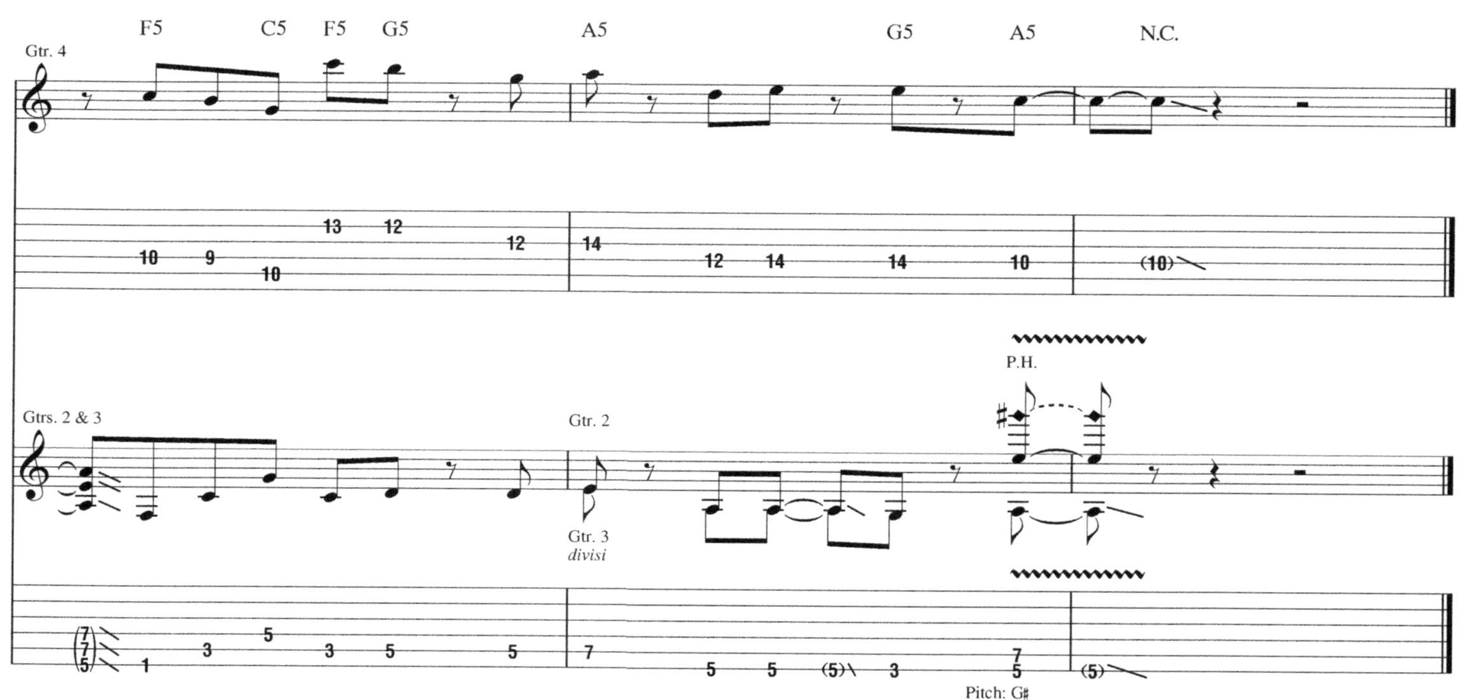
Gtr. 4
F5 C5 F5 G5 A5 G5 A5 N.C.
Gtrs. 2 & 3
Gtr. 2
Gtr. 3
divisi
P.H.
Pitch: G♯

Willing Well I: Fuel for the Feeding End

Words and Music by Claudio Sanchez, Michael Todd, Joshua Eppard and Travis Stever

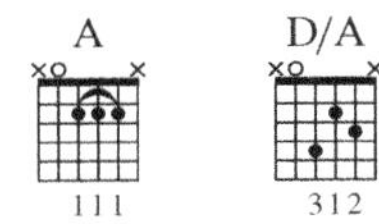

Tune down 1/2 step:
(low to high) E♭-A♭-D♭-G♭-B♭-E♭

Intro
Fast ♩ = 166

N.C.

*A5

Riff A

(Detuned Kybd. effects)
20 sec.

Gtr. 1 (elec.)

mf
w/ dist.

Gtr. 2 (elec.)

mf
w/ dist.
string noise

P.M. – ┤

*Chord symbols reflect basic harmony.

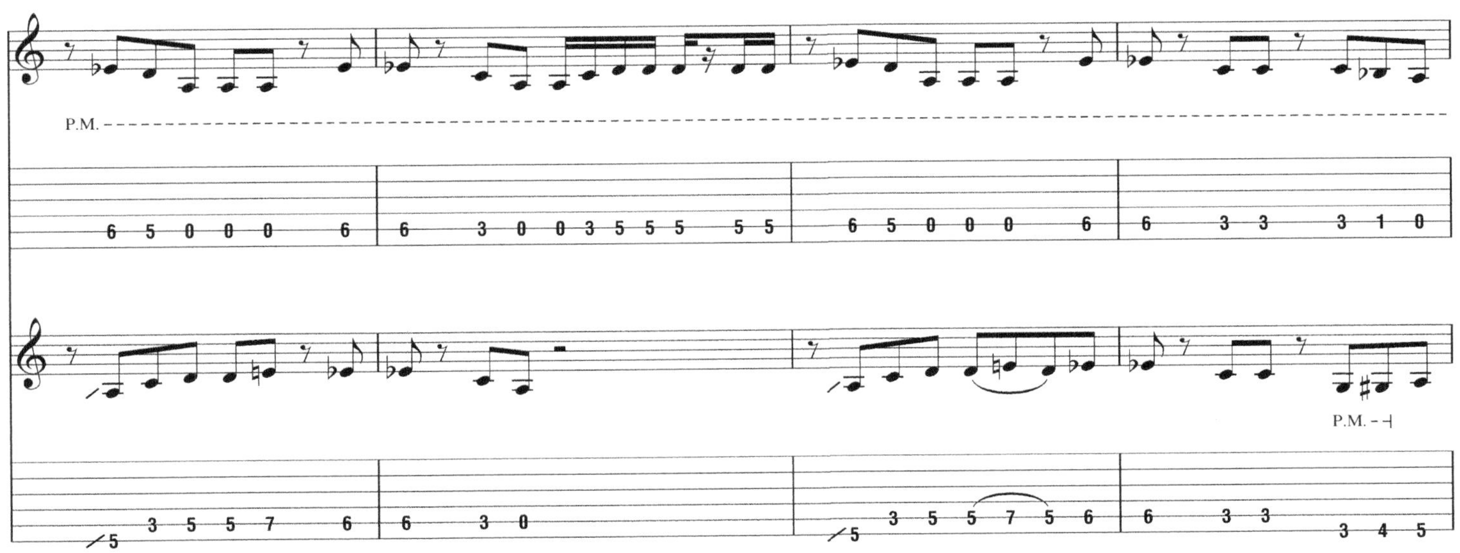

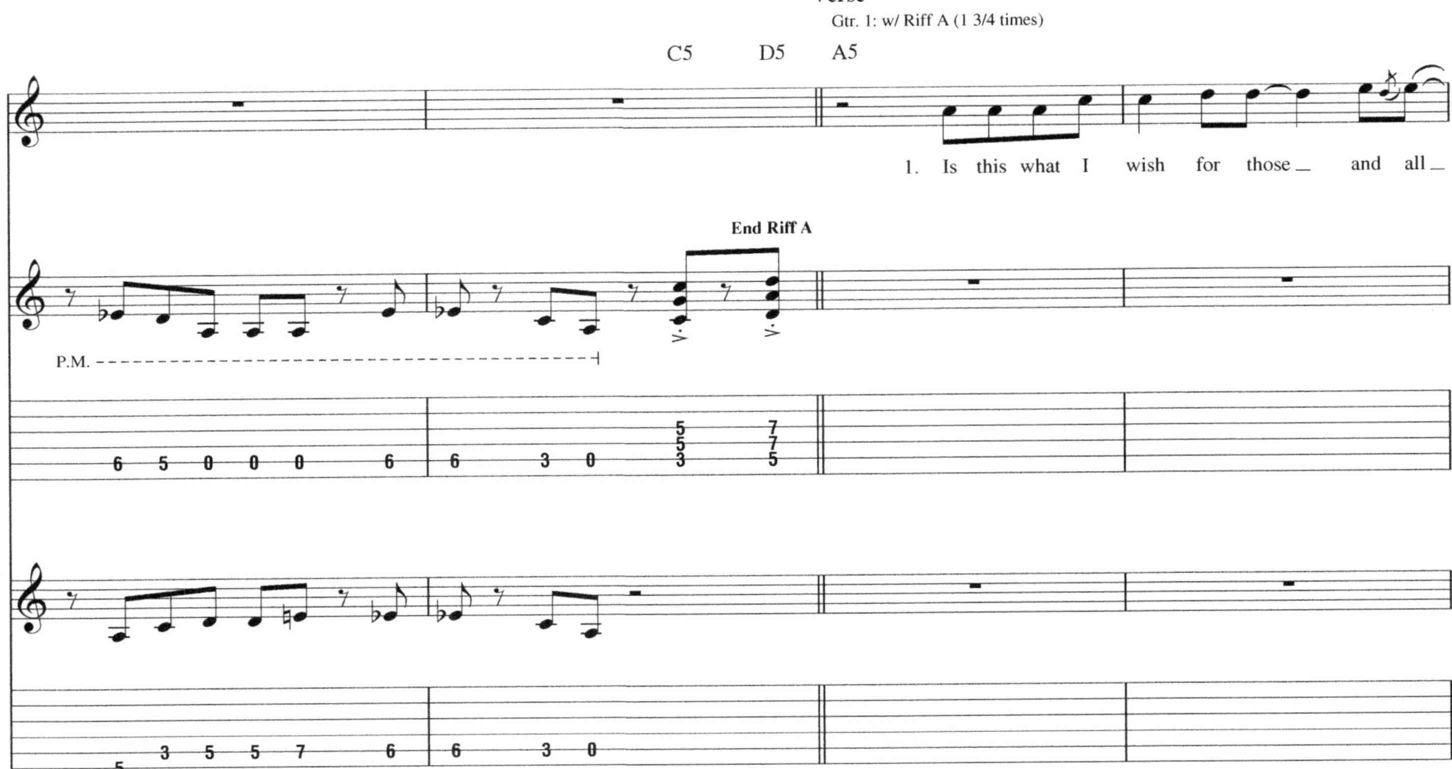
Verse
Gtr. 1: w/ Riff A (1 3/4 times)
C5 D5 A5
1. Is this what I wish for those and all
End Riff A
P.M.

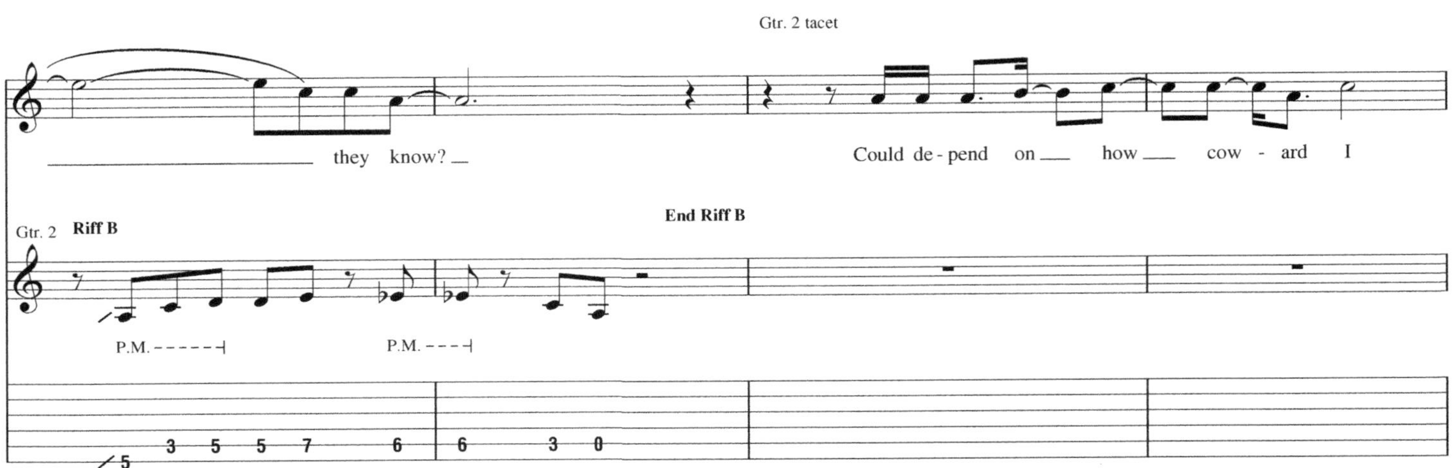
Gtr. 2 tacet
they know?
Could de-pend on how cow - ard I
Gtr. 2 Riff B
End Riff B
P.M.
P.M.

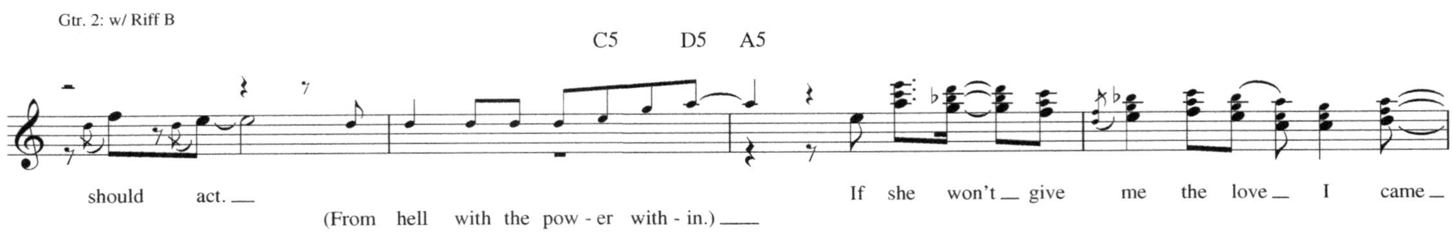
Gtr. 2: w/ Riff B
C5 D5 A5
should act.
If she won't give me the love I came
(From hell with the pow - er with - in.)

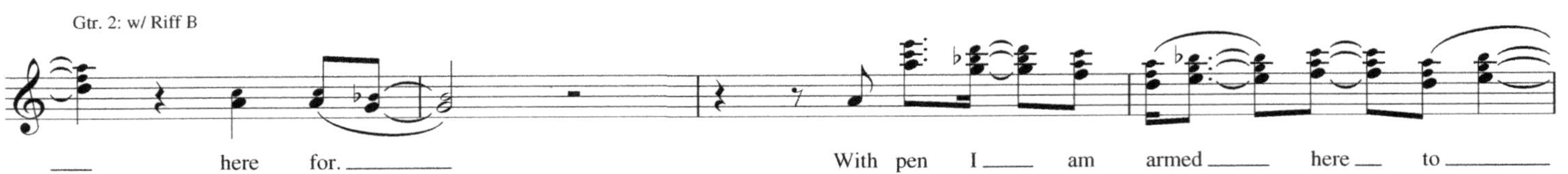
Gtr. 2: w/ Riff B
here for.
With pen I am armed here to

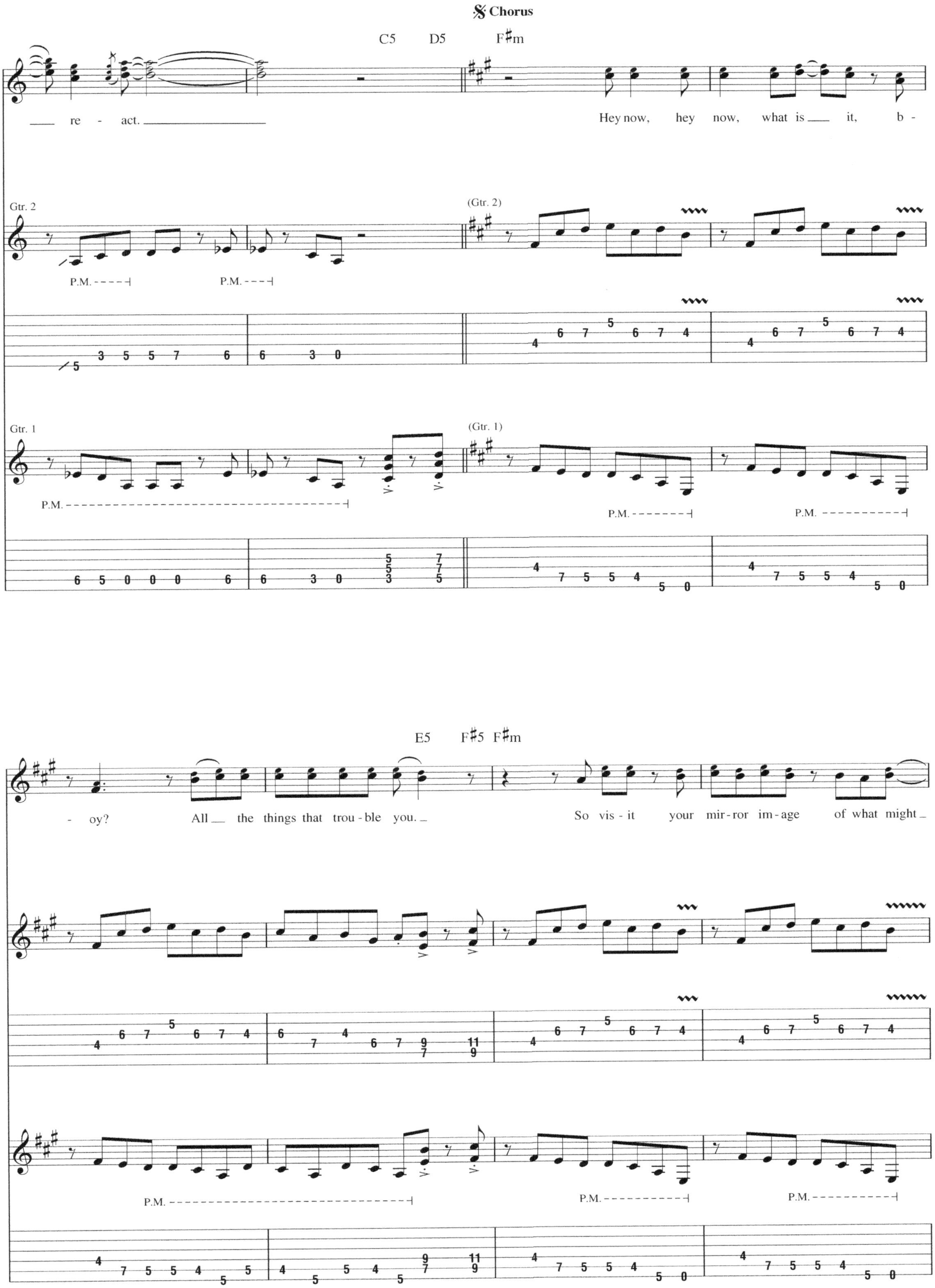

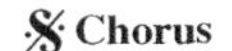

C5 D5 F♯m

re - act.

Hey now, hey now, what is it, b-

Gtr. 2

(Gtr. 2)

P.M. P.M.

Gtr. 1

(Gtr. 1)

P.M. P.M. P.M.

E5 F♯5 F♯m

- oy? All the things that trou - ble you. So vis - it your mir - ror im - age of what might

P.M. P.M. P.M.

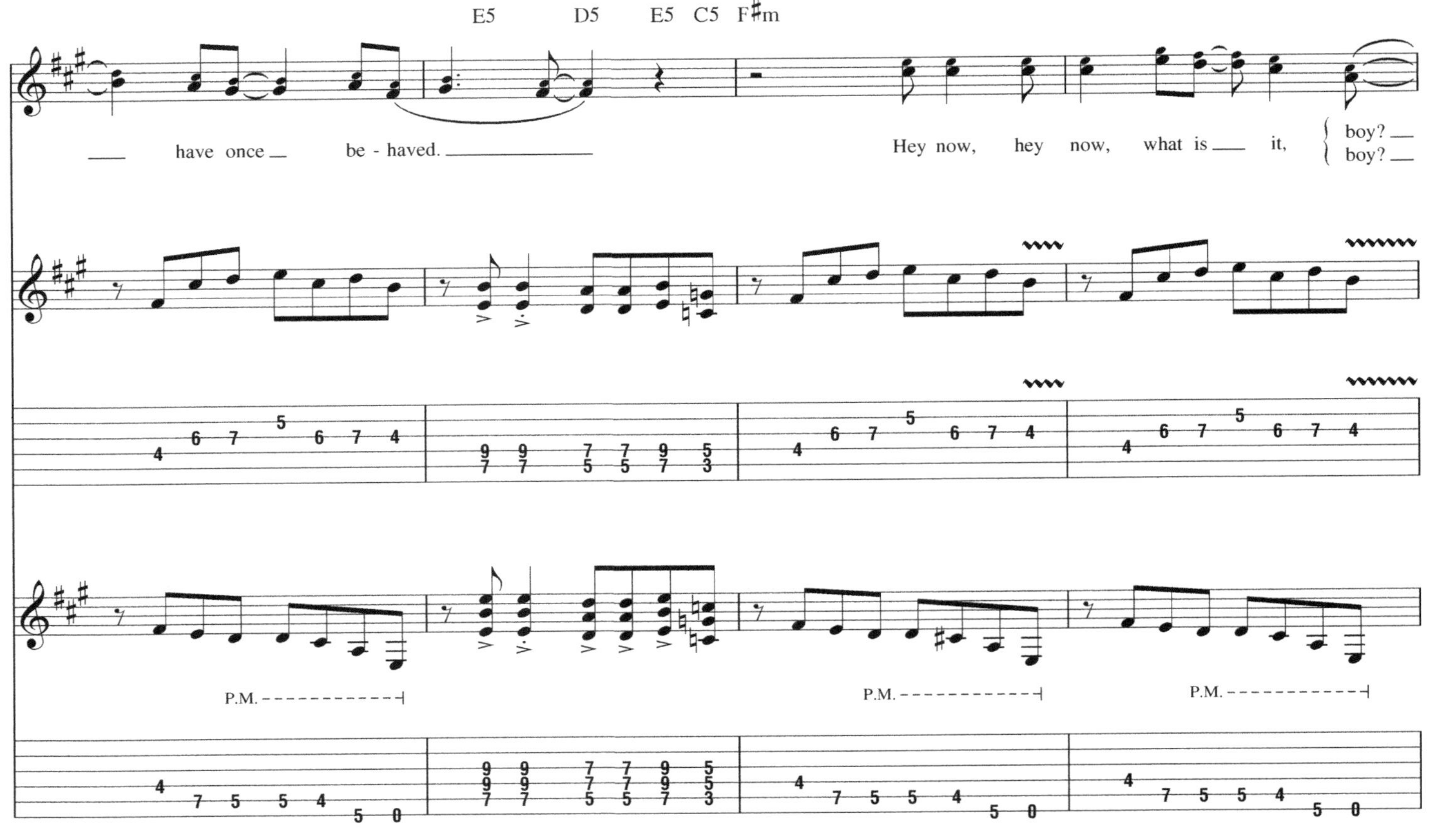

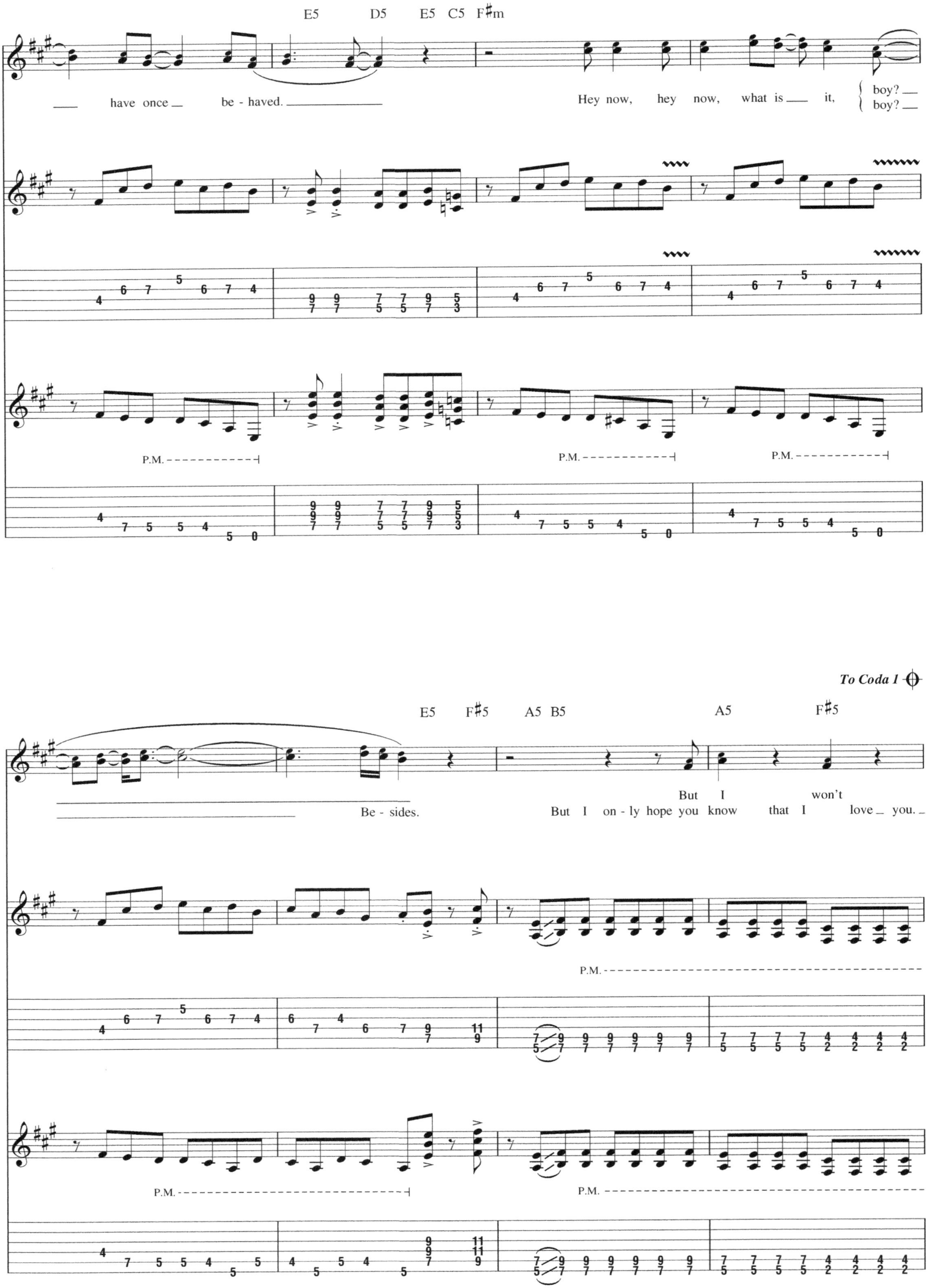

To Coda I

E5 F♯5 A5 B5 A5 F♯5

But I won't

Be - sides. But I on - ly hope you know that I love you.

P.M.

P.M.

P.M.

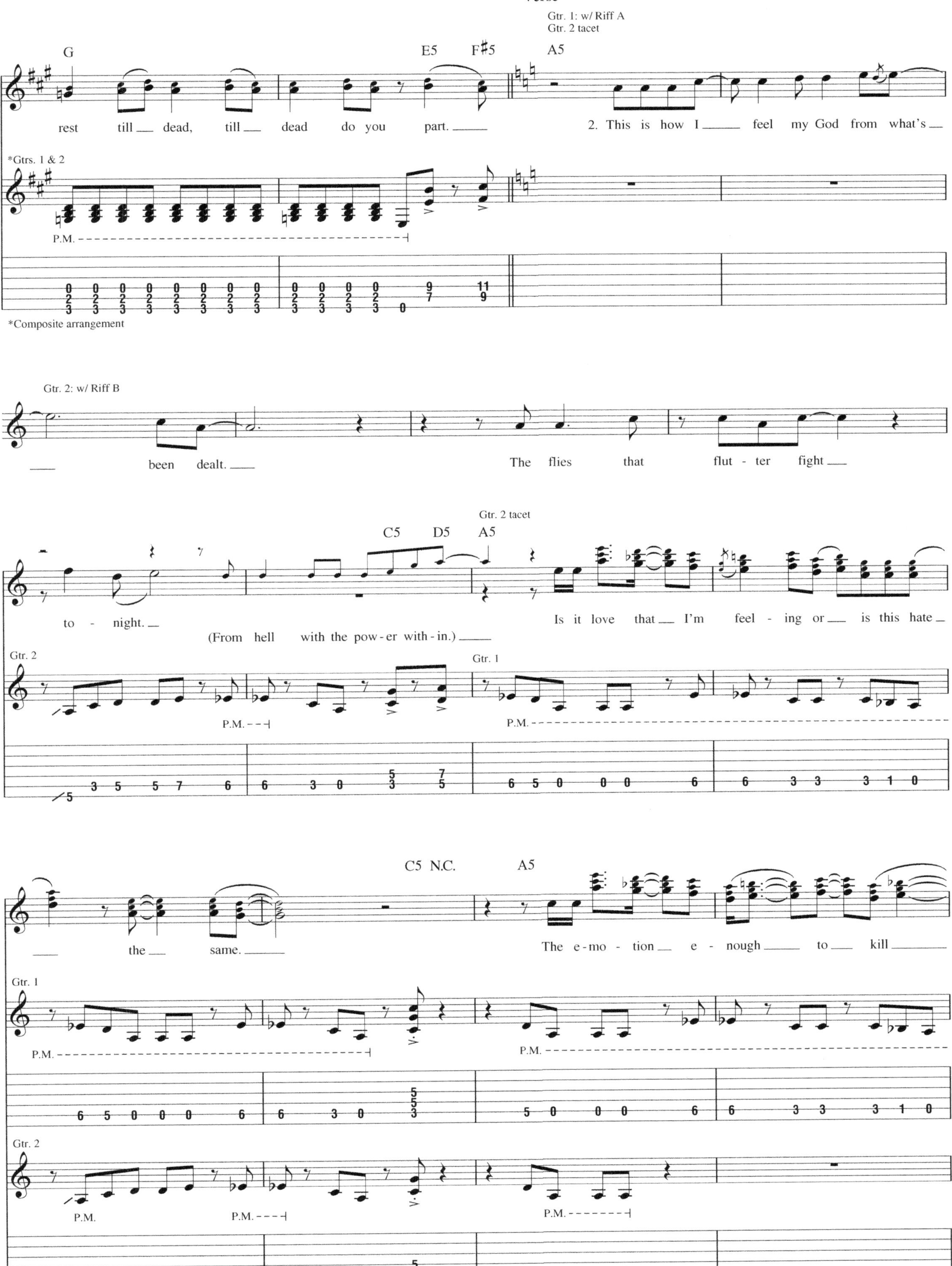
Verse
Gtr. 1: w/ Riff A
Gtr. 2 tacet
G
E5
F♯5
A5
rest till dead, till dead do you part.
2. This is how I feel my God from what's
*Gtrs. 1 & 2
P.M.
*Composite arrangement
Gtr. 2: w/ Riff B
been dealt.
The flies that flut - ter fight
C5
D5
A5
Gtr. 2 tacet
to - night.
(From hell with the pow - er with - in.)
Is it love that I'm feel - ing or is this hate
Gtr. 2
P.M.
Gtr. 1
P.M.
C5
N.C.
A5
the same.
The e - mo - tion e - nough to kill
Gtr. 1
P.M.
P.M.
Gtr. 2
P.M.
P.M.
P.M.

D.S. al Coda 1

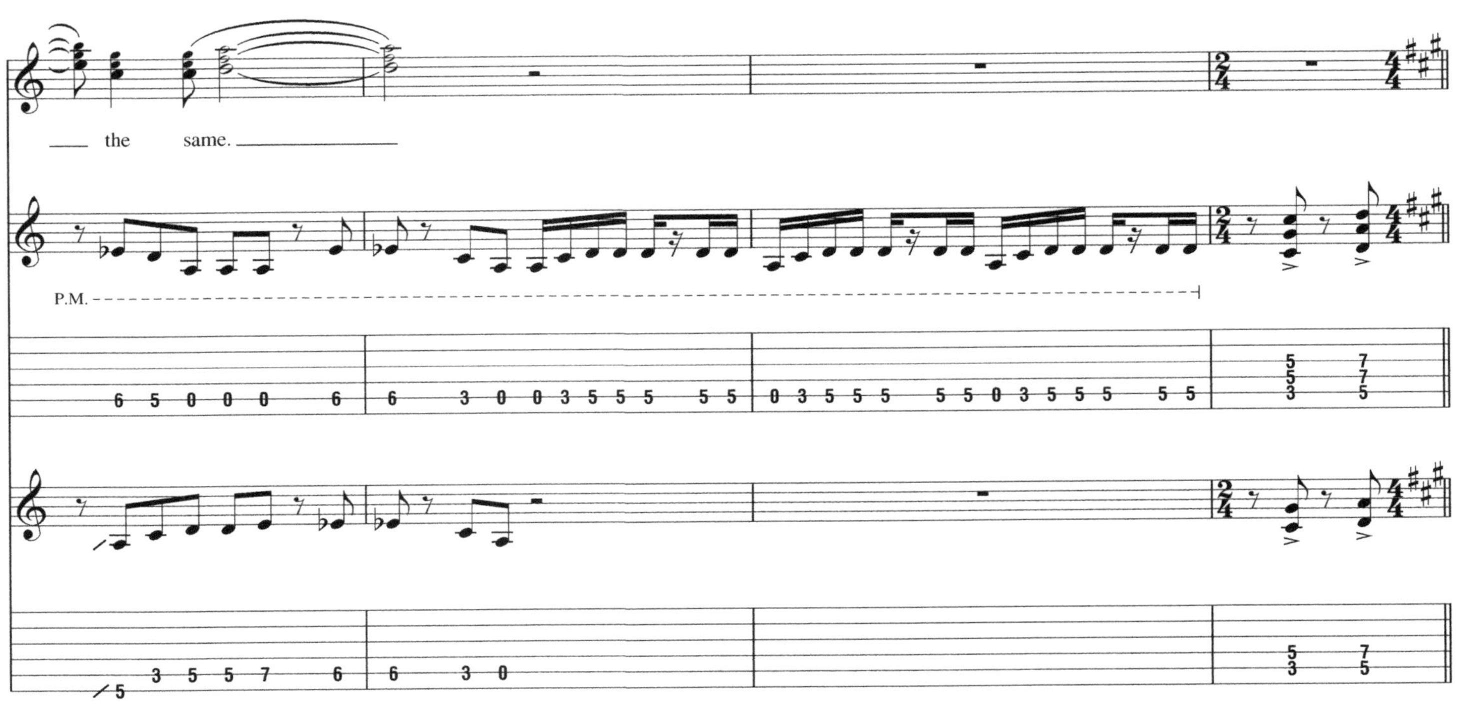
C5
D5
the
same.
P.M.

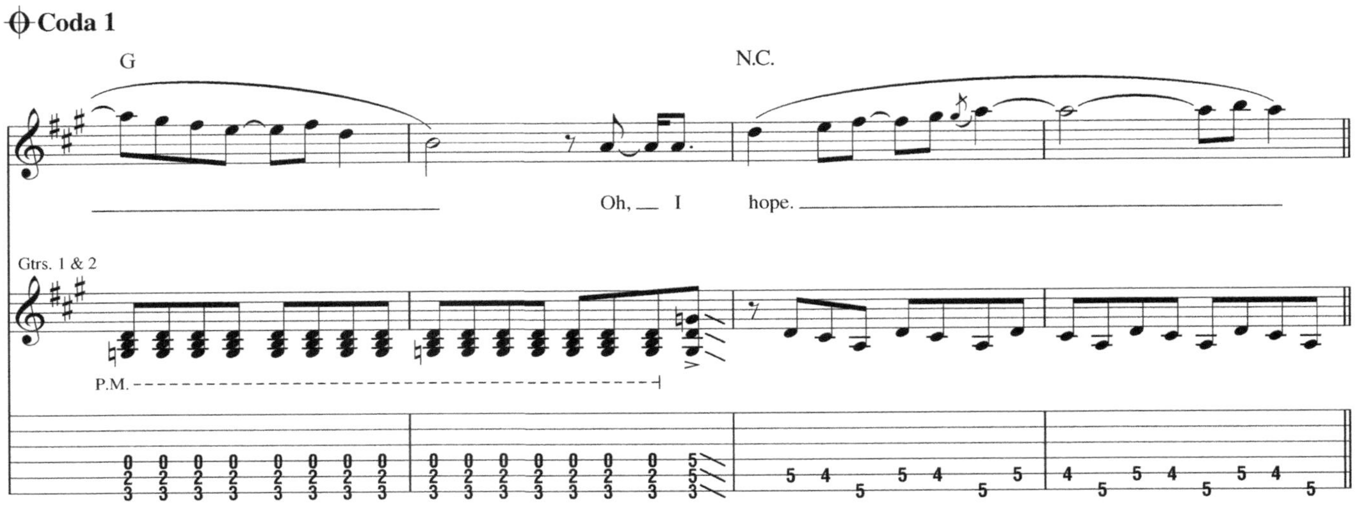
Coda 1
G
N.C.
Oh, I
hope.
Gtrs. 1 & 2
P.M.

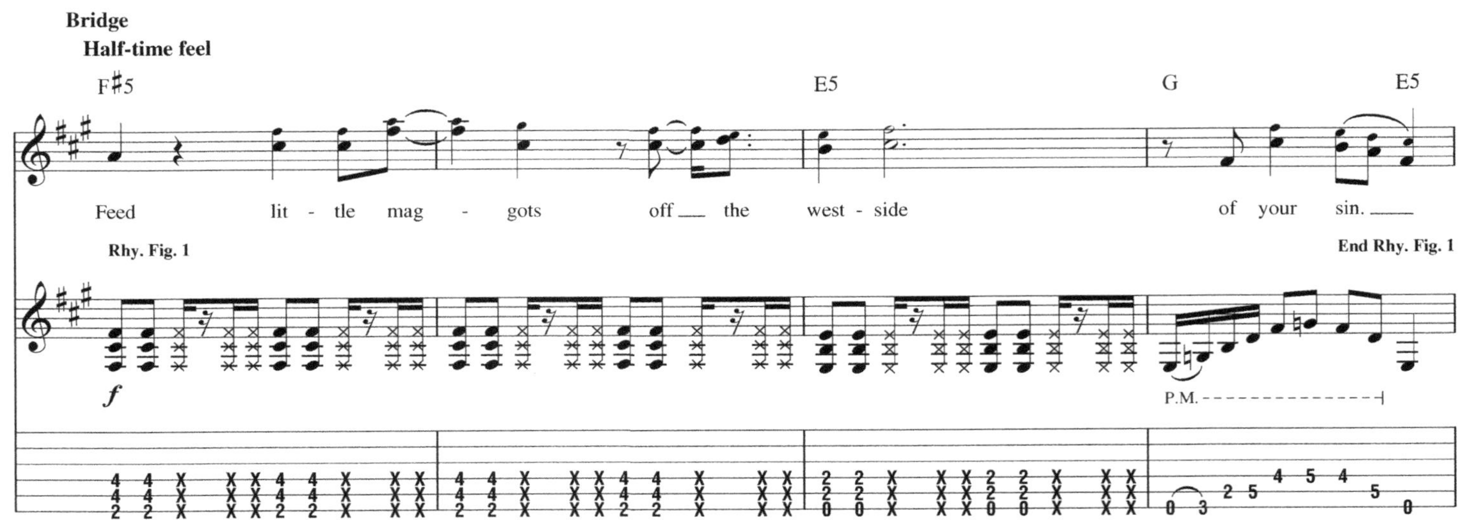
Bridge
Half-time feel
F♯5
E5
G
E5
Feed
lit - tle mag - gots
off the
west - side
of your
sin.
Rhy. Fig. 1
End Rhy. Fig. 1
f
P.M.

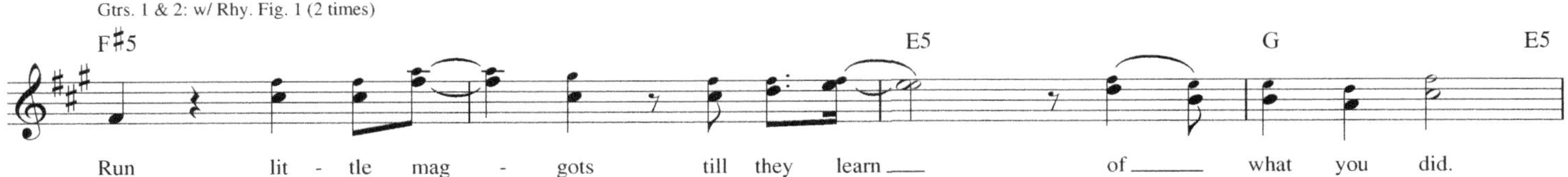

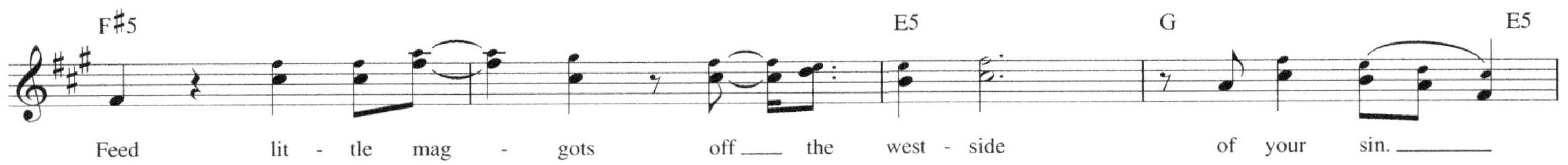

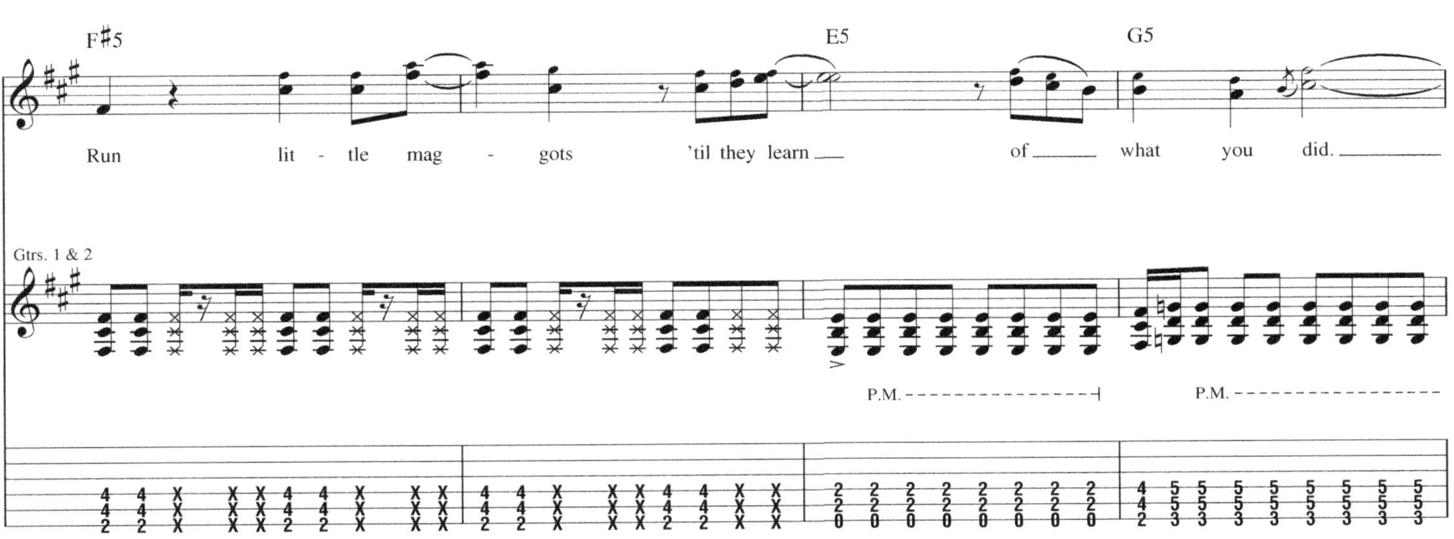

Interlude

End half-time feel

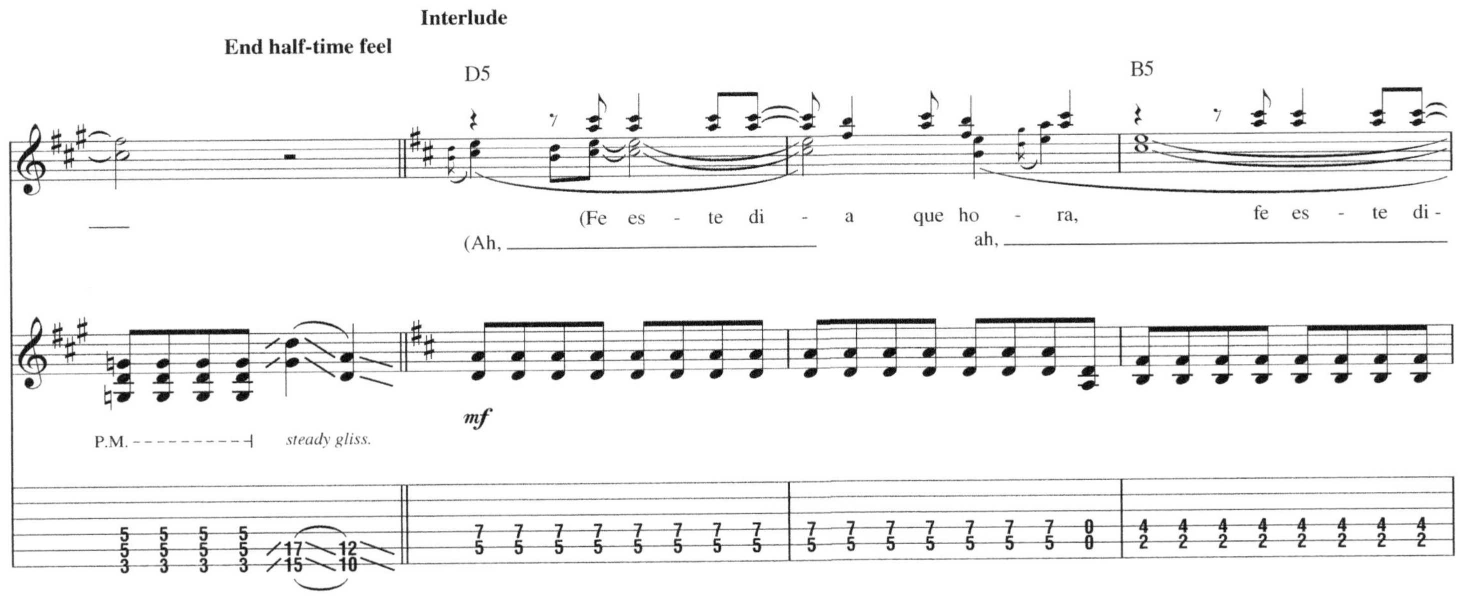

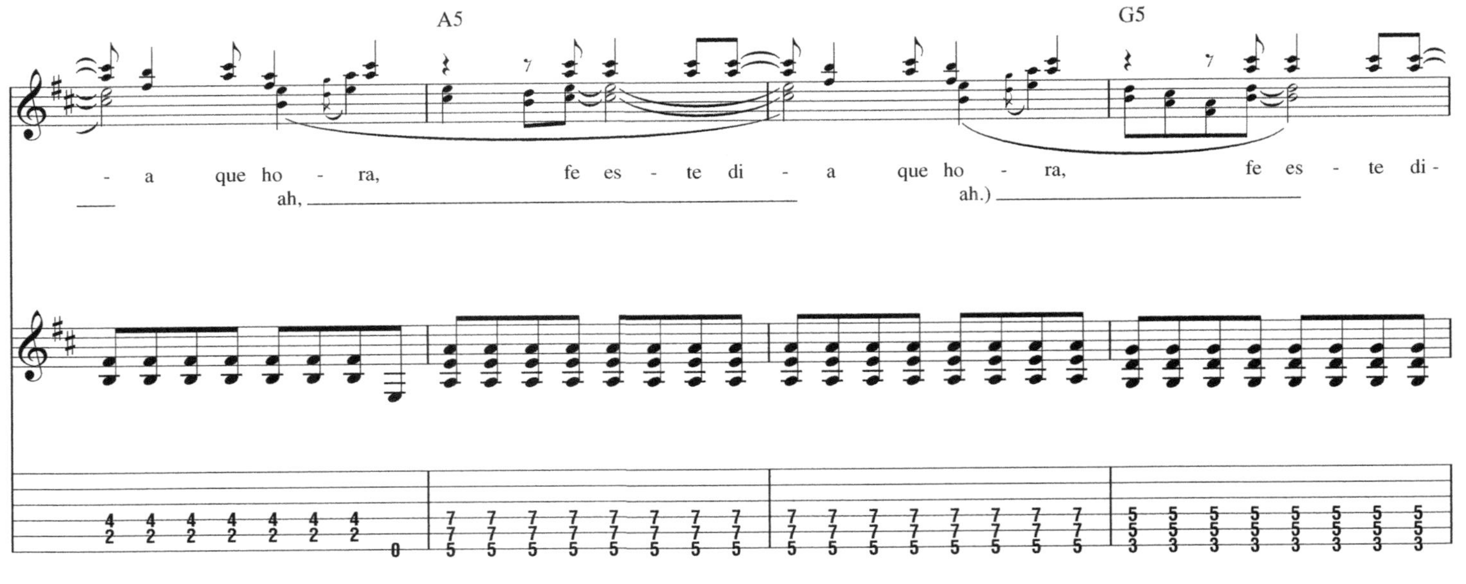
A5
G5
- a que ho - ra, fe es - te di - a que ho - ra, fe es - te di -
ah, ah.)

Bridge

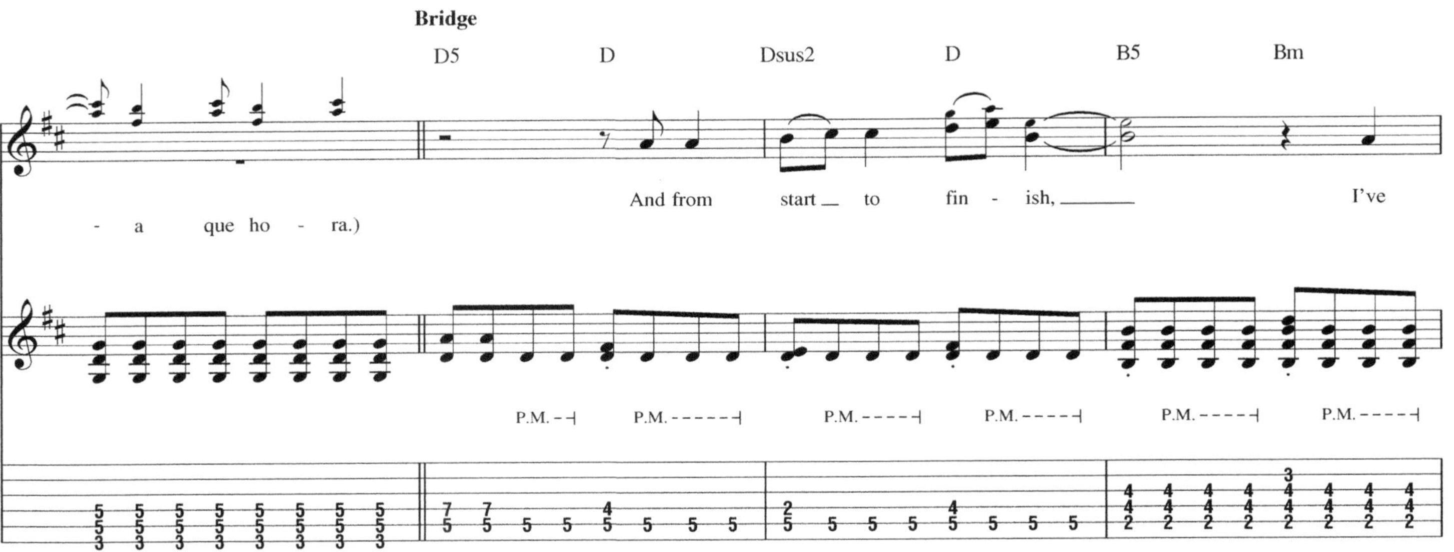
D5
D
Dsus2
D
B5
Bm
And from start to fin - ish, I've
- a que ho - ra.)
P.M.

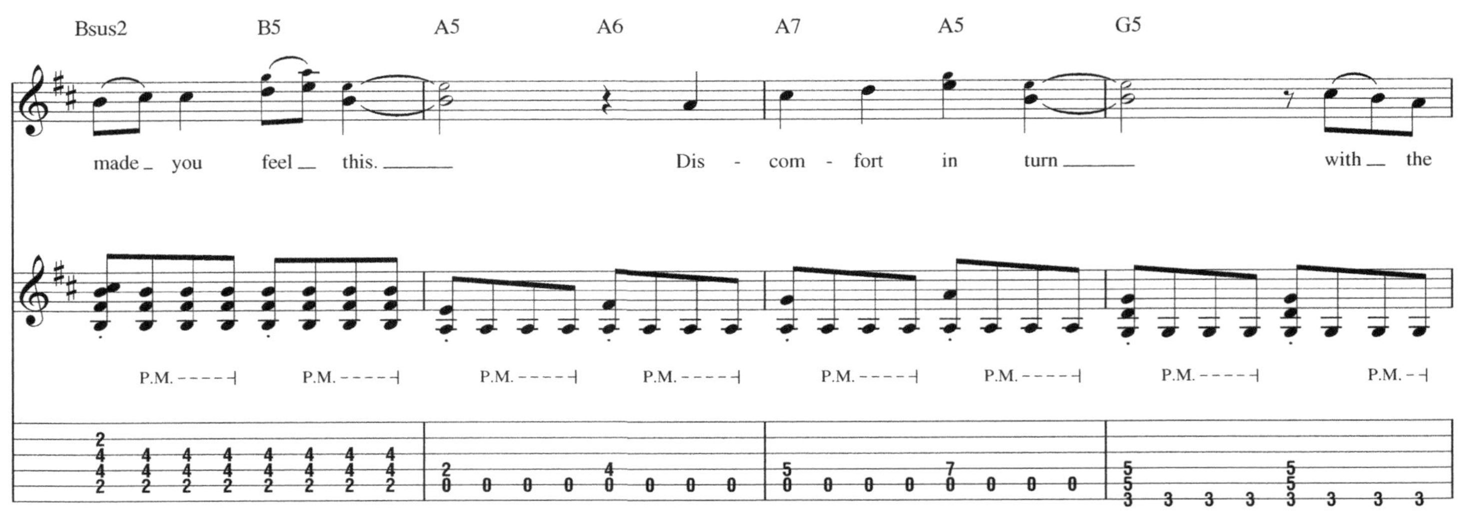
Bsus2
B5
A5
A6
A7
A5
G5
made you feel this. Dis - com - fort in turn with the
P.M.

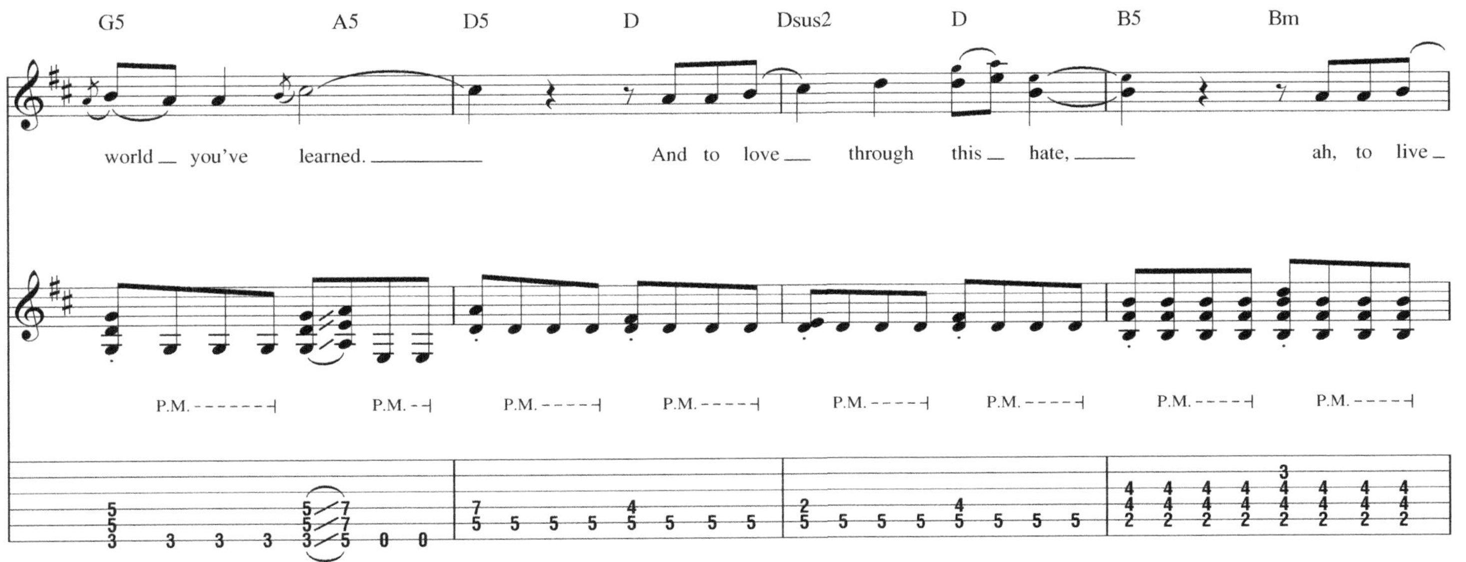

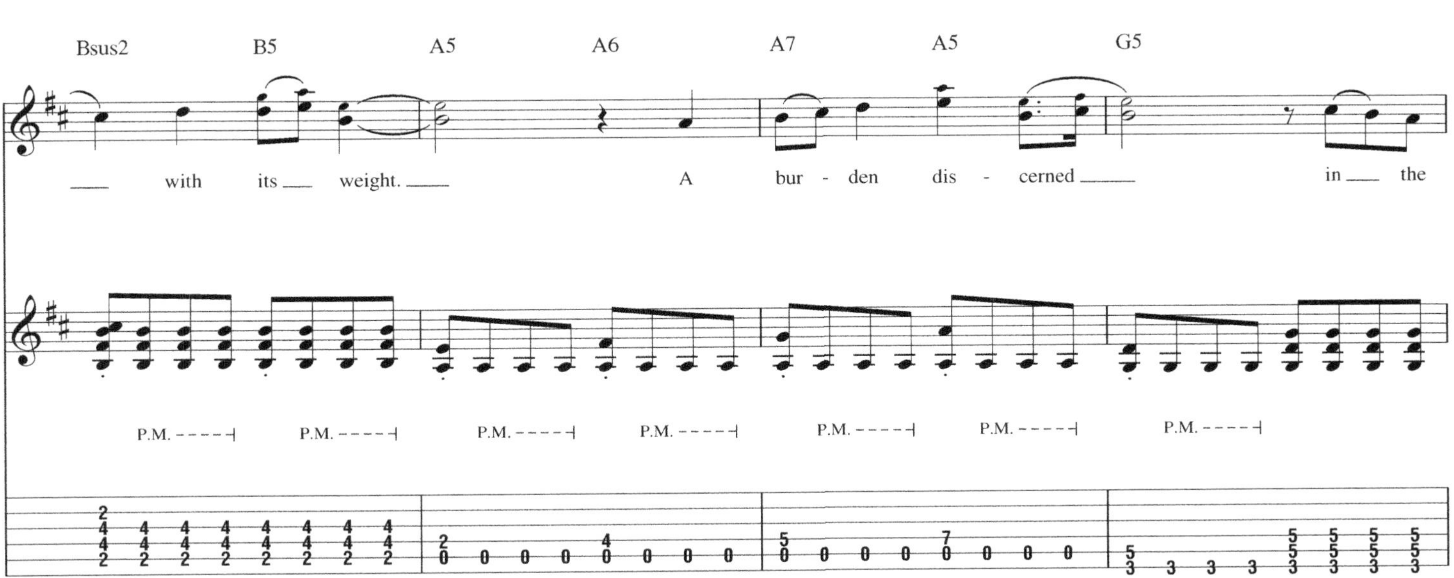

Half-time feel

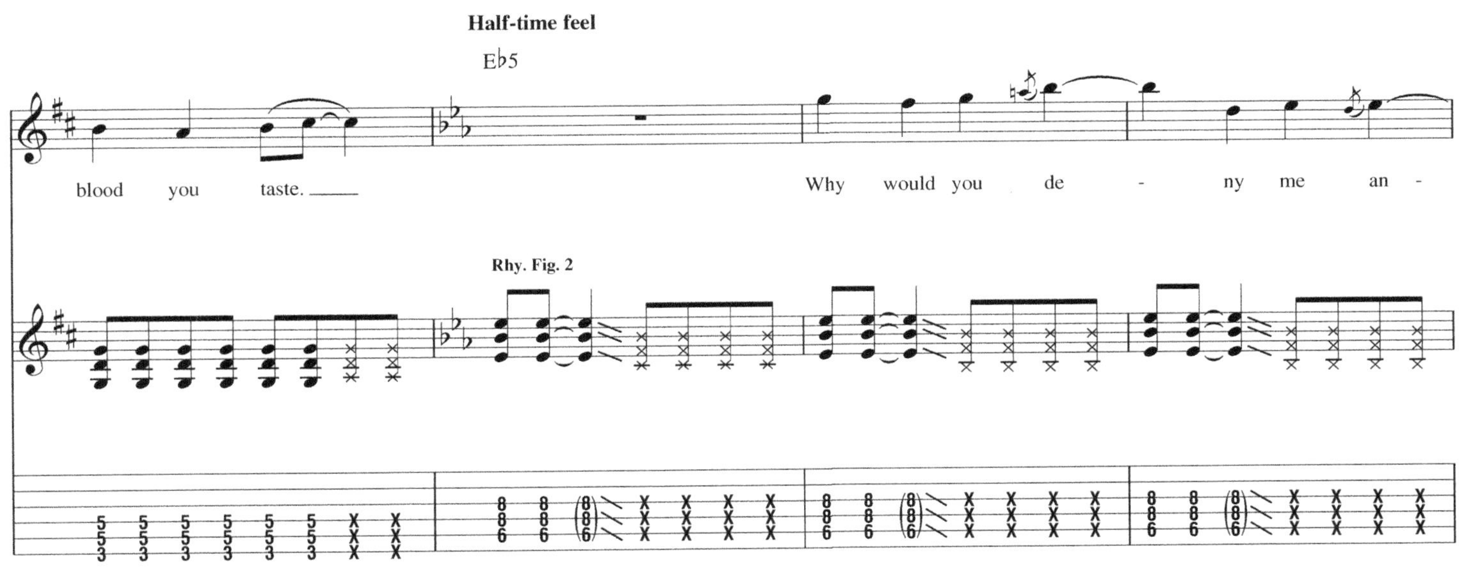

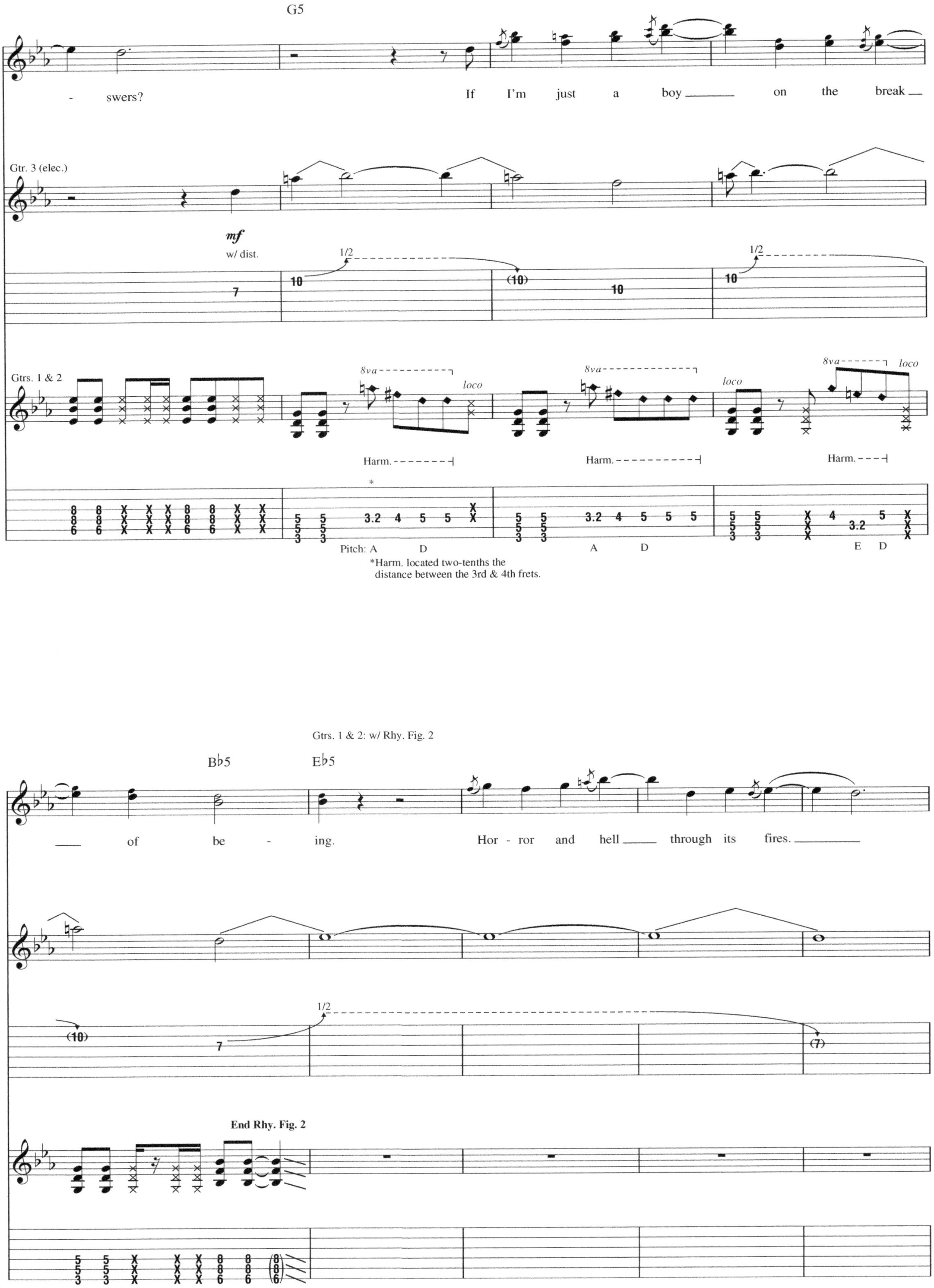

G5

-swers? If I'm just a boy on the break

Gtr. 3 (elec.)

mf
w/ dist.

1/2   1/2

Gtrs. 1 & 2

8va loco 8va loco 8va loco

Harm. Harm. Harm.

Pitch: A D A D E D

*Harm. located two-tenths the distance between the 3rd & 4th frets.

Gtrs. 1 & 2: w/ Rhy. Fig. 2

B♭5 E♭5

of be-ing. Hor-ror and hell through its fires.

1/2

End Rhy. Fig. 2

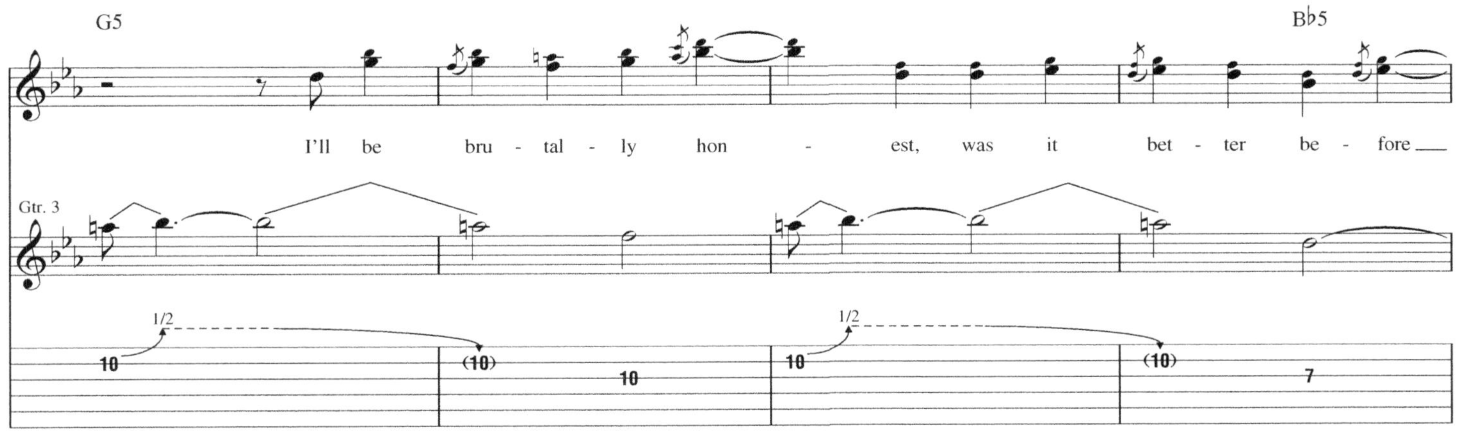
G5
B♭5
I'll be bru - tal - ly hon - est, was it bet - ter be - fore
Gtr. 3
1/2
10
(10)
10
1/2
10
(10)
7

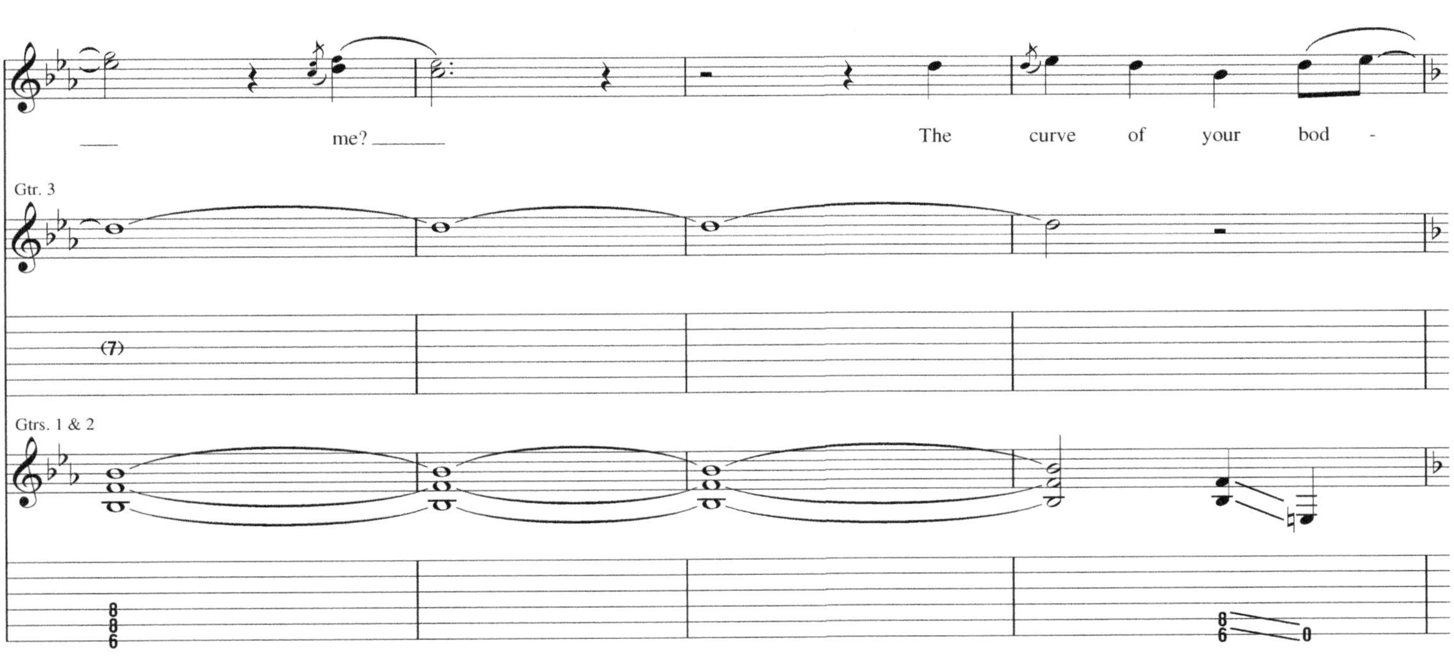
me?
The curve of your bod -
Gtr. 3
(7)
Gtrs. 1 & 2
8
8
6
8
6
0

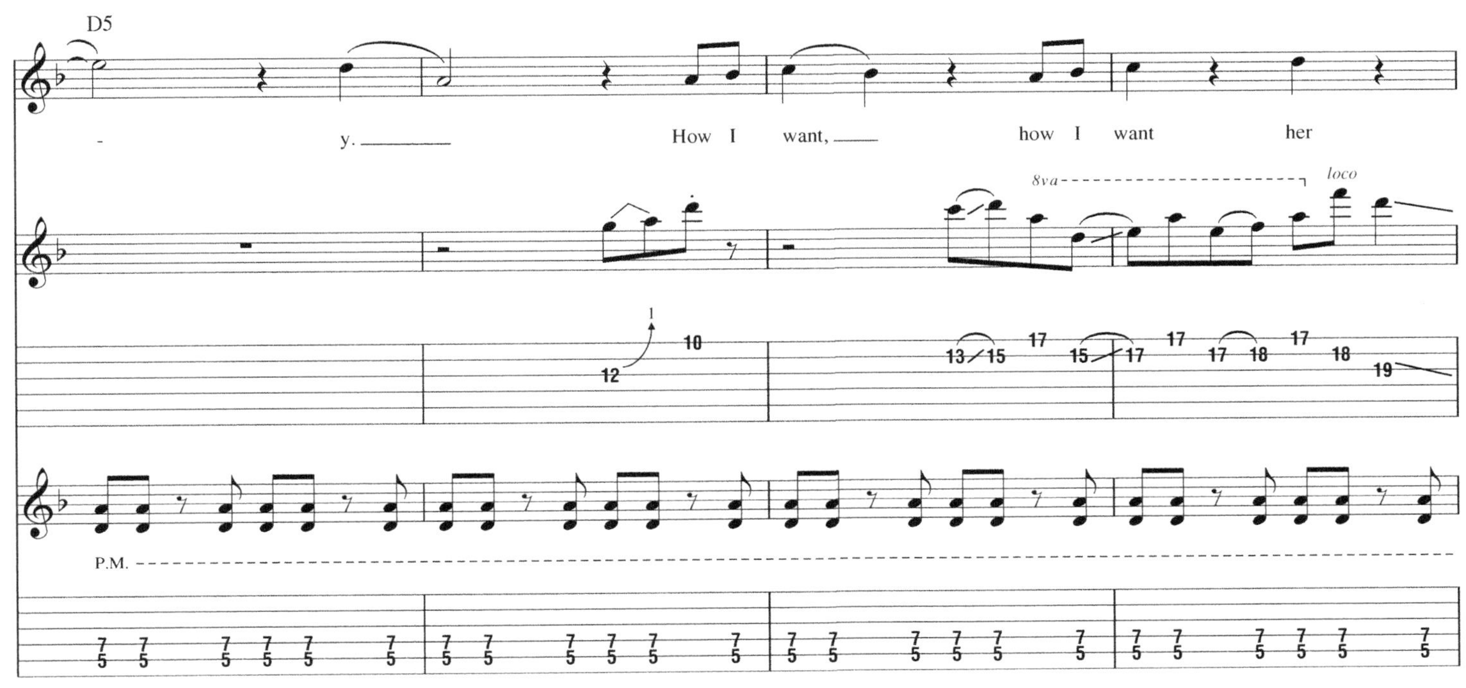
D5
- y.
How I want,
how I want her
8va
loco
1
12
10
13
15
17
15
17
17
17
18
17
18
19
P.M.

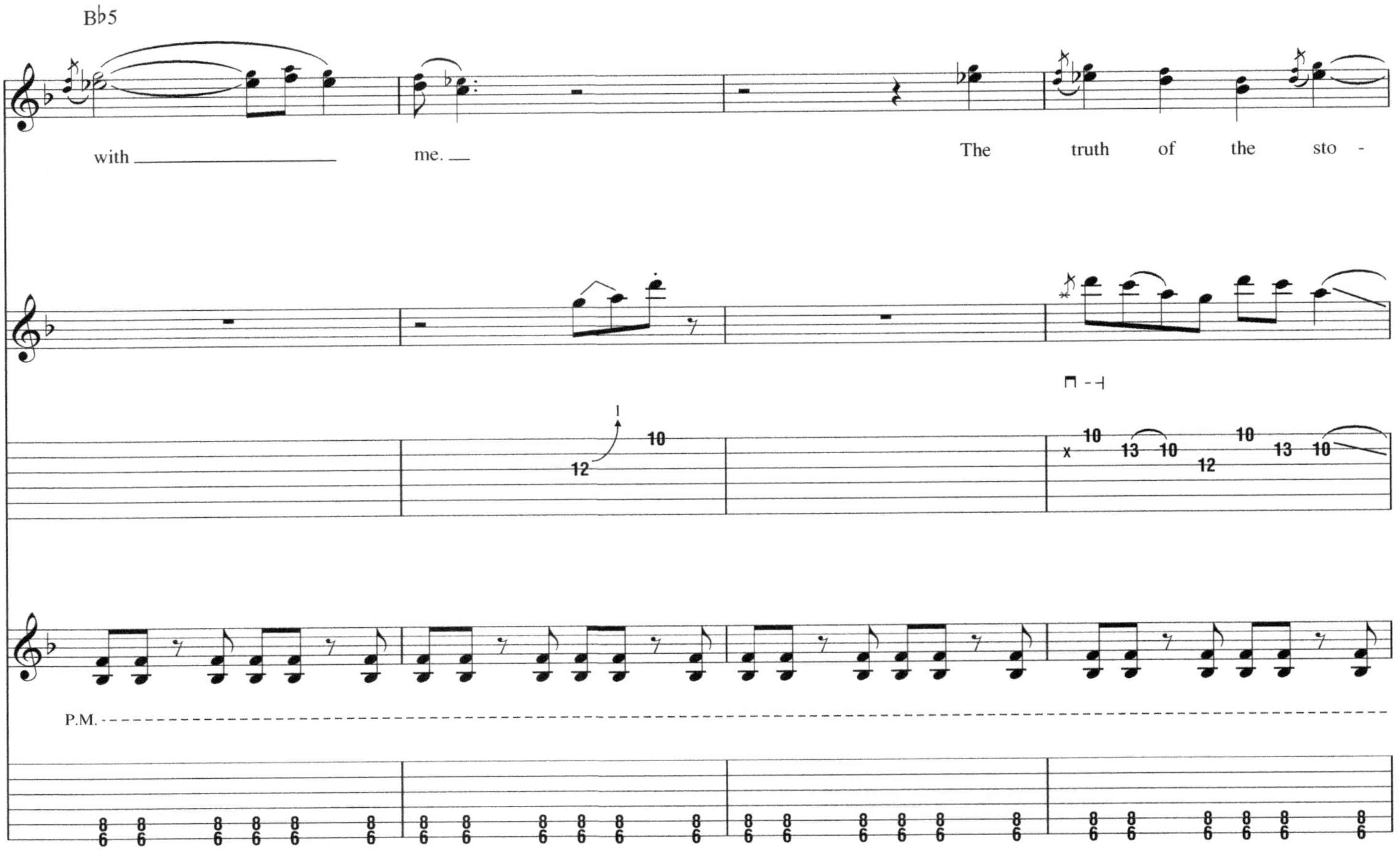

B♭5

with ___ me. ___ The truth of the sto -

P.M.

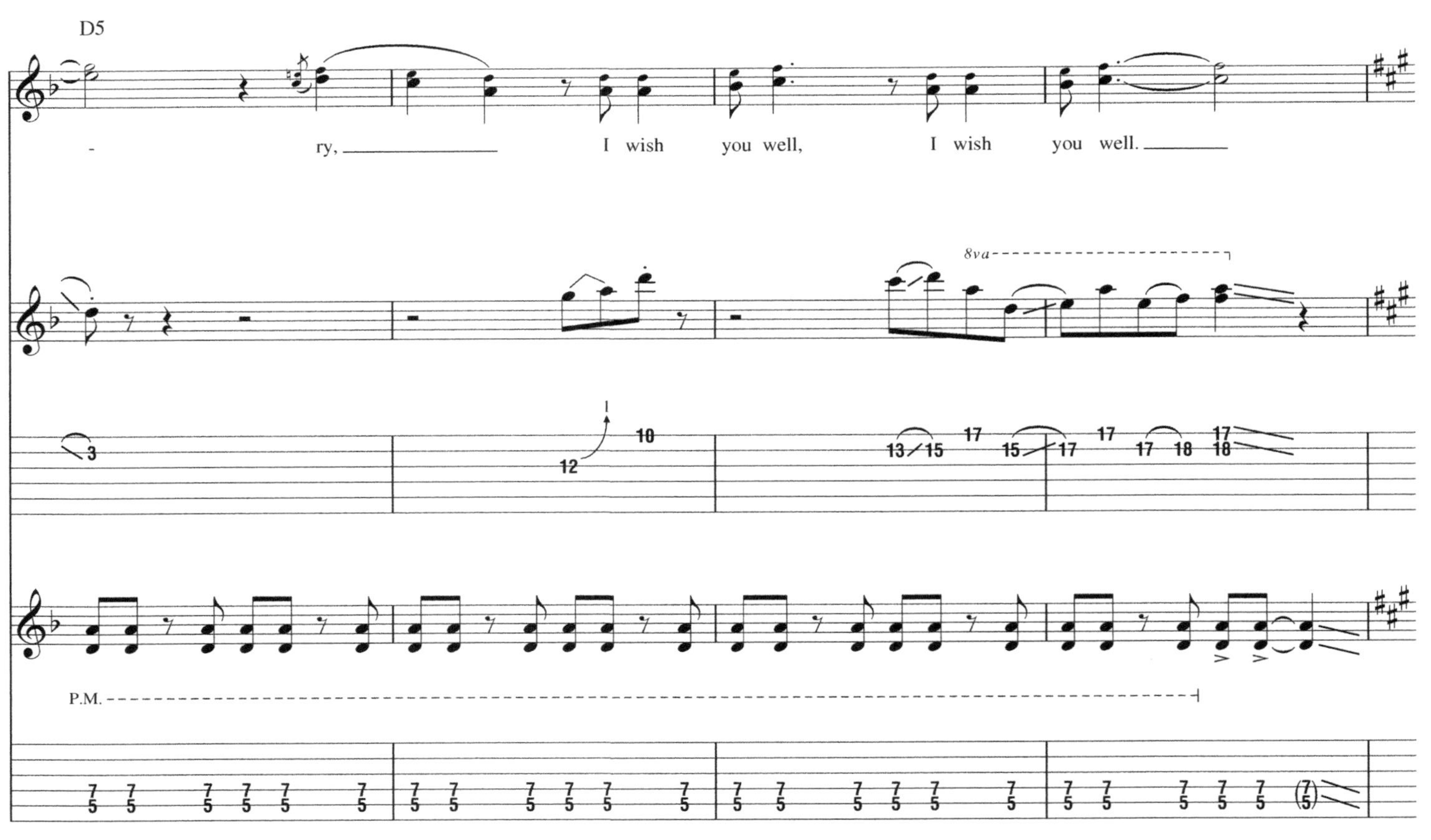

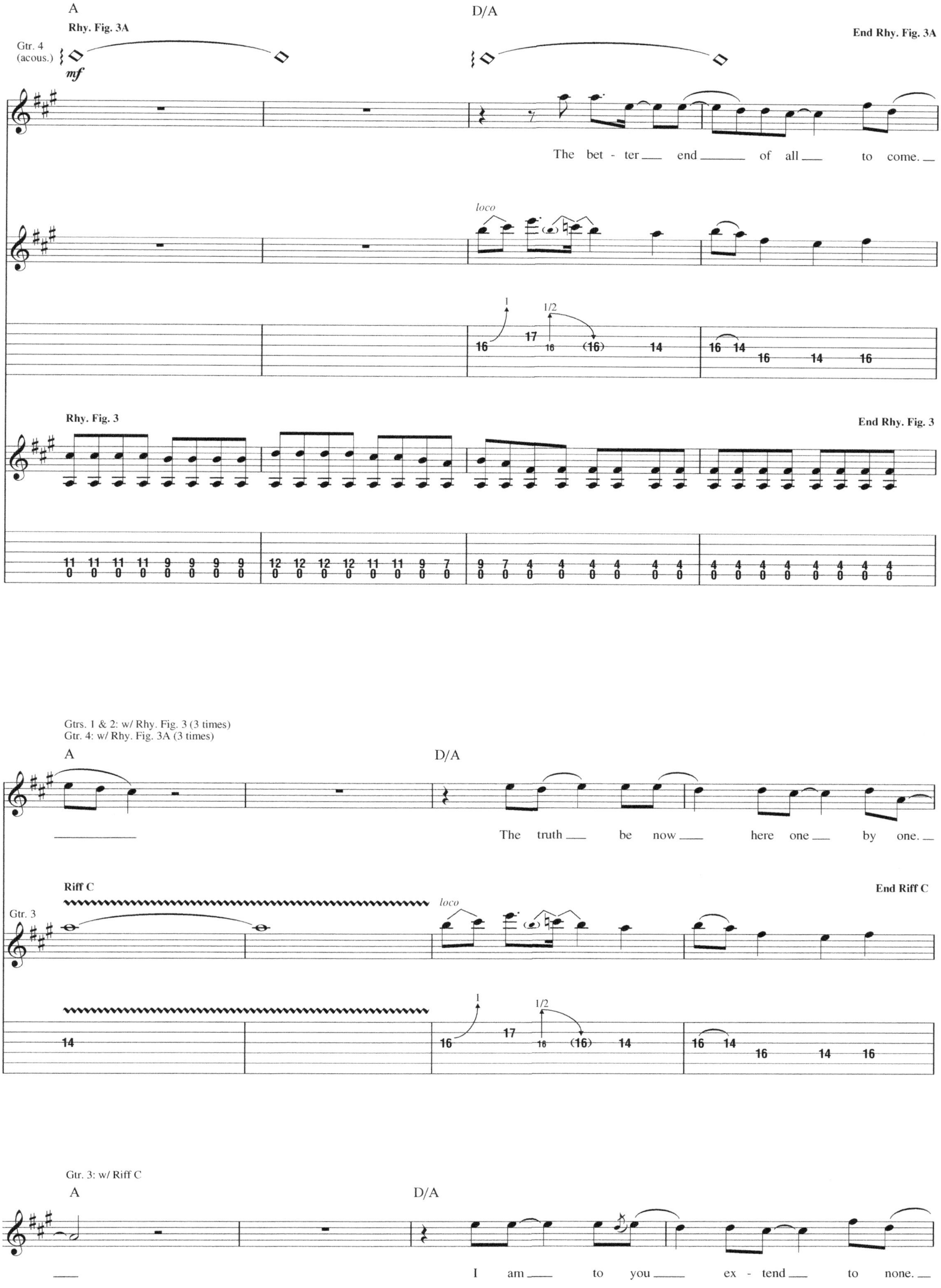

A D/A

Rhy. Fig. 3A

Gtr. 4 (acous.)

mf

End Rhy. Fig. 3A

The bet - ter end of all to come.

loco

Rhy. Fig. 3

End Rhy. Fig. 3

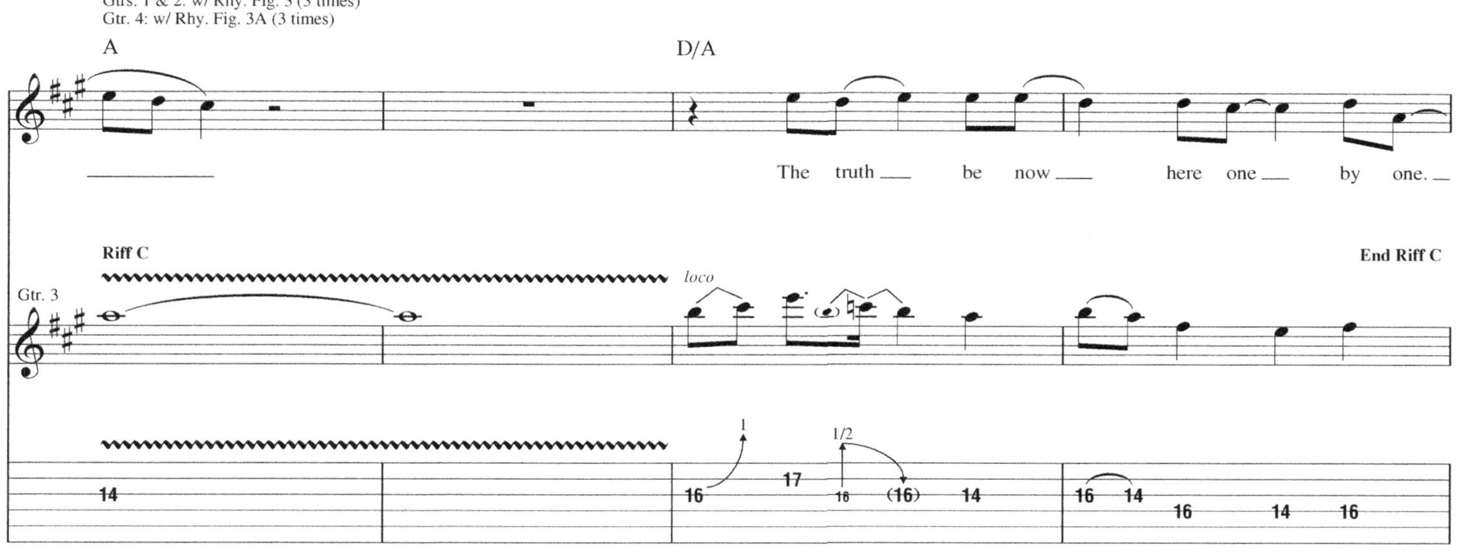

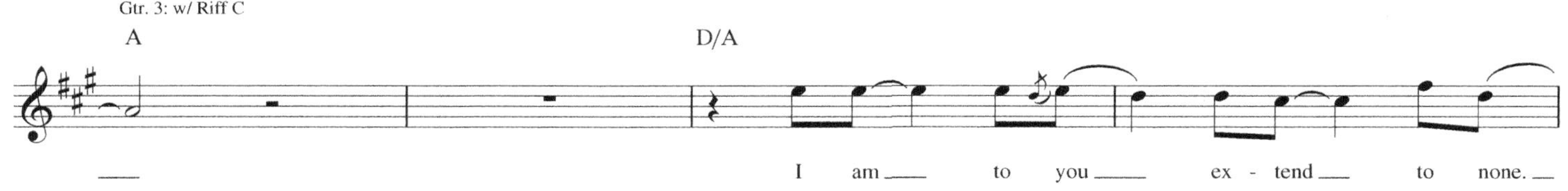

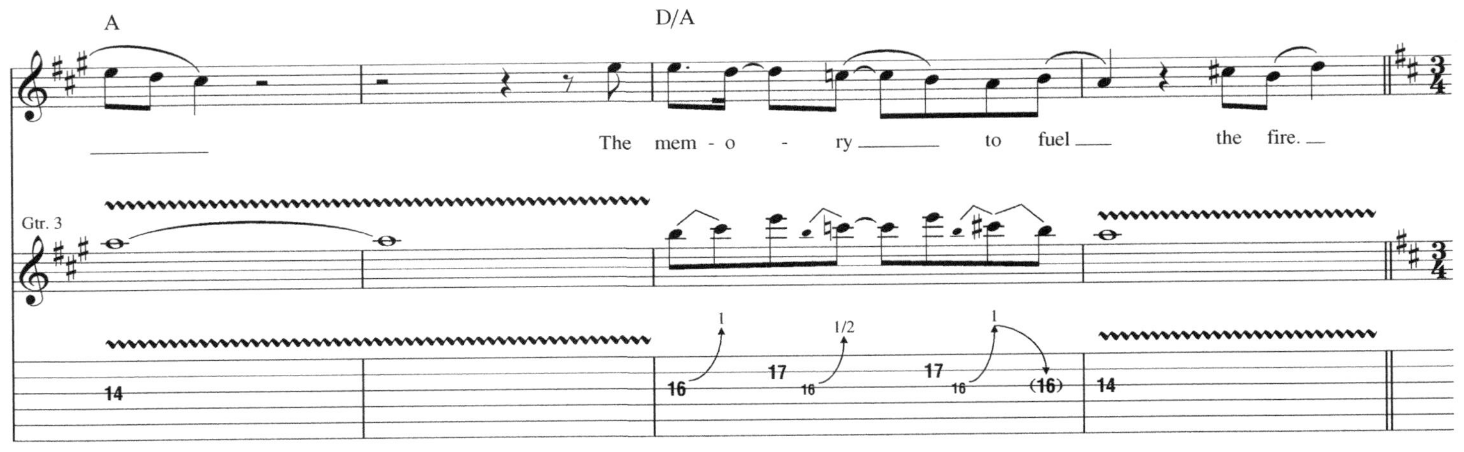

Guitar Solo

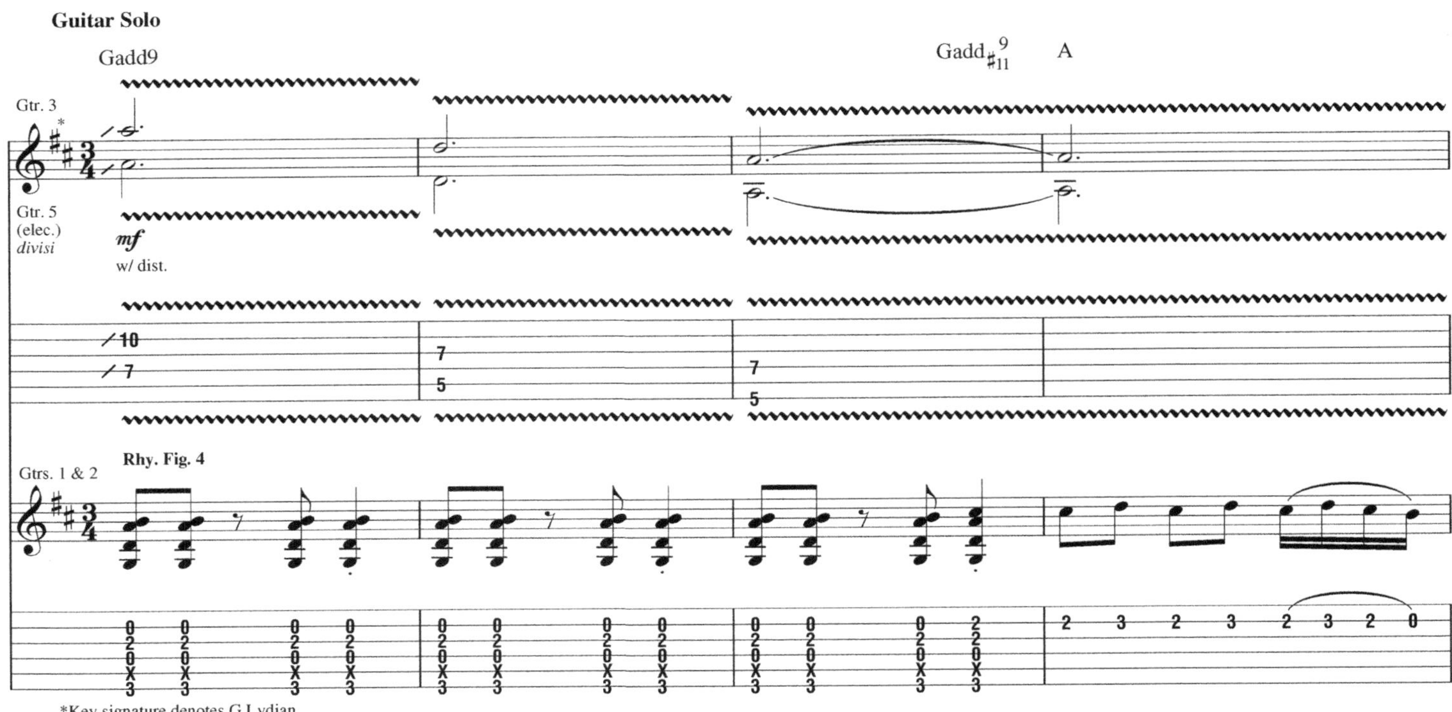

*Key signature denotes G Lydian.

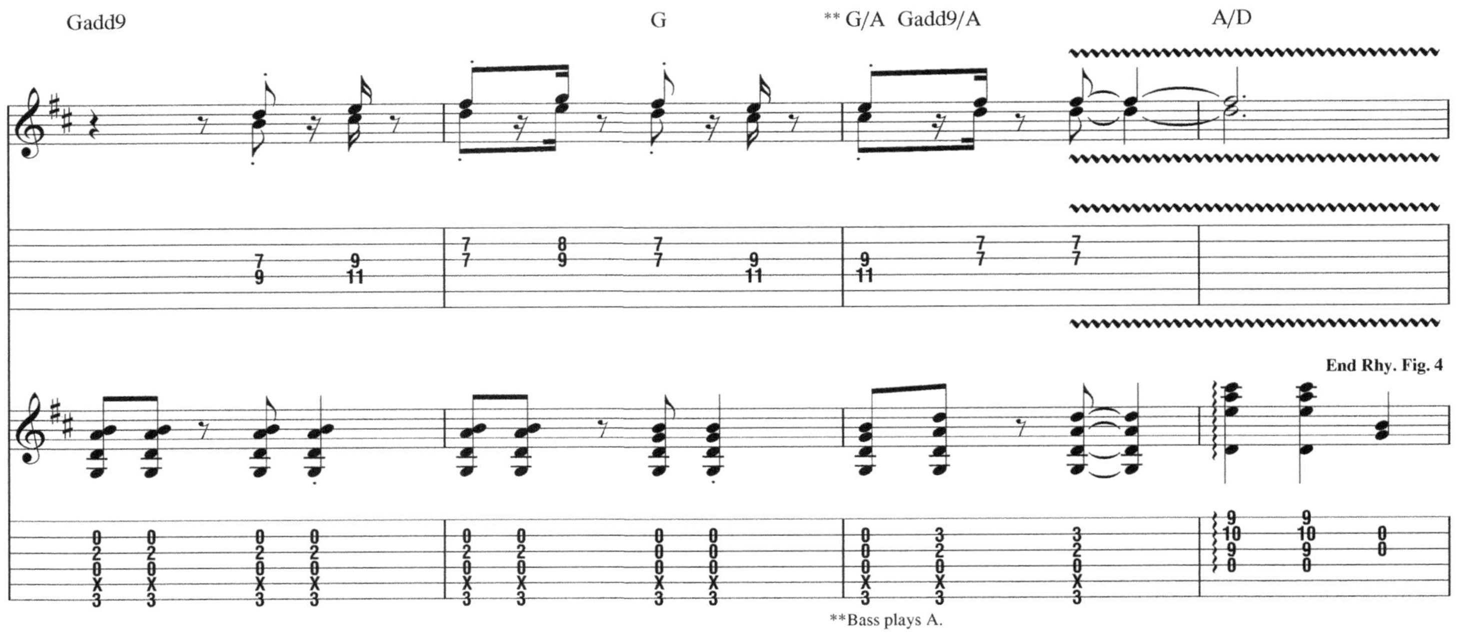

**Bass plays A.

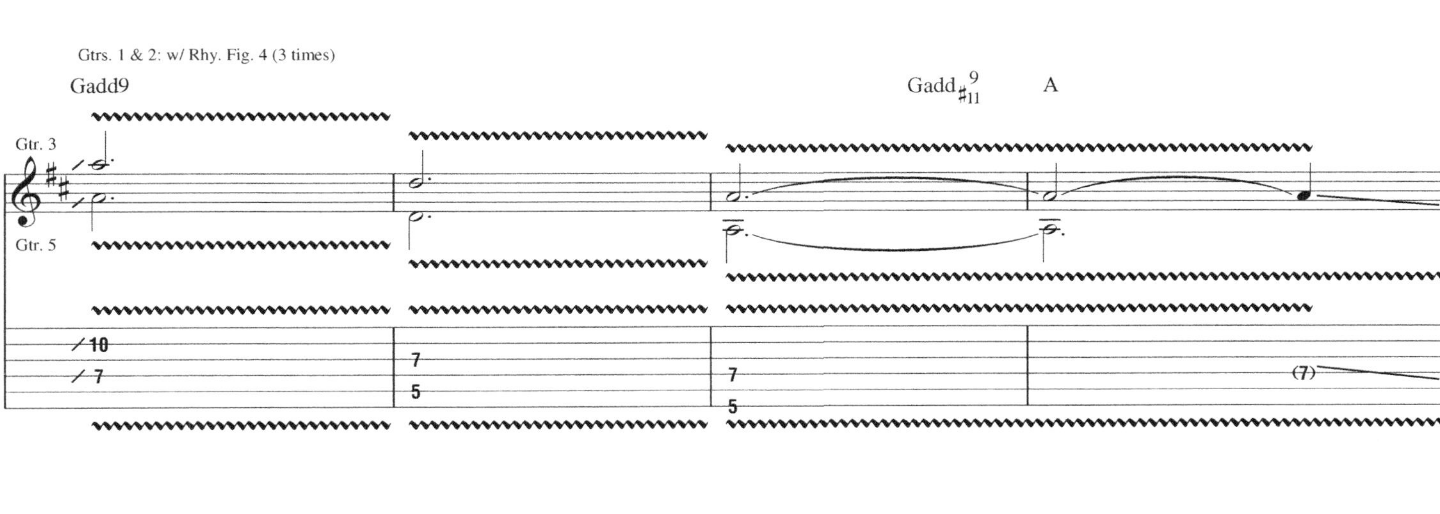
Gtrs. 1 & 2: w/ Rhy. Fig. 4 (3 times)
Gadd9
Gadd#11 9
A
Gtr. 3
Gtr. 5

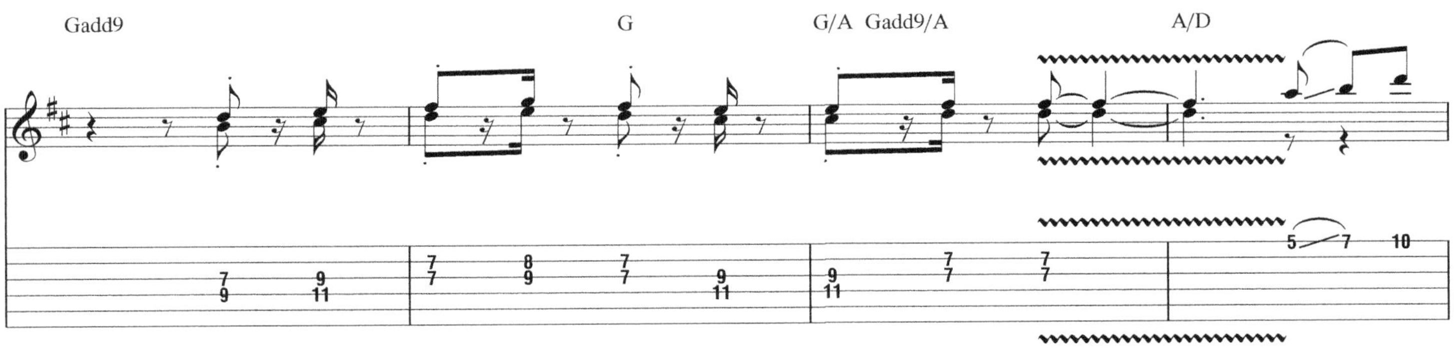
Gadd9
G
G/A Gadd9/A
A/D

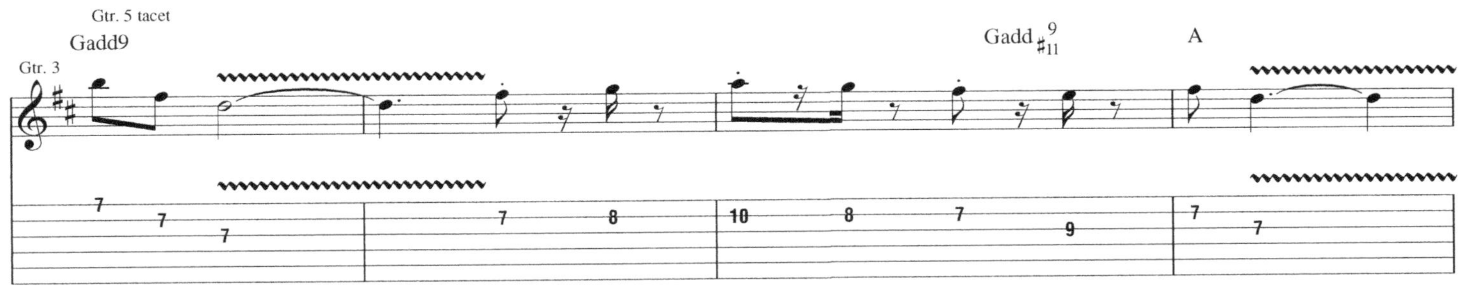
Gtr. 5 tacet
Gadd9
Gadd#11 9
A
Gtr. 3

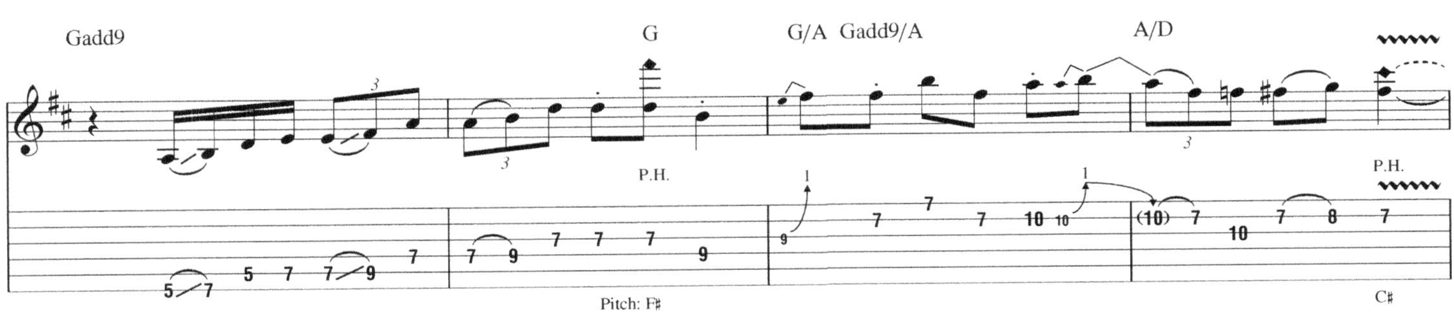
Gadd9
G
G/A Gadd9/A
A/D
P.H.
Pitch: F♯
C♯

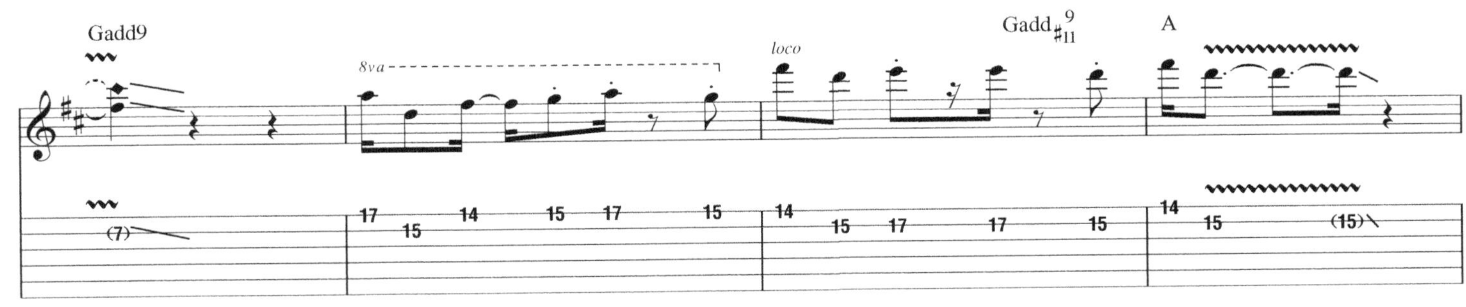
Gadd9
8va
loco
Gadd#11 9
A

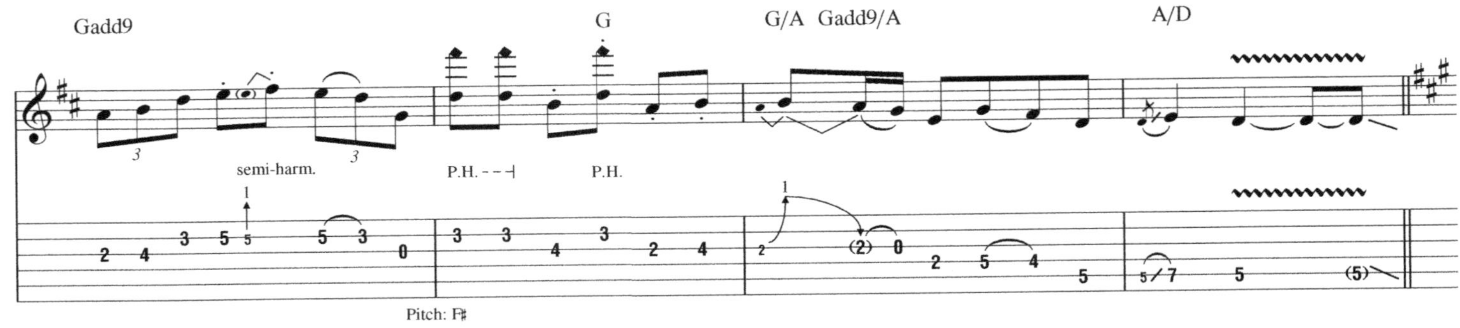
Gadd9
G
G/A Gadd9/A
A/D
semi-harm.
P.H.
P.H.
Pitch: F♯

Bridge

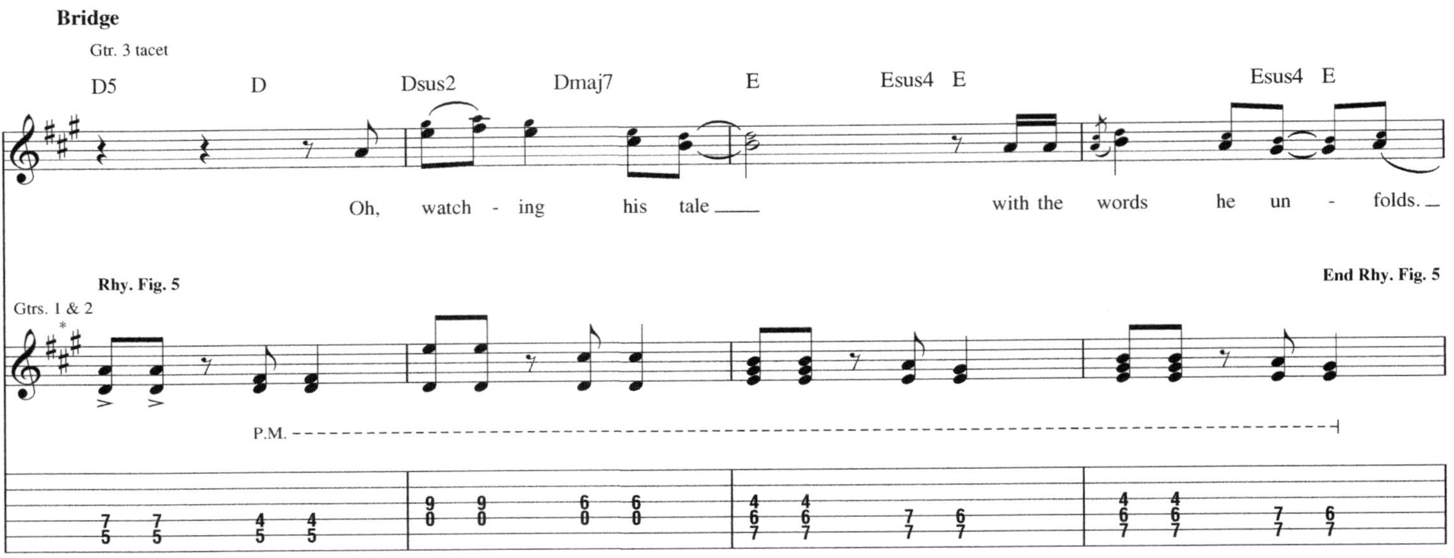
Gtr. 3 tacet
D5 D Dsus2 Dmaj7 E Esus4 E Esus4 E
Oh, watch - ing his tale with the words he un - folds.
Rhy. Fig. 5
End Rhy. Fig. 5
Gtrs. 1 & 2
P.M.
*Key signature denotes D Lydian.

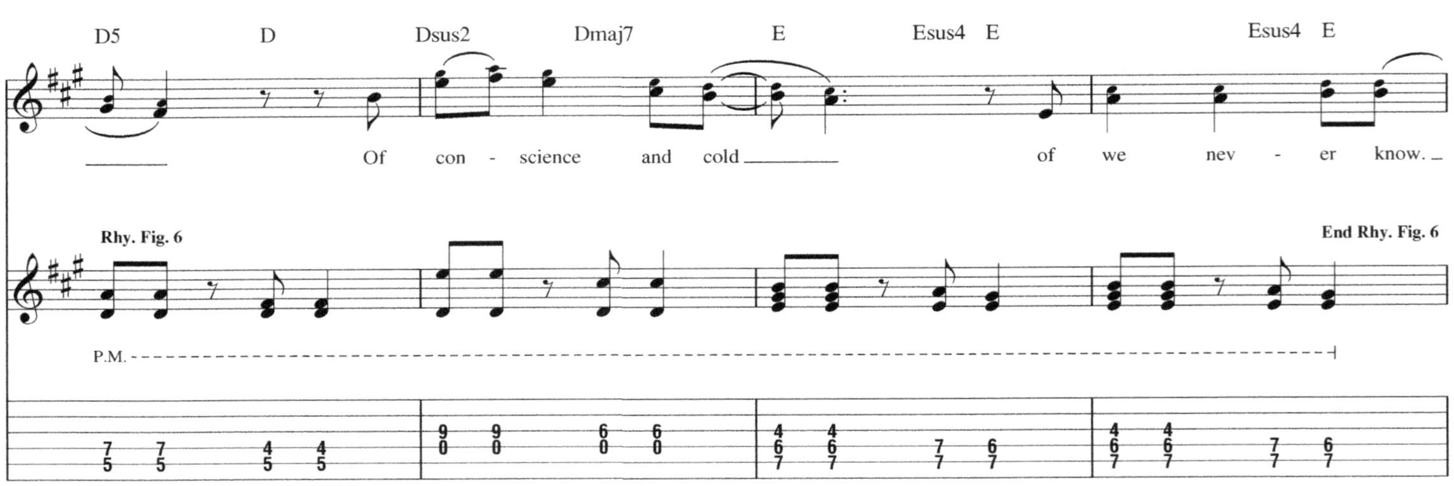
D5 D Dsus2 Dmaj7 E Esus4 E Esus4 E
Of con - science and cold of we nev - er know.
Rhy. Fig. 6
End Rhy. Fig. 6
P.M.

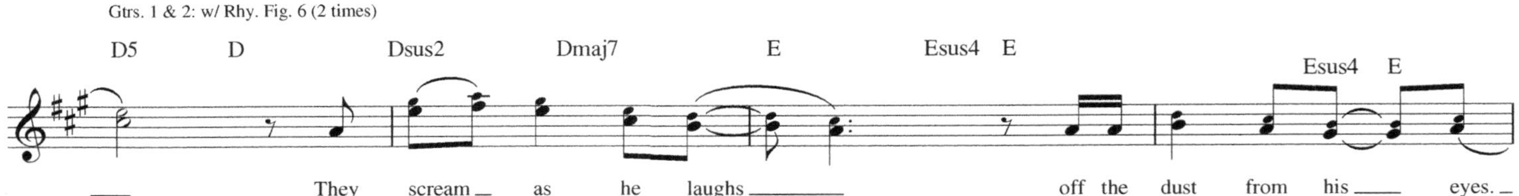
Gtrs. 1 & 2: w/ Rhy. Fig. 6 (2 times)
D5 D Dsus2 Dmaj7 E Esus4 E Esus4 E
They scream as he laughs off the dust from his eyes.

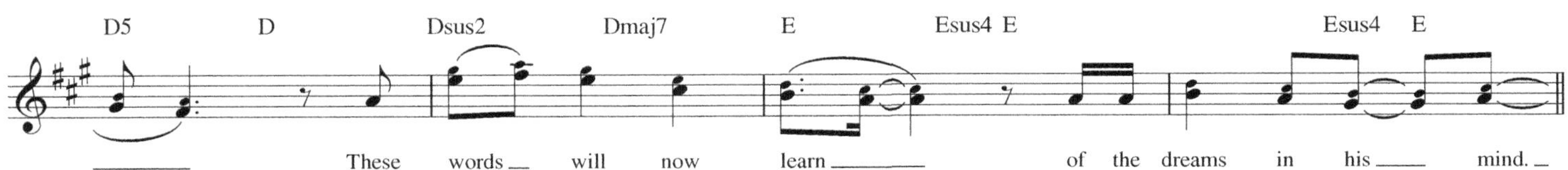
D5
D
Dsus2
Dmaj7
E
Esus4 E
Esus4 E
These words will now learn of the dreams in his mind.

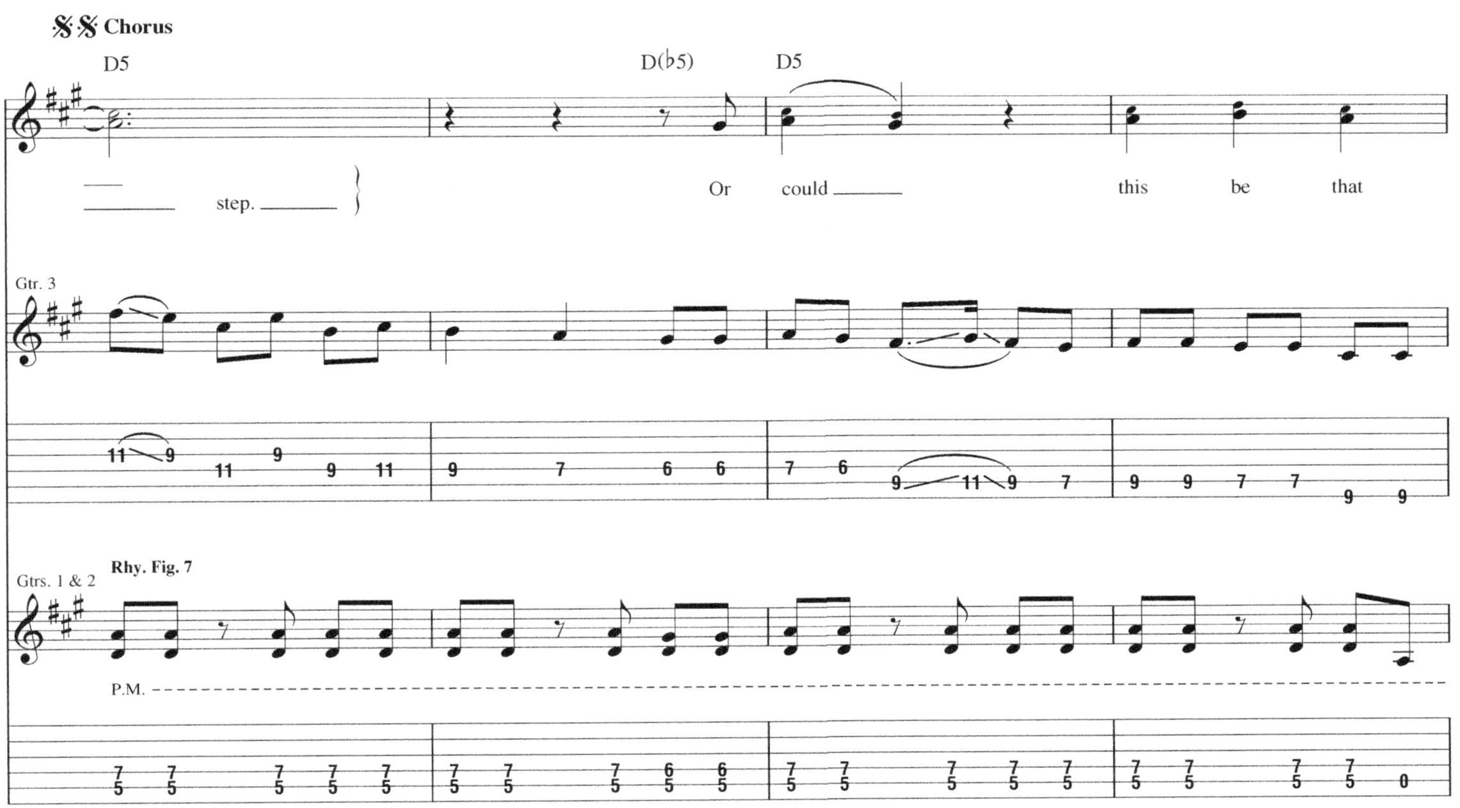
Chorus
D5
D(♭5)
D5
step.
Or could this be that
Gtr. 3
Gtrs. 1 & 2
Rhy. Fig. 7
P.M.

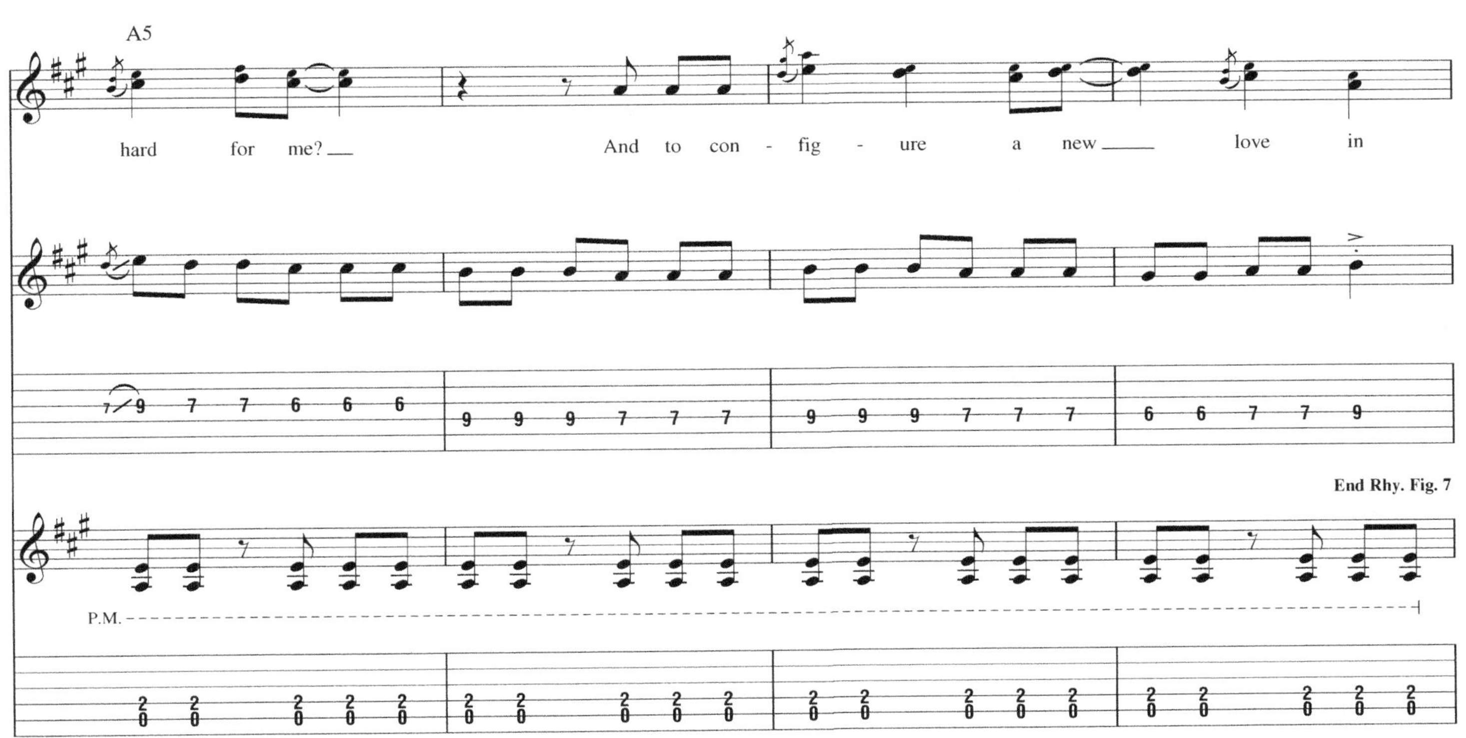
A5
hard for me?
And to con - fig - ure a new love in
End Rhy. Fig. 7
P.M.

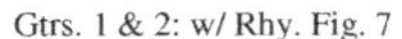
Gtrs. 1 & 2: w/ Rhy. Fig. 7

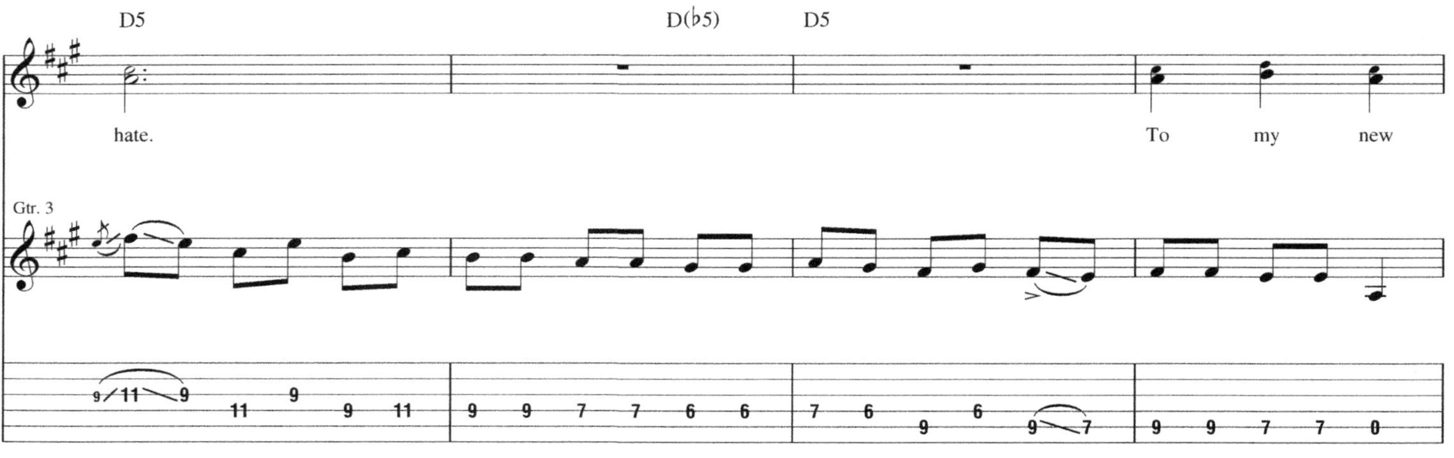
D5
D(♭5)
D5
hate.
To my new
Gtr. 3

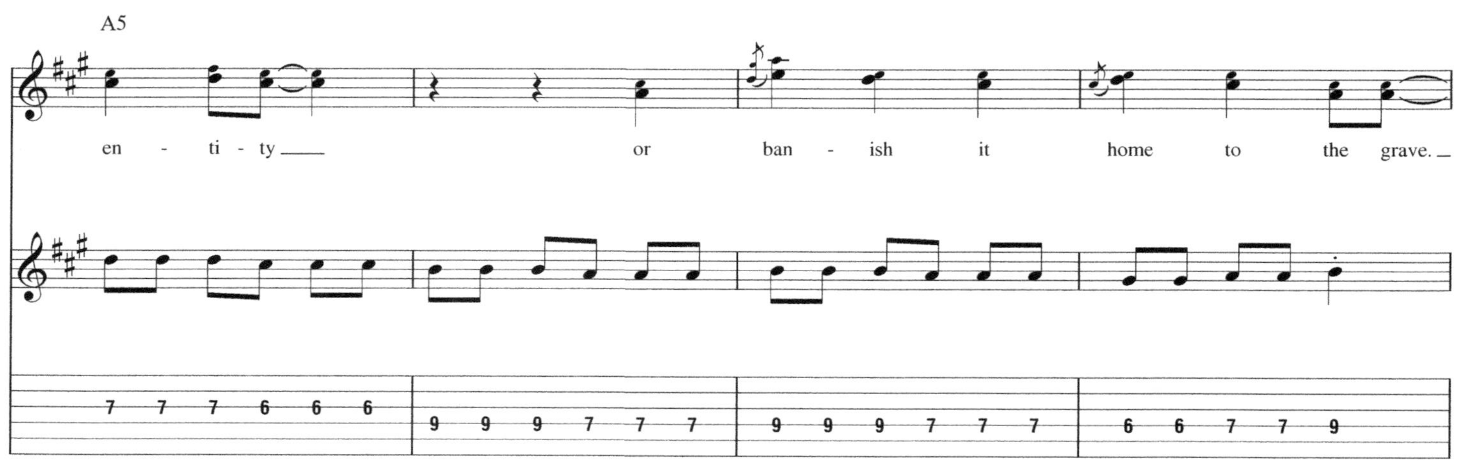
A5
en - ti - ty
or ban - ish it home to the grave.

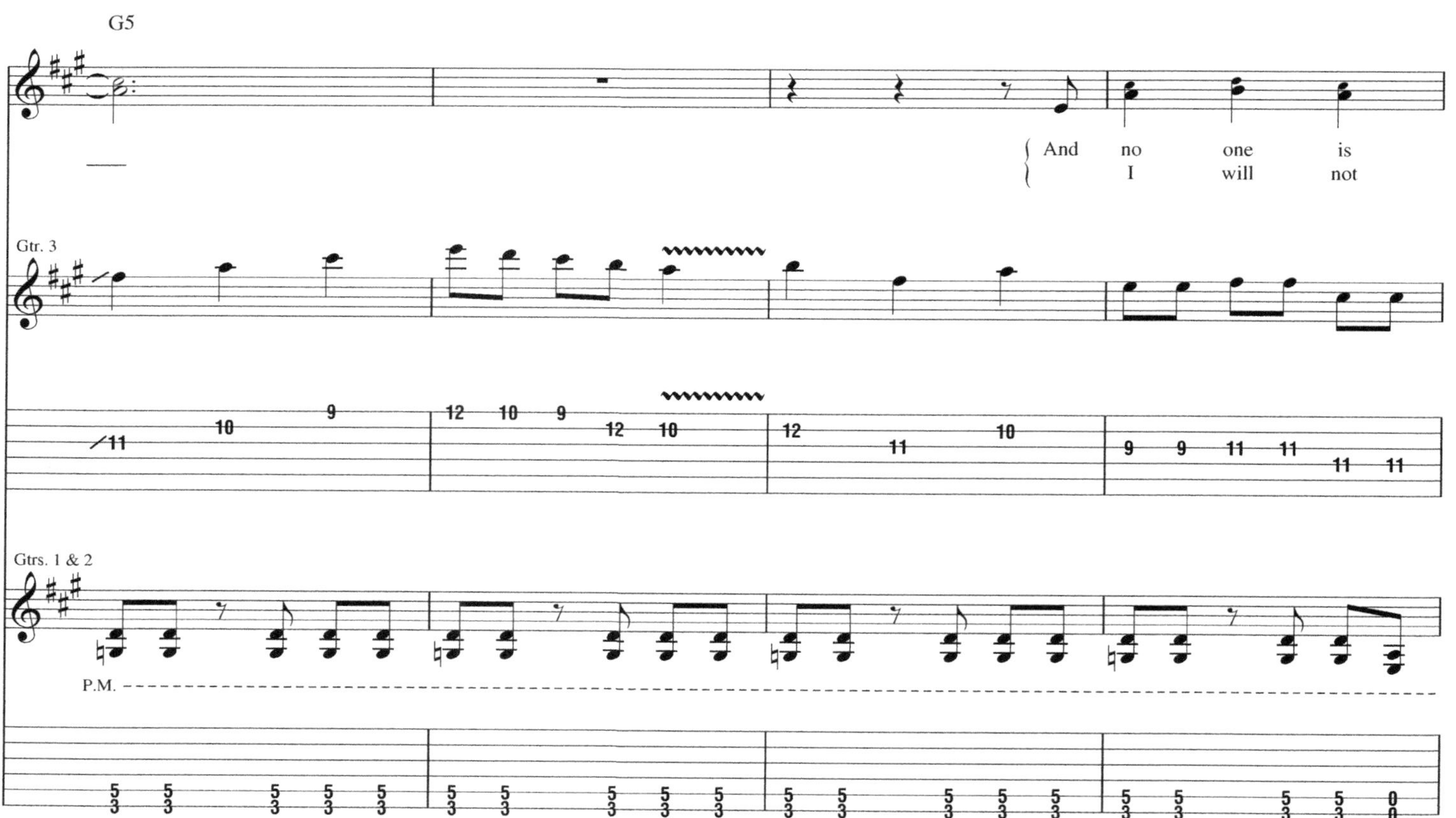
G5
And no one is
I will not
Gtr. 3
Gtrs. 1 & 2
P.M.

To Coda 2 𝄌

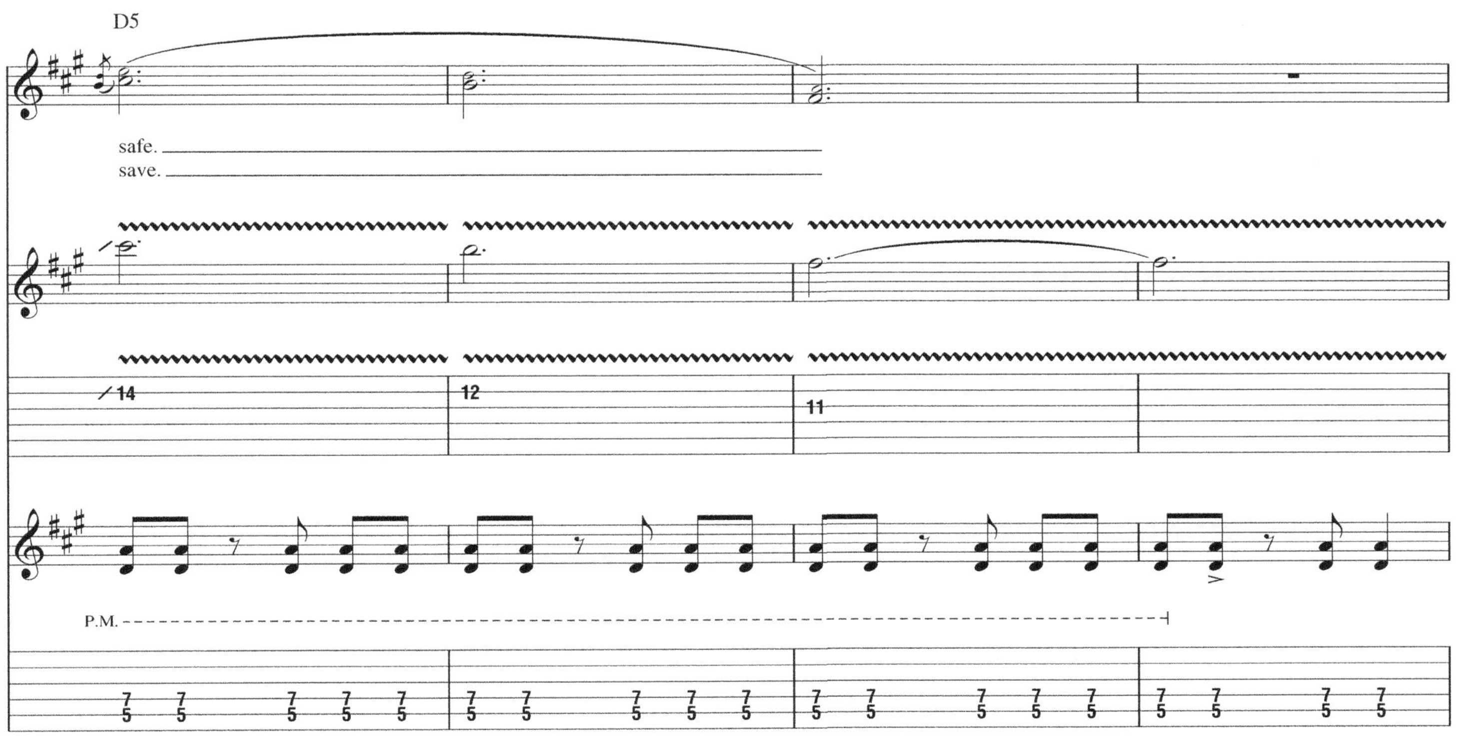
D5
safe.
save.
14
12
11
P.M.

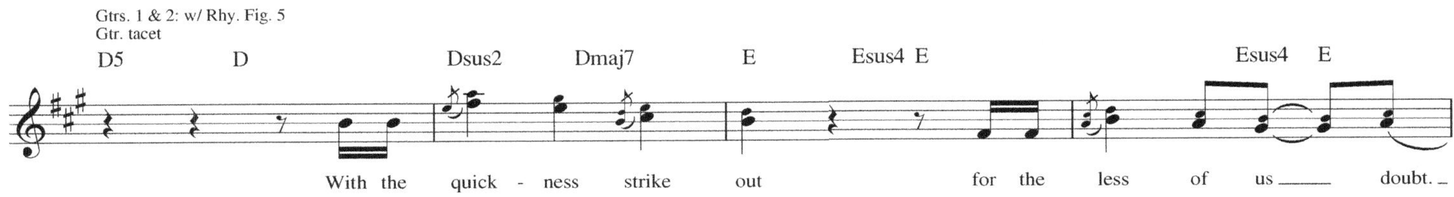
Gtrs. 1 & 2: w/ Rhy. Fig. 5
Gtr. tacet
D5 D Dsus2 Dmaj7 E Esus4 E Esus4 E
With the quick - ness strike out for the less of us doubt.

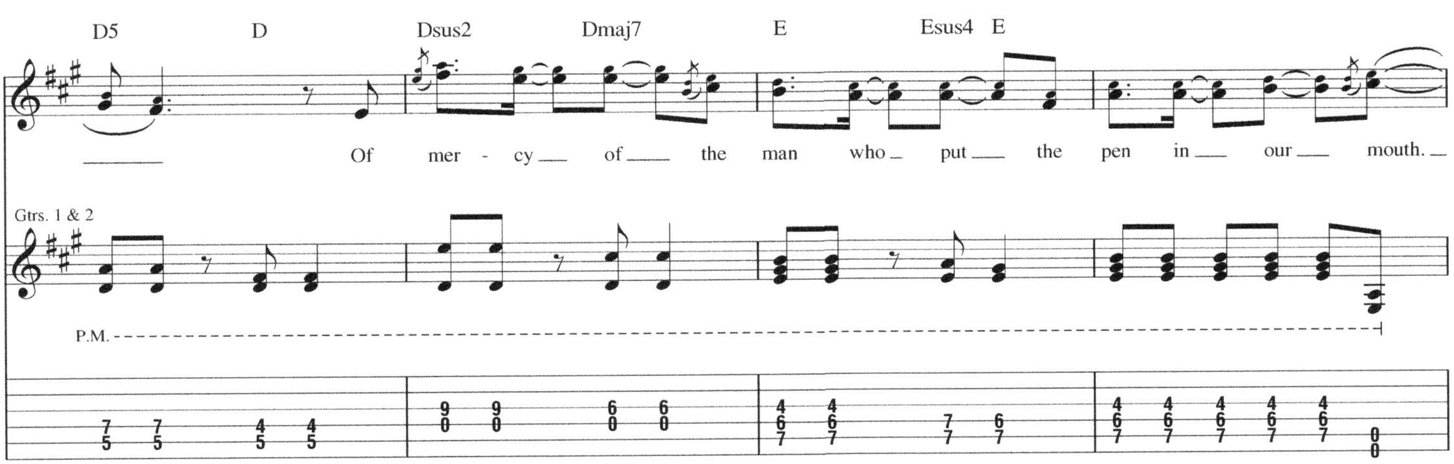
D5 D Dsus2 Dmaj7 E Esus4 E
Of mer - cy of the man who put the pen in our mouth.
Gtrs. 1 & 2
P.M.

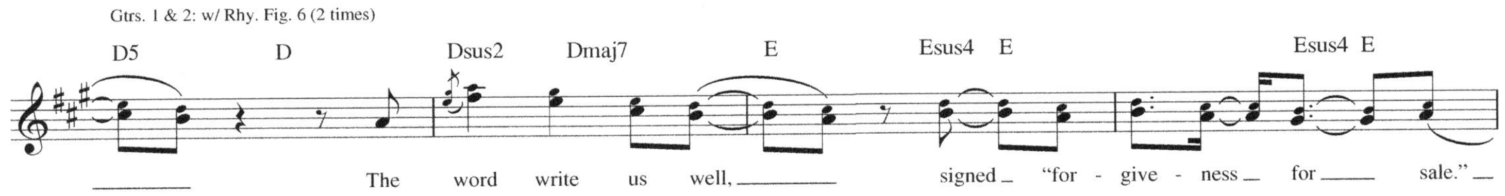
Gtrs. 1 & 2: w/ Rhy. Fig. 6 (2 times)
D5 D Dsus2 Dmaj7 E Esus4 E Esus4 E
The word write us well, signed "for - give - ness for sale."

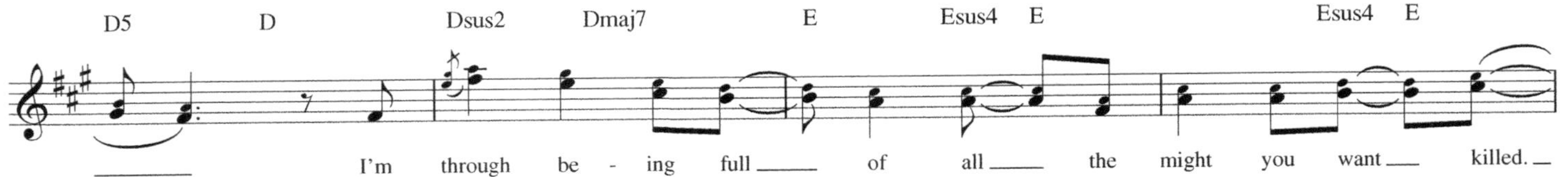
D5
D
Dsus2
Dmaj7
E
Esus4
E
Esus4
E
I'm through be - ing full of all the might you want killed.

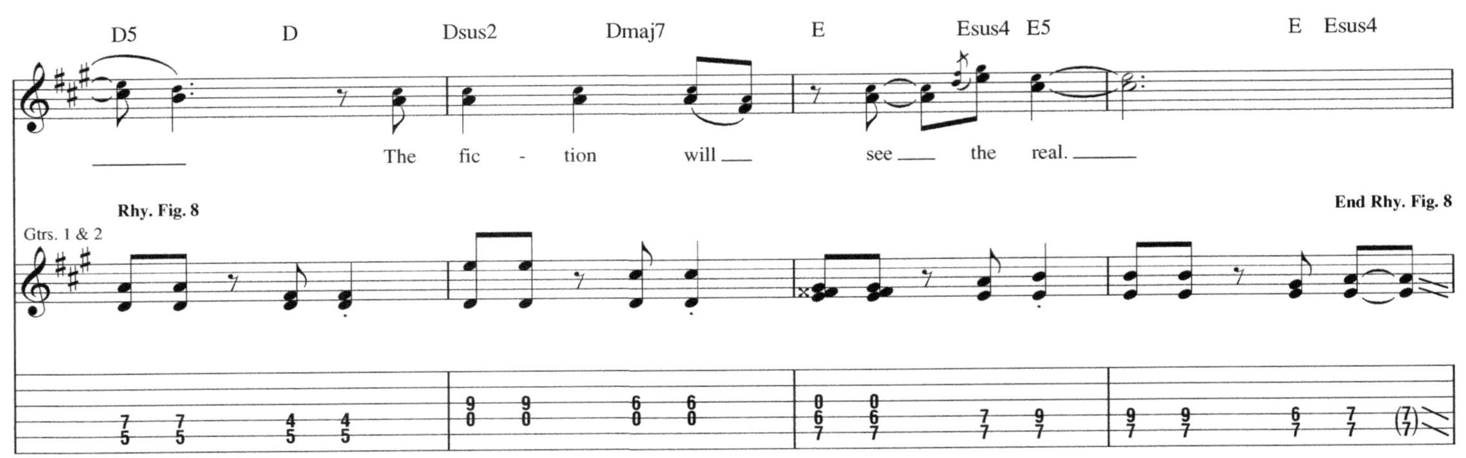
D5
D
Dsus2
Dmaj7
E
Esus4
E5
E
Esus4
The fic - tion will see the real.
Rhy. Fig. 8
Gtrs. 1 & 2
End Rhy. Fig. 8

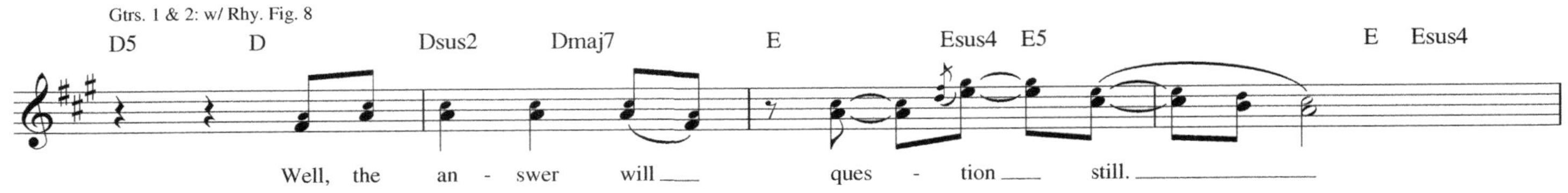
Gtrs. 1 & 2: w/ Rhy. Fig. 8
D5
D
Dsus2
Dmaj7
E
Esus4
E5
E
Esus4
Well, the an - swer will ques - tion still.

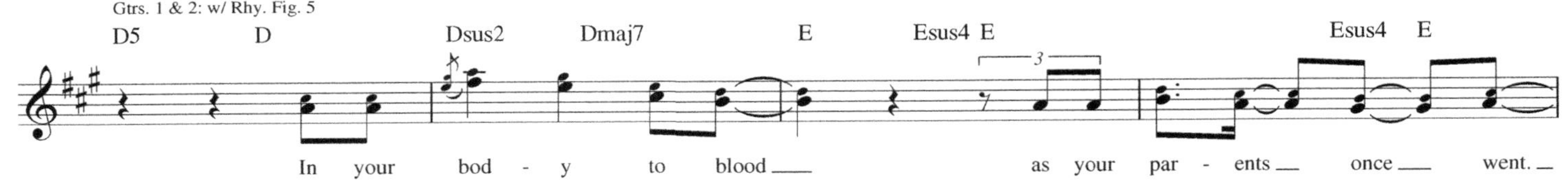
Gtrs. 1 & 2: w/ Rhy. Fig. 5
D5
D
Dsus2
Dmaj7
E
Esus4
E
Esus4
E
In your bod - y to blood as your par - ents once went.

D.S.S. al Coda 2

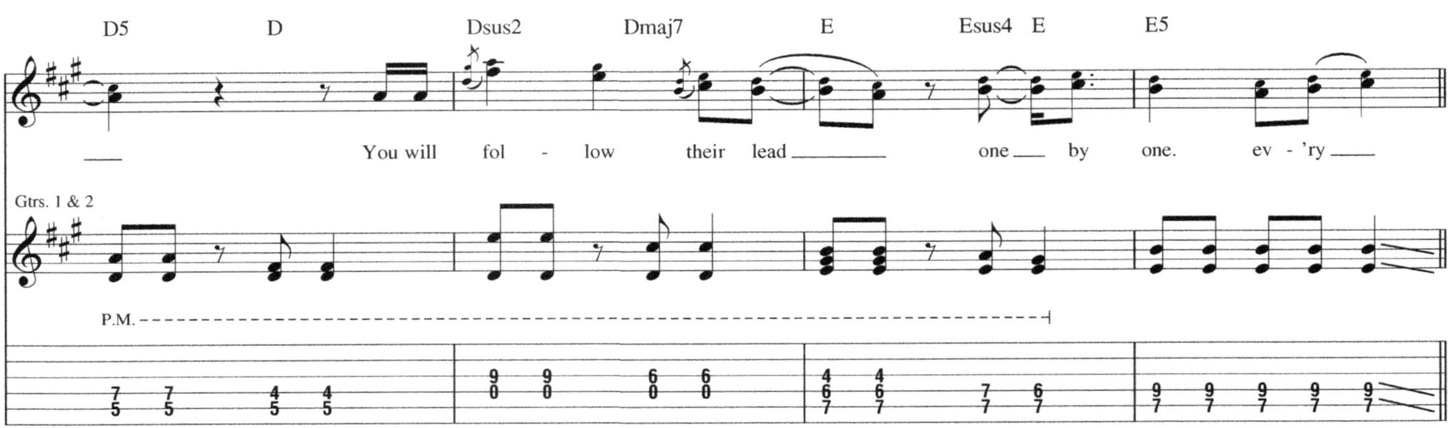
D5
D
Dsus2
Dmaj7
E
Esus4
E
E5
You will fol - low their lead one by one. ev - 'ry
Gtrs. 1 & 2
P.M.

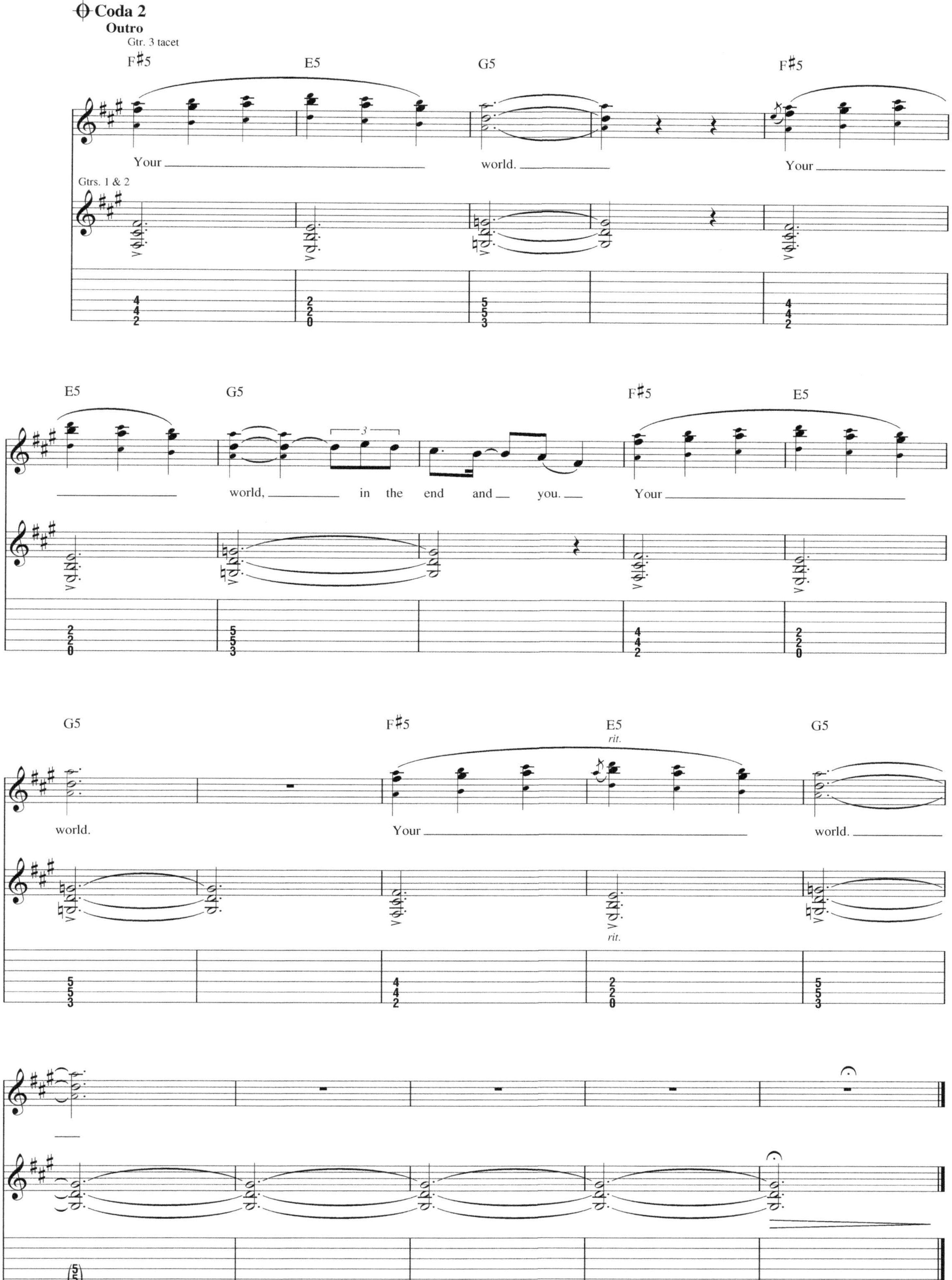
Coda 2
Outro
Gtr. 3 tacet
F♯5
E5
G5
F♯5
Your
world.
Your
Gtrs. 1 & 2
E5
G5
F♯5
E5
world,
in the end and you.
Your
G5
F♯5
E5
rit.
G5
world.
Your
world.
rit.

Willing Well II: From Fear Through the Eyes of Madness

Words and Music by Claudio Sanchez, Michael Todd, Joshua Eppard and Travis Stever

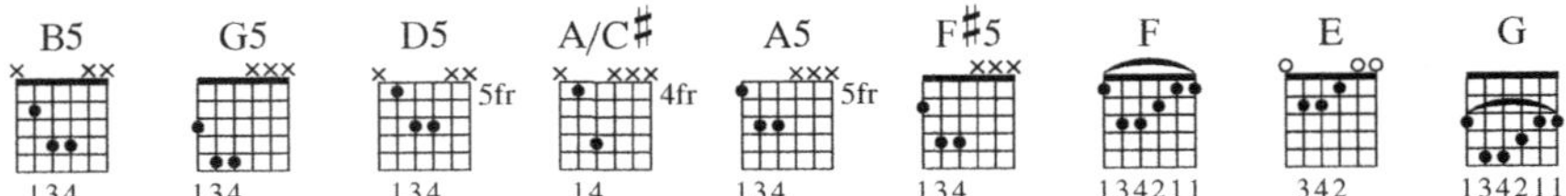

Tune down 1/2 step:
(low to high) E♭-A♭-D♭-G♭-B♭-E♭

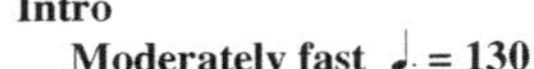

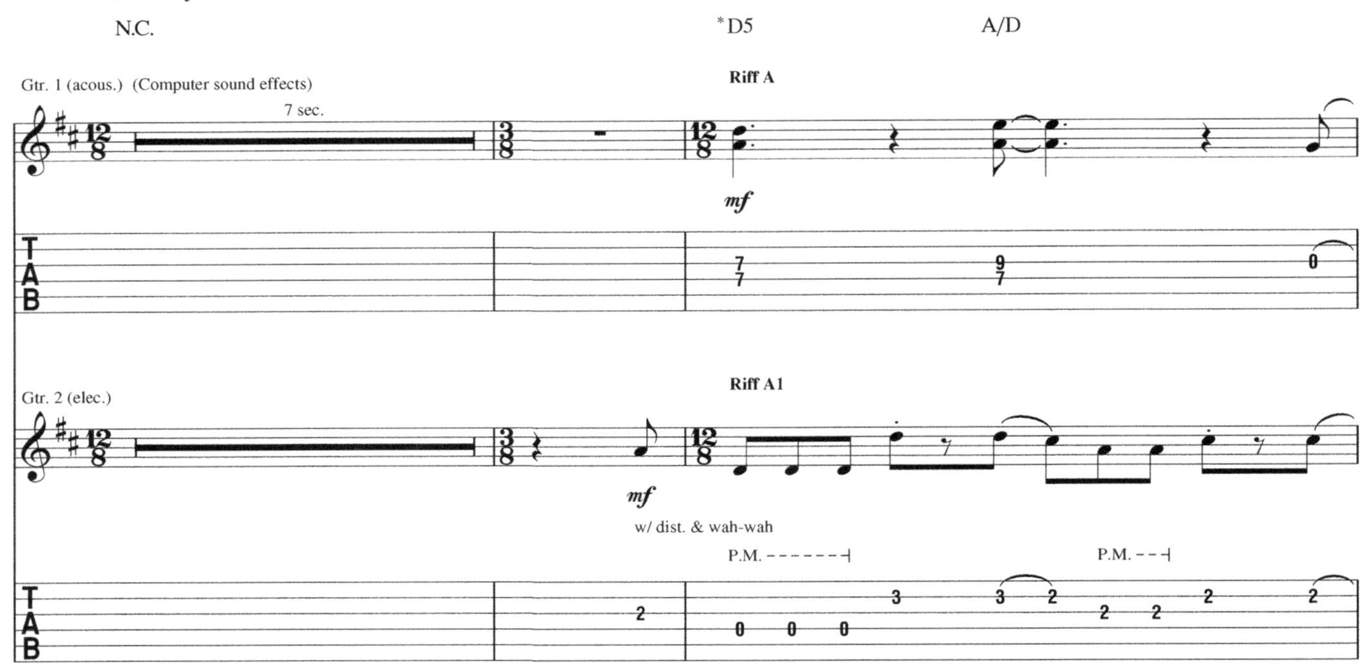

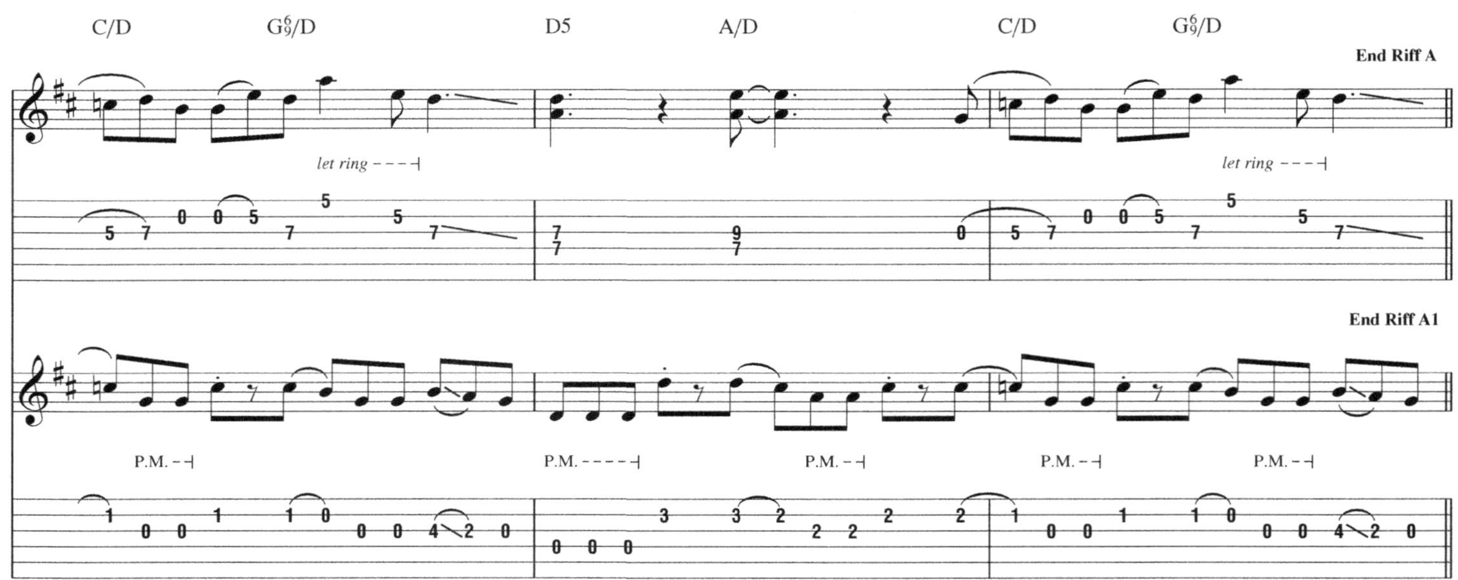

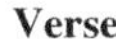
Verse
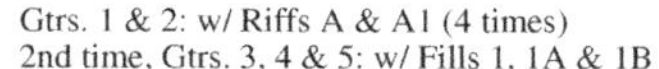
Gtrs. 1 & 2: w/ Riffs A & A1 (4 times)
2nd time, Gtrs. 3, 4 & 5: w/ Fills 1, 1A & 1B
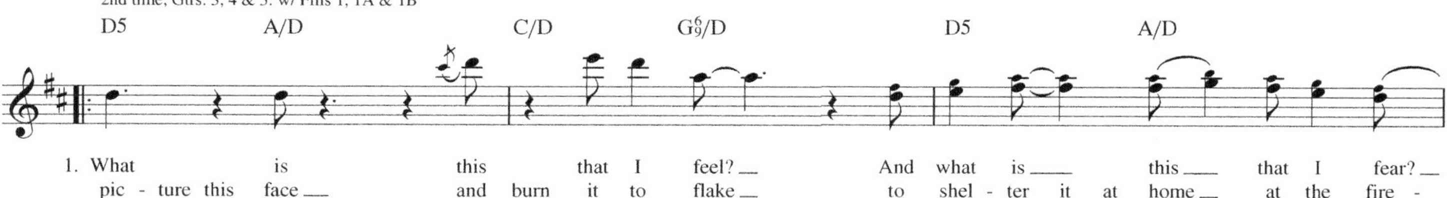
D5
A/D
C/D
D5
A/D
1. What is this that I feel? And what is this that I fear?
pic - ture this face and burn it to flake to shel - ter it at home at the fire -
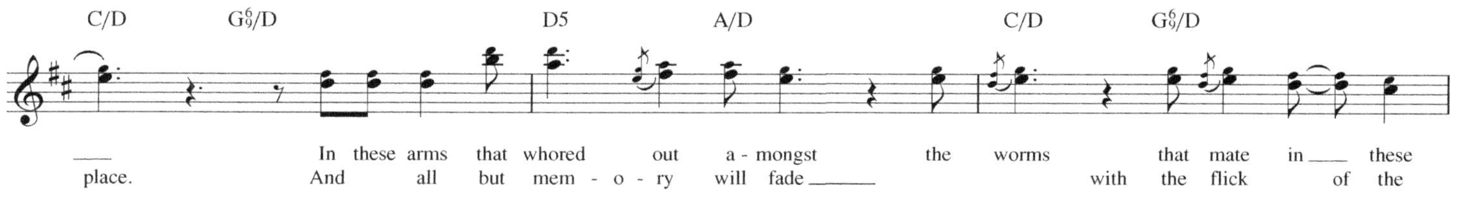
C/D
D5
A/D
C/D
place.
In these arms that whored out a - mongst the worms that mate in these
And all but mem - o - ry will fade with the flick of the
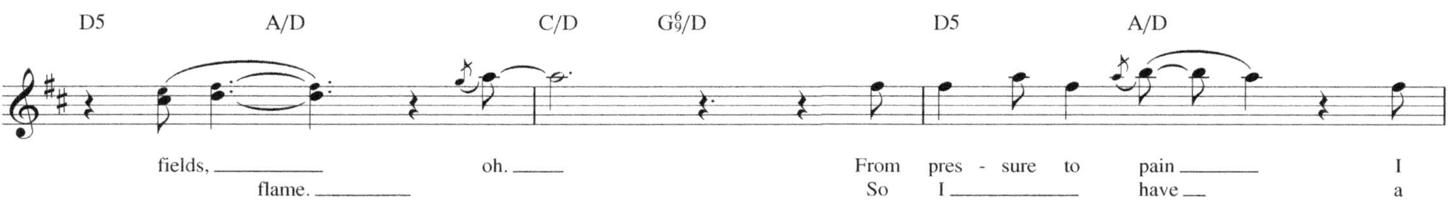
D5
A/D
C/D
D5
A/D
fields, oh. From pres - sure to pain I
flame. So I have a
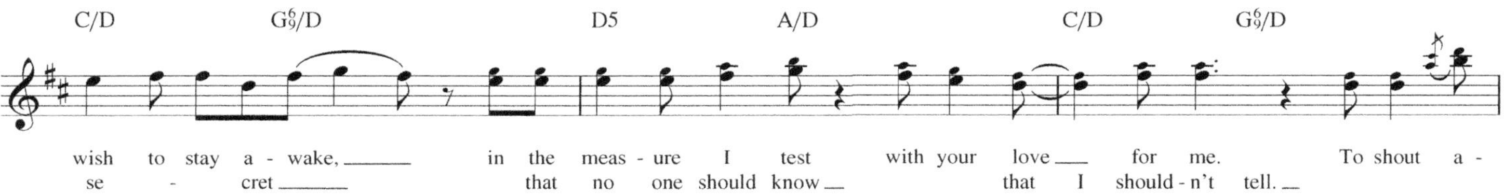
C/D
D5
A/D
C/D
wish to stay a - wake, in the meas - ure I test with your love for me. To shout a -
se - cret that no one should know that I should - n't tell.
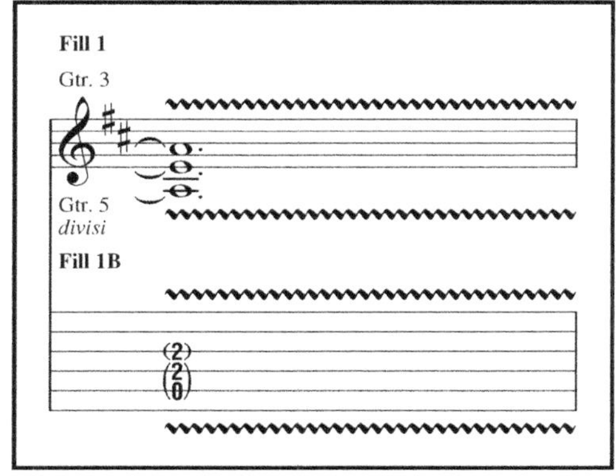
Fill 1
Gtr. 3
Gtr. 5
divisi
Fill 1B
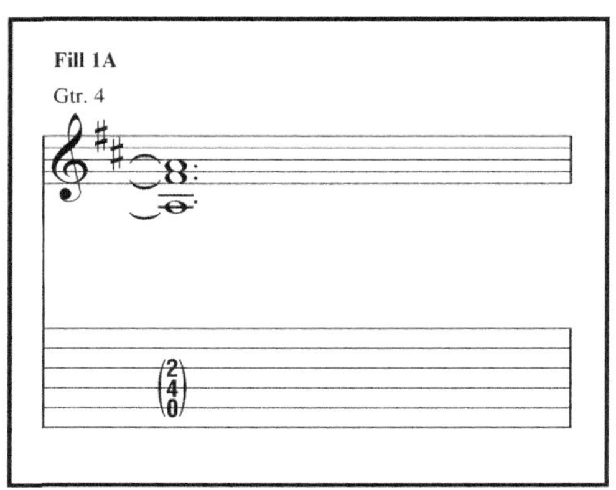
Fill 1A
Gtr. 4

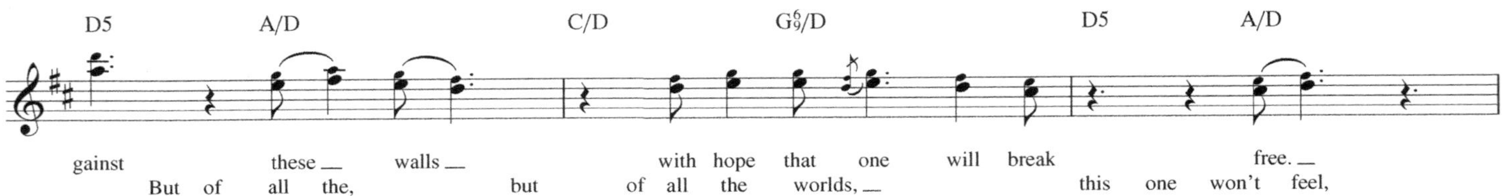

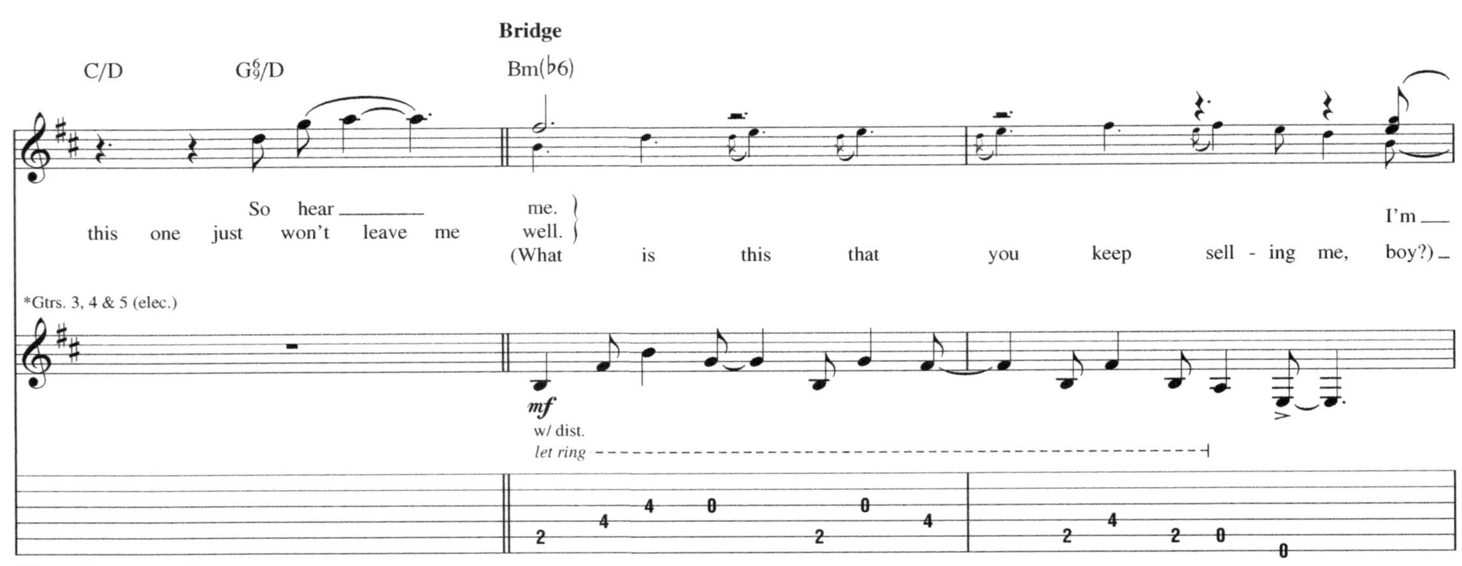

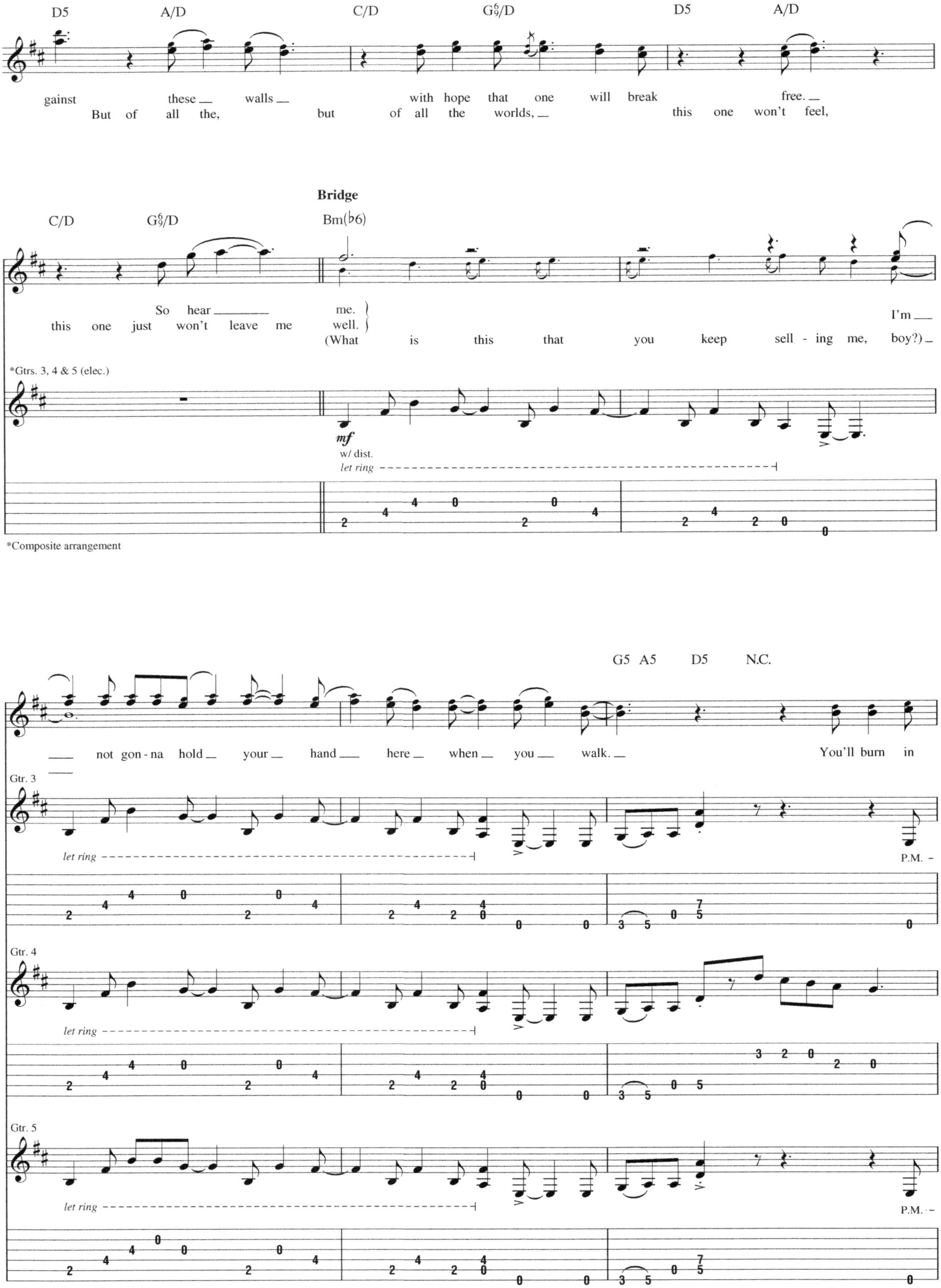

*Composite arrangement

G5 A5 D5 N.C.

not gon - na hold your hand here when you walk. You'll burn in

Gtr. 3

let ring

P.M.

Gtr. 4

let ring

Gtr. 5

let ring

P.M.

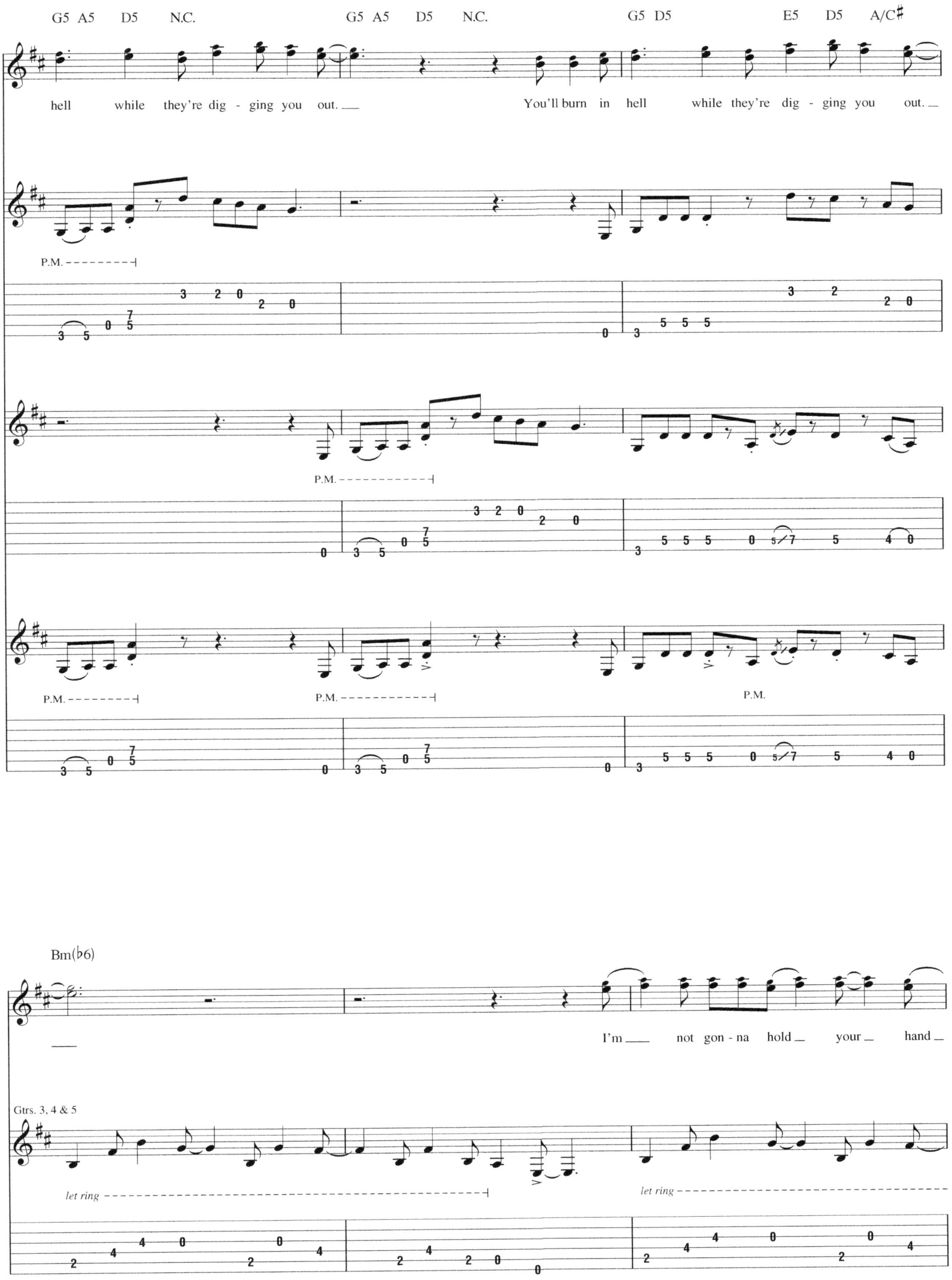

G5 A5 D5 N.C. G5 A5 D5 N.C. G5 D5 E5 D5 A/C♯

hell while they're dig - ging you out. You'll burn in hell while they're dig - ging you out.

P.M.

P.M.

P.M. P.M. P.M.

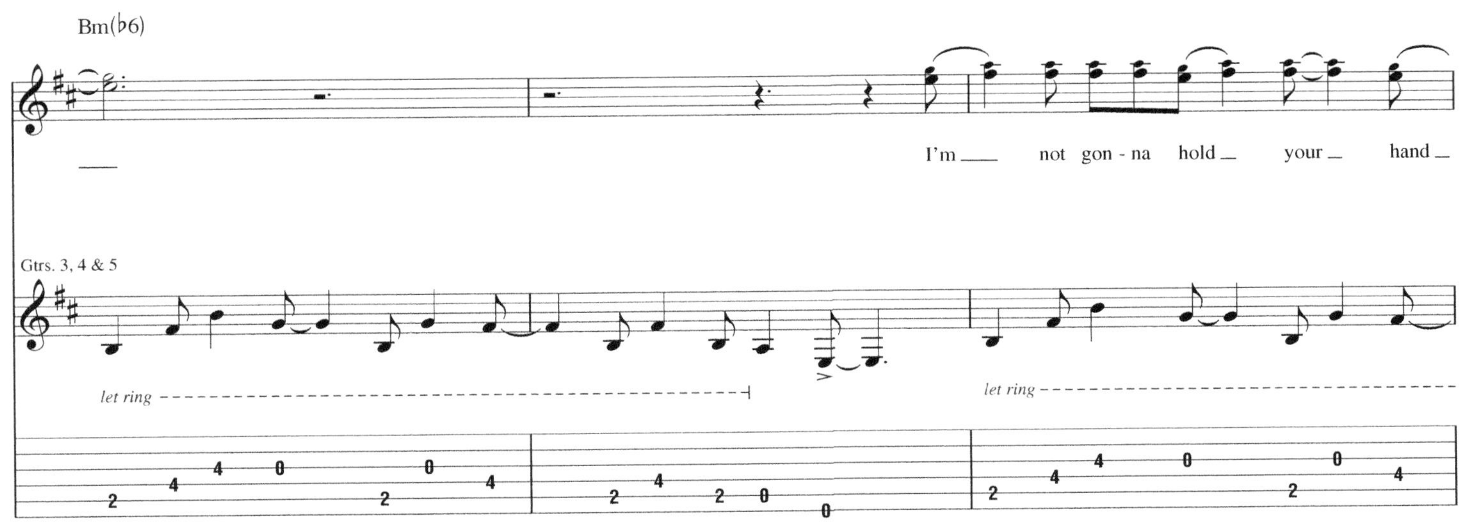

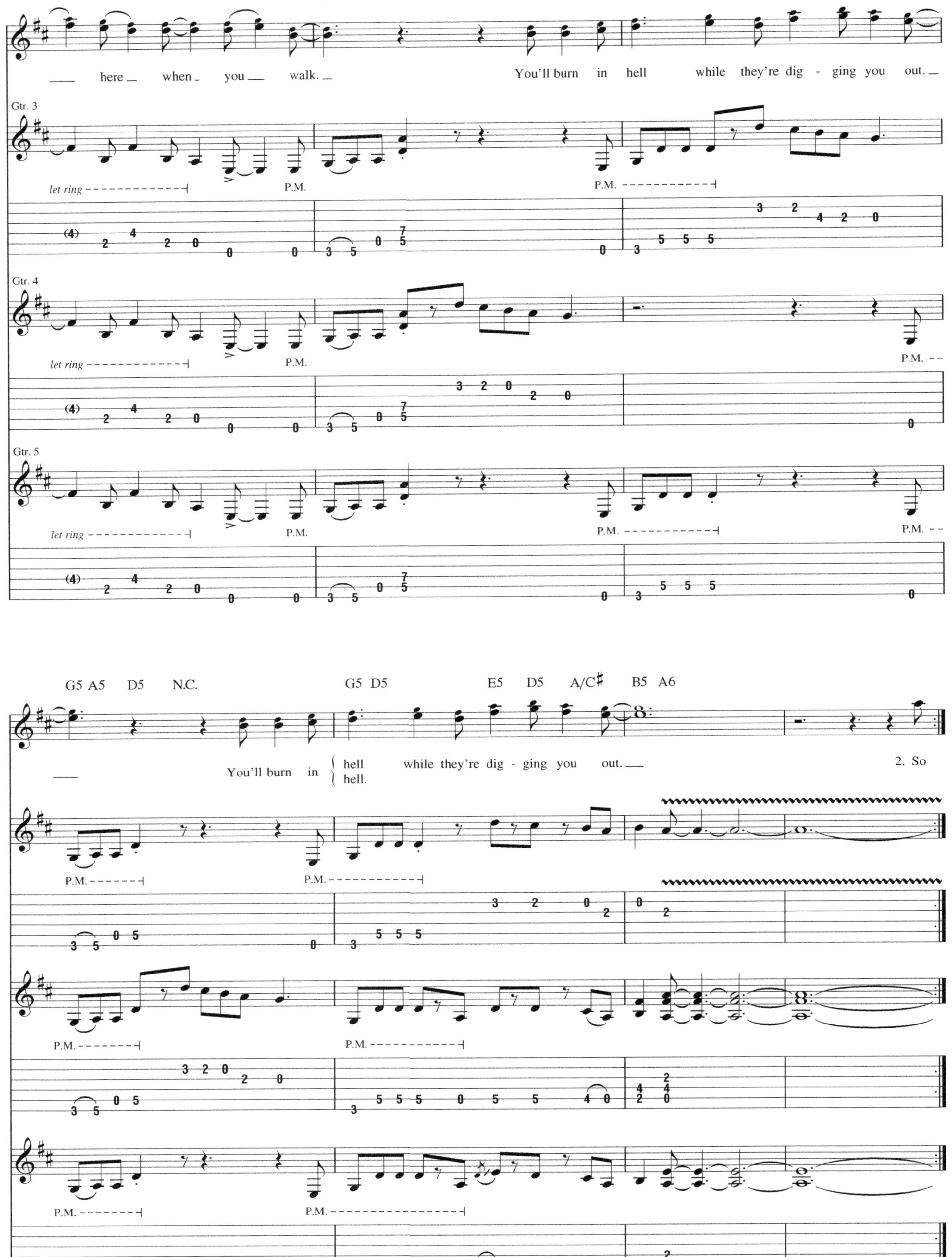
G5 A5 D5 N.C.
G5 D5 N.C.
here when you walk.
You'll burn in hell while they're dig - ging you out.
Gtr. 3
let ring
P.M.
Gtr. 4
Gtr. 5
G5 A5 D5 N.C.
G5 D5 E5 D5 A/C♯ B5 A6
You'll burn in hell while they're dig - ging you out.
hell.
2. So

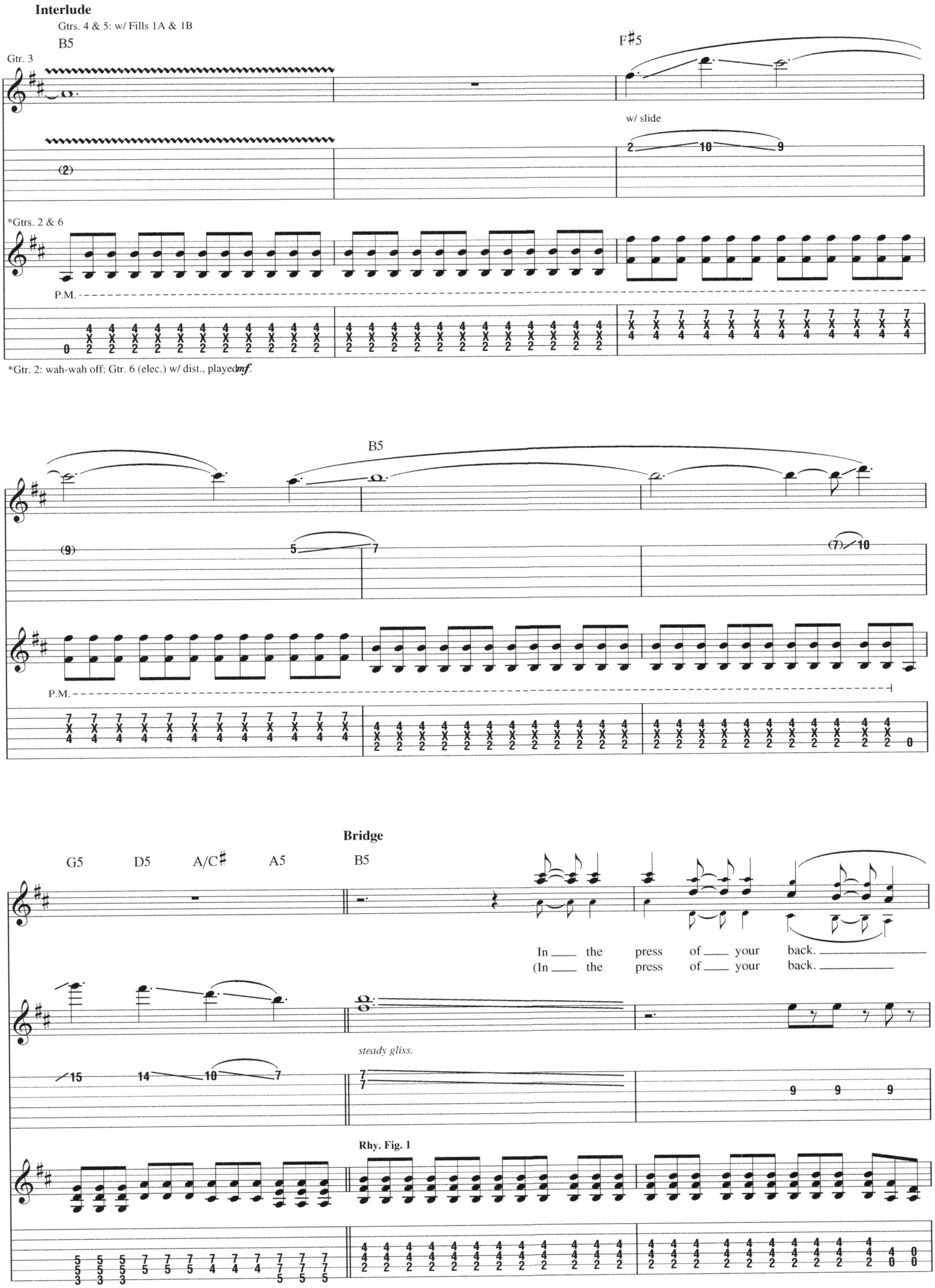

Interlude

Gtrs. 4 & 5: w/ Fills 1A & 1B

B5 F#5

Gtr. 3

w/ slide

*Gtrs. 2 & 6

P.M.

*Gtr. 2: wah-wah off; Gtr. 6 (elec.) w/ dist., played *mf*.

B5

P.M.

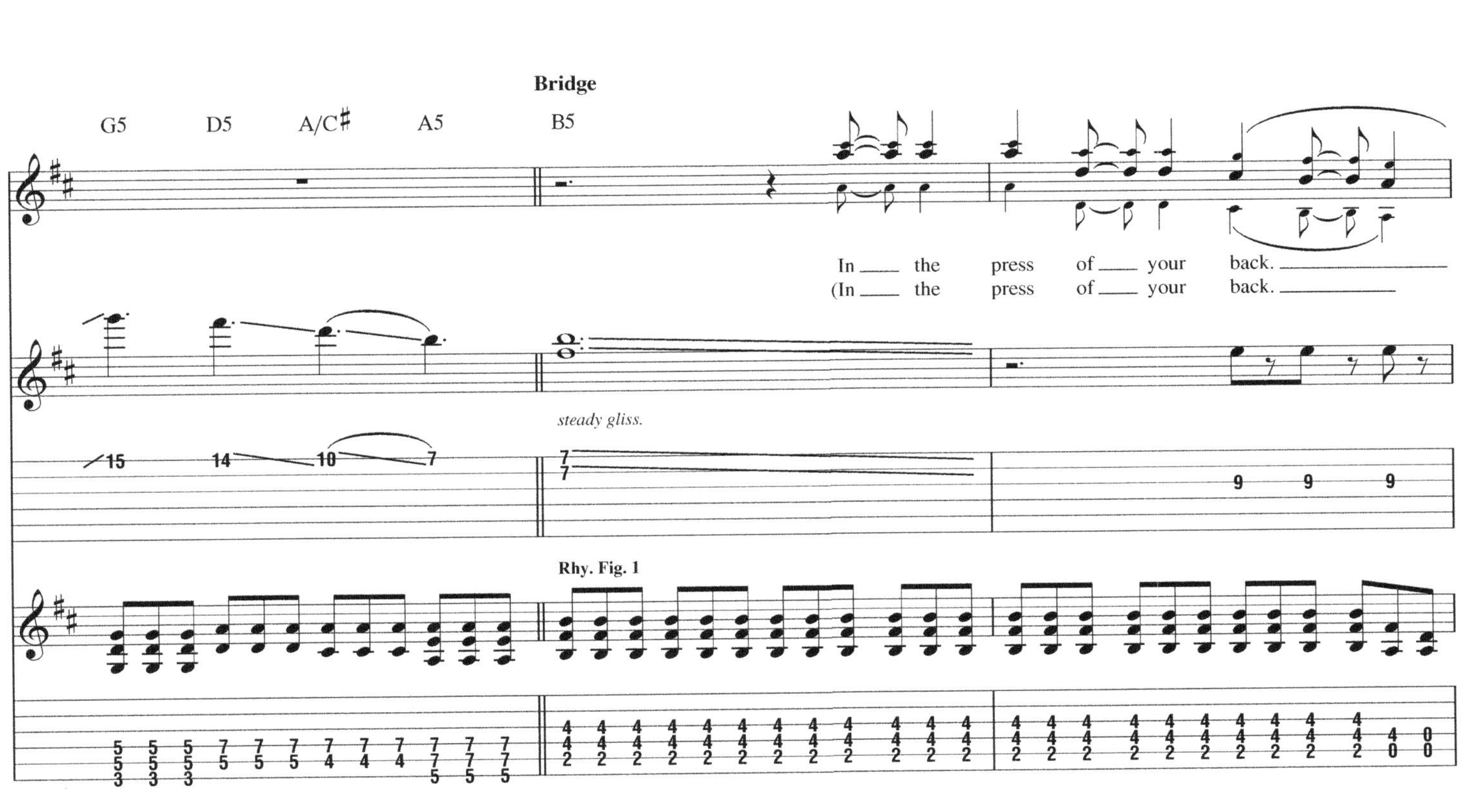

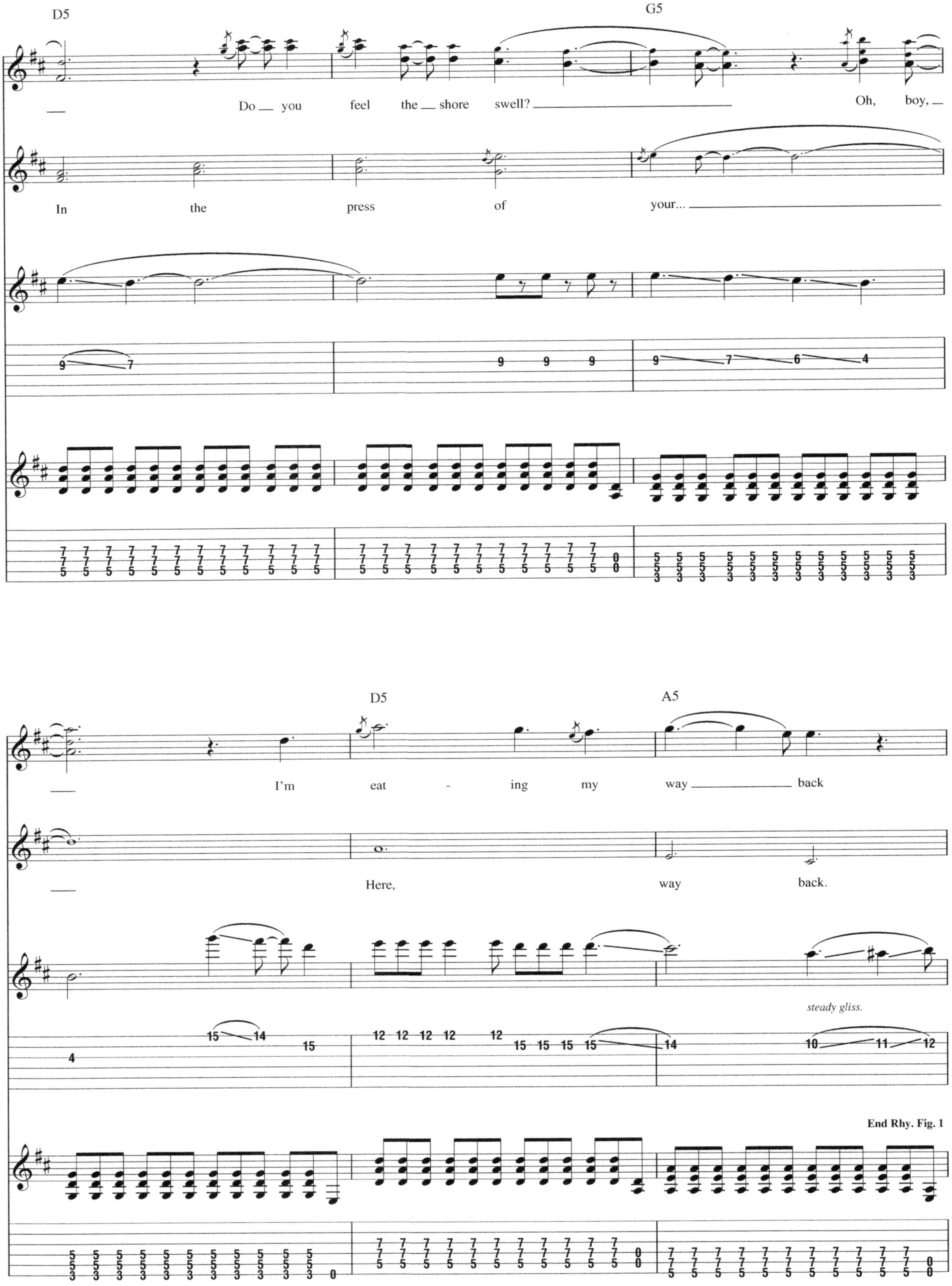

D5 G5

Do you feel the shore swell? Oh, boy,

In the press of your...

D5 A5

I'm eat - ing my way back

Here, way back.

steady gliss.

End Rhy. Fig. 1

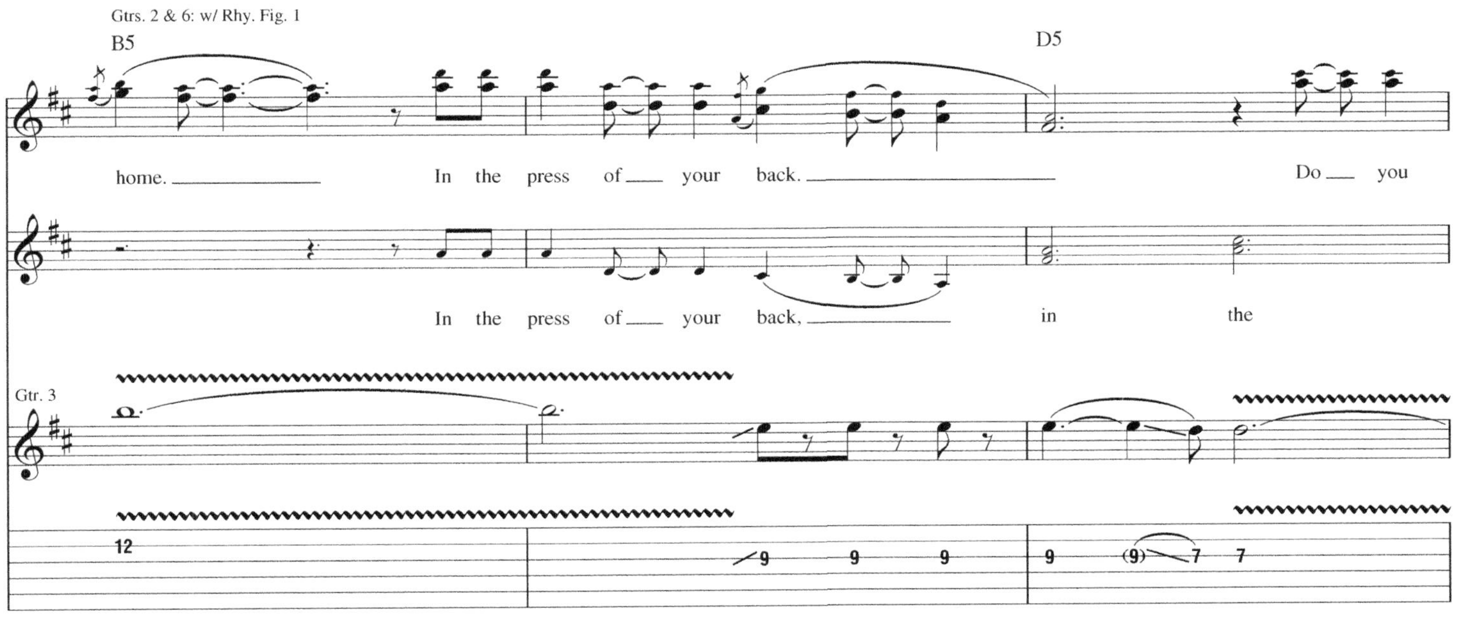
Gtrs. 2 & 6: w/ Rhy. Fig. 1
B5
D5
home. In the press of your back. Do you
In the press of your back, in the
Gtr. 3

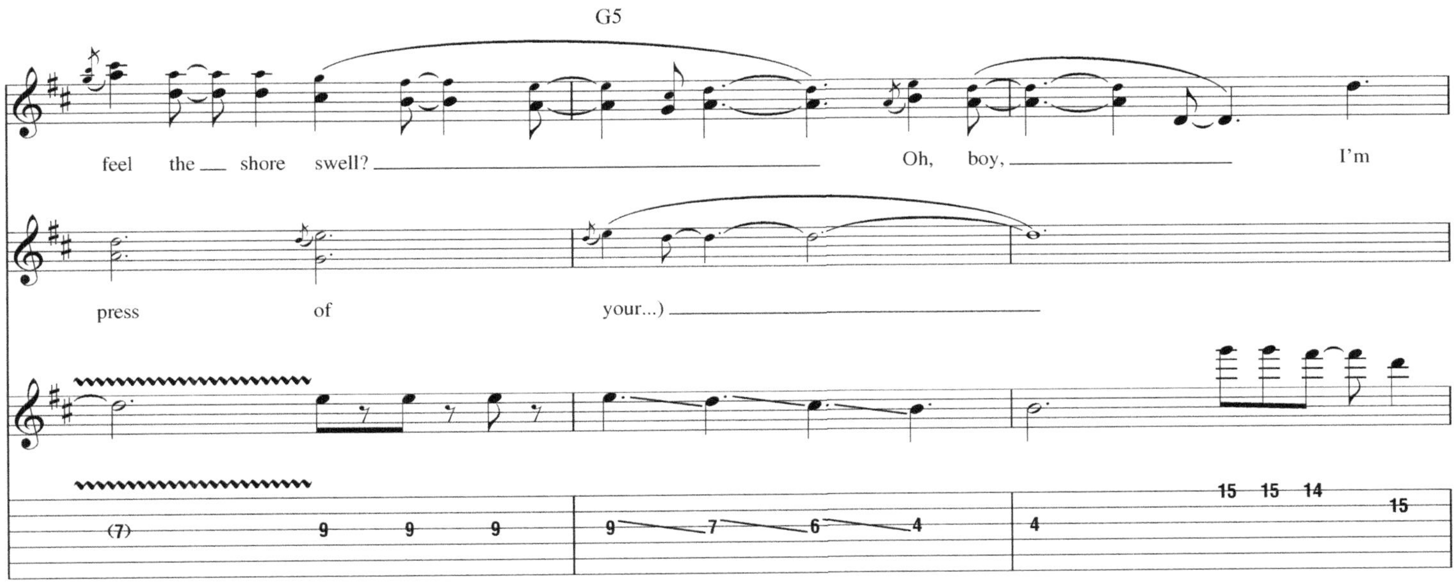
G5
feel the shore swell? Oh, boy, I'm
press of your...)

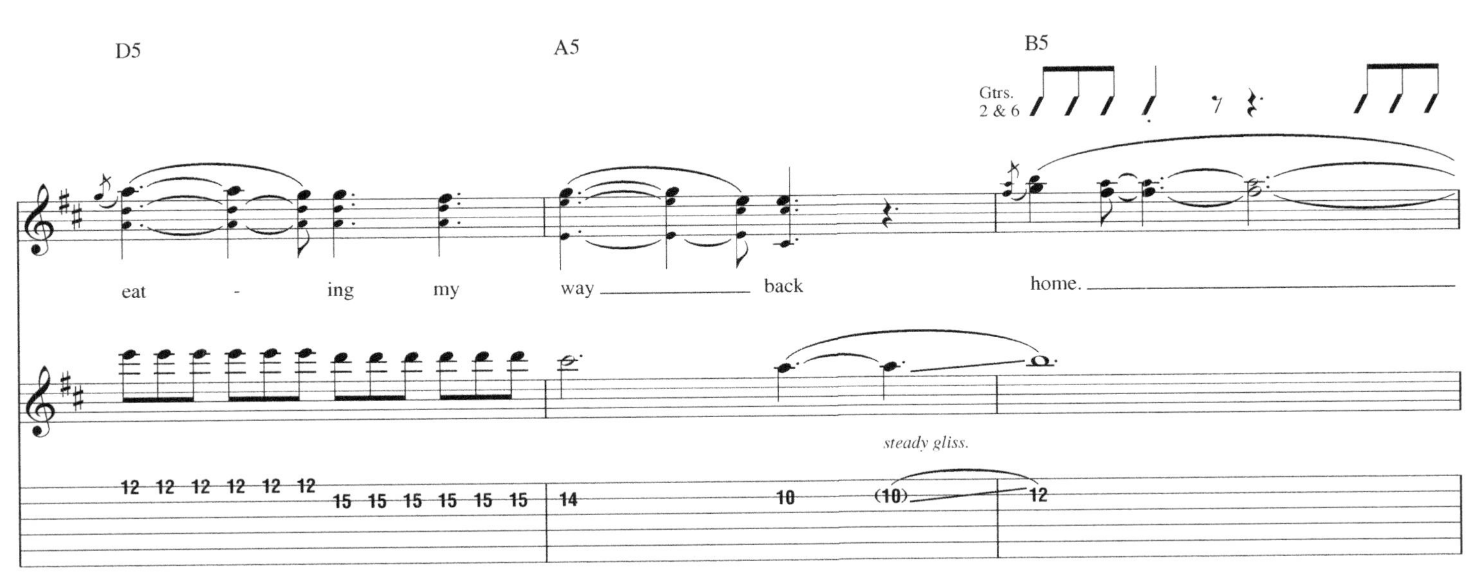
D5
A5
B5
Gtrs. 2 & 6
eat - ing my way back home.
steady gliss.

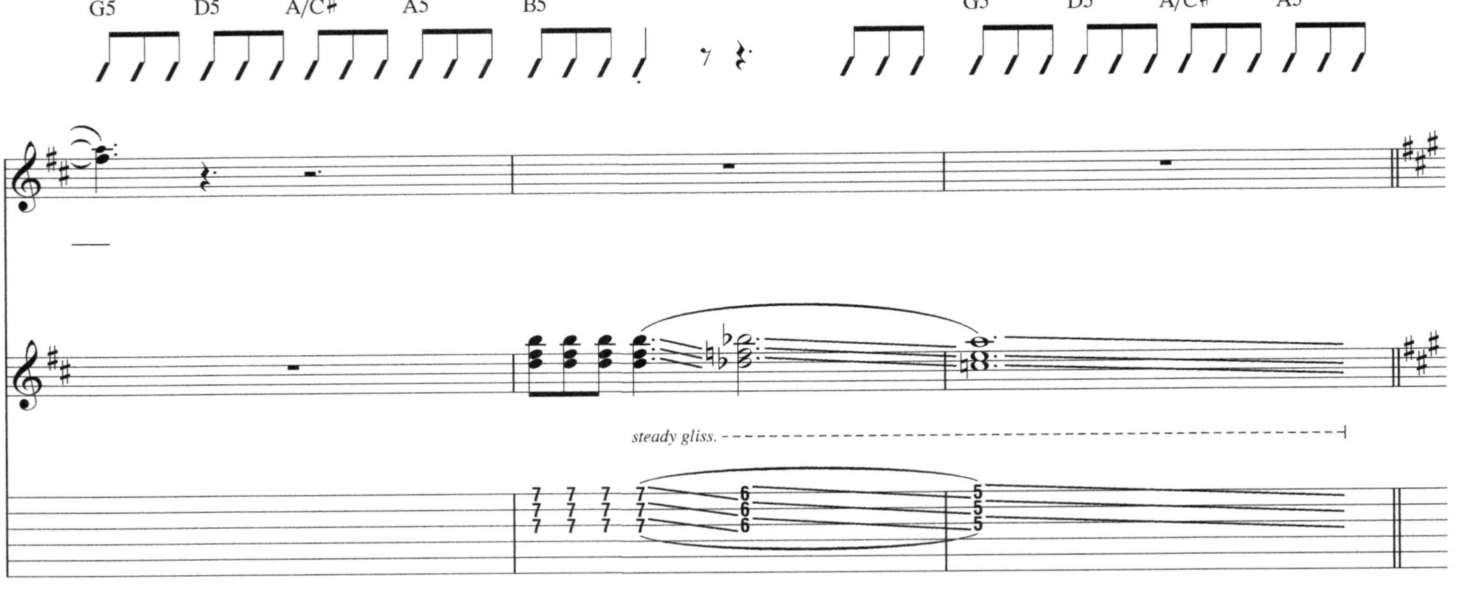

Interlude

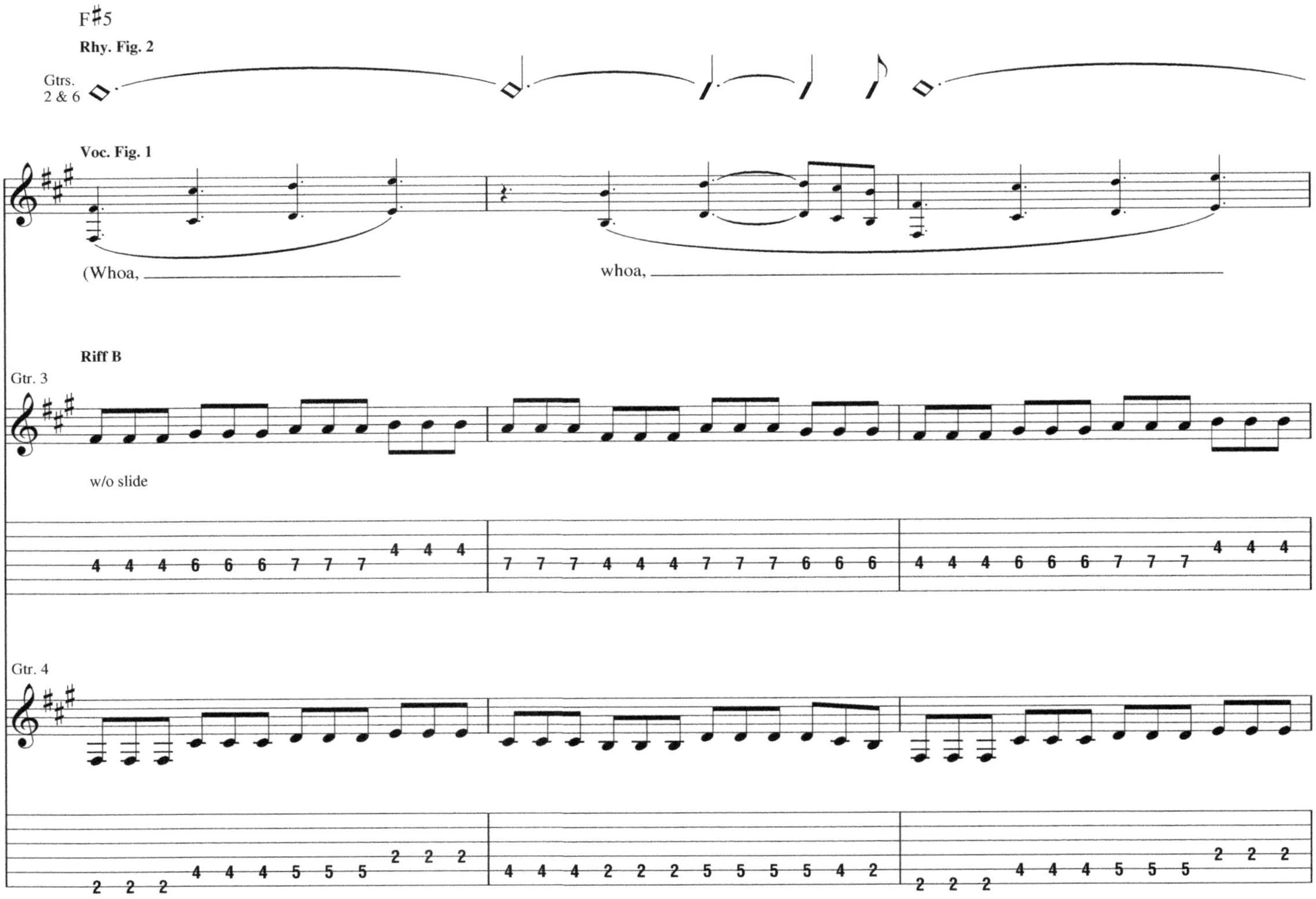

F♯5

Rhy. Fig. 2

Gtrs. 2 & 6

Voc. Fig. 1

(Whoa, whoa,

Riff B

Gtr. 3

w/o slide

4 4 4 6 6 6 7 7 7 4 4 4 | 7 7 7 4 4 4 7 7 7 6 6 6 | 4 4 4 6 6 6 7 7 7 4 4 4

Gtr. 4

2 2 2 4 4 4 5 5 5 2 2 2 | 4 4 4 2 2 2 5 5 5 5 4 2 | 2 2 2 4 4 4 5 5 5 2 2 2

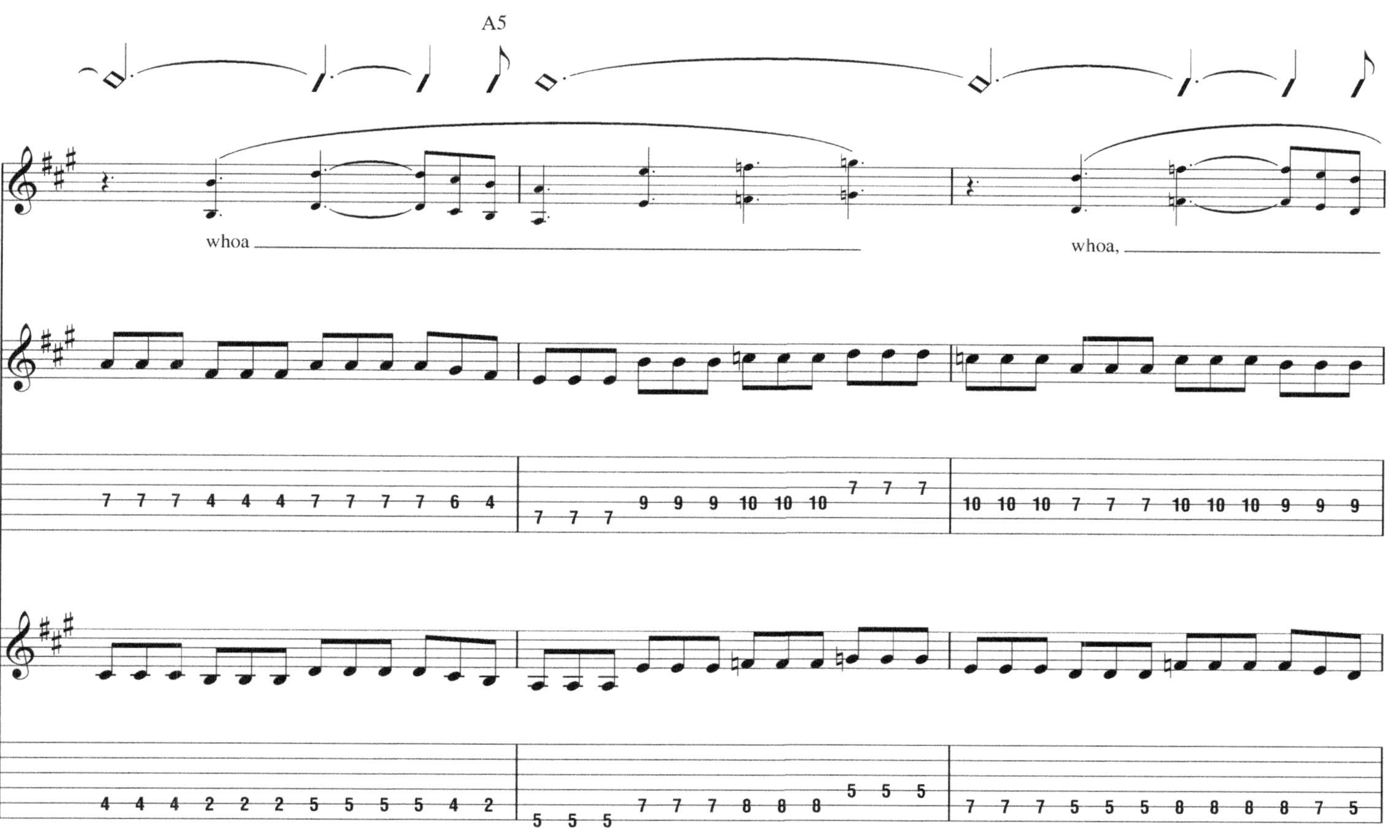
A5
whoa
whoa,

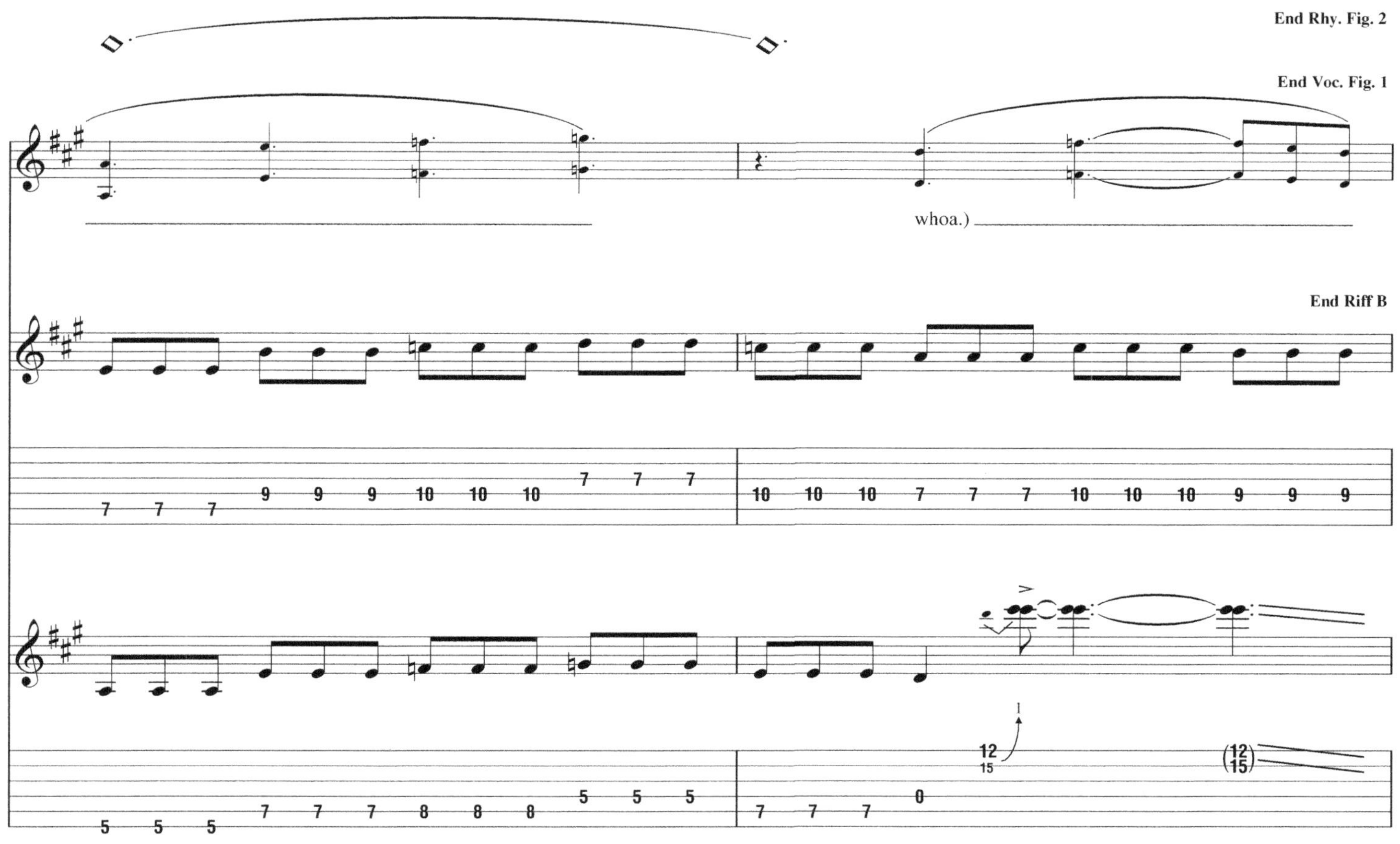
End Rhy. Fig. 2
End Voc. Fig. 1
whoa.)
End Riff B

Bkgd. Voc.: w/ Voc. Fig. 1
Gtrs. 2 & 6: w/ Rhy. Fig. 2
Gtr. 3: w/ Riff B

F♯5

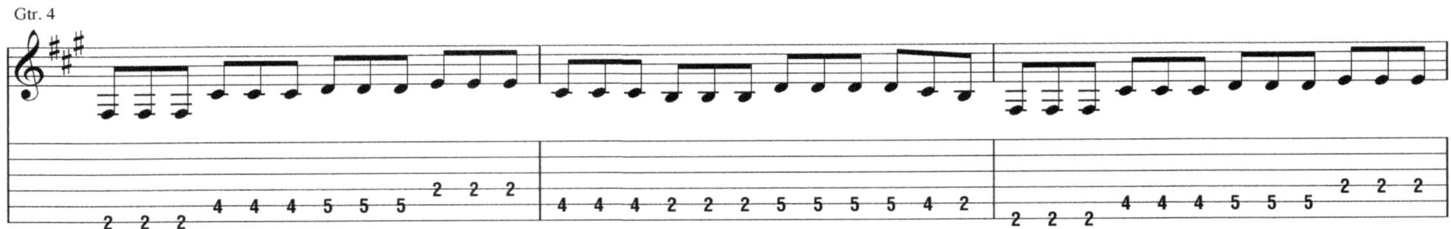

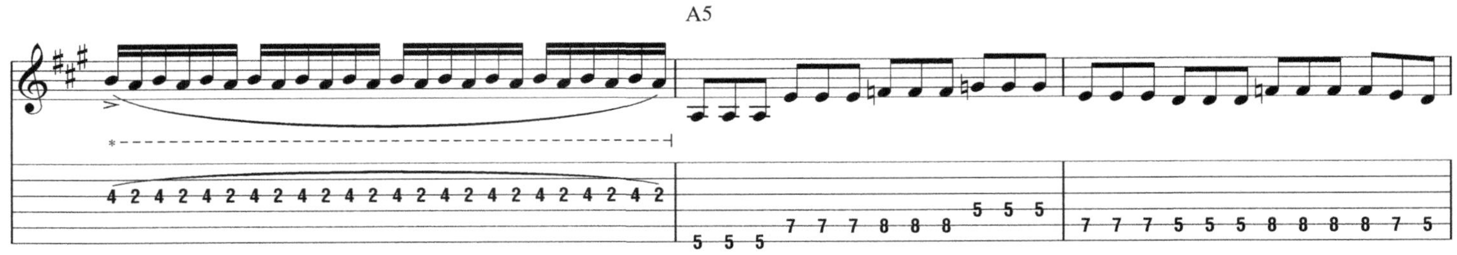

*Gradually brush pick-hand index finger along string length while trilling to produce random harmonics.

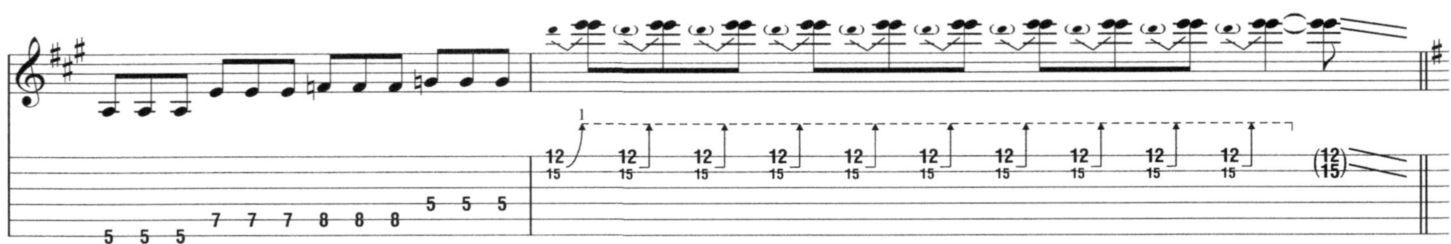

Bridge

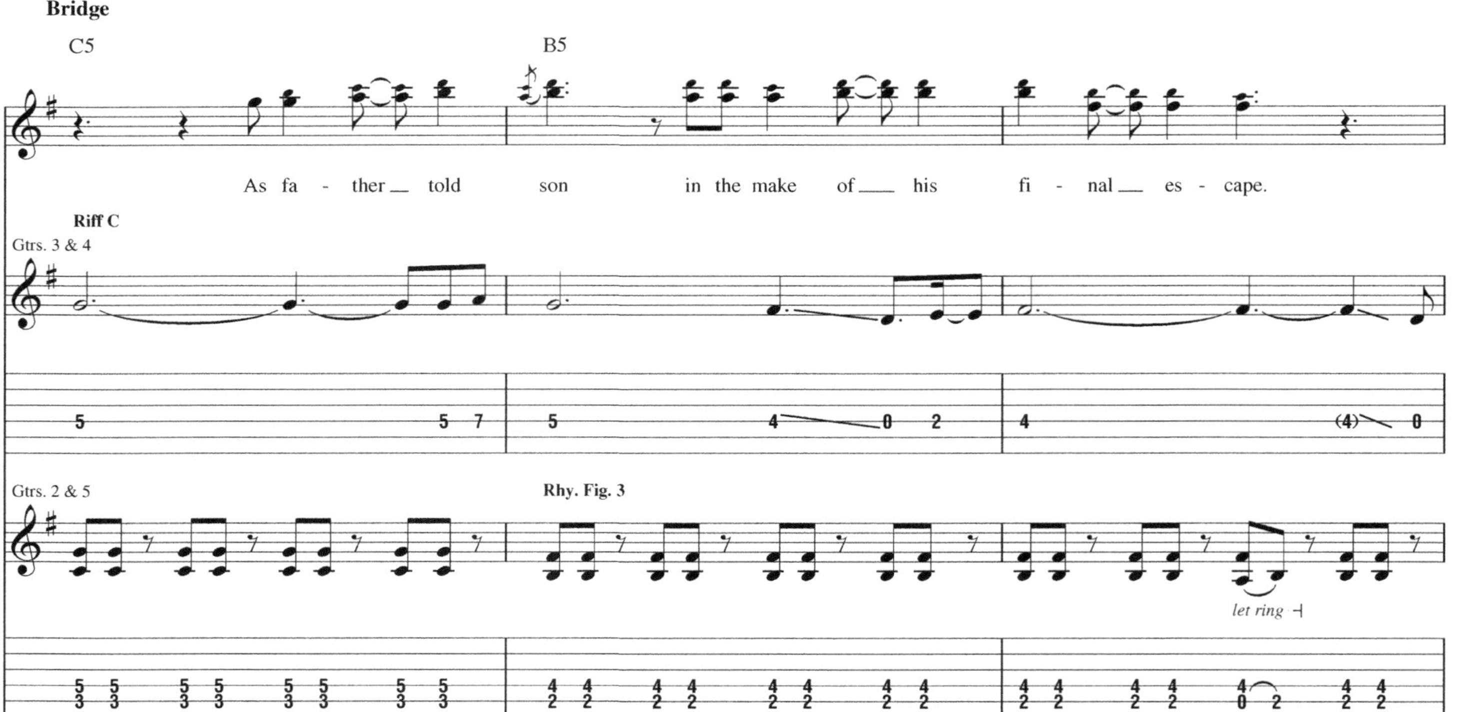

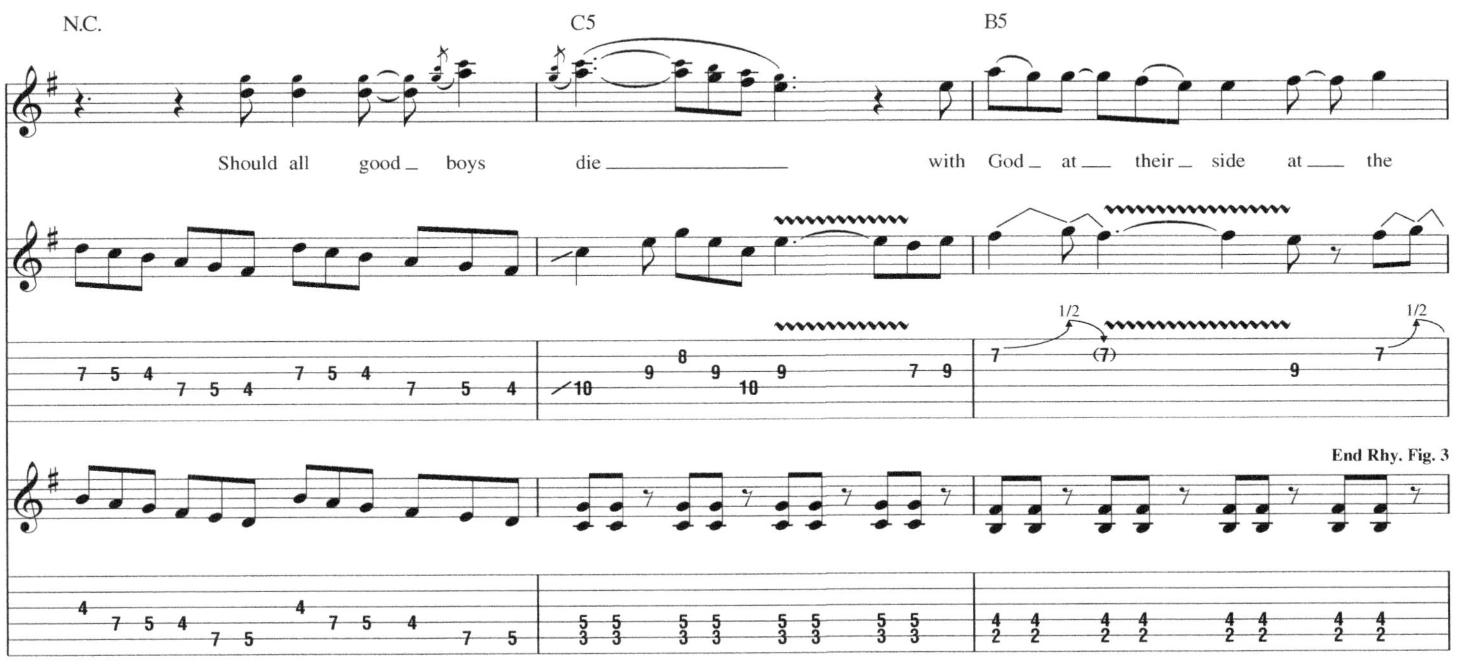
N.C.
C5
B5
Should all good boys die with God at their side at the
1/2
1/2
End Rhy. Fig. 3

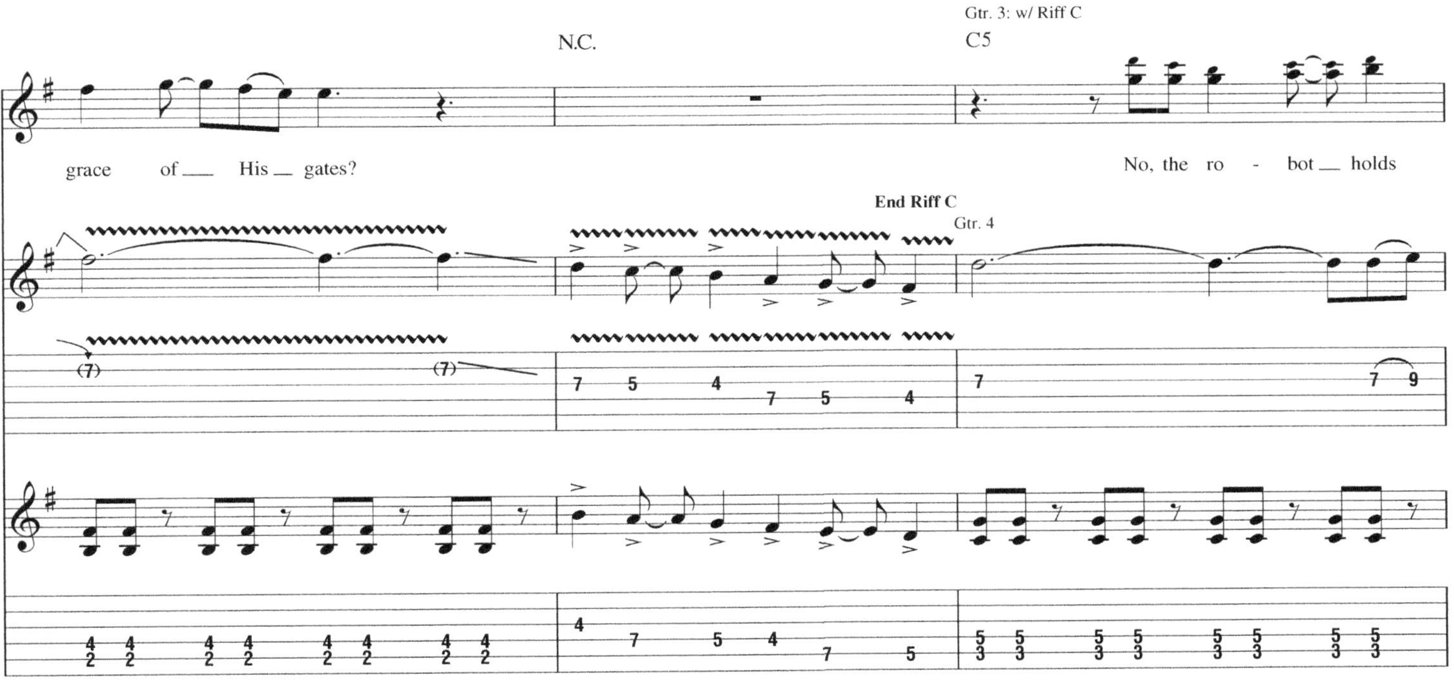
N.C.
Gtr. 3: w/ Riff C
C5
grace of His gates?
No, the ro - bot holds
End Riff C
Gtr. 4

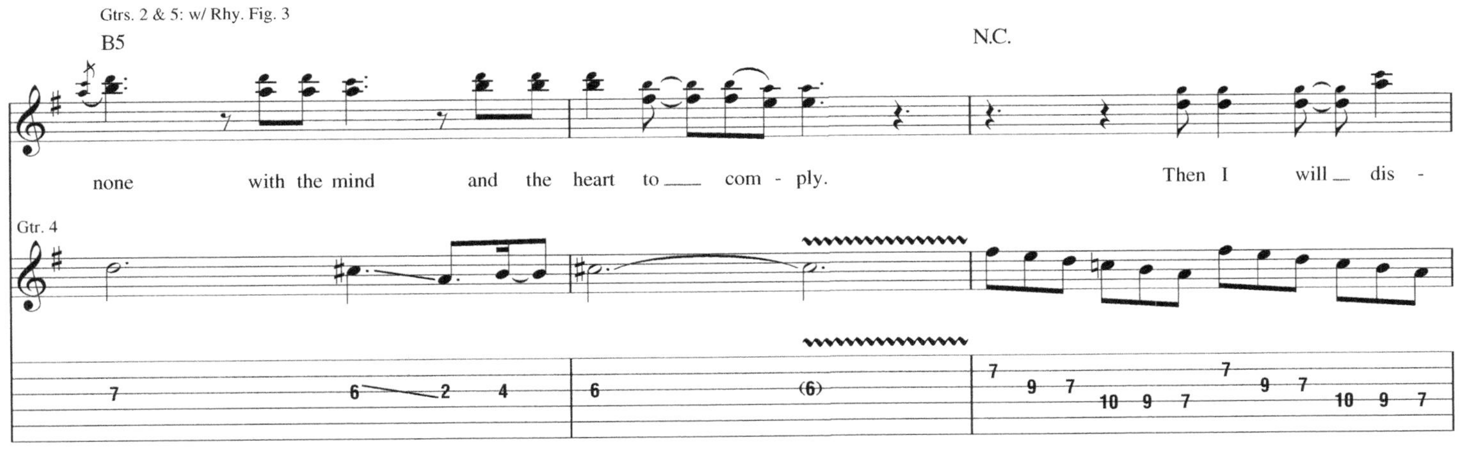
Gtrs. 2 & 5: w/ Rhy. Fig. 3
B5
N.C.
none with the mind and the heart to com - ply.
Then I will dis -
Gtr. 4

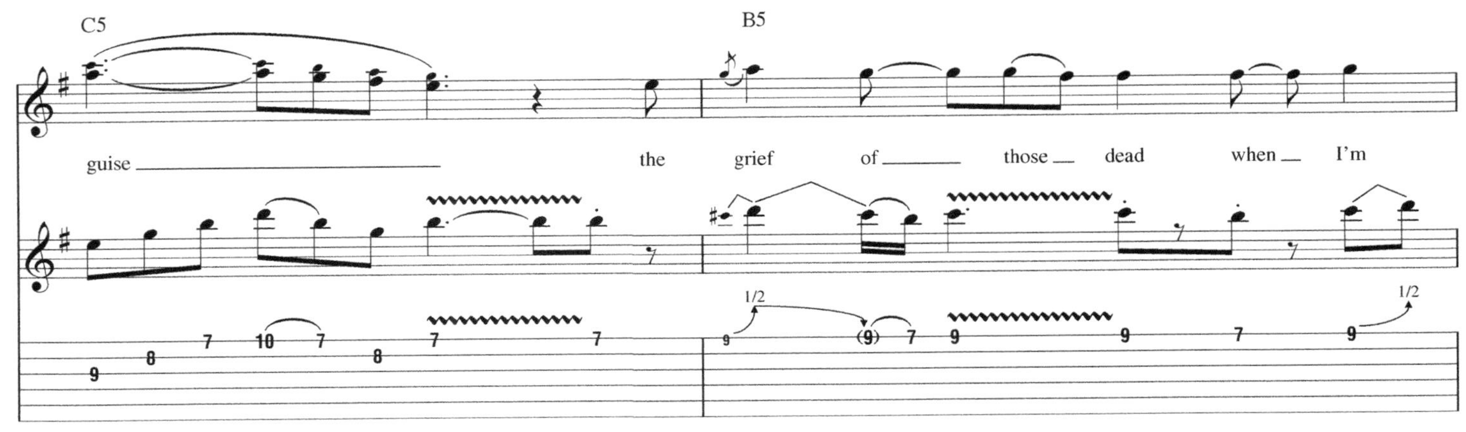
C5
B5
guise
the grief of those dead when I'm
1/2
1/2

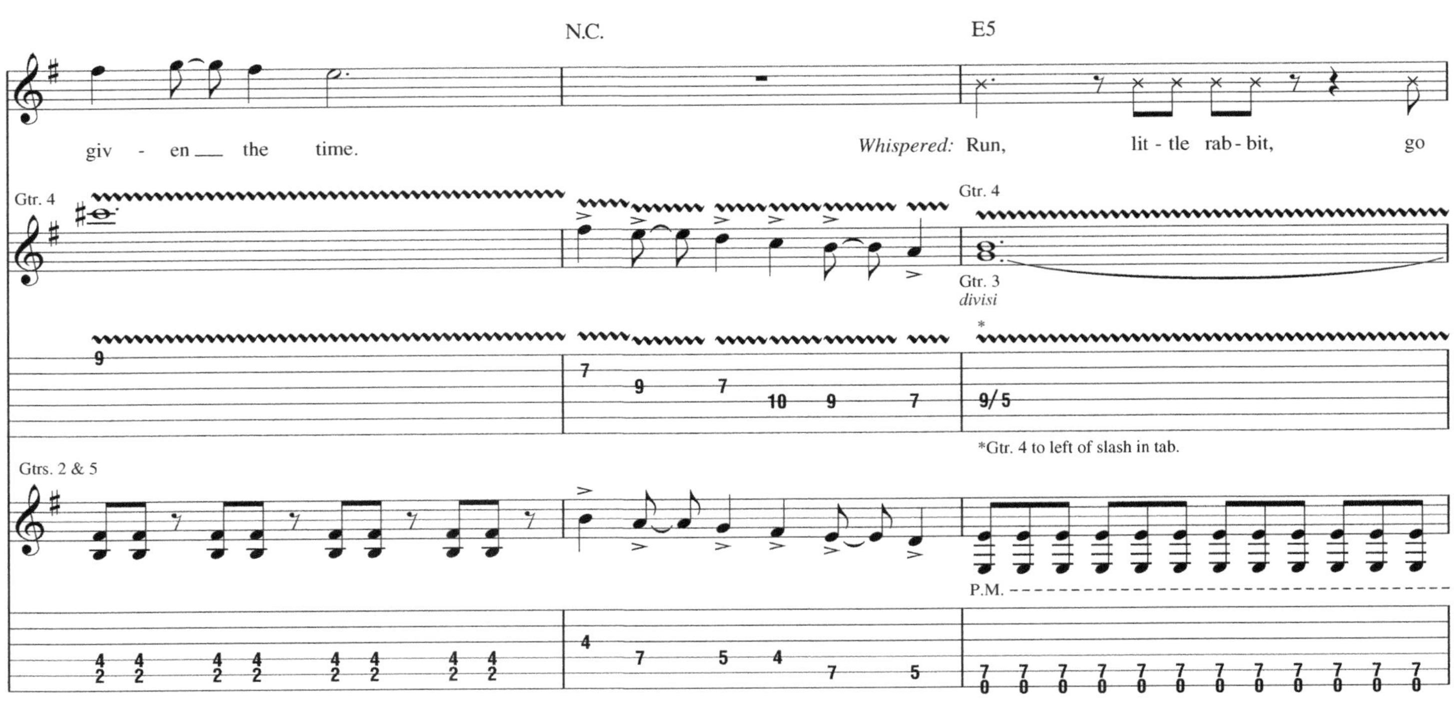
N.C.
E5
giv - en the time.
Whispered: Run, lit - tle rab - bit, go
Gtr. 4
Gtr. 4
Gtr. 3
divisi
*Gtr. 4 to left of slash in tab.
Gtrs. 2 & 5
P.M.

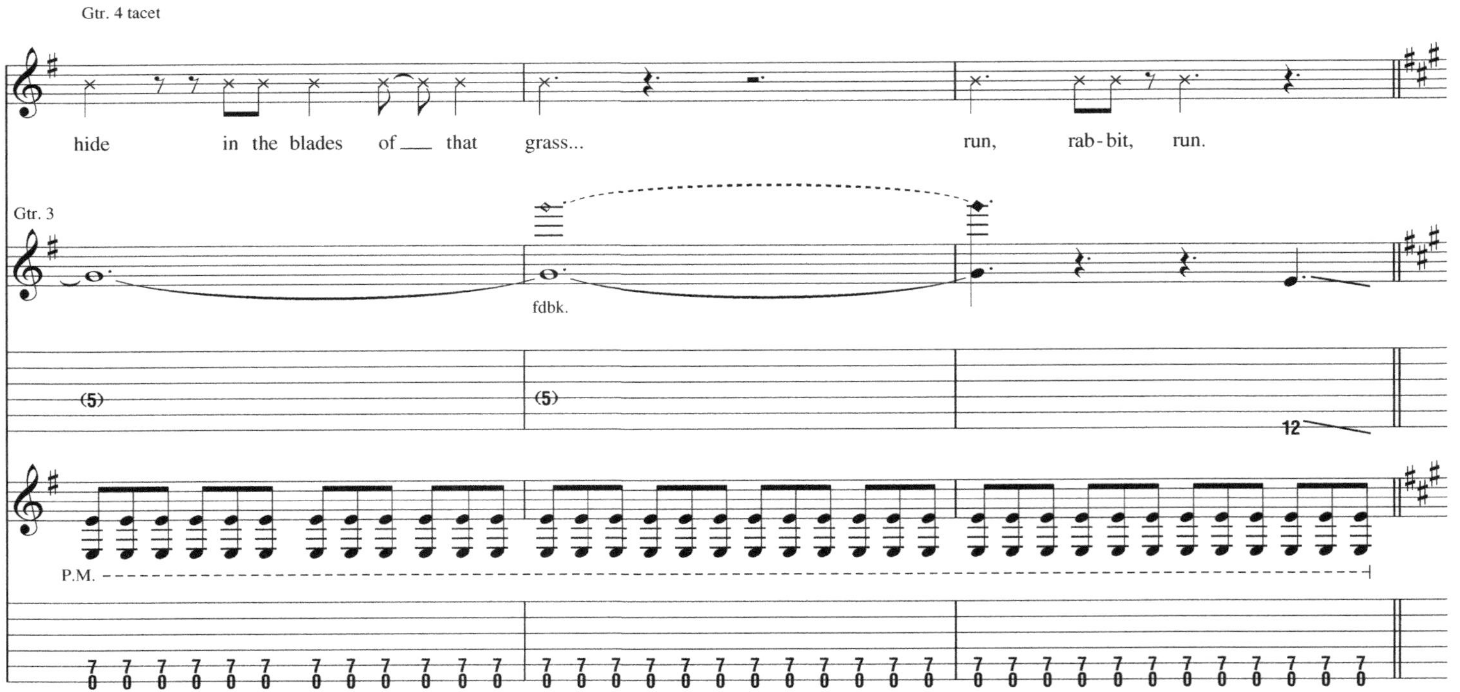
Gtr. 4 tacet
hide in the blades of that grass...
run, rab - bit, run.
Gtr. 3
fdbk.
P.M.

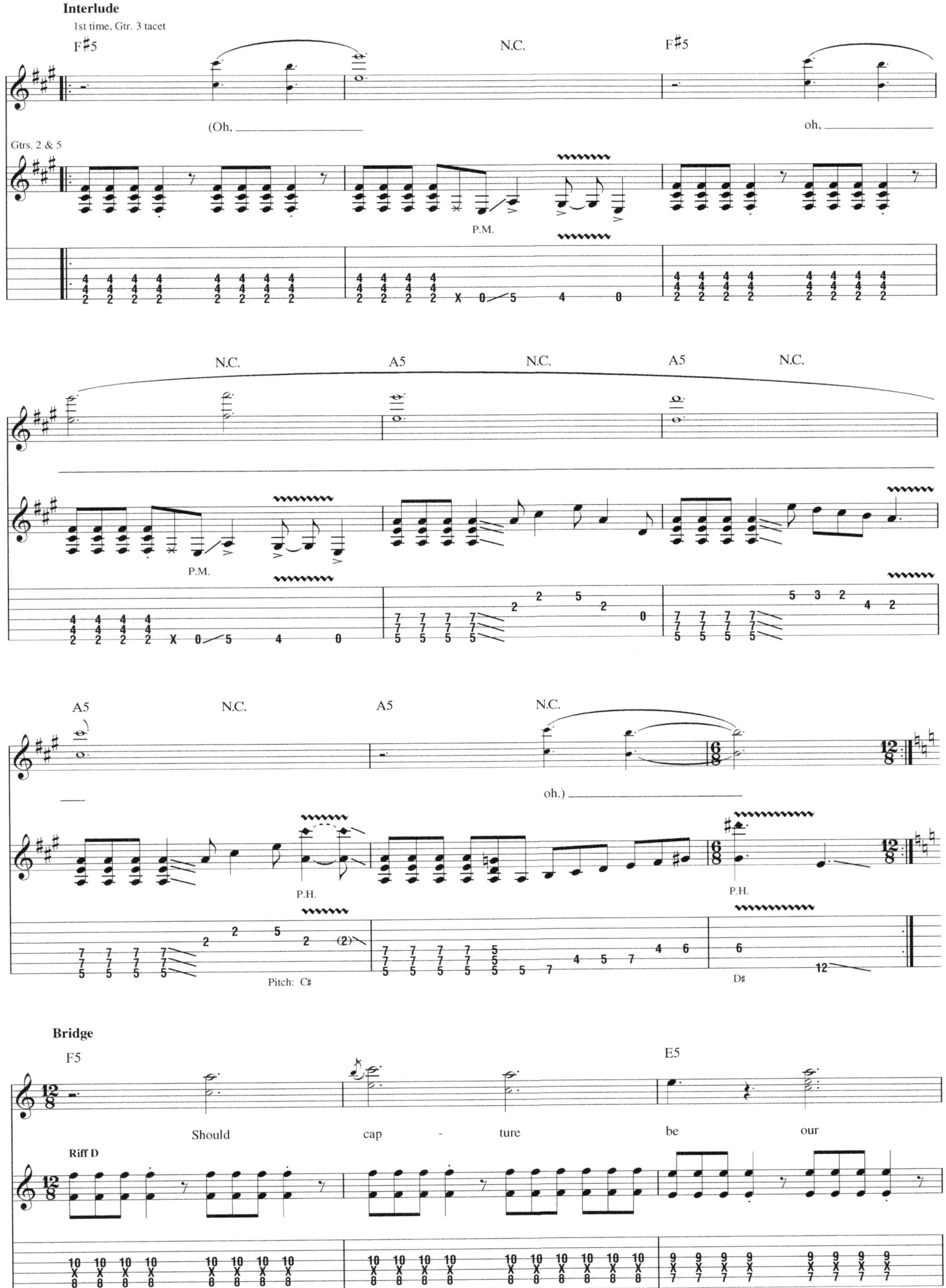
Interlude
1st time, Gtr. 3 tacet
F♯5
N.C.
F♯5
(Oh,
oh,
Gtrs. 2 & 5
P.M.
N.C.
A5
N.C.
A5
N.C.
P.M.
A5
N.C.
A5
N.C.
oh.)
P.H.
P.H.
Pitch: C♯
D♯
Bridge
F5
E5
Should
cap - ture
be
our
Riff D

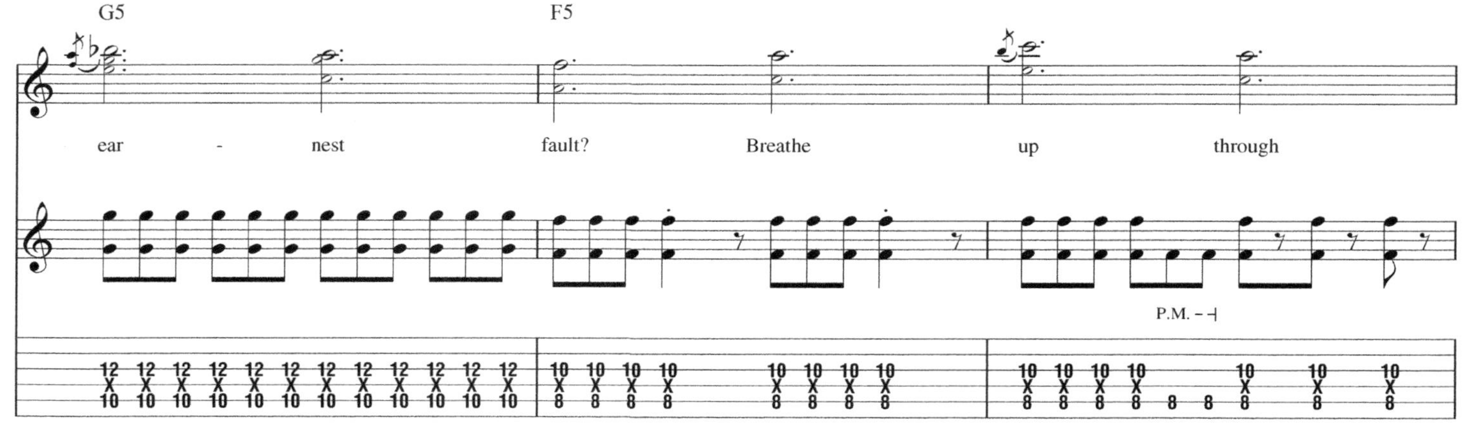

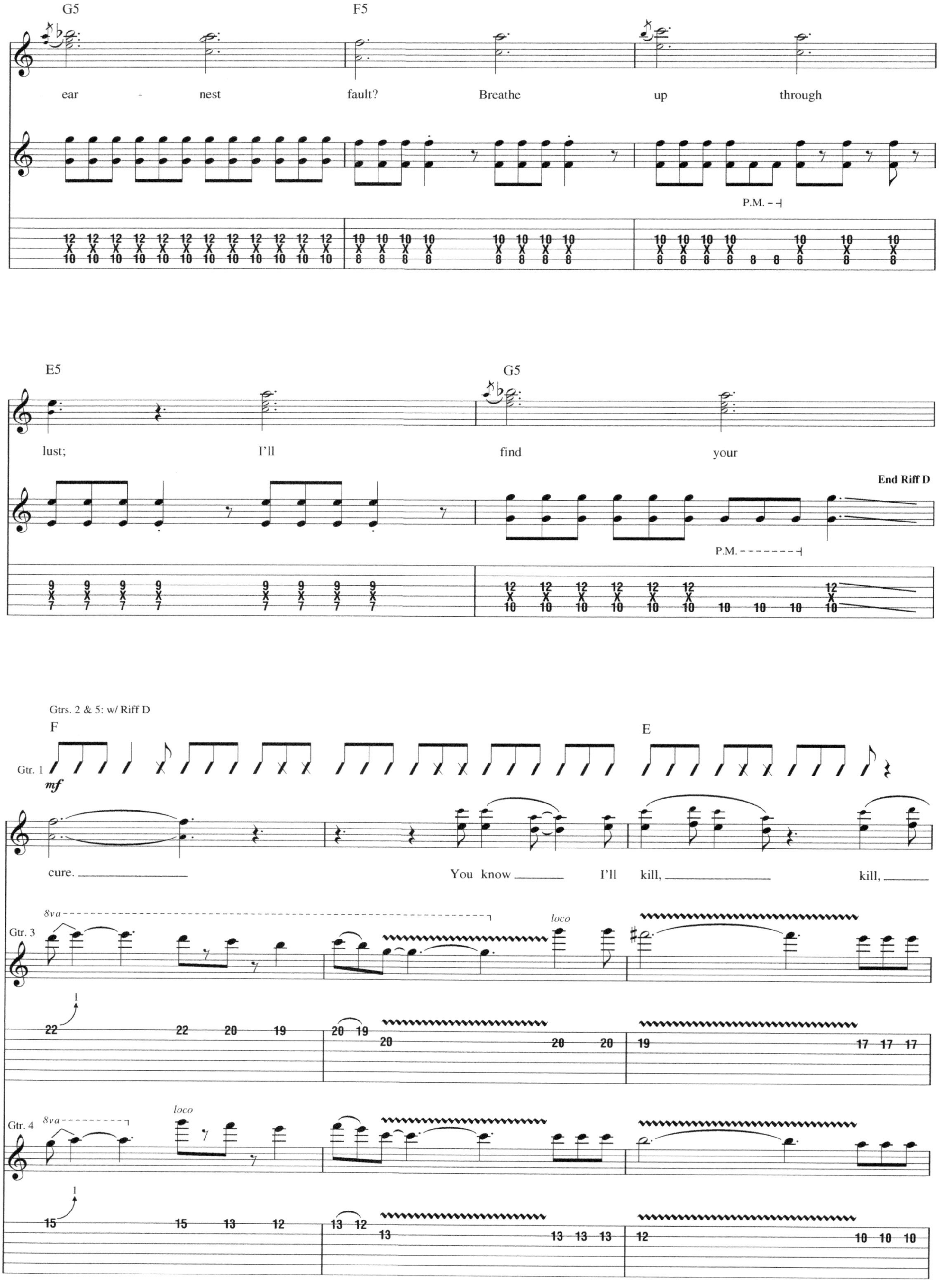

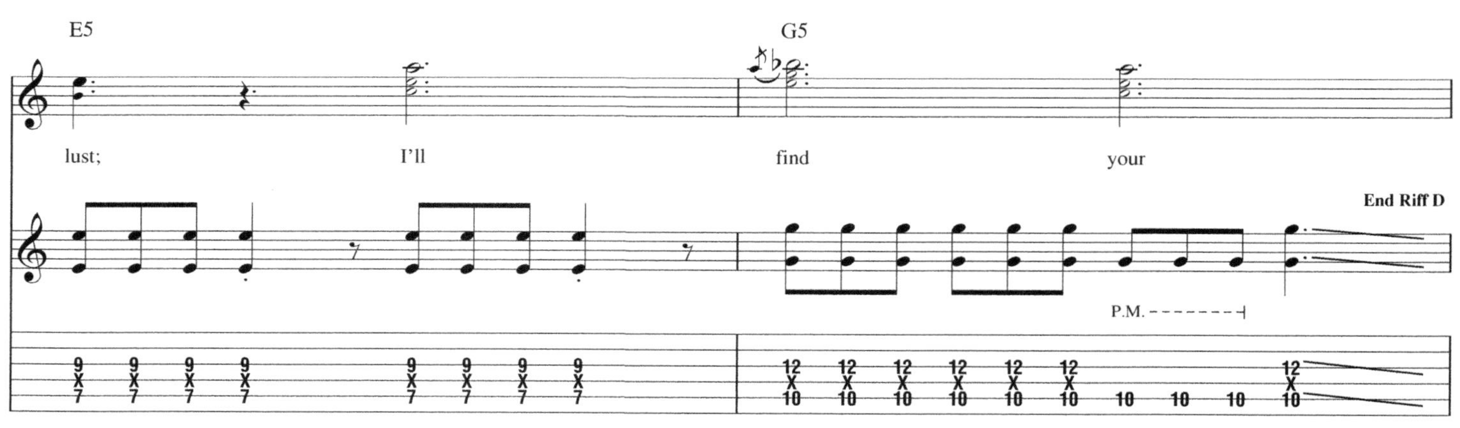

Gtrs. 2 & 5: w/ Riff D

F E

Gtr. 1

mf

cure. You know I'll kill, kill,

Gtr. 3

8va loco

Gtr. 4

8va loco

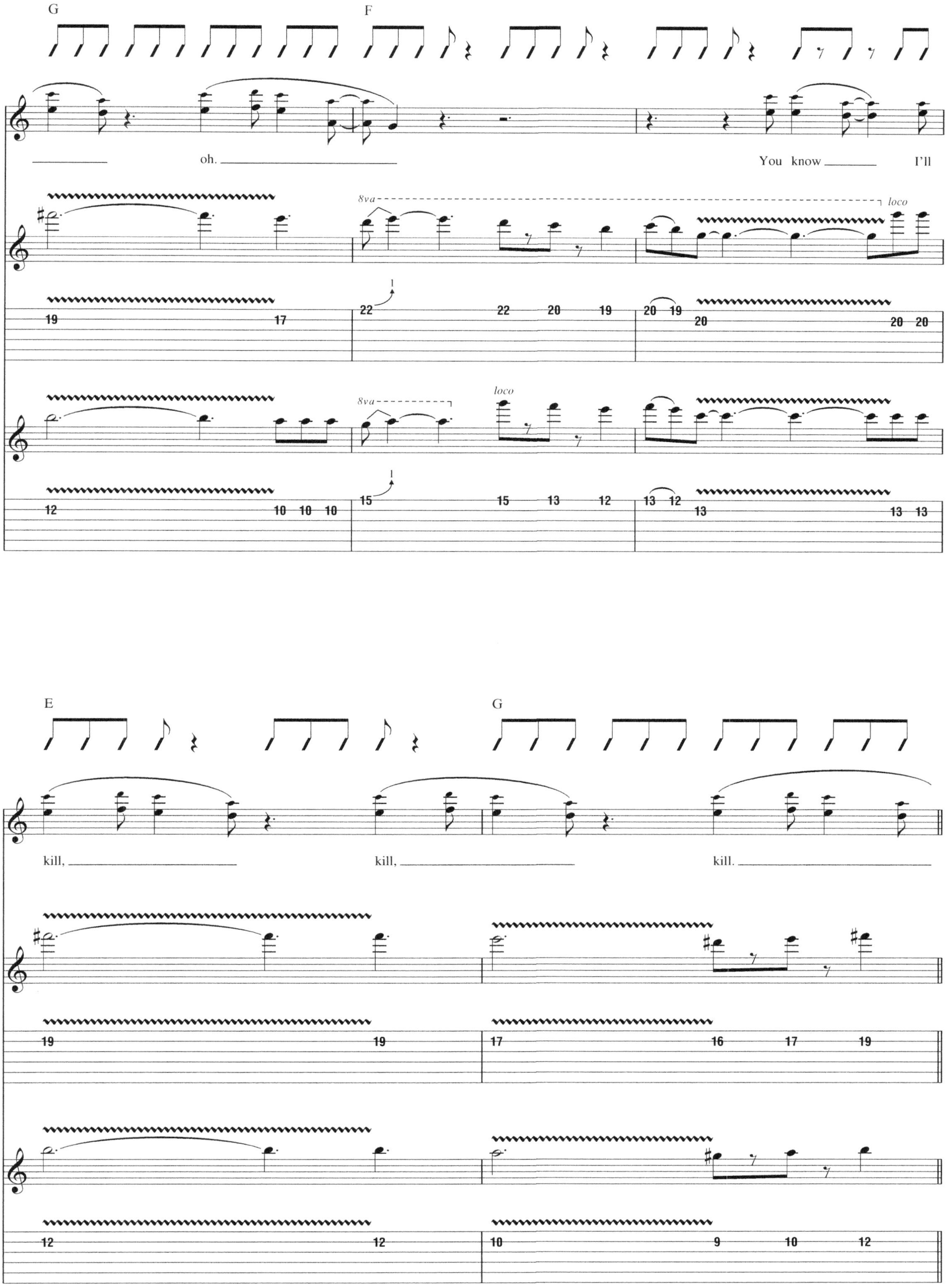

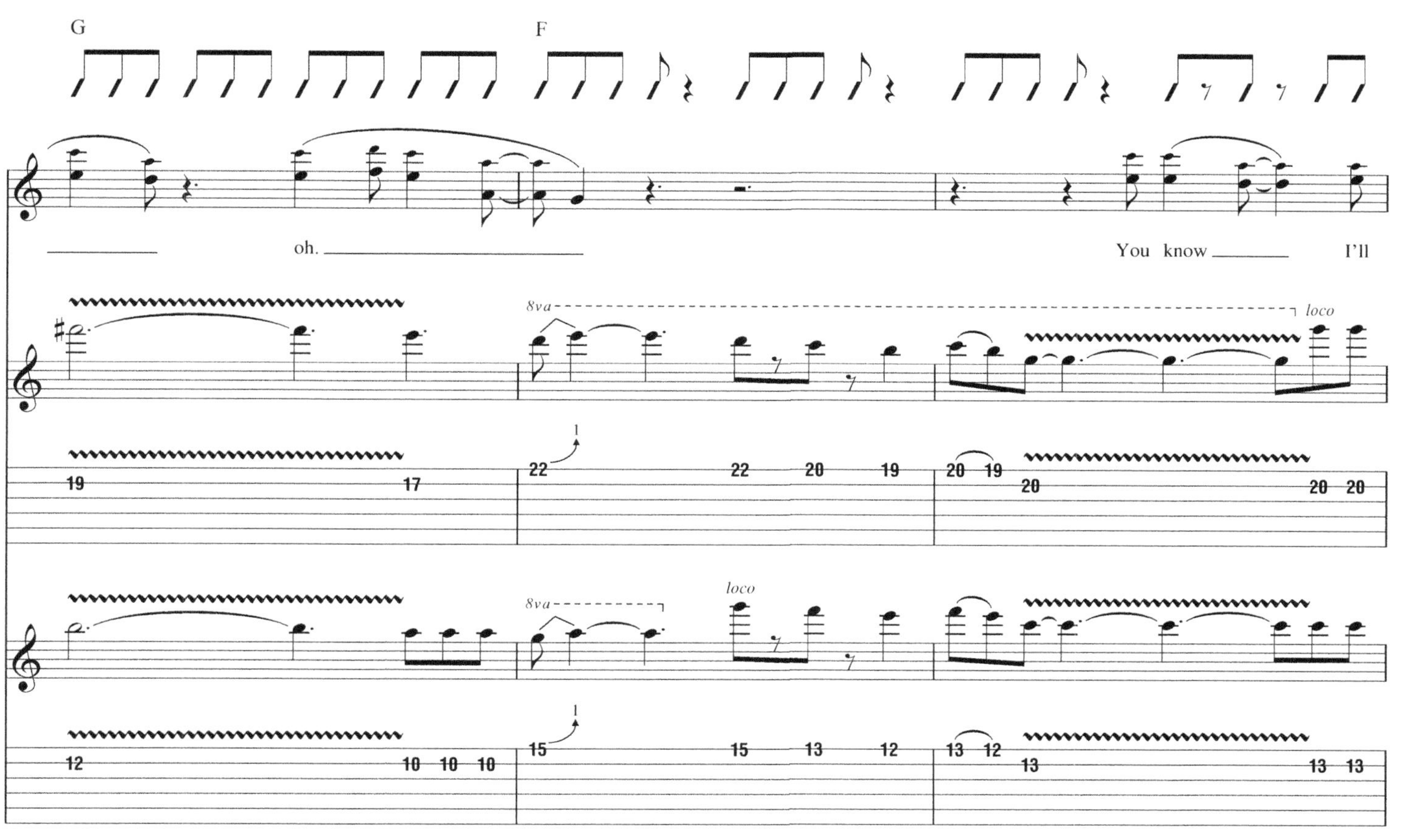

E G

kill, kill, kill.

19 19 | 17 16 17 19

12 12 | 10 9 10 12

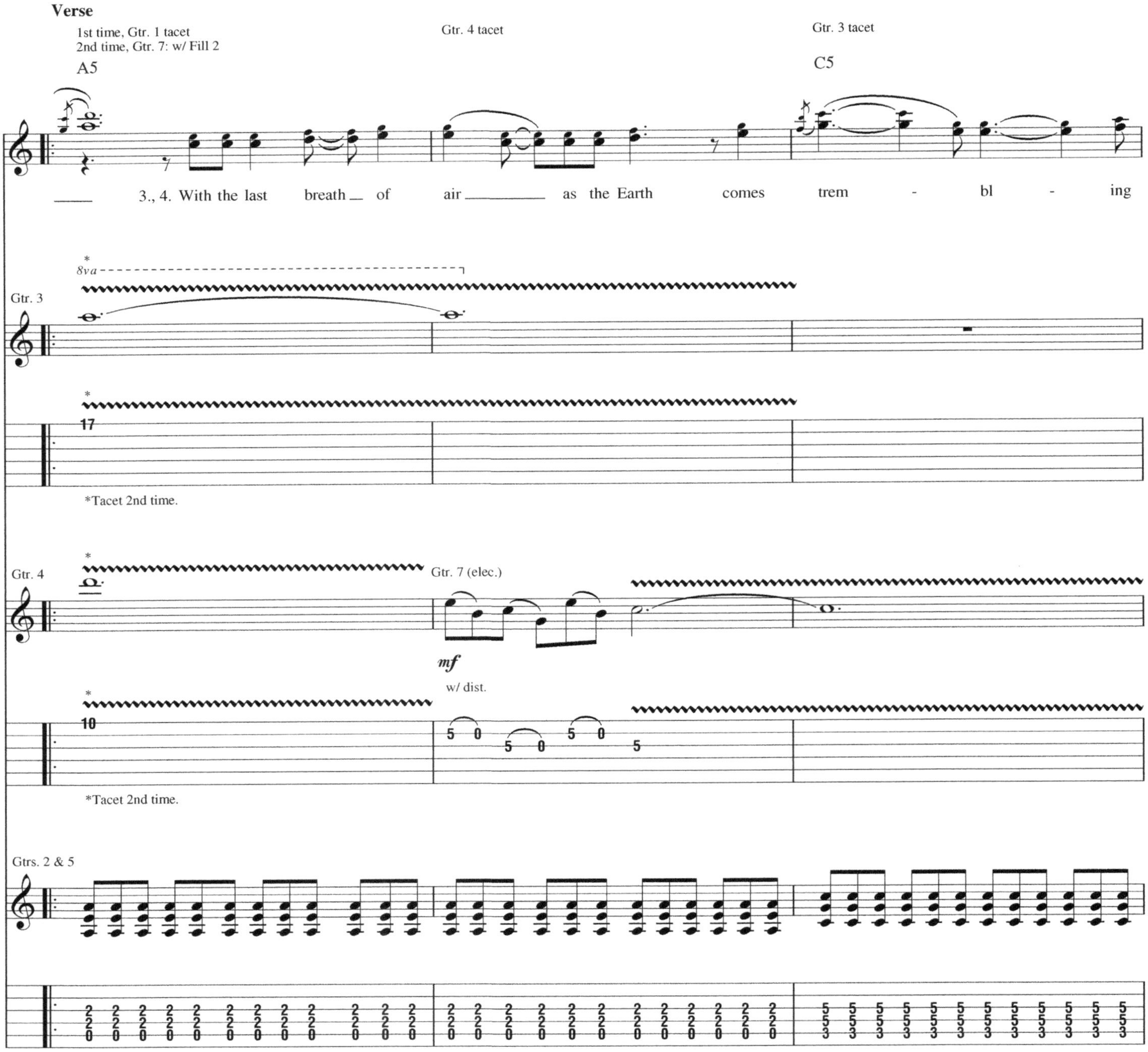

Verse

1st time, Gtr. 1 tacet
2nd time, Gtr. 7: w/ Fill 2

Gtr. 4 tacet

Gtr. 3 tacet

A5 C5

3., 4. With the last breath ___ of air ___ as the Earth comes trem - bl - ing

Gtr. 3

*8va

*Tacet 2nd time.

Gtr. 4

Gtr. 7 (elec.)

mf

w/ dist.

*Tacet 2nd time.

Gtrs. 2 & 5

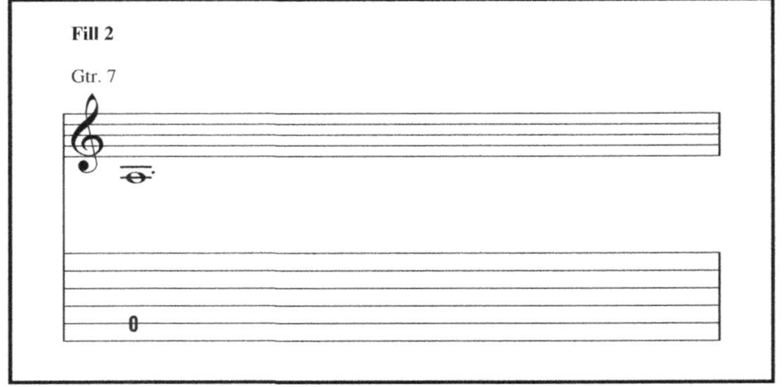

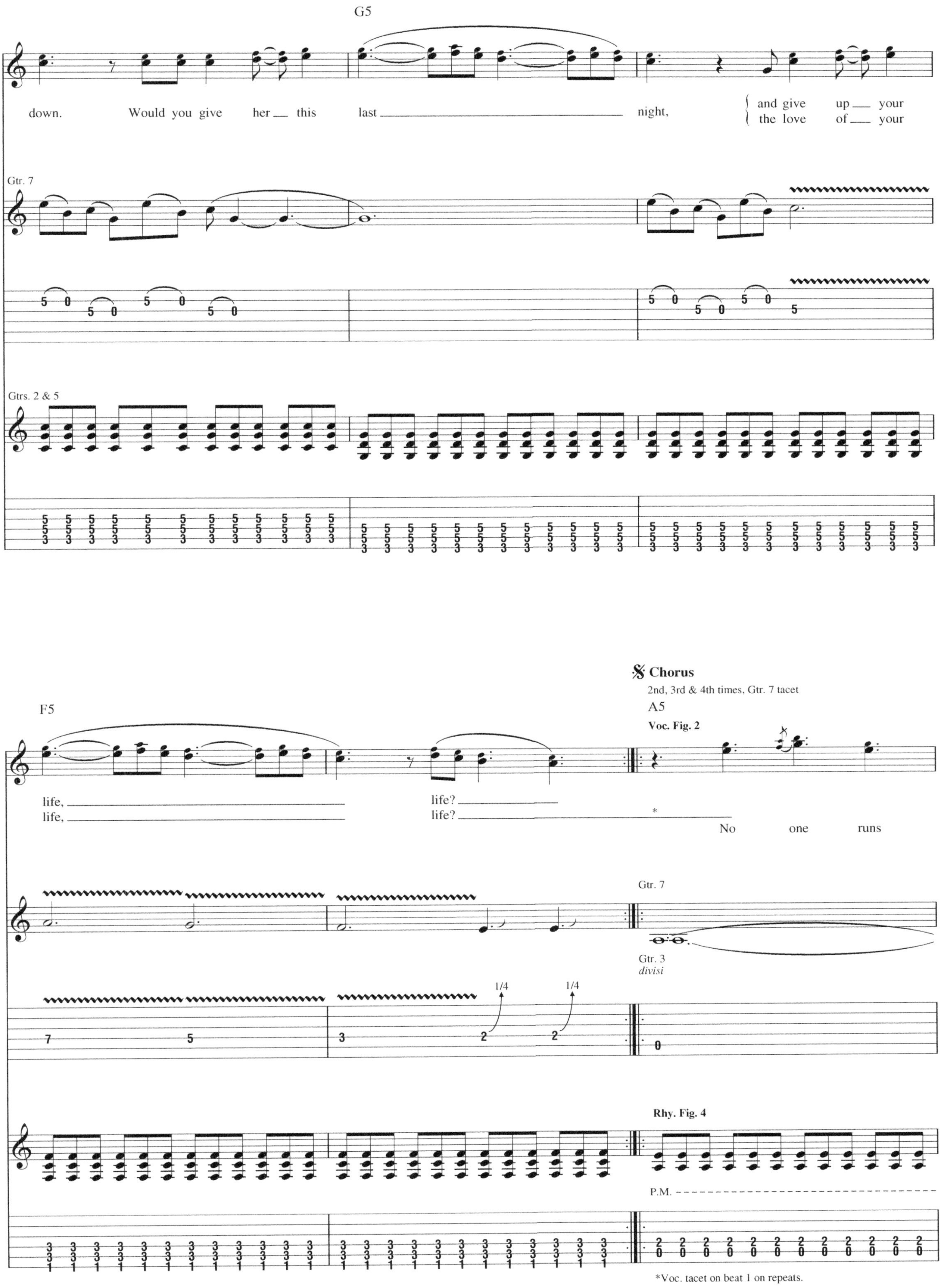

G5

down. Would you give her this last night, { and give up your / the love of your

Gtr. 7

Gtrs. 2 & 5

F5

life, life?
life, life?

𝄋 Chorus

2nd, 3rd & 4th times, Gtr. 7 tacet

A5

Voc. Fig. 2

No one runs

Gtr. 7

Gtr. 3
divisi

1/4 1/4

Rhy. Fig. 4

P.M.

*Voc. tacet on beat 1 on repeats.

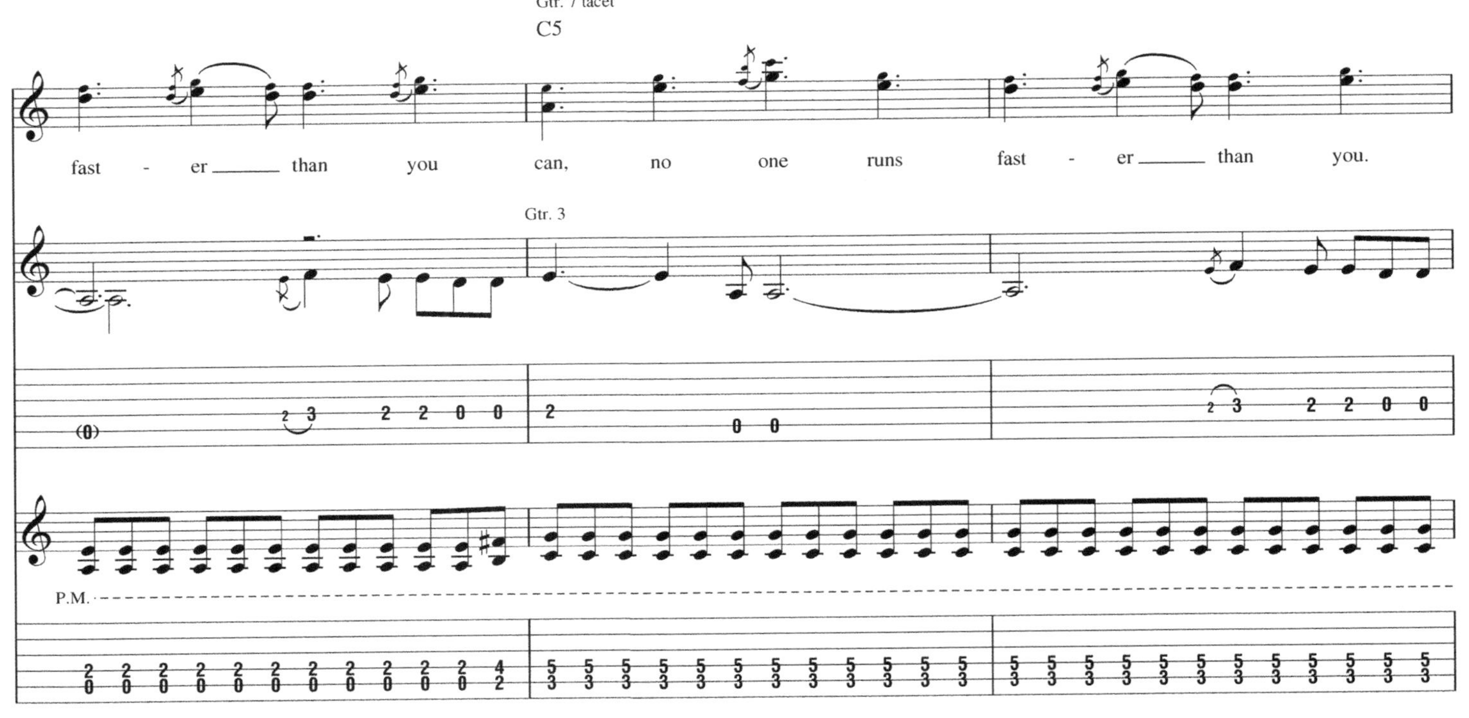
Gtr. 7 tacet
C5
fast - er than you can, no one runs fast - er than you.
Gtr. 3
P.M.

To Coda

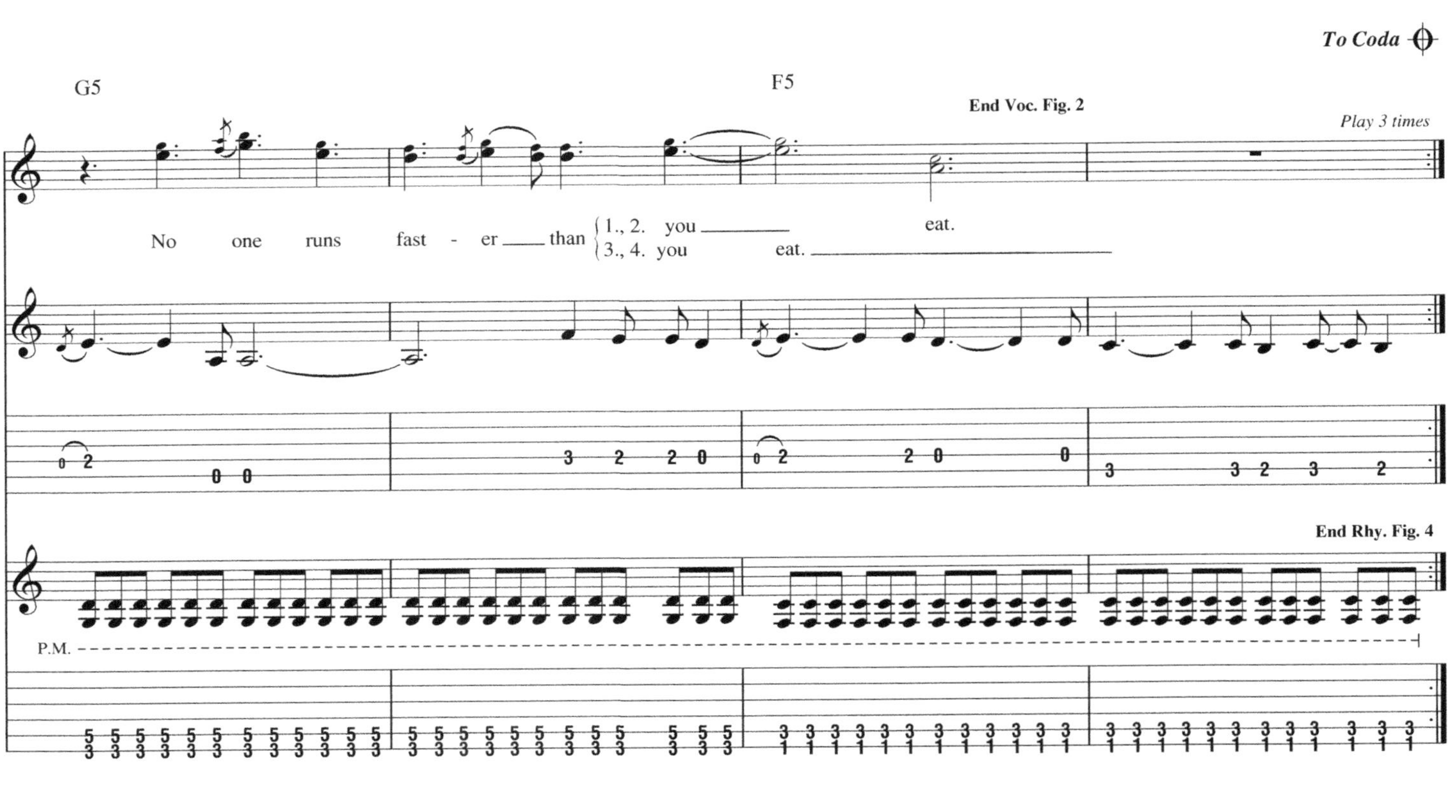
G5
F5
End Voc. Fig. 2
Play 3 times
No one runs fast - er than
1., 2. you eat.
3., 4. you eat.
End Rhy. Fig. 4
P.M.

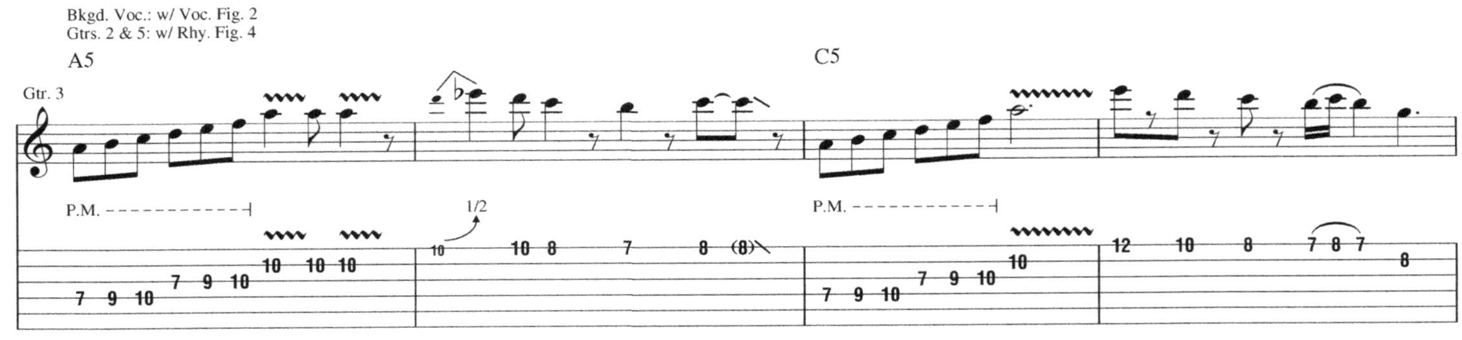
Bkgd. Voc.: w/ Voc. Fig. 2
Gtrs. 2 & 5: w/ Rhy. Fig. 4
A5
C5
Gtr. 3
P.M.
1/2

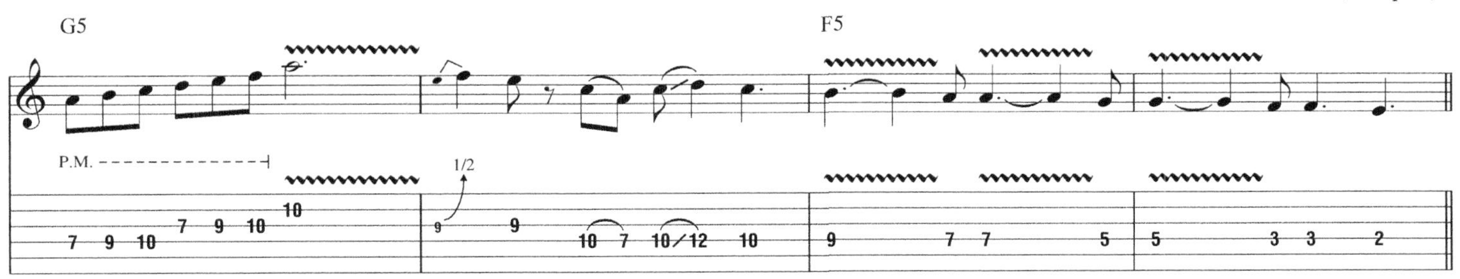
D.S. al Coda
(no repeat)
G5
F5
P.M.
1/2

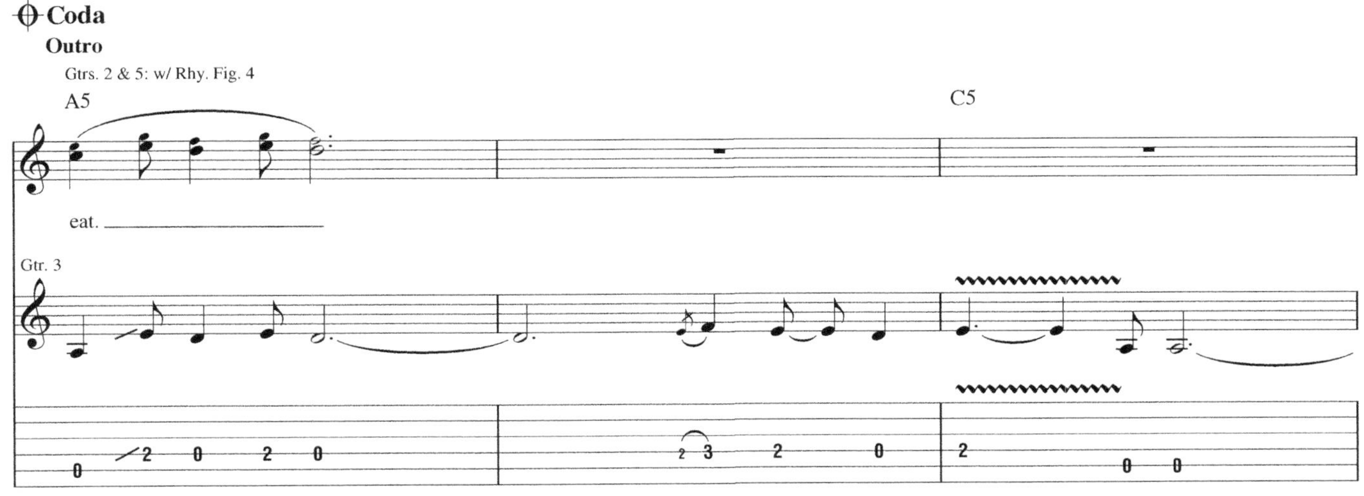
Coda
Outro
Gtrs. 2 & 5: w/ Rhy. Fig. 4
A5
C5
eat.
Gtr. 3

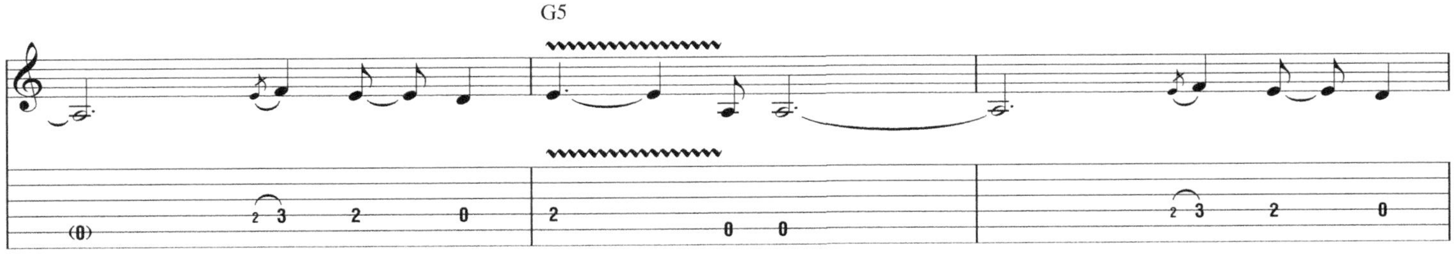
G5

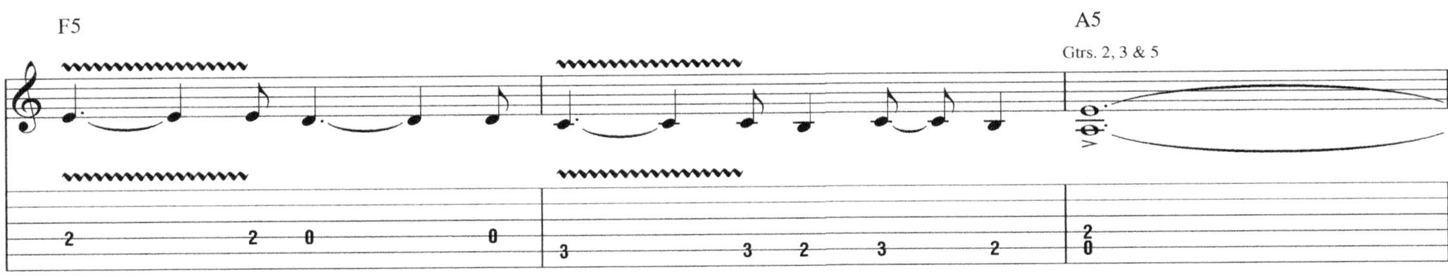
F5
A5
Gtrs. 2, 3 & 5

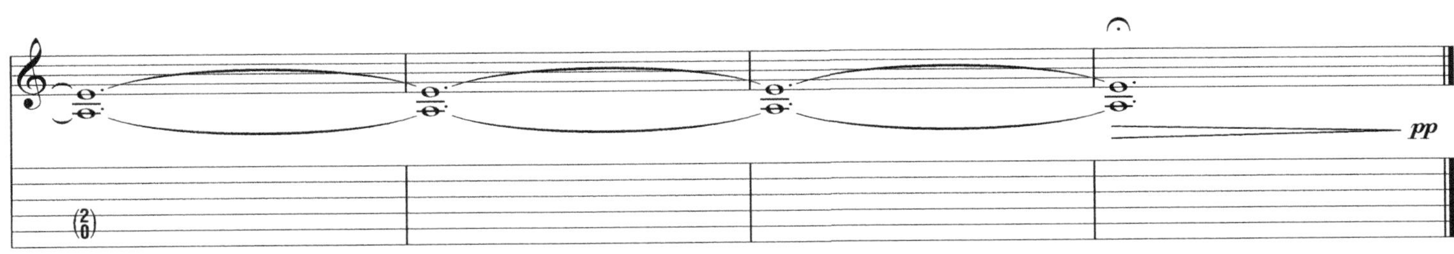
pp

Willing Well III: Apollo II: The Telling Truth

Words and Music by Claudio Sanchez, Michael Todd, Joshua Eppard and Travis Stever

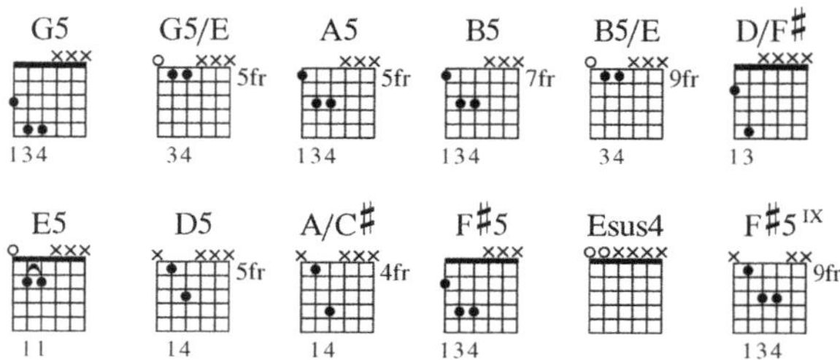

Tune down 1/2 step:
(low to high) E♭-A♭-D♭-G♭-B♭-E♭

Intro

Moderately fast ♩ = 160

N.C.

* F♯7♭9(no3rd)

Riff A1

(Sound effects) 27 sec.

(Drums & Bass)

Gtr. 2 (clean)

mf

Fill 1

End Fill 1 **Riff A**

Gtr. 1 (slight dist.)

mf

P.M.

Riff A2

Gtr. 3 (clean)

mf

*Chord symbols reflect overall harmony.

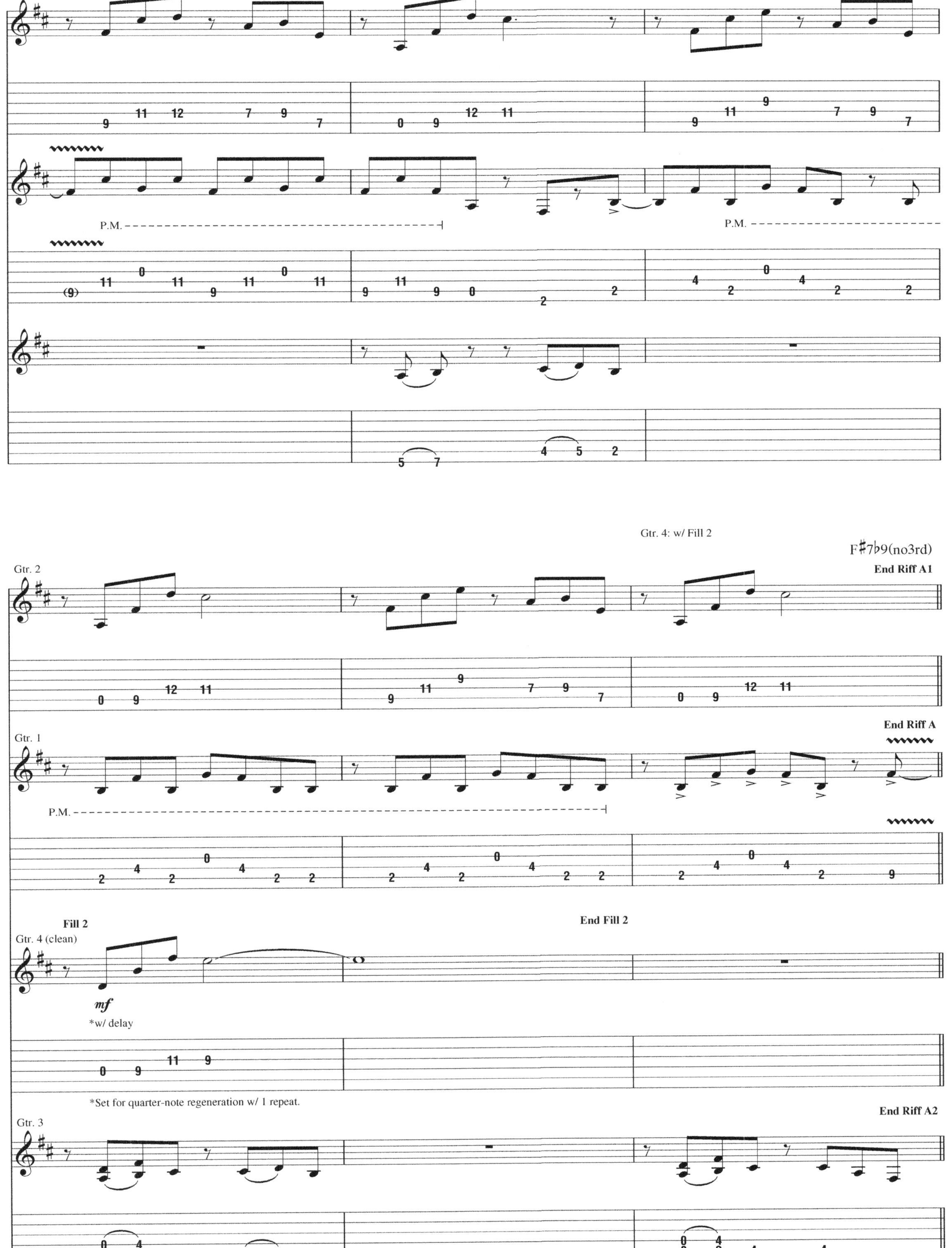

Bm11♭6
P.M.
P.M.
Gtr. 4: w/ Fill 2
F♯7♭9(no3rd)
Gtr. 2
End Riff A1
Gtr. 1
End Riff A
P.M.
Fill 2
Gtr. 4 (clean)
End Fill 2
mf
*w/ delay
*Set for quarter-note regeneration w/ 1 repeat.
Gtr. 3
End Riff A2

Verse

1st time, Gtr. 1: w/ Riff A (1 1/2 times)
1st time, Gtr. 2: w/ Riff A1 (1st 6 meas.)
Gtr. 3: w/ Riff A2 (2 times)
2nd time, Gtrs. 1 & 2: w/ Riffs A & A1 (1 7/8 times)
2nd time, Gtr. 5 tacet
2nd time, Gtr. 6: w/ Fill 6

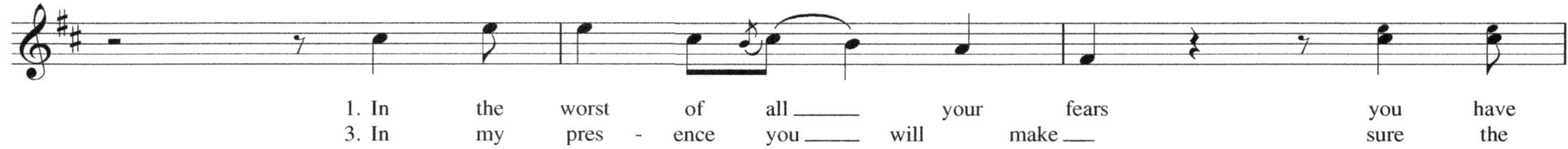

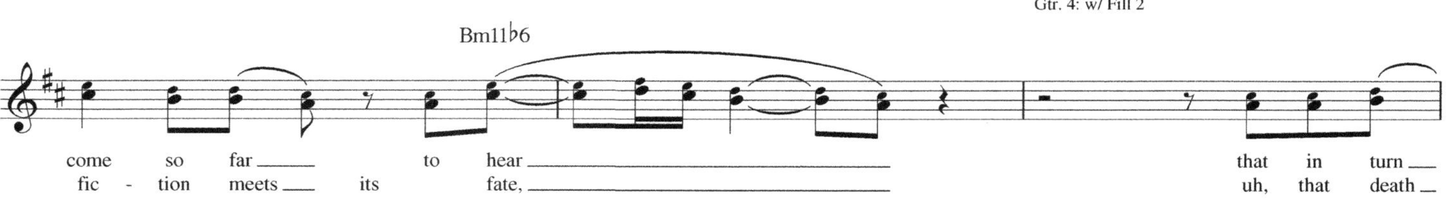

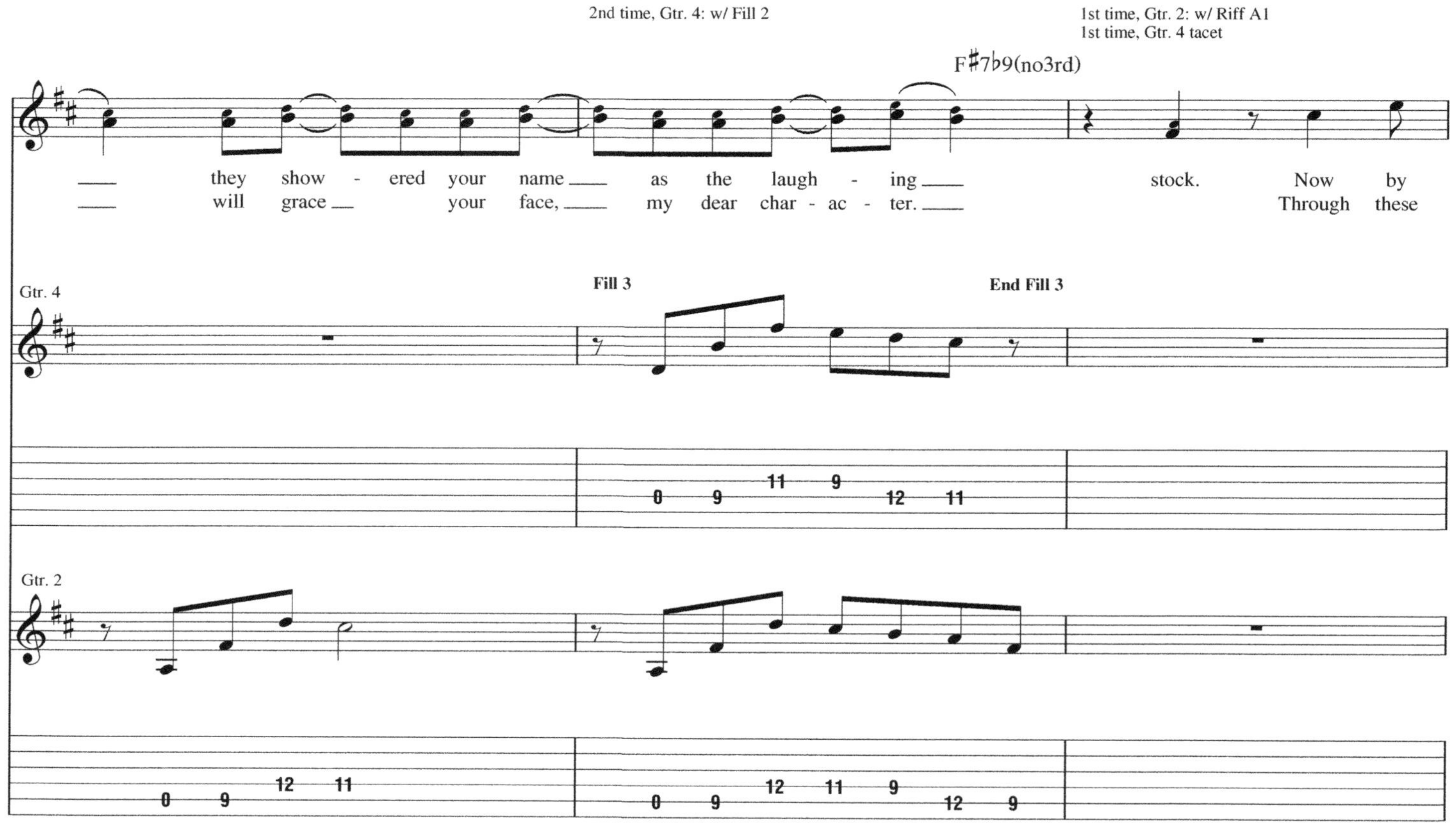

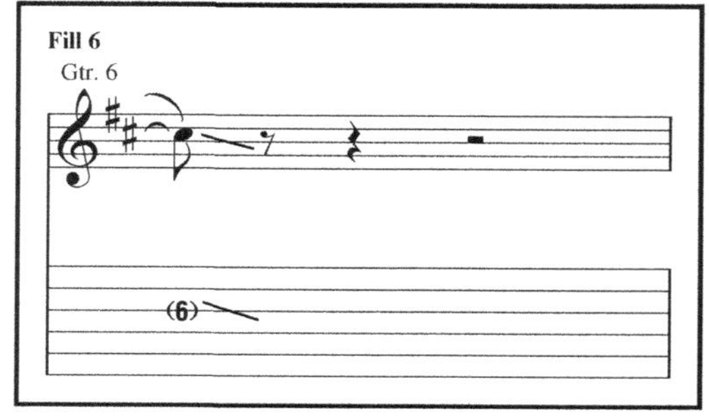

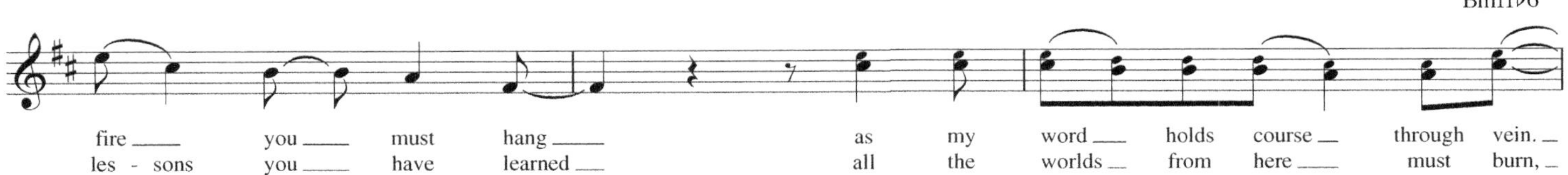
Bm11♭6
fire you must hang as my word holds course through vein.
les - sons you have learned all the worlds from here must burn,

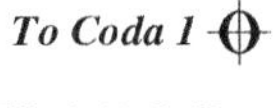
To Coda 1

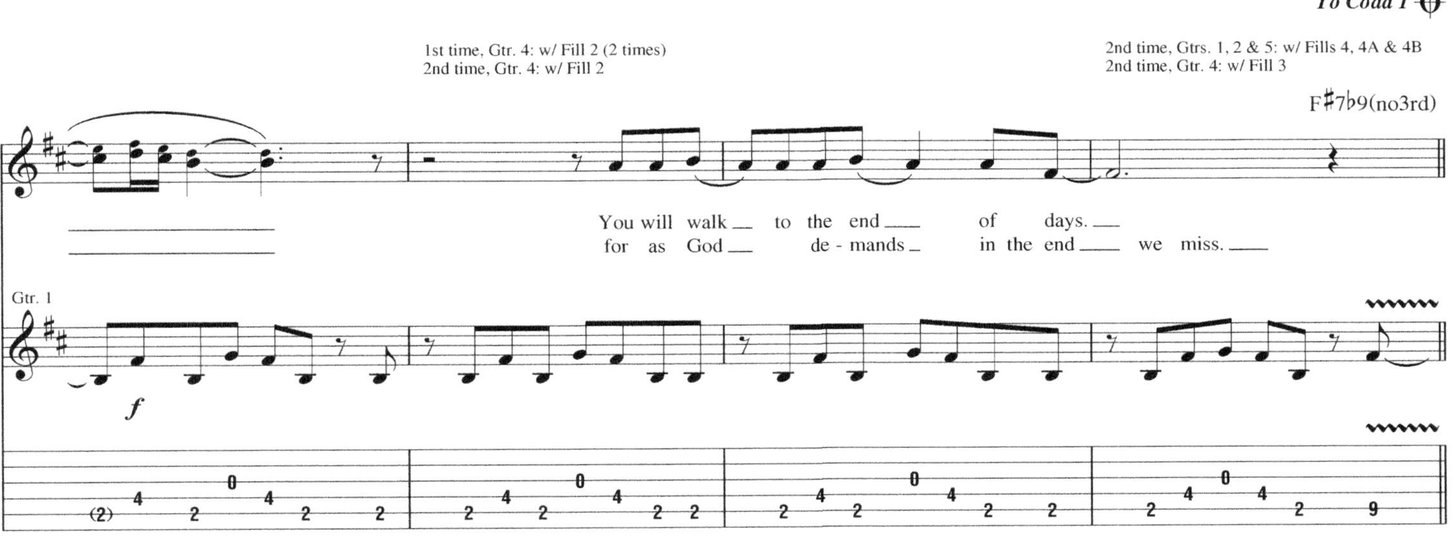
1st time, Gtr. 4: w/ Fill 2 (2 times)
2nd time, Gtr. 4: w/ Fill 2
2nd time, Gtrs. 1, 2 & 5: w/ Fills 4, 4A & 4B
2nd time, Gtr. 4: w/ Fill 3
F♯7♭9(no3rd)
You will walk to the end of days.
for as God de - mands in the end we miss.
Gtr. 1
f

Verse

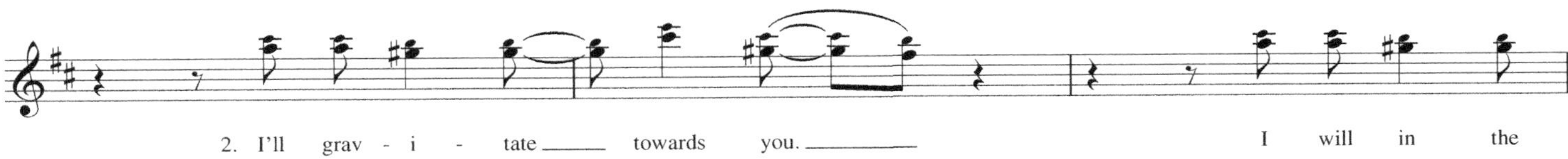
Gtrs. 1 & 2: w/ Riffs A & A1 (1 7/8 times)
Gtr. 3: w/ Riff A2 (2 times)
2. I'll grav - i - tate towards you. I will in the

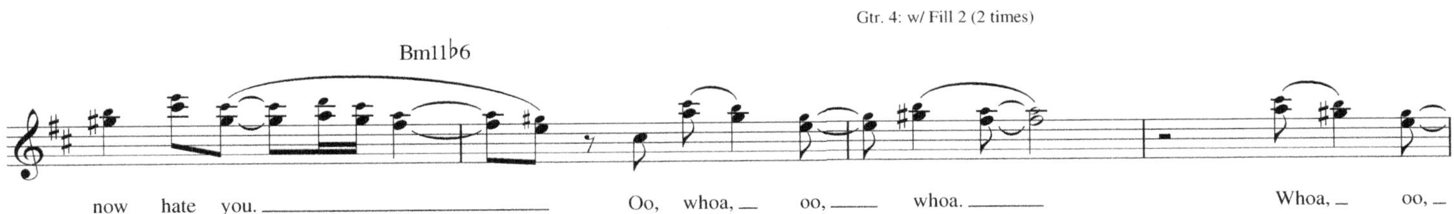
Gtr. 4: w/ Fill 2 (2 times)
Bm11♭6
now hate you. Oo, whoa, oo, whoa. Whoa, oo,

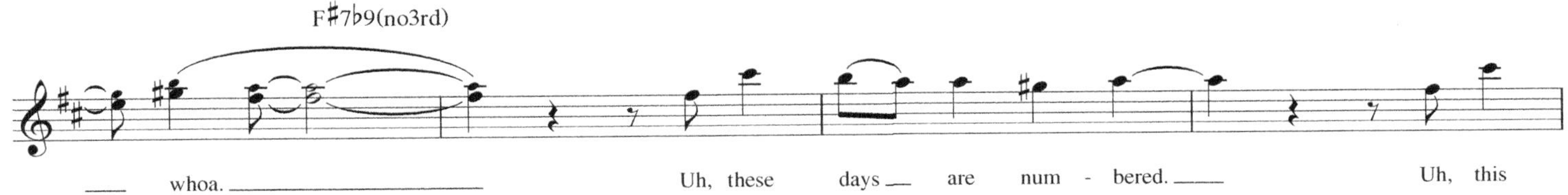
F♯7♭9(no3rd)
whoa. Uh, these days are num - bered. Uh, this

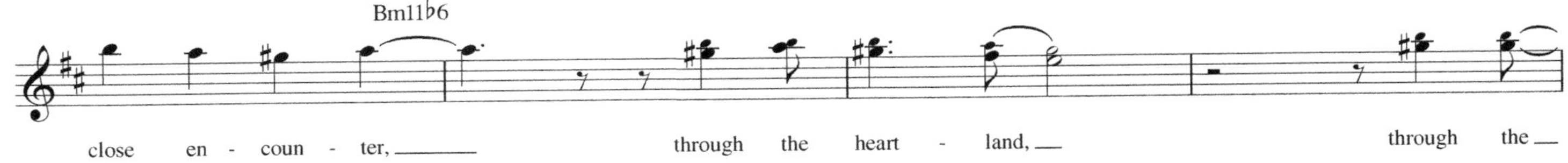

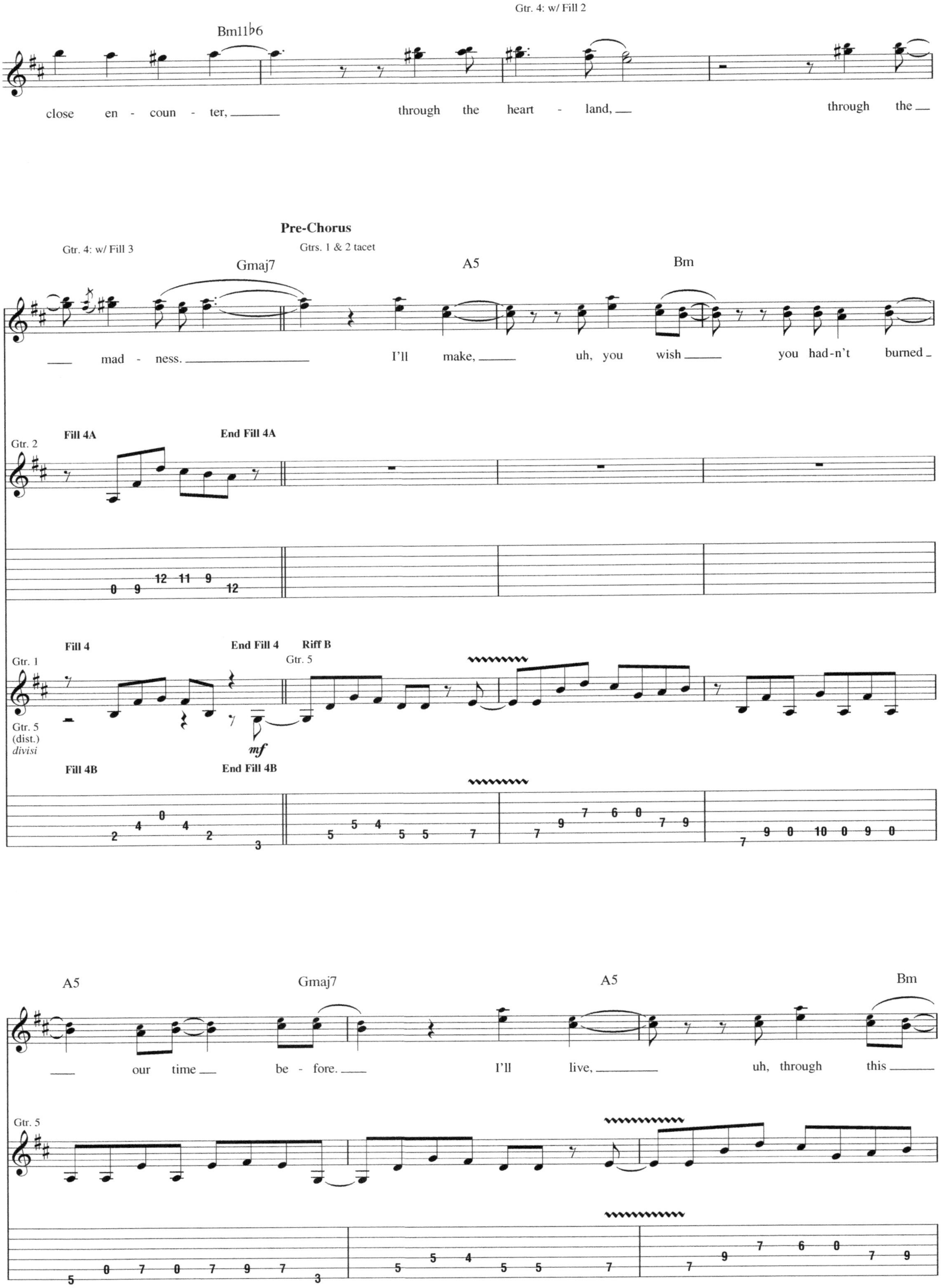

Pre-Chorus

Gtr. 4: w/ Fill 3
Gtrs. 1 & 2 tacet

Gmaj7 A5 Bm

mad - ness. I'll make, uh, you wish you had-n't burned

Gtr. 2
Fill 4A
End Fill 4A

Gtr. 1
Fill 4
End Fill 4
Riff B
Gtr. 5
Gtr. 5 (dist.) *divisi*
mf
Fill 4B
End Fill 4B

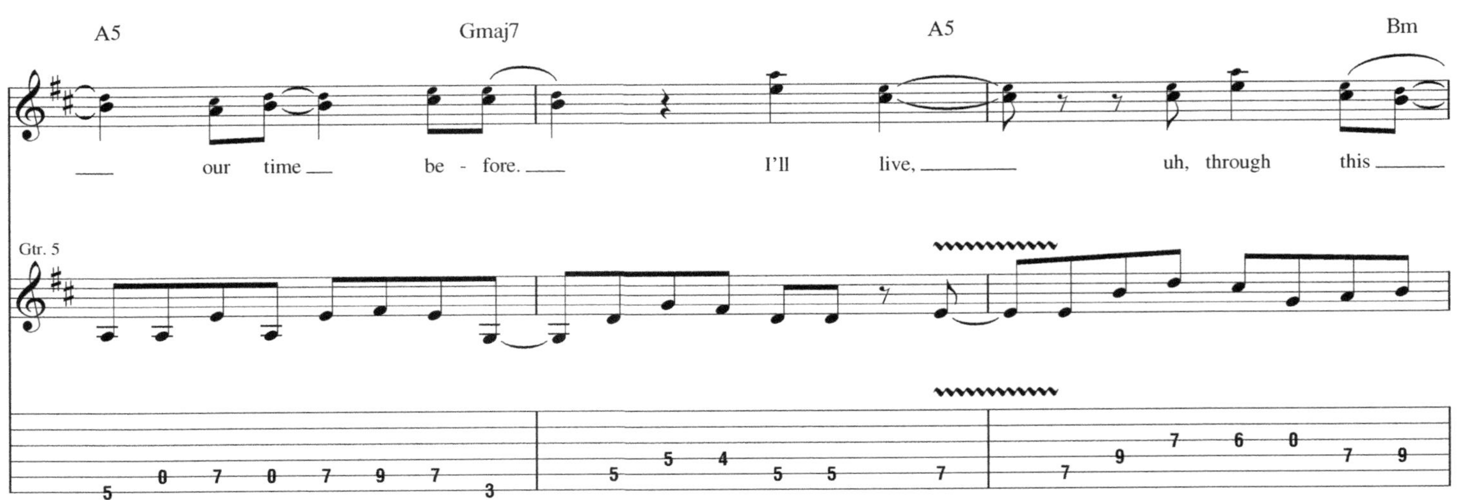

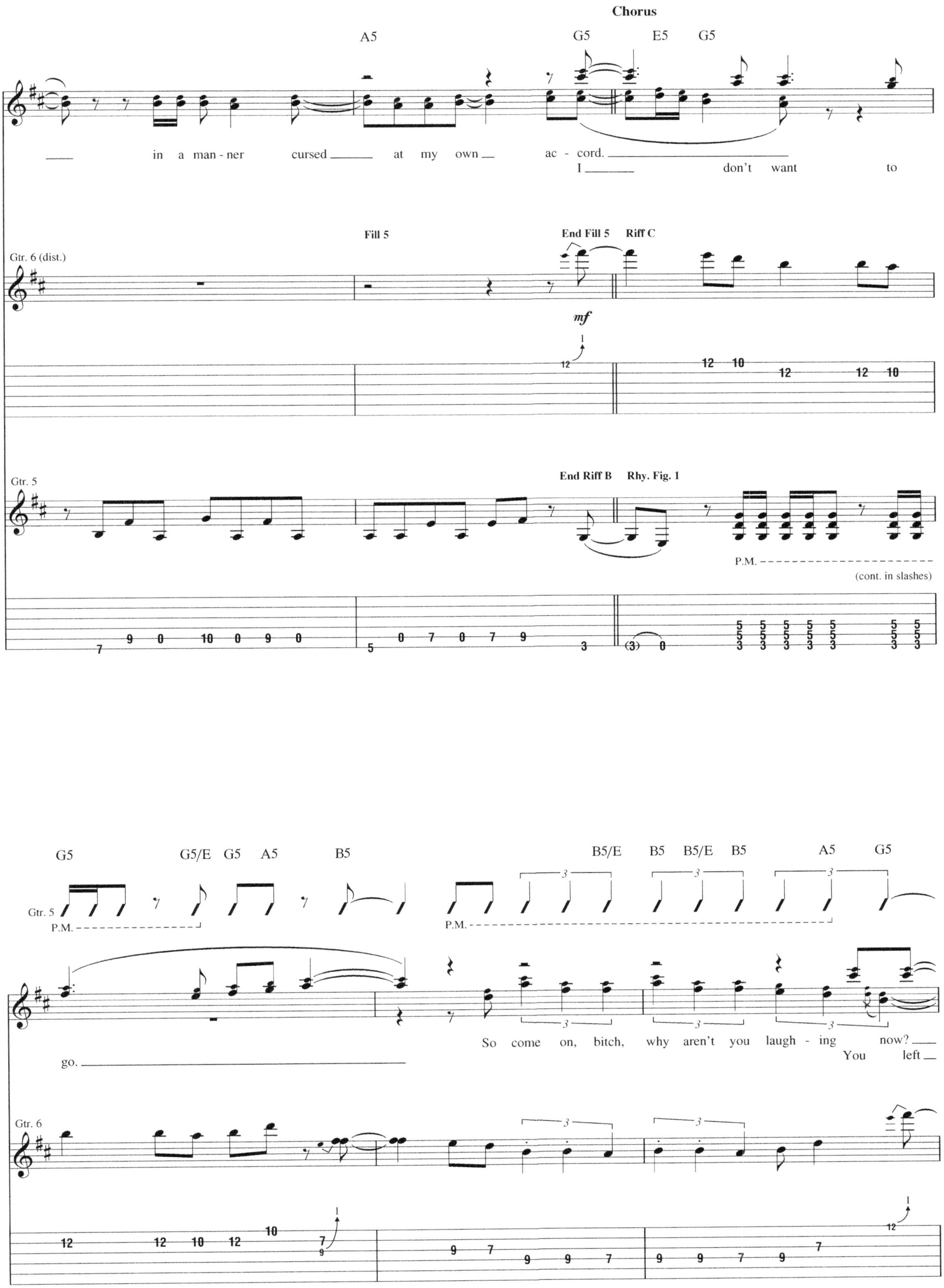

Chorus

A5 G5 E5 G5

in a man - ner cursed at my own ac - cord.

I don't want to

Gtr. 6 (dist.)

Fill 5

End Fill 5 Riff C

mf

Gtr. 5

End Riff B Rhy. Fig. 1

P.M.

(cont. in slashes)

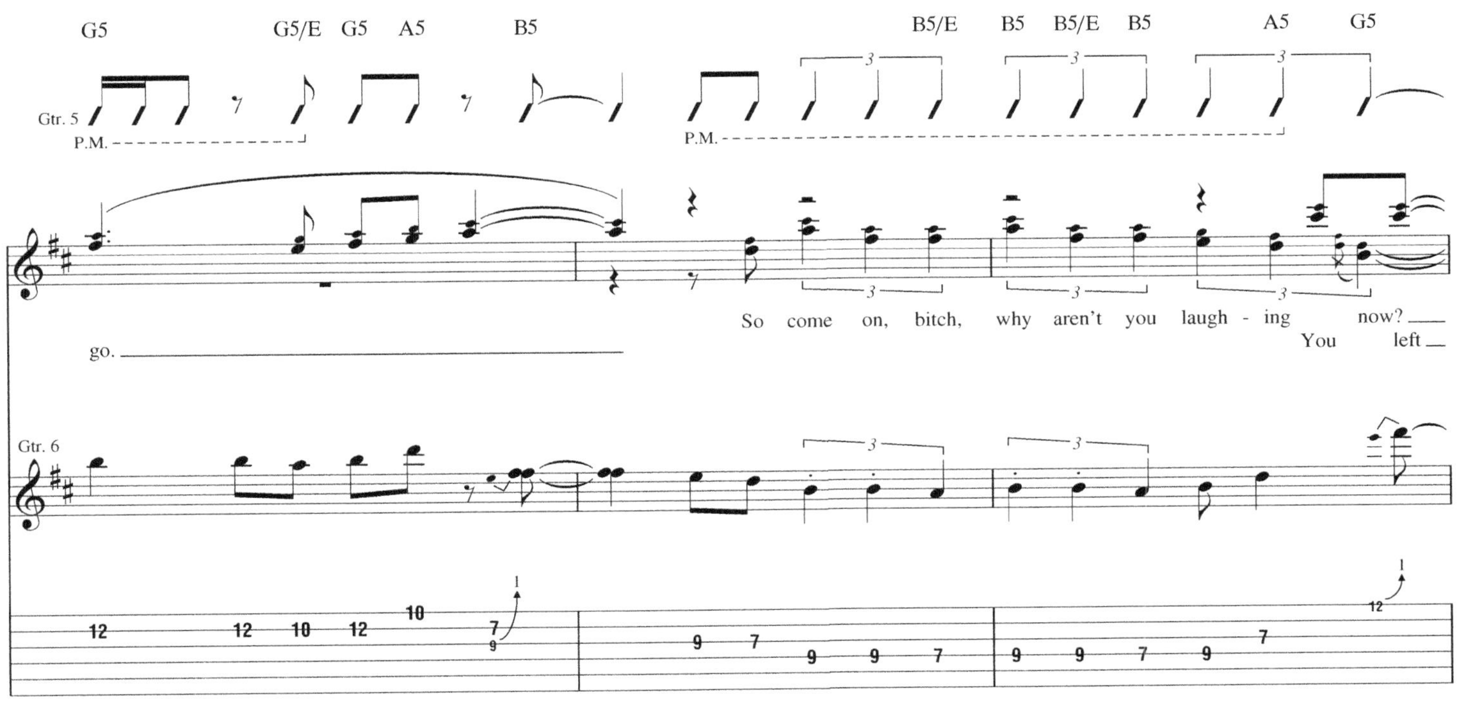

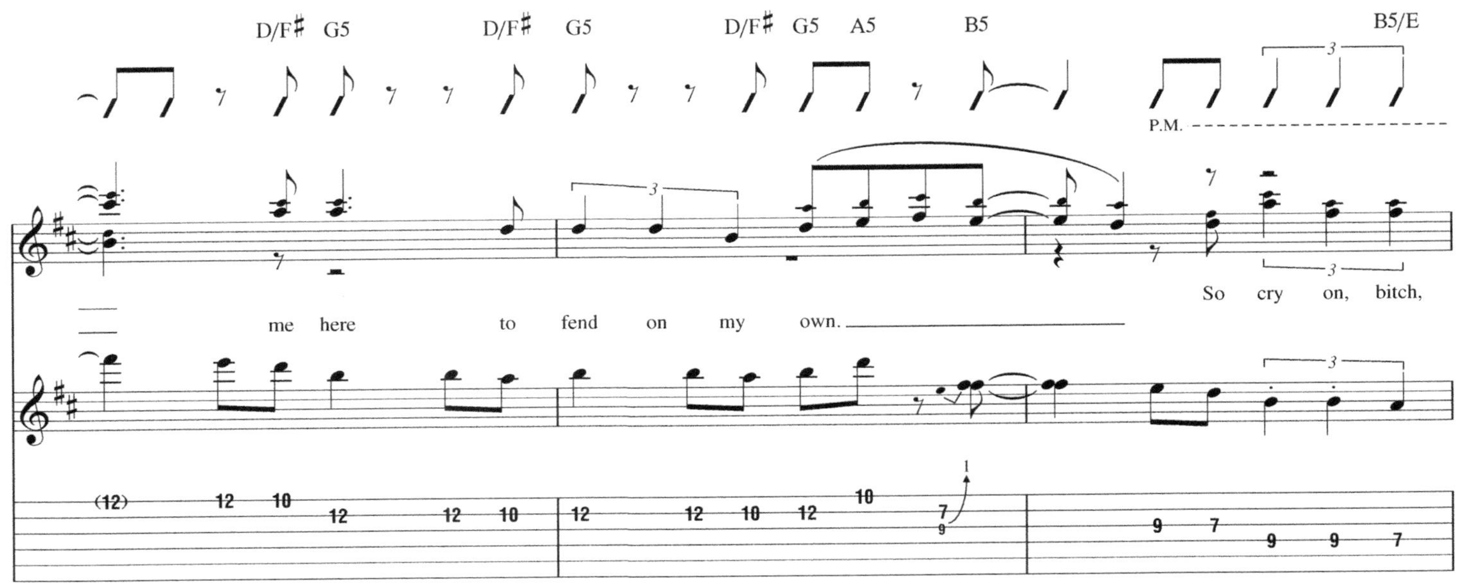
D/F♯ G5 D/F♯ G5 D/F♯ G5 A5 B5 B5/E
P.M.
me here to fend on my own.
So cry on, bitch,

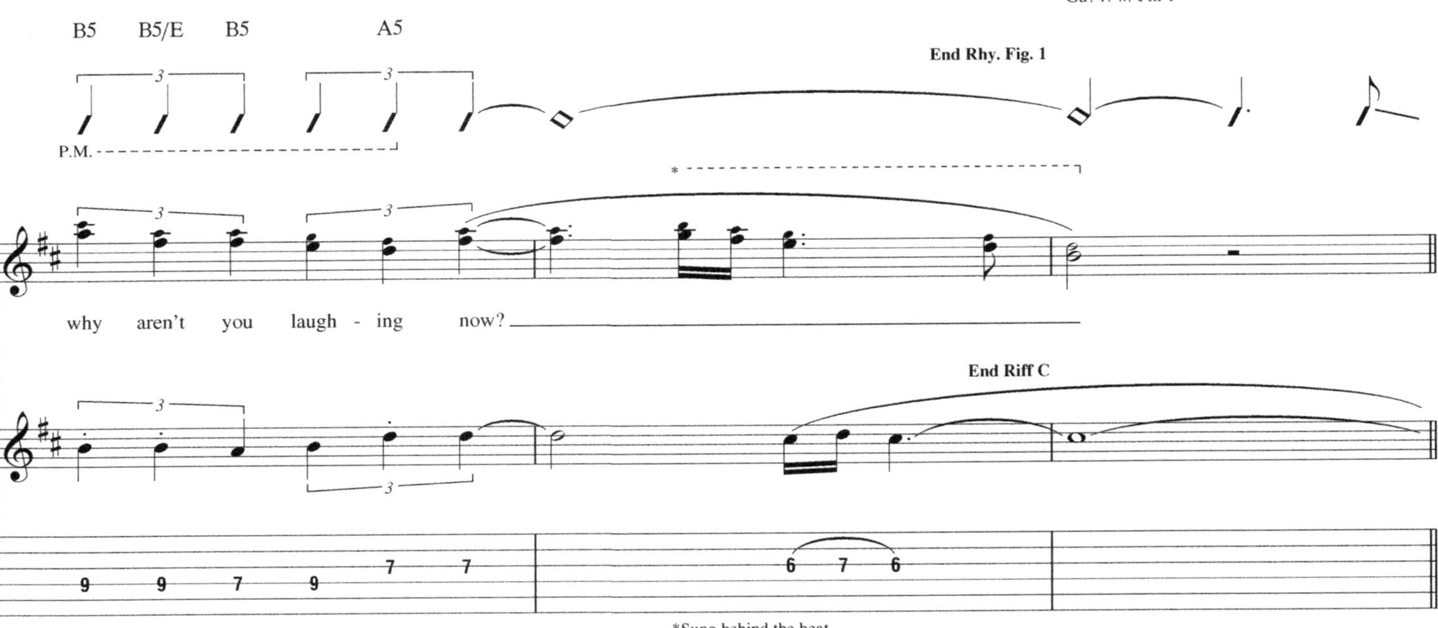
D.S. al Coda 1
Gtr. 1: w/ Fill 1
B5 B5/E B5 A5
End Rhy. Fig. 1
P.M.
why aren't you laugh - ing now?
End Riff C
*Sung behind the beat.

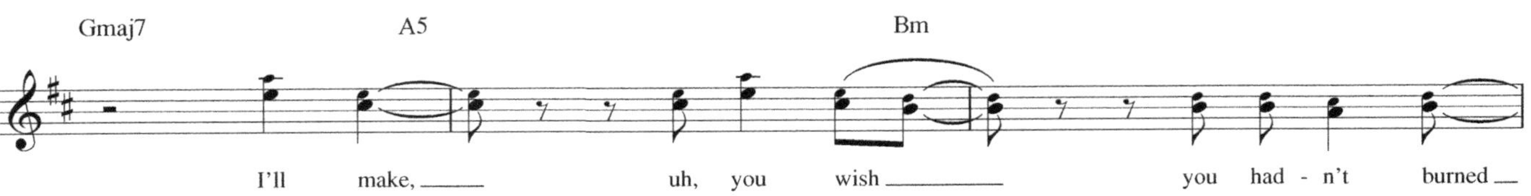
Coda 1
Pre-Chorus
Gtr. 5: w/ Riff B
2nd time, Gtr. 2 tacet
Gmaj7 A5 Bm
I'll make, uh, you wish you had - n't burned

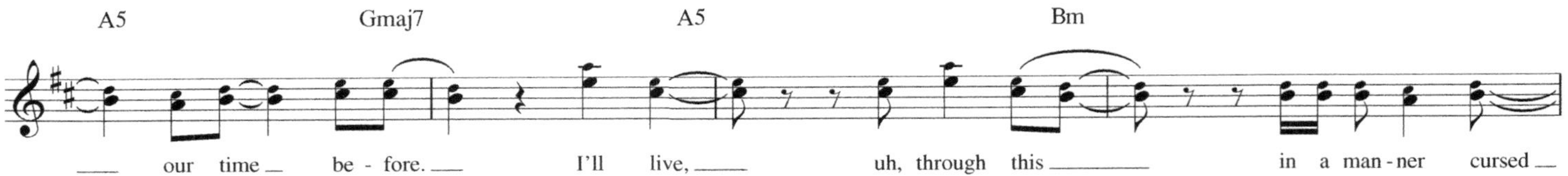
A5 Gmaj7 A5 Bm
our time be - fore. I'll live, uh, through this in a man - ner cursed

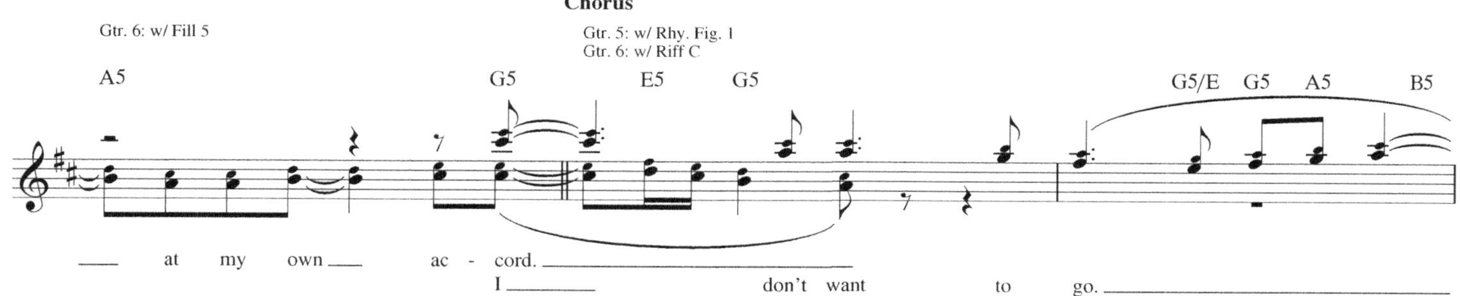
Chorus
Gtr. 6: w/ Fill 5
Gtr. 5: w/ Rhy. Fig. 1
Gtr. 6: w/ Riff C
A5
G5
E5
G5
G5/E G5 A5 B5
at my own ac - cord.
I don't want to go.
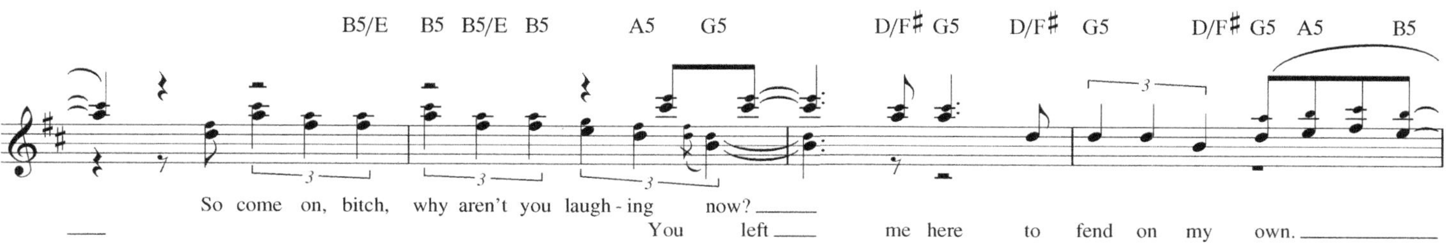
B5/E B5 B5/E B5 A5 G5 D/F♯ G5 D/F♯ G5 D/F♯ G5 A5 B5
So come on, bitch, why aren't you laugh - ing now?
You left me here to fend on my own.
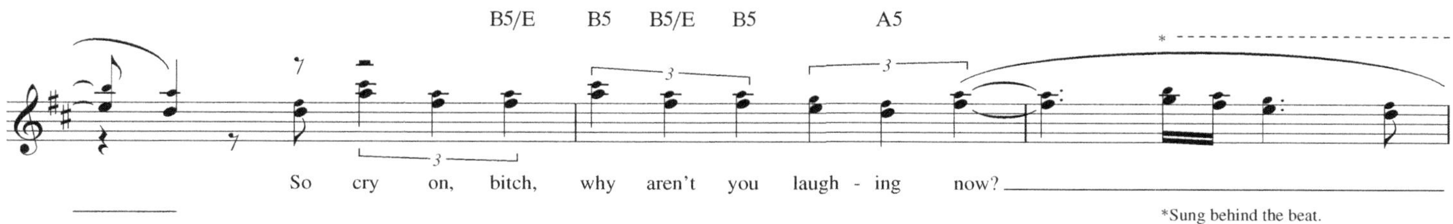
B5/E B5 B5/E B5 A5
So cry on, bitch, why aren't you laugh - ing now?
*Sung behind the beat.
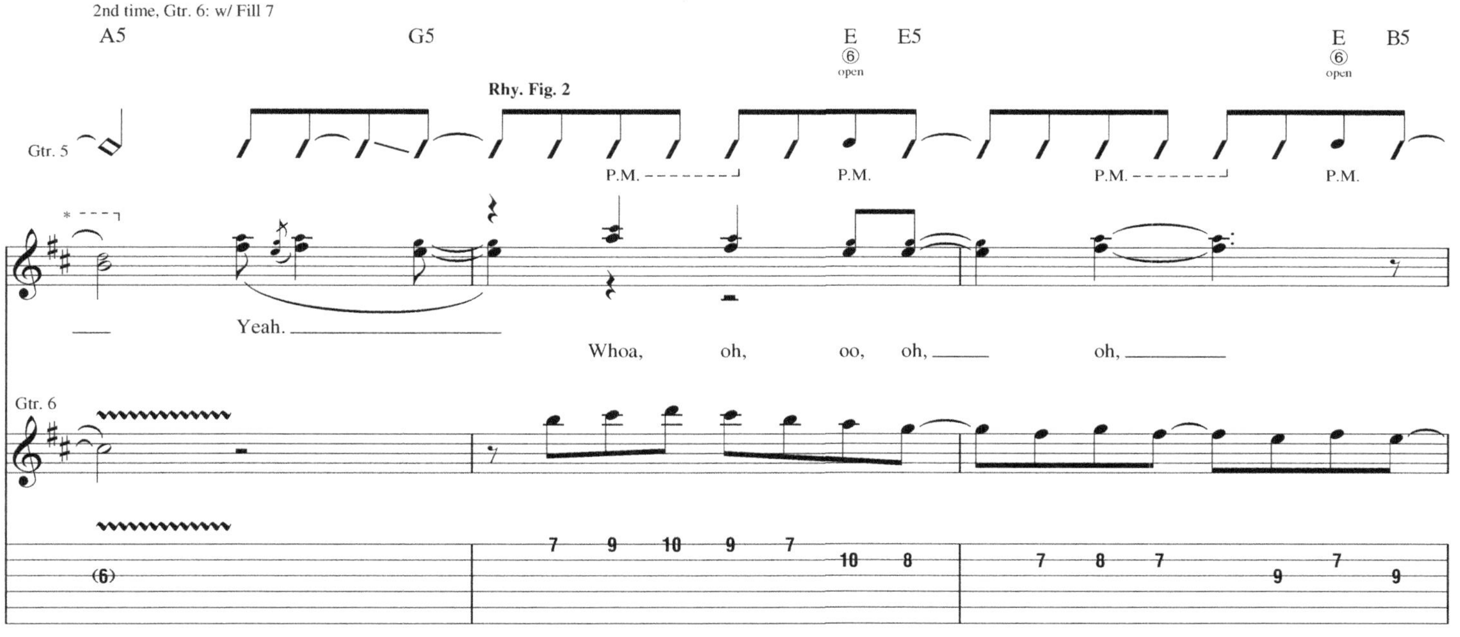
2nd time, Gtr. 6: w/ Fill 7
A5 G5 E E5 E B5
open
Rhy. Fig. 2
Gtr. 5
P.M.
Yeah.
Whoa, oh, oo, oh, oh,
Gtr. 6
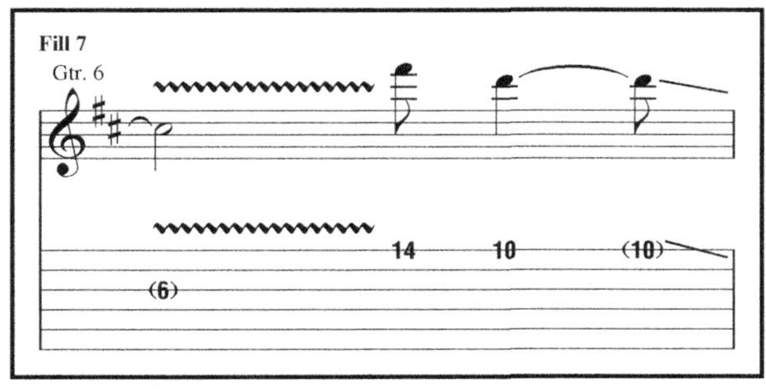
Fill 7
Gtr. 6

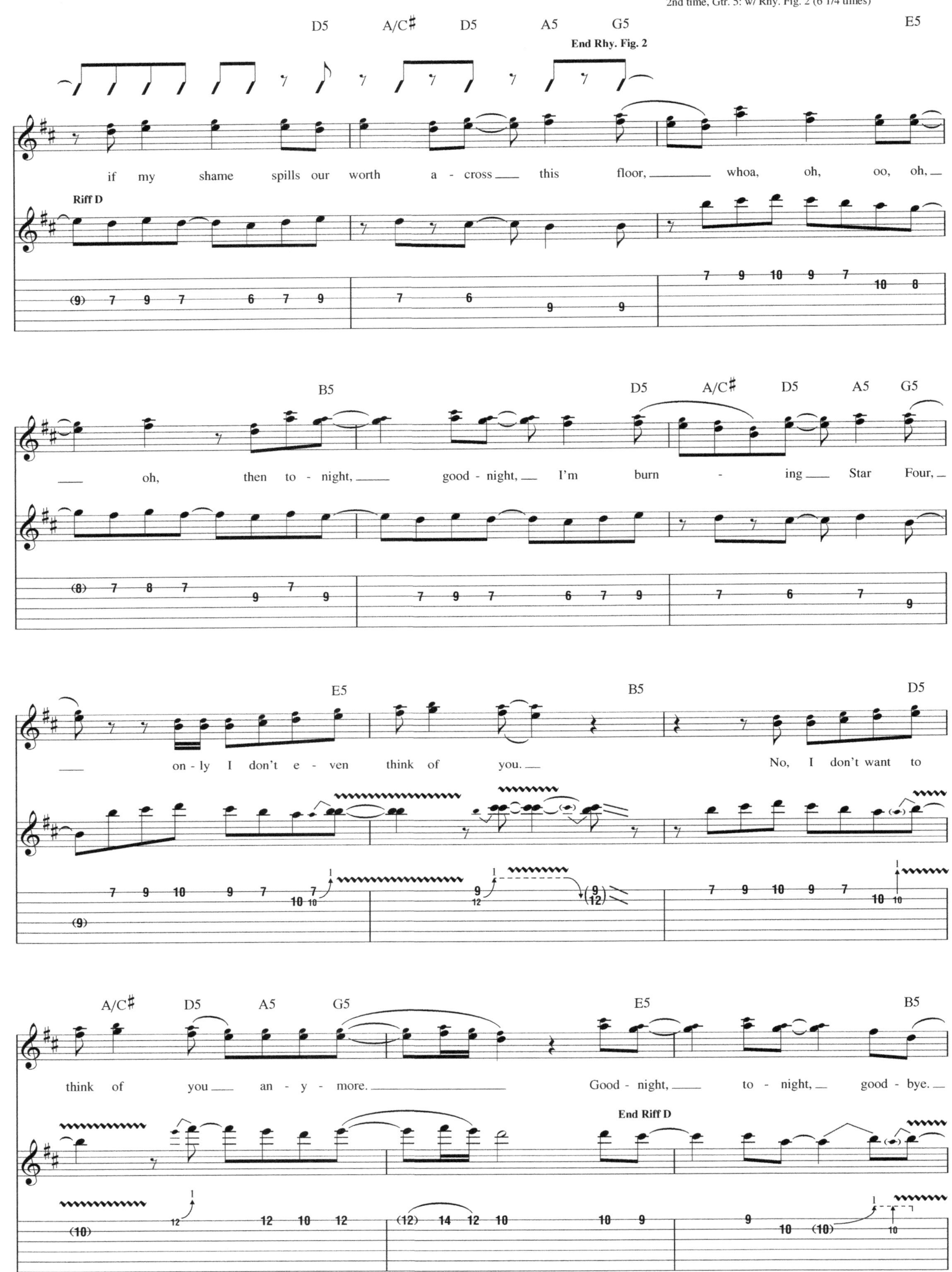
1st time, Gtr. 5: w/ Rhy. Fig. 2 (2 3/4 times)
2nd time, Gtr. 5: w/ Rhy. Fig. 2 (6 1/4 times)
D5
A/C♯
D5
A5
G5
E5
End Rhy. Fig. 2
if my shame spills our worth a - cross this floor, whoa, oh, oo, oh,
Riff D
B5
D5
A/C♯
D5
A5
G5
oh, then to - night, good - night, I'm burn - ing Star Four,
E5
B5
D5
on - ly I don't e - ven think of you.
No, I don't want to
A/C♯
D5
A5
G5
E5
B5
think of you an - y - more.
Good - night, to - night, good - bye.
End Riff D

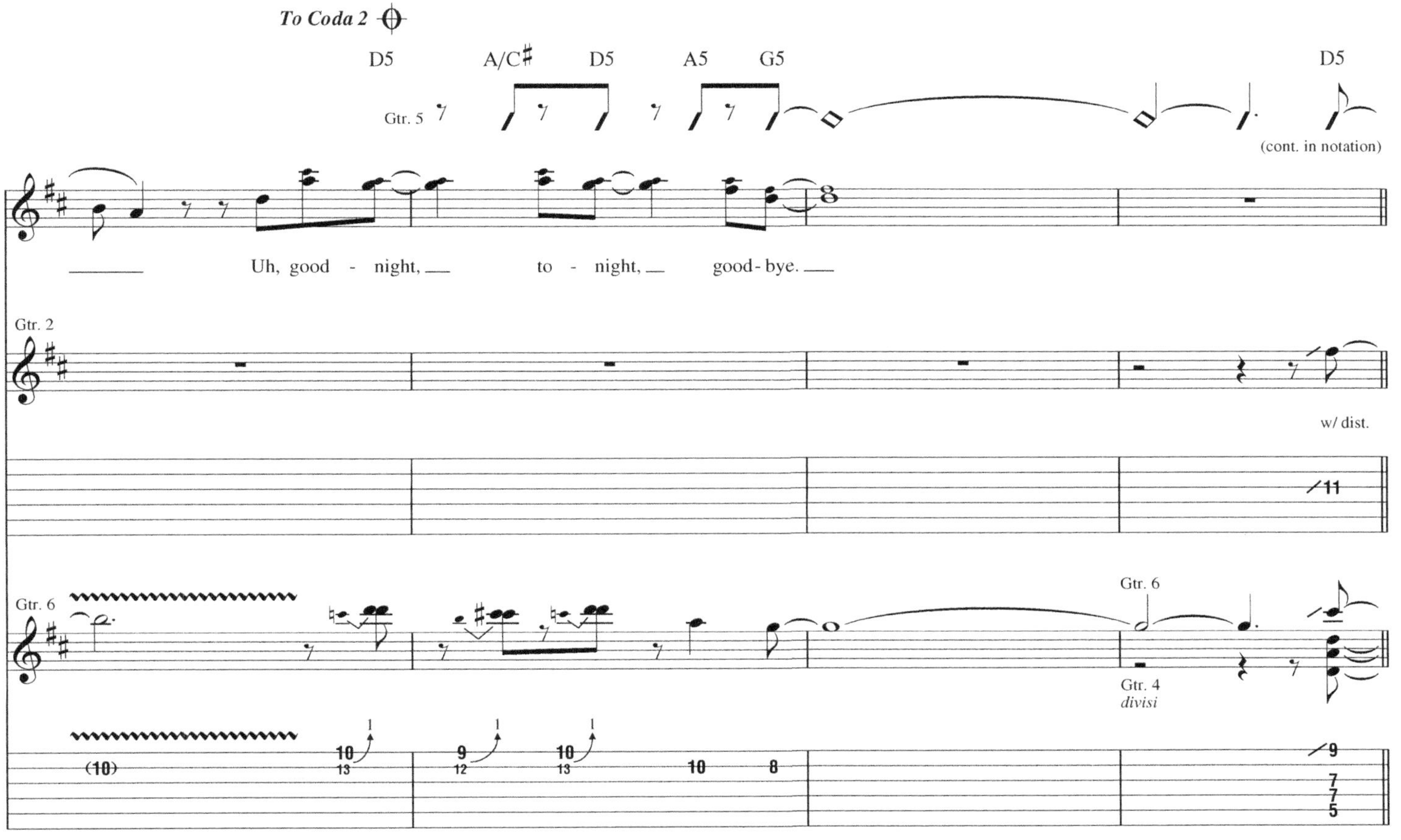

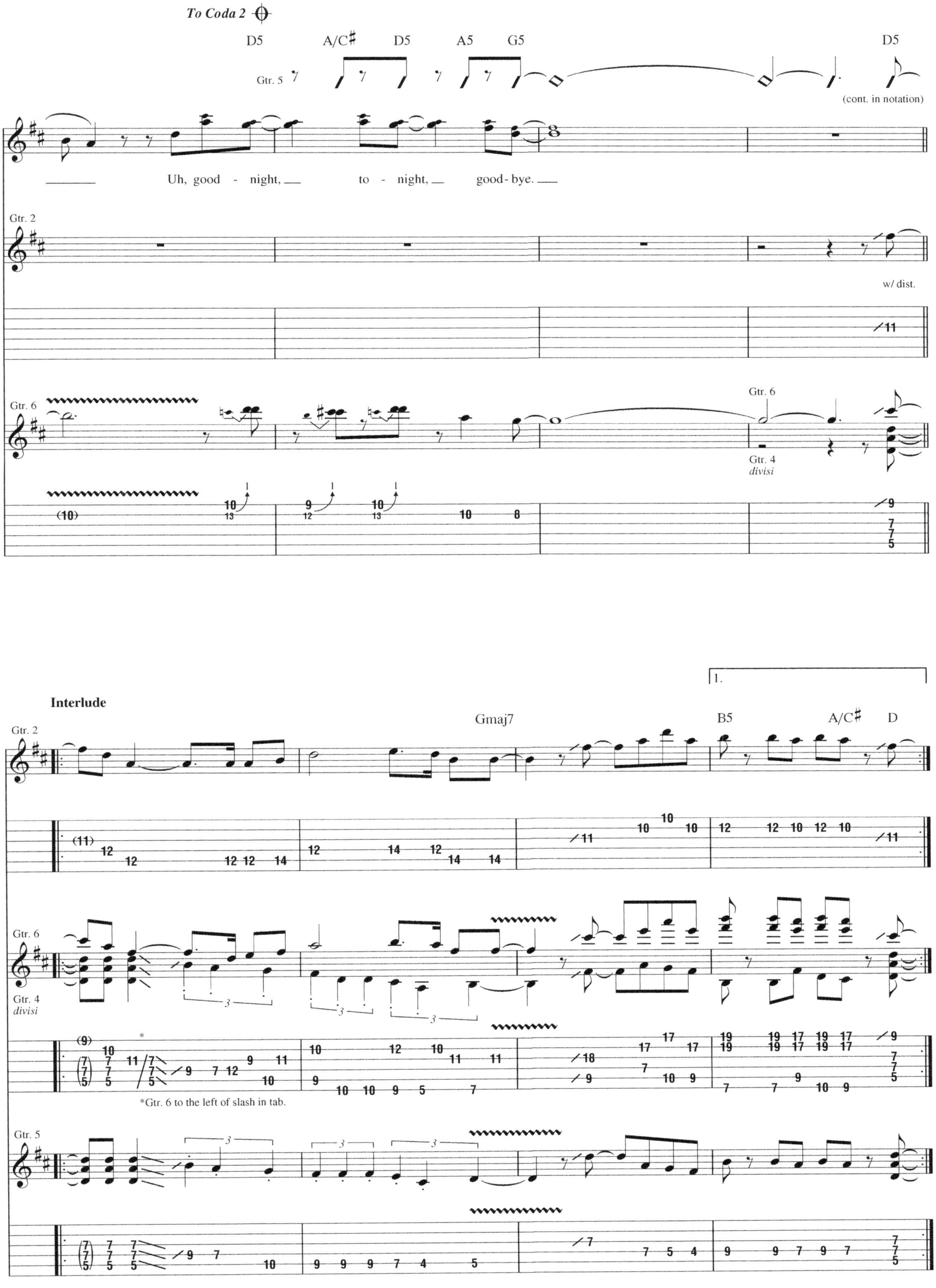

Interlude

1.

Gmaj7 B5 A/C♯ D

Gtr. 2

Gtr. 6

Gtr. 4
divisi

*Gtr. 6 to the left of slash in tab.

Gtr. 5

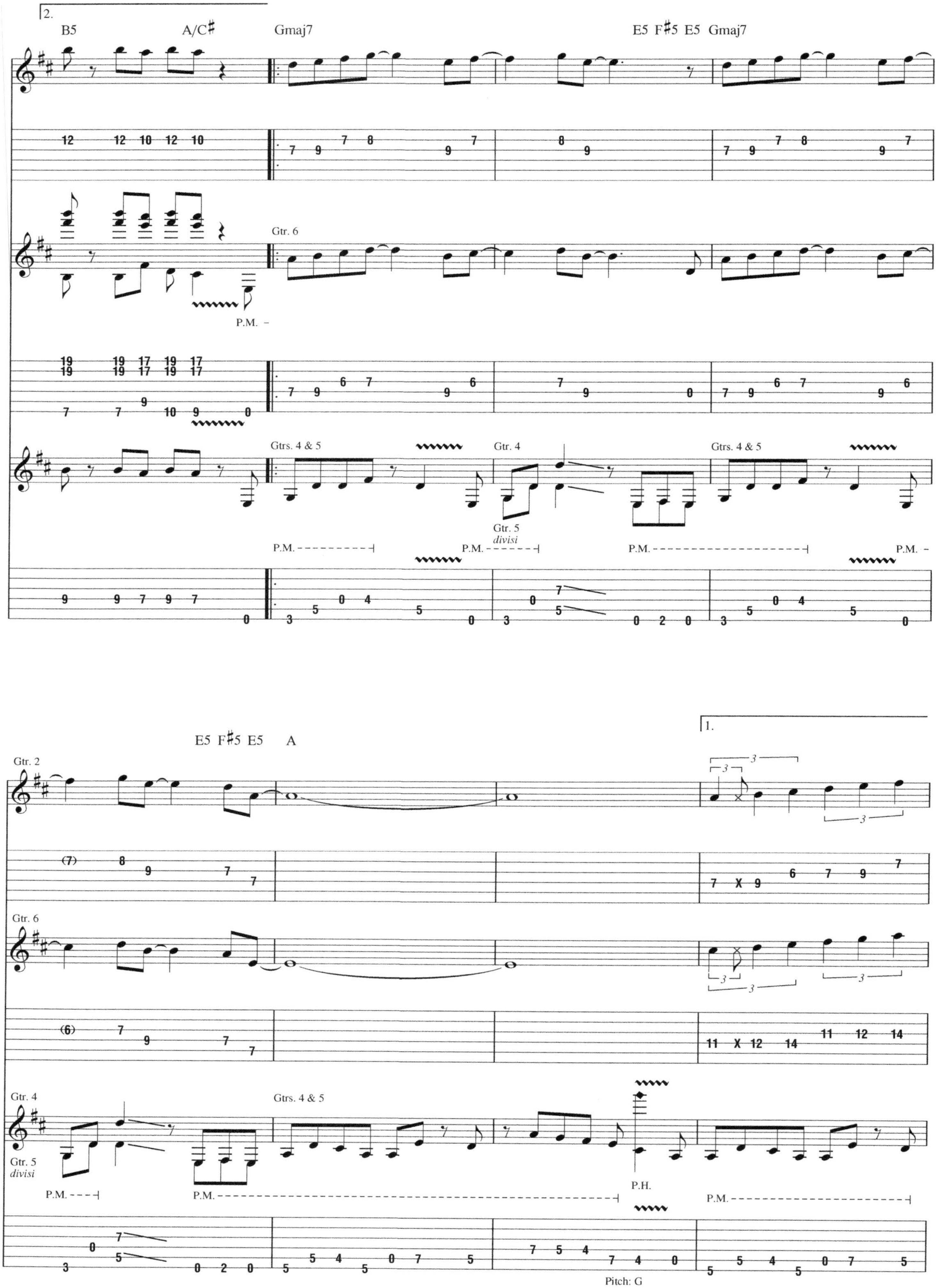

2.

B5 A/C♯ Gmaj7 E5 F♯5 E5 Gmaj7

Gtr. 6

P.M.

Gtrs. 4 & 5

Gtr. 4

Gtr. 5
divisi

P.M.

E5 F♯5 E5 A

1.

Gtr. 2

Gtr. 6

Gtr. 4

Gtr. 5
divisi

Gtrs. 4 & 5

P.H.

P.M.

Pitch: G

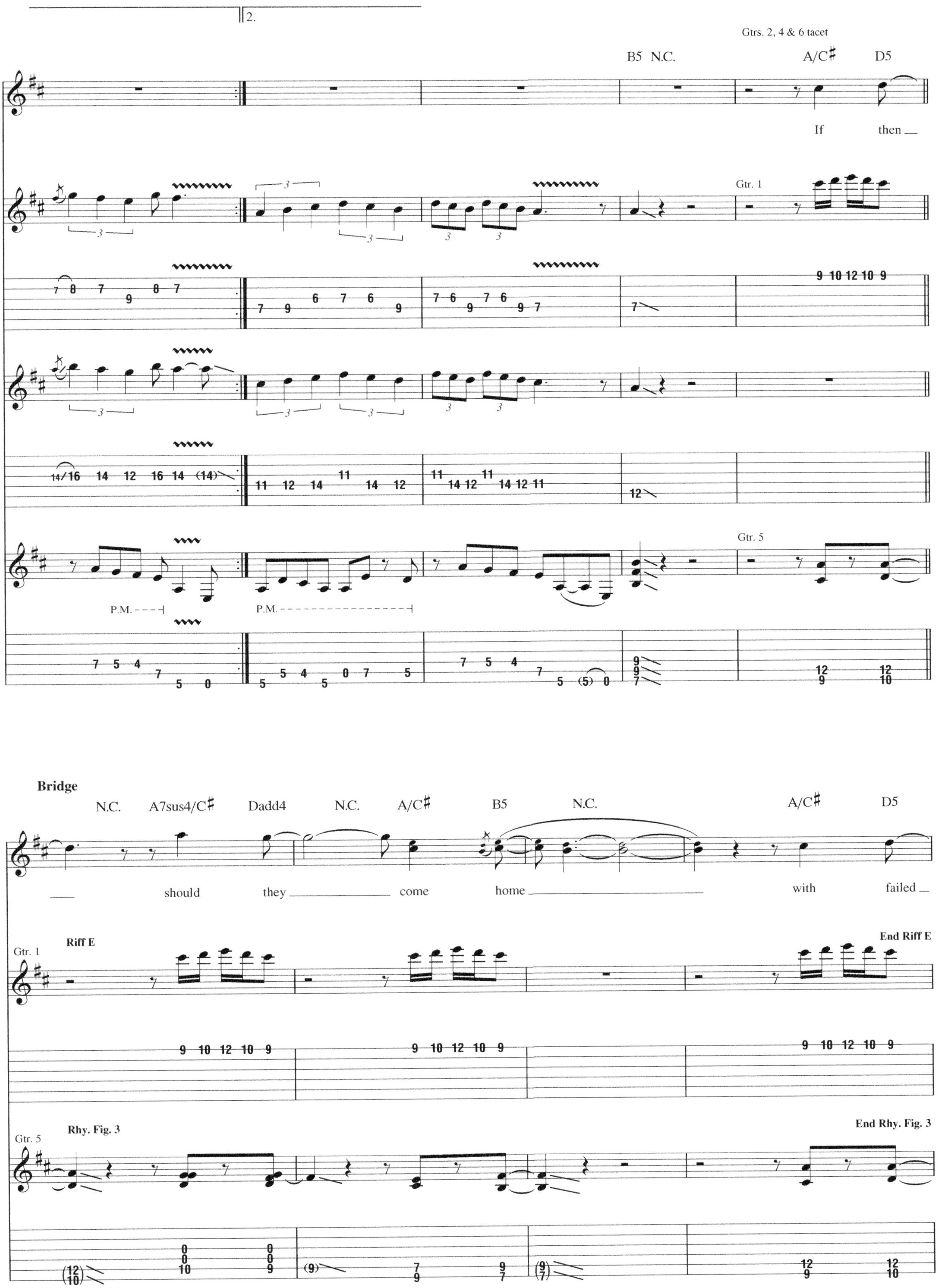

2.

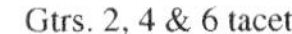

B5 N.C. A/C♯ D5

If then

Gtr. 1

Gtr. 5

P.M.

P.M.

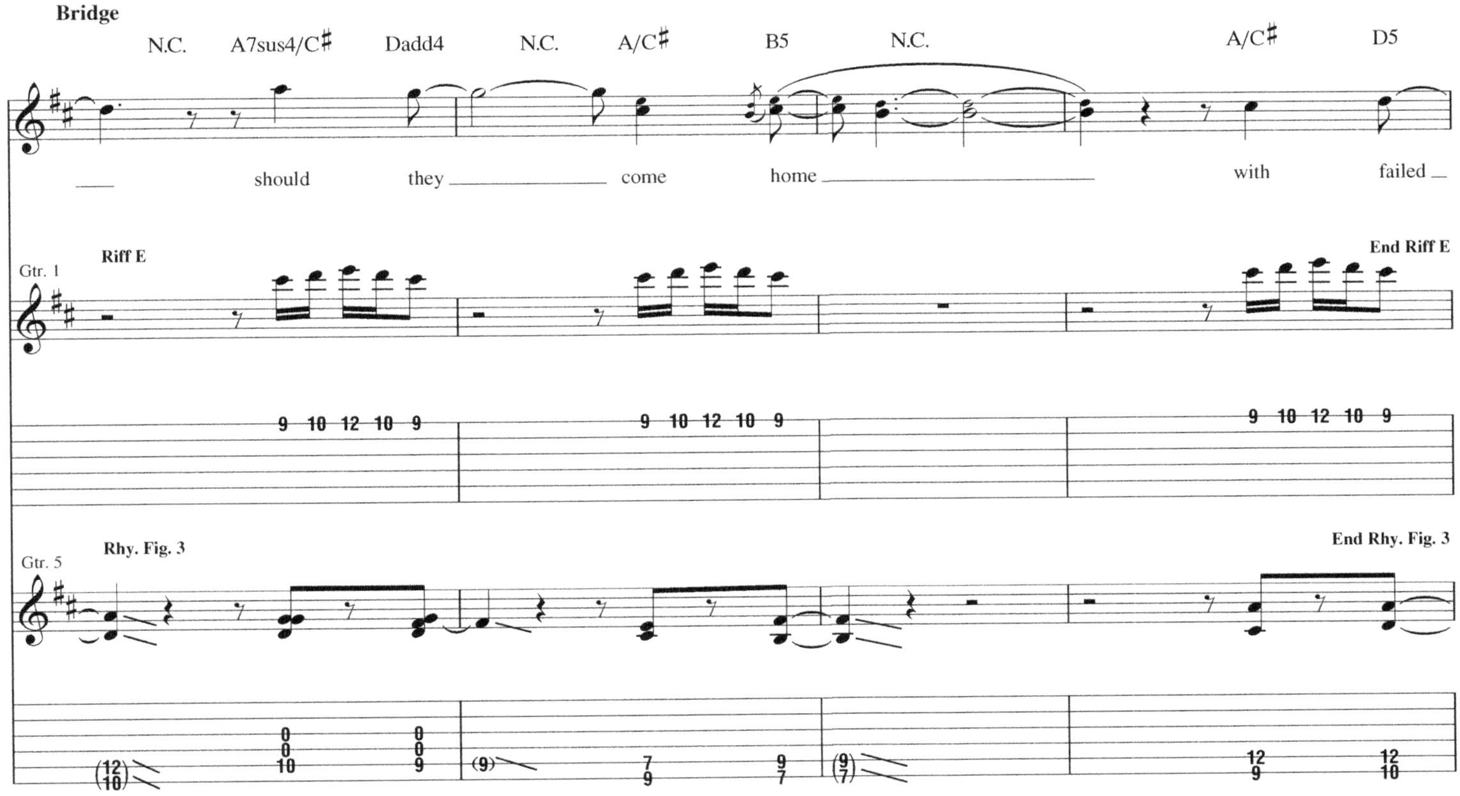

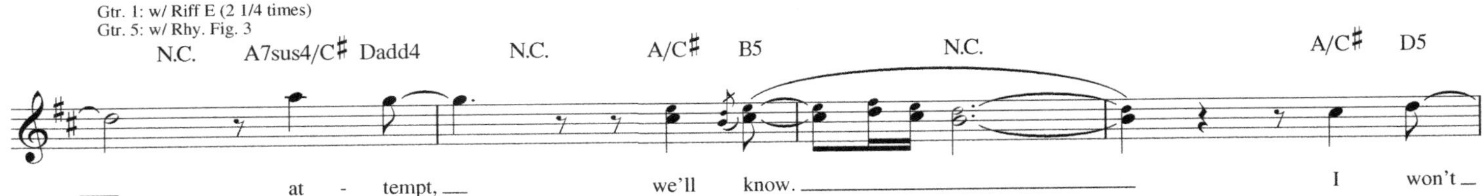

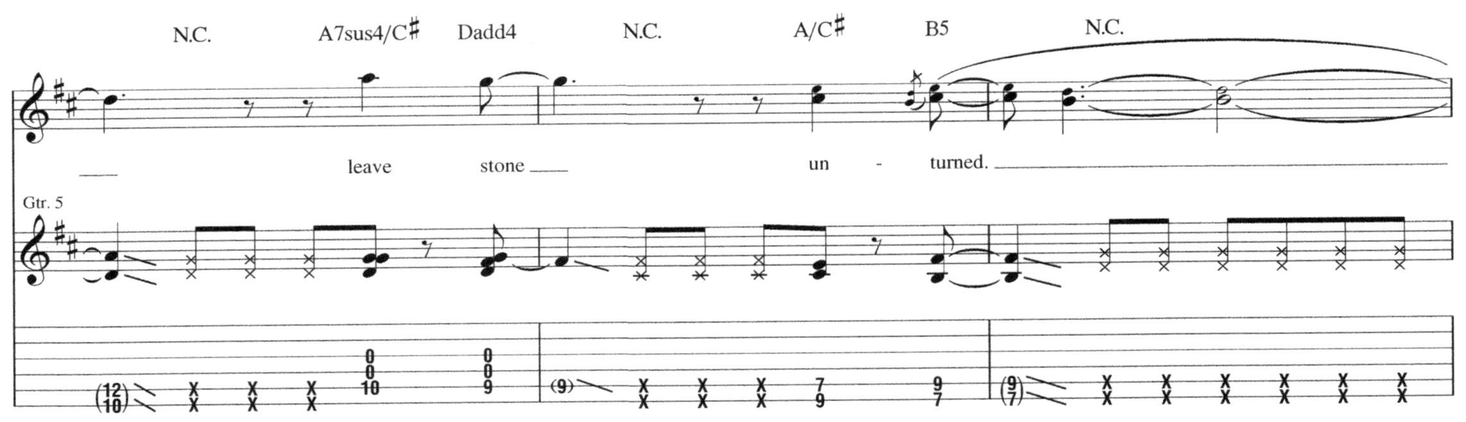

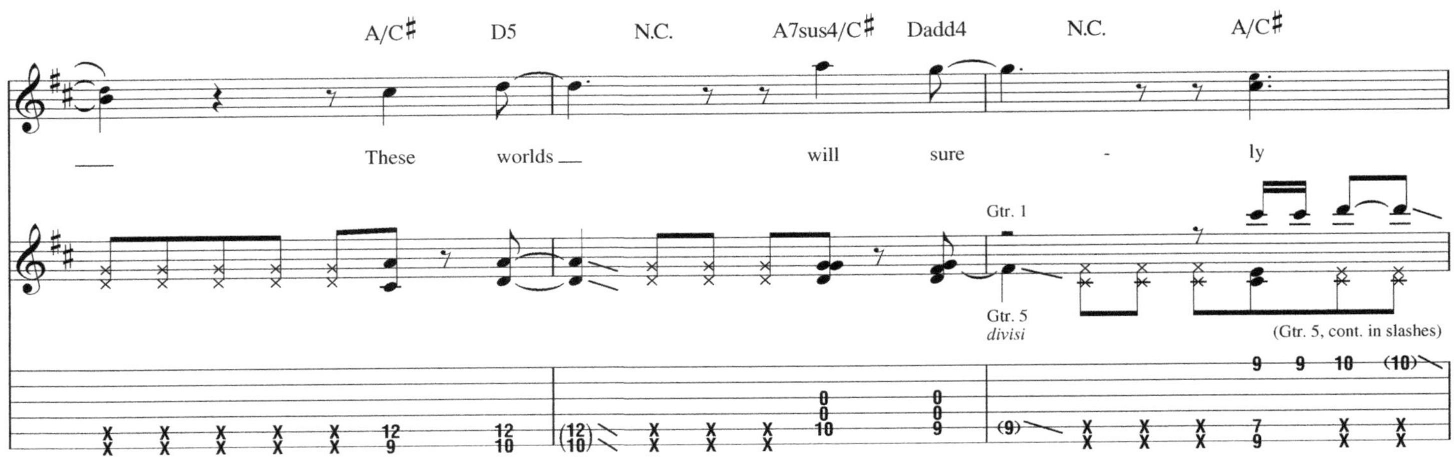

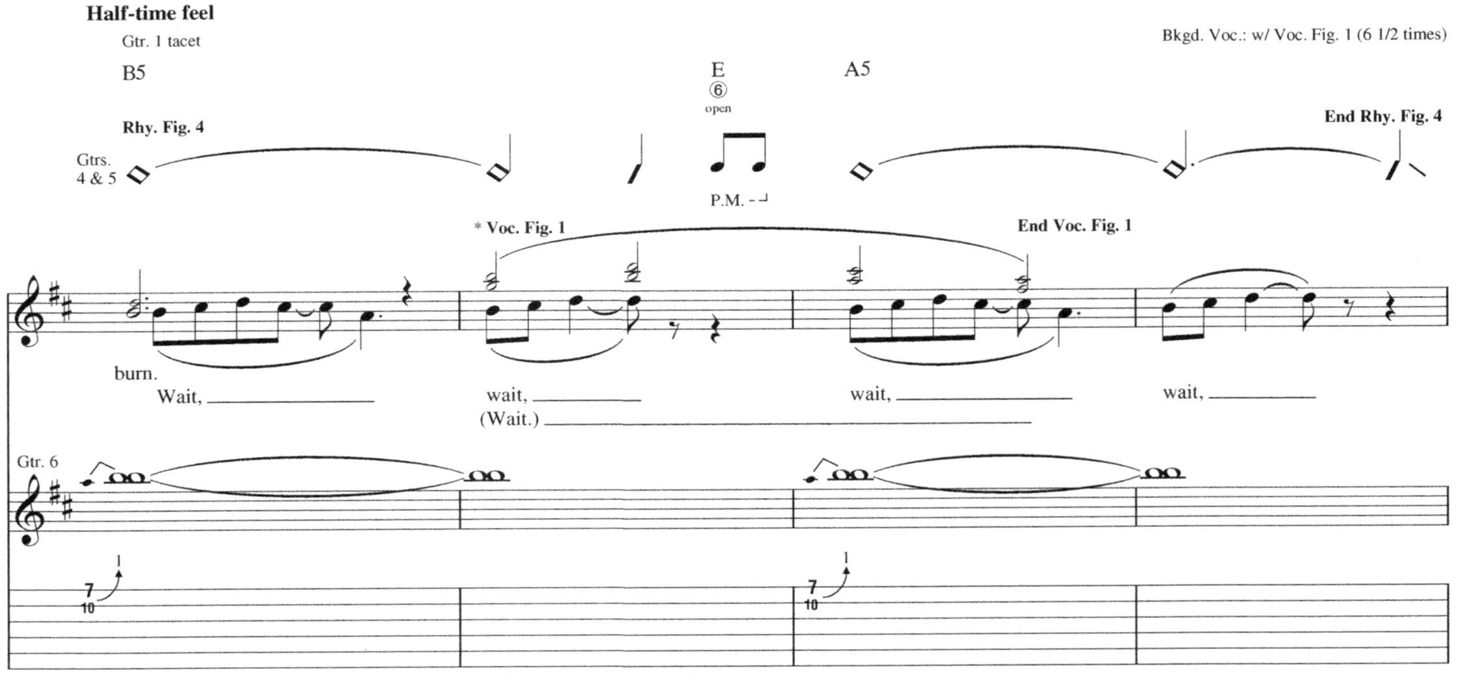

*Refers to upstemmed voc. only.

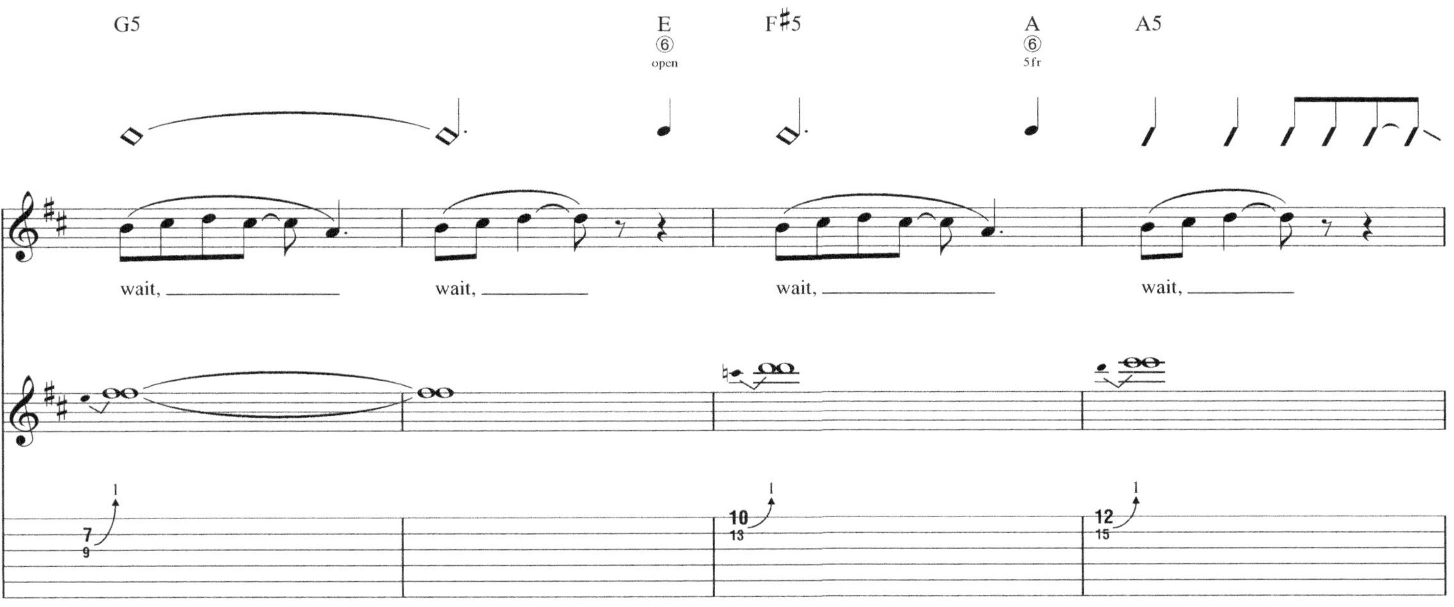
G5
E
⑥
open
F♯5
A
⑥
5fr
A5
wait,
wait,
wait,
wait,

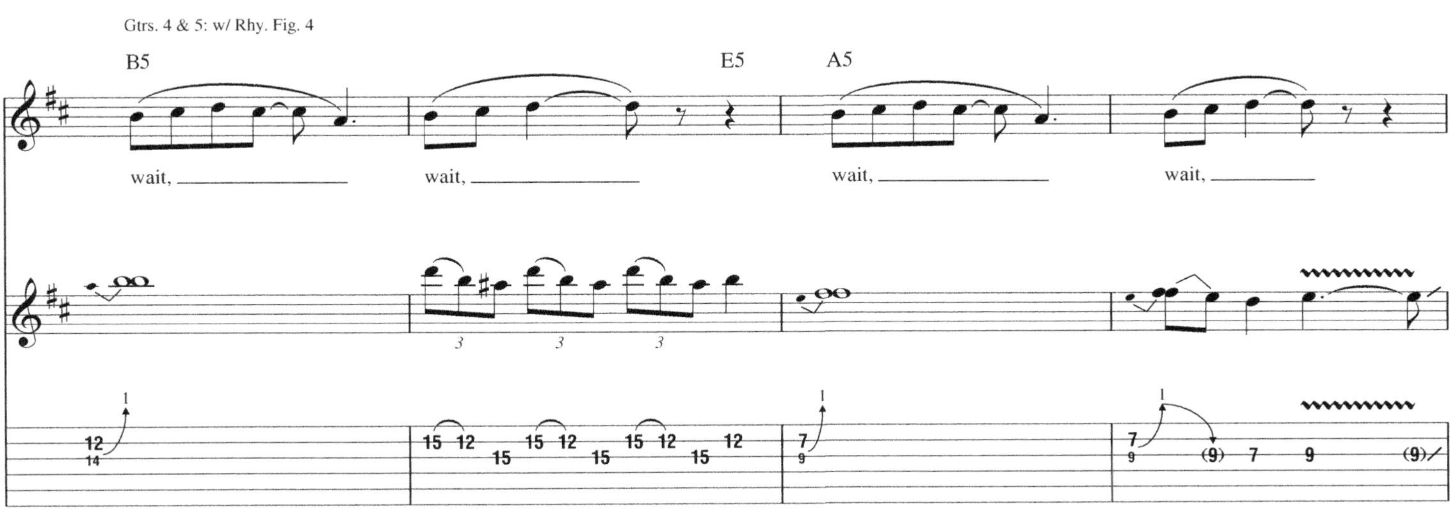
Gtrs. 4 & 5: w/ Rhy. Fig. 4
B5
E5
A5
wait,
wait,
wait,
wait,

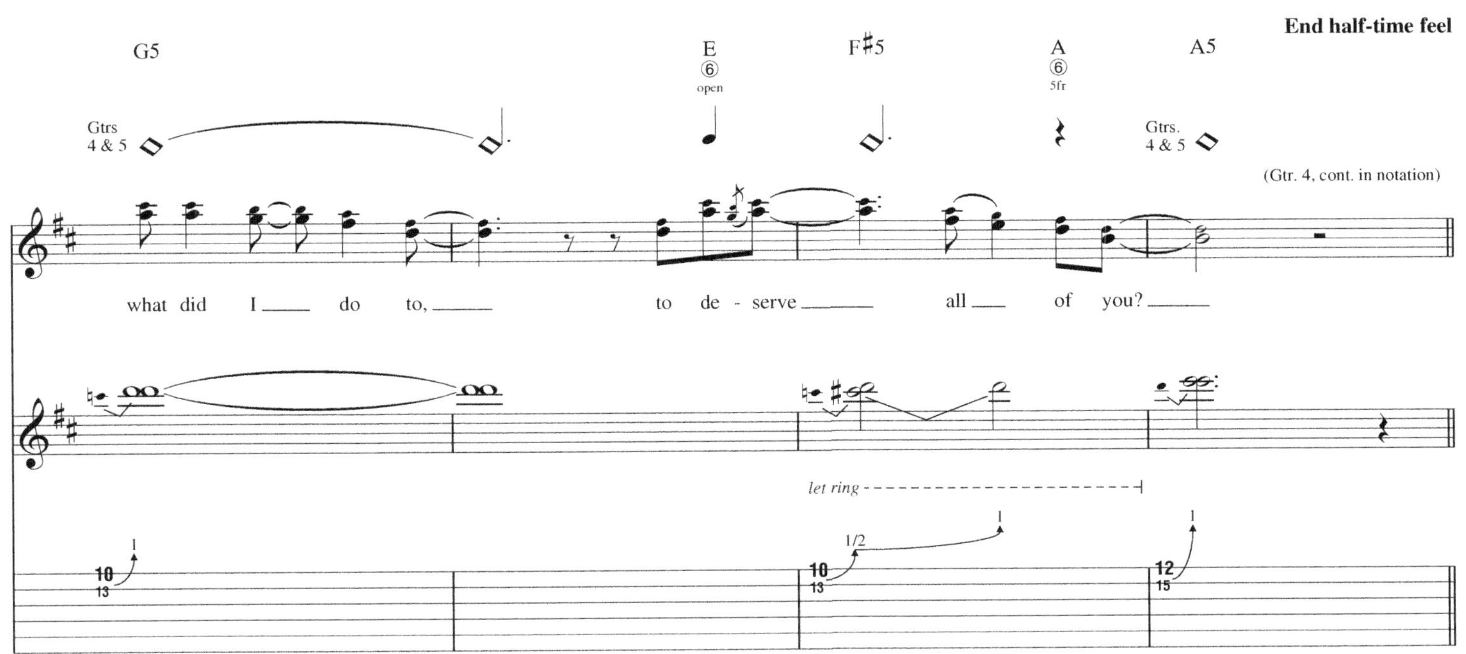
End half-time feel
G5
E
⑥
open
F♯5
A
⑥
5fr
A5
Gtrs
4 & 5
Gtrs.
4 & 5
(Gtr. 4, cont. in notation)
what did I do to, to de - serve all of you?
let ring

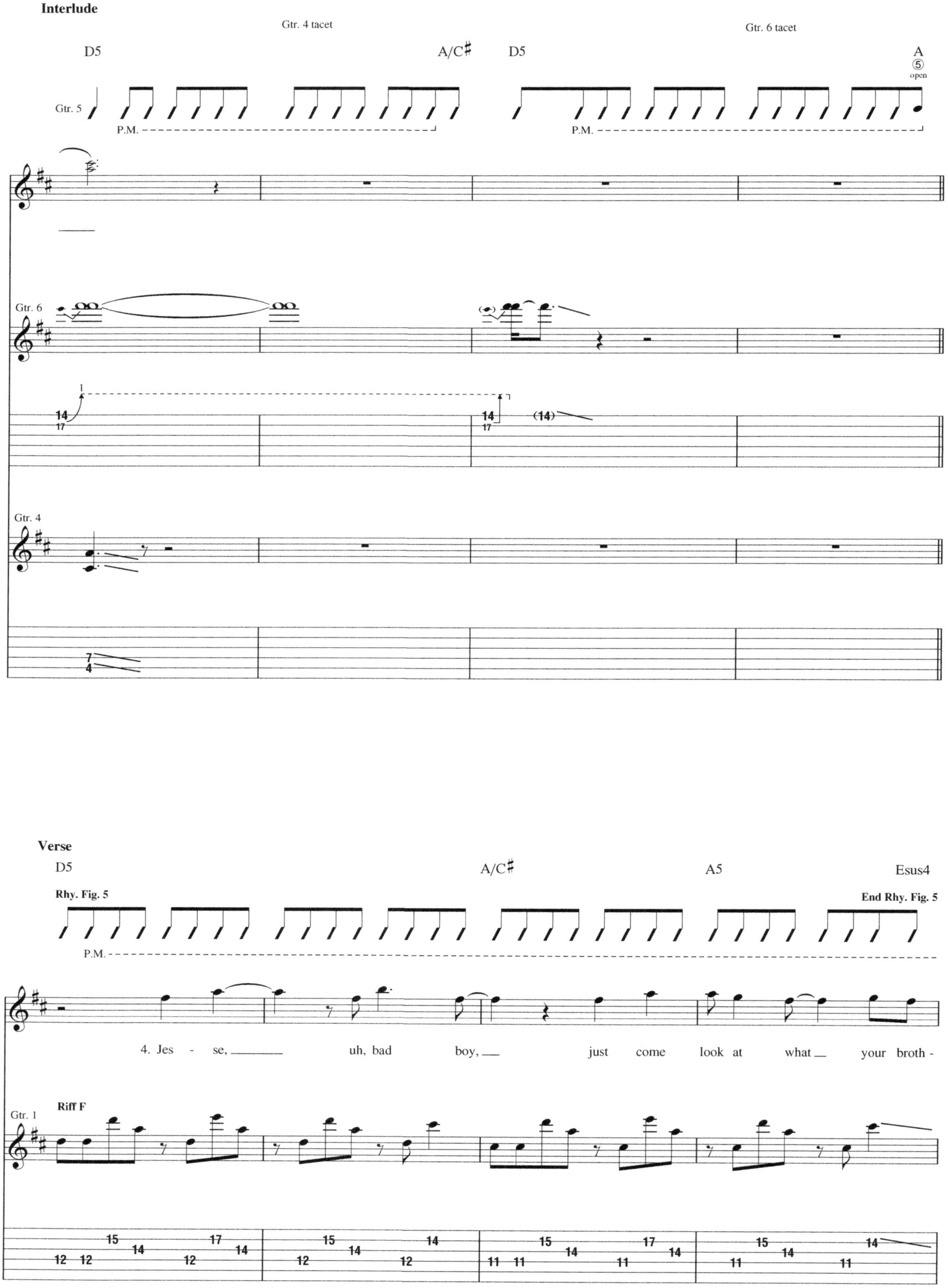

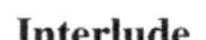

Interlude

Gtr. 4 tacet

Gtr. 6 tacet

D5 A/C♯ D5 A ⑤ open

Gtr. 5

P.M.

P.M.

Gtr. 6

1

14 17 14 17 (14)

Gtr. 4

7 4

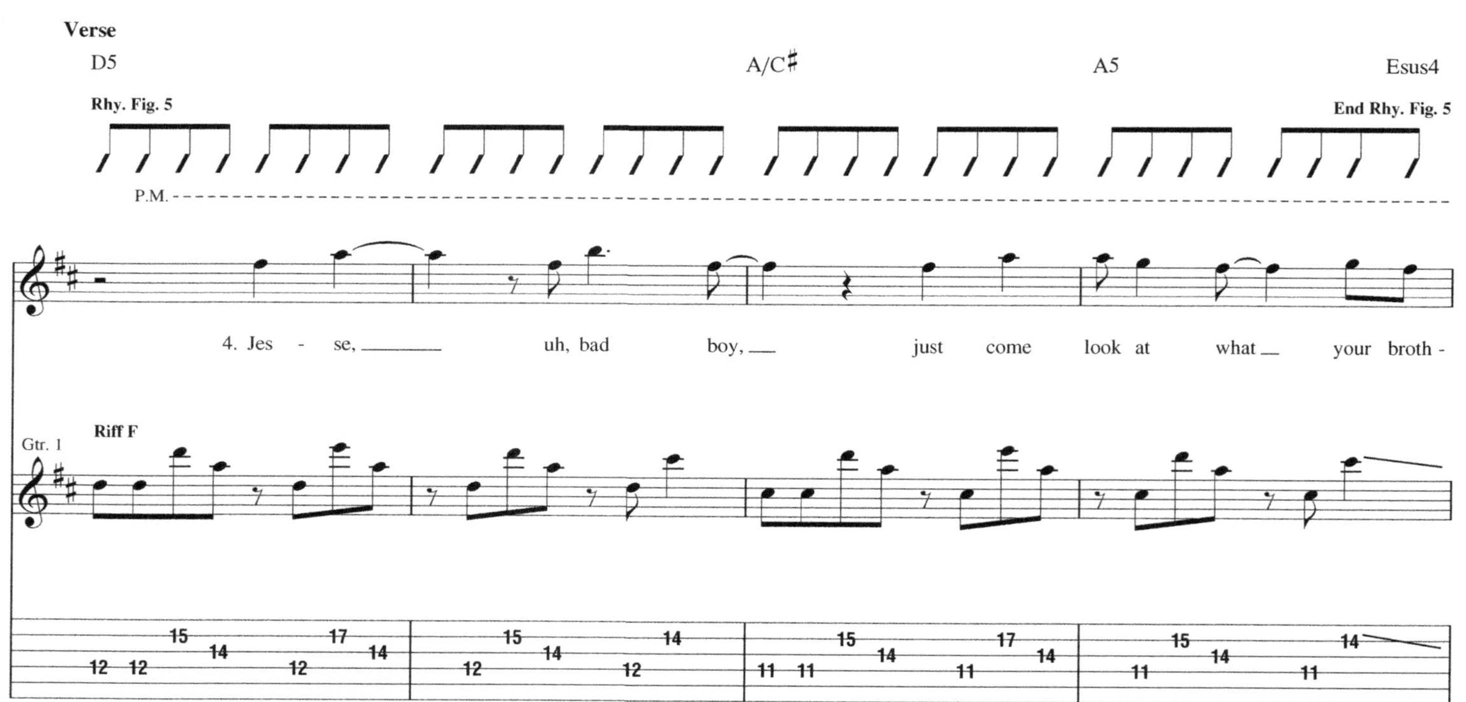

G5
Esus4

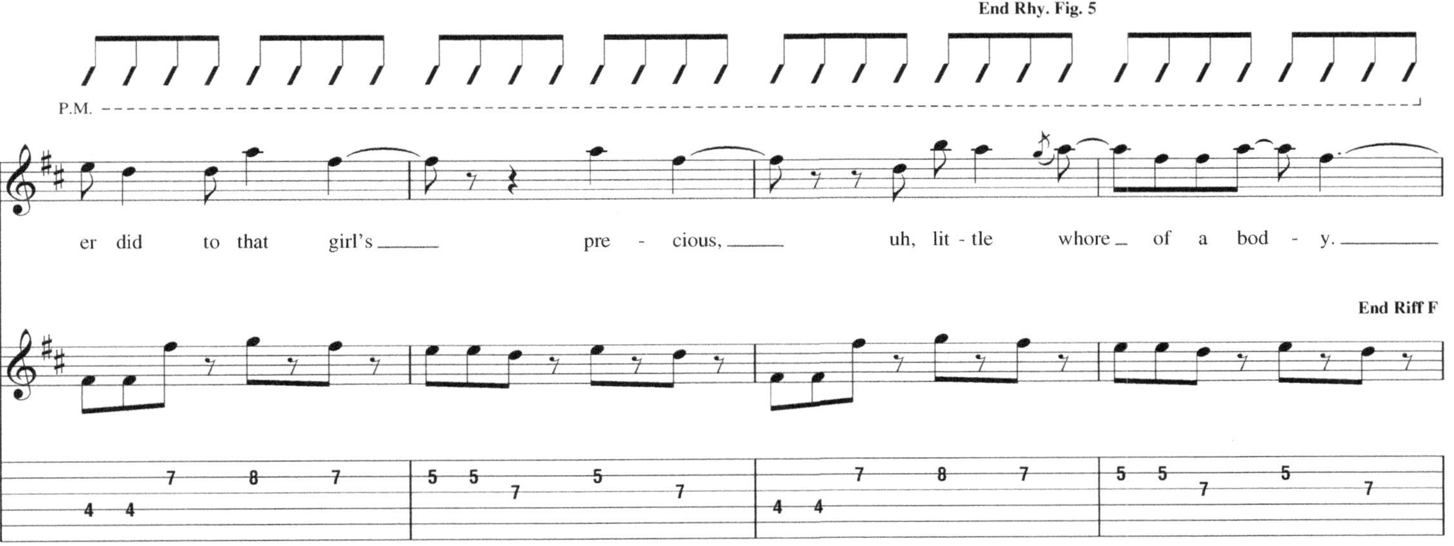
End Rhy. Fig. 5
P.M.
er did to that girl's precious, uh, lit-tle whore of a bod-y.
End Riff F

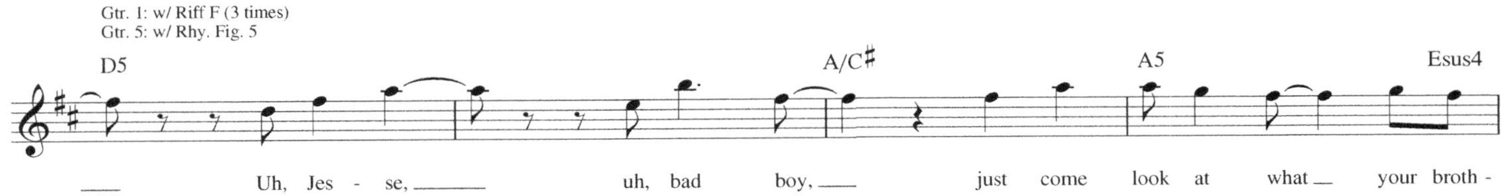
Gtr. 1: w/ Riff F (3 times)
Gtr. 5: w/ Rhy. Fig. 5
D5
A/C♯
A5
Esus4
Uh, Jes-se, uh, bad boy, just come look at what your broth-

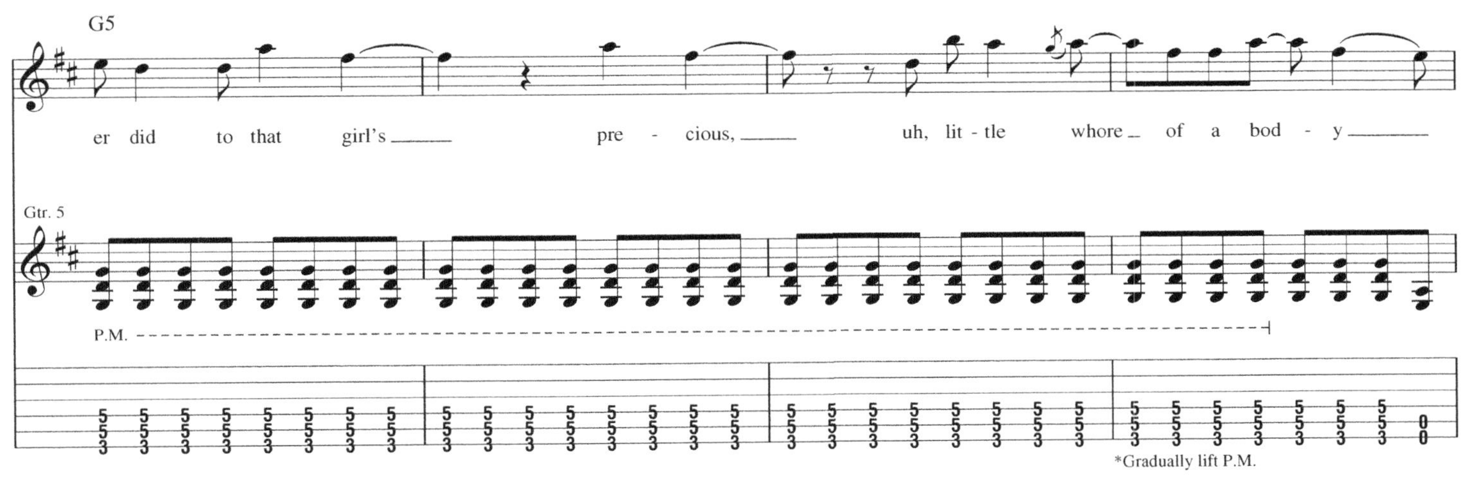
G5
er did to that girl's precious, uh, lit-tle whore of a bod-y
Gtr. 5
P.M.
*Gradually lift P.M.

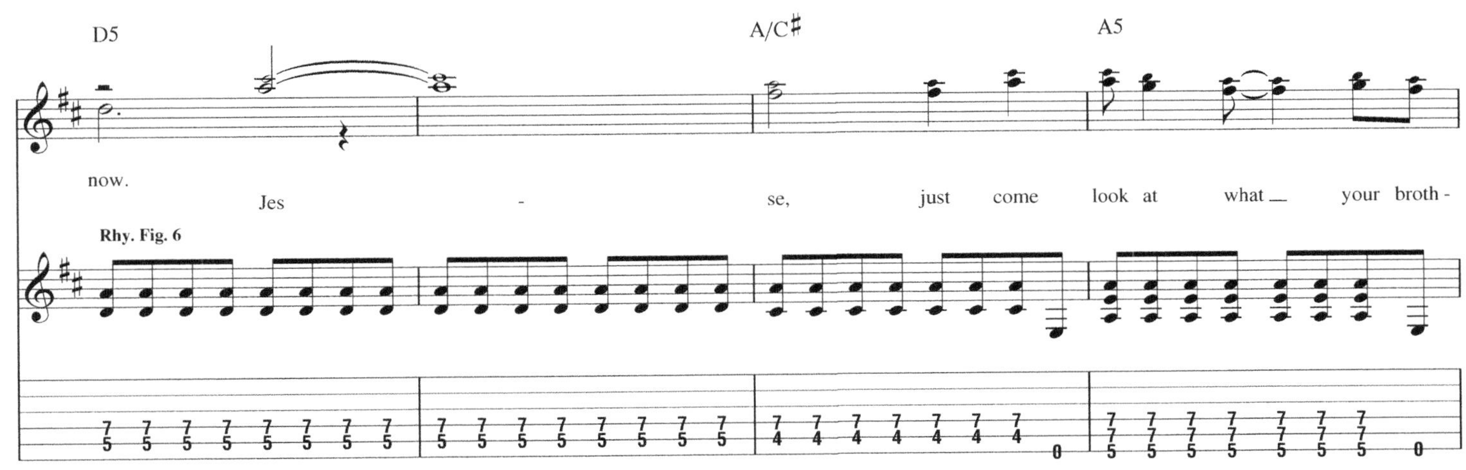
D5
A/C♯
A5
now.
Jes-se, just come look at what your broth-
Rhy. Fig. 6

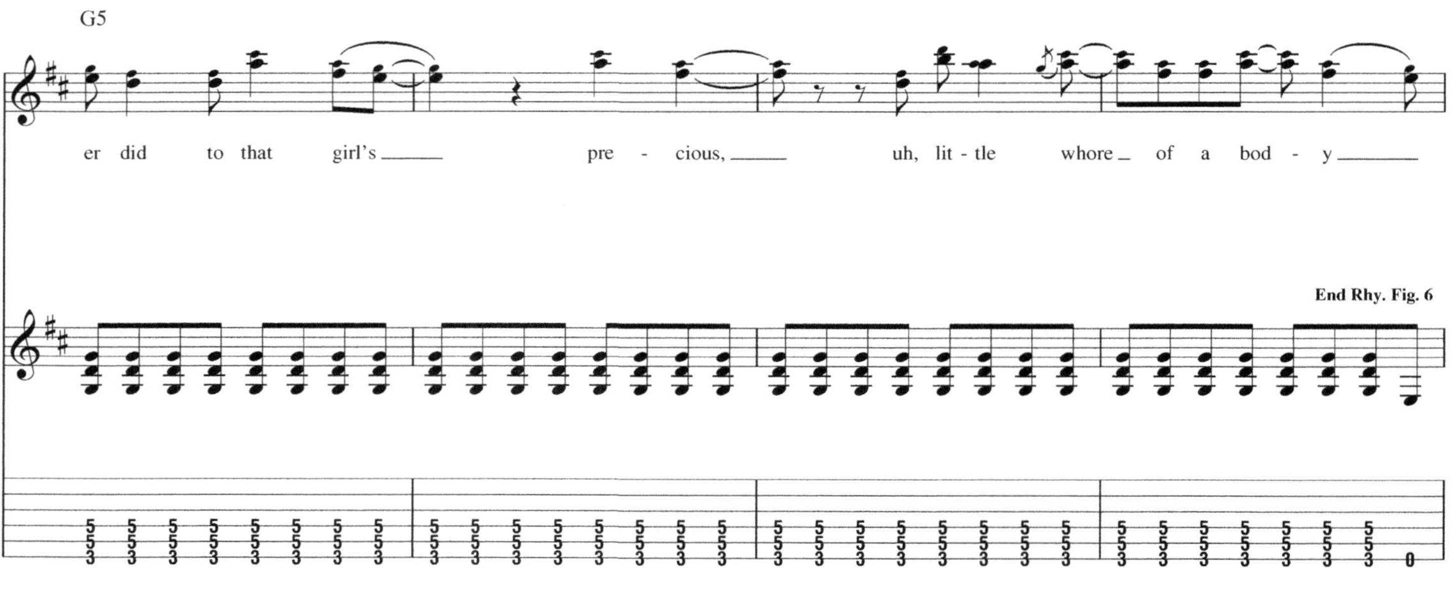
G5
er did to that girl's precious, uh, lit-tle whore of a bod-y
End Rhy. Fig. 6

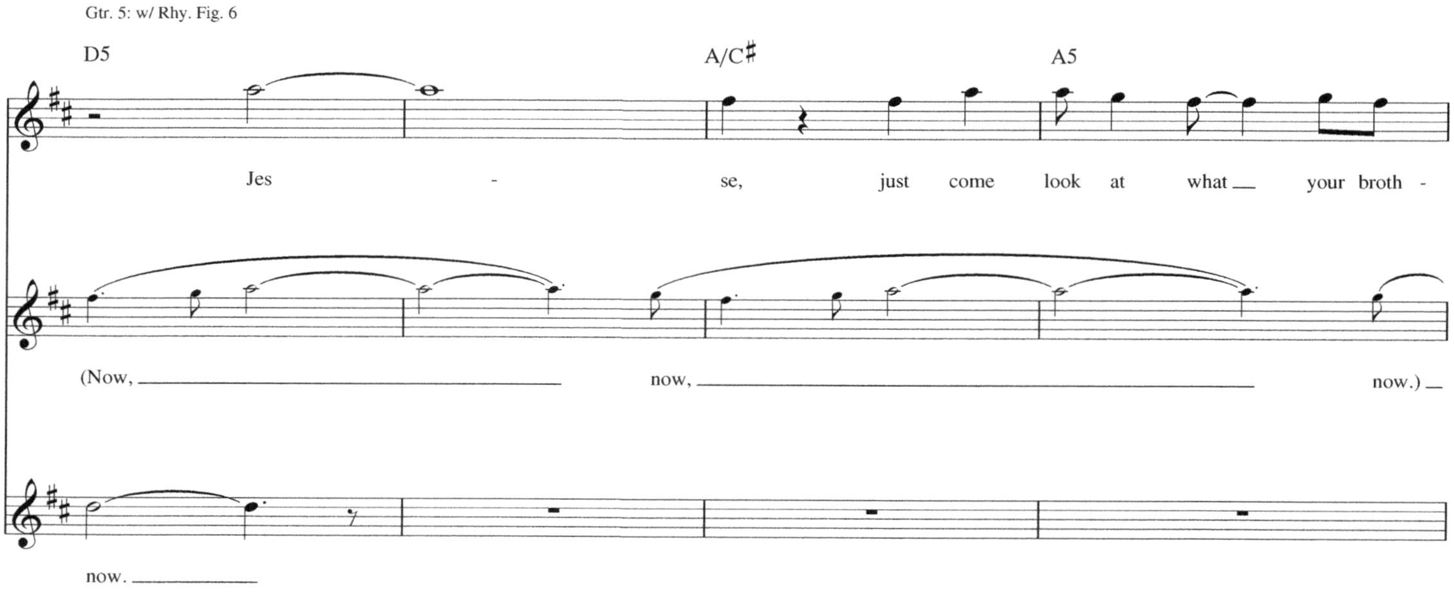
Gtr. 5: w/ Rhy. Fig. 6
D5
A/C♯
A5
Jes - se, just come look at what your broth -
(Now, now, now.)
now.

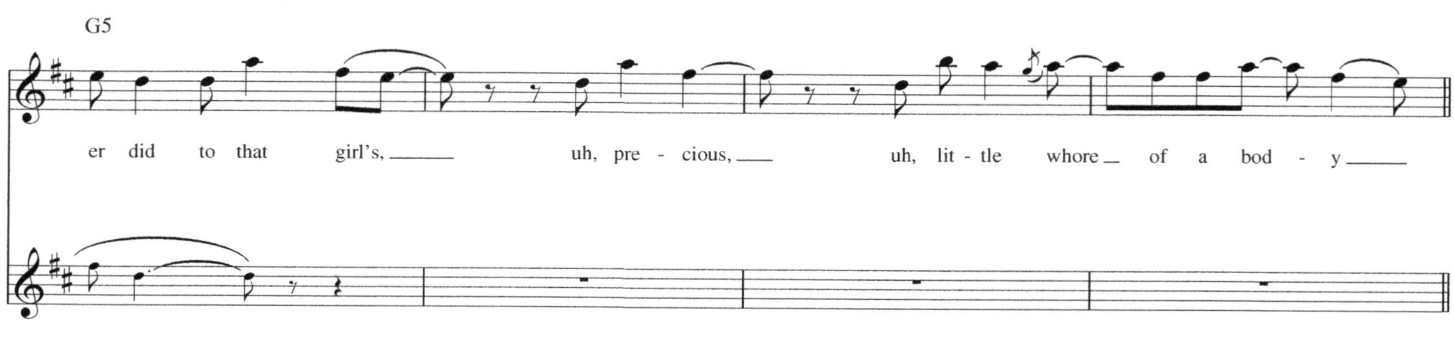
G5
er did to that girl's, uh, pre - cious, uh, lit - tle whore of a bod - y

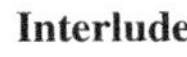
Interlude

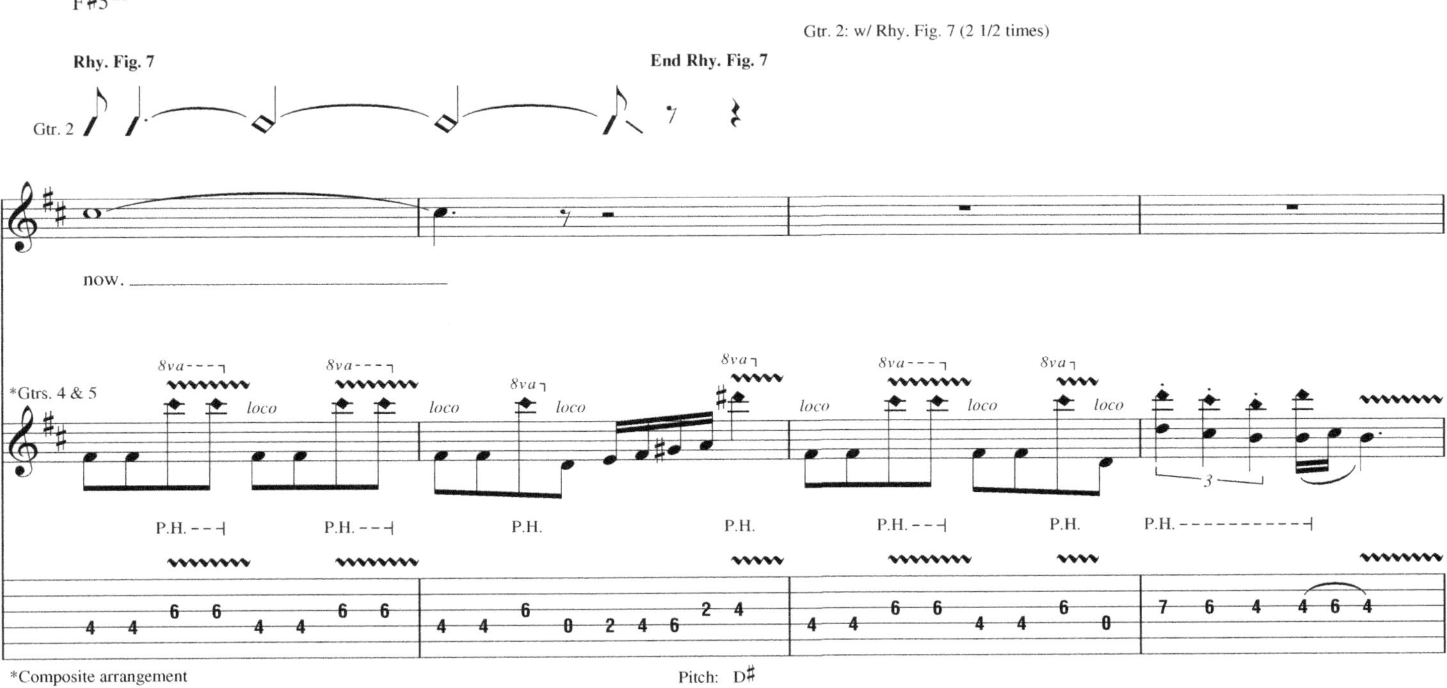
F♯5 IX
Gtr. 2: w/ Rhy. Fig. 7 (2 1/2 times)
Rhy. Fig. 7
End Rhy. Fig. 7
Gtr. 2
now.
*Gtrs. 4 & 5
8va
loco
P.H.
*Composite arrangement
Pitch: D♯

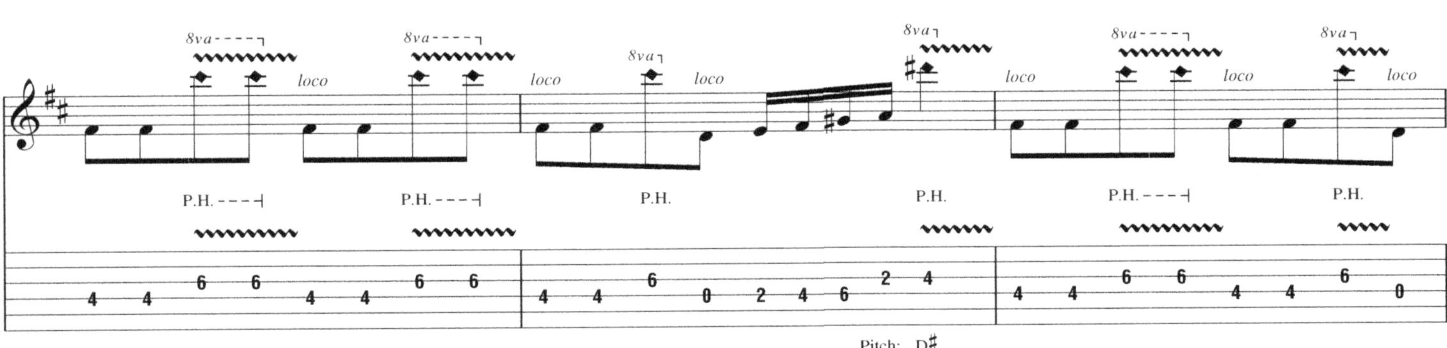
8va
loco
P.H.
Pitch: D♯

D.S.S. al Coda 2

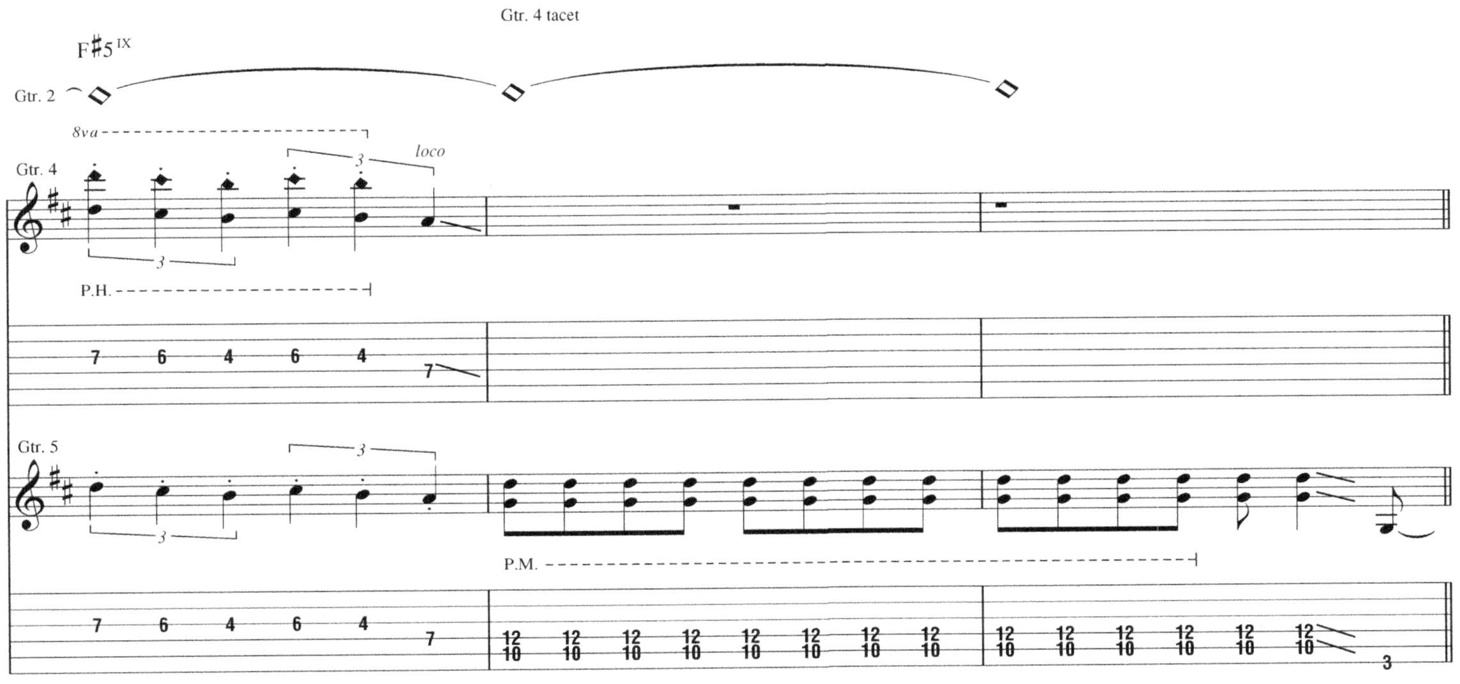
Gtr. 4 tacet
F♯5 IX
Gtr. 2
8va
loco
Gtr. 4
P.H.
Gtr. 5
P.M.

Coda 2

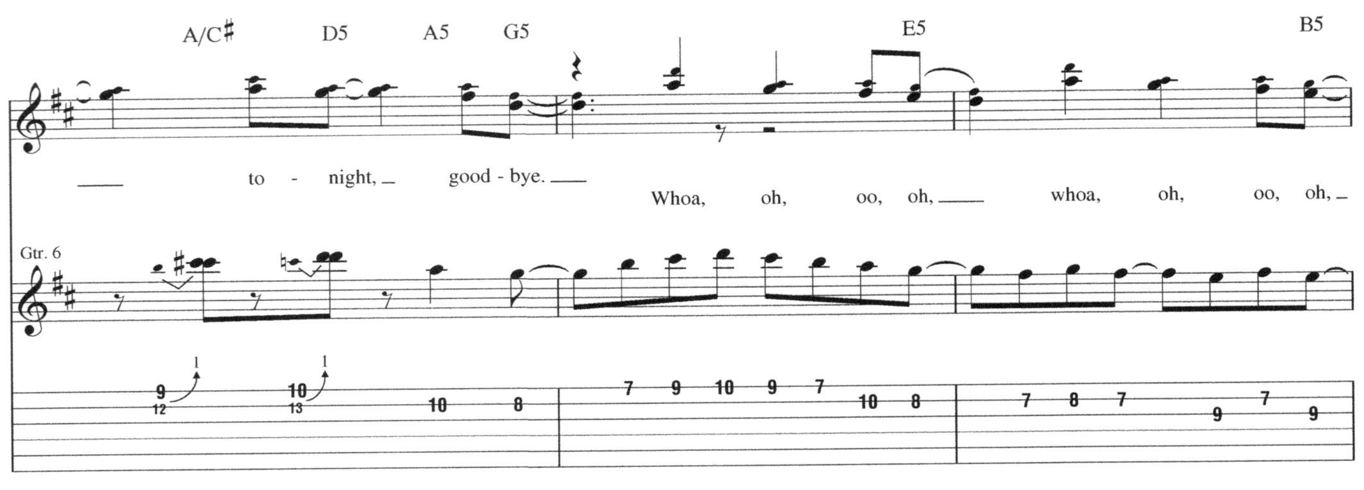
A/C♯
D5
A5
G5
E5
B5
to - night,
good - bye.
Whoa, oh, oo, oh,
whoa, oh, oo, oh,
Gtr. 6

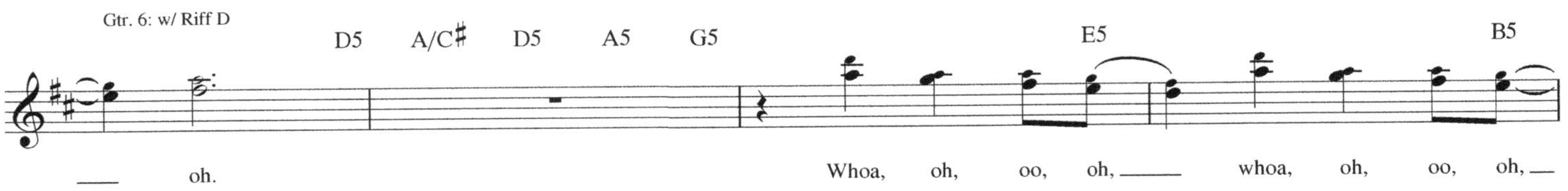
Gtr. 6: w/ Riff D
D5
A/C♯
D5
A5
G5
E5
B5
oh.
Whoa, oh, oo, oh,
whoa, oh, oo, oh,

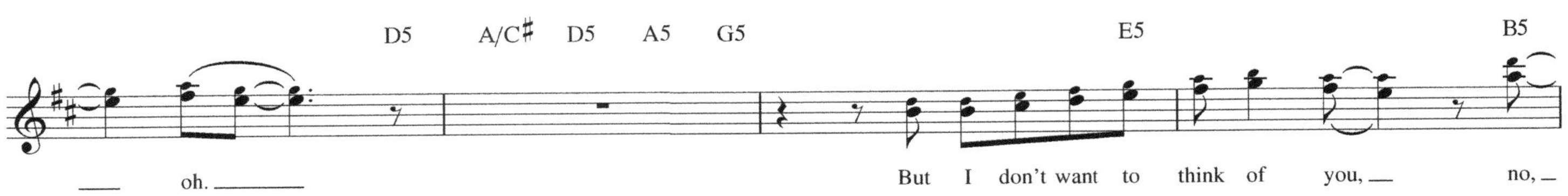
D5
A/C♯
D5
A5
G5
E5
B5
oh.
But I don't want to think of you,
no,

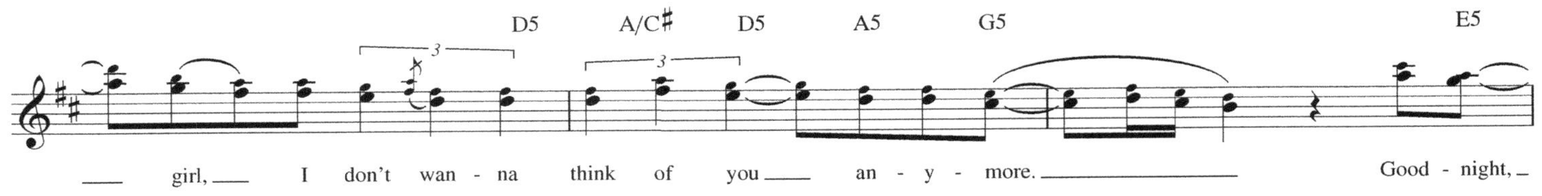
D5
A/C♯
D5
A5
G5
E5
girl, I don't wan - na think of you an - y - more.
Good - night,

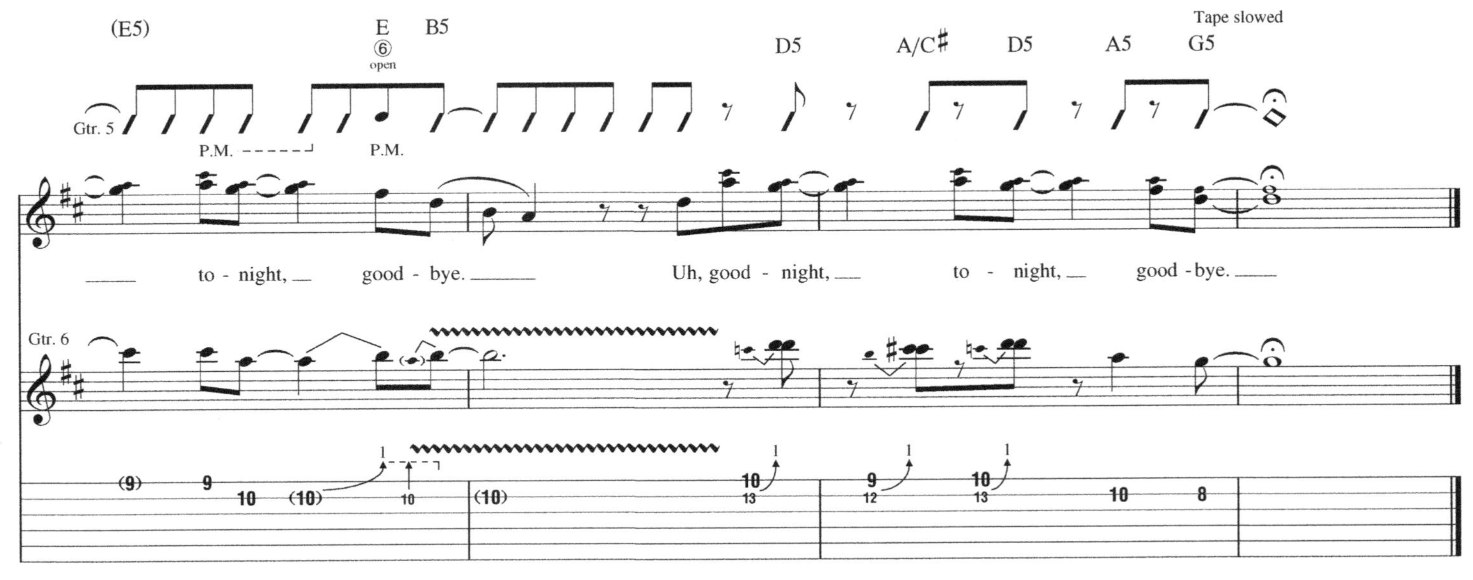
(E5)
E
open
B5
D5
A/C♯
D5
A5
G5
Tape slowed
Gtr. 5
P.M.
P.M.
to - night, good - bye.
Uh, good - night,
to - night,
good - bye.
Gtr. 6

Willing Well IV: The Final Cut

Words and Music by Claudio Sanchez, Michael Todd, Joshua Eppard and Travis Stever

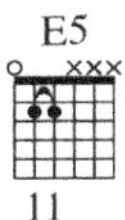

Tune down 1/2 step:
(low to high) E♭-A♭-D♭-G♭-B♭-E♭

Intro

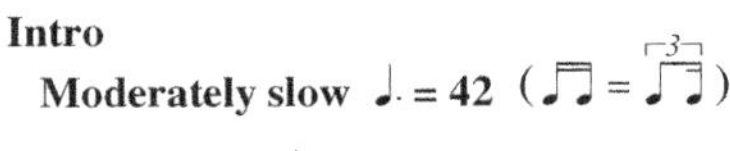

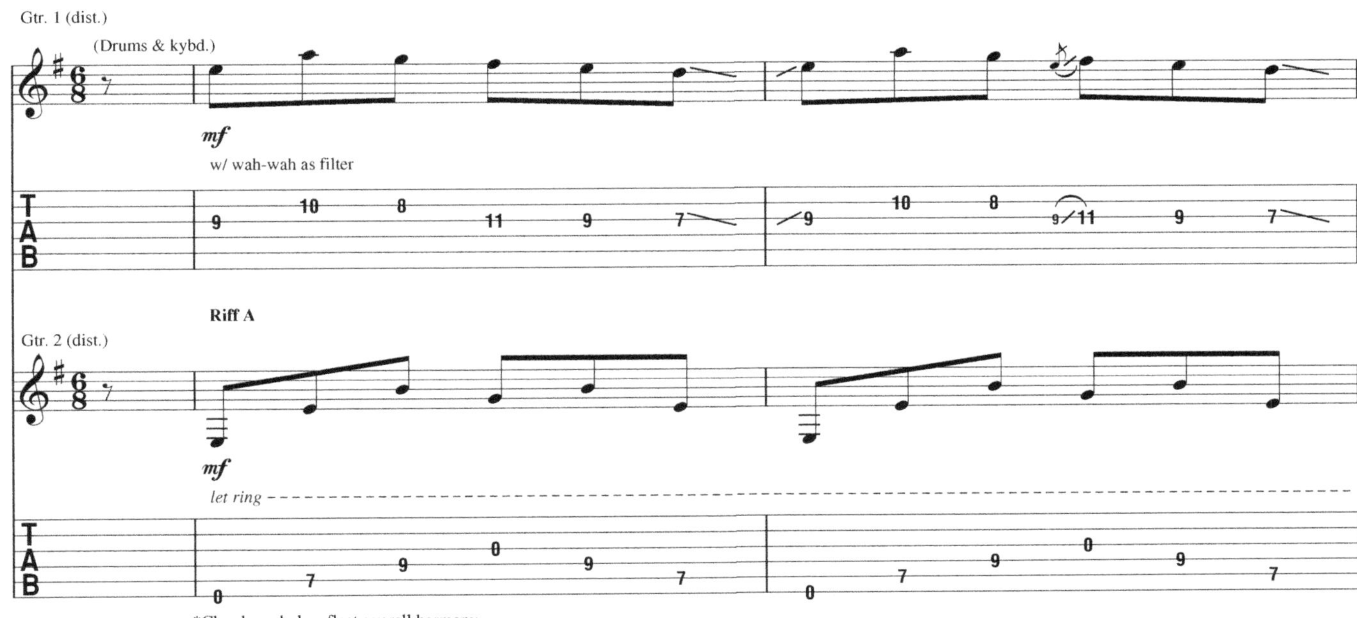

*Chord symbols reflect overall harmony.

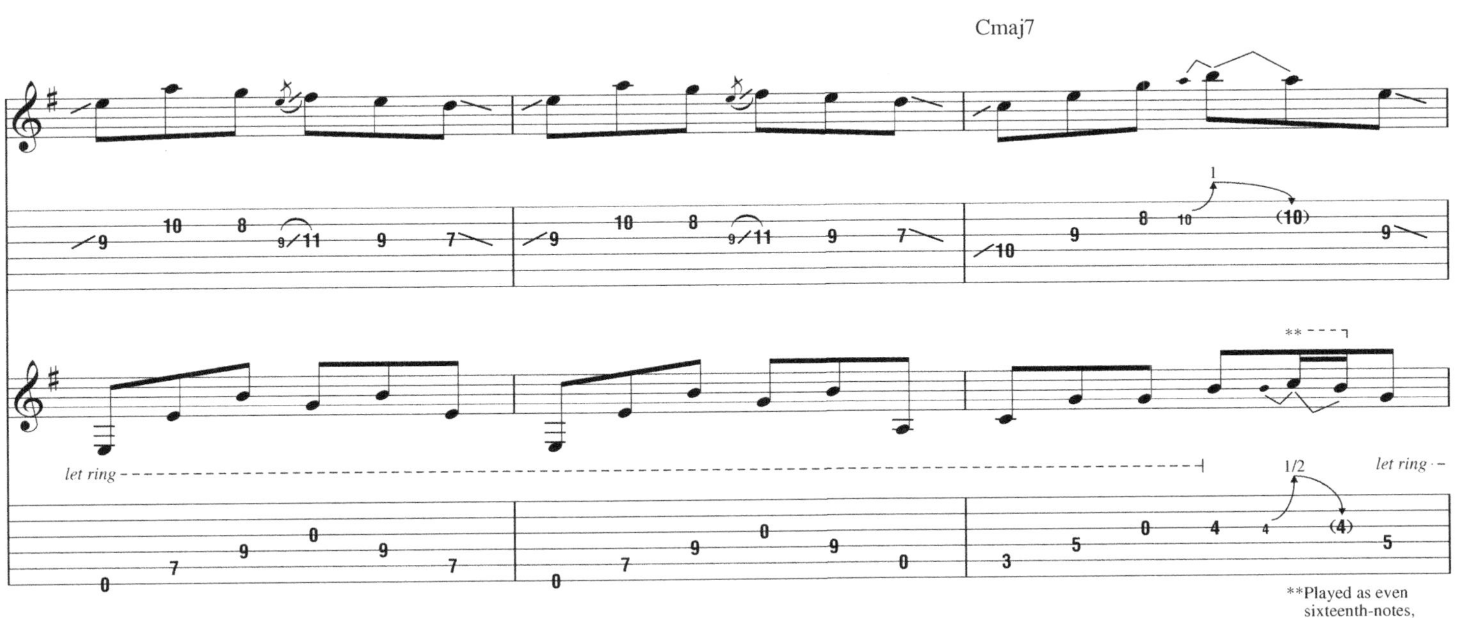

**Played as even sixteenth-notes, next 4 meas.

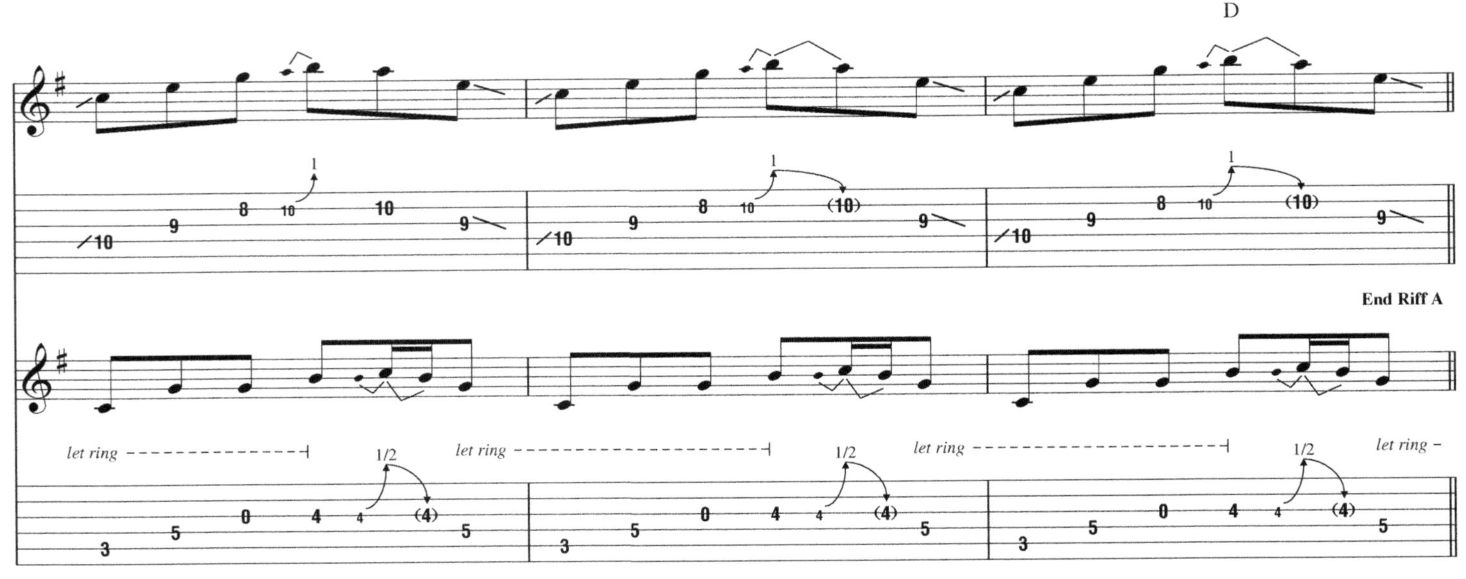
D
End Riff A
let ring
1/2
let ring
1/2
let ring
1/2
let ring

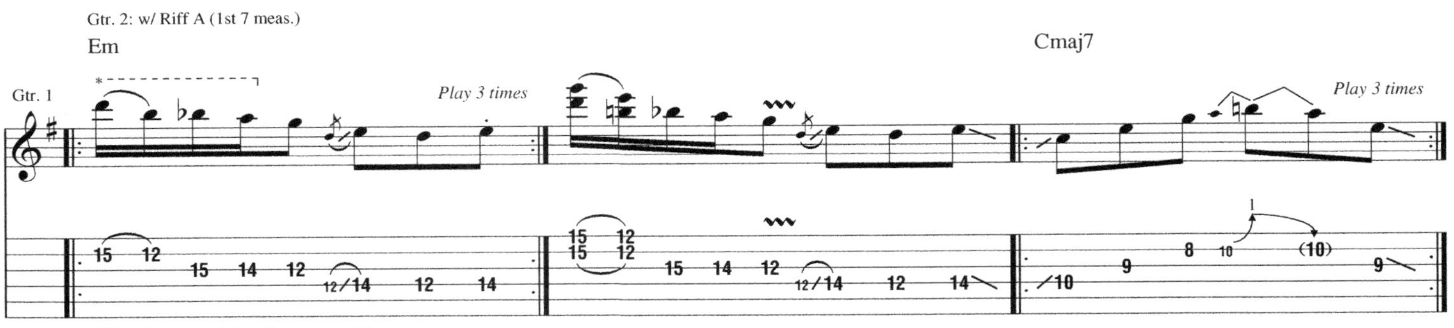
Gtr. 2: w/ Riff A (1st 7 meas.)
Em
Cmaj7
Gtr. 1
Play 3 times
Play 3 times
*Played as even sixteenth-notes, next 4 meas.

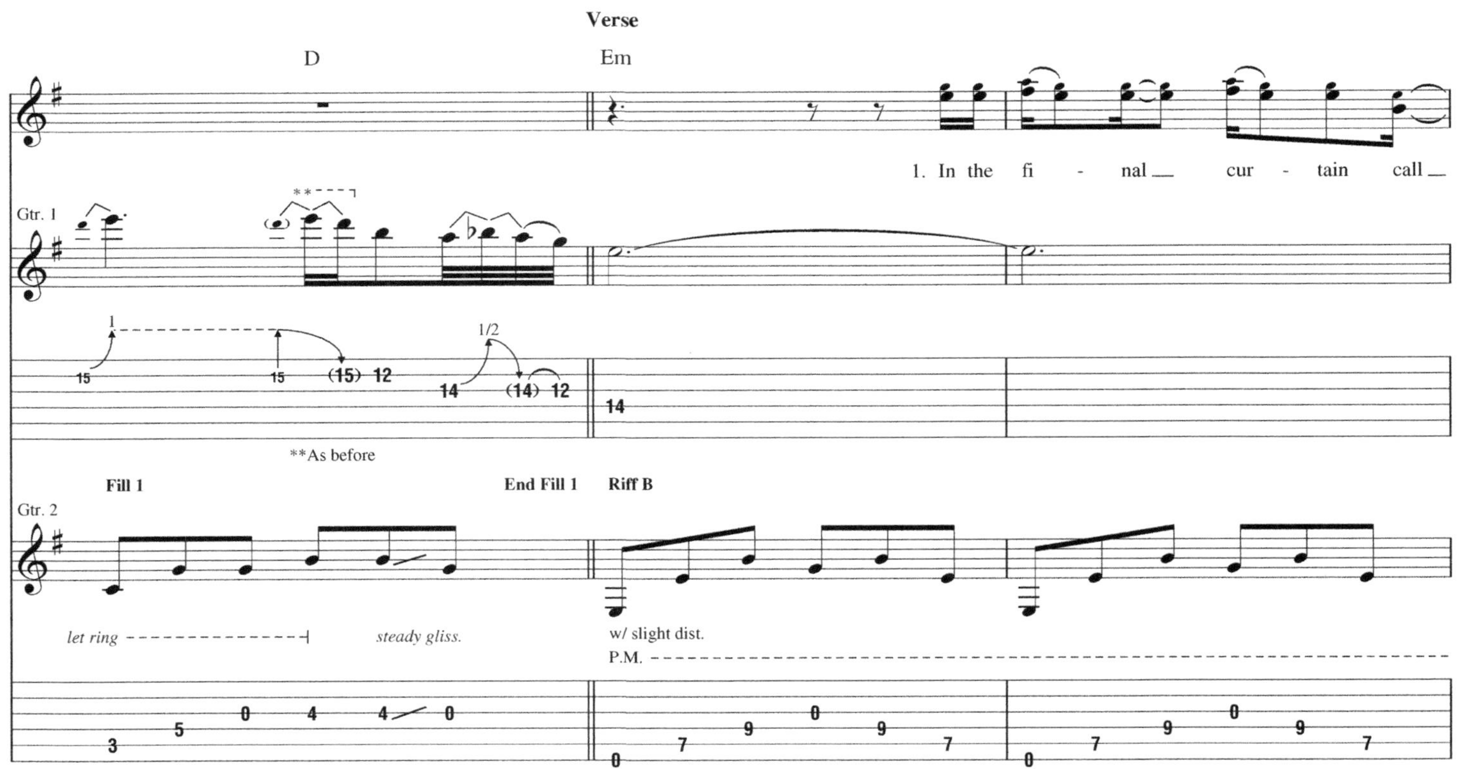
Verse
D
Em
1. In the fi - nal curtain call
Gtr. 1
**As before
Fill 1
End Fill 1
Riff B
Gtr. 2
let ring
steady gliss.
w/ slight dist.
P.M.

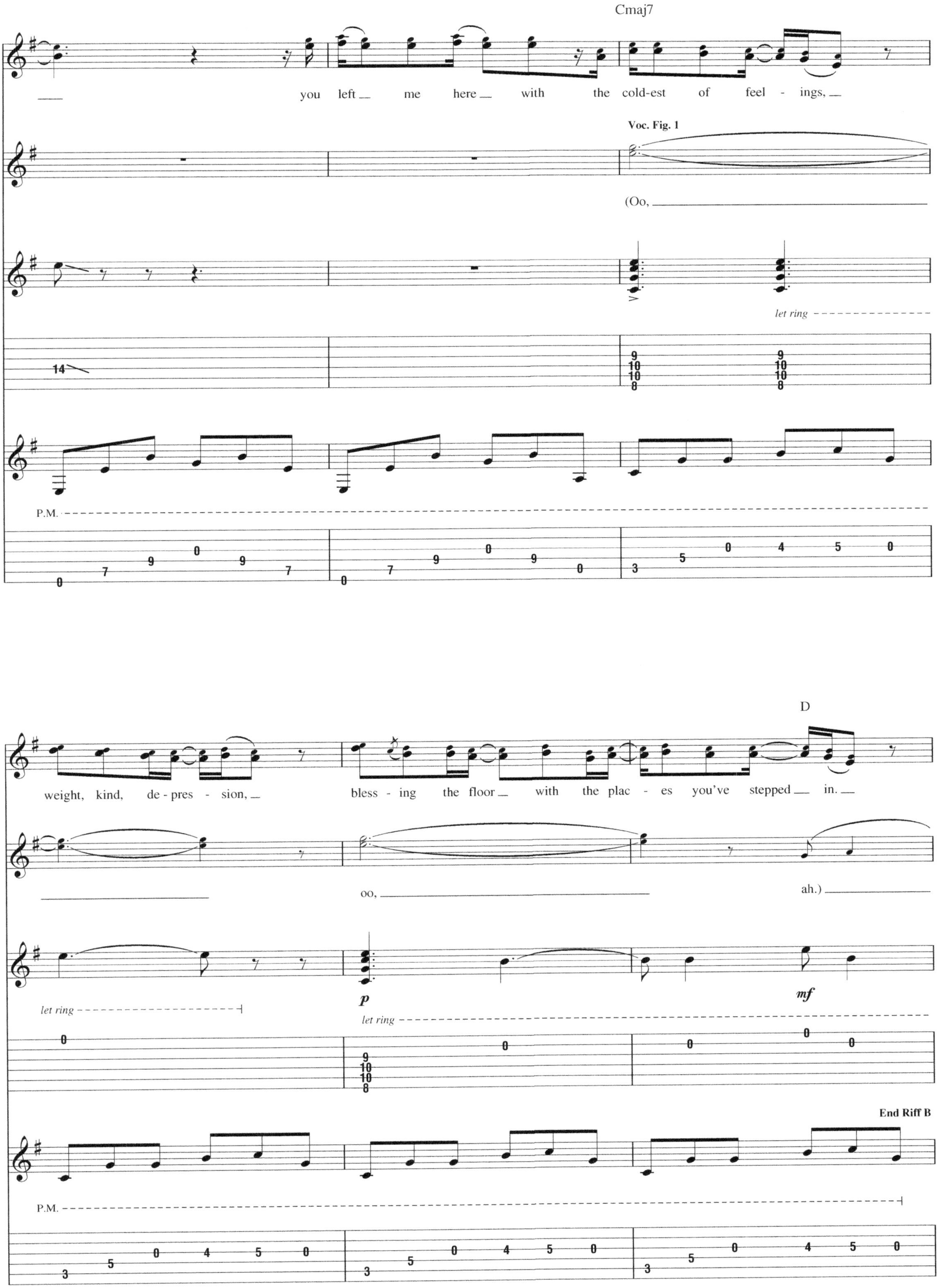

Cmaj7

you left me here with the cold-est of feel - ings,

Voc. Fig. 1

(Oo,

let ring

14

9 10 10 8 9 10 10 8

P.M.

0 7 9 0 9 7 0 7 9 0 9 0 3 5 0 4 5 0

D

weight, kind, de - pres - sion, bless - ing the floor with the plac - es you've stepped in.

oo, ah.)

let ring

p

let ring

mf

0 9 10 10 8 0 0 0 0

End Riff B

P.M.

3 5 0 4 5 0 3 5 0 4 5 0 3 5 0 4 5 0

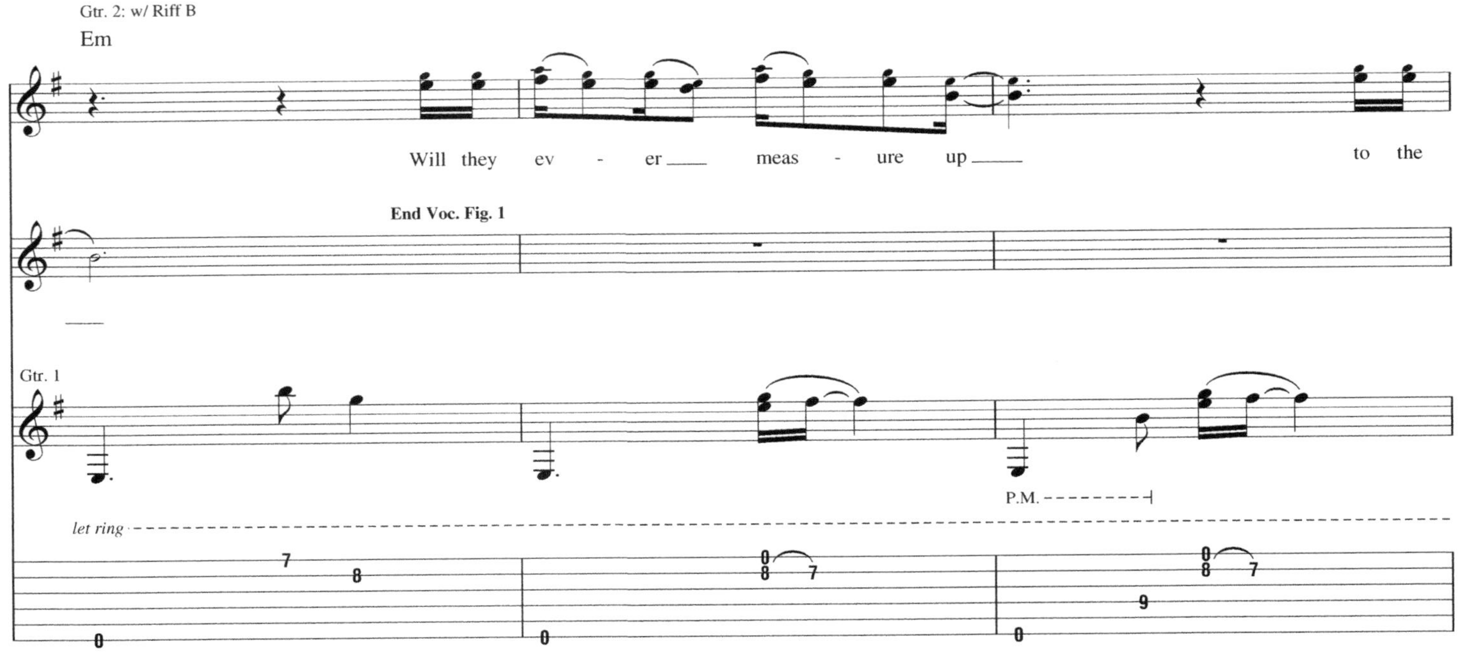
Gtr. 2: w/ Riff B
Em
Will they ev - er meas - ure up
to the
End Voc. Fig. 1
Gtr. 1
P.M.
let ring

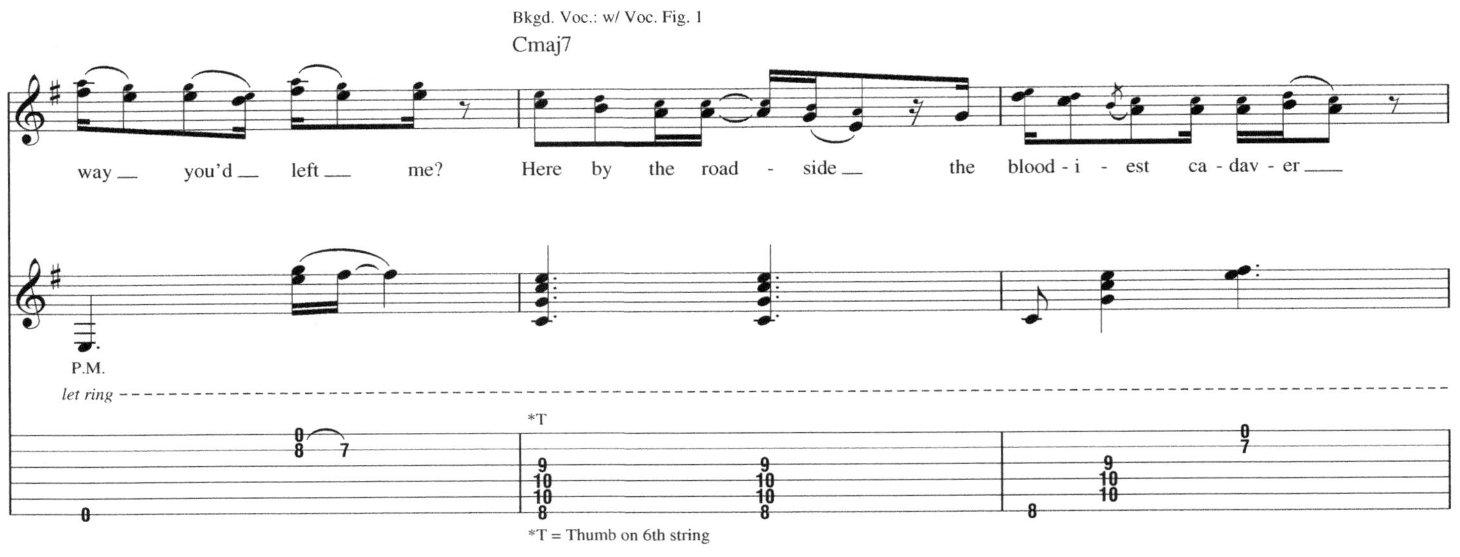
Bkgd. Voc.: w/ Voc. Fig. 1
Cmaj7
way you'd left me? Here by the road - side the blood - i - est ca - dav - er
P.M.
let ring
*T
*T = Thumb on 6th string

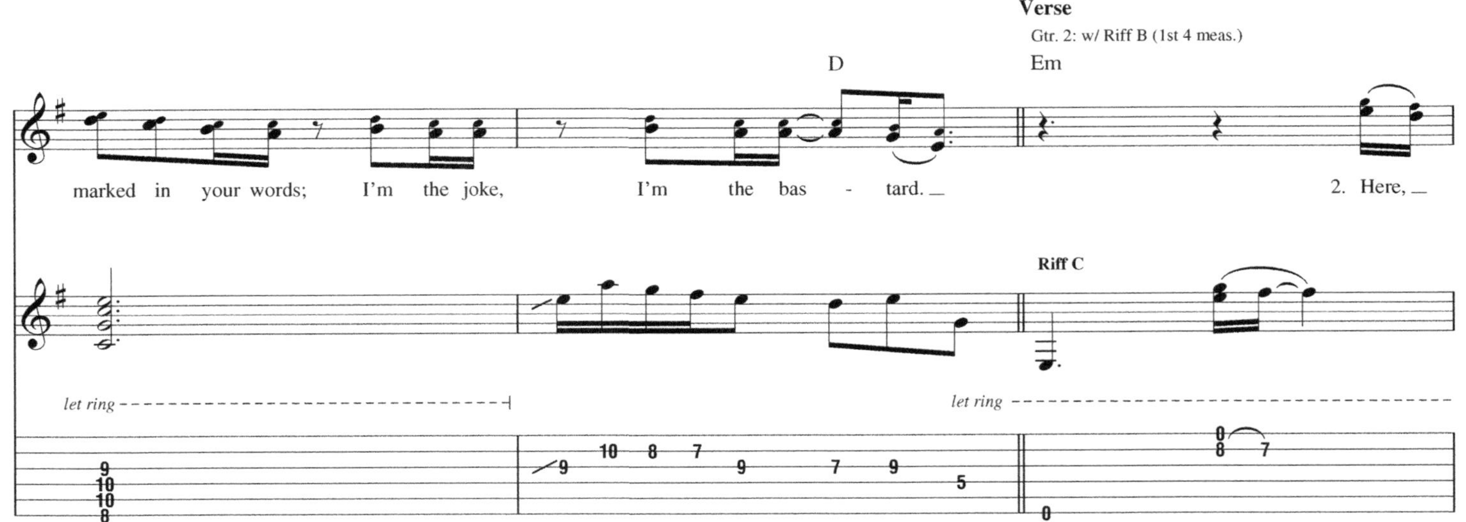
Verse
Gtr. 2: w/ Riff B (1st 4 meas.)
D
Em
marked in your words; I'm the joke, I'm the bas - tard.
2. Here,
Riff C
let ring
let ring

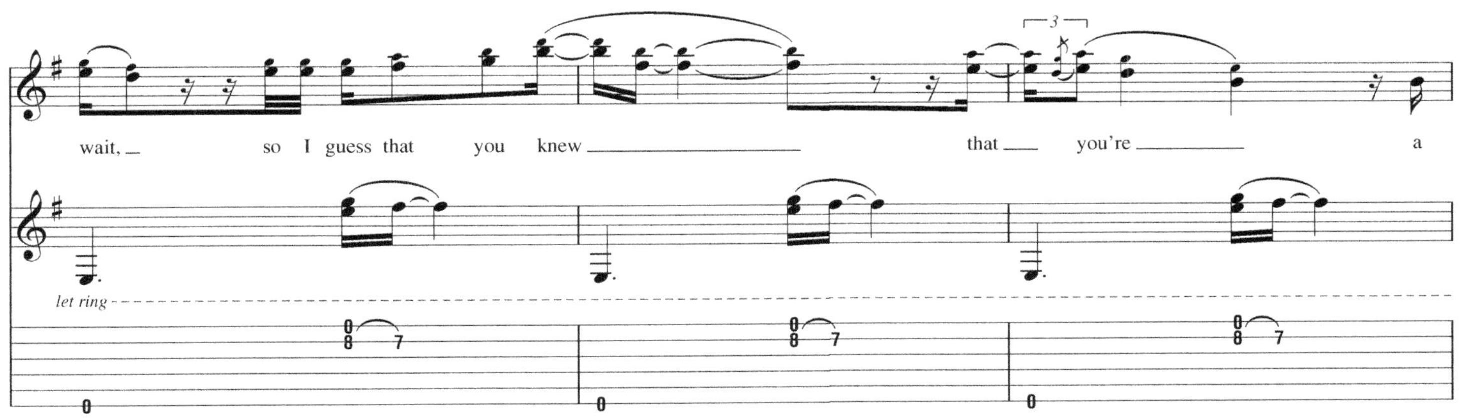
wait, so I guess that you knew that you're a
let ring

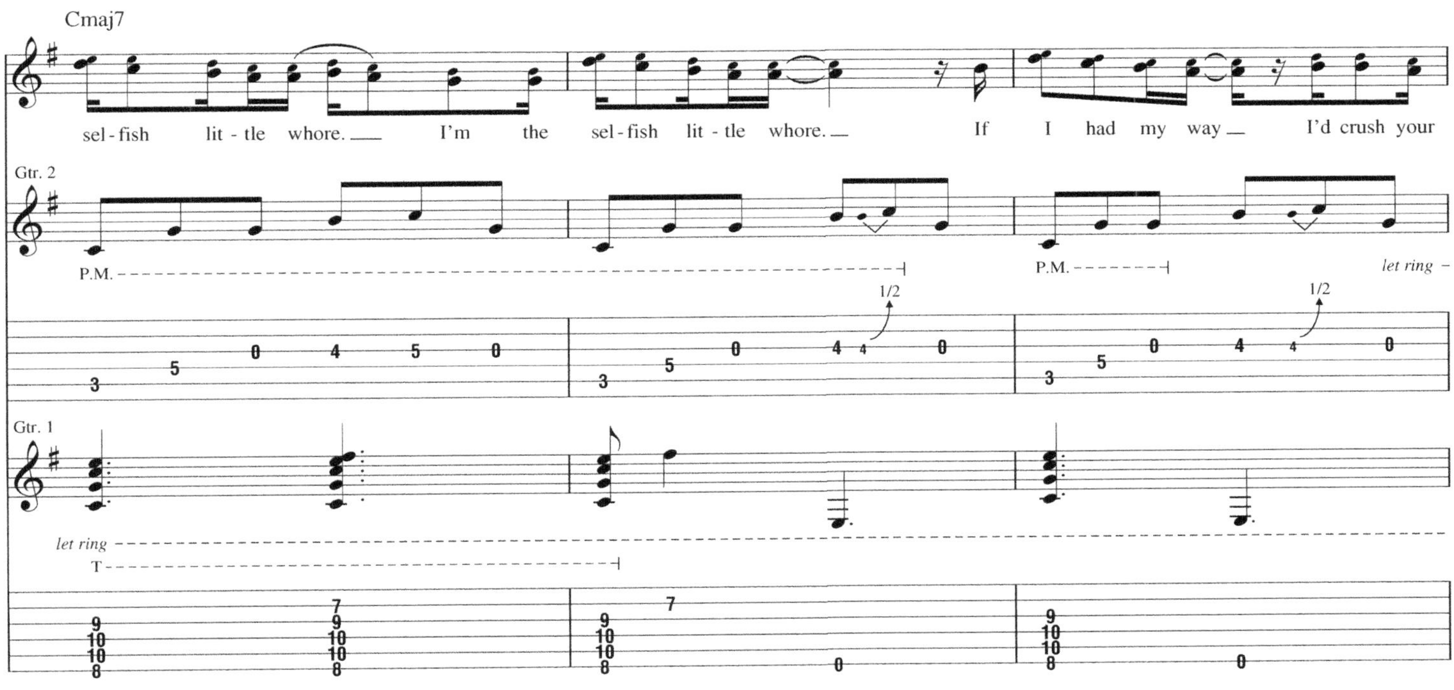
Cmaj7
sel-fish lit-tle whore. I'm the sel-fish lit-tle whore. If I had my way I'd crush your
Gtr. 2
P.M.
P.M.
let ring
1/2
1/2
Gtr. 1
let ring
T

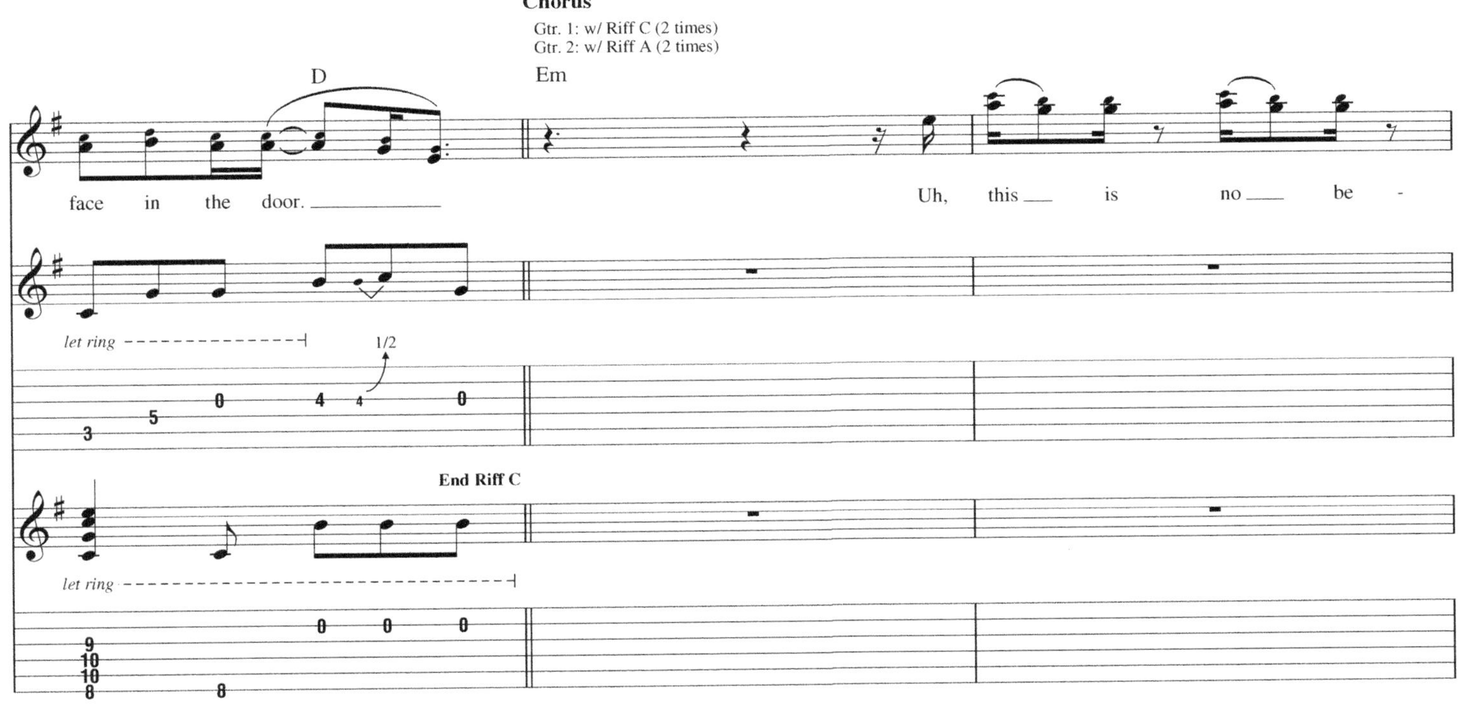
Chorus
Gtr. 1: w/ Riff C (2 times)
Gtr. 2: w/ Riff A (2 times)
D
Em
face in the door. Uh, this is no be -
let ring
1/2
End Riff C
let ring

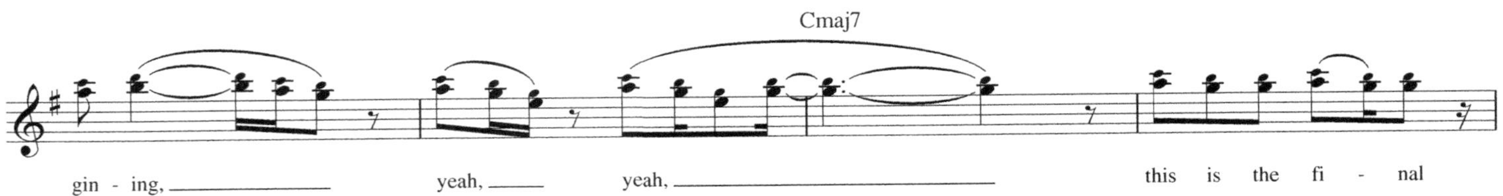
Cmaj7
gin - ing,
yeah,
yeah,
this is the fi - nal

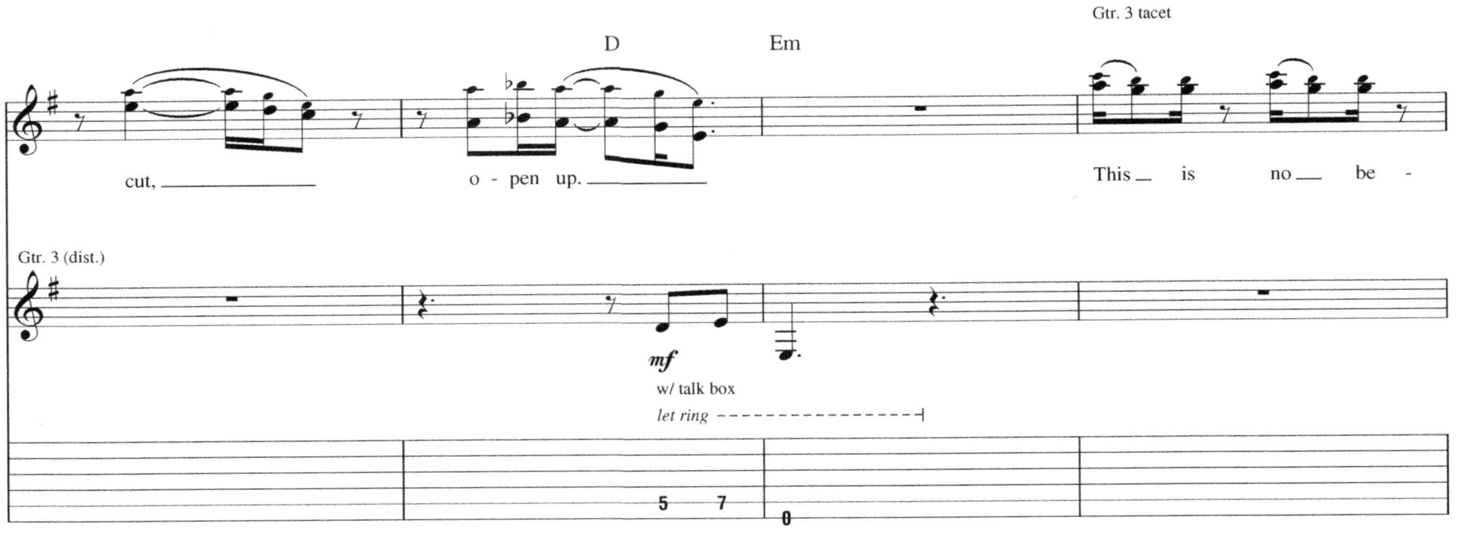
Gtr. 3 tacet
D
Em
cut,
o - pen up.
This is no be -
Gtr. 3 (dist.)
mf
w/ talk box
let ring
5 7
0

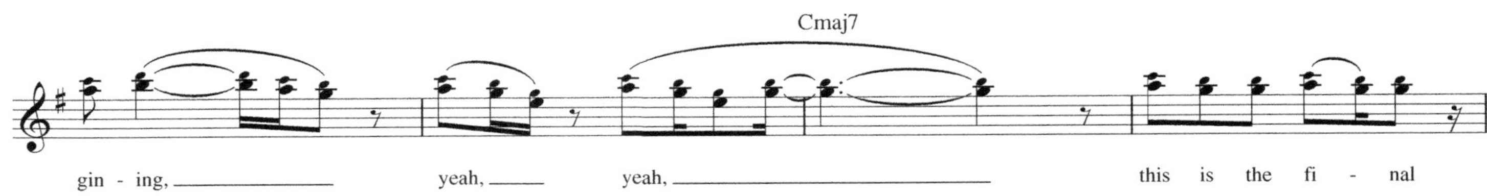
Cmaj7
gin - ing,
yeah,
yeah,
this is the fi - nal

Guitar Solo

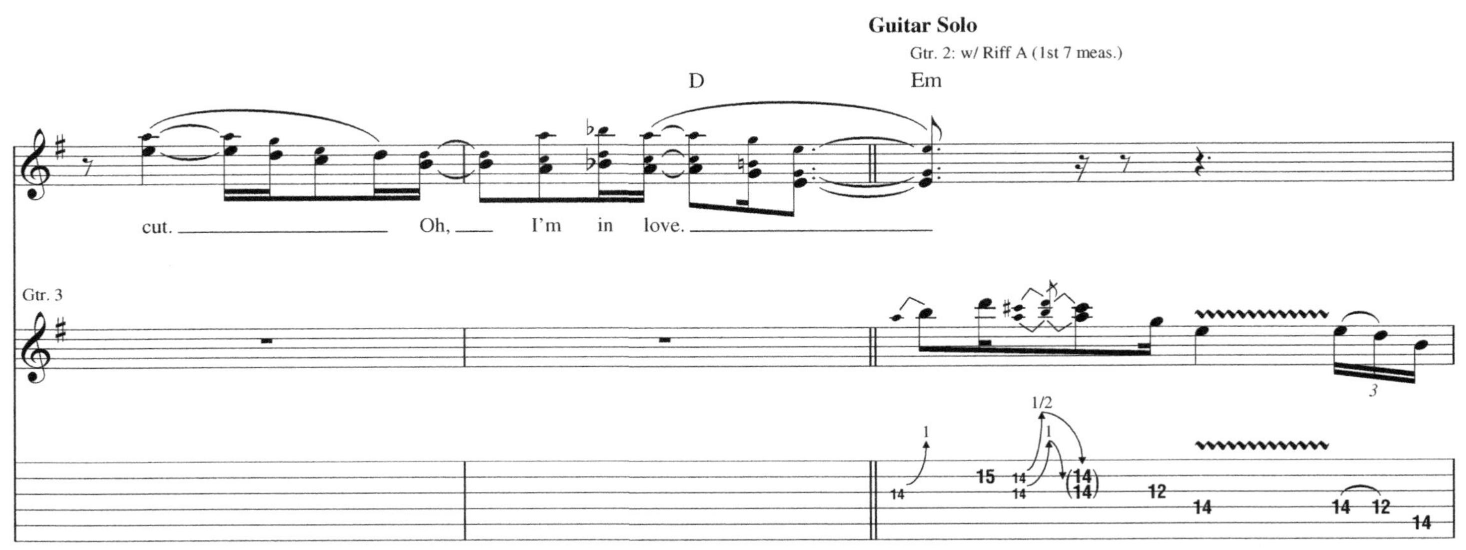
Gtr. 2: w/ Riff A (1st 7 meas.)
D
Em
cut.
Oh, I'm in love.
Gtr. 3
1
1/2
1
14
15
14
14
(14)
(14)
12
14
14
12
14
3

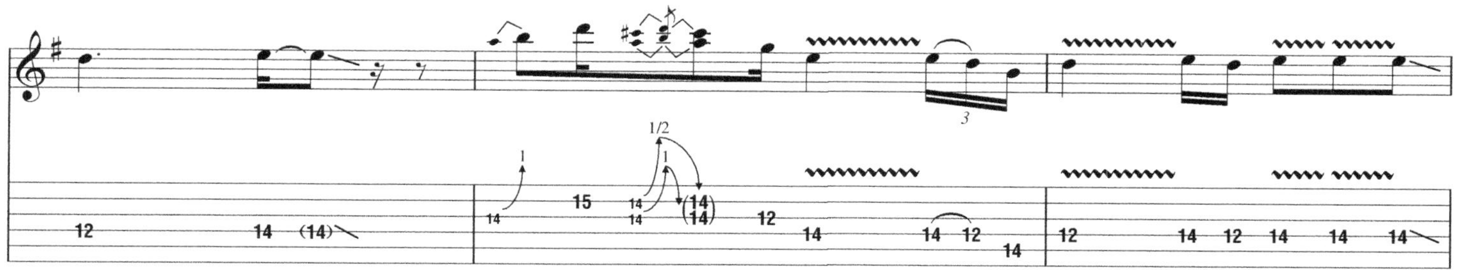

1
1/2
1

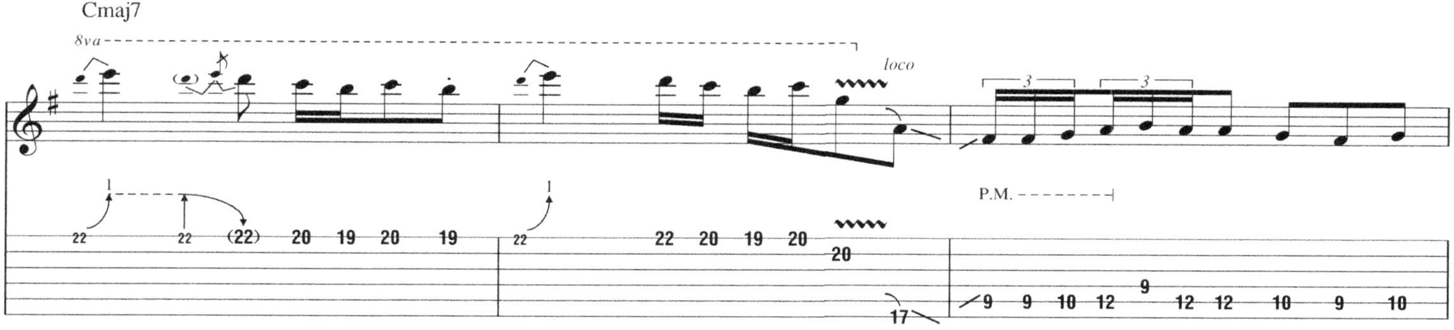

Cmaj7
8va
loco
P.M.

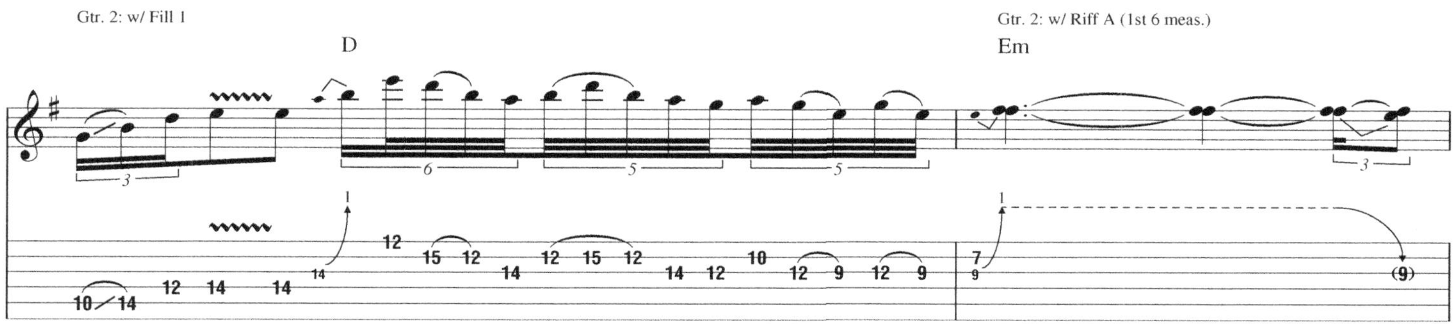

Gtr. 2: w/ Fill 1
D
Gtr. 2: w/ Riff A (1st 6 meas.)
Em

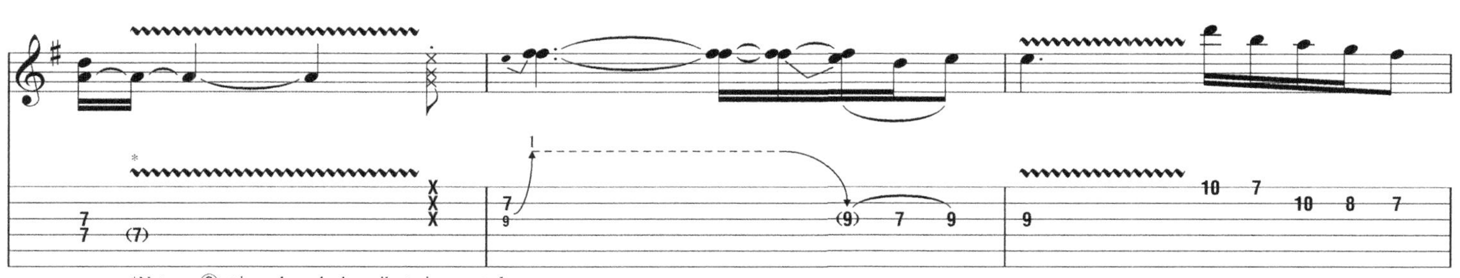

*Note on ③ string released when vibrato is executed.

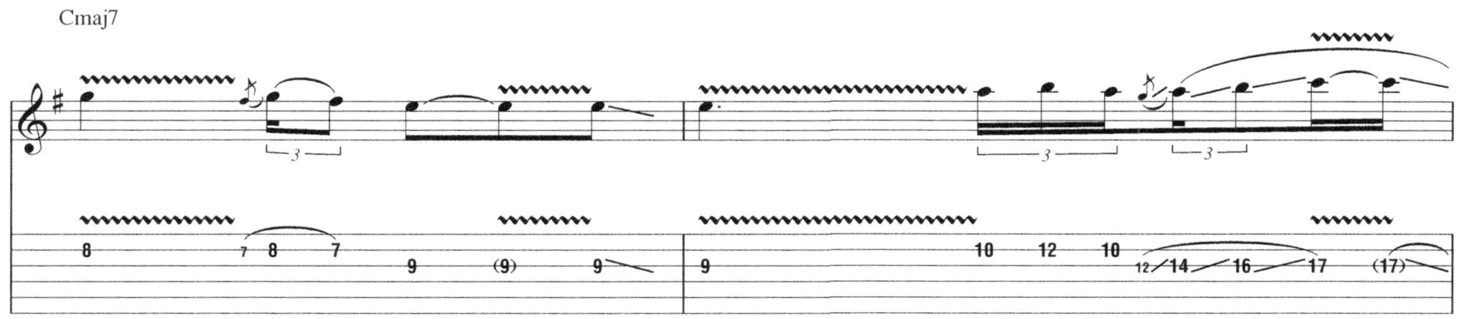

Cmaj7

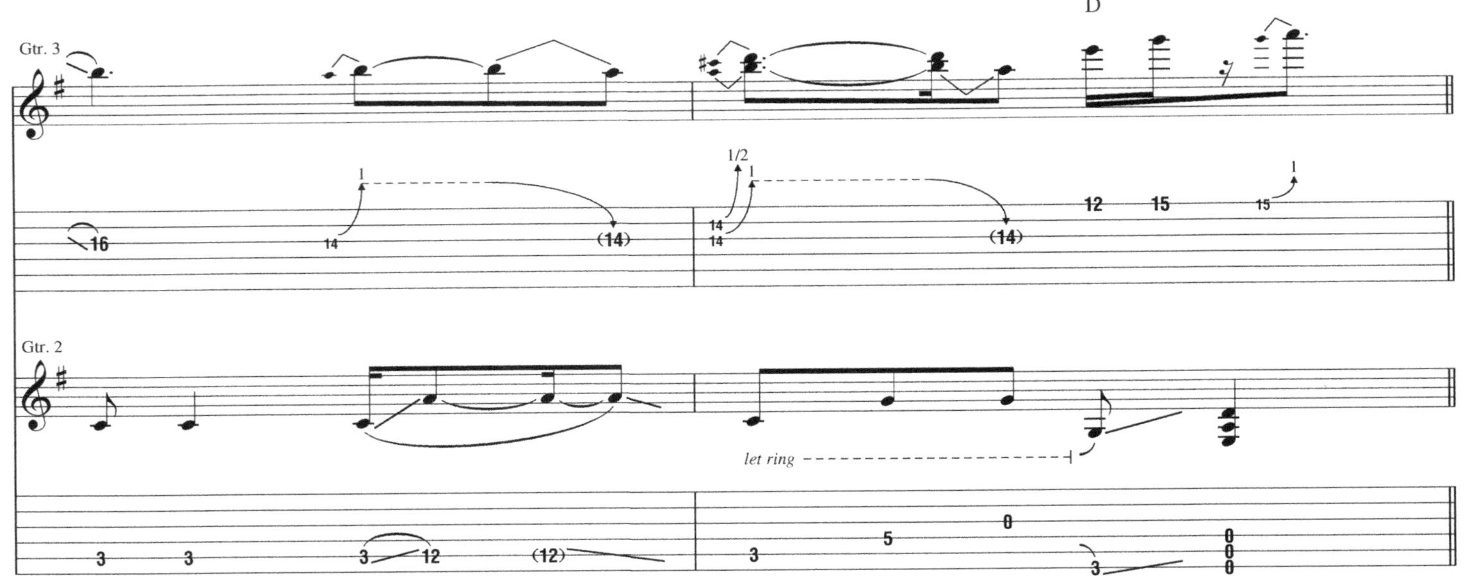
Gtr. 3
D
Gtr. 2
let ring

Guitar Solo
Gtr. 1: w/ Riff C (4 times)
Gtrs. 2 & 3 tacet
Em
Gtr. 4 (clean)

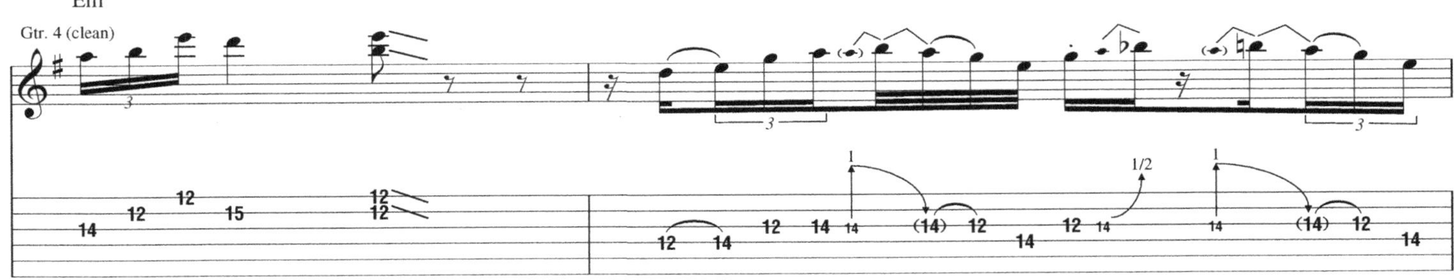

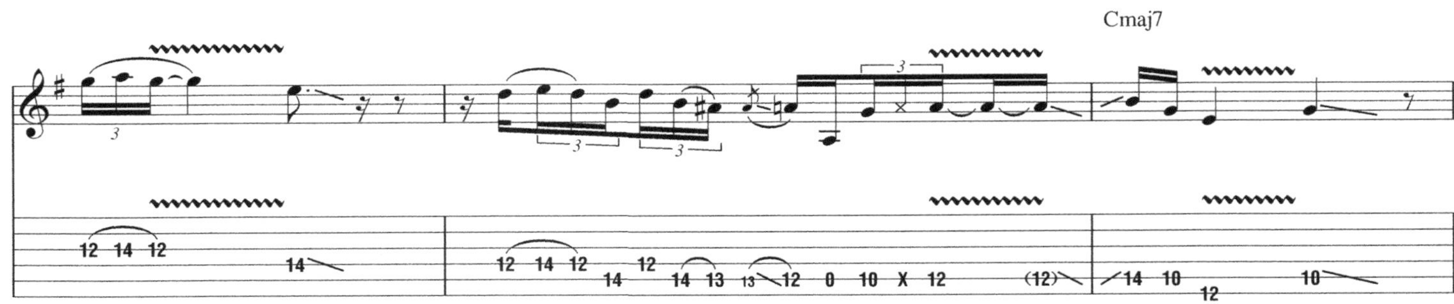
Cmaj7

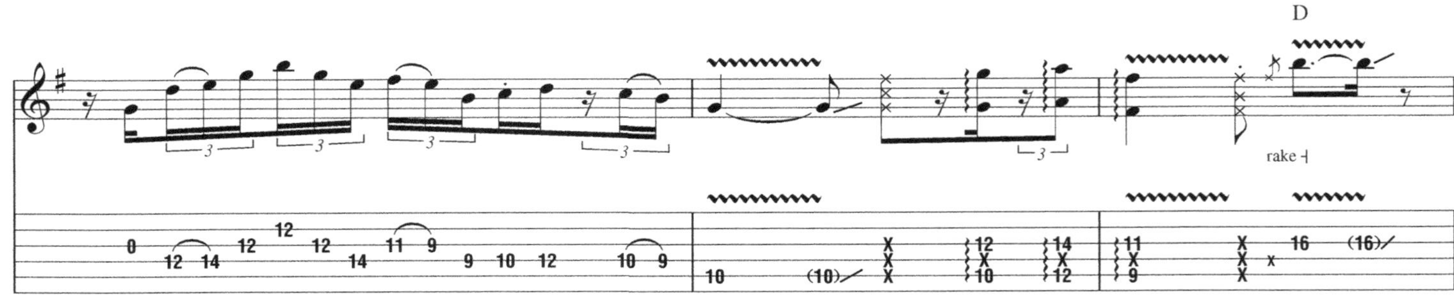
D
rake

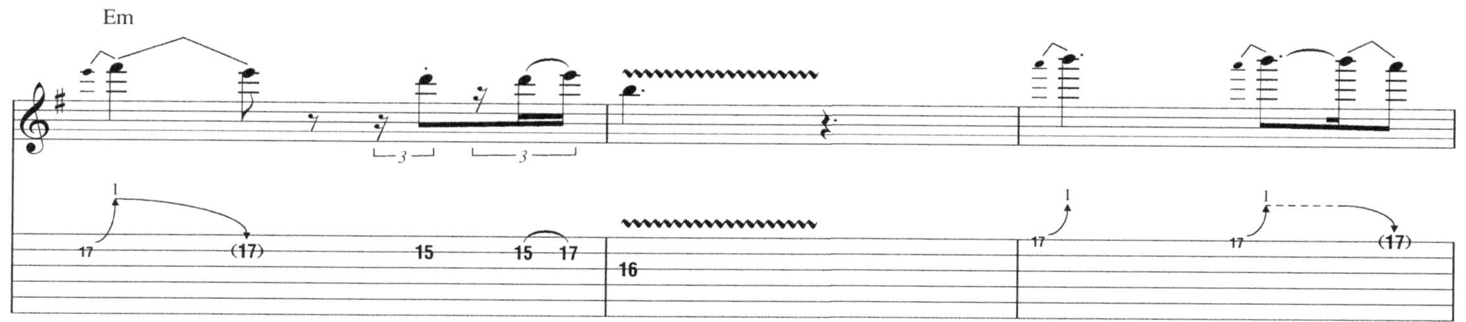
Em

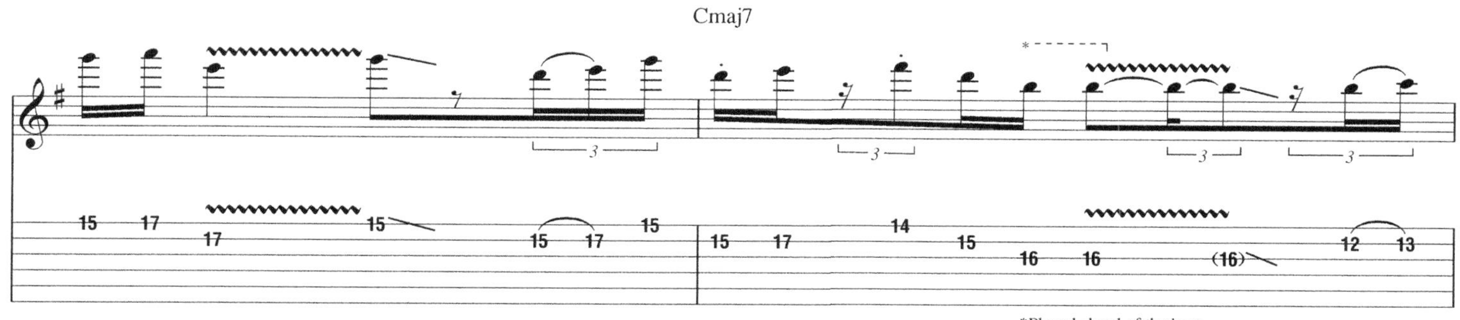
Cmaj7
*Played ahead of the beat.

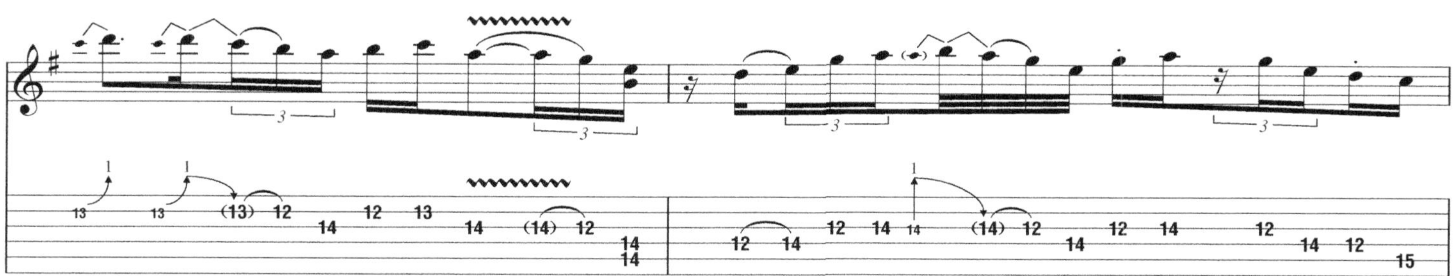

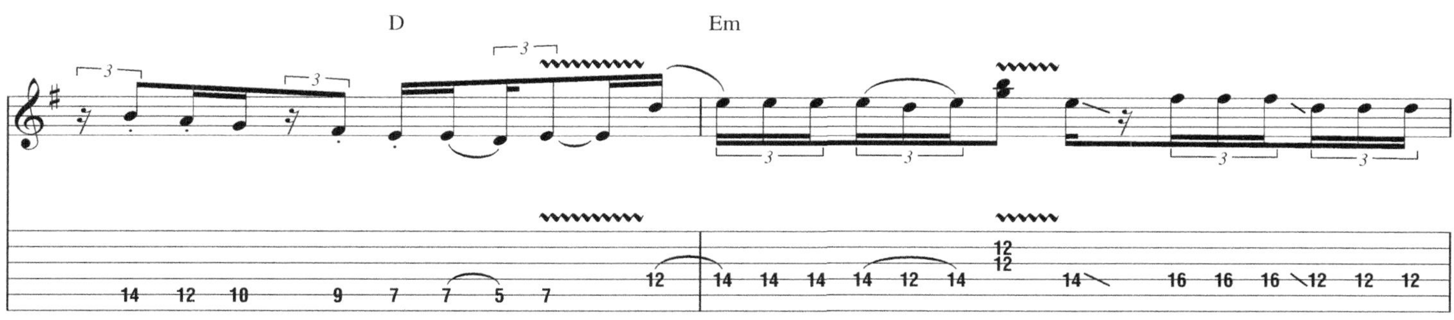
D
Em

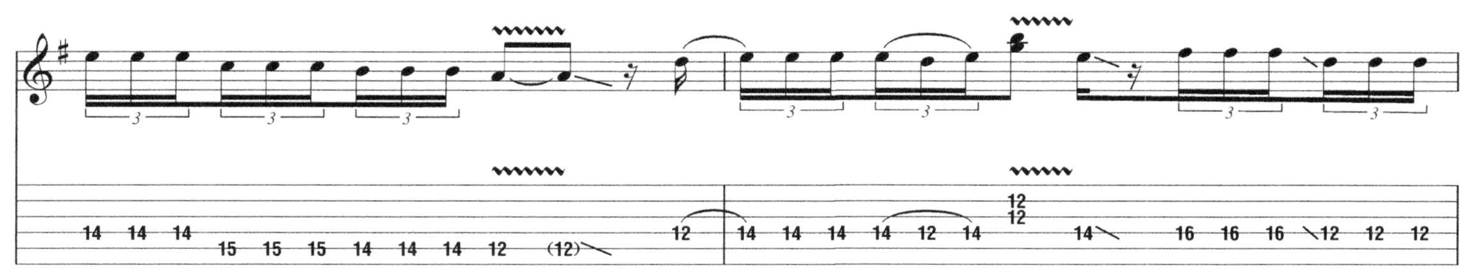

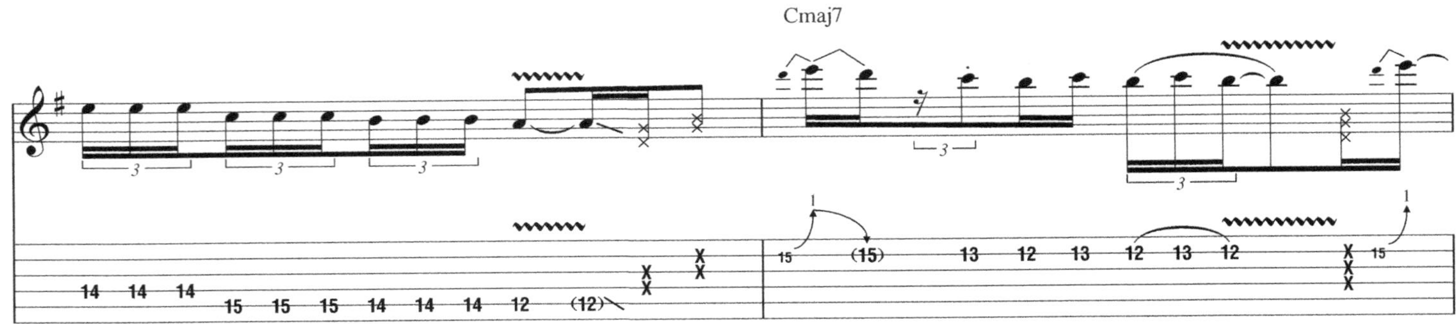
Cmaj7

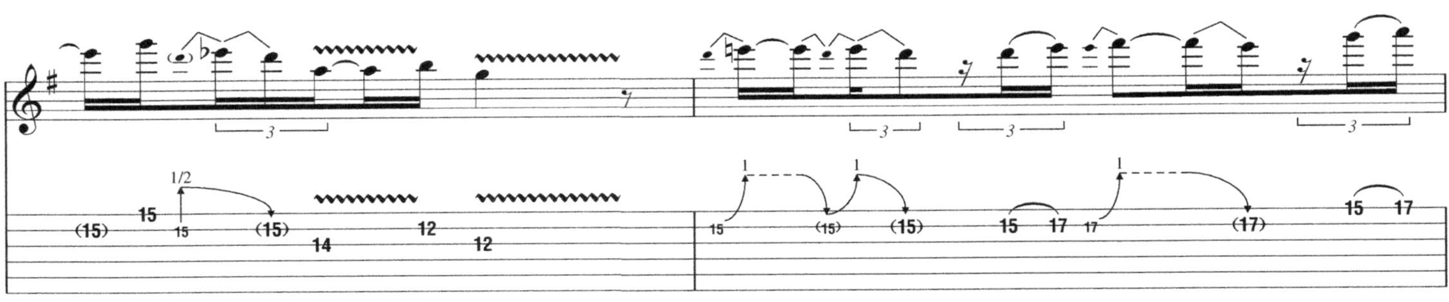

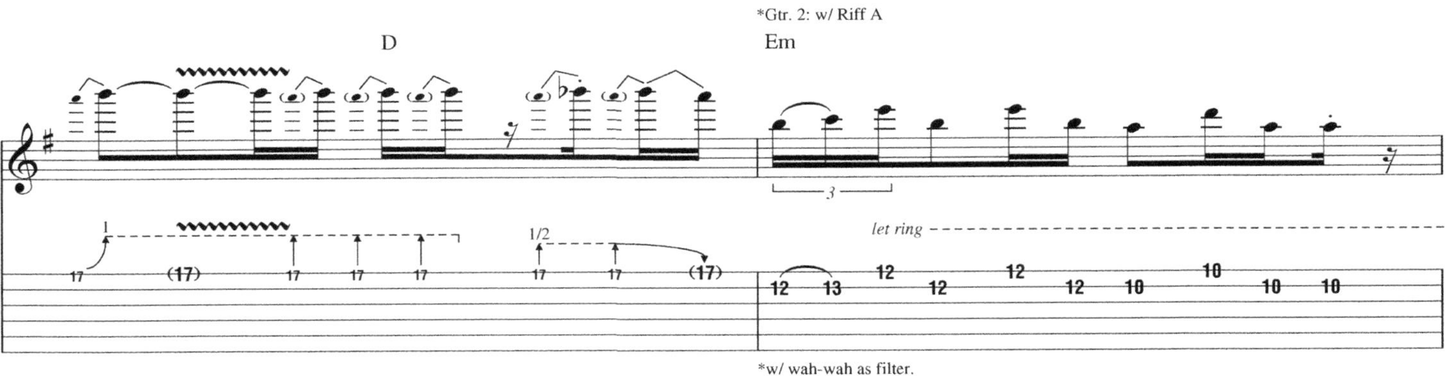
*Gtr. 2: w/ Riff A
D
Em
let ring
*w/ wah-wah as filter.

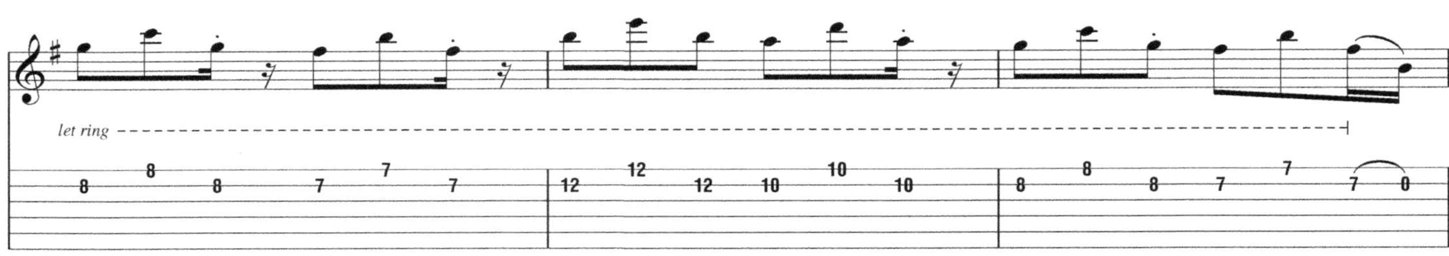
let ring

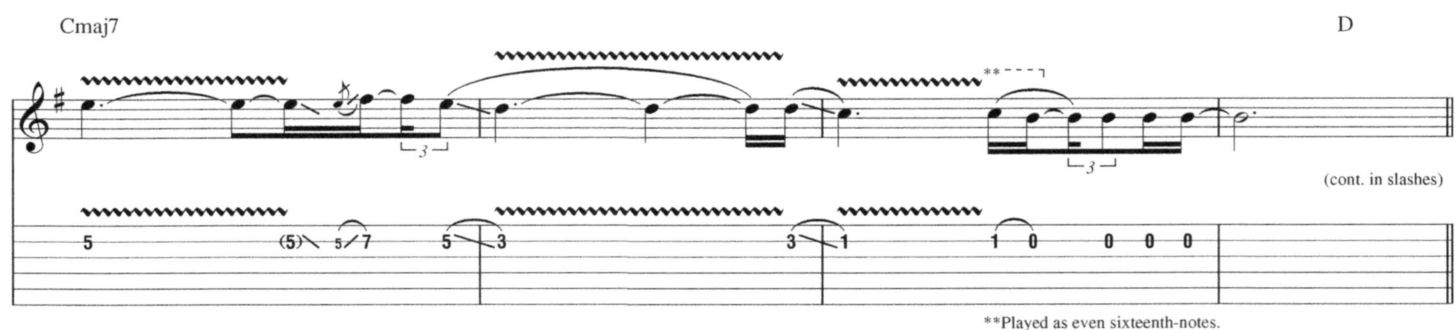
Cmaj7
D
(cont. in slashes)
**Played as even sixteenth-notes.

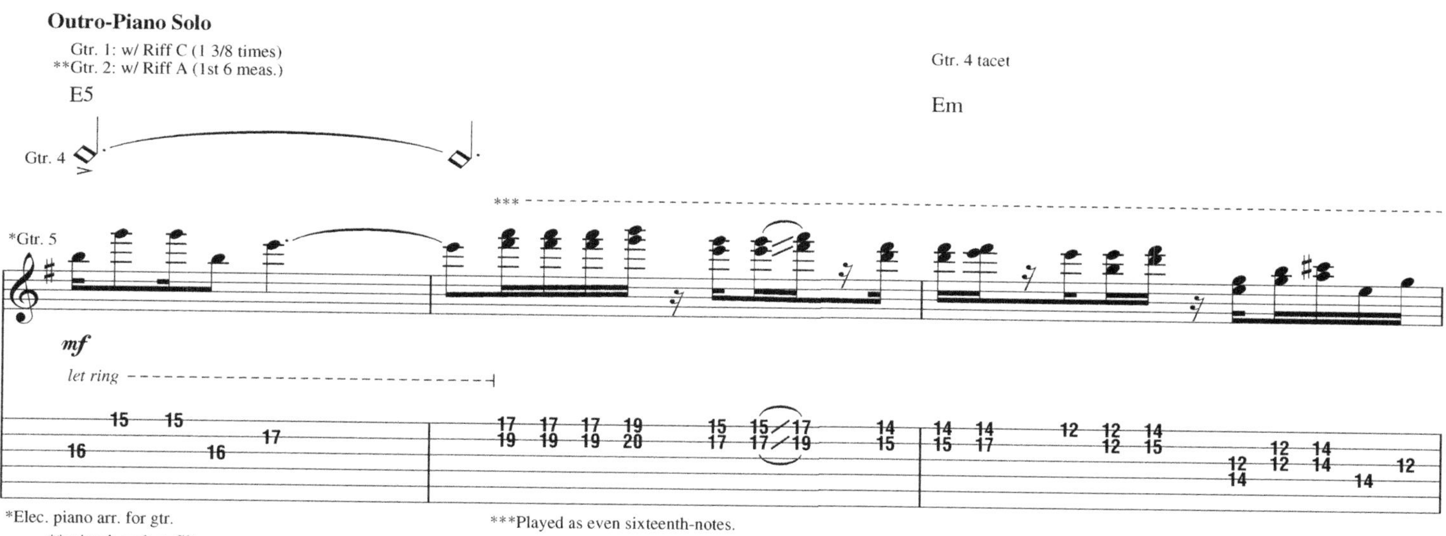
Outro-Piano Solo
Gtr. 1: w/ Riff C (1 3/8 times)
**Gtr. 2: w/ Riff A (1st 6 meas.)
E5
Gtr. 4
Gtr. 4 tacet
Em
*Gtr. 5
mf
let ring
*Elec. piano arr. for gtr.
**w/ wah-wah as filter.
***Played as even sixteenth-notes.

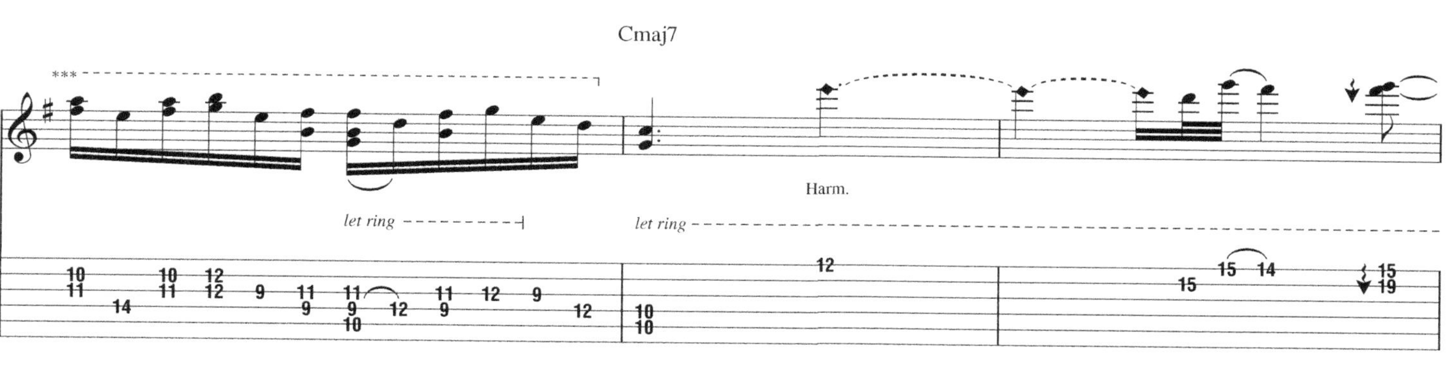
Cmaj7
Harm.
let ring
let ring

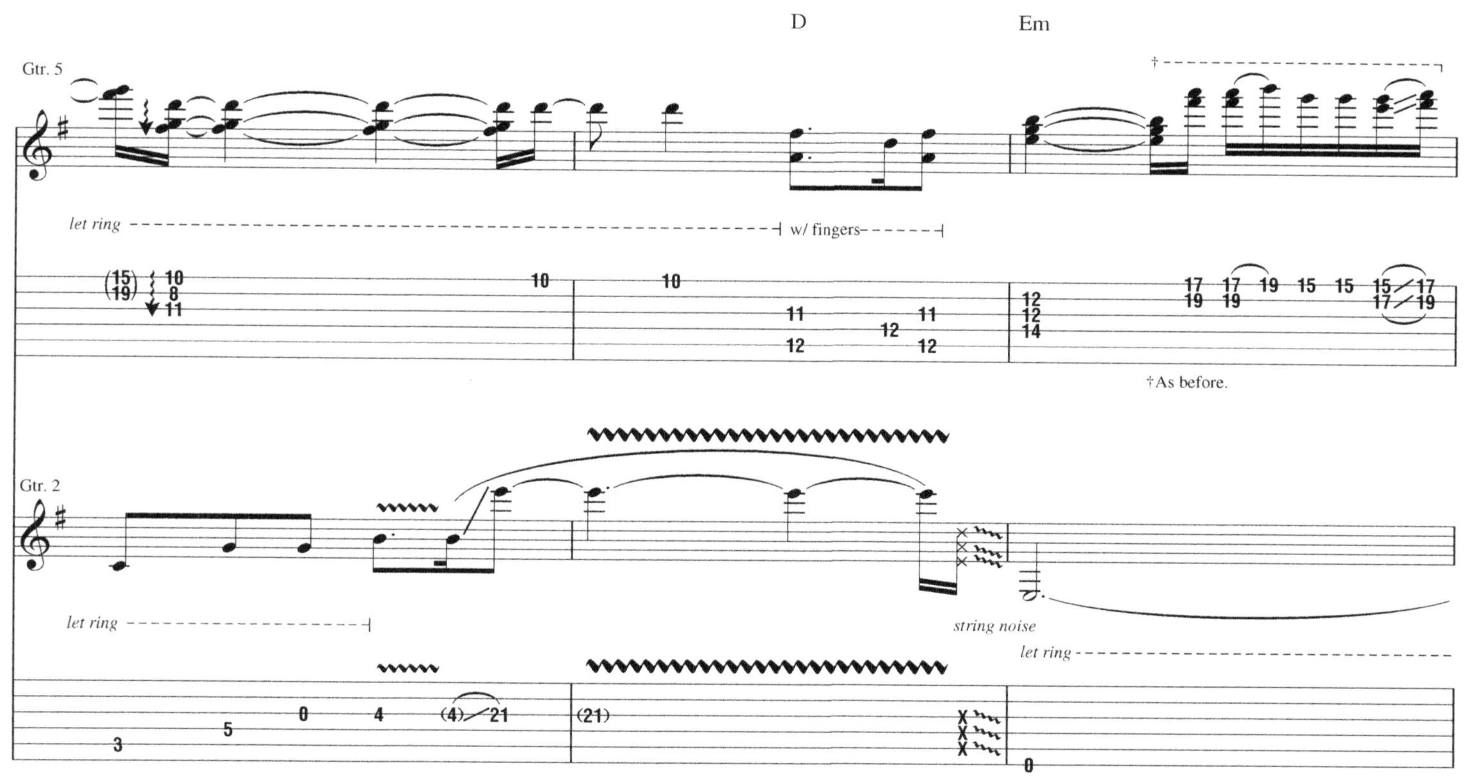
D
Em
Gtr. 5
let ring
w/ fingers
†As before.
Gtr. 2
let ring
string noise
let ring

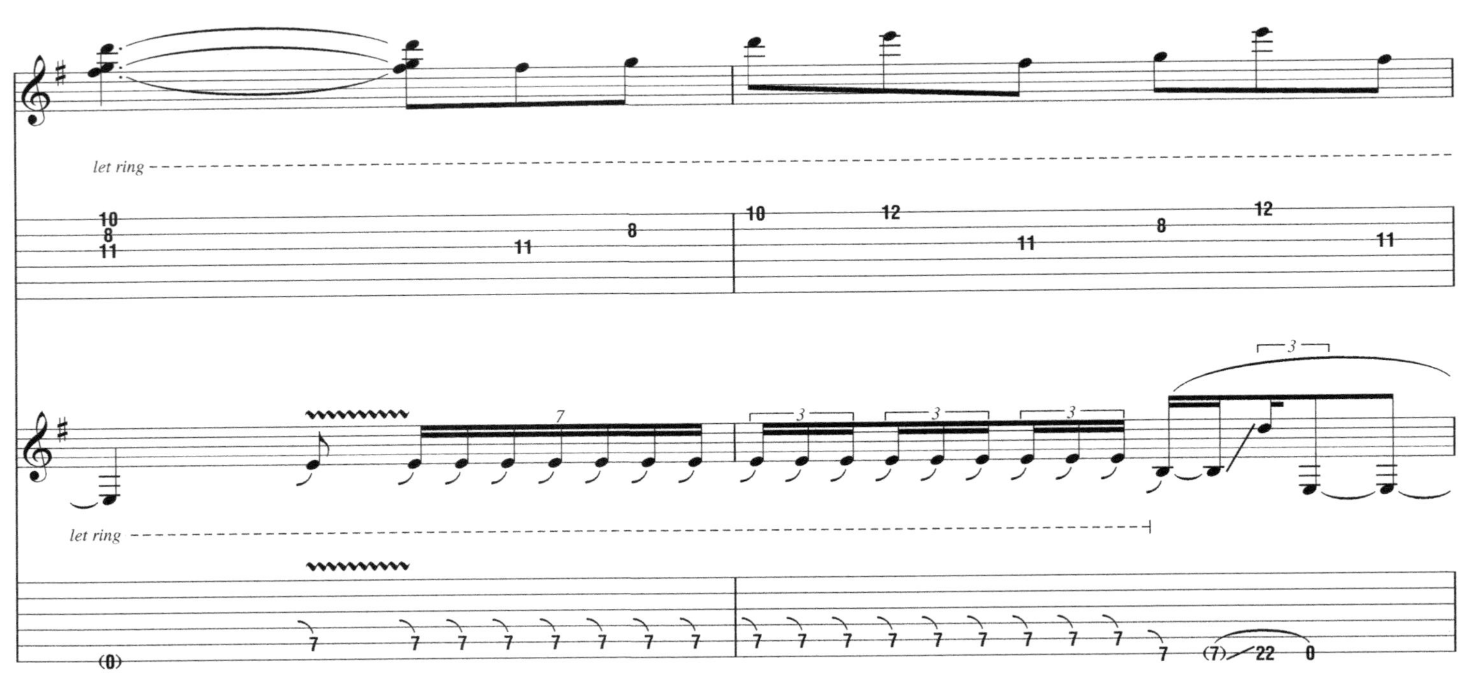

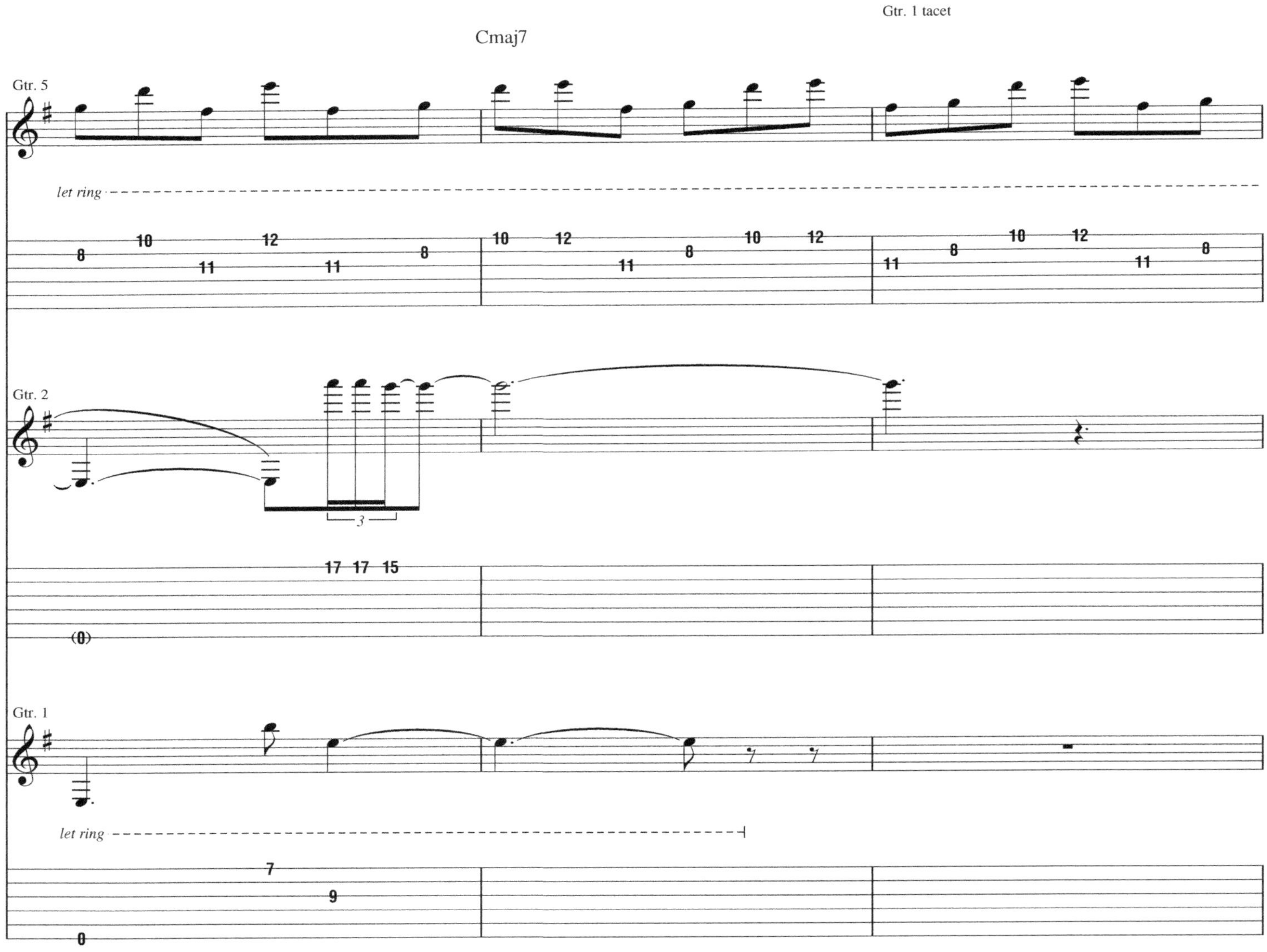

Gtr. 1 tacet

Cmaj7

Gtr. 5

let ring

Gtr. 2

Gtr. 1

let ring

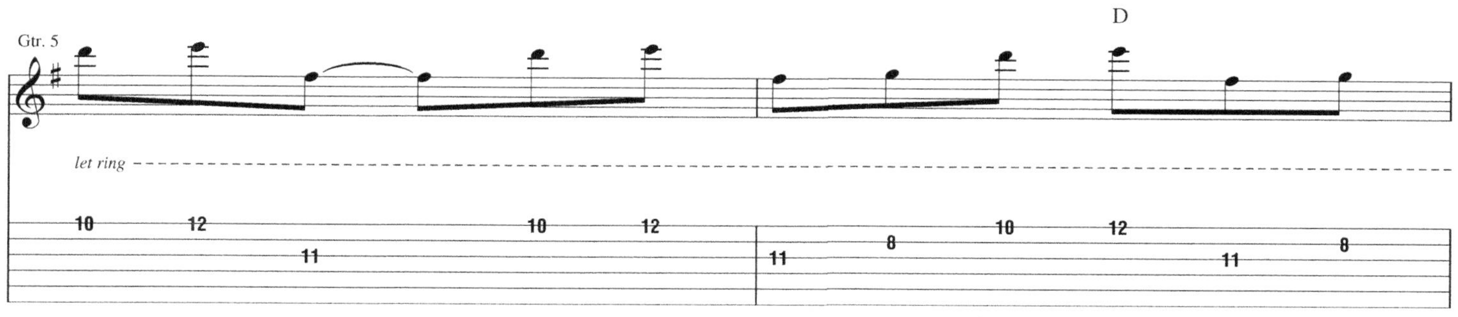
Gtr. 2 tacet
D
Gtr. 5
let ring

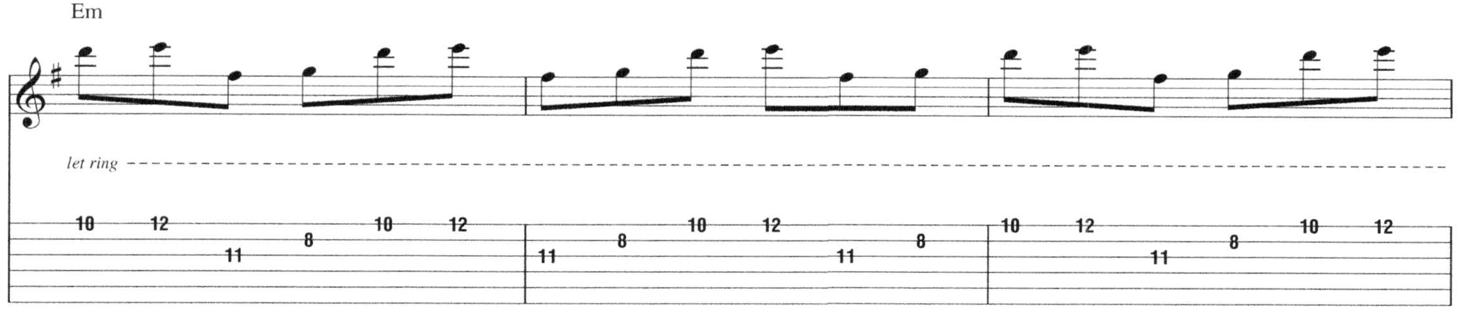
Em
let ring

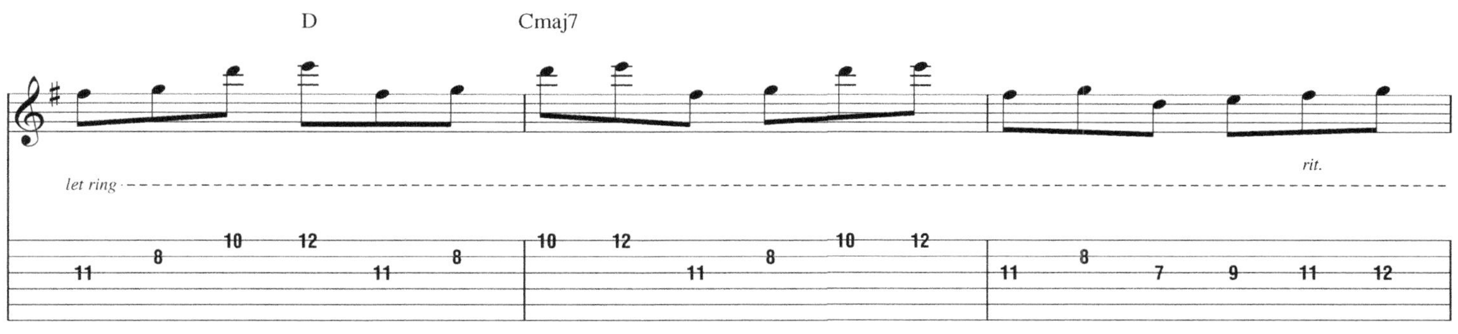
D
Cmaj7
rit.
let ring

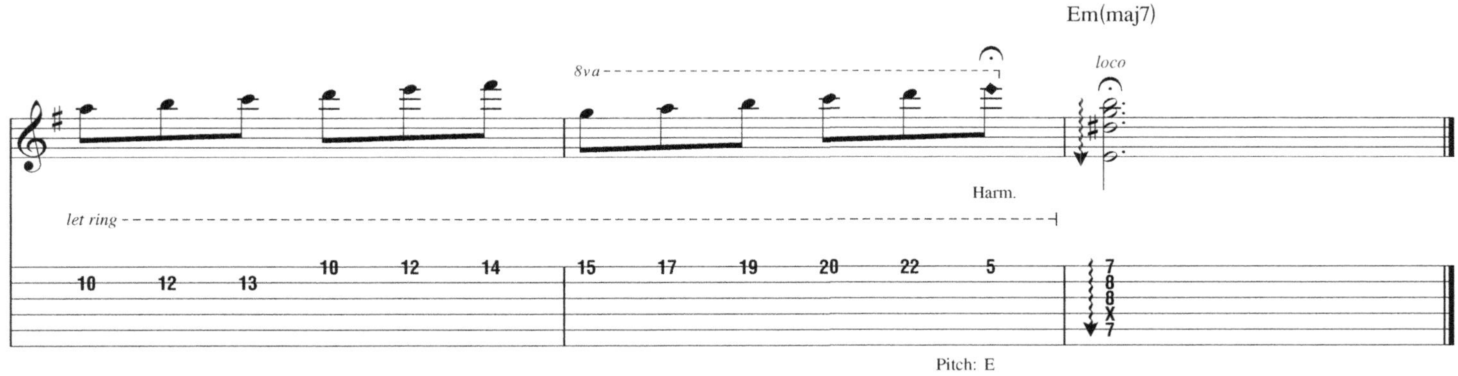
Em(maj7)
8va
loco
Harm.
let ring
Pitch: E

Guitar Notation Legend

Guitar Music can be notated three different ways: on a *musical staff*, in *tablature*, and in *rhythm slashes*.

RHYTHM SLASHES are written above the staff. Strum chords in the rhythm indicated. Use the chord diagrams found at the top of the first page of the transcription for the appropriate chord voicings. Round noteheads indicate single notes.

THE MUSICAL STAFF shows pitches and rhythms and is divided by bar lines into measures. Pitches are named after the first seven letters of the alphabet.

TABLATURE graphically represents the guitar fingerboard. Each horizontal line represents a a string, and each number represents a fret.

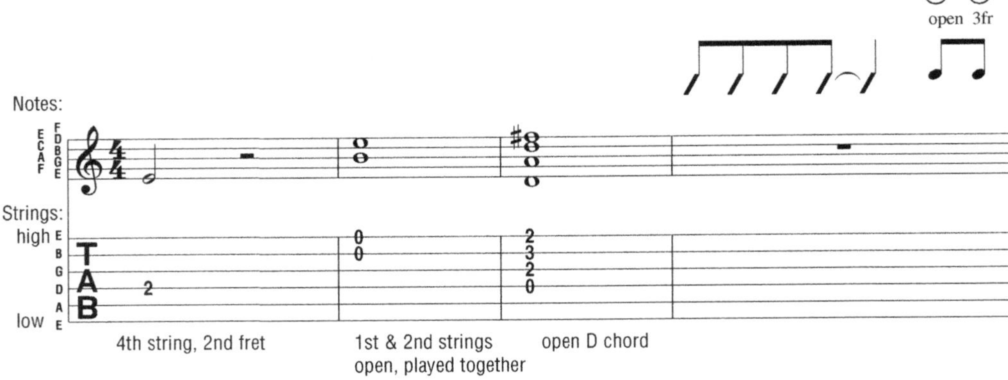

Definitions for Special Guitar Notation

HALF-STEP BEND: Strike the note and bend up 1/2 step.

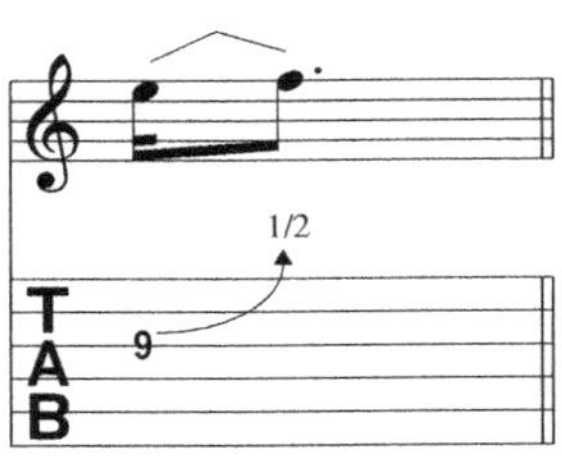

WHOLE-STEP BEND: Strike the note and bend up one step.

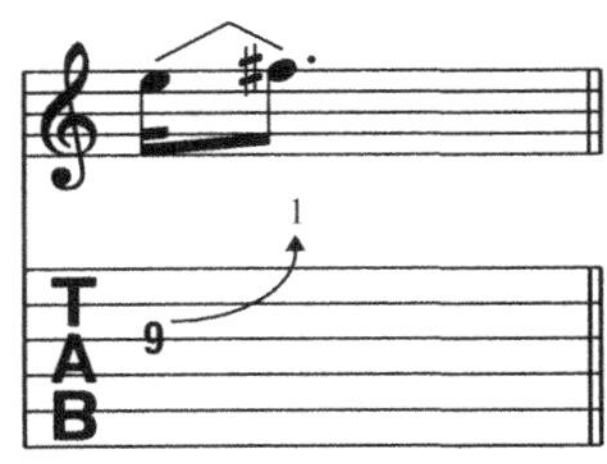

GRACE NOTE BEND: Strike the note and immediately bend up as indicated.

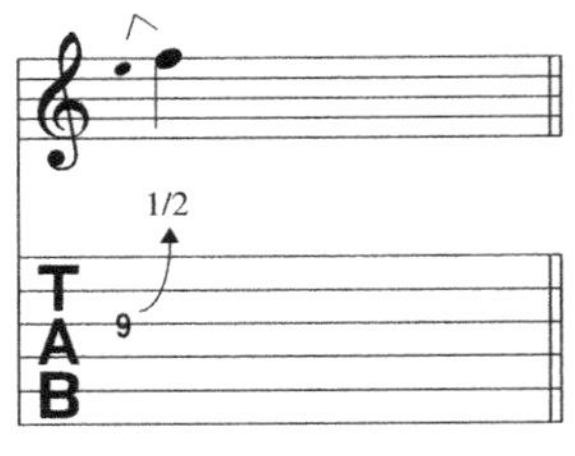

SLIGHT (MICROTONE) BEND: Strike the note and bend up 1/4 step.

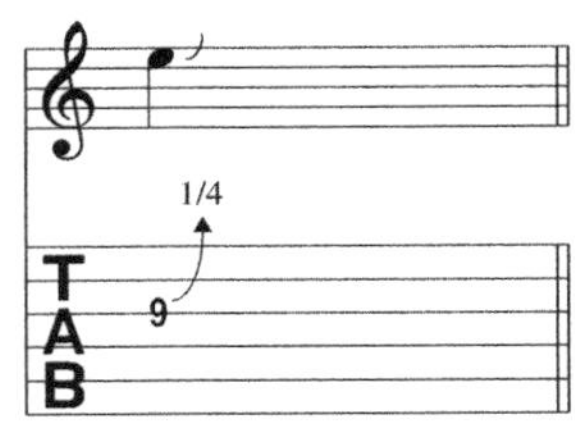

BEND AND RELEASE: Strike the note and bend up as indicated, then release back to the original note. Only the first note is struck.

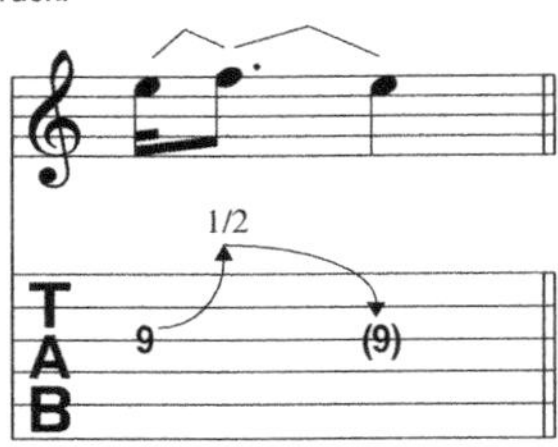

PRE-BEND: Bend the note as indicated, then strike it.

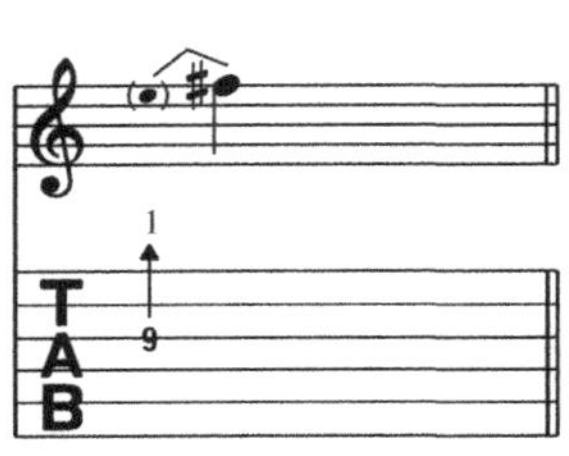

PRE-BEND AND RELEASE: Bend the note as indicated. Strike it and release the bend back to the original note.

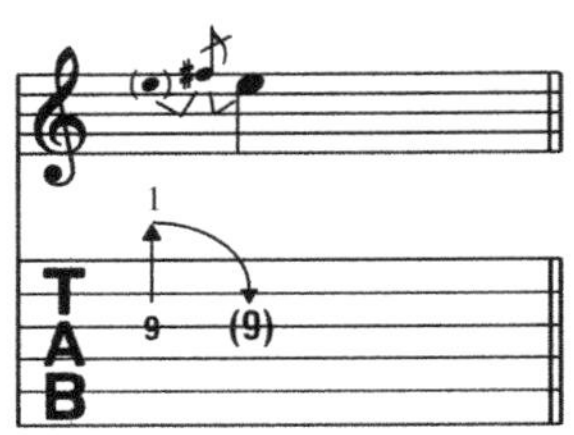

UNISON BEND: Strike the two notes simultaneously and bend the lower note up to the pitch of the higher.

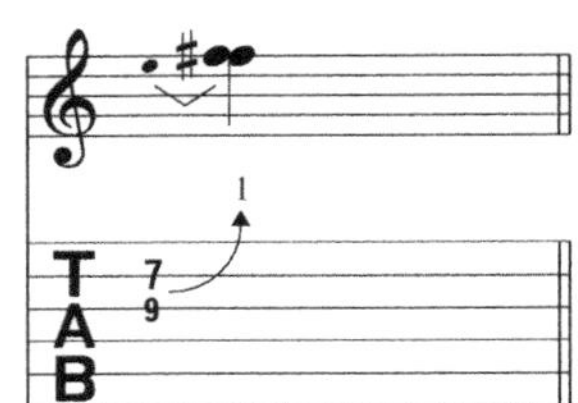

VIBRATO: The string is vibrated by rapidly bending and releasing the note with the fretting hand.

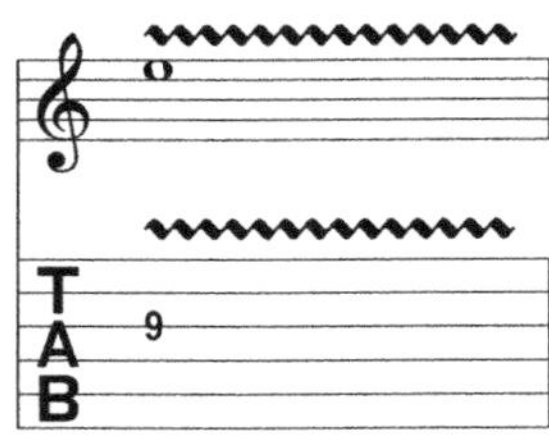

WIDE VIBRATO: The pitch is varied to a greater degree by vibrating with the fretting hand.

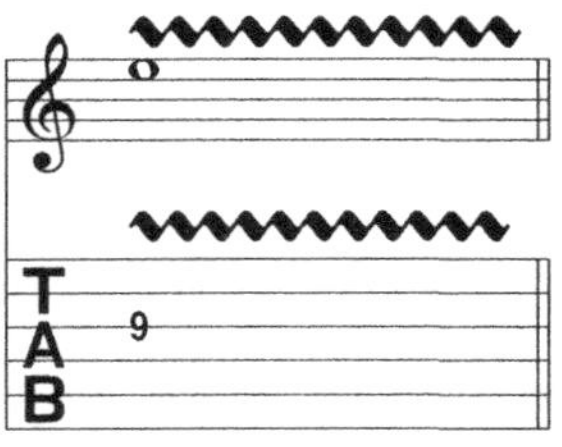

HAMMER-ON: Strike the first (lower) note with one finger, then sound the higher note (on the same string) with another finger by fretting it without picking.

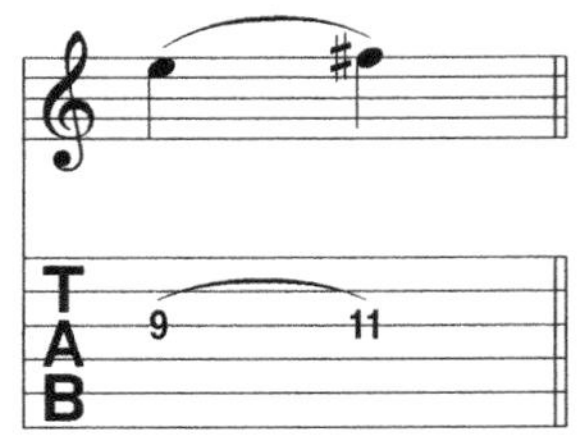

PULL-OFF: Place both fingers on the notes to be sounded. Strike the first note and without picking, pull the finger off to sound the second (lower) note.

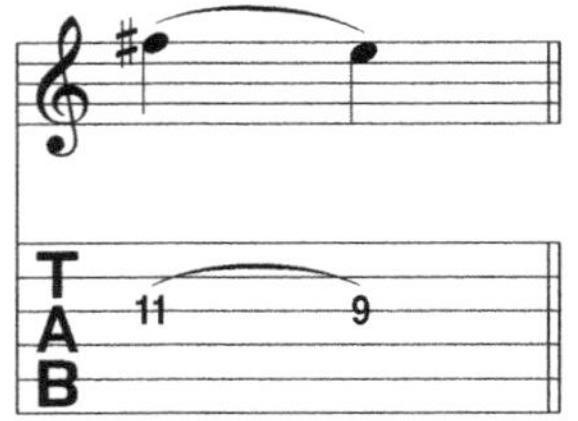

LEGATO SLIDE: Strike the first note and then slide the same fret-hand finger up or down to the second note. The second note is not struck.

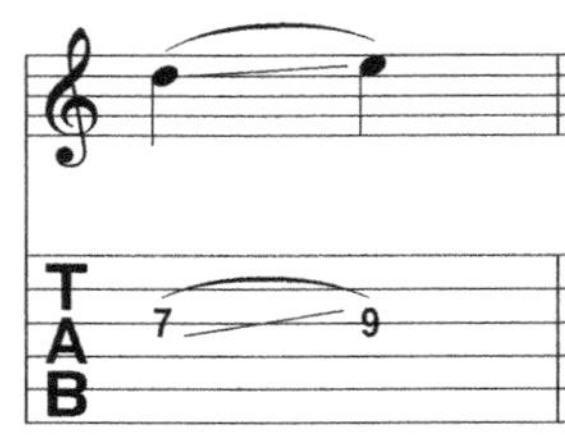

SHIFT SLIDE: Same as legato slide, except the second note is struck.

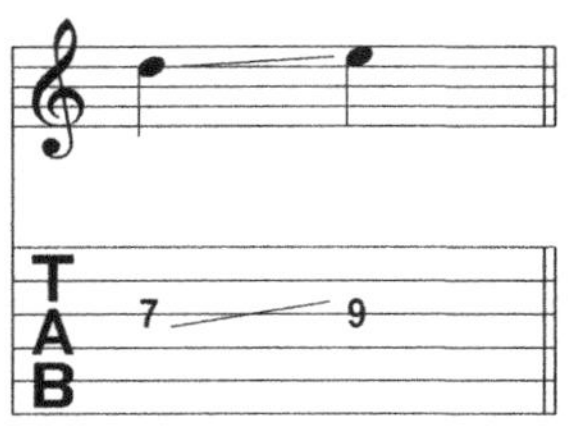

TRILL: Very rapidly alternate between the notes indicated by continuously hammering on and pulling off.

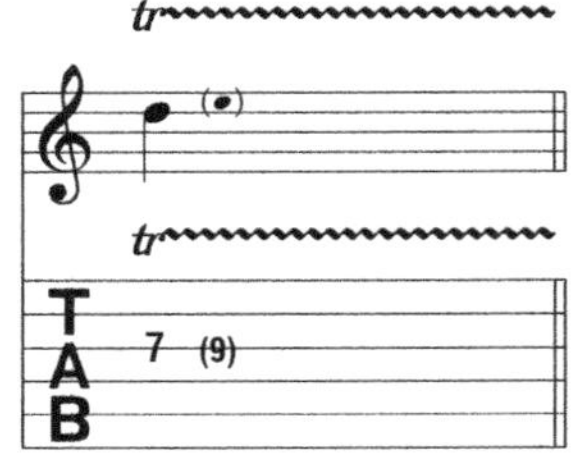

TAPPING: Hammer ("tap") the fret indicated with the pick-hand index or middle finger and pull off to the note fretted by the fret hand.

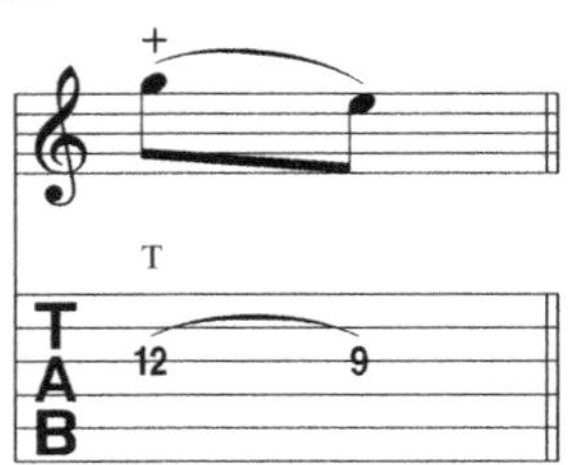

NATURAL HARMONIC: Strike the note while the fret-hand lightly touches the string directly over the fret indicated.

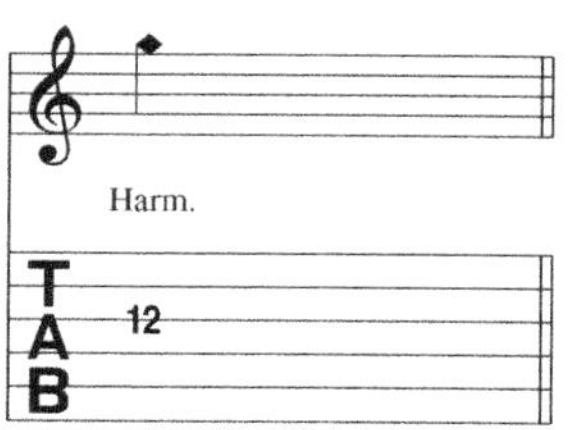

PINCH HARMONIC: The note is fretted normally and a harmonic is produced by adding the edge of the thumb or the tip of the index finger of the pick hand to the normal pick attack.

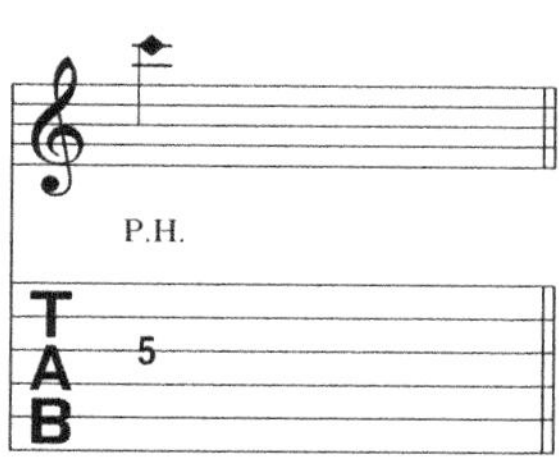

HARP HARMONIC: The note is fretted normally and a harmonic is produced by gently resting the pick hand's index finger directly above the indicated fret (in parentheses) while the pick hand's thumb or pick assists by plucking the appropriate string.

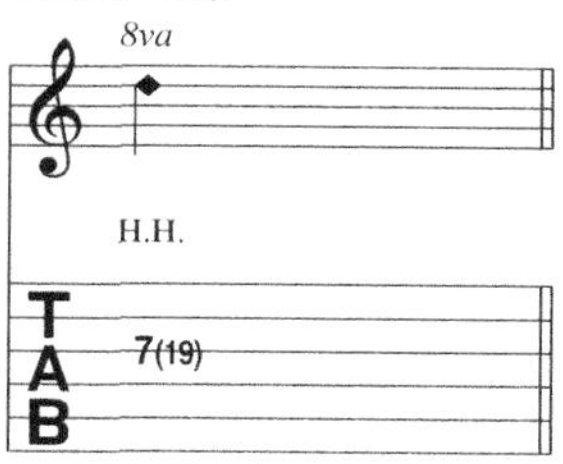

PICK SCRAPE: The edge of the pick is rubbed down (or up) the string, producing a scratchy sound.

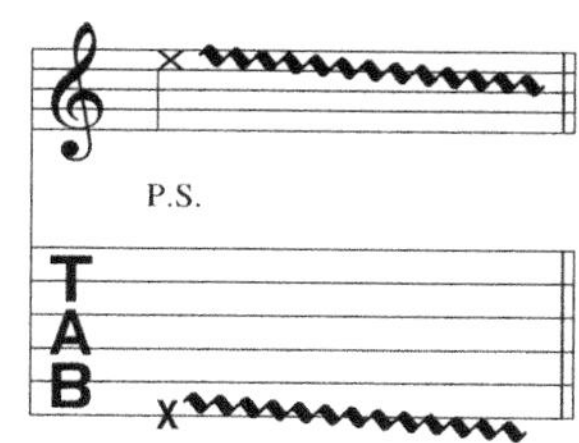

MUFFLED STRINGS: A percussive sound is produced by laying the fret hand across the string(s) without depressing, and striking them with the pick hand.

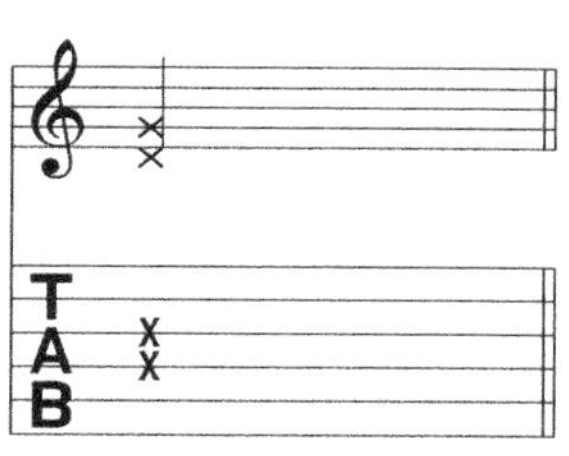

PALM MUTING: The note is partially muted by the pick hand lightly touching the string(s) just before the bridge.

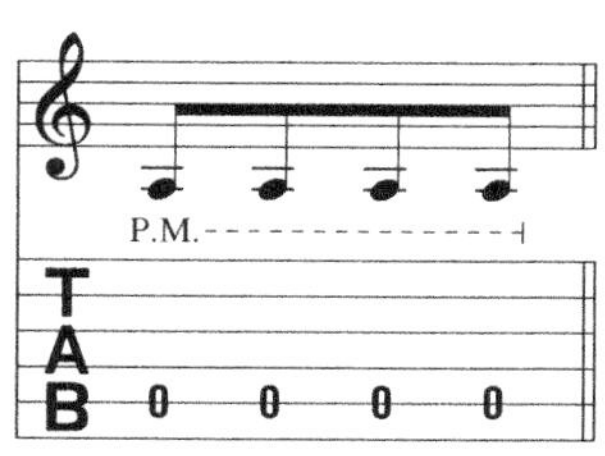

RAKE: Drag the pick across the strings indicated with a single motion.

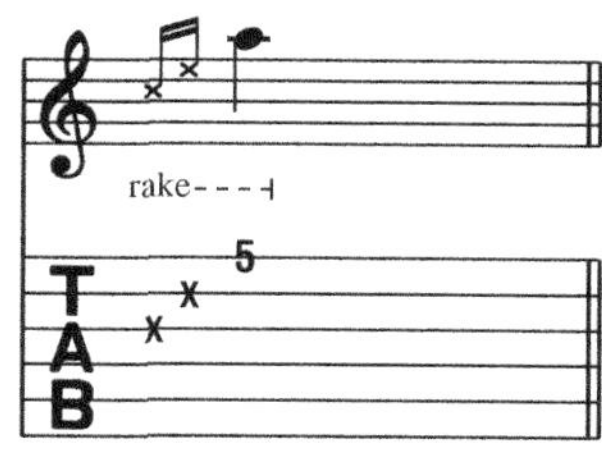

TREMOLO PICKING: The note is picked as rapidly and continuously as possible.

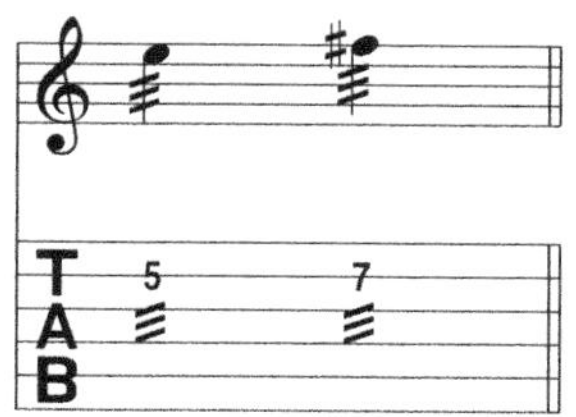

ARPEGGIATE: Play the notes of the chord indicated by quickly rolling them from bottom to top.

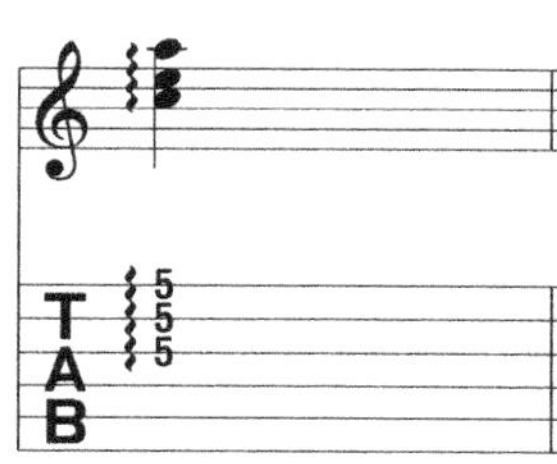

VIBRATO BAR DIVE AND RETURN: The pitch of the note or chord is dropped a specified number of steps (in rhythm) then returned to the original pitch.

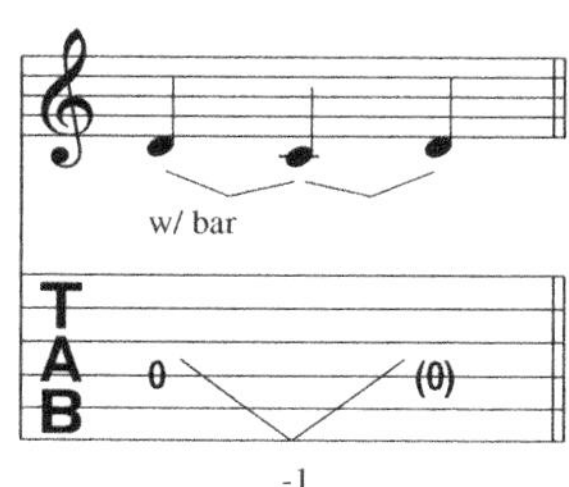

VIBRATO BAR SCOOP: Depress the bar just before striking the note, then quickly release the bar.

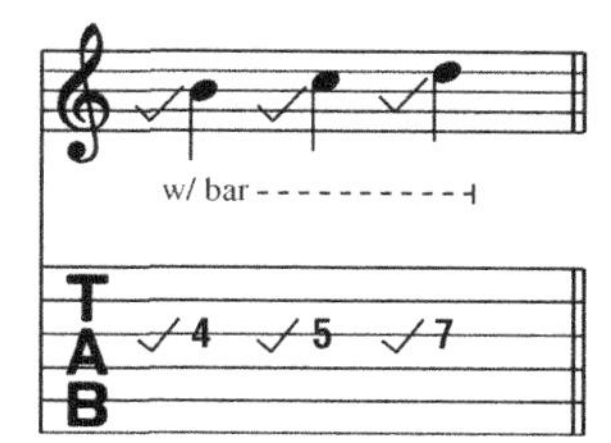

VIBRATO BAR DIP: Strike the note and then immediately drop a specified number of steps, then release back to the original pitch.

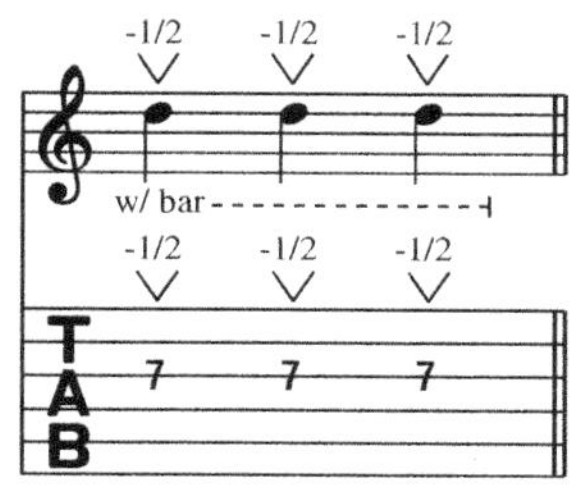

Additional Musical Definitions

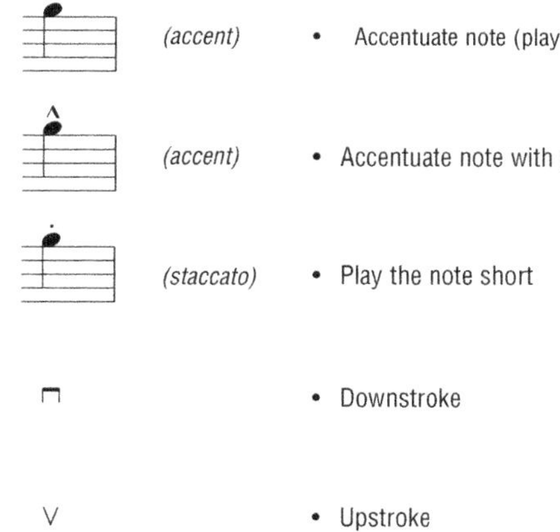

- *(accent)* • Accentuate note (play it louder)
- *(accent)* • Accentuate note with great intensity
- *(staccato)* • Play the note short
- ⊓ • Downstroke
- V • Upstroke
- ***D.S. al Coda*** • Go back to the sign (𝄋), then play until the measure marked "***To Coda,***" then skip to the section labelled "**Coda.**"
- ***D.C. al Fine*** • Go back to the beginning of the song and play until the measure marked "***Fine***" (end).

- **Rhy. Fig.** • Label used to recall a recurring accompaniment pattern (usually chordal).
- **Riff** • Label used to recall composed, melodic lines (usually single notes) which recur.
- **Fill** • Label used to identify a brief melodic figure which is to be inserted into the arrangement.
- **Rhy. Fill** • A chordal version of a Fill.
- tacet • Instrument is silent (drops out).
- • Repeat measures between signs.

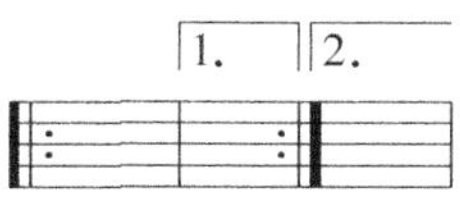

- • When a repeated section has different endings, play the first ending only the first time and the second ending only the second time.

NOTE: Tablature numbers in parentheses mean:
1. The note is being sustained over a system (note in standard notation is tied), or
2. The note is sustained, but a new articulation (such as a hammer-on, pull-off, slide or vibrato begins), or
3. The note is a barely audible "ghost" note (note in standard notation is also in parentheses).

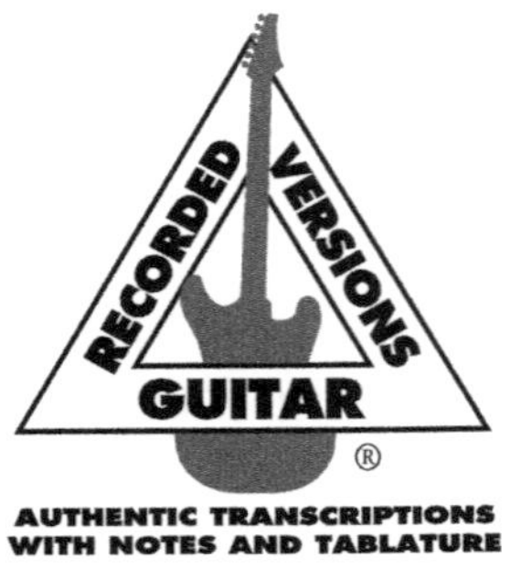

GUITAR RECORDED VERSIONS®

Guitar Recorded Versions® are note-for-note transcriptions of guitar music taken directly off recordings. This series, one of the most popular in print today, features some of the greatest guitar players and groups from blues and rock to country and jazz.

Guitar Recorded Versions are transcribed by the best transcribers in the business. Every book contains notes and tablature unless otherwise marked. Visit **halleonard.com** for our complete selection.

Will Ackerman
00690016 The Will Ackerman Collection $22.99
Bryan Adams
00690501 Greatest Hits $24.99
Aerosmith
00690002 Big Ones $24.95
00690603 O Yeah! $27.99
Alice in Chains
00690178 Acoustic $19.99
00694865 Dirt $19.99
00660225 Facelift $19.99
00694925 Jar of Flies/Sap $19.99
00690387 Nothing Safe $24.99
All That Remains
00142819 The Order of Things ..$22.99
Allman Brothers Band
00694932 Definitive Collection, Volume 1 ....$27.99
00694933 Definitive Collection, Volume 2 ....$27.99
00694934 Definitive Collection, Volume 3 ....$29.99
Duane Allman
00690958 Guitar Anthology $29.99
Alter Bridge
00691071 AB III $29.99
00690945 Blackbird $24.99
00690755 One Day Remains $24.99
Anthrax
00690849 Best of Anthrax $19.99
Arctic Monkeys
00123558 AM $24.99
Chet Atkins
00690158 Almost Alone $22.99
00694876 Contemporary Styles ..$19.95
00694878 Vintage Fingerstyle $19.99
Audioslave
00690609 Audioslave $24.99
00690884 Revelations $19.95
Avenged Sevenfold
00690926 Avenged Sevenfold $24.99
00214869 Best of: 2005-2013 ..$24.99
00690820 City of Evil $24.95
00123216 Hail to the King $22.99
00691051 Nightmare $22.99
00222486 The Stage $24.99
00691065 Waking the Fallen $22.99
The Avett Brothers
00123140 Guitar Collection $22.99
Randy Bachman
00694918 Guitar Collection $22.95
The Beatles
00690489 1 (Number Ones) $24.99
00694929 1962-1966 ....$24.99
00694930 1967-1970 ....$27.99
00694880 Abbey Road $19.99
00694832 Acoustic Guitar $24.99
00691066 Beatles for Sale $22.99
00690903 Capitol Albums Vol. 2 .$24.99
00691031 Help! $19.99
00690482 Let It Be $19.99
00691030 Magical Mystery Tour ..$22.99
00691067 Meet the Beatles! $22.99
00691068 Please Please Me $22.99
00694891 Revolver $19.99
00691014 Rock Band $34.99
00694914 Rubber Soul $22.99
00694863 Sgt. Pepper's Lonely Hearts Club Band $22.99
00110193 Tomorrow Never Knows $22.99
00690110 White Album Book 1 ..$19.99
00690111 White Album Book 2 ..$19.99
00690383 Yellow Submarine $19.95

The Beach Boys
00690503 Very Best $24.99
Beck
00690632 Beck – Sea Change ...$19.95
Jeff Beck
00691044 Best of Beck $24.99
00690042 Blow by Blow $22.99
00691041 Truth $19.99
00691043 Wired $19.99
George Benson
00694884 Best of $22.99
Chuck Berry
00692385 Chuck Berry $22.99
Billy Talent
00690835 Billy Talent $22.99
00690879 Billy Talent II $19.99
Black Crowes
00147787 Best of $19.99
The Black Keys
00129737 Turn Blue $22.99
Black Sabbath
00690149 Black Sabbath $17.99
00690901 Best of $22.99
00691010 Heaven and Hell $22.99
00690148 Master of Reality $19.99
00690142 Paranoid $17.99
00690145 Vol. 4 ....$22.99
00692200 We Sold Our Soul for Rock 'n' Roll $22.99
blink-182
00690389 Enema of the State $19.95
00690831 Greatest Hits $24.99
00691179 Neighborhoods $22.99
Michael Bloomfield
00148544 Guitar Anthology $24.99
Blue Öyster Cult
00690028 Cult Classics $19.99
Bon Jovi
00691074 Greatest Hits $24.99
Joe Bonamassa
00158600 Blues of Desperation $22.99
00139086 Different Shades of Blue $22.99
00198117 Muddy Wolf at Red Rocks $24.99
00283540 Redemption $24.99
Boston
00690913 Boston $19.99
00690932 Don't Look Back $19.99
00690829 Guitar Collection $24.99
David Bowie
00690491 Best of $19.99
Box Car Racer
00690583 Box Car Racer $19.95
Breaking Benjamin
00691023 Dear Agony $22.99
00690873 Phobia $19.99
Lenny Breau
00141446 Best of $19.99
Big Bill Broonzy
00286503 Guitar Collection $19.99
Roy Buchanan
00690168 Collection $24.99
Jeff Buckley
00690451 Collection $24.99
Bullet for My Valentine
00691047 Fever $22.99
00690957 Scream Aim Fire $22.99
00119629 Temper Temper $22.99
Kenny Burrell
00690678 Best of $22.99
Cage the Elephant
00691077 Thank You, Happy Birthday $22.99

The Cars
00691159 Complete Greatest Hits .$22.99
Carter Family
00690261 Collection $19.99
Johnny Cash
00691079 Best of $22.99
Cheap Trick
00690043 Best of $19.95
Chicago
00690171 Definitive Guitar Collection $24.99
Chimaira
00691011 Guitar Collection $24.99
Charlie Christian
00690567 Definitive Collection ..$22.99
Eric Church
00101916 Chief $22.99
The Civil Wars
00129545 The Civil Wars $19.99
Eric Clapton
00690590 Anthology $34.99
00692391 Best of $22.95
00694896 Blues Breakers (with John Mayall) $19.99
00138731 The Breeze $22.99
00691055 Clapton $22.99
00690936 Complete Clapton $29.99
00690010 From the Cradle $22.99
00192383 I Still Do $19.99
00690363 Just One Night $24.99
00694873 Timepieces $19.95
00694869 Unplugged $24.99
00124873 Unplugged (Deluxe) ..$29.99
The Clash
00690162 Best of $19.99
Coheed & Cambria
00690828 IV $19.95
00139967 In Keeping Secrets of Silent Earth: 3 ....$24.99
Coldplay
00130786 Ghost Stories $19.99
00690593 A Rush of Blood to the Head $19.95
Collective Soul
00690855 Best of $19.95
Jessee Cook
00141704 Works Vol. 1 ....$19.99
Alice Cooper
00691091 Best of $24.99
Counting Crows
00694940 August & Everything After $19.99
Robert Cray
00127184 Best of $19.99
Cream
00694840 Disraeli Gears $24.99
Creed
00288787 Greatest Hits $22.99
Creedence Clearwater Revival
00690819 Best of $24.99
Jim Croce
00690648 The Very Best $19.99
Steve Cropper
00690572 Soul Man $22.99
Crosby, Stills & Nash
00690613 Best of $29.99
Cry of Love
00691171 Brother $22.99
Dick Dale
00690637 Best of $19.99
Daughtry
00690892 Daughtry $19.95
Alex de Grassi
00690822 Best of $19.95

Death Cab for Cutie
00690967 Narrow Stairs $22.99
Deep Purple
00690289 Best of $22.99
00690288 Machine Head $19.99
Def Leppard
00690784 Best of $24.99
Derek and the Dominos
00694831 Layla & Other Assorted Love Songs ..$24.99
Ani DiFranco
00690384 Best of $19.95
Dinosaur Jr.
00690979 Best of $22.99
The Doors
00690347 Anthology $22.95
00690348 Essential Collection ...$16.95
Dream Theater
00160579 The Astonishing $24.99
00122443 Dream Theater $24.99
00291164 Distance Over Time ..$24.99
Eagles
00278631 Their Greatest Hits 1971-1975 ....$22.99
00278632 Very Best of $34.99
Duane Eddy
00690250 Best of $19.99
Tommy Emmanuel
00147067 All I Want for Christmas $19.99
00690909 Best of $24.99
00172824 It's Never Too Late $22.99
00139220 Little by Little $24.99
Melissa Etheridge
00690555 Best of $19.95
Evanescence
00691186 Evanescence $22.99
Extreme
00690515 Pornograffitti $24.99
John Fahey
00150257 Guitar Anthology $19.99
Tal Farlow
00125661 Best of $19.99
Five Finger Death Punch
00691009 5 Finger Death Punch $19.99
00691181 American Capitalism ..$22.99
00128917 Wrong Side of Heaven & Righteous Side of Hell .$22.99
Fleetwood Mac
00690664 Best of $24.99
Flyleaf
00690870 Flyleaf $19.95
Foghat
00690986 Best of $22.99
Foo Fighters
00691024 Greatest Hits $22.99
00691115 Wasting Light $22.99
Peter Frampton
00690842 Best of $22.99
Robben Ford
00690805 Best of $24.99
00120220 Guitar Anthology $29.99
Free
00694920 Best of $19.99
Rory Gallagher
00295410 Blues (Selections) $24.99
Danny Gatton
00694807 88 Elmira St $22.99
Genesis
00690438 Guitar Anthology $24.99
Godsmack
00120167 Godsmack $19.95
00691048 The Oracle $22.99
Goo Goo Dolls
00690943 Greatest Hits Vol. 1 ....$24.99

Grateful Dead
00139460 Guitar Anthology $29.99
Green Day
00212480 Revolution Radio $19.99
00118259 ¡Tré! $21.99
00113073 ¡Uno! $21.99
Peter Green
00691190 Best of $24.99
Greta Van Fleet
00287517 Anthem of the Peaceful Army $19.99
00287515 From the Fires $19.99
Patty Griffin
00690927 Children Running Through $19.95
Guns N' Roses
00690978 Chinese Democracy ...$24.99
Buddy Guy
00691027 Anthology $24.99
00694854 Damn Right, I've Got the Blues $19.95
Jim Hall
00690697 Best of $19.99
Ben Harper
00690840 Both Sides of the Gun .$19.95
00691018 Fight for Your Mind ...$22.99
George Harrison
00694798 Anthology $22.99
Scott Henderson
00690841 Blues Guitar Collection $24.99
Jimi Hendrix
00692930 Are You Experienced? .$27.99
00692931 Axis: Bold As Love $24.99
00690304 Band of Gypsys $24.99
00690608 Blue Wild Angel $24.95
00275044 Both Sides of the Sky $22.99
00692932 Electric Ladyland $27.99
00690017 Live at Woodstock $29.99
00119619 People, Hell & Angels $24.99
00690602 Smash Hits $24.99
00691152 West Coast Seattle Boy (Anthology) $29.99
00691332 Winterland $22.99
H.I.M.
00690843 Dark Light $19.95
Buddy Holly
00660029 Best of $22.99
John Lee Hooker
00690793 Anthology $29.99
Howlin' Wolf
00694905 Howlin' Wolf $22.99
Billy Idol
00690692 Very Best of $22.99
Imagine Dragons
00121961 Night Visions $22.99
Incubus
00690688 A Crow Left of the Murder $19.95
Iron Maiden
00690790 Anthology $24.99
00691058 The Final Frontier $22.99
00200446 Guitar Tab $29.99
00690887 A Matter of Life and Death $24.95
Alan Jackson
00690730 Guitar Collection $29.99
Elmore James
00696938 Master of the Electric Slide Guitar ..$19.99
Jane's Addiction
00690652 Best of $19.95
Jethro Tull
00690684 Aqualung $22.99
00690693 Guitar Anthology $24.99
00691182 Stand Up $22.99

John 5
00690898 The Devil Knows My Name $22.95
00690814 Songs for Sanity $19.95
00690751 Vertigo $19.95

Eric Johnson
00694912 Ah Via Musicom $24.99
00690660 Best of $27.99
00691076 Up Close $22.99
00690169 Venus Isle $27.99

Jack Johnson
00690846 Curious George $19.95

Robert Johnson
00690271 New Transcriptions $24.99

Janis Joplin
00699131 Best of $19.95

Judas Priest
00690427 Best of $24.99

Kansas
00690277 Best of $19.99

Phil Keaggy
00690911 Best of $24.99

Toby Keith
00690727 Guitar Collection $19.99

The Killers
00690910 Sam's Town $19.95

Killswitch Engage
00120814 Disarm the Descent $22.99

Albert King
00690504 Very Best of $24.99
00124869 In Session $22.99

B.B. King
00690492 Anthology $24.99
00130447 Live at the Regal $17.99
00690444 Riding with the King $24.99

Freddie King
00690134 Collection $19.99

Marcus King
00327968 El Dorado $22.99

Kiss
00690157 Alive! $19.99
00690356 Alive II $22.99
00694903 Best of $24.99
00690355 Destroyer $17.99
00291163 Very Best of $24.99

Mark Knopfler
00690164 Guitar Styles $24.99

Korn
00690780 Greatest Hits Vol. 1 $24.99

Kris Kristofferson
00690377 Collection $19.99

Lamb of God
00690834 Ashes of the Wake $24.99
00691187 Resolution $22.99
00690875 Sacrament $22.99

Ray LaMontagne
00690977 Gossip in the Grain $19.99
00691057 God Willin' & The Creek Don't Rise $22.99
00690890 Til the Sun Turns Black $19.95

Jonny Lang
00690658 Long Time Coming $19.95

John Lennon
00690679 Guitar Collection $24.99

Linkin Park
00690922 Minutes to Midnight $19.99

Los Lonely Boys
00690743 Los Lonely Boys $19.95

The Lumineers
00114563 The Lumineers $22.99

George Lynch
00690525 Best of $24.99

Lynyrd Skynyrd
00690955 All-Time Greatest Hits $24.99
00694954 New Best of $24.99

Yngwie Malmsteen
00690577 Anthology $29.99

Marilyn Manson
00690754 Lest We Forget $19.99

Bob Marley
00694956 Legend $19.99
00694945 Songs of Freedom $29.99

Maroon 5
00690657 Songs About Jane $19.95

Pat Martino
00139168 Guitar Anthology $24.99

John McLaughlin
00129105 Guitar Tab Anthology $24.99

Mastodon
00690989 Crack the Skye $24.99
00236690 Emperor of Sand $22.99
00691176 The Hunter $22.99
00137718 Once More 'Round the Sun $22.99

Andy McKee
00691942 Art of Motion $24.99
00691034 Joyland $19.99

Don McLean
00120080 Songbook $19.99

Megadeth
00690481 Capitol Punishment $22.99
00694952 Countdown to Extinction $24.99
00691015 Endgame $24.99
00276065 Greatest Hits $24.99
00694951 Rust in Peace $24.99
00691185 Th1rt3en $22.99
00690011 Youthanasia $24.99

John Mellencamp
00690505 Guitar Collection $24.99

Metallica
00209876 Hardwired... To Self-Destruct $22.99

Pat Metheny
00690562 Bright Size Life $24.99
00691073 Day Trip/ Tokyo Day Trip Live $22.99
00690646 One Quiet Night $24.99
00690559 Question & Answer $24.99
00690565 Rejoicing $19.95
00690558 Trio 99-00 $24.99
00690561 Trio Live $22.95
00118836 Unity Band $22.99
00102590 What's It All About $24.99

Steve Miller Band
00690040 Young Hearts: Complete Greatest Hits $24.99

Ministry
00119338 Guitar Tab Collection $24.99

Wes Montgomery
00102591 Guitar Anthology $24.99

Gary Moore
00691092 Best of $24.99
00694802 Still Got the Blues $24.99

Alanis Morissette
00355456 Jagged Little Pill $22.99

Motion City Soundtrack
00691005 Best of $19.99

Mountain
00694958 Best of $19.99

Mudvayne
00690794 Lost and Found $19.95

Mumford & Sons
00691070 Sigh No More $22.99

Muse
00118196 The 2nd Law $19.99
00151195 Drones $19.99

My Morning Jacket
00690996 Collection $19.99

Matt Nathanson
00690984 Some Mad Hope $22.99

Night Ranger
00690883 Best of $19.99

Nirvana
00690611 Nirvana $22.95
00694895 Bleach $19.99
00694913 In Utero $19.99
00694883 Nevermind $19.99
00690026 Unplugged in New York $19.99

No Doubt
00120112 Tragic Kingdom $22.95

Nothing More
00265439 Guitar & Bass Tab Collection $24.99

The Offspring
00690807 Greatest Hits $22.99

Opeth
00243349 Best of $22.99

Roy Orbison
00691052 Black & White Night $22.99

Ozzy Osbourne
00694847 Best of $24.99

Brad Paisley
00690933 Best of $27.99
00690995 Play $24.99

Christopher Parkening
00690938 Duets & Concertos $24.99
00690939 Solo Pieces $19.99

Les Paul
00690594 Best of $22.99

Pearl Jam
00694855 Ten $22.99

Periphery
00146043 Guitar Tab Collection $24.99

Carl Perkins
00690725 Best of $19.99

Tom Petty
00690499 Definitive Collection $22.99

Phish
00690176 Billy Breathes $24.99

Pink Floyd
00121933 Acoustic Collection $24.99
00690428 Dark Side of the Moon $19.99
00142677 The Endless River $19.99
00244637 Guitar Anthology $24.99
00239799 The Wall $24.99

Poison
00690789 Best of $19.99

Elvis Presley
00692535 Elvis Presley $19.95
00690299 King of Rock 'n' Roll $22.99

Prince
00690925 Very Best of $24.99

Queen
00690003 Classic Queen $24.99
00694975 Greatest Hits $25.99

Queens of the Stone Age
00254332 Villains $22.99

Queensryche
00690670 Very Best of $24.99

The Raconteurs
00690878 Broken Boy Soldiers $19.95

Radiohead
00109303 Guitar Anthology $24.99

Rage Against the Machine
00694910 Rage Against the Machine $22.99
00119834 Guitar Anthology $24.99

Rancid
00690179 And Out Come the Wolves $24.99

Ratt
00690426 Best of $19.95

Red Hot Chili Peppers
00690055 BloodSugarSexMagik $19.99
00690584 By the Way $24.99
00690379 Californication $19.99
00182634 The Getaway $24.99
00690673 Greatest Hits $22.99
00691166 I'm with You $22.99
00690255 Mother's Milk $19.95
00690090 One Hot Minute $22.95
00690852 Stadium Arcadium $29.99

The Red Jumpsuit Apparatus
00690893 Don't You Fake It $19.95

Jerry Reed
00694892 Guitar Style of $22.99

Django Reinhardt
00690511 Definitive Collection $24.99

Jimmie Rodgers
00690260 Guitar Collection $22.99

Rolling Stones
00690014 Exile on Main Street $24.99
00690631 Guitar Anthology $29.99
00690186 Rock and Roll Circus $19.95
00694976 Some Girls $22.95
00690264 Tattoo You $19.95

Angelo Romero
00690974 Bella $19.99

David Lee Roth
00690685 Eat 'Em and Smile $22.99
00690694 Guitar Anthology $24.95
00690942 Songs of Van Halen $19.95

Rush
00323854 The Spirit of Radio $22.99

Santana
00173534 Guitar Anthology $27.99
00690031 Greatest Hits $19.95

Joe Satriani
00276350 What Happens Next $24.99

Michael Schenker
00690796 Very Best of $24.99

Matt Schofield
00128870 Guitar Tab Collection $22.99

Scorpions
00690566 Best of $24.99

Bob Seger
00690659 Greatest Hits Vol. 2 $17.95
00690604 Guitar Collection $22.99

Ed Sheeran
00234543 Divide $19.99
00138870 X $19.99

Kenny Wayne Shepherd
00690803 Best of $24.99
00151178 Ledbetter Heights $19.99

Shinedown
00692433 Amaryllis $22.99

Silverchair
00690196 Freak Show $19.95

Skillet
00122218 Rise $22.99

Slash
00691114 Guitar Anthology $29.99

Slayer
00690872 Christ Illusion $19.95
00690813 Guitar Collection $19.99

Slipknot
00690419 Slipknot $19.99
00690973 All Hope Is Gone $24.99

Smashing Pumpkins
00316982 Greatest Hits $22.99

Social Distortion
00690330 Live at the Roxy $22.99

Soundgarden
00690912 Guitar Anthology $24.99

Steely Dan
00120004 Best of $24.99

Steppenwolf
00694921 Best of $22.95

Mike Stern
00690655 Best of $24.99

Cat Stevens
14041588 Tea for the Tillerman $19.99

Rod Stewart
00690949 Guitar Anthology $19.99

Stone Sour
00690877 Come What(ever) May $19.95

Styx
00690520 Guitar Collection $22.99

Sublime
00120081 Sublime $19.99
00120122 40 oz. to Freedom $22.99
00690992 Robbin' the Hood $19.99

SUM 41
00690519 All Killer No Filler $19.95
00690929 Underclass Hero $19.95

Supertramp
00691072 Best of $24.99

Taylor Swift
00690994 Taylor Swift $22.99
00690993 Fearless $22.99
00115957 Red $21.99
00691063 Speak Now $22.99

System of a Down
00690531 Toxicity $19.99

James Taylor
00694824 Best of $19.99

Thin Lizzy
00694887 Best of $19.99

.38 Special
00690988 Guitar Anthology $22.99

Three Days Grace
00691039 Life Starts Now $22.99

Trans-Siberian Orchestra
00150209 Guitar Anthology $19.99

Merle Travis
00690233 Collection $22.99

Trivium
00253237 Guitar Tab Anthology $24.99
00123862 Vengeance Falls $22.99

Robin Trower
00690683 Bridge of Sighs $19.99

U2
00699191 Best of: 1980-1990 $24.99
00690732 Best of: 1990-2000 $24.99
00690894 18 Singles $22.99

Keith Urban
00124461 Guitar Anthology $19.99

Steve Vai
00690039 Alien Love Secrets $24.99
00690575 Alive in an Ultra World $22.95
00690172 Fire Garden $24.95
00690343 Flex-Able Leftovers $19.95
00156024 Guitar Anthology $34.99
00197570 Modern Primitive $29.99
00660137 Passion & Warfare $27.50
00690881 Real Illusions: Reflections $27.99
00690605 The Elusive Light and Sound, Vol. 1 $29.99
00694904 Sex and Religion $24.95
00110385 The Story of Light $24.99
00690392 The Ultra Zone $19.95

Van Halen
00700555 Van Halen $19.99
00295076 30 Classics $29.99
00700092 1984 $24.99
00700558 Fair Warning $22.99

Jimmie Vaughan
00690690 Best of $19.95

Stevie Ray Vaughan
00690024 Couldn't Stand the Weather $19.99
00690116 Guitar Collection $24.95
00694879 In the Beginning $19.95
00660136 In Step $22.99
00660058 Lightnin' Blues 83-87 $29.99
00690550 Live at Montreux $27.99
00217455 Plays Slow Blues $19.99
00694835 The Sky Is Crying $24.99
00690025 Soul to Soul $19.95
00690015 Texas Flood $19.99

Volbeat
00109770 Guitar Collection $22.99
00121808 Outlaw Gentlemen & Shady Ladies $22.99

T-Bone Walker
00690132 Collection $19.99

Muddy Waters
00694789 Deep Blues $24.99

Doc Watson
00152161 Guitar Anthology $22.99

Weezer
00690071 The Blue Album $19.99
00691046 Rarities Edition $22.99

Paul Westerberg & The Replacements
00691036 Very Best of $19.99

Whitesnake
00117511 Guitar Collection $24.99

The Who
00691941 Acoustic Guitar Collection $22.99
00690447 Best of $24.99

Wilco
00691006 Guitar Collection $22.99

Stevie Wonder
00690319 Hits $22.99

The Yardbirds
00690596 Best of $22.99

Yes
00122303 Guitar Collection $22.99

Dwight Yoakam
00690916 Best of $19.95

Frank Zappa
00690507 Apostrophe $22.99
00690443 Hot Rats $22.99
00690624 One Size Fits All $27.99
00690623 Over-Nite Sensation $24.99

ZZ Top
00121684 Early Classics $27.99
00690589 Guitar Anthology $24.99
00690960 Guitar Classics $19.99

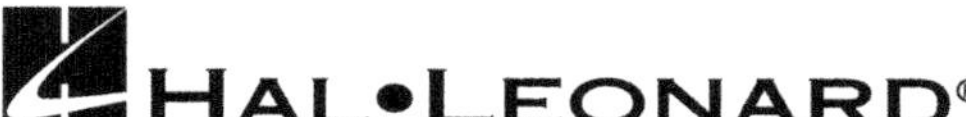

Complete songlists and more at **www.halleonard.com**

Prices and availability subject to change without notice.

HAL•LEONARD®

GUITAR PLAY-ALONG

Complete song lists available online.

This series will help you play your favorite songs quickly and easily. Just follow the tab and listen to the audio to the hear how the guitar should sound, and then play along using the separate backing tracks. Audio files also include software to slow down the tempo without changing pitch. The melody and lyrics are included in the book so that you can sing or simply follow along.

INCLUDES TAB

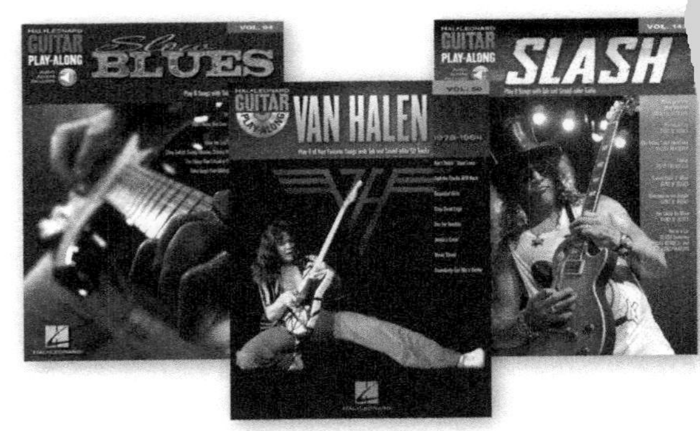

VOL. 1 – ROCK .... 00699570 / $16.99
VOL. 2 – ACOUSTIC .... 00699569 / $16.99
VOL. 3 – HARD ROCK .... 00699573 / $17.99
VOL. 4 – POP/ROCK .... 00699571 / $16.99
VOL. 5 – THREE CHORD SONGS .... 00300985 / $16.99
VOL. 6 – '90S ROCK .... 00298615 / $16.99
VOL. 7 – BLUES .... 00699575 / $17.99
VOL. 8 – ROCK .... 00699585 / $16.99
VOL. 9 – EASY ACOUSTIC SONGS .... 00151708 / $16.99
VOL. 10 – ACOUSTIC .... 00699586 / $16.95
VOL. 11 – EARLY ROCK .... 00699579 / $15.99
VOL. 12 – ROCK POP .... 00291724 / $16.99
VOL. 14 – BLUES ROCK .... 00699582 / $16.99
VOL. 15 – R&B .... 00699583 / $17.99
VOL. 16 – JAZZ .... 00699584 / $15.95
VOL. 17 – COUNTRY .... 00699588 / $16.99
VOL. 18 – ACOUSTIC ROCK .... 00699577 / $15.95
VOL. 20 – ROCKABILLY .... 00699580 / $16.99
VOL. 21 – SANTANA .... 00174525 / $17.99
VOL. 22 – CHRISTMAS .... 00699600 / $15.99
VOL. 23 – SURF .... 00699635 / $16.99
VOL. 24 – ERIC CLAPTON .... 00699649 / $17.99
VOL. 25 – THE BEATLES .... 00198265 / $17.99
VOL. 26 – ELVIS PRESLEY .... 00699643 / $16.99
VOL. 27 – DAVID LEE ROTH .... 00699645 / $16.95
VOL. 28 – GREG KOCH .... 00699646 / $17.99
VOL. 29 – BOB SEGER .... 00699647 / $16.99
VOL. 30 – KISS .... 00699644 / $16.99
VOL. 32 – THE OFFSPRING .... 00699653 / $14.95
VOL. 33 – ACOUSTIC CLASSICS .... 00699656 / $17.99
VOL. 34 – CLASSIC ROCK .... 00699658 / $17.99
VOL. 35 – HAIR METAL .... 00699660 / $17.99
VOL. 36 – SOUTHERN ROCK .... 00699661 / $19.99
VOL. 37 – ACOUSTIC UNPLUGGED .... 00699662 / $22.99
VOL. 38 – BLUES .... 00699663 / $17.99
VOL. 39 – '80s METAL .... 00699664 / $16.99
VOL. 40 – INCUBUS .... 00699668 / $17.95
VOL. 41 – ERIC CLAPTON .... 00699669 / $17.99
VOL. 42 – COVER BAND HITS .... 00211597 / $16.99
VOL. 43 – LYNYRD SKYNYRD .... 00699681 / $19.99
VOL. 44 – JAZZ GREATS .... 00699689 / $16.99
VOL. 45 – TV THEMES .... 00699718 / $14.95
VOL. 46 – MAINSTREAM ROCK .... 00699722 / $16.95
VOL. 47 – JIMI HENDRIX SMASH HITS .... 00699723 / $19.99
VOL. 48 – AEROSMITH CLASSICS .... 00699724 / $17.99
VOL. 49 – STEVIE RAY VAUGHAN .... 00699725 / $17.99
VOL. 50 – VAN HALEN: 1978-1984 .... 00110269 / $19.99
VOL. 51 – ALTERNATIVE '90s .... 00699727 / $14.99
VOL. 52 – FUNK .... 00699728 / $15.99
VOL. 53 – DISCO .... 00699729 / $14.99
VOL. 54 – HEAVY METAL .... 00699730 / $16.99
VOL. 55 – POP METAL .... 00699731 / $14.95
VOL. 56 – FOO FIGHTERS .... 00699749 / $17.99
VOL. 57 – GUNS 'N' ROSES .... 00159922 / $17.99
VOL. 58 – BLINK 182 .... 00699772 / $14.95
VOL. 59 – CHET ATKINS .... 00702347 / $16.99
VOL. 60 – 3 DOORS DOWN .... 00699774 / $14.95
VOL. 62 – CHRISTMAS CAROLS .... 00699798 / $12.95
VOL. 63 – CREEDENCE CLEARWATER REVIVAL .... 00699802 / $16.99
VOL. 64 – ULTIMATE OZZY OSBOURNE .... 00699803 / $17.99
VOL. 66 – THE ROLLING STONES .... 00699807 / $17.99
VOL. 67 – BLACK SABBATH .... 00699808 / $16.99
VOL. 68 – PINK FLOYD – DARK SIDE OF THE MOON .... 00699809 / $16.99
VOL. 71 – CHRISTIAN ROCK .... 00699824 / $14.95
VOL. 72 – ACOUSTIC '90s .... 00699827 / $14.95
VOL. 73 – BLUESY ROCK .... 00699829 / $16.99
VOL. 74 – SIMPLE STRUMMING SONGS .... 00151706 / $19.99
VOL. 75 – TOM PETTY .... 00699882 / $17.99
VOL. 76 – COUNTRY HITS .... 00699884 / $16.99
VOL. 77 – BLUEGRASS .... 00699910 / $15.99
VOL. 78 – NIRVANA .... 00700132 / $16.99
VOL. 79 – NEIL YOUNG .... 00700133 / $24.99
VOL. 80 – ACOUSTIC ANTHOLOGY .... 00700175 / $19.95
VOL. 81 – ROCK ANTHOLOGY .... 00700176 / $22.99
VOL. 82 – EASY ROCK SONGS .... 00700177 / $17.99
VOL. 84 – STEELY DAN .... 00700200 / $19.99
VOL. 85 – THE POLICE .... 00700269 / $16.99
VOL. 86 – BOSTON .... 00700465 / $16.99
VOL. 87 – ACOUSTIC WOMEN .... 00700763 / $14.99
VOL. 88 – GRUNGE .... 00700467 / $16.99
VOL. 89 – REGGAE .... 00700468 / $15.99
VOL. 90 – CLASSICAL POP .... 00700469 / $14.99
VOL. 91 – BLUES INSTRUMENTALS .... 00700505 / $17.99
VOL. 92 – EARLY ROCK INSTRUMENTALS .... 00700506 / $15.99
VOL. 93 – ROCK INSTRUMENTALS .... 00700507 / $16.99
VOL. 94 – SLOW BLUES .... 00700508 / $16.99
VOL. 95 – BLUES CLASSICS .... 00700509 / $15.99
VOL. 96 – BEST COUNTRY HITS .... 00211615 / $16.99
VOL. 97 – CHRISTMAS CLASSICS .... 00236542 / $14.99
VOL. 98 – ROCK BAND .... 00700704 / $14.95
VOL. 99 – ZZ TOP .... 00700762 / $16.99
VOL. 100 – B.B. KING .... 00700466 / $16.99
VOL. 101 – SONGS FOR BEGINNERS .... 00701917 / $14.99
VOL. 102 – CLASSIC PUNK .... 00700769 / $14.99
VOL. 103 – SWITCHFOOT .... 00700773 / $16.99
VOL. 104 – DUANE ALLMAN .... 00700846 / $17.99
VOL. 105 – LATIN .... 00700939 / $16.99
VOL. 106 – WEEZER .... 00700958 / $14.99
VOL. 107 – CREAM .... 00701069 / $16.99
VOL. 108 – THE WHO .... 00701053 / $16.99
VOL. 109 – STEVE MILLER .... 00701054 / $19.99
VOL. 110 – SLIDE GUITAR HITS .... 00701055 / $16.99
VOL. 111 – JOHN MELLENCAMP .... 00701056 / $14.99
VOL. 112 – QUEEN .... 00701052 / $16.99
VOL. 113 – JIM CROCE .... 00701058 / $17.99
VOL. 114 – BON JOVI .... 00701060 / $16.99
VOL. 115 – JOHNNY CASH .... 00701070 / $16.99
VOL. 116 – THE VENTURES .... 00701124 / $16.99
VOL. 117 – BRAD PAISLEY .... 00701224 / $16.99
VOL. 118 – ERIC JOHNSON .... 00701353 / $16.99
VOL. 119 – AC/DC CLASSICS .... 00701356 / $17.99
VOL. 120 – PROGRESSIVE ROCK .... 00701457 / $14.99
VOL. 121 – U2 .... 00701508 / $16.99
VOL. 122 – CROSBY, STILLS & NASH .... 00701610 / $16.99
VOL. 123 – LENNON & McCARTNEY ACOUSTIC .... 00701614 / $16.99
VOL. 124 – SMOOTH JAZZ .... 00200664 / $16.99
VOL. 125 – JEFF BECK .... 00701687 / $17.99
VOL. 126 – BOB MARLEY .... 00701701 / $16.99
VOL. 127 – 1970s ROCK .... 00701739 / $16.99
VOL. 128 – 1960s ROCK .... 00701740 / $14.99
VOL. 129 – MEGADETH .... 00701741 / $17.99
VOL. 130 – IRON MAIDEN .... 00701742 / $17.99
VOL. 131 – 1990s ROCK .... 00701743 / $14.99
VOL. 132 – COUNTRY ROCK .... 00701757 / $15.99
VOL. 133 – TAYLOR SWIFT .... 00701894 / $16.99
VOL. 134 – AVENGED SEVENFOLD .... 00701906 / $16.99
VOL. 135 – MINOR BLUES .... 00151350 / $17.99
VOL. 136 – GUITAR THEMES .... 00701922 / $14.99
VOL. 137 – IRISH TUNES .... 00701966 / $15.99
VOL. 138 – BLUEGRASS CLASSICS .... 00701967 / $17.99
VOL. 139 – GARY MOORE .... 00702370 / $16.99
VOL. 140 – MORE STEVIE RAY VAUGHAN .... 00702396 / $17.99
VOL. 141 – ACOUSTIC HITS .... 00702401 / $16.99
VOL. 142 – GEORGE HARRISON .... 00237697 / $17.99
VOL. 143 – SLASH .... 00702425 / $19.99
VOL. 144 – DJANGO REINHARDT .... 00702531 / $16.99
VOL. 145 – DEF LEPPARD .... 00702532 / $17.99
VOL. 146 – ROBERT JOHNSON .... 00702533 / $16.99
VOL. 147 – SIMON & GARFUNKEL .... 14041591 / $16.99
VOL. 148 – BOB DYLAN .... 14041592 / $16.99
VOL. 149 – AC/DC HITS .... 14041593 / $17.99
VOL. 150 – ZAKK WYLDE .... 02501717 / $16.99
VOL. 151 – J.S. BACH .... 02501730 / $16.99
VOL. 152 – JOE BONAMASSA .... 02501751 / $19.99
VOL. 153 – RED HOT CHILI PEPPERS .... 00702990 / $19.99
VOL. 154 – GLEE .... 00703018 / $16.99
VOL. 155 – ERIC CLAPTON UNPLUGGED .... 00703085 / $16.99
VOL. 156 – SLAYER .... 00703770 / $19.99
VOL. 157 – FLEETWOOD MAC .... 00101382 / $17.99
VOL. 159 – WES MONTGOMERY .... 00102593 / $19.99
VOL. 160 – T-BONE WALKER 00102641/ $17.99
VOL. 161 – THE EAGLES ACOUSTIC .... 00102659 / $17.99
VOL. 162 – THE EAGLES HITS .... 00102667 / $17.99
VOL. 163 – PANTERA .... 00103036 / $17.99
VOL. 164 – VAN HALEN: 1986-1995 .... 00110270 / $17.99
VOL. 165 – GREEN DAY .... 00210343 / $17.99
VOL. 166 – MODERN BLUES .... 00700764 / $16.99
VOL. 167 – DREAM THEATER .... 00111938 / $24.99
VOL. 168 – KISS .... 00113421 / $17.99
VOL. 169 – TAYLOR SWIFT .... 00115982 / $16.99
VOL. 170 – THREE DAYS GRACE .... 00117337 / $16.99
VOL. 171 – JAMES BROWN .... 00117420 / $16.99
VOL. 172 – THE DOOBIE BROTHERS .... 00119670 / $16.99
VOL. 173 – TRANS-SIBERIAN ORCHESTRA .... 00119907 / $19.99
VOL. 174 – SCORPIONS .... 00122119 / $16.99
VOL. 175 – MICHAEL SCHENKER .... 00122127 / $17.99
VOL. 176 – BLUES BREAKERS WITH JOHN MAYALL & ERIC CLAPTON .... 00122132 / $19.99
VOL. 177 – ALBERT KING .... 00123271 / $16.99
VOL. 178 – JASON MRAZ .... 00124165 / $17.99
VOL. 179 – RAMONES .... 00127073 / $16.99
VOL. 180 – BRUNO MARS .... 00129706 / $16.99
VOL. 181 – JACK JOHNSON .... 00129854 / $16.99
VOL. 182 – SOUNDGARDEN .... 00138161 / $17.99
VOL. 183 – BUDDY GUY .... 00138240 / $17.99
VOL. 184 – KENNY WAYNE SHEPHERD .... 00138258 / $17.99
VOL. 185 – JOE SATRIANI .... 00139457 / $17.99
VOL. 186 – GRATEFUL DEAD .... 00139459 / $17.99
VOL. 187 – JOHN DENVER .... 00140839 / $17.99
VOL. 188 – MÖTLEY CRÜE .... 00141145 / $17.99
VOL. 189 – JOHN MAYER .... 00144350 / $17.99
VOL. 190 – DEEP PURPLE .... 00146152 / $17.99
VOL. 191 – PINK FLOYD CLASSICS .... 00146164 / $17.99
VOL. 192 – JUDAS PRIEST .... 00151352 / $17.99
VOL. 193 – STEVE VAI .... 00156028 / $19.99
VOL. 194 – PEARL JAM .... 00157925 / $17.99
VOL. 195 – METALLICA: 1983-1988 .... 00234291 / $19.99
VOL. 196 – METALLICA: 1991-2016 .... 00234292 / $19.99

Prices, contents, and availability subject to change without notice.

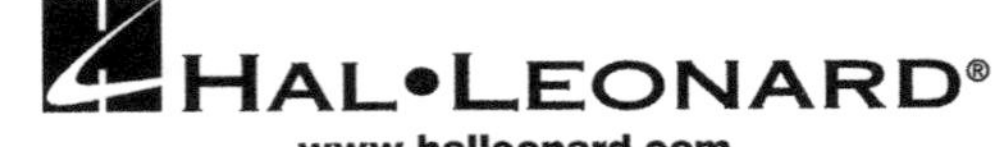

www.halleonard.com

0820
173